JOURNEY

of a

PROPHET

Jesus Tells His Story

Kaarin Alisa

SECOND EDITION

8TH CHAKRA PRESS

8th Chakra Press books may be ordered through booksellers or by contacting:

8th Chakra Press
http://www.8thchakrapress.com/
2885 Sanford Ave SW #28596
Grandville, MI 49418
1 (503) 914-5856

Because of the dynamic nature of the Internet, any web addresses or links contained in this book may have changed since publication and may no longer be valid. The views expressed in this work are solely those of the author and do not necessarily reflect the views of the publisher, and the publisher hereby disclaims any responsibility for them.

The author of this book does not dispense medical advice or prescribe the use of any technique as a form of treatment for physical, emotional, or medical problems without the advice of a physician, either directly or indirectly. The intent of the author is only to offer information of a general nature to help you in your quest for emotional and spiritual wellbeing. In the event you use any of the information in this book for yourself, which is your constitutional right, the author and the publisher assume no responsibility for your actions.

ISBN: 978-0-9980541-1-7 (sc)
ISBN: 978-0-9980541-2-4 (e)

SECOND EDITION
Published: September 20, 2018

Material previously published under the titles:
Journey of a Prophet: Jesus Tells His Story
Bare Bones: The Unabridged Life of Yeshua son of Joseph from Galilee

Dedicated to Conscious Choice

Table of Contents

Table of Figures

Foreward

by Don Joseph Goewey

I am one of those you might call a Recovering Christian, which means a soul trying to overcome the way his brain was programmed to feel ashamed of himself. I'm a Baby Boomer, born after the Second World War, and I was indoctrinated to Christianity in the 1950s when fire and brimstone infused the catechism of the day. The term recovering Christian often gets a laugh but the experience one is attempting to recover from is no joke. It's the experience of being disheartened by a fearful orientation to God and Jesus, which often leads to a generalized feeling of unworthiness and disconnection that thwarts spiritual growth.

I was sent to Catholic catechism at the tender age of seven, an innocent still able to see the diamond shining at the center of my life, with no concept of fault or flaw or sin, as far from damnation as a morning in Spring. Three years of catechism classes with convent nuns changed all that. It spun tendrils of doubt around my sense of safety and belonging and replaced my feeling for God and Jesus with dread. Even worse, it distorted what was sacred for me, starting with my mother, and turned the wonder of the infinite sky above me into the fear of being condemned for eternity in an inferno someplace below me.

I will admit, however, that Catholicism was not a total bust. The human heart has a kind of spiritual GPS that navigates its way to whatever light is shining and available. The one sanctuary my spirit secured in the middle of poor Sister Bernadette's spiritual wasteland was Mary, the mother of Jesus. I looked to her for help in getting out of whatever trouble I had gotten into (she never failed) and I rested during hard times in the unconditional acceptance I felt her extending to me, regardless of my mistakes. Mary was enough to keep me believing in a power and grace greater than myself that cared about me and was looking after me.

Then, in my late thirties, when I was married with four children, my life was hit with a perfect storm of stress and it seemed nothing could save me, not even Mary. I was fired from a job I'd spent a decade climbing the career ladder to reach, and nine days later I was diagnosed with a brain tumor that the doctors warned could render me unable to ever work again. Surgery was scheduled six weeks out since the tumor was slow growing, and I spent the first two weeks waiting in abject terror. It was wearing me down to the point that my wife was worried I wouldn't be strong enough to tolerate brain surgery. Finally, in desperation, I went to see my long-time psychotherapist to find a way to shift my fear. She was a superb therapist, with a Ph.D. from Stanford, so I was surprised when, without much ado, she referred me to a spiritual adviser she described as "a kind, trustworthy and absolutely authentic human being who channels a spirit named Yeshua that is also known as Jesus."

"Jesus," I said. "You're joking."

"No, I'm not," my therapist said. "Trust me; this can do more for your situation than anything I can do."

I resisted at first; it was just too weird for me. But my desperation for relief from the gawd-awful terror toppled my resistance and I went. The adviser's name was Kaarin, the author of the book you're holding, and the help she channeled to me changed my life as well as the outcomes from my perfect storm of stress.

I remember how relieved I felt when this gracious redheaded, beaming faced woman welcomed me into her home with a heart-warming smile. The little kid in me who once liked horror movies was afraid she might look like Maleva, the old gypsy fortuneteller with the dark penetrating eyes and jangling necklace from the movie The Wolf Man. Kaarin was quite the opposite. She offered me tea and we talked pleasantly for a few minutes and as strange as I felt about this undertaking, I immediately liked her. She explained to me that the spirits she channeled were simply beings who made themselves available to anyone who chooses to call on them for information and greater understanding about the life they're living.

The first session I had with Yeshua, aka Jesus, began exquisitely. It had been raining hard all day and as Kaarin took her posture to begin to channel, the rain stopped and the sun came out. The change caught my attention and I looked out the picture window across the high grass of the orchard outside just as the sun broke through with a beam of light. The beam of light skipped its way across the grass, turning droplets of water to diamonds, and when the light burst through the window it lit up Kaarin's face just as Yeshua said hello and, for a moment, another face flashed in Kaarin's. Sometime later, a friend showed me a picture of Christ that hangs in the Ananda centers founded by Yogananda nearly a hundred years ago. Yogananda introduced millions of westerners to meditation and he said that Christ appeared to him on occasion and this painting by an artist from the Midwest was what Christ looked like. I was blown over. The face in the painting was the same face I had seen that day.

Yeshua's brother James also channeled through and there was so much we talked about, but it all boiled down to "be love, give love, receive love." Yeshua said that nothing else mattered. In terms of resolving my perfect storm of stress, Yeshua and James told me that the crisis afforded me a chance to learn how to transmute fear into clarity, and thus open to learning from the crisis all its large and subtle manifestations. They said that learning to make this shift was all I needed to do to bring myself through the crisis safe, healed and whole. They taught me that in letting go of my fears and doubts, it was very important to recognize that although I didn't want to be dominated by fear or negative concepts of the future, it was important to understand that these painful waves of emotion that passed through me were valid and needed to be acknowledged. When resisted they touched other trigger points, feeding new fears and doubts, but when embraced they washed through restoring clarity. I followed their prescription. I let go of fear in this way and I went about my day loving the world and my life as much as I possibly could. The surgery was a complete success, sparing me a life of disability - and I even got my job back. One might call it a miracle. I do.

Yeshua urged me, as he does you in this book, to call upon him, and not to worry about achieving some kind of clairvoyance to find him. He encouraged me to have faith that when I called, he would be there and would give on whatever level I was able and willing to receive. I've done so for the past thirty years and I can say, unequivocally, he has never failed to respond to my call for help.

Preface

by Kaarin Alisa

When I was a little girl and the pain of life was overwhelming, I'd lie in bed at night and weep. My childhood wasn't easy. Even at the young age of eight I remember thinking how much better it would be if my life was over, if I could just die.

In those dark moments, with the demons dancing 'round my bed, a familiar man would come and sit with me in my sorrow. His warm and unusually tender hand would stroke my hair and he spoke to me in a soft, deep voice, wrought with love and a hint of grief.

He told me his name was Yeshua; that other people called him Jesus, but that I could call him by his familiar name, Yeshua. He always made me feel better, by his touch and by his tone; he told me of the days to come when I would have much work to do in the world. And that this life I had such a difficult time embracing, was to be filled with adventures. He promised he would always be with me, whether or not I could see him, and that all I need do was call his name.

Sometimes he'd sing a small tune, other times tell a short story, but it was his tenderness and constancy that saved me. He never asked anything of me. Rather he gave without regard for payment of any kind. He seemed always to light-up when I calmed down, as if his reward was to see my pain ease.

I never questioned why he was there. I took it on faith that he was with me, like a guardian angel. I never wanted for his presence – when I needed it he was magically by my side.

They were dark, yet they were simple days. I don't miss the pain of them, but even now, I can remember the comfort, the joy of being in his presence in such an innocent way. I didn't question, I didn't falsify, I merely accepted. And it was to prove to be the beginning of a relationship of love that has served me through these many long and varied years. Even the times I egoistically denied his presence, he never left, understanding that I would again one day remember and welcome his loving company.

This book is about this man called Yeshua, this man of love and constancy. It is the story of his life as he has relayed it to me. Ultimately, it is about who he is to all of us. It's about the incredible journey of a man that holds this entire universe in his grace and has never given up on us.

This is his story and it's an honor to be able to help him tell it.

Preface

by Yeshua son of Joseph

My name is Yeshua, though you might call me Jesus. I was born in Galilee over 2000 years ago by your calendar. I was born from the womb of Mariam, whom you might call Mary; raised by the loving and wise hands of her and Yosef, my adopted father, whom you might call Joseph.

Born into the royal family David of antiquity, I was raised with a measure of comfort. Also born into a Nazorean community, a splinter of the Essene, a then accepted sect of Judaism, I was raised with great attention to my spiritual attainment.

Most importantly to this story is the very real, very human life I led that took me from a knowledge-starved boy, to an eastern adept, to a leader of my people in thirty short years. It is the humanity of my story I wish to share with you. The joys, the pains, the triumphs and the pitfalls, all of which I very humanly lived. It has been a full and rich life.

If I could choose only one word to describe my childhood, it would be the word blessed. Not because every drop of time was happy, but because the immense blessings of love, health, and happiness overrode the brevity of every pain, bruise, or shame. I was blessed beyond measure, from the moment I slipped from my mother's womb, until the day I came of age.

Most likely, right now, you live in an automated, mechanized, and digitized world. Whether you were born in a hospital, a birthing center, or a home, you no doubt came from your mother into a world quickly filled with chemical smells and artificial light. You framed your young days by one or more artifices that may have included:

- dreading the long number of hours you spent with a surrogate instead of a parent, or perhaps the opposite,
- fearing the number of days until you had to again visit a doctor who prodded you, then stuck you with a long, painful needle,
- wondering what time the alarm by your parent's bed would abruptly sound and he or she would force you into action,
- counting the years until you were old enough to sit without a car-seat, then sit in the front seat, then finally sit in the driver's seat,
- tapping out the minutes until one class ended and, like it or not, you had to attend another class,
- anxiously awaiting your favorite show on television, or the latest summer blockbuster to be released,
- stressing about when the spinning 'wait' icon on your screen was going to stop spinning,

+ and plodding through the many more reports to complete, meals to serve, boxes to stack, or emails to answer before the weekend saved you.

Blessed was I, I had none of these.

The measurements of time have played a huge part in your life, and because of this fact, time took on a hyper-dimensional quality. It became a static and ever increasingly unkind overseer that, by the time you were a functioning adult, you spent at least half of your life yearning for the clock to speed-up, slow-down, or stop; in any case, your focus was on that devil time. Now, you may be plagued by the desire to retire, move to a grass hut on a tropical isle, or find some other way to run away from that cruel host time.

If you've been lucky, you found your way to a sanctuary, an internal process or external practice that reframed your days to include a small measure of 'timeless' interaction, hopefully with yourself first, and with nature and others second. But for you, that sanctuary was not guaranteed.

If you've not been lucky, you may have immersed yourself in a less optimal way of running from time; drugs, alcohol, sex, gambling, eating, spending, or incapacity wrought by any other of the myriad of excesses that nurture unconsciousness. Unfortunately, these excesses, when they are excesses and not occasional distractions, only work to give time an even greater capacity to oppress you. Any of these excesses bring the insufficiency of time to a head as you plunge toward death and have to start the cycle over again hoping that next time, next life, you find that bit of sanctuary.

Modern life isn't easy. You have washing machines and computers, refrigerators and televisions, but with that oppression of time bearing in on your life, what ultimate good do they really serve?

Blessed was I, for through my youth, time was not an oppressor, it was barely noticed. In my youth, I:

+ knew my parents intimately and respected them immensely,
+ ate healthful, whole food that was grown within a short distance from my table,
+ had good health that was naturally persistent,
+ was an integral part of the seamless weave of nature around me,
+ woke each day with the sun and happily sprung from my bed to run to my morning devotions,
+ never yearned for the responsibilities of adulthood to come faster, because when I was ready for them they naturally went into effect,
+ studied subjects I was passionate about, so every teaching was welcomed and lasted until I was ready for the next,
+ had no artificial means of entertaining myself, so entertainment came each day and evening, from moments of discovery, hours with my own thoughts, or warm and joyful interactions with people I loved and who loved me,
+ and I welcomed the Sabbath every week, as it came without fail, regardless of what I had or had not accomplished, and nothing, ever, got in its joyous way.

Blessed was I.

I had other blessings as well. Some of these may be more familiar to you as blessings:

- my family owned land and resources, enough to be self-sufficient,
- I lived in a community of like-minded people; all of whom subscribed to peace as an overriding principle of life,
- I had siblings that loved me and helped me learn some important lessons of childhood, like overcoming greed and jealousy and embracing sharing, tutelage, and the good of working for a common goal,
- and, even when danger was present, I knew beyond a shadow of a doubt, that if they could, my parents, my family, and every member of my community would ensure my safety, as I would theirs.

Blessed was I.

I spent my youth in this framework. These were the blessings that molded me, that propelled me into adulthood. To be sure, not everyone in Galilee was as blessed as I. Most children, if they were fortunate enough to have a family, had many of these blessings, and few or none of the oppressive time pressures you in the modern age experience.

We did have an oppressor though, and he came with a big boot and a sharp spear. His name was Rome and he was to be feared. Anyone able to read or go to the movies, probably already has an idea of how oppressive Rome was to many people, not just my own. And it didn't matter which tyrant was in power, or which de-facto prefect or king governed locally, the Roman boot was ever-present and his greedy hand was outstretched, grabbing what it could, always with the threat of death at the end of his fingers.

As I describe my life in this book, take into account the differences I have just outlined. These differences created a framework that made life different at the turn of the millennium into the Common Era.

Along with the differences, it's also important to understand the commonalities. We weren't devoid of technology, and we weren't primitive. We had the same magnificent brains and hearts that you have; time has done little to change that over these few thousand years.

And right now you, by virtue of being in these pages, are in my life. You are integral to the weave of me. You are a welcome part of my current framework. How very blessed am I.

If you come to this story not knowing much of me, I promise you a tale of a life well lived and filled with adventure, drama, and mystery.

If you come to this story filled with dogma that you believe is knowledge of me, and my life, you may wish to stem your own tide of disbelief until the tale has been fully woven for you. The truth of my life, as it formed by the beating of my very human heart, will be unfamiliar to you. The revealing of my life as it truly happened may even anger you if you are unable or unwilling to set aside your preconceived notions of me. Yet I assure you, that which is set in these pages is the truth to the best of my memory.

This is not the first written work I've put together for you. But it is one of the newest. In giving you the truth about my life, I hope many more people will find me, where I am now, fully living and able to accept a relationship with each and every one who desires it. If you desire to know me, you need but ask. Reach out and extend your hand; I will meet it with my own.

You can find me, with or without a religion, a prophet, or a dogma. Throughout the ages, some people have found me through those means, but no religion or particular viewpoint is necessary to find me or to know me. You can find me right here, wrapped lovingly around your life awaiting your heart to connect with mine. It is an invitation that requires nothing of you but an intention to engage with me. I will never ask you to change. You need never change a thought floating in your head, a belief written on your heart, or set aside any part of your current life for me to accept you. Your intention, your willingness to know me is all that matters. And through relationship with me, by the acceptance of the love I will make known to you, you may change, but if so it will be an organic change that stems from within you as a response to our closeness and the love you accept from me.

I turn away no one, and yet you may turn away from me, now or at any time. Your own beauty of being and spiritual divinity does not depend upon any relationship with me. But if you are struggling with life, unable to find peace or happiness, or if you are committed to walking a road to spiritual attainment, I can offer a sounding board, a roadmap, or a healing touch from my embrace. Let my words touch you, human heart to human heart.

This story is written in collaboration with Kaarin Alisa. I trust Kaarin. We have been in a relationship since she was a child. I have asked her many times to help me present this material; it is only now that she has agreed to this project.

Kaarin is dear to me. She's an old friend with an exceptional spiritual clarity, vision, and a genuine lightness of heart. Her very human life of trials and triumphs has led her to a passion and willingness to serve all of humanity. This willingness has also brought her to the ability to hear my words with very little filter.

Kaarin is also integral to the story you now read. She has word-crafted my anecdotes with care. Throughout this book, concurrent with my life story, she will also present to you information that was derived from her discussions with other beings now in spiritual form that were present during the physical phase of my lifetime.

In all these accounts, narratives, and discussions, I have been an integral part of the collaboration and I affirm the authenticity and truth of that which is included herein.

May your life journey be furthered toward your own desired goals by venturing into this book.

I love you.

Yeshua son of Joseph from Galilee

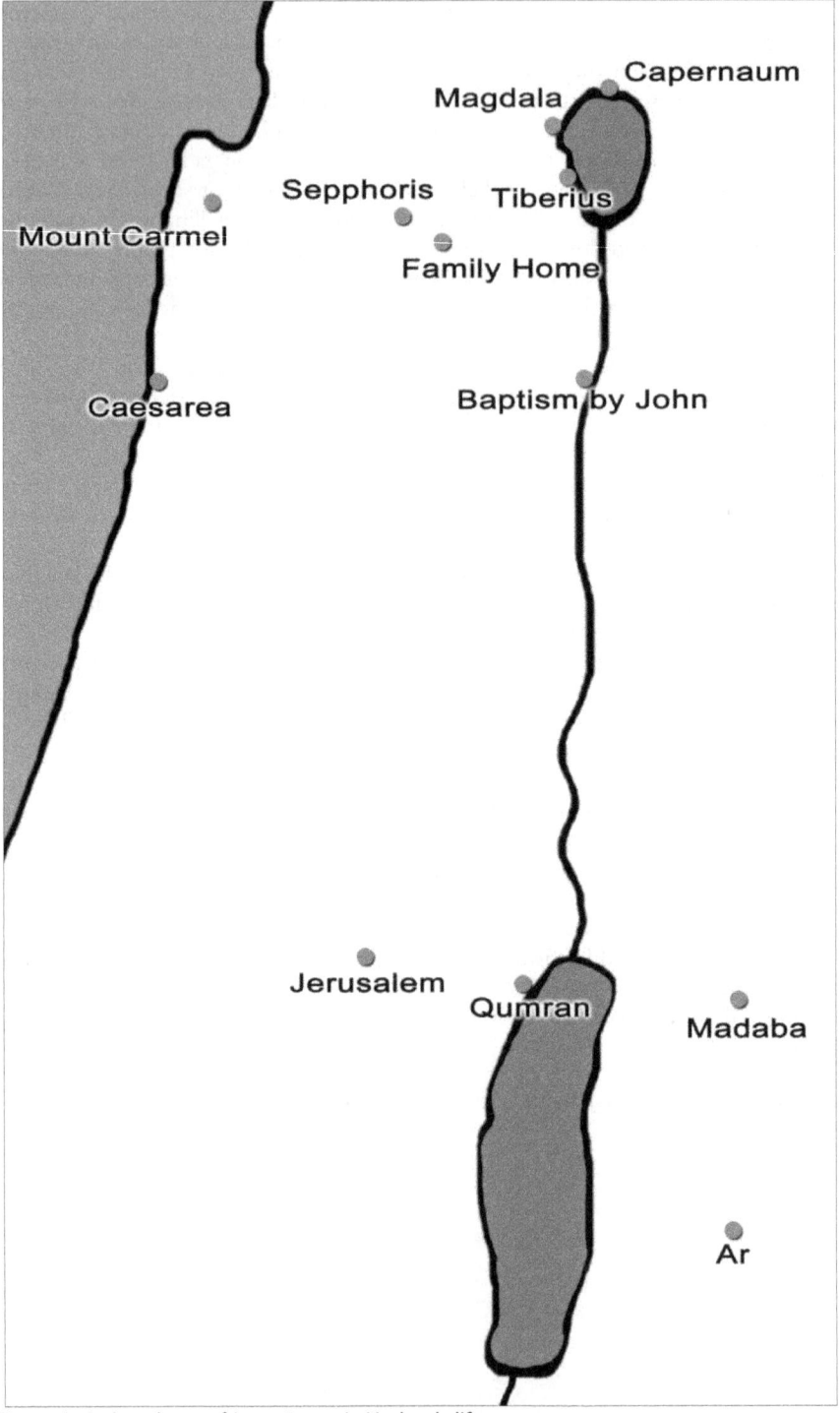

Figure 1: Judea places of importance in Yeshua's life

Childhood

1 · My Rocking Chair

If I want for solace, I come here, to my rocking chair. Its simple construct, with gentle curves and well-worn armrests, envelopes me. This embrace mimics his embrace and he, of course, is my father, my Joseph. In the gentle support of the wood, I find strength, courage, and healing; all of which I need in regular and abundant doses.

I wish I could bring you here to my home where wounds are immediately salved, grief is replaced with joy, and love rules without contest. Many conspired to bring me here and it started a long time before I was born. Walking the path that enabled my life required courage and sacrifice from countless people. To each soul, I'm grateful.

But none more so than Joseph. He's been marginalized in the annals of time; his perceived role reduced to that of a foster father who provided food and shelter, a mere smidgen of his true contribution. I had only fourteen short years to learn from him, to soak in his wisdom and his love. But that wisdom, that love, molded me more than all that came after. He was a leader, and as such a true follower. He led our people, our family, and he followed the call of our needs with his heart and soul born of reason and compassion. Many teachers followed, and many experiences disciplined me, but of them all, Joseph was the finest. His lessons were basic and to this day, I call on them often: love without compromise, protect what is sacred, accept responsibility for your actions, contribute to life with goodness, and embrace that which is divine; in nature, in others, and in yourself.

Joseph's gentle manner was commanding. When he spoke, people listened. He chose his words carefully, as if like Torah, each word conveyed intrinsic value. But more than that, the cadence touched your ear in a way that made you want to listen more carefully.

As each day begins anew, I start my communion with my Creator in the same way. I ask to be humble enough to see my mistakes and courageous enough to correct them. This I learned from Joseph, too.

Then, of course, there's my mother, Mary, who shouldn't be forgotten, not that anyone could. She was unforgettable. Mary wore her soul like most women wear clothes. She oozed love; not sappy love, but unconditional love channeled straight from her Creator. She was tough when needed, strong when circumstances required, and focused like a laser when her mind was set.

She was a woman of few words, knowing her actions spoke more eloquently than her voice ever could. She was educated, poised, and resolute. As her son, her

"We derive our strength from divine love. Our community breaks only if we disregard one member for the fear of our own skin. The Way of Peace teaches that we stand together or we don't stand at all."

- Mary mother of Yeshua -

first-born, I never saw her faith falter. Not even during or following the time of my physical persecution was she anything other than a pillar of strength and divine acceptance.

She was however, deeply affected by circumstances. Never did a tear flow that didn't prompt her compassion. Never did a wound bleed that she didn't reach to soothe. And never did a loved one die that her heart didn't burn to ash and have to find a way to rise like a phoenix to continue to the next day.

These two remarkable people were my parents.

And there were others, family and community members I remember with great love: uncles, aunts, cousins, community elders, farmhands, workers, and friends of all sorts. It was a rich community of people around me, but who was I to them? I don't know. I could recount what they said, or how they acted in my presence, but I don't recall anyone sitting me down and telling me what they thought of me.

I was obviously different from other children. I was taller than other boys, and highly precocious.

When I turned two, my parents made a change to the sleeping arrangements of our home. Where there had been separate beds and a cradle in my parent's room, now there was only one bed, and instead of sleeping in the cradle, I was moved to another room.

The family grew rapidly after that. Before I was three James was born, and by five, Ruth joined us. Jude came the year after that and Sarah was born two years later.

Little Shelah, small and fragile, was born two years after Sarah. Unfortunately, her health never held strong and she died before her majority, after I left home for my studies in the east.

All these siblings made for a lively household. The sound of children seemed ever-present. There was always someone with whom to share an adventure, or to tease, or to discover a truth about life. Sometimes those truths came with laughter, sometimes with tears, but always with love.

When I was three, my only living grandparent, Anne, died. I fondly remember her face. Wrinkled and filled with solemnity most of the time, my heart burst with joy when, upon seeing me, her eyes lit and her mouth unfolded into a wide smile. She loved me and I her.

My brother James was my fondest companion. I never made a better friend. He was intelligent, but being two years younger, he could never catch up. It started a competition that lasted until I left home. He was vigilant to do me one better if he could. Truthfully, there were plenty of things James did better than I. If he'd spent more time uplifting his own talents, than trying to outdo mine, he would've had a smoother childhood.

Like me, he was taller than most children. Years later, when I came home from my wanderings, James stood nearly as tall as I and looked very similar in appearance. Some might've said we were twins the resemblance was so strong. As a child, the resemblance seemed normal; however, as an adult, I found it unusual. I knew by then that I wasn't a product of my mother and father's genetics, but James supposedly was, and I couldn't figure out how he came out looking so much like me instead of more like our other brother, or Joseph's sons from his first family.

Unable to hold myself back from the things I loved, I devoured the wise books of my ancestors. I needed knowledge. My mind took it in like dry sand takes in water. My curiosity about the world was so strong that even the field workers grew weary of my questions. I wanted to know how everything worked. The why of it all was my ever-present quest.

But as quick and agile as my mind was, my hands were less agile. I could do most anything I set my mind to, but when it came to mundane tasks, the results of my efforts were often mediocre. I could build a beautiful chair, but it might wobble. I could prune a tree, but I might take twice as long as someone else. I could sweep the floor, but often, poor Josea, our cook, housekeeper, and wife of Herodes our trusted foreman, would regret asking for my help, because she would have to sweep again nearly right away.

My brain may have functioned in some way that in your modern time would be a diagnosable disorder, I can't say, but the fact remained that when it came to learning and using my mind, I excelled; and when it came to doing the mundane, I didn't.

All in all, my unquenchable thirst for knowledge was exactly to plan.

2 · Present Danger

For the most part, life was pleasant around our community. But even as early as three or four, I understood there were dangers that could confront us at any moment.

The main part of our property was surrounded by a stone wall. There were two gates in the wall where traffic could pass. The northwestern gate was used only when heavy goods were being transported by cart. Otherwise, we kept it fortified. The southern gate was the main entrance, with a road through it that wound up the hill to the porch of our house. Construction was being done close to that road on new homes and buildings needed to run the farm efficiently. Normally, the gate was open and people passed through as needed without question.

But from time to time, Joseph would post men there and at watch stations around the property. When this happened, fear was palpable and children were admonished to stay near or inside the buildings. I was too young to understand the full ramifications of it all.

When I was five, I had the misfortune of witnessing the horrifying effects of this danger for the first time. James was a toddler and Mary was pregnant with Ruth.

It began at morning meal. A rider came, excited and out of breath. Joseph immediately called the community together. All work stopped and I was sheltered inside the gathering room of our home with Mary and several other women and children. Men were dispatched to fortify the gates, while others rode away on horseback.

After a time, friends who lived outside the walls were escorted up the hill and sequestered into the buildings. As soon as this was accomplished, a hush fell over the community. The adults seemed consumed with worry. When I questioned Mary, she told me not to worry, that we were people of peace and that God would watch after us.

Over the next few hours, people around me periodically lowered their heads in prayer. But no one spoke; the quiet remained. Even the children, who would normally squirm with the desire to run and play, cowered under the cloaking arms of the adults. We were afraid, but we didn't know of what.

A commotion began. Through the big windows I saw down the hill. A large party of men on horses came to the gate. They were dressed strangely, in short costumes that glinted in the sun, unlike anything I'd ever seen. Our neighbors at the gate tried to prevent their entrance, but they pointed sharp-bladed poles at them. After a few moments, the gate opened. Soon, I would come to understand these poles for what they were; terrible instruments of destruction.

The strange men came up the hill. Mary shook as she held James and me tightly to her side, tears dripping down her cheeks.

Two men dismounted and spoke with Joseph. Their voices got loud and their manner animated. As they talked, several others dismounted and brandished their spears at Joseph and Herodes. Mary gasped and I heard Joseph say in a clear voice, "Please, we're people of peace. I'll work with you. We'll comply with the law."

The man in charge waved at his men to pull back their spears. They gestured toward the houses and menaced Joseph. Joseph nodded at Herodes and he walked to his house with two strangers and asked a friend to come out. I knew the man. His name was Jacob and I liked him. He often came up the hill to help Herodes work the fields. He had a wife and two children. As he came forward, one of the strangers grabbed Jacob by the arm and flung him to the dirt.

Joseph stepped forward, "Please, calm yourselves. I'm sure we can clear this up without violence." The man in charge raised his hand to Joseph and I thought he was going to strike him, but he stopped when Joseph stood unguarded and without flinching.

Jacob's wife tried to run to him. Herodes stopped her as the strangers paced back and forth in front of Jacob, peppering him with questions.

Jacob answered their questions, but I could feel his fear. His eyes got big and his head shook back and forth, fervently denying something. I heard Joseph shout, "Please, Officer! He says he didn't do this! Surely we can listen to his story with an open mind!"

Instead, the officer raised his arm in the air. He shouted something in a strange language and let his arm fall quickly to his side. As he did, two men lunged forward and thrust their weapons through Jacob's chest. I saw a heavy stream of blood spurt from him. Jacob's wife screamed and a jolt of electric fear shot through my spine. The strangers extracted their spears with a violent shaking motion that caused Jacob's body to bob about like a rag and fall to the side, lifeless. Joseph fell to his knees, arms wrapped around his heaving chest, gasping for breath.

Herodes let go and Jacob's wife ran to cradle her now motionless husband. Her cries were loud as a trail of bright red blood flowed from Jacob down the road like water from a spring.

Joseph picked himself up in a deliberate fashion. The man in charge strutted slowly in a circle, his hands clasped behind his back, a perverse smile on his lips. He leaned into each face present and peered toward every building. I swear his eyes met mine through the window.

He motioned for the others to mount up, as he came close to Joseph, shouting into his face, and made a sideways chop with his hand that I interpreted to mean 'it's done.' He mounted and they all rode away.

When the strangers cleared the gate, Joseph knelt with Jacob's wife. He wrapped his arms around her and wept over Jacob's body for a long time.

It was my first encounter with those who were called Romans, and if I was a different person, one who couldn't, or wouldn't learn to live the way of peace, my heart would've been blackened on that day. It's the reason why, even though I didn't usually agree with the actions of the rebel Zealots, I always understood their position.

"Taken individually, Romans might've been good people... but banded together under the cloak of their Emperor, they became lustful savages with no regard for life."

- James brother of Yeshua -

3 · Bit of Love

In my first years, as I learned to navigate the world, I was followed and counseled by beings who had no physical form. If I was ever alone, without my parents, or in need, they came to my aide with suggestions and messages of wisdom and love. They gave me no name, so the 'Unseen' stuck as their name in my personal lexicon.

Other people couldn't see or hear them. As far as I could tell, they made no audible sound, and yet I heard them through some mechanism in my brain other than my ears. And in many ways, it's a good thing others couldn't hear them, because the comments they made were often sarcastic and embarrassing. They teased me like my family did.

There were usually three of them. One was rather normal looking, an elderly man with a long beard and staff, but the other two were odder. Of them, one stood about four feet tall and had a long, curved neck. The other was only a few feet tall and had a habit of floating around me like a bee around a flower. They were my companions. Their oddities didn't faze me; it was part of my normal.

Children chided me if I forgot and mentioned something one of the Unseen did or said. Joseph patiently helped me learn to accept this part of my life. I was different from other children in many ways, and this was just one of those differences.

It's hard to be different, especially when you're young. Often, people fear differences, and children can be cruel with their teasing. I usually didn't take hurt from it. I credit Joseph for that. He spent hours working with me, to help me understand that my differences were purposeful and blessed. I had a mission in life that only my continued growing and learning would uncover. To Joseph's credit, he did the same with each of his children. He knew, as I came to know, that we each have a special place in the weave of life. To uncover and bring to fruition that mysterious passion is a magnificent journey best nurtured.

Sometimes I heard other adults speak to Joseph about me and they used the term 'Great Teacher.' When I began my formal schooling in the sacred texts, that term resurfaced. I couldn't relate to it. I couldn't fathom being spoken about in the texts of my ancestors. It seemed fanciful and preposterous even to entertain the idea.

When I asked Joseph what someone meant by calling me that, Joseph said I should always follow my own counsel and that of the Unseen around me. That I was the best judge of my place in life's passion. But even when he said that, and he said it often, I sensed he was holding back.

Early on, I studied the Hebrew texts, as well as texts from a different religion,

"Looking to his side at something I couldn't see, his eyes twinkled... he was obviously not alone."

- James son of Zebedee -

an older religion called Bon. My community was Essene, an established sect of the Jewish religion, but we were also Nazorean. In the language of the teachings that term meant, 'the devoted ones who went west.' It was a term brought from the east, and given to us through these Bon texts. At one time, people all through the continent and beyond adopted early Bon tenets, and I understood that many people still revered the Bon principles, though they lived a great distance from us.

These Bon texts taught that the first Great Teacher walked on earth over 35,000 years before me. He arrived already a man from a realm outside our earth plane. He stayed on this earth for many years and after he decided to go home, the philosophies he espoused became the Bon religion. Reportedly, he also left behind writings that his devotees eventually codified as the first Vedic texts. The Great Teacher vowed that he would return as a child one day and continue the teachings.

The Nazorean Essene always believed they were the chosen few who would make a safe place for the Great Teacher to begin his new life. And here I was, being called the Great Teacher, born a Nazorean, with invisible people following me around. Yes, I was different, but I wasn't willing to accept prophecy as law for my life. I was intelligent, talented, blessed with gifts others didn't possess, and too in love with the freedom I felt to let prophecy define me.

Later, when I was twelve and settled enough for rabbinical study, I unilaterally tossed aside the prophecies that inferred I was special. I accepted my differences as cherished gifts to further my own desires, not someone else's. Instead, I threw myself into my studies, and yet people around me couldn't help but notice that I was driven by a passion to learn.

It was around the age of seven that I began talking to James about the Unseen. He was barely five, just beginning to read, but he was fascinated by their antics.

The common language spoken around my community was Aramaic and the Unseen communicated with me in that language. An ancient form of Aramaic was also the language of the Bon texts I studied. The next language I learned was Hebrew, so I could study Torah along with its sacred commentary, and converse about it with the elders. I also learned Hieratic in written form, so I could study sacred texts of Egypt.

The Unseen had a name for me though, that was separate from my name Yeshua. They called me by a common Aramaic word that in English sounds much like the word bit. The word had several meanings, depending upon how one used it in speech, adding simple sounds and inflections to the word. The way the Unseen said the word it roughly meant 'promised steward.'

One day I told James about their name for me. Since he was learning how to read, I thought he would find it interesting, but he laughed too loud and too long. You see, the most common use of the word bit was 'house.' He carried on about me being called a house. He made joke after joke about it. He'd come up behind me, pull up my robe, and say he was looking for the bedroom. Or he'd step on my foot and ask if I'd swept the floor. It continued like this for days. Then he got it in his head to reverse the letters. Unfortunately, the reversal of 'bit' is roughly 'tab,' which meant 'vomit.' That prompted a whole string of pranks such as holding his nose around me as if I stank. He was relentless.

Finally, I had enough of the pranks and I went to Joseph. "How can I get him to stop?"

Joseph looked at me with a twinkle in his eye. He chuckled and said, "Why do you worry so about his pranks?"

"They make me feel small," I said quickly.

"Ah," Joseph nodded his head, "and you think it's your brother making you feel small?"

"Well…" I was about to blurt, yes, but I realized I'd better think about his question before I answer. I could tell he was prompting me to reconsider my thoughts. So I sat pondering the question and after some ruminating, I decided that my initial reaction was correct. So I said, "Yes. I do think he's making me feel small."

"I'm pleased that you thought about your answer before you spoke, however," he put his hand on my shoulder, "if I were you I'd look closer to home for the culprit." He chuckled and went about his business.

What could that mean? I was the only thing closer to home to me than my brother. I thought, 'I make me feel small?'

———✹———

A few days later James was again deep into his antics, snorting when he was near and making fake vomiting noises. It dawned on me that I didn't need to shrink from his noise; I could join it. So I said, "You better be careful, because when I vomit, I really blow!" I opened my mouth and mimed as if to vomit in his direction.

He squealed with delight and ran to hide. I hadn't expected this turn. I found him hiding behind the back cistern and pretend vomited all over him. He squeaked and laughed like a tickled baby as we tumbled on the ground.

To my surprise, it stopped. James got what he wanted and never teased me about my Unseen name again. In fact, several months later, he began to use it and it became his lifelong preferred name for me. It was, and still is, an in-joke for us that means absolute brotherhood.

"There will always be more of yourself to find than the judging part of yourself will see."

- James brother of Yeshua -

4 · There Were Others

The Unseen weren't the only odd beings I interacted with as a child. Shortly after my eighth birthday, I met someone even odder.

Joseph asked if we could go for a walk. I was delighted. Just us, out for a walk, was a rare treat. We walked into the back acreage and talked as we strolled. The grain was tall and beginning to turn color into that radiant gold it displays just before it gives over its fruit.

Mary was pregnant again and he asked if I had any questions about that. I wasn't ignorant about these things. When you live around farm animals, you see the cycle of procreation and birth up close. Joseph and I already had conversations about it and I understood that unlike animals, these matters were personal, even sacred to people.

"Only one question right now," I said.

"And?" He placed his hand on my back as we walked.

"Will it be another brother?"

Joseph chuckled, "Well, that's something I can't know until the child is born."

This answer perplexed me, "But you told me once you knew I'd be a boy before I was born. Why did you know with me and can't know now?"

Joseph stopped walking and looked down at me. "That's a great question."

I smiled, considering it a compliment.

"Perhaps your question is a good way for me to introduce the reason I asked you out here today." He placed his hand on my head. "There's someone I'd like you to meet."

I looked at him. "Meet? Out here?"

"Yes, out here. Only a few people ever get to meet this person. Do you see that tree over there?" He pointed to a majestic oak tree standing in the field.

"Yes, I see it."

"Well, someone is waiting beneath that tree. He's an old friend of mine and will become a trusted friend of yours, in time."

I couldn't see anyone. The tree looked as empty of people as our entire walk had been. "There's no one there," I said.

"Ah, well, your eyes deceive you."

I looked again and still I saw no one. "I'm confused," I confessed as I strained to see what I was missing.

"Yes, of course you're confused. Don't strain your eyes. You won't be able to see him yet. We have to talk first."

I stared toward the oak; my mind looking for anything to help me see what Joseph could see and I couldn't.

"Yeshua, listen to me."

I pulled my attention from the tree and back to Joseph.

"Before you were born," he said, "I met this very special person. He helped me understand that it was my honor and privilege to marry your mother." Joseph's attention was laser focused. "He's also the one who told me you'd be a boy. At first this person frightened me, but in time I came to understand he was one of the most important allies I could possibly have."

"Why did he frighten you?"

"Well, frankly, because he's different."

I thought about that for a moment, "What's wrong with him?"

Joseph laughed, "There's nothing wrong with him, it's what was wrong with me."

I gave Joseph a strange look, so he knelt to be at eye level with me. He put his hands on my arms, "Now listen to me very carefully. This being is not entirely like us. But he's kind and intelligent and works diligently on our behalf. He's our ally and my friend."

Now, he'd really caught my attention, "Is he like the Unseen?"

"No. He has a body, but he has ways about him that are different. Like right now, he can remain invisible if he wishes it."

"So, if he wants me to see him, then I can?"

"Yes, my boy, that's correct."

I was filling with excitement, "And I get to meet him now?"

Joseph nodded, "That is, if you think you can. It may take all your strength to walk past your fear when you see him. Do you think you can do that?"

"Father!" I cried, "Remember the Unseen? They're very strange!" I mimicked the little one flying around me like a bee.

Joseph laughed, "Well, perhaps your experience has prepared you better than I was prepared when I met him." He stood, "His name is Philar."

"Philar?"

"Yes, Philar. Are you ready?"

I took a deep breath. I could barely hold my composure, "Yes!"

We walked to the tree and Joseph said, "Philar, Yeshua is ready to meet you."

Suddenly I saw him sitting on a rock. He was different looking. The differences weren't subtle, but neither were they grotesque. He had no hair, and his neck was thick, but his eyes radiated intelligence and compassion.

"Hello, Yeshua," he said, "how're you today?"

I stepped back and gasped. "You can talk!"

"Yes, we're a little different from one another, but I have a mind and a soul just like you."

I moved in closer, looked him all over, and held out my hand, "Nice to meet you."

Philar returned my handshake. I was surprised his hand was warm and his grip solid. My insides churned. I was frightened, and excited, but I didn't want it to show, so when my body started shaking I tried to ignore it. Joseph could see it, though. He put his hand on my back, "It's alright, Yeshua, if you're frightened. It's a natural reaction."

"I'm not frightened," I insisted.

Philar looked at Joseph and I could tell he was holding back a chuckle. He

"I had another visit last night. My angel came with news. He says I'll be with child soon."

- Mary mother of Yeshua -

looked at me with love in his eyes, "It's a pleasure to meet you face to face. I've only seen you at a distance before this."

"You've seen me before?"

"Yes, I've watched your growth with great interest."

"Why?" I blurted.

"Because you're the reason I'm here."

"Why me?"

Philar took a deep breath and let it out with a sigh. It sounded like the muffled rattle of a carrion bird. "I'm a friend of your family," he said, "I hope to become your friend, too." I noted that his answer evaded my question. Like Joseph, he was holding back things he didn't want to say. He continued, "I'm not from here, as you can probably tell."

"Where do you live?"

"Right now I live here, but I'm not from here originally."

"I've read about angels," I said as my mind tried to find a way to pigeonhole Philar, "are you an angel?"

"You could call me an angel if you like," Philar answered, "many have."

"But why? You talk like a human. Why aren't you human?"

He smiled, "Because my parents weren't human."

That made me laugh and I relaxed. I leaned against Philar's leg, "I like you." Philar tipped his head and the muscles around his neck flexed and bulged. I asked, "Why am I meeting you?"

He looked me directly in the eye and said, "Because I'm going to help you."

"Help me how?" I quickly asked.

"Help you live your life well."

I looked at Joseph, "Joseph does that." Joseph smiled.

Philar continued, "But Joseph can't be with you always."

I frowned when I heard this. My head whipped around to Philar again, "What do you mean?"

"I mean that I and my friends are here to help you and we'll be able to follow you wherever you go, for the rest of your life. Joseph may not be able to do that, he has other responsibilities." I stepped away from Philar and fumbled for Joseph's hand.

"It's alright, my boy," Joseph said, "I'm not going anywhere."

Philar said, "Yeshua, I'm your friend. I'm here so we can get to know one another."

I squeaked out, "Alright."

"Maybe that's enough for today, Philar," Joseph said as he pulled me close.

"Perhaps you're right," Philar said as he stood. He was tall, at least a full forearms length taller than Joseph. He said, "Thank you for meeting me today, Yeshua. We'll meet again soon. Goodbye," and he disappeared.

I gasped. Joseph wrapped his arms around me, "I'm proud of you, Son, you handled that well."

I looked around to see if I could discern his presence. "He's still here, isn't

"They're not like us, Joseph. They are legions not of this earth."
- Jacob, Essene Elder -

he?"

"He may be… he may be," he said patting my shoulder, "and I suppose of all of it, that's the hardest to get used to. He or his friends may appear at any time, and you'll have no warning that they're near before they do." I shuddered with understanding as we turned and began our slow walk home.

"One more thing," Joseph added as we walked, "this is our secret. Most people don't experience life the way you do. The Divine Creator reveals his magnificent diversity of creation only to those he selects, not to everyone. You must promise to tell no one. Not even James, or Mary. Do you understand?"

It was unsettling, but I said, "Yes, I understand," and as I looked across the field, I had the feeling that a big change had just come into my life; a change that was inevitable and made me feel sad, though I didn't know why.

5 · Power of a Frog

Each morning I bounced from bed with joy, curiosity, and wonder. I'd sprint to the creek for morning baptism. We were lucky to have a spring-fed creek on our property. Many people didn't. But, baptism could be easily managed from collection cisterns, and here in our community, many adults only used cistern water as it was warmer and easier to access.

Morning baptism was unique to the Essene. In Galilee, people lived according to the requirements of their situation and station. Most farmers, herders, artisans and their families didn't cleanse their bodies every day. And when they did, it was less thorough than your modern methods of bathing, using no, or nearly no cleansing agents, like soap. Soap and other luxuries were just that; expensive luxuries. Outside the Essene community, among those with access to fresh water, once a week or so seemed to be normal. For those without regular access to fresh water, even once a month might be difficult to manage.

But as an Essene, morning baptism was about consecrating one's life to the Holy Spirit; an imperative every day. It's how we kept our moral and spiritual principles ever-present. If water wasn't available, there were special prayers and procedures to sustain consecration until it was.

Baptism was a ritual. One's body might be relatively clean after the ritual, but the ritual itself had little to do with what you would call cleanliness. Any cleanliness of the body arose as a side effect, if you will, from the desire for the body to remain an appropriate vessel for spiritual attainment. And the key to that was the proper use of the mind.

Every morning we stripped our minds of their troubles. We gave our thoughts to the Holy Spirit and asked for forgiveness of our failings. We confessed to our Creator whatever we did that was unholy and readied ourselves to greet each day with integrity of spirit and action. We didn't always succeed, but each day was a new opportunity to transform.

Part of morning baptism was silence. From the moment we rose we didn't speak until our baptism was complete. This helped mold me into a contemplative person and this propensity has served me immensely. Necessity sometimes caused morning silence to be disturbed, but intention was at the heart of it. Maintaining silence was one of my favorite parts of the routine.

But not so for James. He hated morning silence. One day, James seemed particularly bent on disturbing my silence. He set about breathing in my ear, with a hot, moist breath that tickled.

I tried to ignore him and was somewhat successful. He tried tickling the back

"Yeshua is fully expressed life in humility... he is compassion connected through humanity like the roots of a great tree."

- Miriam wife of Yeshua -

of my neck with a plant stalk. When that didn't work, he flicked water at my face. I continued to ignore him as best I could and he stopped. I naively assumed he went about his business. A few minutes later though, he grabbed the neck of my robe and slipped a frog down my back. The slimy wriggling of the frog caused me to jump up and shout. I danced in the creek trying to get the frog to drop. Unfortunately, the frog caught in my underclothes, and it wouldn't drop no matter how I gyrated.

I was livid. A string of slanders at James came pouring from my mouth. As I whirled around, I saw Mary standing on the bank just a few feet from me. This last twist caused the frog to loose itself and drop into the water.

"What are you doing?" Mary said in a stern tone that I was all too familiar with; a tone that meant I was in trouble.

"It's James! He dropped a…"

"I don't care what James did or didn't do!" Mary waggled her finger in my direction, "Keeping silence is your responsibility. It's not your brother's fault if you can't control yourself."

"But you didn't see the…"

"Yeshu'men'horah!" she barked, using a name she called me when she was displeased with my behavior, "Since when do you backtalk me?"

I clamped my mouth shut and knew I was beyond redemption. Bottom line, I was at fault. Only an emergency was reason to open one's mouth, and a frog was not an emergency. I understood this and yet, I immediately set about contemplating how I was going to repay James.

The rest of the day was uneventful, other than James giving me wide berth. He seemed to be afraid of a wild and undisciplined retribution. There had been times when that was true, but I was learning to be more measured in my approach to life. His avoidance of me didn't keep us from crossing paths a few times and at each juncture, I strived to treat him as if nothing had happened. It confused him, which, of course, was my intention. I was going to do something to pay James back, but it wouldn't be this day.

After supper, Joseph took me aside to address the incident. As usual, he was calm and even as he discussed my transgression. I didn't try to defend myself, I took full responsibility. Joseph looked at me, not with displeasure, but in a way that caused me to think he might be amused by the display at the creek as reported to him.

"I thought you rather enjoyed silence," he said.

"I do," I said, "I look forward to it."

"What happened today that caused you to break silence in such a dramatic fashion?"

"I was annoyed."

"Hmm. About what?"

I didn't want to give-up my desire for revenge. I knew it was ill-tempered, and

I didn't want Joseph to talk me out of it. The singular desire to get back at James was too sweet to relinquish. So I said, "I'd rather not say."

Joseph was experienced at raising boys, having had two sons he stewarded to adulthood in his first family. I'm certain he sensed the seeds of revenge sprouting in my young head. Joseph sighed one of his long sighs that generally preceded him meting out penance. I dropped my gaze and waited, but he surprised me, "Anyone can become annoyed from time to time. I know you to be generally well disciplined. So... let's put this behind us." He slipped his hand beneath my chin and raised my face. He locked eyes upon mine and said, "Can we do that? Can we let this matter go?"

My heart began to race. My desire to get even was too sweet to relinquish. So I feigned, "Yes, Father."

Joseph's brow furrowed. "I'll take you at your word," he said with authority, and dropped the subject, moving our conversation onto something else. I was relieved, but also uneasy that I had just blatantly lied to him.

6 · Your Time to Cry, James

Several days went by and each morning I kept silent during baptism, but I held my feelings of revenge close. Confessing them would've given them room to leave, and I was stubbornly intent upon keeping them. The thoughts of revenge grew, until it wasn't about paying James back in kind. It was about teaching him a lesson that he wouldn't soon forget.

A dangerous desire to see James cry consumed me. He loved nature, especially creatures. He'd take-in hurt animals and try to nurse them back to health. He wasn't always successful, but his desire was sincere. His sincerity persuaded Joseph and Mary to tolerate what sometimes became a burden on the household. Odd animals appearing in odd places were expected.

Right then, James was nursing a bird with a damaged wing. His kind manner as he patted and fed his animal was normally endearing to me, but when I saw him these last few days, I was incensed. I thought, 'How dare he have such compassion for this animal and treat me so badly.'

The importance of my original irritation at James grew out of proportion. What should've been a temporal annoyance quickly forgiven, became a near-mortal wound in my mind. Everything became fodder for my musings of how and when I would strike. And I decided to strike at the very heart of him, so my thoughts began to include the use of James' bird.

Before I continue, it might be important to mention that as an Essene, I was mostly a vegetarian; as was our community. Unlike other Jewish sects, the only animals we ate were fish, either dried, or fresh when they were available, which was rare since we lived inland. We drank fresh milk and stored it dried for cooking. We ate cheese and other milk products, but we didn't eat common animals such as cattle, sheep, goat, deer, or birds. It had little to do with a moral objection to killing, and we used leather for bags, sandals, straps, and sundry other items. Our objections to eating meats were twofold. The first was the same as with daily baptism, to provide a cleaner body; a better vessel for our spirit on earth. The second reason was to respect life, to understand that all life was sacred, and not to be taken without need. Therefore, if we could eat well and healthfully without killing animals, then we shouldn't kill them.

When an animal in our care died, we processed its body to maximize the gain from its flesh. If there was usable meat, if the death met Mosaic standards, we gave the meat to people in need outside our community. Certain types of hair, feather, and fur would go to the weavers. Skin was processed into leather, and large bones

"Guard your desires. They are the basis for your thoughts and your thoughts are the substance of your life experience. Like it or not, what you consistently wish for yourself or others finds its way to your doorstep."

- Yeshua son of Joseph -

were dried and crushed for use as a raw material.

There were certain animals however, that were treated a little differently. Some dogs, cats, goats or other animals that had garnered a familial intimacy with their people might be treated with more care as a spiritual being, than as a resource for reclamation. They might be laid to rest in a manner more closely aligned with how people were treated. It wasn't proscribed by Hebraic law, but was often done by custom.

Given this, death was a rarity. It wasn't an everyday occurrence. We might see a larger animal kill and eat a smaller one in the wild, but that was somewhat removed. When death did occur in our community, whether an animal or a person, it was a notable event.

So, getting back to James and my plot of revenge: I decided to steal and hide James' bird. I wanted to see James hurt, to fear for loss, and to… well… cry. It burned in me so strongly I thought of nothing else. The idea that the bird might come to harm never entered my mind. Revenge, as is so often said, is a consuming passion that blinds the holder.

So, on the morning of the fifth day after the event in the creek, I exacted my plan. While James was at baptism, I stole his bird and ran with it in a bag to one of the outbuildings. I found a pile of seed sacks and carefully nestled the bird in its bag among the sacks. It looked safe enough. I went back to the house and waited.

James returned from his baptism and we gathered for morning meal. All through the meal, my family laughed and the sun shone its brilliant light upon us, but for me it was all in preparation for that one moment; the moment James found his bird gone. I played it over in my mind. How he would cry. I could see his face contorted with pain in my mind's eye and I practically shook with glee at the imaginings.

Finally, James rose from the meal with a bit of bread and water to take to his feathery charge. I waited and waited. Nothing. Finally, I couldn't contain myself. I had to go see. I found James sitting on the floor with the empty box on his lap. He looked at me and said, "Where do you think he went?"

"Who?" I asked.

"The bird. I left him here and now he's gone." James was truly perplexed.

I sat next to him and said, "Maybe he flew away?"

"No," James offered, "he was doing better, but not better enough to fly."

I was dumbfounded. I expected James to be upset, but he was merely perplexed. I looked at James hoping to see some hint of upset, of pain. I found only concern on his face; a heartfelt concern for the little one he was nursing.

All of a sudden, my world collapsed. Looking at James with the eyes of love and compassion looking back at me, I realized how wrong I'd been to want to cause him pain. He was my brother, I loved him, and I'd been unspeakably cruel in thought and deed.

I started to cry. James thought I was crying for the bird, so he said, "It's all right, Bit. I'm sure we'll find him. You can help me look."

"I dogged him relentlessly. He was my brother, but he was so often enigmatic. I was obsessed with garnering his attention. I'm sure it was frustrating to be on his end of all the childishness. That said, he wasn't always gracious in his reaction. He could take a lot, and he could serve it back as well."

- James brother of Yeshua -

His words made me cry harder and it all blurted out. I told him the whole story of my anger, my desire for revenge, and that I'd stolen his bird.

James put his hand on my knee and said, "I'm sorry, I didn't mean to get you in trouble. I just wanted you to pay attention to me."

The look of forgiveness in James eyes made me feel horrible. I didn't want him to spend another moment without his patient. "Let's go get him. I'll show you where he is." I led him to the outbuilding expecting to find the bag safely tucked among the seed sacks, but it wasn't there.

I was mortified, "I put him right here… I don't understand." All I wanted to do was restore the balance I'd so rudely interrupted. I became frantic.

Then I saw it. Just outside the back door, I saw a corner of the sack on the ground. I ran to the door expecting to rectify my mistake, but I stopped dead in my tracks when I saw the scene before me. One of the cats we kept on hand to help control field mice had ripped through the sack and was devouring the bird. Feathers were strewn and the sack was coated with a spray of the bird's blood.

I shrieked. The cat ran leaving the half-consumed carcass on the bloodied bag. James followed behind me and when he spied the mess, he shrieked too. I looked at James and to my horror, his face was filled with the contorted pain I'd earlier so desired to see, but now seared into my heart like a red-hot poker.

I grabbed James and tried to console him, but there was no consolation to be given and none to be had. Because of me, my brother hurt and I was guilty of that and causing a beloved life to be lost. I'd left the bird out like a strapped animal ready for the slaughter and I had no idea how I would atone for either offense.

Hearing our cries, two members of the community found us hovering over the bloodied bag, tears streaming down our faces. They paced us back to the house and into the arms of Joseph and Mary.

7 · Who's Crying Now?

James and I sat on a bench, sniffling, our arms slung around each other's back. We'd been crying for the better part of the morning. Joseph sat patiently in front of us. Mary stood behind him with Ruth and Jude holding her knees and little newborn Sarah in her arms. Everyone's eyes were upon us as we relayed the story. Joseph sat silent for a long time.

"My boys," he finally said, "this has been a difficult morning." I looked at him, my eyes pulsing with pain from the tearful wringing I'd given them. I couldn't say a word. After a moment, Joseph continued, "Yeshua, I think the first order of business is your apology – to me."

"I'm sorry," I squeaked out.

"Do you know what you're apologizing for?"

"Yes," I said with precious certainty, "I lied to you."

"Indeed you did." Joseph nodded, "That was your first mistake."

James looked at me in shock, "You lied to Father?" I hung my head and tried to keep from crying more.

Joseph continued, "And I assume you've already apologized to James?"

"Yes, many times."

Joseph's eyes narrowed, "Did you mean it?"

"Yes," I squeezed out, sounding like a rusty knife grating across stone.

"James, do you accept your brother's apology?" James nodded.

"As do I," Joseph sighed and said, "Boy, part of me is glad you experienced this."

"Glad?" I inquired.

"Yes." Joseph continued, "You see firsthand what the passion of vengeance can do to a soul."

"Yes," I squeaked, "I do-oo-oo-oo," as I began to sob again.

"The teachings of confession and forgiveness are to help you navigate through a world filled with transgressions," he explained. "In so doing, you keep free of these burdens."

I looked at Joseph through my tears and his face told all. In it, I saw the same forgiveness and compassion I'd seen in James' face. I felt sick to my core at what I'd done.

"I won't do this again, Father."

"Indeed, I believe you. You carry a heavy burden now, my son."

"Yes," I burbled through my sobs. "What do I do?"

"That's the kind of father I want to be to this boy... I want to uplift him. To help him see his mistakes through the fruit of his actions and help him rectify them through responsibility."

- Joseph father of Yeshua -

"Here's my decision." Joseph looked at me with a stern set to his eyes, "First, today, you'll again perform your baptism, and you'll do it properly. You'll confess your deeds to Creator as you've confessed them here to us." His eyes narrowed, "Then you'll keep silence all day and until your baptism is complete again tomorrow. Do you understand?"

"Yes."

"Good. And continue to confess your burden each morning until you feel forgiveness from it. That's when the burden will be lifted."

"Alright," I sniffled.

"And one more thing; as penance to your brother, I suggest you do your own chores as usual and help James with his chores starting tomorrow and for three days." I agreed. I looked at James and he nodded in agreement, too.

———

As Joseph commanded, I confessed each morning. And as he suggested, I helped James with his chores, not for three days, but I helped him for two more; one day of help for each day I wanted him to hurt. It took me several weeks of confession to find my burden lifted. When it did, the weight that left me was surprising. The way I felt before vengeance consumed me, now felt freer and lighter than I imagined.

8 · Mediterranean

Later that year, Joseph came to me with a proposition. "My boy, I need to make a journey by boat for business. Would you like to come with me?"

"By boat?" I asked with excitement.

"Yes."

I felt my insides churn with anticipation, "Where?"

"Well," Joseph bent closer and said in a conspiratorial voice, "Egypt."

I shrieked, "Egypt?" I was beside myself with glee. I'd just begun studying Hieratic and this was like manna from heaven, almost too good to be true, "Why?"

"I've some new business," Joseph explained, "and I thought we might see up close how our western brethren live."

"When? When?" I questioned as I bounced in place, barely able to contain myself.

Joseph laughed, "How about next week?"

Before I knew it, Joseph, a few associates, and I were boarding a boat in Caesarea and heading toward the Nile. When we arrived at the sea, the first thing to catch my attention, of course, was the Mediterranean itself; a magnificent body of water unlike anything I'd ever seen. The water was an astonishing color, something between blue and green, but so saturated a hue, I felt drawn to melt into it.

Of course, there were the odors. Caesarea was wholly different from any place I'd been yet, very Roman by all accounts, but near the docks, the smells were overpowering. Fishing vessels emptied their nets, flooding the air with fishy emissions. Sea flora lay on the warm rocks to bake in the sun. And people were anointed with scented oils, a luxury only the inhabitants of a prosperous city like this could afford.

Once on the boat and pushed off from the dock, I was delighted with the feeling of gliding. I learned how to navigate walking on deck with the odd rocking. It made some people queasy, but I had no trouble at all. It was thrilling.

I remember the feeling I had when we entered the open sea and, for the first time, I couldn't see land in any direction. I felt like a true adventurer; as if on another world, going places no one had ever been before. Of course, this feeling only lasted until we saw land again, but it filled me with a lust and passion for travel that never left me.

After three days', we sailed into the delta region and slowed to make our way toward Alexandria. We had to slow down because the mouth of the delta was filled with boats; moving too quickly would put every craft at risk of colliding. The boats

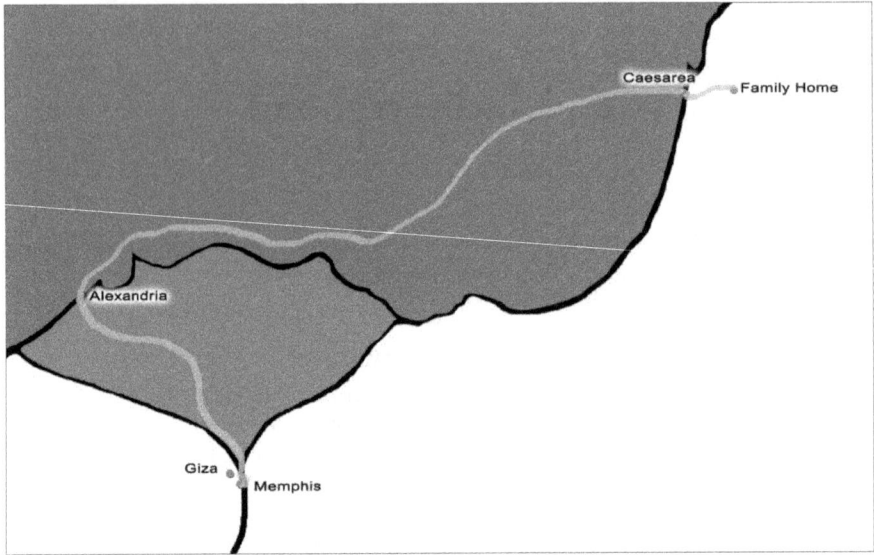

Figure 2: Yeshua's travel route to Memphis, Egypt

were varied in size and shape. Some were so small they could only carry one or two people. Others were so large I imagined an entire regiment would fit onboard. I saw cargo ships, passenger sails, fishing boats, military ships, barges; some made of reed, but most of wood. The diversity fired my imagination.

Navigating into the docks brought us very close to the Alexandrian Lighthouse, a magnificent creation that stood taller than any building I'd seen yet. Each night, during our stay here, I saw the beacon shine from its tower like the welcoming hand of God.

Once our boat docked, we began our foot journey into the great city. Alexandria was big, close to the size of Jerusalem. Unlike Jerusalem, with its crooked and narrow alleyways, streets here were orderly, wide, and laid out in a perpendicular grid pattern. But wider didn't mean vacant; the streets were busy and congested with commerce like any other prosperous town.

One of our associates knew how to navigate the byways to the Jewish quarter where we'd stay. Walking through the streets was pleasant. The weather was similar to that of Galilee with cooling, sea breezes in the afternoon.

When we got to the Jewish quarter, the differences in dress from those in my homeland surprised me. Yes, we were all Jewish, but our brethren here were mostly Hellenist. Their ancestors were a mixture of Greek and Egyptian, emphasis on the Greek. Their dress was more colorful and the styles had more flair. Women adorned themselves with scarves, silver, gold, and other jewelry, even more so than in Sepphoris. Many men wore hair ornaments and colorful shawls or loose-fitting vests hung over their robes. The diversity was pleasant to the eye.

Unfortunately, I didn't understand the language. I had a good ear though and shortly realized that they were speaking two different languages. One of them, Joseph could partially speak, but of the other he was as ignorant as I. Luckily, or more likely by design, our associate spoke both.

We stayed for several days in the home of a nice family. The children were all older than I, but I enjoyed their company. They taught me how to play a game on a squared board. It had pieces that moved according to simple rules, the object being to capture the enemy and dominate the board. It was fun for a while, but it was a war game and as such, didn't interest me further than the immediate enjoyment of playing with new friends. The oldest son also taught me how to play a flute made from a hollow reed stalk. I'd never seen one like it and I enjoyed the sweet sound it made. In just those few days together, I wasn't able to blow more than a handful of good notes, but to my surprise and joy, when we departed, he gave me the flute as a present. He said, "This is to bind our hearts." That flute gave me pleasure for years.

Each day we bought fresh food. Joseph always bought more than was needed. Half his purchases were plenty for the entire household and neighbors who joined us for supper each night. I assumed this overage compensated for any imposition our visit created. Later, I asked Joseph about it and he said these people were very poor and the business we'd bring might keep several families from disaster. That made my heart swell with pride for Joseph and the way he did business. I couldn't have had a greater teacher of responsible generosity.

On the Sabbath, we walked across the 'Divide' to the local synagogue. The Divide was part of a manmade canal that meandered through the city, providing a means of rapid transport between quarters. At times, the canal was open to the air, and at other times, it disappeared under the streets. In the Jewish quarter, the canal came through in two places. One leg of the canal was mostly subterranean, meandering under the business district to provide basement access for unloading cargo. The other leg was fully exposed. This was the section called the Divide that we crossed by bridge.

I was excited to attend an unfamiliar synagogue. At home, the community room at our house functioned as the synagogue. On the Sabbath, many neighbors came to worship and pray. It was always a joyous celebration of our faith. Meeting like that, at the home of a neighbor, was common in small communities.

Here, the synagogue was a separate building that existed as school, place of worship, and community gathering center. This was more common in cities. The gathering was pleasant and I enjoyed the service; strictly conservative Hellenist, and not exactly like Essene or Pharisaic gatherings I'd experienced. It wasn't until I was older that I understood more of the political issues that stood between the Hellenist sect and the priests in Jerusalem. If I'd known then, that the people I was worshipping with this day wouldn't be accepted at the Temple, I would've been shocked. Nothing in their manner of worship, or the contrivances of their rituals, was less than sacred. Their hearts struck me as holy, and as filled with the love of our Creator as any I'd known.

"The Roman mind was far different from the Jewish mind. Nothing reflected that better than the cities of each culture. Jewish cities grew organically from life as situations arose, making the streets crooked, the buildings diverse, and the organization haphazard. But Roman cities grew from a plan, where the streets were laid out according to some mathematical equation that made variance rare and gave everything a patina of discipline. It's a wonder we co-existed at all."
- James brother of Yeshua -

9 · The Nile

When business was complete, we boarded a barge to travel up the Nile to Memphis. I was eager to see the Nile of course, but more so, and if possible, to visit sacred buildings and temples. Joseph was clear, we were here for reasons of business; any side trips to satisfy my curiosity would be taken only if time and opportunity permitted. But I craved to see the carved writing I'd heard about.

Our barge snaked through the countryside. I was intrigued with the sheer size of the river. It was wide, so wide that it looked more like a sea than a river. We traveled for days and I was astounded to hear that we were seeing only a very small portion of it.

The flood season was barely over and the river was near its deepest annual depth. We were going against such a strong current that our barge had to augment the paddles with sails to overcome the force of the flow. The captain assured us the journey could be made more quickly on land, but the dangers would be greater. Especially now, after the flood season, predator animals could be desperate for food and would attack without provocation. And, as if the local wildlife wasn't enough danger, bands of marauders looked for any opportunity to attack travelers, usually with fatal results. So we sailed on, regardless of the slow pace.

On the second day, we encountered a herd of hippopotamus. These creatures intrigued me, but their size intimidated me, especially when they came near. I wasn't the only one with fear; the captain steered as far from them as possible. He told florid stories of barges overturned by angry hippos; the thought frightened me.

But the hippos were nothing compared to the crocodiles. Crocodiles had been a natural fixture of the landscape since we entered the river; they were intimidating, but the beasts near Alexandria were small compared to those further south on the delta. These fearsome creatures were longer than three men stacked head to toe. Some of their teeth were as long as my forearm. In daydreams, I gruesomely envisioned encountering one on land with inevitable results; my body ripped and shredded by those huge teeth set in those powerful jaws.

Each night, near sunset, we moored the barge and camped on land to build a fire for cooking, and also to spread out for sleeping. The men took turns staying awake through the night to watch for dangers.

On the fourth night, a fierce howling awakened us. I'd never heard anything like it, several voices overlapping. The captain hastened us back to the boat. I was glad because the clamor grew frighteningly close over the course of a few hours. At one point, we heard what sounded like a klatch of men laughing; but not a happy laugh, more an evil laugh. I couldn't see what was making the sound. All of a sudden, there was a fearsome scuffle, with growling and yelping. I realized animals were making the noise, not men.

During this entire time, my brain raced with wild imaginings about the beasts responsible for the horrible noise. By the time the bedlam stopped, my mind's eye had seen monsters larger than hippos, longer than crocodiles, and fiercer than either. But when I revealed my concerns about these imagined beasts to the captain, he politely explained that it was a cackle of wild hyena. He said they usually lived on the plains, but after the floods, the displaced animals might wander closer to the river than usual. When he described the stature of a hyena, I had to laugh as they were closer to the size of dogs. Joseph mentioned that hyenas were also native to Galilee, I'd just never seen them before.

When the sun finally rose, we retrieved the rest of our belongings. We spotted the bloody remains of a donkey being picked over by carrion birds just a short distance from camp. The hyena had eaten their meal, and we were relieved it wasn't one of us.

A week into our journey, we sailed toward a sight that surpassed my grandest dreams. On the horizon towered the triangular spires of the Giza Plateau pyramids. We were several days' sail from them and they already dominated the landscape. I'd heard stories from men who'd been here, but the excitement I felt about visiting was nothing compared to the excitement of being within their reach. Their polished sides were so smooth that at sunset, they reflected the light with such brilliance that I could no more look directly at the spires than at the sun itself. It was glorious and made me feel close to my Creator.

I was disappointed that we wouldn't stop at Giza, but as we neared those pyramids, I saw there were other pyramids beyond. It was then that I realized how far from home I was and just how different life was near this great river. Watching the brilliant stars in the heavens as we camped at night, I imagined what it was like for our ancestors to call this land their home. People were basically the same, but the land and all else that dwelled on it here, the plants, trees, animals, even the insects, were so very different from Judea.

As we coursed up the Nile, I began to have a strange feeling in the pit of my stomach, an apprehension of misfortune to come. I was only nine, but when the apprehension overcame me, I felt oddly older, already a man.

"I was born from Egyptian royalty. I wasn't born in Egypt, because Nefertiti's descendants fled that country when her dynasty collapsed. I'm told I look very much like her."

- Miriam wife of Yeshua -

10 · Memphis

We sailed into Memphis harbor at midday with the sun blazing at its apex above us. The harbor was little more than a small mud dock. The town was large and spread out making this dock seem tiny in comparison. Something wasn't right.

Joseph approached the captain and asked if this was the main harbor. The man merely grunted and said, "Yes, yes. This is Memphis." For the first time on our trip, things were awry and the uneasy feeling in my belly persisted.

We began to make our way into the metropolis. None in our party had been here before, so unlike arriving in Alexandria, we didn't have clear directions to our destination. It wasn't long, however, only a little way down the road, when we realized we were approaching a temple. The scale of the temple was overwhelming. It felt constructed for giants, not people. The pillars rose above our heads some ten spans of a man's height.

"This is not where we want to be," Joseph said ominously as we neared the grand entrance to the temple complex. The external walls, colorfully decorated and filled with carved writing, intrigued me. I tried as best I could to decipher some of it as we walked past, but the meanings eluded me.

On the far side of the complex was a garden lush with plants and ponds, and sprinkled with statues of deities that were half-human, half-animal. We paused at one of the larger statues of a woman with the head of a lioness, when suddenly the Unseen encircled me in a protective fashion.

From behind, we heard a woman speaking perfect Aramaic, "Greetings travelers. You look to be far from home."

I turned to see her dressed in lavish robes with a headdress of gold circling her brow. She was striking with large eyes sheathed in paint. Joseph gasped. When he did, the woman stepped closer to us and a look of surprise came over her.

"Joseph?" She blinked and cocked her head to one side. All the color drained from her face.

"Salome. It's been a long time," Joseph said, "I didn't know you were in Memphis." Joseph stepped closer to me and put his arm around my shoulder.

She regained her composure and smiled, "Yes, I'm the head-priestess of the temple here."

"Congratulations on your position," Joseph said as his hand squeezed my arm.

"Thank you." She looked at me, "Who is this young man?"

Joseph did something I'd never experienced him do before. He lied, "This is my grandson, Jeremiah."

"Ah, he's a handsome boy." She placed a finger on my cheek, "He has a light about him."

Joseph pulled me away from her finger, "Yes, I'm beginning his apprenticeship as merchant trader. We're here on business."

The priestess looked me up and down. Her face turned dark and her voice deepened, "Joseph, you shouldn't try to deceive me. This is Mary's boy, isn't it?"

Joseph's hands urged me behind him. "No, this is my grandson." He stood his ground between us. For a moment, they looked at one another, unmoving. The atmosphere crackled with tension.

Finally, the woman smiled and took a step back, "Well, he has a great spirit. You're blessed to have such fine progeny."

"Thank you."

"I won't hold you any longer. Is there anything I can do to assist you?"

"Thank you for the offer, but no, we're taken care of."

"Very well, goodbye Joseph," and with that she walked back toward the temple court.

When she was out of sight, Joseph urged our party through the garden and deeper into the town itself. He was anxious and it didn't escape me that his behavior toward the woman was uncharacteristic in total. Not only had he lied to her, he hadn't introduced her to anyone else in our party.

We made inquiries, searching for the people we came to meet. It became clear though, that we were far from our destination. We walked all afternoon and it was nearly sundown before we found the Jewish section of town. Once there, however, it took little time to locate the correct people. They welcomed us as warmly as the families in Alexandria. To our displeasure, we learned that these people lived within a stone's throw of the main harbor; a large, bustling harbor the captain obviously steered us from.

That night, Joseph didn't let me move more than a few inches from him and he insisted that we sleep on the same cot. When we were finally in bed, I asked, "Who was that woman?"

He wrapped his arms around me, "She lived at Carmel... the same time your mother and I were there."

"Why are you afraid of her?"

Joseph was silent for several minutes. He finally said, "Because I know what she's capable of. She would murder if it suited her goals."

"Murder?"

"Yes, my boy, murder." I closed my eyes and said a prayer that the sun would rise to find us safe.

We did awaken safe and Joseph was noticeably less stressed. The people we stayed with were friendly and I was comfortable in their home, and as in

"Salome had been raised in the orphanage. Her mother was Jewish, but her full parentage was unknown. Once she became a sister however, she submitted to obey the Sisterhood above all. She had a keen mind and received an excellent education. She was proficient in scribing three languages, a rarity for a woman. And she had her eye firmly set on the powerful Head-Mistress position. As far as she was concerned, if the sisterhood asked, she would kill for it."

- Joseph father of Yeshua -

Alexandria, we shopped each day for more food than could be immediately consumed.

Things changed a few days later though. I was playing a hoop game with neighboring children when I began to feel dizzy. I tried to ignore it, but the dizziness persisted. By the time we convened for evening meal, I wasn't well. I stumbled to the table and couldn't eat. Very soon after supper, I collapsed from fever.

I know Joseph brought a healer, because I remember an older, dark-skinned man massaging my neck and under my arms. He examined inside my mouth, in my ears and eyes, and around my feet and hands.

I slipped in and out of consciousness for several days. Yet, each time I awoke, Joseph was lovingly by my side, looking after my every need. I remember his doting on me, carrying me to the latrine, and using a wet cloth to wash my face. But I don't think I even uttered a word, as my body was unresponsive to my commands.

On one afternoon, I awoke to find Joseph and one of the other men in our party propping me up with pillows. Joseph had a cup of warm liquid for me to sip. I knew what he wanted, but I could barely manage to move my lips to take sips. More than half of what left the cup spilled down my chest instead. My fever persisted.

Later, I came to consciousness enough to hear Joseph in conversation, "I'm so afraid for him."

"Do we know what the problem is?" another man asked.

"No," replied Joseph, "not specifically, but I have no doubt it was caused by Salome."

"Who is she?"

"Oh, you can't know everything about the time before Yeshua was born. Some of those days were dark indeed." Joseph paused, "There are forces… people… who didn't want him born… they murdered for that outcome."

"Surely not!"

"Oh yes. Salome was one of those people."

"I wondered why you tried to hide his identity from her."

"I would do anything to keep her from him," Joseph sighed, "but I'm afraid it hasn't been enough. If he doesn't come out of this soon, we'll lose him." I could hear Joseph weep. I wanted to comfort him, but my body simply wouldn't respond.

"I don't recall seeing Yeshua ill. I had sniffles from time to time, but not my brother. There was the time he was poisoned while he was in Egypt, but other than that his health was generally excellent."

- James brother of Yeshua -

11 · Can You Talk?

This time when I woke, it was Philar leaning over me. "Yeshua, can you talk?" he queried. I tried to form a word, but my throat was raw. I gulped back saliva and tried to clear my throat. What came out was a raspy grunt.

"Oh, that's good!" I heard Joseph exclaim.

"Yes," said Philar, "it's promising. At least his fever is down."

"Yeshua? Can you move your hand?" asked Joseph. I tried to move my hand and I must have been partially successful, because they both laughed with appreciation.

Philar said, "You may not be able to respond yet, my boy, but we're working to make you well."

Joseph added, "I love you so much." This I knew, but it was nice to hear right then.

My recovery was slow going and it took weeks for me to be able to do anything on my own. When I did regain full use of my faculties I was fatigued, but grateful. It's a terrible and frightful thing to have your body betray you and not function correctly.

On the first day out of bed, Philar came to me again. "I'm glad you're up. How're you feeling?"

"I'm tired, but glad to be out of bed."

"I imagine you are."

"What happened?"

"You were poisoned."

My eyes widened, "Poisoned?"

"Yes," Philar tipped his head downward, "and I must apologize."

"What for?"

"I should've been more diligent in protecting you."

"But I'm ok, so it's alright," I smiled.

"Yes, it's alright now. We'll endeavor to be more careful from now on."

Philar was obviously sorry for what he considered a grave mistake. I observed that he must have a full range of emotions, just like humans. I was still getting to know him and this surprised me. "Philar?"

"Yes?"

"I mean, that if Philar and his associates are not angels, they're not human either. I have no idea what they are. They have technology that is beyond anything I understand and they are thoroughly capable of anything they suggest."
- Jacob, Essene elder -

"Thank you."

Philar shook his head and smiled. He placed his hand on my shoulder. "You are eternally welcome."

I was young, as I mentioned, just nine years old. It was easy to shake off this event and continue as if nothing happened. The fact that someone wanted me dead didn't have an impact on me. In my mind, I'd been ill. Many people get ill and it was good to be well again.

Joseph completed his business and we spent a few extra days wandering among the temples by the pyramids. Joseph didn't want us to go, but I wanted it so much he couldn't bring himself to refuse me. Philar promised his people would be with us the entire time, guarding, so Joseph relented.

It was thrilling. The pyramids were huge, and the temples with their grand columns and carved reliefs held me rapt for hours. The priests seemed to like me and tolerated our presence well. They gave me clues and I began to make a correlation between some of the carved writings and the language of Hieratic I was learning. It was pitifully few, but it excited me to have these small breakthroughs of understanding.

I could've stayed there for days, weeks, but Joseph was eventually insistent that we leave. It wasn't long after that, only a day or two, that we began our uneventful trek back to Galilee, but I left enraptured by Egypt; its sounds, smells, buildings, creatures, people… all of it. I guess you could say that Egypt got into my blood.

12 · My Will Be Done

When we arrived home, Joseph took Mary aside to discuss what happened. Mother's arms crossed over her chest in a resolute manner. "Do you think they followed you into Galilee?"

"It'd be imprudent for us not to assume so," Joseph replied.

So, for the next several years, I was treated to a never-ending parade of Other following me around. I rarely saw them, but I soon fostered the ability to discern their presence with my inner eye. It was a knowing that came over me when they were near. An almost electric charge that stimulated some sensory apparatus inside me that told me I wasn't alone. After a time, I could discern, not merely that they were present, but also, how many and where they were. It was good for me. It forced me to develop these inner-sight abilities in ways that perhaps I wouldn't have if not for this event and its aftermath.

Other abilities, even more unusual, spontaneously began to assert themselves. For example, I realized that my will was more powerful than other children's. If I put my mind to something happening in a particular way, it generally happened just as I willed it. Joseph was clear with me on the proper use of will. Even still, there were times I'd make something happen for someone else, just because I thought it was what he or she needed. The ability to do so was seductive, but it usually turned out quite poorly.

One time I willed for everyone to love a box James built and for him to receive great praise for it. The box wasn't very special; it was functional, but not grand. But everyone acted as if it was grand and James puffed up like a bull in mating season. I thought it would help him gain confidence and it was wonderful to see him happy. I didn't even mind when he jeered at me with taunts like, "I did something better than you-uu."

It was false pride though. It wasn't the truth. James' next several projects didn't receive such praise and he was crushed. He couldn't live up to the 'one box.' He began to feel worse about himself than he had before I intervened.

I confessed to Joseph. Together we spoke with James. He was angry, not so much that I used my will, but that I let him strut about exclaiming his superiority, knowing it wasn't true. He felt betrayed, rightly so, and he felt great shame.

Joseph met with James separately for many weeks. It wasn't easy for James to reconcile the pain my meddling caused. Joseph admonished me severely, "Never presume you know what's best for someone else." He said, "There are things you create for yourself and there are things you co-create with other people. It's the way of peace to allow co-creation full reign. It takes everyone's voice to fill out a

"I suppose the most maddening thing Yeshua ever did was to make his will manifest in other people's lives; especially mine!"

- James brother of Yeshua -

pleasing chorus." It was a lesson I had to learn many times, but when the lesson finally landed home, it stuck like a fly to honey. I follow Joseph's advice on the proper use of will to this day.

Even more astonishing, I developed the ability to manipulate time. At about age eleven, a new family joined our community. They were a kind couple with three children, the oldest being a boy just my age, named Michael. We liked him, and he joined in play with James and me most afternoons.

One afternoon, we were running in the grain fields playing tag. We jumped and ran with gusto. As we careened down a steep gully, Michael suddenly disappeared. The ground had collapsed into a deep hole. When James and I looked down the hole, we saw Michael's leg twisted out to the side in an unnatural position. Something was very wrong.

"Can you move?" I shouted.

"No, it hurts!" he cried out through his sobs. I told James to run back to the farm and get help, but I soon became so concerned for Michael's safety, I ran back to the farm also. Something came over me when I started running. What should have taken minutes, took mere moments.

I alerted the first men I came upon to the problem. They ran for rope, and other provisions needed to get Michael out of the hole. Suddenly, I became concerned for Michael being alone and I needed to get back to him. So I ran to the hole, and again, what should have taken minutes, took almost no time at all.

At the hole, I sat on the edge and talked to Michael, trying to calm him as best I could until the men showed up. When they arrived, James was with them, having encountered them on his way to the farm. James stared at me, incredulous that I could've made the trip there and back before he even got half way.

They got Michael out of the hole. He had a severely broken leg that would take some time to mend. Separately, James was bothered. He looked at me suspiciously, from the corners of his eyes, as if he didn't know who I was anymore.

Later that evening, Joseph took me aside and we reviewed the incident. In going over the events, I realized what I'd done didn't make sense. "It was odd, wasn't it, that I got back before James?" I said to Joseph.

"I would say so, yes," he said.

This bothered me. I couldn't explain it. "What does it mean?" I asked.

"I don't know," Joseph thought about it, then said, "I suspect we're seeing a new ability emerge."

"Oh no," I groaned.

"Don't begrudge what makes you different, my boy." But I did. Every time some new ability showed itself, I had to learn to control it. The process was laborious and I was tired of it.

"Well, be kind to yourself," Joseph added. "Why don't we ask Philar about it and see if he has some clues for us?" I nodded my head, but I felt exhausted. 'Here we go again,' I thought to myself.

§ *"The wise books are filled with stories of men offered opportunities arisen from fantastical circumstances; circumstances that any normal thinking man would reject. Faith is an important part of life."*

- Joseph father of Yeshua -

The next morning after baptism, Philar joined us. "I suspect," he said, "that it has to do with the flow of time."

"Time?" I said.

"Well, time is one of our greatest resources," Philar stated.

"Yeah, but time's out of our control," I said with great sincerity.

"I suggest you're learning that it's a resource dependent upon perception."

"Perception?"

"I suspect that fully comprehending the nature of time may be beyond you at present," Philar explained, "but regardless, you seem to be developing the ability to manipulate it."

I really didn't like hearing that some concept might be beyond my grasp. I had a good brain and I knew how to use it, but I did finally concede that I truly didn't understand. And unlike many of my other abilities, Joseph didn't just suggest I not indulge in its use, he insisted.

"It's dangerous," Joseph said. "You must admit that other people can see its effects firsthand. It calls attention to you in a way that could be dangerous. I must insist that you refrain from using this ability until such time as you better understand it." Upon reflection, I could see the wisdom of his request. I promised I would refrain. It would be some years before I broke that promise.

13 · Libraries of Knowledge

By the time I turned twelve, I was deep into my rabbinical studies. When I reached my majority and had to make my professional ambitions known, to no one's surprise I chose to become a Temple priest, at least to work toward that goal. The elders around me approved. Such a goal couldn't be guaranteed. It would mean a lot of study and trips to Jerusalem, but it was my desire.

The study was no issue. I would study the sacred books whether it was my profession or not. The travel wasn't an issue in and of itself, but being able to convince the elders of the Temple in Jerusalem that I warranted a position made me nervous. It meant I had to study the Essene ways of my birth, and become proficient in the Pharisaic ways of most mainstream priests.

There were synagogues guided by priests scattered around Galilee. I'd have to seek one out and gain his tutelage. Joseph suggested we start by requesting the help of Jacob in Sepphoris. Jacob was on the Essene Elder Council and was the Jewish Ambassador reporting to the Romans stationed there. Jacob had been instrumental in preparations leading up to my birth and Joseph trusted him explicitly.

The next day, Joseph and I made the short trip to Sepphoris by foot, since it was only a few miles from our compound. Sepphoris was Herod's glittering jewel of commerce in the heart of Galilee. Larger and more prosperous than Caesarea; Sepphoris was home to the Roman Praetor and claimed a measure of prosperity that brought out the best and worst from its inhabitants.

I'd never met Jacob before. I'd heard about him and read letters he exchanged with Joseph on a number of occasions, but this would be the first time being eye-to-eye with him.

A servant escorted us into Jacob's home, and the opulence overwhelmed me. Our family home was much more humble. This building began with a courtyard, with several arched doorways leading to other portions of the house. The courtyard was decorated with colorful frescoes and pots filled with lush greenery.

The servant led us through one of the arches to a sitting room. It contained

---

"The community spearheaded by Jacob and supporting this newly reformed, yet still deposed, Davidian regime had been very generous. Deeded to Joseph was a large plot of land, practically in the shadow of Mount Tabor, covering most of a hill southeast of Sepphoris. And added to that was a substantial cache of resources for building the appropriate community. Joseph was well provided for."

- On Jacob's work with the Essene Elders to provide for Joseph and his new family -

benches with pillowed covers on them. Low tables were stacked with baskets filled with fruits and biscuits. Scattered around the floor were large pillows where I guessed people could lounge, and the walls were hung with tapestries or painted in colorful designs. I'd never been in a home even remotely like this one and I reasoned that Jacob was quite wealthy.

As we waited, I asked Joseph, "Is Jacob a rich man?"

"Well, I imagine he has more than he needs to live comfortably, but you should know he also gives a great deal of his wealth to the needy. And he works tirelessly toward ushering in the new age that has a great deal to do with you, my son. But we can talk about that another time."

I looked at Joseph and shook my head. I knew there was no use asking more about that right now. So I asked, "Why is his home so opulent?"

"I imagine to placate his Roman employers." Joseph chuckled, "I'm sure he enjoys it as well."

"I should think it would make him feel strange to live like this when so many of our brothers are destitute."

"Yeshua," Joseph shook his head, "don't judge a man by his possessions, in either direction, whether you think he has too little, or too much. It's a man's heart and the actions he takes from its bidding that define him."

As I contemplated Joseph's admonition, Jacob came into the room. The moment I saw him I liked him. He was warm and open and made me feel at home immediately. Joseph and he embraced in a tight hug, then turned to me.

"Jacob," Joseph said with pride, "please meet our marvelous boy, Yeshua."

Jacob grabbed me and gave me just as tight a hug as he'd given Joseph. "I'm so pleased to finally meet you. You mean so much to me, as your father knows." He looked at Joseph, his face beaming.

Jacob took a step back and dipped his chin in homage to me, "I'm honored to meet you." I was bewildered to be treated with such respect by such an important man, when I was just a boy. My face must have shown my bewilderment because Jacob laughed, "Don't worry, that's for me to understand. You just continue to make us proud."

My face turned red. I know because I could feel the heat of it on my cheeks. Jacob suggested we all sit down.

Joseph explained to Jacob that we'd come to seek help with becoming a Temple priest.

"Well!" began Jacob, "This complicates matters!"

"Why do you say that?" Joseph asked.

"Because I also have a proposal and we may have to be clever to figure out how to accomplish both."

"Continue, please."

"Do you remember some letters you read before Yeshua was born? They were from an unknown party far from here and sealed with a strange emblem."

"Yes, of course. They were perplexing missives."

"Indeed," Jacob nodded, "they were at the time. But I know much more about these people now."

"I'm all ears." Joseph's curiosity was piqued.

"Well, they're a people adherent to a religion I believe you're intimately familiar with; Bon."

Joseph's face reflected his pleasure at hearing they were Bon, "Yes. It's part of my tradition."

"I thought as much." Jacob took in a deep breath, "Well, they live in an area far from here in the northeastern part of the Indus. A place called Kapilavastu. They've recently come under military control by the Kushan, but they are devoutly spiritual people."

"That sounds familiar." Joseph chuckled and looked at me to see if I was paying attention. Of course, I was.

"They run a university," Jacob continued, "and due to their diligence in preserving their spiritual legacy, they have great libraries of knowledge." Now I was acutely attentive. Libraries of historical knowledge? My heart picked up its beat.

"They're committed to helping our cause and quite interested in having some time with our dear boy here."

"In what way do they want to accomplish this?" Joseph asked.

"They've proposed that Yeshua come to their university and study."

Joseph's eyes got big and he swallowed hard, "Oh. I don't know. It's so far away." He glanced at me and his face fell. I'm sure my face reflected the eagerness I felt. "I see you already have desire for this, Yeshua." I didn't open my mouth, I simply continued to hold Joseph's gaze with mine. "Yes, of course." Joseph sighed and turned back to Jacob, "You've said the magic words; libraries of knowledge."

Jacob laughed, "I'll put you in contact with them to work out the details. I'm sure they'd like him to come as soon as possible." He shifted his gaze back and forth between Joseph and me and chuckled, "So, I guess now we have to figure out how to accomplish Yeshua's priestly position before he leaves."

Joseph did work out an arrangement with the Bon Masters in Kapilavastu; I would go there as soon as I was done with my rabbinical study. Jacob found a priest willing to mentor me. I studied with diligence and accomplished in two years, what other young men were expected to accomplish in six. By the time I was fourteen, I was ready to apply for a position with the Temple.

I'd love to say that my stellar achievements and deep knowledge born of study was enough to get me the job, but it wasn't. In the end, it was a substantial donation from the Essene Elders, and a promise that I wouldn't accept the position until I was of a more proper age, that persuaded the priests. Very simply, the position was bought, but I didn't feel badly about it. In my heart, I knew I was prepared and this appointment was perfect.

"The note was sent by unnamed allies before Yeshua was born. It was a strange note from a faraway land and it bore a seal like none I'd seen before. They wanted to offer support for the child that was to come from Mary. I set the note down on the table and thought about it's message. I reasoned that if the Great Teacher was here for all mankind, it follows that others who were taught by him would also be waiting for his return."

- Joseph father of Yeshua -

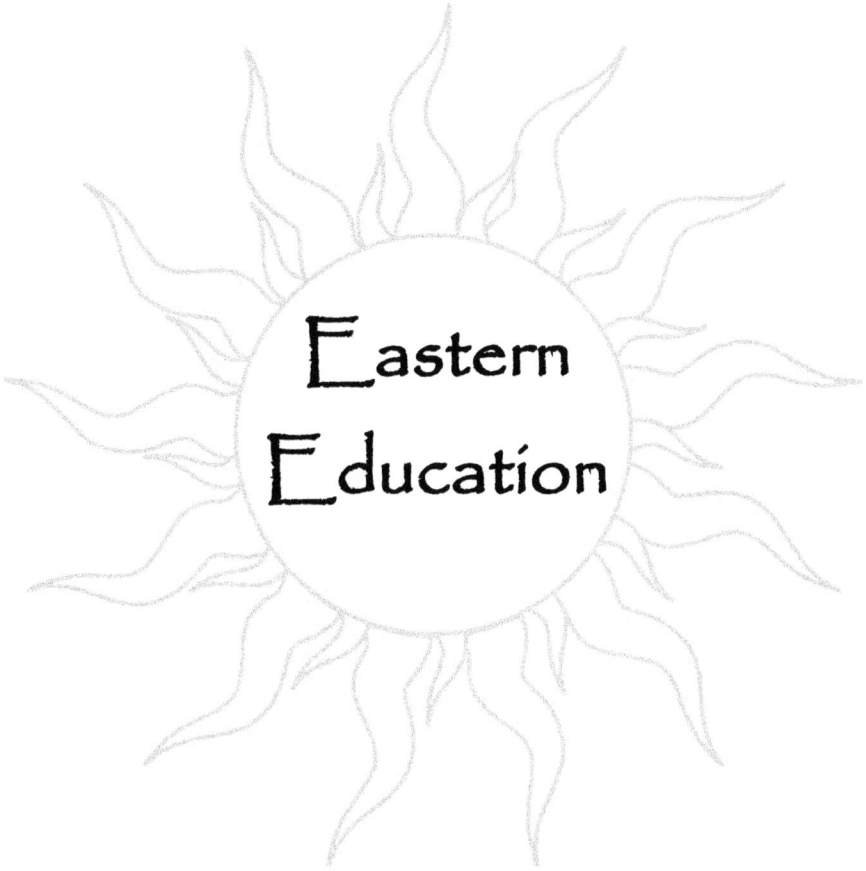

Eastern Education

14 · Gnosis Trumped Everything

Even though the day began like any other, it was a day like no other. It was the day I left home. I didn't know how long I'd be gone or when I'd see my siblings again. But most importantly, looking into the face of my mother, I didn't know when I'd touch her cheek again. I was fourteen. Sure, I was old enough to be considered a man, but that was an arbitrary distinction, not a real one. I was her eldest child, and the sight of her gentle eyes surveying me with such sadness filled me with apprehension. It would surely be years before my feet again touched the yellow soil of my home.

Shelah, the youngest of my parent's brood, was still a toddler, barely taller than my knee. She was a small girl, much like our mother, and she bubbled with glee when I touched her hair.

James stood in the door watching, his usual stance these days. He was uncharacteristically quiet. The next year would be the year of James' majority; he'd choose his profession and I would miss it. That pained me. I hoped he'd follow his heart and turn to his studies. I knew, of course, that Joseph would help him find his way.

The other children were unconcerned with my departure and more excited by the clacking of a grasshopper or some such wonder that only a child's eyes will see.

Father would be walking with me to Aqaba, supporting me on the beginning of my journey. I didn't have to face saying goodbye quite yet. He was my rock, my mentor, my protector, and my heart was heavy when I thought about saying goodbye to him. He was the elder of our village, the leader of our people. I didn't know, nor could I calculate his age, but his hair was fully gray and beautiful lines of wisdom etched his brow and cheeks. He was still vibrant, filled with the vitality and fervor of a man half his age, but for how much longer? I was grateful to know I'd have these next days of concentrated time with him.

Two of the men with us would stay with me for the entire journey. They pledged to see me through as long as they could. Hassim was a man of honor, a widower with a lust for new experience. He was also gray-haired, but surely not as old as Joseph. And Myrrh was a gentle monk from the City of Salt. He was young enough to be robust and strong, and he found the mission to accompany me a great honor and calling. I couldn't comprehend that sentiment, any more than I could when Jacob honored me, but I was happy to have Myrrh's company.

I was a young man, full of myself, but not fully cognizant of my truth. The

"When Yeshua left home, I was lost. If I could've kept him home, I would've. I moped in self-pity for weeks, wondering where I'd again find joy. Everything around me paled in comparison to the light I found in my brother's presence. I did, of course, finally relinquish my addiction to living life in his shadow, but it wasn't easy."

- James brother of Yeshua -

surge of youth's exuberance has a way of blinding the mind to long-range thinking, but I had a tremendous thirst for knowledge. Gnosis trumped everything. I wanted to know all there was to know in the world and I was still young enough to believe it was possible.

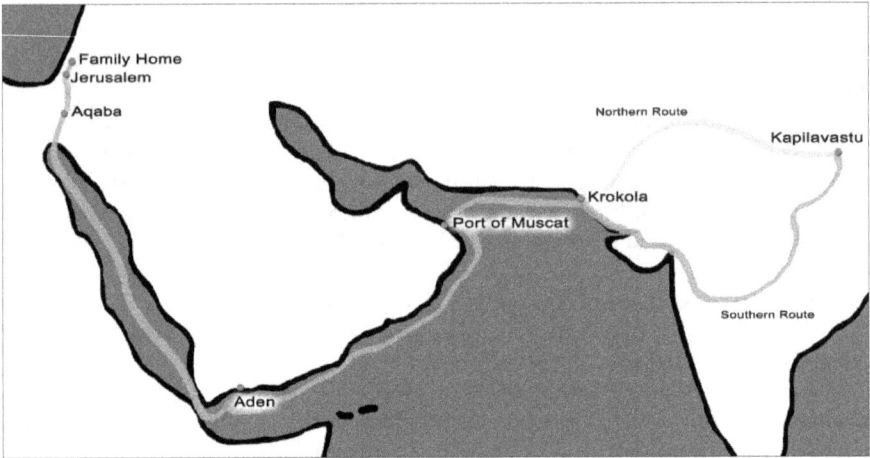

Figure 3: Yeshua's travel route to Kapilavastu

15 · Five Promises

And so it was that we left our community and set out to the south. We were a large party: my pledged companions, a few beasts of burden, and those men that would return to Galilee with Joseph. Hassim, Myrrh, and I had a donkey to carry provisions as well as gifts for people we met along the way. Strapped to my back was everything I'd need for my personal keeping.

I made five solemn promises before beginning this journey. To my highest self and to my Creator, I promised:

- Firstly, to travel with no more than I needed and only as much as I could easily carry. This would protect me from the weary of physical burden.
- Secondly, I promised to propel myself across land with my own feet. By this, I could avoid the burden of laziness from wearying beasts with a body rightly carried by its own volition.
- Thirdly, I promised to remember the covenants of my birth as a Nazorean. This would allow me to remain confident and not incur the burdens of self-doubt and confusion.
- Fourthly, I promised to bring honor to my family, to my creed, and to my ancestors, through right ways of thought and action. If I kept to this, I would remain free of the burdens of selfishness, deceit, and narcissism.
- And fifthly, I promised to return to my home and to my family. By returning, I wouldn't incur the burden of remorse at forsaking my sacred roots.

I sincerely meant to honor and keep all five promises.

We spent the next days walking south to Jerusalem. I'd been to Jerusalem a number of times and always found it an exciting place. Family greeted us warmly whenever we arrived and the bustle of people in the streets with their diverse activities excited me. I loved Jerusalem, but like Sepphoris and my own home, I would return one day and have my fill of them again. Right now, I was ready to experience something completely different.

We stayed in Jerusalem two nights – long enough for Joseph to make business connections with several important men. Joseph also made plans to visit with his eldest son Adam on the way home. We then climbed back onto the road heading south to Aqaba.

Adam was one of my half-brothers. Joseph and his first wife had raised three children, Adam, Simon, and Desiree, well before he married my mother. Joseph's first wife died after the children were adults. That grief swayed Joseph to become a monk at Mount Carmel, which is where he met my mother.

On the road to Jerusalem, Joseph and I debated ideas, talked about family, and imagined wistful futures. We laughed and enjoyed a comradery I would later miss. On the road to Aqaba, however, Joseph had more serious subjects to discuss. The conversation started with, "My Son, there's a great chance we'll never see each other again…" and proceeded from there. He took the opportunity to speak with me about subjects he hadn't previously broached.

He revealed to me more about his decision to be my adopted father and what it meant to him to fulfill that responsibility. He'd never before told me how close he came to denying the role. Philar had been quite influential in persuading Joseph to wed Mary. I offered prayers of thanks for Philar and his loyalty to us.

Joseph also spoke of his deep faith, both in the source of all things, and in me and my journey. He imparted to me a vision he had of my eventual return to our homeland and what he believed might be my larger mission. Unfortunately, youth kept me from understanding his full meaning. How could I, at such a tender age, understand even one tenth of the magnitude and breadth of my eventual work? Nevertheless, I did catch his fervor and his faith, and they have stayed with me until this very day.

Joseph braved the topics of sexuality and other physical excitements such as unhealthy eating, alcohol, narcotics, and self-eroticism. He wanted to help me understand these temptations, since I was likely to encounter most of them outside the protected environment of home and family. He gave me his cautions and his sanctions; following the Nazorean thought that life was to be lived with gusto, albeit with moderation. He confessed in detail his own fall into gambling and drinking when he was young. His account of his loss of dignity was compelling and painful to imagine. But, of course, I was certain I was immune to such earthly attachments. Life, however, would eventually prove me wrong.

Above all, he stressed the wonders of the human heart and its capacity to love and govern the spiritual journey through life. He urged me to remember always that within my breast was the most sophisticated organ in all creation. That if I ever lost my way, all I had to do was follow my heart and it would lead me back to home.

I listened and absorbed his words as a dry sponge soaks up water. I barely spoke, knowing this might well be the last time I'd have the pleasure of listening to his sage advice. I wanted to fathom fully the man who was my trusted guardian and spiritual compass.

Weeks later, when we arrived in the thriving port town of Aqaba, I realized just how much more I wanted from him, versus how little time I had left to receive it. But I put our upcoming goodbye as far from my mind as I could. The thought frightened me.

The first thing we did when we reached Aqaba was to secure passage on a ferry that would take my party down the Gulf of Aqaba to the Red Sea. There, we'd transfer to a merchant ship to make the long journey to Krokola. The ferry would depart the next morning, so we procured lodging at an inn near the port.

Aqaba was a modern settlement with architectural influences from many

"My father was a man of strong faith, a Davidian priest. He impressed all his progeny with a desire to return the David family to our rightful royal station. It was his mission in life to work for the time when such would be true… I carry this desire in me… it's from him."

- Joseph father of Yeshua -

cultures. The foreign decorations and styles mesmerized me. I was familiar with Egyptian architecture, from my journey to Egypt, but to see that so generously mixed with Persian and Quraysh influences was a delight to the eye.

Fresh water was plentiful here and aqueducts were constructed to carry water through the town and down many narrow stair-stepped alleys. The sound of flowing water was everywhere, and many gardens were set aside for the flowering of plants. In Galilee, Samaria, and Judah, gardens were plentiful, but they were generally planted conservatively, with fruit trees, or other edible plants. Here, many of the gardens seemed to have no other purpose but to be beautiful and fragrant.

When we finally got to bed, my exuberance continued. I was bursting from new sights and sounds, smells and ideas. I kept Joseph up most of the night, assailing him with questions. Mostly to continue to listen to his words and keep trying to fill that capacity I held for his wisdom.

When the sun finally rose over the eastern hill-line, I was exhausted, but ready to greet this unprecedented day. We gathered our resources and lined up at the dock ready to board the flat-block ferry. Several other parties lined up with us and for the first time in my life, I actually began to get a sense of the size of the world. How much activity happens in any given moment that we never have knowledge of? My perception of life to that point was pitifully narrow in comparison.

Joseph was brushing a tear from his eye. I realized this was the moment I was dreading. "Stay with me longer," I pleaded, "come with us to the sea."

Joseph looked away for a moment, and said, "I can't do that. I have to get home to the others. They still need me."

"I need you."

"No, you cling to me," he said. "You love my presence because I shower you with acceptance, but you don't need me."

"No, that's not true."

"Yes... it is. You're a man... a man destined to be deep in service to others. You need none but your connections to the Unseen and the Others around you. Keep them in your vision and you'll always fare well." After a moment of silence, he continued, "I love you. I've always loved you. I will always love you. No matter what you do, where you go, how high you climb... or how low you fall, I will always be your loyal supporter. From wherever I sit, or wherever I watch, I'll extend a hand of caring. And I will always hold you in my heart." With that, he laid upon my palm a small wooden ornament on a leather thong. It was a perfectly shaped, and lovingly-crafted heart.

I immediately placed the thong over my head and let the heart fall to the middle of my chest. As soon as it touched my skin, tears began to flow down my cheeks. I grabbed Joseph's arms and I didn't want to let go.

I didn't... want... to let go...

"You must, through continued effort, push into new frontiers of thought with faith and love. Push against those hidden barriers to new thought through which few beings have already passed."

- Yeshua son of Joseph -

16 · The Ship to Krokola

Upon reaching the Red Sea, we boarded a large merchant ship similar to some I'd seen on the Mediterranean, with a tall mast toward the center front of the ship that supported a billowing sail. Below deck was a compartmented hold where one could secure cargo and animals, and where people could rest and remain safe from inclement weather. Finally, the ship left port, and we were on the way to Krokola.

The first days on the ship were long and frustrating. I was excited about where we headed, but I mourned the loss of Joseph as a companion. My mood was dark. I knew I had to climb out of it as soon as possible, but the sadness prevailed for many days.

The ship was crowded; the captain, being an enterprising man, filled her to capacity. People, animals, and cargo were shoulder to shoulder with one another. There were numerous stops along the Red Sea, but none where I could debark for more than a few minutes to walk off the stiffness in my legs and find a respite from the crunch. Cargo would leave, cargo would board, passengers would change, but the cramped quarters were a constant. Finally, after what seemed an eternity of crowded days, the ship made its way through the mouth of the Red Sea and into the Sea of Arabia. Not long after turning to the east, the ship ported for a full day at Aden. I was relieved to walk on land again.

Aden was an old port town of mixed cultures. Influences from the entire trade route from Rome to China were evident in the people, the architecture, and the goods for sale in the marketplace. There were commodities like spices, dried fruit, jade ornaments, and silk from the east, and gold baubles, papyrus paper, game boards, and ivory from the west. Meandering by the many merchant stalls, my mood brightened and by the time I boarded the ship at nightfall, I was again filled with the excitement of travel.

When we set sail just after sunrise, I noticed we were less crowded and the passengers had changed substantially. One of the newly boarded was a young man close to my age. He was stockier and shorter than I, with dark skin and black hair. He was from Axum and with other members of his family, taking valuable trade goods to the Kushan area of the Indus. It was possible that once we docked at Krokola, our paths across land would be coincident for a good distance.

I spent many hours as our ship sailed up the coast of Arabia, getting to know this young man. His name was Madib, and I was fascinated by his stories of the Indus. He'd been there two times previous. I noticed Hassim made a point of getting to know Madib's family as well.

All seemed copacetic until the morning we pushed off from the Port of Muscat. I awoke with a thundering sound in my ears. I felt something was wrong. Nothing on the boat seemed to answer my question of what the noise had been. Myrrh and Hassim hadn't heard the noise, so I scuttled the question into my belly and decided I'd learn more about its cause later, if important. But I felt unsettled, a feeling I couldn't shake for the remainder of the day.

That night I sat on deck by myself, staring at the stars, still wrestling with feeling unsettled. Suddenly, a familiar Other appeared in front of me. I still found these sudden visits startling.

"Yeshua," he began, "there's something you must know."

My breathing became rapid. I said, "Please tell me."

"You and your party are in danger."

I looked around to see if anyone else was there, "Right now?"

"No, but soon after you leave this vessel."

My mind raced, "What kind of danger?"

"Grave danger." I stared at him, not knowing what to do, waiting for him to continue, "We can protect you, but you must follow our directions."

"Of course. Tell me what to do," I said.

He explained his plan, that when we reach Krokola, and before we set out on our land journey, I was to complain of a stomachache and ask to visit a healer. The healer would give me a liquid to drink. I shouldn't drink the liquid, but secret it upon my person for a later time. After the healer, I was to stay in Krokola an additional two days, ostensibly to recover. When the two days were complete, I could go about my journey, but I was to insist to Hassim that we take the southern route, not the northern route.

"I'll tell Hassim your directions," I said.

The Other was adamant, "No, don't tell anyone of our meeting tonight."

"What's the danger?"

"Your new traveling companions aren't what they seem."

I was shocked, "Madib?"

"Yes, Madib."

"Please tell me more."

He looked behind me, "There's little more I can tell you at this time. Just remember, we can protect you if you follow our directions. The most important thing is you mustn't travel further with those people. Your subterfuge should cause enough confusion to give you a chance to get away from them, at least long enough to reach your destination."

"I'll do that, of course. You've never failed me."

"I must go. We'll contact you again in a few days." He vanished, and as I was still looking through the spot where he stood a moment before, a familiar voice sounded.

"Can't sleep?" Madib asked.

"No, I can't, the stars are so beautiful tonight," I answered, but I was nervous now, unable to settle down. First, the loud noise in the morning, next the unsettled feeling all day, and now this surprising visit from the Other with such ominous news. It was enough to keep me up most of the night. To my surprise and displeasure, Madib stayed up with me.

"Our most basic physical sense is smell followed by sound. When we're born, we have little understanding of the world around us until we begin to catalog odors and noises in our environment. Our brain keys to those first sounds and smells. When your intuitive sense wants to alert you to danger in the most basic way possible, it might choose to use a sense this fundamental to survival to push it into your consciousness."

- Yeshua son of Joseph -

17 · Subterfuge

Once we arrived in Krokola, I did exactly as the Other suggested; I complained of a stomachache. It was unlike me, so complaining of a pain or problem was of great concern to both Hassim and Myrrh. I also felt guilty for lying to them, so my disturbed demeanor probably backed up the idea that I wasn't well. Hassim immediately found a healer.

Events progressed as the Other suggested. The healer examined me, rubbed my belly with a cream, had me smell a series of pots with pungent oils in them, and gave me a liquid to drink. And as instructed, I didn't drink the liquid, stashing it in my bag instead.

Hassim secured rooms for the night. Madib and his family did the same, saying they hoped to leave with us the next day. But the next day I again did as the Other suggested and by the third day, as I complained of residual fatigue, they decided to go about their business without us. I was relieved beyond measure. Myrrh and Hassim both thought it odd that they had waited for us at all.

That night as I was lying in bed awaiting sunrise, the Other again appeared. This time it was Philar. He said, "Very good, young one. You've been successful in your subterfuge."

I countered, "I've done what you asked, but it feels bad. I don't like lying to the men charged with my safe-keeping."

"I understand your difficulty," Philar said, "I assure you there was no other way to get you safely away from them."

He stepped closer to me, so I asked, "Do you still want me to insist on the southern route?"

"That's good, yes." He sat down on the edge of my bed, "Since we have a few minutes together, do you have any questions for me?"

I couldn't remember a time when Philar offered to answer my questions without a sense of haste. I didn't know where to start. It took me a moment to slow down my thoughts. When I did I had many questions, but the most pressing was this, "What is it about Madib and his family that's so dangerous?"

Philar took in a deep breath and answered, "They aren't what they seem. They were sent on this expedition with orders to befriend you."

"Orders… to befriend me?" I was surprised, "Why?"

"To kill you."

I gasped, "Who would issue such orders?"

Philar sighed, a sound that was heavy, raspy, and labored. I'd come to dislike that sound as it generally preceded him saying something I didn't want to hear. "Young one, there are powerful people who don't want you to live. This should be no surprise. Have you forgotten what happened in Egypt? You've been sheltered in your homeland. Now that you're again traveling openly, you're more vulnerable. That is… until you become more educated."

I regarded Philar with a skeptical eye. What he said was difficult to understand.

I was barely fourteen. I hadn't done anything yet. "How is it possible that I have such desperate enemies? How do they even know of me?"

"There are many who've opposed you since before you were born." He looked at me in a manner that I interpreted as fatherly. "You're held in high regard through many lands that you can't yet fathom. Where I come from you're regarded as a promise to humanity."

"I understand I have a mission, but I haven't even begun that."

"Don't worry; just as we've always been here, we'll continue to be. You need just walk your path and stay focused. All will be well."

I didn't like that answer. It's what you say to a child, to keep them from becoming fearful. "Why do you talk to me as if I were a child still?"

Again, Philar sighed with intent, "You're still a child in my eyes. But I will endeavor to speak more frankly with you."

"Thank you." I wanted to make good use of this opportunity, so I regarded my words carefully. "If Madib's people are under orders, why did they stop so easily?"

"Oh, they haven't stopped, merely regrouped. They became concerned that you'd uncover their motives if they stayed in town, but you'll encounter them again."

"When?" I asked.

"Probably in Kapilavastu."

"What would happen if we take the northern route tomorrow?"

"You'd meet them on the path. They're camping just outside town, waiting for you. You've told them your intended route. They assume you'll follow through as stated."

I became drowsy without warning. I wanted to ask a plethora of interesting questions, but my eyes were heavy and my mind sluggish. I didn't realize it at the time, but later I recognized this sudden plunge toward sleep. It was Philar's doing, I'm sure to help me, so I wouldn't lay awake ruminating all night, and probably also to lessen the number of questions he needed to answer. But before I was completely asleep, I divulged a question I'd felt burning in me for a long time. "Tell me please," I asked, "who's my Father?"

And as I plunged toward unconsciousness, I heard Philar's reply, "If you're asking who raised you as his own, cared for your every need, and loves you with his soul, you know the answer; it's Joseph. You already know your mother didn't conceive you the way babies are normally conceived. So, if you're asking whose seed gave you life, there's no answer you'll understand other than divine intervention." He paused to fuss with my blanket, pulling it up and tucking it around my shoulders. It made me feel safe and cared for. "So, if you're asking who helped the divine with that intervention, my boy… it's I." My last sight before sleep engulfed me was the face of Philar, looking upon me with simple love and satisfaction.

"Have you ever noticed that people who are 'open-books' tend to appear happier? They smile more and make friends more easily. Holding secrets, about yourself or others, is one of the most stressful activities a person can undertake. If you want to be happier in life, strive to have less to hide."

- Yeshua son of Joseph -

18 · The Southern Route

As requested, I insisted on the southern route to Kapilavastu. Hassim was resistant; it added time to our travels. The northern route was much faster, following the valleys northeast and proceeding directly through Delhi and on to our destination. But I insisted on seeing the lush, tropical valleys of the interior I'd heard so much about. Hassim finally agreed and we were back on the road.

It was a long trek, taking several months at the height of summer. It was hot and humid most of the time. I enjoyed the countryside, the jungles, and even the sudden showers of warm rain that landed on us.

The landscape changed regularly; one day might be steep mountains with lush jungles, another day might be high plains with low, bushy vegetation. At various times we stopped to pay our respects at different shrines and temples. We were Jewish, yes, but we were of the Essene. More importantly, we were Nazorean, and as such, we revered several traditions, including those of the Buddhas, the first of course being the Great Teacher, and the most recent of which was the Great Master Gautama Buddha. Some of the temples we visited were awe-inspiring in their greatness. While Jewish places of worship were mostly of similar architecture and layout, these temples varied widely from one another with ornate decorations, carvings, and statues. Most often, these carvings depicted ancient stories from the various traditions. If we didn't recognize them by sight, someone would always give us a rousing rendition of the plight of the gods and humans depicted.

Many of the statues and temples were hung with cloth blankets and drapes of bright, warm colors. People worshipped with alms and candles as devotionals. The distinctive scents raised the spirits and inspired faith. This was a completely new world. It was stimulating and aroused my imagination.

We also met with people of the various Hindu faiths. I was familiar with the beliefs of some of those faiths, having been taught that the Great Teacher imparted the initial Vedic texts many thousands of years previous. Yet here, some Hindu worshipped the Vedic teachers and masters as deities such as Indra, Vishnu, and Lakshmi.

I found it baffling that people separated these traditions. I held them all as sacred; I endeavored to see the divinity and wisdom in the entirety of the teachings together. But here, if you weren't animist, you were Buddhist, or Hindu, as travelers from Persia were mostly Zoroastrian and we from Judea were Jewish. All of these systems of belief stemmed from many of the same texts and traditions, from the same wisdom, from the same divine presence. I began to ponder certain questions that turned into a study of mine: What exactly gave people the need to separate from the wider truth and narrow their devotionals? More importantly, what made people want to hand down to their children a narrow perspective when the wider perspective was free to be had?

At most of the temples, Buddhist and Hindu, animals such as elephants, monkeys, and peacocks roamed freely with the people, both inside the temples and on the grounds. These animals were afforded great respect, unlike what I was used to in Galilee, where most animals, if they weren't tethered to humans as work mates, were raised for food. In Judea, animals that lived in the wild had a healthy fear of man, avoiding us at almost any cost. But people here were mostly vegetarian as I was, so the animals had little fear and interacted willingly with me if I approached them. I soon found that if I wasn't careful at meals, there were always a few nimble monkeys hanging around to snatch anything that looked tasty. I found their behavior at once surprising and endearing.

The three of us were having a good time on the road. Laughter was quick and plentiful and we met wonderful and openhearted people. Hassim admitted to me one morning that he was very happy we'd taken the southern route; he was having the time of his life.

So was I.

"Believe in the great mysteries. Thrive in your journey through the unknown. Life's path is grandest when it unveils itself, little by little, as a lover would on her wedding night."

- Yeshua son of Joseph -

19 · Slow Down Time

During our travels to Kapilavastu, there was one incident of note that threatened our safety. We were crossing the great flood plains of the Ganges; the lush tropical lands were behind us, as was the sacred river. We'd crossed it by ferry the day before. Here the land consisted of dry and wet tributaries and vast fields of shrubs and grass. Sparsely grown trees dotted the landscape. It was late summer and we were probably about a week from our destination.

As we walked past one trickling tributary, a fast moving monsoon bore in on us with wind like I'd never experienced. My thin body nearly toppled several times. Heavy rain pummeled us unexpectedly. A light rain was easy to deal with – just keep walking. But this rain was strident. We found an earthen rise with a handful of trees and rocks and planned to huddle there until the wind and rain stopped. After more than an hour of this driving rain, we began to feel a shudder in the ground that was familiar to Hassim. He sent Myrrh up one of the trees and to his horror, Myrrh spied a wave of water – a flash flood – moving quickly in our direction.

He yelled at us to climb. Hassim had difficulty climbing, but with my help, he made it halfway up a tree. The beast was on its own. All I could do was untether it before I quickly climbed a third tree. I hoped the beast could swim and save itself somehow. It was unclear if the trees would survive, but it was our only chance.

We wrapped ourselves around the trunks, and while holding on for our lives, a roaring wall of mud and debris-laden water hit. It was frightening. The water nearly engulfed us. I was my height times two up the tree and the water hit above my knees. It sped by us with unexpected strength and made the trees bow. The donkey was carried away instantly. As far as I could see in every direction, there was only water where there was nothing but ground a few minutes before. It was a massive amount of water; a sight I'll never forget.

My tree held, Hassim's tree held, but Myrrh's didn't. Myrrh was upstream from me, so when his tree snapped and he was thrown into the water, he came toward me. If I didn't act, and act fast, Myrrh would be swept away by the current.

I was blessed, for as soon as I asked for help, the Unseen answered. They instructed me to ride out on a branch and grab Myrrh as he passed by. To accomplish that, they told me to slowdown time. I wasn't keen to use this ability. Joseph was clear that these oddities of behavior I possessed were no joke – nothing to use lightly. But this was an emergency. So I willed time to slow down. The water

"Yeshua had the great good fortune of his Unseen companions from birth. The good fortune was in his ability to see them and interact with them without veil. As a child, I was envious of this ability. However, in later life I realized we all have this great good fortune of unseen attendants ready and willing to help us at every juncture. The only difference being that we have to find a way to lift the veil that separates us from those helpers."

- James brother of Yeshua -

slowed and I glided out to the end of the branch. It was easy with the water moving at a slower pace, even though the rain was still falling.

Myrrh was coming toward me. I shouted to him to let go of the tree. He did, but he began thrashing. I realized too late that he didn't know how to swim. I shouted again for him to relax and let the water bring him to me. But he kept thrashing. When he finally got close to me, his head went under the water.

I was beside myself with fright. One of the Unseen yelled, 'Slow time more!' I did, and now time was moving at a turtles' pace, but Myrrh was still below the water. The Unseen yelled, 'Find him!'

So I took a deep breath and slid in. I kept my grip on the branch and I saw part of Myrrh's leg and robe caught in the foliage. At least he was here and not downstream.

I tried to pull his body above the waterline, but he was caught badly. I stripped off his robe and got his head into the air, but he wasn't breathing. Everything was moving very slowly now except me. If I could get him up on the tree, maybe I could get him breathing again. Then I saw the damage. Blood was flowing from a gash to his right temple. He must have hit the tree in the fall.

I pulled Myrrh onto a higher branch and held him tight. I didn't know what else to do. The Unseen said, 'He has water in his lungs. It has to come out!'

"How?" I shouted to be heard over the roar of the rain and the water, forgetting that my Unseen companions heard thought as loudly as spoken words.

'Turn him over so his face is below his chest.' I did that. 'Raise his arms above his head.' I did that.

Suddenly, Myrrh was coughing, water gushing from his mouth. Now all I had to worry about was the wound. I ripped a piece of cloth from my robe and bound it around his head to apply pressure to it. With all my strength, I held onto the tree with one arm and onto Myrrh with the other, and I prayed thanks to my Divine Creator as I released my hold on time. The water went back to its rush. I looked at Hassim. He stared at me jaw-dropped and wide-eyed, his face white from fright and shock. I was concerned that part of his shock was my altered-time display. All I could do now was wait for the water to subside. Dealing with any reaction from Hassim would be nothing compared to how I'd feel if Myrrh had been swept away by the current.

20 · Consequences

We hung in the trees for about an hour, until the rain subsided and the water began to recede. When it did recede, it did so quickly, and the patch of higher ground where we once huddled became visible. I shouted to Hassim to stay put. The first priority was to get Myrrh to the ground. Myrrh was semi-conscious, unable to respond, and shaking.

I eased us both out of the tree and laid him on the wet ground. I freed his robe from the foliage and laid it over him, though I'm not sure how much good it did as the robe was still wet.

I helped Hassim ease down. He was shaking too, and refusing to talk. The most he could muster was a praise of thanks to God. He wouldn't take his eyes off me.

I sat Hassim next to Myrrh and demanded of my mind to formulate a course of action. It was apparent that I was the least fragile physically, and of the three of us, I was the only one not in shock, or so I thought. But I was deeply affected by these events, more than I realized. I faced an unfamiliar and difficult situation. We were alive, that was our grace, but we needed to stay alive and the road to that pleasant outcome seemed elusive.

Taking stock of our resources took but a moment. With the beast gone, most of our provisions were gone. We had what I was carrying on my back: a bag for water, an extra robe, a towel, a comb for my hair, a bark for my teeth, some fruit and nuts, a few trinkets I'd picked up along the way, and a slip of now wet scrolls. I also had some money and one nefarious item – the potion I'd stashed away in Krokola.

Hassim saw what I was doing. He pulled from a leather purse hidden under his robe, some coins, a small stack of letters for delivery in Kapilavastu, a little ocarina, and a pendant on a fob that had belonged to his deceased wife.

Even though they didn't seem to help our current situation, I thanked Hassim for his reveal and handed him a piece of fruit. As he slowly and deliberately ate, he calmed; his breathing became less shallow and color returned to his cheeks. He was, however, not saying a word and not moving his eyes off me.

Myrrh was another story. He was breathing irregularly and while the shaking of his body had subsided, it was not gone altogether. And he was still not fully conscious. But sitting here on the wet ground silently watching the waters recede began to settle my mind.

Taking stock, the resources we had were pitifully light. We had enough food for no more than one day, splitting what I was carrying between three people, and nothing with which to make a fire. And nothing with which to dig or cut. I was traveling with a knife, but somehow it was lost. We were in the middle of nowhere and several days away from our destination. It would soon be night and I wasn't sure how to attend to Myrrh. It was possible his head injury was worse than it looked.

As I tried to piece the picture into a plan, Hassim said, "I can't know."

I said, "You can't know what?"

"I can't know anything," he replied, "I can't know."

I was unable to understand his meaning. "I'm not following you."

He paused, then asked, "Who are you?"

"It's me, Yeshua. Hassim, don't you recognize me?"

"I don't know you."

"You know me, I'm your charge. I'm Yeshua, Joseph's son," but his eyes glazed over and I thought it best to wait.

As I was trying to come up with a solution, I became aware that we weren't alone. Standing behind Hassim were three Other. One put a finger to his mouth signaling me to be quiet, and put Hassim to sleep.

"There, that's for the best," he muttered, "We're here to help."

I sighed in relief, "What can I do? We have no food to speak of, no way to keep warm. I've no means to move Myrrh." Looking into this Other's eyes, I could feel my composure begin to deteriorate, "Help."

"Yes, we'll help. I'm Colum. Don't fear; we'll move you soon, but first we need to look after the head injury."

"Please," I gestured toward Myrrh, "I'm afraid for him."

The two Other behind Colum began assessing Myrrh's condition. I felt helpless, but having the Other here seemed a Godsend.

Colum came closer, "Philar says you have a potion with you."

"Yes!" I picked up the small flask and handed it to him. My desperation began to subside and as soon as it did, confusion overtook my mind.

"Ah, good, good." Colum took the flask and turned it over to his companions. They quickly poured the liquid down Myrrh's throat. He sputtered, but swallowed the bulk of it.

Colum looked at me, "This will help stabilize him for the journey."

"Journey?" I asked.

"Yes, we're going to transport you to your destination."

"But... how?" My confusion grew, "I see no carts, or... or beasts?"

"Calm yourself."

"Did you know we'd have trouble?" My mind raced. But before I spun completely out of control, Colum smiled and put me to sleep too.

When I woke, I was on the ground under a tree. Hassim and Myrrh were lying unconscious next to me. In this place, everything was dry and warm. I sat up and when my eyes fully adjusted to the light, I saw Colum sitting a few feet away.

"Welcome back, young one. You're now at Kapilavastu."

"If we define ourselves based on what we think, believe, and do, we can easily take exception with how the world treats us. But, if we build a definition of ourselves on the beauty and value of our soul, we can never take exception with the world around us, because the world around us is merely an extension of the magnificence we stem from."

- Yeshua son of Joseph -

"How?"

He didn't answer my question. Instead, he said, "Your confusion is natural." Colum stood and looked across the meadow. He pointed, "On the other side of this field is a river. If you follow the river upstream, it becomes a lake. After about five minutes' walk, you'll pass some buildings, at which point you'll come to the main gate of the university. Proceed through the gate and ask to speak with the Schoolmaster. When you find him, tell him who you are and that your companions are hurt and need help. He'll know what to do."

"How will I explain getting here?"

"With truth, young one, with truth. You were caught in a flood. Your party was overcome. You don't know how you got this far, but help is needed now."

"I will, thank you."

"I'll wait here until you return. No more harm will befall your friends. Hurry."

I did as Colum outlined. Once inside the gate, I was grateful that I'd learned a small amount of a local language on the trek. I could be understood just enough to be led to the Master of the University. I must have looked a mess when I finally found him. He looked me up and down with concern. "Young man, do you need help?"

"Yes, I do. Are you the Schoolmaster here?"

"Yes, I'm Huume." He placed his hand on my shoulder in a fatherly fashion that was reassuring.

"I'm Yeshua son of Joseph and I think you're expecting me."

Huume took a deep breath and pulled me into his embrace, "Oh, my boy, just this morning I became so concerned for you. I'm relieved you've arrived." He looked around us, "But where are your companions?"

"They're outside the city, both are hurt. We were caught in a flood. We need help."

"Hurt?" He shouted across the common to a man I assumed was a priest by his garb. Speaking to him in a language I didn't understand, a flurry of activity was set in motion. Within a few minutes, I was escorting a group of men and a cart to where my party laid waiting. And as promised, no more harm had come to them.

"Truth is relative. My truth and your truth may not be a perfect match, but they are both truth and as such, must be respected. I cannot ignore my truth and expect to be happy. But neither can I ignore your truth and expect you to stay."
- Yeshua son of Joseph -

21 · Kapilavastu

I sat on a bench next to Huume. Abundant orchards and lush gardens surrounded the university and a pastoral, mirrored lake flanked the entire settlement. More than a hundred brothers lived in and around the university. Some of the brothers taught, others worked the orchards or tended the fields. Some were doctors, cooks – in short, every specialty needed to run this operation. They mixed well with the townspeople and everything seemed tranquil.

"This is our humble village," Huume said. "This is where the Great Master Gautama Buddha lived his young life."

"It's beautiful here," I remarked.

"Yes. And I think you'll find your studies stimulating."

I looked at my feet, then at Huume. I felt awkward and unsure how to address him. "Master?" I said.

"There's no need to call me Master. Please call me Huume."

"Alright… Huume," I cleared my throat, "I've been thinking about what you said yesterday, about my name being hard to pronounce."

"Yes, it doesn't flow easily from the tongue here, like it might in your homeland."

"I like my name, but I'm already different enough. I don't need to call that out with a name others will dislike."

"What do you think of my suggestions?"

"Well, I really like the sound of Issa."

"That's a good choice. It means 'the beloved one.' People smile when they hear it." He smiled at me, "Alright, Issa, so be it." His face reflected a deep serenity. Everyone I'd met here had a peace about them that was compelling. I wondered if, after a time, my face would reflect the same serenity. I couldn't fathom it right now, but the possibility intrigued me.

So far, we'd been here a mere handful of days and in that time, the health of my companions increased. Myrrh was still in the infirmary, but when I visited each day, I saw him improving. His brain had been injured from the blow he suffered during the flood, but he could walk and talk and we hoped he would fully recover. Hassim was excited by the new surroundings and made a private, quiet space for himself in the library. There he could study the subjects he was interested in at his own pace. He and I never talked about the flood, nor of what he witnessed. Once he recovered from shock, he seemed resolved about the incident, or perhaps his shock had wiped the events from his memory. Either way, it seemed for the best, so I let it go.

"There was a freedom in assuming a new name when I traveled to the east. It gave me permission to begin anew."

- Yeshua son of Joseph -

And so it was, that I jumped into this new life with hope, promise, and a new name: Issa.

This was an international university. Students came from diverse cultures and spoke different native languages. In its wisdom, the university declared one language, Sanskrit, the primary language of the school. All teachers and students were required to know it. It was the most common language used in the local sacred texts and so was familiar, if not fully known, to almost everyone who might want to study here. And even though it wasn't the only language I'd need to learn here, learning it first would give me the greatest base of commonality to people. It was easy; I had a flair for language and soon I was conversing quite well.

My companions and I were assigned to a small, one-room bungalow next to the university. Hassim and I moved in immediately. Myrrh would join us when he was well enough to leave the infirmary. The room had three cots, each with a small table, and together we shared a set of shelves. It was plenty for us, comfortable, and within a short walk of the library and classrooms.

I soon learned the university had several nicknames. Officially, its name reflected the locale, the University at Kapilavastu. But the students, especially those that had been there for years, called it other names, some that were synonymous with catacombs. These nicknames mocked the boring and monotone teaching style of some of the brothers, and by the time I was fully immersed in my classes, I wholeheartedly agreed with the sentiment. So, I began my scholastic career, however short it turned out to be, at the Combs.

Our schedules were simple. Each workday, Hassim sequestered himself in the library, and Myrrh worked in the fields in the morning, and monitored classes in the afternoon. I attended classes in the morning, and spent the afternoons studying. Along with these activities, we folded into the spiritual life of the community. We added to our morning baptism, group chanting sessions with the brothers, midday prayers, and pre-supper meditations. These were not required of students, as many were not Bon, but we were of like mind and wanted to take advantage of the spiritual support. I loved every minute of it.

In the evenings, we were free to visit with friends, read, write, play games, or join whatever social activities arose. As the months flew by, I learned a number of social skills, from playing a stringed instrument, to performing traditional songs and dances, to mastering strategy games. I even learned how to use and decipher a personal oracle from China called I Ching.

This new life suited me well.

"We received many letters from Yeshua while he was away at the university. I often had to fight my own jealousy over his good fortune to go off to school. But after I got home from my trip to Europe, I no longer envied him. I felt I was the lucky one to have the love of family with me."

- James brother of Yeshua -

22 · Madib Returns

One fateful afternoon, some friends and I were in the outdoor commons debating the shortcomings of some of our less illustrious teachers. As adolescent boys will do, we boisterously laughed at jokes we shouldn't even have cracked.

Out of the corner of my eye, I saw a group of visitors with carts wander past. Visitors and supply trains came often, so it wasn't anything to be concerned about. But my attention became piqued when the Unseen popped up, unbidden and pensive. A young boy ran to me shouting, "Issa, Issa, they say they know you." I also noticed telltale signs of the Other watching me. This meant danger was near. The hair on my arms stood on end.

The boy tugged on my sleeve, "Come, Issa," but I was riveted in place.

Two friends slapped my back. One said, "Hey, what're you waiting for? Let's see who's here. Maybe it's someone from your home."

I made myself walk toward the visitors, but a jolt of fear nearly knocked me over when I saw the grinning face of Madib.

"Yeshua," he shouted as he ran to embrace me. His touch made my stomach wrench. "We weren't sure what to make of your new name." Madib exclaimed loudly, "We almost couldn't find you!"

I patted his shoulder and pulled back from his embrace. "What brings you to our village?" I asked.

"We were near and thought to look you up, that's all."

I mustered a weak smile. Madib glanced at his family members in a way that made my intuition scream at me to be careful. I politely introduced them to my Combs friends. A few moments later I said, "Let me go find the schoolmaster and see if we can make you a place to stay for the night. I'll be back shortly."

I ran toward the library, and when I was out of sight, I ducked between two buildings, waiting for the Other to appear. I was desperate for help and the next minute was unbearable; it felt more like an hour. Philar spoke behind me, causing me to jump with fright, "Calm yourself, Issa. We'll protect you."

"It's like you said," I blurted, "they caught up with me."

"Don't worry," Philar restated, "you're safe. I have a plan. Take a deep breath and listen." I took in not just one, but several deep breaths, and tried to focus on what Philar had to say. It wasn't easy. He continued, "These people are nefarious. They're wanted by the authorities for other crimes."

"Oh?"

"Yes, we've been following them for weeks. We thought they wouldn't come

"Always pay attention to the little things around you. They may be harbingers of larger events to come; events you might miss if you aren't paying attention to the clues."

- Yeshua son of Joseph -

here, but since they did, we'll take this opportunity to have them captured."

"Captured?" I inquired.

"Yes, for their crimes."

I calmed more, and said in a sarcastic tone, "How do we make that happen?"

Philar put his arm around my shoulder and explained more of the plan, but it all came down to me soliciting Huume to contact the Kushan authorities. Philar's plan made sense. He assured me that every moment, whether I perceived it or not, the Other protected me.

———✦———

As expected, I found Huume in the library. I urged him to his office to speak privately, and told him there was danger.

"What's this?" Huume's face reflected a sudden concern, "Sit down, Issa." Huume sat and motioned for me to do the same. "What are you talking about?"

Without revealing Philar's true identity, I relayed the story that my allies had alerted me to this danger and helped me escape these men in Krokola. "Hassim and Myrrh don't know anything about this, Huume. I'm telling you because taking you into my confidence is a plan my ally feels will keep me safe."

"I see," Huume said, but I could see the confusion on his face. "Give me a moment to consider this." I waited patiently, but I felt the pull of time. Too long of a delay would surely cause Madib and his family to become suspicious. Finally, Huume asked, "Can I speak with the man who concocted this plan?"

"I'm afraid not."

Huume sighed, "This is a difficult thing you ask of me. We don't like to involve these Kushan in anything that happens here."

"I understand. I grew up with the Romans always at our back."

Huume nodded, and continued, "I know you have enemies, Issa, just as you have allies. I'm not ignorant of what this means." He paused again, obviously wrestling with the decision. To my relief, he said, "Alright, I'll trust this. Your safety is paramount." He stood, "I'll contact the authorities. In the meantime, let's assign the visitors to quarters where they'll be seen if they try to leave." He turned again to me, "Be careful Issa."

I left Huume's office, picked up Hassim from the library, and walked back to where Madib's party was waiting. All went well the rest of the evening.

———✦———

Later that night, alone in our bungalow, Myrrh confessed he was nervous. Hassim concurred. Myrrh did something he'd never done before; he pushed his cot

"There are always three things left to do. Even when you see pages of a to-do list in front of you. In any moment, the list reduces to just three things if you correctly identify what's important. And yet, you can do only one of them well at that moment. Patience is learning to attend to the one that is in the forefront, doing it, and letting the other two go until each, in turn, either disappears or slides to the forefront."

- Yeshua son of Joseph -

in front of the door in such a way that if anyone tried to come into the room, he'd awaken.

"I don't know why," Myrrh said to us, "I just feel safer this way." Neither Hassim nor I objected.

The next morning, we woke, safe, and performed our morning rituals, but I didn't go off by myself, I stayed glued to Myrrh and Hassim. When it was time for breakfast, we went together; we even went to the latrine together. My companions didn't know everything I knew, but their intuition told them I was in danger.

Madib's group joined us for breakfast, all the while behaving as if they were our best friends. I marveled at their ability to treat me so dearly, knowing I was merely a mark they hunted. That they could smile to my face, while they envisioned spilling my blood. It was a lesson about human nature I wouldn't forget.

After breakfast, several brothers stayed with us in the dining hall as we talked about our various travels. I'm sure Huume told them to stay; otherwise, they'd have had no reason to ignore their regular duties.

Just before midday prayers, our bunch and Madib's party gathered in the outdoor commons. We talked about this and that, trying to keep the conversation light, but I didn't feel light. I was anxious for this situation to resolve. As we talked, I felt an energetic change descend on the area. I heard the muted sound of horse hoofs, more horses than normal. I saw brothers scurrying, which was unusual given that they were normally unhurried. An unnatural hush settled in around us. Madib's party became nervous; they fidgeted in their seats as if they were sitting on sand grit.

Suddenly, three men jumped toward us from behind a building, each brandishing a bladed weapon. From the opposite side three more armed men ran forward. It was the Kushan. Madib's group was surprised. For a moment, it looked as though they might bolt, but it was of no use; a swath of men stepped out of hiding, and it was obvious we were surrounded.

Madib yelled something in his native tongue and grabbed Hassim, pulling him to his chest in a tight grip. His uncle grabbed me and slipped a small knife to my throat. He yelled, "Stop, or I'll kill him."

As if out of nowhere, Madib's uncle tumbled to the ground unconscious, with me landing on top of him. As I scrambled to my feet, Myrrh grabbed Hassim to keep him from freefalling, as Madib joined his uncle on the ground, unconscious. The rest of Madib's men stood in shock as the Kushan rushed forward to shackle them.

I was immeasurably grateful that the whole business was over. In the aftermath, none could understand what happened. It was unfathomable to all but me. It was the Other that caused Madib and his uncle to go unconscious. But of course, I told no one.

Later, Huume told me that the Kushan authorities were grateful for his assistance. Madib's party was wanted for several crimes, including arson, kidnapping, and murder. Because of the capture, the University received a reward of more money than it usually collected from students in an entire year. Huume had made an ally of the local authorities, a relationship that would serve him in the years to come.

———⚜———

That night, my friends threw me a party. I had a sudden mystique about me, having to do with criminals threatening to assassinate me. I didn't mind the attention. In fact, my ego loved it. Being fawned over felt good.

But when the party was over and I climbed into bed, I was still shaken from the incident. I realized that the things Philar told me were true. His words rumbled through me in a way they never had before, and I had to ask myself a tough question, "Who am I, really?"

"I never believed, when I witnessed my brother's life threatened, that his light could be extinguished; not until he was captured by the Romans and tortured. In my mind, he was untouched and untouchable. He'd recounted a few stories of danger from his travels, but something about his presence, once he finally came home for good, was so compelling. His every cell oozed peace and love; too much to imagine his light was in any way vulnerable."

- James brother of Yeshua -

23 · Death

A few other notable events took place that year. The first was a series of letters I received from James. He'd reached his majority and remained undecided about his path. It was unfortunate, because he'd receive pressure to decide quickly. I supported him taking his time, but many didn't.

Our cousin Joseph from Jerusalem was a high-ranking member of the Sanhedrin. He was also a well-established merchant with heavy ties to Rome and regions north of the Mediterranean. Joseph was concerned about James finding a suitable path and wanted to welcome him into the business as an apprentice and eventually as a partner. After some lengthy conversations with our father, he invited James to accompany him on a trip into those northern regions to see how he took to the merchant life.

At first, James's letters were effusive about the people and places he encountered, but about half way through the trip, the tenor of his letters changed. He complained about life on the road and longed to be home again. Bottom line is that by the time he got home, his mind was made up. He wanted to become a scholar. Not just that, but he also wanted to become a monk and disavow marriage.

This was a hard thing. As a Jewish male, it was a commandment from the Almighty to marry and multiply. Becoming a monk straight out of childhood, without trying one's hand at a family first, was frowned upon.

I asked James his reasons. His answer was adamant. He was sure, beyond a doubt, that he'd never he happy as a husband, nor would any wife be happy with him. It was hard to imagine that, at the age of thirteen, one could be so sure of such a thing. I was fifteen and I didn't have a clue how I'd feel being a husband, or what that would even require of me. Nonetheless, I felt James' resolve. I wondered how Joseph would handle the matter. Only time would tell.

The year progressed and as Huume foretold, my studies were stimulating. By the end of that year, I'd advanced more than two years in the curriculum.

That's when another event occurred; one that was more difficult to accept. Near the end of the scholastic year on a clear, crisp morning, Myrrh was working in the fields as usual, when something terrible gripped him. He lost consciousness and

"My decision to not marry brought grief to my family. There were instances as an adult when I wondered if I'd made a mistake. But looking back, it was the best choice. In the first place, I had no passion for sex. More importantly though, as a young adult I was strident in my judgments of the behaviors of others, and I would've made life unbearable for a wife."

- James brother of Yeshua -

fell to the ground, his body shaking violently. The brothers carried him to the infirmary, but there was nothing to do but wait.

A few weeks later on a cool afternoon, he recovered consciousness for a short time. He was anxious to speak with me. "Yeshua," Myrrh began, "I want you to know I'm happy."

I was puzzled, "What do you mean? Happy about what?"

"I'm dying."

"No, you'll recover," I became agitated, "we'll figure this out."

"No, I know I'm leaving, and soon. I just needed to talk with you one more time before I go."

"No, Myrrh, don't, please, hold on."

He laid his hand on my arm, "Don't be sad. Be happy with me." I looked at him, speechless. How could he ask me to be happy with the thought he was dying? He continued, "I've been home, just now, home... with all that is." I grabbed his hand and squeezed. "I've seen God. He welcomes me," Myrrh said as his eyes glazed over.

"Please stay Myrrh..."

"He says I've done well." His eyes rolled back and I was afraid it was the end, but his eyes came back to center and he said, "I've always known accompanying you was my greatest path and deepest honor. At this moment, I feel that one-thousand fold." His hand cupped mine, "I'm going home with my head held high. Thank you for the opportunity to do something important with my life."

He smiled as I held his hand. Slowly but surely, each muscle relaxed until there was no spirit left to animate them. Gentle Myrrh went home, his face serene.

I was devastated.

24 · Insa'alet

It wasn't like me to become an emotional whirlwind, but this was no ordinary day. I'd lost my companion. I began to wail, unable to control the sound erupting from me.

Some brothers rushed in and found Myrrh's body dead on the cot and me roaring. I was inconsolable. I couldn't believe that I wasn't able to stop Myrrh from dying. I broke from their embrace and ran from the infirmary, sprinting into the orchards, all the time bellowing from the pain of it.

My mind spun. The thought of what just happened was nearly unimaginable. 'Why this?' I thought, 'Why him? Why now?' And as I asked these questions, a well of grief opened up in my breast and I fell to the ground sobbing.

I sobbed for hours as these same inevitable, yet worthless questions continued to assail my consciousness. When the sobs finally calmed, I opened my eyes and saw Huume standing a short distance from where I lay. Concern shrouded his normally tranquil face. When he realized I knew he was present, he stepped over and knelt on the ground, "What can I do for you, Issa?"

I was exhausted. I looked into his face and said, "I have no idea."

Huume wrapped his arm around my back and softly prodded me to a standing position. His warm presence supported me as we walked back to my quarters and settled me into the cot. He perched on the edge of a stool, his hand resting on my shoulder until sleep overtook me.

When I woke many hours later, I spied Myrrh's empty cot and realized he'd never be in it again. This time when the tears started, there was no wailing. There was only a river of grief staining my sight with despair. It felt horribly unfair.

Hassim shared my grief, but was more resolved than I to the finality of death. After all, he'd lost his wife. He confessed he'd lost a child to death as well. He'd lost parents and friends, a whole cadre of people throughout his life. This was the way of it. Hassim explained that death was never easy; it usually came without warning and rarely left anything but a hole in its wake.

The doctor explained that Myrrh's death was a result of his injury sustained during the flood. In some ways, it was comforting to have a reason, something to point to and blame. In another way though, I felt guilty. That injury happened

"Death of a loved one is one of the hardest things a person will ever encounter in life. Everyone handles it differently on the outside, but on the inside, everyone must reconcile with death's effects. To not accept death, is to turn your back on life."

- James brother of Yeshua -

while he was in service… to me.

A few days later as I moped, Huume suggested I visit the Temple at Insa'alet. Apparently, the Temple Master had expressed a desire to meet me and Huume thought it might do me good to get away.

So, I strapped a bag to my back, and accompanied the next supply train that came through our village on its way to Mustang Province. Mustang Province was north, on the other side of Annapurna. Thankfully, I wouldn't be traveling all the way to Mustang, as the temple was along the way, this side of the peaks.

The terrain was easy going, albeit treacherous in parts. These men working the supply train were rugged individuals who stopped rarely and slept little. Even with youth on my side, keeping pace was a challenge. At times, we walked through green valleys, at other times we traversed narrow paths with steep drops to one side. The trail went up and down in elevation, but the net effect was up.

Because of our quick pace, we arrived at the temple on a sunny afternoon just a few days after we began. The brothers at the temple were delighted to receive the supplies and they welcomed me with wholehearted enthusiasm.

Staying at the temple was healing. I accompanied the brothers through their days. This included long hours of meditation and deep reflection. Silence was rarely broken and even though the food was austere in substance, it fed my spirit as deeply as the meditation and prayer.

A few weeks into my stay, the Temple Master tapped me on the shoulder during a meditation and asked me to accompany him to one of the lookouts. From there, we could see across the valley to the rugged, snow-covered peaks of Annapurna. This temple sat high in the mountains, but these tremendous peaks rose even higher. They pulsed with energy and looked treacherous. I could hardly imagine the men with the supply train continuing over them to Mustang.

Even though these peaks were overwhelming in their majesty, I felt the presence of the Master at my side. The authority of his presence was fearsome and palpable. Yet, at the same time, the calming qualities of joy and peace emanated from him.

"I've been following your progress, young Issa." His voice was just as powerful as his presence: strong and clear, yet soothing.

"I'm honored, Master."

"There's no honor in being watched. Honor is what you claim from fulfilling your inner calling."

"I'll remember that."

"Issa, I know you're struggling with death; one of life's greatest mysteries."

As soon as he said this, hidden tears I hadn't touched in days resurfaced, "Yes, my companion Myrrh died. He was such a gentle man."

After a moment, the Master said, "Gentle men are part of God's army."

I looked at the Master, "What do you mean?"

"Ah," he chuckled, "haven't you noticed that those who are especially gentle of spirit die sooner?"

I thought about it, and said, "No, Master, I hadn't noticed."

"Then this marks the beginning of your lesson." Suddenly, my mind filled with perverse thoughts of the people I knew dying around me, falling limp off their breakfast stools or lifelessly dropping mid-stride. I had to fight the temptation to reel in fear from the notion of this lesson just beginning. "Issa," he continued, "death isn't the end. We all must endure this shift. Death marks the movement from one plane of existence to another. It's to be celebrated for the completion of one aspect of spirit and the joyous beginning of another."

"But I didn't get to say goodbye properly," I lamented, "I was full of fear when he left."

"You think your words are what follow him?"

I thought for a moment, "When I left home, it's the words of my loved ones that followed me. They sustain me through days when I miss them. When I yearn for their company, their words accompany me instead."

The Master said, "You're mistaken."

How was I mistaken? What could otherwise be true? My mind skittered through my brain looking for a place of connection to any concept it could find.

"Young Issa, continue your search for a thought more to your liking. When your search is exhausted and you're ready to find truth, let me know." With that, he turned and left me feeling as if I had just flunked my greatest test.

25 · Restricted Library

I had many more conversations with the Temple Master as the days progressed. I was unaccustomed to his teaching style. It felt brutal. But after several days of being told I was wrong and being left alone with my fragmented thoughts, I realized it was a gauntlet I needed to run. My mind was agile, my brain responsive, but my ego was weak. It was addicted to being right.

Being bathed in grief presented a wide opportunity for me to grow. Regardless of how I felt when these lessons began, within a short time I felt myself change. I became comfortable with uncertainty, ambiguity, malformed hypotheses, and questions without answers. After two months of this ego scrubbing, I learned that I was better off when I accepted that the only thing I had real hope of knowing was myself.

As is so often true of people who are quick-witted and agile, my ego held itself above others. I'd become arrogant and felt entitled. My overblown ego came close to breaking on that cool afternoon when Myrrh died. I howled and screamed in defiance of what happened. I couldn't accept that something so dire could or would happen against my will. Luckily, rather than soothe my disturbed ego, the Temple Master broke it open. Like the taming of a wild horse, breaking was beneficial.

By the time I got back to the Combs, I was ready for school to continue. Perhaps I wasn't as far along my road as my ego might have wished, but I was a sight further down the path. And it didn't take long for me to miss Insa'alet.

The next year was relatively uneventful. Academically, I sailed past other students, nearly completing enough subjects to graduate. The brothers told me no one had ever progressed so fast. But it wasn't enough for me. The subject matter of most classes was flat. I knew in my heart there was more to know and I suspected the brothers were actively hiding knowledge.

I went to Huume more than once and inquired about where the older and more esoteric texts were. Each time he acted as if he didn't know what I meant. I

"There were times when Yeshua's affect in the world appeared arrogant to many people. His excessive intelligence sometimes translated into platitudes or actions that reeked of a dry or cold affect. Knowing him as I did, I understood this was usually a result of being distracted. But when the demands settled down and his heart fully engaged, he usually recognized his less than desired behavior and was quick to apologize or otherwise rectify mistaken actions and impressions."

- Miriam wife of Yeshua -

was persistent, however, and near the end of the school year, he finally admitted that there was indeed a second library. It was restricted, only open to a select few. When I asked him how I could become one of those few, he replied, "It can't be earned, it can only be revealed." I had no idea exactly what 'revealed' meant, the reference was obscure, but the way he said it conjured pictures in my mind of dark rooms and arcane secrets. The mystery of it inflamed my desire. I wanted to go so much further than the brothers had taken me. There are no words to describe how much I desired access to that hidden knowledge.

Soon after, Hassim went home to Judea. I didn't want him to go, he was the last person there with ties to my home, my family; the last person with whom I spoke Aramaic.

Hassim loved his time in Kapilavastu. He enjoyed his quiet corner of the library, but a letter arrived from one of his daughters explaining that her husband died and she needed him to come home. Her children were young enough to need a father figure and she needed a protectorate. So Hassim agreed to make this the next phase of his life. The trek home would be hard for him, but he'd take it slow, accompanied by the man who brought the letter; and this time they'd go on horseback, taking the shorter route. I had every faith he'd arrive at his daughter's unharmed.

That same rider also delivered a second letter, this one to me, from James. By now, James was fourteen and Joseph had asked him to sit with his thoughts and that if by the time he was fifteen he still wanted to be a monk, Joseph would consent. In preparation for what James felt was an eventuality, he applied, and was accepted, to the community at Qumran, the same place Myrrh had lived.

Qumran was called the City of Salt, an Essene monastery located east of Jerusalem near the banks of the Dead Sea. Salt was primarily academic and the brothers there were strict in their devotions. Salt was an element used primarily for cleansing and preservation, and as the name might imply, the brothers at Salt concentrated on the study and preservation of 'The Word' in all its many textual forms.

This would suit James. Unlike me, he thrived when the rules were clearly defined and austere in nature. Of the companions he might make in that community, I thought of Myrrh and knew that if only a fraction of the brothers at Salt were as gentle and kind as Myrrh, James would be in good company.

He asked for my blessing. I would give that, of course, but he shared something else with me; something he was reluctant to talk about, but felt he needed to say. While he was traveling with our cousin, James had a series of waking visions. Each vision had come to him when he wasn't expecting it, when he was otherwise performing some mundane task.

These visions showed him deep in study, living a monastic life. The last few visions revealed he and I walking the land and teaching people. The visions were compelling enough, but they also left him with a body of knowing. This knowing began with the understanding that marriage wouldn't suit him. It would be a distraction, not a joy. He confessed that he was so uninterested in sex that the notion of marital relations didn't intrigue him; it repulsed him. This knowing clarified that his eventual calling in life was to take his place by my side.

I didn't know what to make of this. I didn't know what I'd eventually do. When I wrote my reply though, I suggested that he tell our father about the visions. They were eerily similar to what Joseph shared with me when we were on the road to Aqaba.

The next academic year began, but there was no placement for me in the current class roster. Instead, Huume assigned me to a tutor to oversee my curriculum and I studied on my own in the library. My friends, all good and dear young men, gave me a hard time. They likened my sequestering to a culling of the herd, when the herder pulls the weaker animals so the pack is less vulnerable to predator attack. It was good for my ego to have their constant ribbing. It helped me stay in check.

One day, Huume asked if I'd meet him in his office. When I got there, three brothers joined us. They were older brothers, only one of which had been my teacher.

"Issa, thank you for joining us," Huume began.

"Yes, of course," I said as I looked at their faces. They were solemn, but not sad. I couldn't imagine I was in trouble, so I just waited.

The brothers glanced at each other for a few moments, then Huume continued, "Well, Issa... it's been revealed that you're to have access to the restricted library."

"Uh... what?" I exclaimed. Truly, I didn't expect this, though I wanted it more than anything.

Huume chuckled, "I'm sure you heard me. Never have these sacred texts been revealed to someone so young. You're just seventeen."

One of the other brothers said, "I must say, Issa, I'm shocked by this reveal. I have faith... and I comply with my consent to giving you this privilege... but it makes me nervous."

"I understand," I said as the gravity of this advantage began to sink in. "I respect your honesty. I'm prepared to be responsible with your trust."

"You'd better be," he said with some force.

Huume interrupted, "Issa, we all feel nervous, but we agree, if your access has been revealed then it must be for the good."

"Thank you," I said as my insides vibrated with excitement.

Huume added, "There are rules... you'll have to learn them. The first is that you don't talk about this with other students... or anyone for that matter. You're sworn to secrecy."

"I understand."

"I hope you do." Huume looked around at the men in the room, "Well, I suppose we should take him to the stacks and give him what he needs to be responsible with this knowledge."

"If there is only one thing better than knowing, it's not-knowing. Consider that more understanding can be gained in the state of not-knowing than all the knowing in the world will open to you."

- Yeshua son of Joseph -

"Agreed," the other men said nearly in unison.

Within moments, we were walking through a hidden door and down a flight of stairs into a room that astonished me. I felt the vibrancy of these ancient documents practically jump off the shelves. The brothers led me through a series of rules and vows. This satisfied them that I knew how to act with this knowledge: how to use it, and how to protect it.

They handed me a door key. When they placed it in my palm, I became light headed and almost passed out. Huume steadied me and said, "Whoa there, ground yourself. You'll need strength to start your new studies."

Everyone laughed, even me, and I was pleasantly surprised by my ego. Instead of feeling as if this was a right, I felt humility and simple appreciation for this honor. I remembered the Temple Master say, 'Honor is what you claim from fulfilling your inner calling.' How clear things can become in hindsight.

26 · The Natural World

I dove into my studies. This restricted library gave me access to older and more esoteric texts that stimulated my learning goals at lightning speed. It was exhilarating.

There existed not just texts written by the Great Teacher and the Great Master Gautama Buddha, and their devotees, but volumes of works from millennia past. These books contained information about the land and people the Great Teacher came from, about the creation of this Earth, and about the creation and rise of humanity. There were volumes on the nature of our hearts, our brains, and these mysterious bodies in which we dwell. They wrote about civilizations that had come and gone, as well as their technologies that illuminated possibilities. Surely not the least of the subjects regarded the physics that govern life. Each new wave of knowledge and understanding brought a new wave of questions. I felt insatiable – in the midst of a gnosis revolution.

I spent hours reading and absorbing this information, some days only leaving the library long enough to touch my feet to the earth and feel the sun on my skin; just enough to stay vital and grounded, if that was even possible during this orgy of knowledge reunion.

I say reunion because, at some point I became hyper-aware that rather than learning this knowledge for the first time, I was remembering things I knew before I was born. I learned that my ego was a temporary shell created through my thoughts and experiences; it was not my self. My self was a being that lived and experienced many things before I incarnated as Yeshua.

At night during sleep, I dreamed of events in which I was interacting with people I knew now, but in unfamiliar places and behind unfamiliar faces. I began to walk through my dreams in a lucid, mystical fashion, as if I was standing outside my dreams and directing their flow consciously.

I woke each morning, barely able to settle myself for baptism and prayers. I ran to the books, and missed meal after meal, in an attempt to have more time learning.

I wanted food less and less. I was never a big eater, but now I consumed less than half of what I had just weeks before. I seemed to find sustenance from the ideas, as if the very air within my lungs gave me the building blocks for sustaining life.

Something must have shown on my face. People began to treat me differently.

"I love the sun. Without it, all opportunity for life in our three-dimensional world would perish. It's not the only force our Divine Creator put into play for our benefit, but it is essential. Touch your spirit, touch your heart, every day, and let the sun do the same."

- Yeshua son of Joseph -

They no longer coddled me as a child. They made way when I passed and were often silent in my presence. I paid it no mind; I didn't care what they saw. I cared only for what I was learning.

It was as if time and space came to a halt and I was standing on a precipice preparing to lift my feet off the ground and fly across the divide that keeps man on Earth and the spirits in the heavens.

But as the natural world would have it, time and space crashed in on me one deceptively calm, autumn afternoon as I rushed back to the library. I glanced across the commons and a young woman took my breath away. For the first time in months, something outside my books caused me to take notice, and it hit me like an elephant at full charge.

I'd awakened the fullness of life's passion in my heart with my gnosis revolution and now some of that passion redirected and pulsed through my body, screaming at me with a primal beat. She was beautiful.

As I stood mesmerized, I saw her move in my vision in slow motion as I imagine a cat sees the movements of the prey it's intent on capturing. I felt desires I was unaccustomed to feeling. The sudden sensations of my body rooted me to the ground. I forgot where I was going and why I was here in the commons in the first place. I thought only of looking at her. Something unfamiliar made its way into my thoughts and I instantly changed from a learned mystic to a common youth looking upon the face of physical desire without a foundation to understand it.

It was the first time I encountered physical lust. Joseph tried to prepare me, but no one can prepare a person for the gripping torment brought on by the hormones of lust, especially a healthy and inexperienced young man. Only experience brings it home. She suddenly consumed my every waking thought.

I tried to get back to my learning, but it was no use. The sight of her moving across the commons continually replayed in my mind until I finally thought, 'enough of this,' and had to search for her. The desire to meet her felt beyond my control.

As I wandered the settlement, I found she lived in the northern quadrant of the community. It was a good distance from the commons, or the library for that matter, and if I had any hope of meeting her 'coincidently' I'd have to wait conspicuously in an area where I usually spent no time. Not just spent no time, but I couldn't even think of another reason to be there at all.

I went to Huume and asked about her in a way I thought wouldn't attract attention, but Huume was a perceptive man and he caught my game within moments.

"You're infatuated with this girl, aren't you?"

I decided to open this gate of ignorance, "I'm lost. I don't know what's happening to me. I see pictures of her in my mind and have thoughts about her I can't control."

"Are some of those thoughts erotic in nature?"

I bent my head and hugged my chest. I didn't want to admit it. But if I had any hope of getting this under control I'd better say something. "Yes, they are," I instantly felt a red-hot flush of shame move through my face.

Huume could tell I was struggling, "There's nothing to be ashamed of. Believe me. What you're feeling is natural. What you're feeling hurts no one. It's how you choose to act that defines you."

These comments were sane. I concluded I was in wise hands and sat down. "What do I do?"

Over the next several weeks, Huume taught me how to use my mind to change how the energy of passion moved through my body. Not to make me passionless, but to subdue the intensity of my physical reactions so I could interact with life appropriately. I felt like a clumsy monkey, like this was something other men must instinctively know, but was fundamentally missing in me.

What a letdown this experience was from the nearly godlike feelings I had before I saw her. In perfect fashion I experienced how, when you push yourself out of balance, a balancing event will occur. I had to be brought back down to earth and this experience did that with a great big thud.

When I was finally able to walk through an entire day without being overwhelmed by lust, I asked Huume, "So, now, can you tell me her name?"

Huume regarded me with a slant eye, "Tell me about the last few days first."

I recounted my days and promised Huume, not only was I handling my energy appropriately, I was eating appropriate amounts of food. He wasn't the only person that noticed how much body mass I'd lost in the last months. After listening, he seemed satisfied, "Her name is Seleya." Learning her name was all I could handle. I immediately had to call it a night.

"I have been fortunate to love and be loved by many extraordinary women: my mother, sisters, and good friends – wives and widows, teachers and healers. The absence of even one would be a diminishment to me. Yet in the area of romance, only two women ever captured my heart. The first was very young and destined to leave me. The second very wise and destined to stand with me. From each I received gifts and for each I am grateful. I hope that in some way, I've given to them in as great a measure as they've given to me."
- Yeshua son of Joseph -

27 · Tutoring Seleya

A few days later, I was working on a theory in the library, this time in the regular library. I set my gnosis revolution aside to concentrate on rebuilding balance. As I was reading a Vedic text on the healing aspect of community, the scent of sweet blooming flowers caught me.

When I looked up from the table, I saw Seleya, books in hand, sit down at the other end. She didn't look at me, but rather moved her attention directly into the pages of her texts. I hadn't considered that she might walk into my space. I rationalized that if I didn't pursue her, I was safe. To my pleasant surprise, her presence aroused my thoughts, but didn't overwhelm me.

That was, however, the end of my theorizing for the day. My nose was busy memorizing the sweetness of her scent and my ears listened to the soft sound of her sighs. I pretended to be locked into my texts, but I was wholly locked into her.

The next thing I felt was Huume's hand on my shoulder, "How are your studies today, Issa?"

"They're going well," I tried to sound normal. "I'm enjoying this new stack of texts you passed me."

Huume said, "I could use some help if you have a moment." I felt a flood of relief to have a good reason to walk away.

"Of course," I said as I eagerly followed Huume to his office.

As soon as we were alone Huume asked, "Tell me, how are you doing?"

"I don't know what to do," I blurted, "I could leave for the afternoon."

"Hmm. So what you want to do is give in to your fears and run away?"

"Yes, exactly," I said. Huume laughed. After some discussion, I decided to face my fears and introduce myself.

Huume was right, I was afraid. I hid, working up the nerve to say hello. This wasn't like me. I judged myself harshly for being weak to my fears. Shame assaulted me, but I finally stepped forward and said, "Hello."

Seleya looked up from her book, "Hello."

If I could've run from the room, I would've. Instead, I took a deep breath and said, "I've seen you around. My name is Issa."

"I haven't seen you until now," she answered.

Now I really wanted to run. Instead, I said, "Well, I do keep to myself, mostly studying."

"I'm studying too. My father wants me to learn certain subjects, so I'm here."

"Your father sounds like a good man that he wants you to be educated."

"I've nothing to say about my father except that he's determined."

I wanted to be helpful, "Well, I've been here studying for several years now, so if you want any guidance, just let me know."

I started to walk back to my books when she said, "I'm sorry, my name is Seleya. Please have a seat."

"Hi, Seleya, sure," and I sat. I can't adequately explain the pins of excitement I felt sitting next to her. We began talking about the subjects she was here to learn. It seemed a rather rarified set of topics on her curriculum, but all were things I knew well and could easily help with. Speaking with her about ordinary things outside of my intimate dilemma helped me center and balance. I spent the rest of the afternoon helping her pick out texts that would cover the basics of her disparate topics.

"Obviously these are just the basics," I said, "as you finish each we can discuss it in more detail. Then I can move you to the next level of learning."

"Thank you." She looked at me with bright eyes.

For a moment, her eyes held me in silence. I finally said, "You're welcome. Well, it's almost time for supper; I should go."

"Yes, of course," she added with some sadness, "I always eat in my room." We both stood another minute, staring in silence. Finally she asked, "Can we meet again tomorrow? I can ask you questions about what I read."

"Um, sure. Yes. I can meet you here after midday prayers."

Huume was right again, I was more comfortable facing my fears and beginning a dialog. I found her to be bright, inquisitive, and gentle. And I went to sleep that night with her scent on my tongue.

The next day, as promised, I met with Seleya. Her questions were sensitive and intelligent; her thoughts interesting and her observations poignant.

As the days progressed, I delighted in how quickly her mind assimilated knowledge. And I was charmed by her sense of humor. I gladly anticipated seeing her eyes twinkle and her cheeks flush when we met each day.

We began taking some of our discussions out for walks, through the orchards and by the lake. From time to time, our conversations turned to subjects that were more personal. I learned about where she came from and how she lived when she wasn't here. Her community followed a caste system and her family was at the lowest end of the highest caste. She didn't know why her father needed her to study these subjects, but she was enjoying the opportunity to learn.

"There are too many societies in this world who are afraid to allow their women an equal role. This is as detrimental to community as any other form of discrimination. In particular, any society that holds separate one segment of its population, where the basis of exclusion to privileges such as education, healthcare, remuneration, and political voice is solely an attribute of a person's body, is a society that will become ill and suffer great pain. Moral and economic collapse becomes inevitable."

- Yeshua son of Joseph -

I was enjoying just being with her. My original flush of lust made room for a genuine affection to emerge.

One day she didn't show for our meeting. I waited half the morning and decided to go find out what happened. As I came near her building, I saw a handful of tethered horses and unfamiliar men tending to them. I didn't go closer reasoning these were people from her village and I went back to the library sad to have missed her.

Several days later, she was still missing from the library. I went again to her building, but the same scene assaulted me. I just had to wait.

Nearly a week went by. I was reading at our table when she was again delivered to my joy. I could smell her before I saw her. When she came into my vision however, her face was sullen and an older, stark-looking woman accompanied her. When Seleya got closer, I saw long red welts on her cheek that had the shape of fingers.

I wanted to run to her and hold her, find out what happened, but before I could, I felt Huume's hand on my shoulder. He said, "May we help you?"

The older woman spoke, "Yes, I'm Rasa, Mistress to Seleya. I've been told that this boy has been speaking with her daily."

Huume took the conversation in hand, "Yes, I believe he has. He's one of our brightest students and he's been tutoring Seleya."

"He must stop," she declared. These words crushed me.

"I appreciate your request," Huume said. "May I ask why? He's been instrumental in her progress." Seleya looked at me with tears in her eyes.

Rasa continued, "Something is happening between them that's not proper. Their association must end."

I couldn't hold myself back, "There's nothing improper between us." Huume squeezed my shoulder in an attempt to get me to shut-up. I locked my teeth together.

Huume said, "I've seen nothing that appears improper, but of course your request will be honored."

Rasa said sharply, "Good. I trust it will be so." She gave me a look of absolute distaste, as if my very presence on this Earth was anathema to her. She took Seleya by the hand and pulled her out of the library.

Huume took me to his office, "Tell me right now, has anything improper happened between you? If so, you must confess."

"No, I can't imagine. I've been very proper. I haven't touched her. I haven't even told her how I feel."

Huume was not consoled. "Well… this community can't afford a scandal. So you must do as she requests. Stop tutoring Seleya."

"But did you see her face? Something awful happened to her."

"That's not our business. Let it go. And let her go."

I was downhearted. Try as I might I couldn't get Seleya off my mind. And for the next month, when Seleya came into the library, Rasa was with her. Not once did Seleya appear to be happy. I kept my nose to the books and my heart in my hand.

"Have you ever watched a child play when they didn't know you were watching? When left alone, most children will assume some affect that doesn't reflect reality, as you know it. They'll pretend to be someone different, or have a larger experience of things or people around them than you can see. If you've noticed this, does it make you question their sanity? Probably not, because this type of play is how children learn about themselves and grow. So then, why stifle this same behavior in yourself? Truthfully, in your most quiet and private moments, don't you sometimes see more, feel more, be more, imagine more? Isn't this how you become more?"

- Yeshua son of Joseph -

28 · Vengeance Strikes

A day arrived when Seleya showed up alone. She didn't look at me and I didn't approach her. It was excruciating to sit by and know she was in ears distance of my voice and not be free to reach out to her with compassion, or brotherly love, or any of the more complex feelings I held.

A few days later, Seleya pulled texts from a different set of shelves and I became quite curious about what new subject she was studying. So after she left for the evening, I searched those shelves and found something altogether surprising. She was studying the Vedic sutras on human eroticism and sexuality.

I'd stayed away from this subject because I thought it wouldn't be beneficial for me. But since I saw that Seleya was studying it, I decided to do the same. As I originally suspected, this information was not beneficial to finding balance, but it didn't take me long to read them. When I completed the last volume, I went to Huume.

"I read the texts on sexuality," I said.

"I'm glad you did," he said, "now you know all there is to know outside of experience."

I said, "Alright," and that was the end of that conversation.

<hr/>

In the Essene community, families arranged marriages. A young man was expected to marry well before his twentieth birthday. Most were married before their seventeenth. A young woman was expected to begin seeking marriage by her twelfth birthday, married before her fifteenth. After reading the texts on sexuality, I couldn't imagine marriage that young. At eighteen, I was already past the prime age of marriage and until I read these texts, I was as naive as anyone could be. My first experience of lustful arousal hadn't even come until I was seventeen and that by an accident of community.

Perhaps other young men of my community found their sexual awakening earlier than me. However, I know my experience was common and if others had awakened earlier, they would've been given council in temperance, encouraged to not dwell on what they couldn't yet have.

After reading the texts on sexuality, I could only imagine that marriage between two inexperienced and naive people must be frightening and confusing. Merely contemplating it was such for me. I know these words may seem strange or odd to you, but I wasn't born into a sexualized society. Sex was sacred, not for public discussion as it is in the time of this writing. Rather, its mysteries weren't even contemplated until marriage was imminent.

But marriage was not imminent for me. I had more knowledge than I had the physical capability to explore.

A few weeks later, as spring was fully upon us, Seleya left her seat in the library. I was curious and followed her from a distance. My intent was unclear. Did I want to talk to her? Did I want to protect her? Or did I want more?

She walked into one of the fruit groves and sat beneath a tree. After a few minutes, she began to weep. I felt shame watching her without her permission, especially as she expressed such personal intimacy as tears. So, I made my presence known. It startled her, but she called me over to her side.

"Issa, please let me explain."

"I need no explanation. I'm sorry I followed you. It's not my intention to intrude on your privacy." She looked at me with her tearful eyes and they appeared more beautiful than ever. I felt her longing. I asked, "What's going on though? Who hit you?"

She looked at me with surprise. "My father!" she blurted.

I was shocked. "Your father did that?"

"It wasn't the first time, and certainly not the worst."

My experience of a father was Joseph – a gentle, loving, kind mentor who wanted nothing more than my complete wellbeing and safety. This news rocked my sense of the world and reminded me how much I missed my home and family. "I can't imagine a father hurting you like that."

"It's alright, Issa. It is what it is. But it matters little because soon I won't be in his house."

"What do you mean?"

"I'm to be married." It was a second blow. It should've been clear to me from the topic of her new studies, but it wasn't. Now it was clear and grief filled me.

"Oh, Seleya…" I pulled my knees up to my chest and buried my head in them. I couldn't stop the tears and I didn't want her to see me cry.

She blurted, "It's my fault, this… prohibition on our studying together."

"How can it be your fault?"

"Father told me of the marriage plans and my feelings for you spilled out." Now it began to make sense, why Rasa's sudden accusation of impropriety. "That's when he hit me," she added.

But now, hearing Seleya confess to having feelings for me, a new sense of overwhelm arose. I pulled my head out of my knees and looked fully upon her face. I confessed, "I care so much for you."

Before I could catch myself, Seleya and I embraced in a kiss. We became frantic for one another. I knew this was wrong, but I couldn't control my hands or my lips. I smothered her face, her neck, with kisses, and she the same on me.

Whatever improprieties might have followed, they weren't to be as the next thing I felt was the sting of a whip. When I heard the 'crack' and felt its sting across

> "At Qumran, I became familiar with many men who confessed terrible familial dysfunction. Violence and sexual misconduct weren't the norm in Jewish families overall, but were common to families of the monks. Many of these men became monks because they had no good image of family and didn't want to perpetuate the pernicious patterns they were taught."
>
> *- James brother of Yeshua -*

my legs, I was shocked and alarmed. Seleya screamed, wrestled out of my arms, and rose to run, but a large man with vengence on his face grabbing her by the arm and pulling her to the ground at his feet.

He snarled something in an unfamiliar language. I stood and backed away from him a pace. Seleya screamed, "Issa, run!" But I wouldn't, I wasn't about to run from the consequences of my actions, now or ever.

Hearing her words, the large man cracked his whip again, this time over Seleya and it struck across her chest and shoulder. Red stains begin to grow on her clothes.

"Stop whipping her!" I shouted. The man looked me in the eyes and growled as if he were a large, angry bear. I stepped forward and held my ground, yelling, "Let her go!"

The pitch of our voices carried past the grove. I heard footsteps and shouts of people rushing toward us. By the time they reached us, the man with the whip had pulled Seleya up to stand at his side, his brutal hand crushing her soft arm.

"What goes here?" one of the monks asked. I couldn't speak.

Another monk said, "What's happening?"

The angry man snarled again in the other language. One brother seemed to understand and put his arms around Seleya. He said firmly, "She needs medical attention. Let her go so we can attend to her." The angry man let go of her arm and I was concerned it was broken. She passed out and a brother picked her up and carried her toward the settlement.

I stood, panting, wondering what would happen next. The angry man looked at me; his face glowed bright red and saliva drooled from his mouth he was so enraged. This had to be Seleya's father. He raised his arm and I braced for the lash of the whip, but the brothers wrested the whip from his hand before he could use it.

One of them said, "Let's go sort this out." They escorted the man away and motioned for me to follow.

29 · Rehashed and Punished

By the time the events between Seleya and me were rehashed to everyone's satisfaction, I was emotionally wrung out and raw. One healer tended to the large, partially broken welts on my legs and another healer attended to Seleya. I couldn't see her, but Huume filled me in on her ordeal.

She did have a broken arm and several large gashes across her legs, shoulder, and chest. The Healer was concerned that some of them would leave scars. Although Huume informed me that old scars populated many parts of her body. My heart gushed with pain thinking of Seleya repeatedly enduring the lash of the whip.

Rasa wasn't willing to accept our story, that we'd met this once and had merely kissed, so Seleya had to endure an examination to determine that she was still a virgin. Rasa, on the urging of Seleya's father, insisted on punishment for our salacious crimes. The brothers had no standing to stop her. So to punish us both, Rasa smeared a caustic cream on Seleya's mouth and other soft body parts and made me sit in the next room so I could hear her cry out and whimper from the pain of it.

I was devastated. To think that my inability to control myself led to such suffering left me in a state of near catatonia. Huume finally walked me to my quarters. He laid me in bed and rolled out bedding so he could stay with me through the night.

That night, my dreams repeatedly relived the event, until I woke with a fever from the experience. Huume attended me with a cool, wet rag.

By the time morning came, I was even more exhausted, but comforted to see Huume still by my side. He left me alone for a short time to pick-up breakfast for us. While he was gone, I wept. From the depths of my soul, I wept.

I punished myself by picking at my food. I was hungry, but my guilt wouldn't let me accept nourishment. After a time, Huume said, "We should talk about this."

"I know."

He asked, "Shall we begin that now?"

"Alright," was my listless response.

"I understand what happened."

"I don't," my voice was small and lacked courage.

Huume continued, "I take some measure of responsibility for this. In forcing the two of you to stay apart, we were actually forcing you together."

I shook my head, "No, the fault is mine."

"Issa, you're young and inexperienced. The elders around you should've taken measures to keep this from happening." I stared at the ground. Huume added,

"You're a fine young man. I think you've suffered enough for what you did. I see no reason you should continue to punish yourself."

"But I do."

———

The next several days I ached to see Seleya. She spent nearly a week in the infirmary, but I was clear that any further contact would risk further suffering and I wasn't willing to instigate that.

———

After leaving the infirmary, Seleya stayed sequestered in her room. Rasa continued to come to the library and carry out texts for Seleya. I didn't help her.

———

One day, Huume told me that Seleya was leaving. Apparently, her marriage was imminent. I could only pray that the man she'd marry was less brutal than her father. I watched from across the open field as they secured her belongings to the cart. When complete, they escorted Seleya out and secured her inside. As they were drawing the horses for the ride, her eyes caught me standing across the way. Even at that distance, I saw her wearied face drip tears as we looked upon each other for the last time.

I never felt more helpless. I resolved that never again would I lose control of myself. Never again would I let the whims and desires of my body dictate my actions. But as the saying goes, never say never.

"It was much easier to let go of my infatuation with Seleya than to forgive the guilt I felt over the pain she suffered from our association. Guilt is a form of self-punishment. If one doesn't find forgiveness within, over time, the pain inflicted from guilt can be far greater than the crime warranted."

- Yeshua son of Joseph -

30 · The Valley of My Heart

The events surrounding Seleya ravaged my emotions. Nothing could've prepared me for the loss of self I felt. I decided to travel again to the Temple at Insa'alet. There, I'd spend days in silence and isolation. One monk agreed to travel with me.

The road was uneventful and relatively easy to pass. Even though snow fell on us each day, we were relieved not to encounter icy patches. When we arrived at the temple, the monks welcomed us warmly. They appreciated our willingness to join in prayers and otherwise respected my desire for isolation, but I couldn't let go of Seleya. Unruly thoughts punctuated my meditations. Grief sat beside me at meals. And when I undressed for morning baptism, I always saw her face in the mirrored, cold waters of the Himalayas.

After more than a month of this, the Temple Master summoned me to his room. I was trepidatious about visiting him in such an intimate setting. All my previous interactions with him had been in a public place. He asked me to sit. I had such a sense of awe in his presence, I wanted only to listen and respond if prompted.

He asked why I was unsettled and listened patiently to my sad story. He asked if she was the first woman I'd felt a physical attraction to. I confessed she was; that before Seleya, I only had eyes for books and knowledge.

He asked to meditate with me. I closed my eyes and saw his spirit take my hand and lead me to a green valley beyond the reach of my physical eyes. He explained this was the valley of my heart. We walked by a stream until we came to a monument; upon a platform was a statue of Seleya.

The Temple Master asked, "Why have you immortalized her with a monument in your heart when she's not available to you?" I thought about his question, but I had no satisfactory answer.

The Temple Master took out a rod, tapped the statue, and it crumbled to dust. He asked, "Why do you erect a statue that has only the appearance of immortality, when it falls to dust at the slightest touch?" I thought about his question, but again I had no satisfactory answer.

He told me to stand on the platform. When I did, a large metal beast came and opened its belly for me to enter. I asked the Temple Master what I should do.

He said, "Turn around and see what's behind you."

As I did, my vision beheld a beautiful and majestic white tiger. A tiger as I

"You have a human heart. You may not listen to it. You may find fault with actions you've taken from its urging. You may even feel it's broken and beyond repair. But you have one, and it's the most sophisticated and magnificent organ in all creation. It has infinitely more power to heal, to love, and to sustain life than your brain has. If you'd fully tap the depth and breadth of your heart and utilize its power, you'd be unbreakable."

- Yeshua son of Joseph -

have never seen, with golden stripes and bright green eyes.

"It's a white tiger."

"Yes, and she wants you," he said.

"What does she want me for?"

"She wants one of two things; either she wants to eat you, to take your life, or… she wants to be your companion, your blessing upon your journey."

"How do I know which?"

"You'll know when it's time. I see this for your future, young one. The answer to this question could be your greatest gift and your hardest choice. When the time comes, you can choose to climb into the belly of the beast and embrace dispassion, or you can embrace the White Tiger and pray she wants to be your companion."

I didn't fully understand his prophecy, but I stared into the eyes of the tiger, and saw only compassion. I wasn't afraid of her. My heart opened and embraced her, as if I already knew she was to be part of my life.

The Temple Master continued, "For the superior man, there is no greater joy in life than to know the companionship of the great White Tiger. Let us now depart." He took my hand, led me back to my seat, and I opened my eyes to the warmth of the Master's quarters. He asked, "How do you feel?"

I surveyed my heart, and found no pain. "I feel fine, Master."

"Very well. I suppose you won't be staying with us much longer."

"I suppose I won't, Master." I rose to leave, but he had more to say.

"Young one, hear my words. A day will come when you have the choice to climb into the belly of the metal beast and embrace dispassion, walking the decaying road to your end without companionship, or to turn and embrace the White Tiger. But hear my warning, embracing her entails risk. You'll have to risk everything to hope to gain the greatest companion a man can have. Make your choice wisely and until then, don't be so quick to immortalize that which falls to dust."

"I'll remember your words, Master." I bowed and left the room. From that day forward, I never again saw Seleya's face in the waters of my baptism.

31 · A Proposition

Once I settled back into my studies, Huume took me aside, "Issa, I've been watching your growth for several years now. You're a fine, able, and committed student."

I smiled at the compliment. "Thank you, as you know, knowledge is my passion."

"I've noticed, there's little more to teach you here. Your erudition surpasses most of the Brothers."

My heart gripped for what I feared was coming, "But I don't want to leave yet."

Huume said, "I'm not proposing that. It's something else I'd like to suggest." I sighed with relief. Huume watched me closely as he said, "I was impressed with the way you tutored Seleya." He smiled, I assume because I didn't flinch upon hearing her name. He continued, "We have several students who are progressing rapidly and could use an accelerated curriculum."

"Oh, I see."

"I'd like to offer you a position here at the university, as teacher."

I was astonished, "You think I'm ready for something like that?"

"It would be a great responsibility. Some of these children are as hungry as you were when you first arrived. They're in need of a strong hand."

This was a delightful proposal. I said, "I can't think of anything more fulfilling to do right now."

Before I could think twice, I had a teacher's studio. My first task was to review the current curriculum and find ways to accelerate the teachings.

It was a fine task. I was able to add to the curriculum some of my own radical theories. The curriculum I developed split the teaching into phases so that students could begin at different points depending upon their current knowledge set. I devised ways of testing to determine a student's current level without the need for a teacher to guess and risk under- or over-challenging an improperly placed student.

Only one event marred my otherwise idyllic beginning. A rider brought a note from home. It was a short note, but the tragedy it relayed brought me to tears. My little sister, sweet, lithe Shelah, died. She was only eight. When I went to bed that night I was bereft that I couldn't be with them, my dear family. I was so far away. I couldn't brush away a tear, I couldn't hold them warm in my embrace. But overlaying that I again heard the Temple Master's words, 'Haven't you noticed that those who are especially gentle of spirit die sooner?'

I laid on my cot and thought of Shelah, I thought of Myrrh. I thought of how the Master at Insa'alet called them 'God's army.' If these were some of the spirits standing on our side, we were well covered.

By late winter, shortly after my nineteenth birthday, I formally began teaching. I felt like a prince, in a country of my choosing, teaching bright and willing boys about subjects I knew well. It was comfortable and exciting. They ranged in age from ten to fourteen and seemed to get along with me; they respected my knowledge, and were generally well mannered and responsive. When the weather was nice, we held class under the fruit trees, or by the lake. I also took some of the emphasis off the texts and brought in more experiential learning.

After watching me help these boys inundate their fertile minds and assimilate knowledge in new ways, a handful of brothers began incorporating my radical techniques into their own classes.

Before long, the whole university was lit up with bright and diverse minds of capable and assertive youths, both boys and girls. Students were participating in group projects and enlivening their studies with games to open the mind and train the spirit.

And of course, when I wasn't teaching, I had time to continue my exploration of the Master Texts in the restricted library. This year was a fresh and welcome joy after the last year buried under the weight of my preoccupation with Seleya. I was coming into my own and it felt good.

When the next school season began, word of the new curriculum's success had spread, and the university received a large number of new student applications. When this fresh batch of students flooded the Combs, life was truly fulfilling, seeing the success of my labors so richly borne out in their shining faces.

However, by the time the season was nearing completion, I felt a pull toward something new. I'd completed my studies of the Master Texts and Philar assured me life wasn't destined to be lived in this hallowed institution. I didn't know what to do, but surely, I needed a new avenue. I went to Huume.

"I've completed my studies of the Master Texts and I've written a set of addendum texts of my thoughts regarding these treatises and… some associated theories I put together. I'd like you to read them and give me your thoughts."

He seemed pleasantly surprised and said, "Issa, I'd be honored."

I passed the texts to Huume, "But there's something else as well." I paused, not sure about my feelings over what I was about to say. "I think it's nearing time

"Don't despair for those who've died with thoughts like, did they have enough time, did they finish what they came here to do, or do they know how much I loved them? These worries only keep you from thoughts that have more meaning, such as, have I accepted the love they gave me, have I forgiven myself for what I left unsaid or undone between us, or how can I better use the resources I have left to finish what I came here to do?"

- Yeshua son of Joseph -

for me to leave here."

I felt Huume's disappointment spill into the room. He finally said, "I'm sad to hear this… but I'm not surprised." We sat in silence until Huume spoke, "When you came to us, your father had negotiated your extended stay. We were anxious to have you. His letters made it clear though, that you'd one day tell us it was time to move on. We accepted this."

He looked up from his lap and bore his eyes directly into mine, "I know who you are, Issa. And there's no part of me that would try to keep you here. There's so much more for you to do." He paused, "I wasn't sure when you first arrived that you truly were more than a very bright and hungry boy. But watching you over these years… getting to know you… the miraculous change you've instigated in this institution… your radical ideas have changed us all. You've given our university a great gift. I've come to know and accept in my heart of hearts that you are who you were presented to be."

Huume's comments surprised me, "But, I don't know who I am." I blurted, "How is it that you can see for me what I can't see for myself?"

Huume raised a finger into the air and with a wry smile said, "That's a good question." He went to his cabinet and withdrew a small box hidden behind a false door. "I'd been looking for you, Issa." He brought the box back to his seat and opened it. He withdrew two letters, both addressed to me. I was astonished. "Your Father wanted these given to you when the day came that you asked to leave. I don't know what they say. They're for your eyes only." He handed the letters to me and withdrew from the box a band of brilliant green and purple crystal beads. "These beads are from the Temple Master at Insa'alet." Huume's eyes sparkled as he spoke, "He said to give them to you when you were ready for the next phase of your journey."

He held them out to me. They were brilliant in color and clarity. I carefully took them and felt the pulsing energy that ran through them. They were cut from emerald and amethyst. I draped them over my head and let them drop beneath my robe to rest gently next to the wooden heart that Joseph gave me. They felt good against my skin. I looked at Huume, unable to find words.

Huume glanced over his shoulders and pulled from the box one last item, a small leaved note with writing on it. He leaned close. I saw excitement in his eyes. "Issa…" he licked his lips, "this is a map left in our keeping over 500 years ago by the Great Master Gautama Buddha himself. It's been handed down, generation to generation, always in the care of the schoolmaster. It contains directions to a very special place."

With great care and facility, Huume unfolded the note to reveal a map. Strange writing flowed down the right side of the map. Huume proceeded to decipher the script and what it said left me speechless. He read:

"I've always had a non-stop stream of thoughts. Everyone begins that way. Yet, one of my deepest blessings was the ability to turn those thoughts toward the search for deeper truth. Strive to give your thoughts meaning. Give them a job to do that moves you forward. Because, if you can't stop them, or you don't give them a constructive direction, they'll consume you. They'll destroy your peace."

- Yeshua son of Joseph -

"This map is for one person only. No other will be able to follow its marks.

"To the one who will come, there is a road that must be walked. You, who are to follow, will tread the road I also compressed. You will see this path for what it offers.

"I clearly see you in vision; a young man, with sun-streaked hair and sallow complexion. You stand above your peers, in height and in intellect. You'll be born of this Earth in half a millennia time. Those around you will know you by the gifts you bestow.

"I instruct you to take this map so that you may find your way to the Temple of Man. You will learn truths that will reinterpret space for you. You will gain all you need to lead humanity out of its stupor and into true sovereignty.

"Your heart knows you are he.

"Take the road in three weeks' time. Where the map is vague, signposts will appear. Prepare to be absent from this world for a period of three to five years. This is what it will take to prepare you for immortality.

"Be blessed upon your journey young man.

"Siddhartha Gautama"

"It can seem so easy to see a truth about someone else. In fact, it can seem so easy that we may forget to stop and consider whether what we see is truth or another illusion. When we do see truth for a person, it might help them, because contradictory internal beliefs might block them from seeing it for themselves. However, any time you think you see something true for another, you must, before all else, accept that you might be wrong. Great harm can come inadvertently under the guise of truth. Tread softly with your 'knowing' and you have a very real chance at helping others."

- Yeshua son of Joseph -

32 · Map from Antiquity

As soon as Huume finished reading, I must have exclaimed, because Huume hastened a finger to his lips, "Shhh… This isn't for everyone," and quickly folded and shielded the map beneath his robe.

I was distracted; my mind was nursing revolving waves of giddiness, shock, and uncertainty. It was one thing to have the community of my birth believe I was destined to teach and lead my people. It was quite another to have the Great Master Gautama Buddha reach out from the depths of antiquity and leave a map for me to follow.

"H-hu-huume…" I sputtered, "he… he can't be writing about me."

"It must be you. The description is too precise. Who here has sun-streaked hair and pale skin? Who here stands out from the rest by both intellect and height? Who here also came to us with prophecy already following him? Who's been given the gift of a precious crystal prayer-band from the Temple Master at Insa'alet? And who's now known by his great gifts that revolutionized our way of teaching? To the great benefit of our students, I might add."

I was incredulous, "I-I'm just… a simple Nazorean."

"You're anything but simple, Issa."

Uncertainty buffeted me, but what Huume said made sense. There seemed to be a preponderance of signs coming together into one conclusion.

"But… the Temple of Man?" I said, "Truly?"

"It must be. Why else would the Master write about it?"

I knew from my readings that the Great Teacher established the Temple of Man to keep his sacred teachings alive in this realm. It's said to exist in both this realm and in his realm of origin. It remains hidden by design to all but those personally invited. It's the place where the Great Teacher, the originator of Bon, walked home after his sojourn on Earth over 35,000 years before me. Of course, just a half a millennium ago, the Great Master Gautama Buddha is the last human I knew of to walk there – and return.

If this was indeed a map to that temple, I knew I'd quickly set my uncertainties aside and prepare for the journey. If this was a valid invitation to the Temple of Man, I was more than ready, I was eager to accept.

I took the map from Huume to study. It was sparse in clues, but I trusted that,

"I've never received an answer to the question, 'Who am I?' That's because thoughts only illuminate the question, and actions merely demonstrate it. One cannot know the answer to that question, one must be the answer."
- Yeshua son of Joseph -

as stated in the note, I'd be led by signposts along the way. And of course, I trusted the Unseen to assist.

At my quarters, I gently unfolded the first of my two letters from Joseph. In it, he expressed that if I was now ready to leave, he was certain I'd distinguished myself in some fashion. He extolled how proud he was of me. He assured me his heart was with me and that everything was proceeding in perfect fashion. I longed to wrap my arms around him so much that the letter made me cry.

After I reread the first letter a few times, I braved the second. It was of a different emotion. It was a detailed description of a vision given to Joseph on the day I was born. He explained that when he held me in his arms for the first time, I sprang fully-grown in front of him. I took him by the hand and walked him through a progression of my life. What was most disturbing was the very last event in the vision. He said I showed him a pool of blood and said it was my blood. That it had flowed from my body until it was devoid of life-signs. In the vision, Joseph said I told him not to grieve, that though this happens while still young, I would transcend physical laws and live.

This message was at once ominous and cryptic. How could it possibly be true? I folded both letters and put them with the things to take with me. I knew I'd read them many times.

My excitement burgeoned almost immediately. Huume reassigned my students to other teachers and I began preparing for the journey.

When my time was nearly at hand, just two days hence, I wrote one more letter home, explaining that I might be out of touch for years. I asked them to understand and remember that my love for them was eternal.

Immediately after the rider carrying my letter set out upon his western journey, a wayward storm descended from the north. Snow in Kapilavastu was rare, even in the depths of winter. All I could do was hope that the storm would pass before my scheduled day of departure.

The day before I was set to depart, snow was still falling. Regardless, I was resolved to leave on the day instructed, so I began my farewells. It was a tear-filled, yet joyful day. These wonderful people had filled my life with all good things and were etched in my heart forever.

I arose the next morning with great anticipation. When I begin morning baptism, the snow had stopped falling and the entire world sparkled. Crystalline water covered everything. Every surface of every building, every limb of every tree, and every leaf of every bush, was sheathed in clear ice refracting the sun's light into it's pure colors. It was dazzling. Many exclaimed they'd never seen anything like it before.

Midmorning, I stepped from the security of the Combs and began the journey to the Temple of Man. As I promised myself years before, my burdens were light. Upon my back was all I needed and nothing more. And as I walked down the glistening, crystalline-lined road, the echoing strains of the Brothers chanting in prayer followed me. They were praying for my keeping, and for the keeping of all our souls.

I knew not where I headed, nor what I would find. But my heart was filled with new fervor and for the first time in years, I felt at home in my own skin. I was a man now, not a young man, not a boy, and I was stepping into life for the first time on my own. The Holy Spirit had whispered into me with these shafts of brilliant color and propelled my feet on a carpet of strength.

This was day one.

"*Every moment is complete. Each moment gives to you all it has to give and takes from you all you offer in return. When it's done, it's done. When you remember a moment gone by, all that transpires in you as memory is only in you. Nothing from outside yourself is involved in the memory. Memory can stimulate you to create some new emotion, such as, happiness, pain, love, anxiety, but nothing new is happening around you. So the next time a memory makes you happy or unhappy, remember that it's you doing it to you. That moment has come and gone. To glean an emotion from a memory is a choice.*"
- *Yeshua son of Joseph* -

33 · Following the Signs

I carefully followed the map, slowly moving east for more than two months. Each time the marks on the map became vague and obscure, a sign appeared to highlight the way. Sometimes a person offered advice that suggested a course correction. Other times a sacred tree or rock redirected my path. And sometimes, I was simply filled with certainty of the next step to take.

But it seemed that all guidance had ceased. I'd been wandering through these foothills for days. The next and last marking on the map was a large mouth yawning open. But how would I find it? How would I get there? I had no answers.

So, I camped by a lazy, green river. I needed clarity. Weeks before, I ran out of the food I brought from the Combs. The last time I encountered people with provisions, I traded for crisp bread and dried milk. But that was gone now too. The forest was filled with edible plants, so I could keep myself alive. Nonetheless, I was anxious to reach my destination and I had no way of knowing when the next sign would arrive.

On this morning, I slowly waded in and out of the river searching near the bank for food, when I spied a patch of fungi nestled beneath an acacia tree. As I got closer, they sparkled as if they had gold dust sprinkled on them. The dust was pollen falling from the blooms of the tree, but the dust hung in the air around the fungi as if by magic.

I squatted and inspected the fungi more closely. They were purple and I was about to decide they weren't edible, when a green hummingbird flew in and perched upon one of the wide caps. The rapid motion of the bird's wings did little to disturb the gold dust hanging in the air and I was mesmerized.

I realized the brilliant green bird on the deep purple cap mimicked the colors of the band of crystals around my neck. I lifted the necklace from under my robe and looked at the stones. They were indeed the very colors.

When my hands cupped round the stones, I heard the soft sound of movement behind me. I turned and saw a gentle musk deer. The deer walked toward me in short and measured steps, until she stood nearly on top of me. She bent her head and nuzzled my cheek with her cool, moist nose. Then she ate one of the fungi. The hummingbird fluttered up, the breeze from its wings caressed my face, and I felt more at one with this world than at any other time in my life.

So I mimicked the deer's action and plucked a fungus. When I placed it on my tongue, she licked my forehead as if to bless my action. The fungus was at once bitter and sweet. I instantly knew that this was the next sign leading me to the

"Signs and synchronicities; they're pervasive. They permeate life as generously as salt permeates the ocean. Never despair for them, merely open your eyes, for when you look, they appear."

- Yeshua son of Joseph -

Temple of Man.

I swallowed the fungus and lay back on the bank wondering what would happen next. Before I had much time to ponder that question, I wrenched forward and threw-up on the riverbank. I retched for several minutes in a violent fashion I'd never experienced before. I wondered if I'd just poisoned myself when the objects of the world began to change shape.

Regular colors melted away to be replaced by brilliant colors for which I had no name. The sun disappeared behind a cloud and a grey mist descended around me. I felt as though the top of my skull was detached from my head, exposing my brain directly to the elements.

As I tried to make sense of the shifting world, the musk deer changed form into a small, old woman wrapped in a grey and white cloak. She looked kindly, but determined. The hummingbird transformed into a red-tailed falcon and perched upon her shoulder.

The old woman said, "Follow me." She began walking at a vigorous pace and I eagerly followed. We quickly headed into a higher elevation. The mist swirled around us creating a mystical overlay on the already distorted landscape. Luckily, the retching had stopped and for that, I was thankful.

We climbed and climbed. A few times the landscape changed so abruptly that I was unsure if I was still on earth. Periodically, the old woman laughed and the falcon pierced the air with shrill screeches. I made no sound except the loud crackling of twigs and dry leaves beneath my clumsy feet.

After hours of climbing, we stopped on the edge of a deep canyon. I looked over the edge and saw no way to move forward. I thought, 'Where has she led us?' The old woman laughed, a deep belly laugh. I looked at her. She stood facing away from the canyon, her outstretched arm pointing at something behind me. I turned and saw a wide gaping hole in the rock. It was the entrance to a cave and, to my relief and delight, it looked very much like a mouth yawning at me.

The old woman said through her laughter, "I leave you here. If you find your way through the dark, you will see the light." She immediately changed back into a musk deer and bounced off, quickly swallowed by the dense undergrowth of the forest. The falcon transformed back into a hummingbird and disappeared into the canyon.

I was alone again, standing in front of the last marker on the map. The natural colors of the world returned to my vision and I recognized that it would soon be night. I decided to camp and enter the Yawn in the morning. Where was I? I didn't know. What waited inside? I didn't know. I started out on this journey, with nothing but a sparse map and my intuition, and everywhere I found a guiding hand helping me. I was once again reminded that free will and fate are inextricably entwined.

"You couldn't exist without nature, you are nature. When you enter this world through your mother's womb, you're already an integral part of nature. Many humans have a sad propensity to disavow membership in the very community of their birth. Next time you wonder how you could survive in nature, or you fear over what nature might do to you; turn it around. What would you do without it? How could you survive without nature enfolding you? How could you even exist? While you're in a body, you are nature."

- Yeshua son of Joseph -

34 · Entering the Yawn

When morning came, I entered the Yawn. I assumed it'd be dark, but until I was immersed in the cave I didn't realize how dark. There was no light – not even one very dim iota of light. The darkness played tricks with my mind. I turned around by accident and found myself back at the mouth of the Yawn.

I sat in the familiar light of day and pondered my challenge. I had no torch, though I reasoned a torch might keep me from reaching my destination. As I thought this, the Unseen rose into my vision. I asked, "Have you guidance?"

The long necked one said, 'Don't rely on your eyes.' This seemed obvious.

The flying one said, 'You have other senses.'

"What do you mean?" I asked, but they disappeared. So, I picked myself up and again braved the darkness of the Yawn.

I moved slowly, testing each step to see if I was placing my foot on earth or air. I was afraid I'd fall into a crevasse and break a leg or worse. Fears welled up every few minutes and I had to fight them back.

For several hours, I explored the cave with my hands. Finally, I felt the path split into two narrow passages in front of me, but there was no guarantee that either passage would take me to my destination. It was wholly possible that I'd already missed a crucial bend or split in the path. That thought terrified me. I stood deep inside a black cave with no food or water, and I didn't know which way was out. My mind said I was hopelessly lost and in peril of dying. I began to panic.

I sat; my heart racing. Sweat formed on my brow, and my breathing was shallow. Thoughts of doom raced through my mind. No one knew I was here. No one could possibly find me. If the Unseen were talking to me, I couldn't hear them.

This orgy of fear immobilized me for a good period. Eventually, I fell into an altered state. All at once, the room opened up and I 'saw' a 'lighted space' in front of me. Then I saw it, the pool of blood Joseph had described in his letter. Next to the pool stood a man who looked like me, but older. He had multiple wounds on his body, each dripping with blood that flowed into the pool.

The man sat in front of me. As he gazed into my eyes, I felt his countenance merge with mine. I felt the gashes in his skin and the dehydration that permeated his body. Suddenly I became desperate with thirst and had to fight the compulsion to run.

The man said, "Why do you fear so?"

"I'm lost," I answered in nervous haste. "I've no clear path and no light to show it to me."

"You have all you need to find your way," the man said as if my situation presented no more challenge than eating supper.

"How can you know this?" I demanded.

"Because I'm you. Or you're me. Either way we're the same. I'm your future." My mind reeled. If that tortured body was my future, why would I take up this path to begin with? What kind of path would bring me here on the road to the Temple of Man and then deposit me into a future like that? I didn't want any part of it. It frightened me.

The vision of my future-self flanked by a pool of blood started to fade. I thought it might vanish altogether until I realized it was the fractured, fearful nature of my mind that was disrupting the vision. I calmed my mind with a familiar mantra and the vision appeared strong.

The man-who-would-be-me said, "This is what you fear... your own mortality."

"Are you dead?" I asked.

"No, I'm alive," he said.

"But you look like you're dead or dying?"

"You only see the path your fear reveals." He closed his eyes and fell silent, his body posed in a mudra. I was frustrated. What was the meaning of this? What did I need to do? Quite out of character, I felt anger well up in me. I wanted to scream at him, but he just sat there, calm and unyielding.

I looked again and thought that perhaps I needed to mimic his pose, just as I'd mimicked the action of the musk deer. So, I reconfigured my body into the same mudra, closed my eyes, and fell silent. I let the silence carry me, dispelling the fear and anger as best I could.

When I opened my eyes again, the man was now lying wrapped in a shroud as if fully dead. "That's it? Now we're dead?" I shouted in frustration. I felt the fear mount again. I stared at the shroud. "Speak to me!" I yelled in anger, but all I heard were my angry words echoing back.

I caught myself. I thought, maybe this is the next mudra, if there is one, the mudra of death. So I laid down in a death pose. I began to get cold and my heart rate slowed. I felt other processes of my body slow as I got colder and colder.

I tried to open my eyes, but I couldn't. My body wouldn't respond. I felt dead, I acted dead... my mind said, 'I must be dead.'

I saw myself running in a field as a child, Mother walking behind, James a toddler at her side. I was running toward a butterfly. I heard Mother shout, "Don't run, Yeshua. Come here and stay close."

I saw myself a bit older, standing in synagogue beside Joseph. I wasn't tall enough to see Torah unfurled. I strained to see more and Joseph firmly pulled my back up straight, so I was standing without strain. He whispered, "Don't strain, a good man always stands straight."

I was with children taunting me for speaking to invisible people that they thought didn't exist.

That scene faded and I was at supper, family around me. I was proud and bragging about some accomplishment. Joseph came over and said, "You know, I think you deserve something special for that, Son," and he squished a palm-full of honey into my hair. Everyone laughed, except me.

Immediately, I was saying goodbye to Joseph on the docks at Aqaba holding on to him, afraid to let go.

"Fear. I wouldn't have become me without it. And, I wouldn't be me now with it. It's necessary, yet insidiously harmful. The trick is to embrace fear the few times in life it keeps you away from immediate physical harm and eschew it in every other circumstance."

- Yeshua son of Joseph -

The lash of the whip hit me and I saw the seething face of Seleya's father as he made ready to strike me again. The scene shifted and I was sitting in the infirmary, hearing my beloved cry from the pain of her unwarranted punishment.

As tears welled, my present situation overtook me and I saw myself crawling in the darkness, not finding my way, falling victim to thirst, and perishing. I looked at my dead body and wondered at all I'd just seen. I was confused. Just now, when my life marched before me, why hadn't I seen the love or felt the joy that permeated most moments? Where was the laughter, the merriment? Where was the warmth and genuine happiness I shared with these people? Where was… the love?

The Temple Master said, "Death is a passage, not to be feared, but to be embraced." But what was I to embrace? These moments of torment? These moments of fear?

I looked again at my corpse and saw it rot in an accelerated fashion. Beetles walked over me, flesh fell from my bones. I felt no pain. I felt only disappointment at missing the love and the joy of having known wonderful people.

I sat with my corpse rotting on the ground. I buried my hand into the mush of it. I found nothing of substance. What was this life worth now?

It was then that I realized: in truth there is no substance in me. The substance is what I left in the people I touched, in the lives I helped, in the love I shared. And suddenly, as I thought these thoughts, the cave echoed with the sound of laughter. I heard people speak about what a joy it was to know me. People remarked that my kindness and passion had given them hope. Others spoke about how my compassion and love gave them strength to persist. Children exclaimed that they were inspired by my example. I saw Seleya rocking a baby and remembering the young man who was her only love. She reminded herself that kindness and compassion do exist in the world.

As I soaked in the love of these revelations, the man-who-would-be-me reappeared, bleeding from every wound, emaciated from dehydration, "I see you've found what's important."

I looked at him and laughed. "If I have, why're you still bleeding?"

"Each drop of blood," he said, "represents a waterfall of love I've given. Only love has meaning." And as he said this, the cloak of blood and emaciation lifted from him. He stood in front of me transformed, healthy and strong, glowing with a golden aura. "You see, death isn't real."

I stood, "Yes… I get it… It's the love I give that matters." I felt the truth wash over me, "That's the worth and substance of my life. And that doesn't perish when my body does."

"Exactly." He said as he spread his arms, the earthen walls of the cave melted from view, and I stood on a granite walkway. I shielded my eyes from the sudden flood of light. When I was again able to see, a tall, blonde man with green eyes stood before me reaching out his hand.

"Welcome to the Temple of Man, Issa. We've been expecting you."

"Knowing Yeshua moved me to be a better me, and that's the overwhelming response people had, and still have, to him. He moves people to live in greater light just by being in his presence."

- Miriam wife of Yeshua -

Light
of the
Universe

35 · The Temple of Man

I grasped the man's hand and let him guide me to a courtyard of trees flanked by tall buildings. A gentle breeze rustled the leaves, causing them to tinkle like tiny bells. Water flowed from fountains lining the walkways creating a pervasive bubbling sound that lifted my spirit. The ambient temperature was warm enough to be pleasant. And we weren't alone; many people seemed to be going about their lives.

I'd never met a man as tall as the one holding my hand. With my own above-average height, I wasn't accustomed to looking upward at anyone. He had the appearance of a young man close to my age, and in most respects, he looked typically human. However, he had features uncommon in my experience: pinkish-white skin, yellow-blonde hair, and dazzling, emerald-green eyes. I was mesmerized by the entire scene.

Suddenly, the man burst into laughter, "Oh, Issa, you should see your face. I love your surprise. It's so honest." He made me chuckle, and in that moment I finally realized my success, I'd found the Temple of Man. Mere minutes earlier, I'd wondered if I was already dead. Yet here I was, clearly alive and in the light. It was a striking reminder that the dawn immediately follows the darkest of the night.

And as I had that thought, the man said, "Indeed Issa, the darkest hour is always just before the dawn."

Again, I was startled. How did he know my thoughts?

"Hahaha," he laughed, "there are many things for you to learn here. The least of these is mental communication. You're already loud and clear on the transmission side of things, but… you could use some instruction on receiving."

I looked into his eyes. He felt so familiar to me. "What's your name?" I asked.

"My name is Jo," he said as he winked in what felt like a conspiratorial act, but I had no idea what the conspiracy was. Then he said, "Let's walk a bit."

We meandered through the courtyard and past the tall buildings to a cluster of homes. As we strolled past the homes, I noticed that the overriding feelings emanating from them were peace, intimacy, and love. Obvious care had been shown to details that made each dwelling unique.

We paused in front of one that was oddly without decoration. It had no feeling to it, no unique details, like a blank parchment. I wondered who lived here and how it was that they left no imprint.

Jo opened the low gate in front of the house and said, "Issa, can't you guess?

"When I was young, I thought I could hide things from the world; I believed my truth wasn't bearable to others. When I entered the Temple of Man, I learned that in truth, nothing can actually be hidden. Even if other people allow themselves to live with blinders on, which most people do, everything is viewable to the right eyes. Face it, you can't hide."

- Yeshua son of Joseph -

This house is blank because you haven't moved in yet." And in that moment, you could've knocked me over with a soft breath. Not only was it clear that they did indeed expect my arrival, it was abundantly clear that I could no longer hide behind my thoughts. In this place, I was an open book.

The most accurate thing I can say about the Temple of Man is that it's a place of exacting truth and excruciating honesty. Every action is transparent. Sometimes I witnessed new arrivals try to hide their inner recesses, but in nearly no time, their efforts were thwarted by the very nature of this place.

Here, there were no laws, no government, no need for soldiers, or guards. No one carried money or weapons. No one needed to tell you how to act, or what to think. There were no mirrors, or any reflective surfaces other than water, for that matter. Each moment was in all ways, governed by the pull of higher order.

I learned that people who looked thirty could've been three-hundred, and people who looked eighty might be twenty-five. The body was a reflection of inner belief. Inner belief could change rapidly and with it, the outer appearance. Early in my stay, I aged quickly, reflecting my belief that wisdom couples with age. That changed though, and one day I began to grow younger, a reflection of a higher order of belief, one where growing toward death wasn't inevitable.

In experience, I stayed at the Temple of Man for more than eleven years. In earth time, I was away just over two years. The correlation between the timeline of the temple and my place of birth was illusive and inexact. If I'd tried to venture from the temple to my homeland unassisted, I wouldn't be assured when or where I'd land. Accurately piercing the veil that held both worlds separate and connected was a science. A person had to train for years to be able to navigate between the two realms.

Jo was one of those scientists. In time, he became one of my dearest companions. His mind was quick and his spirit overflowed with passion and fire. He winked at me the day we met because he knew the truth that he was of the same soul as my earthly father, Joseph. At every level one can examine, ours proves an intricate and multilayered universe that can only surprise and delight the person who opens and engages its profound mysteries.

36 · The Event

Many beings had the good fortune to study at the Temple of Man. As one, I accepted the challenge before me. I promptly moved into my modest dwelling and began the adventure of living in this unusual new world.

To my astonishment, this was Philar's home, too. When he wasn't visiting on earth, he lived here. Like Jo, he was a scientist, but in a different discipline. Philar was a geneticist. Through many enlightening conversations, I gained a new understanding of my life. The Creator works in mysterious and sometimes scientific ways.

My days were pleasant and I quickly became accustomed to the ways of this place. When I did, Jo introduced me to one of the most illuminated beings I've ever had the fortune of knowing. His name was Man'wa and he became my new mentor.

My sojourn on earth thus far had been one of knowledge – mind knowledge. I knew a lot. And I'd learned the basics of an upright life: integrity, humility, honesty, strength of character, and compassion. And yet, I was a personality inhabiting a body, not yet governed by the truth of my spirit. If I'd lived an ordinary life, I've no doubt I would've been a good rabbi, a strong leader and family man. But I owned a mission, one that encompassed all those roles, and surpassed them in ways I'd not yet begun to understand. Knowledge and understanding are two very different things.

Many years into my studies with Man'wa, I was no longer the person who innocently followed the musk deer to the great Yawn. I hardly remembered him. I'd walked, sometimes stumbled, through layers of lessons that amplified my innate potential. I had abilities other humans didn't seem to possess, but we sharpened them, honed them for their proper use. Other abilities awakened in me that, if it weren't for the wise hand of Man'wa, might have lain dormant forever. Space and time became like raw clay to me. They were resources to use, just as one might use earth, stone, or wood. After years of study, I could actively, and with willful purpose, sculpt reality.

There were truths, both universal and colloquial, that I learned as well, such as the diversity of creation that exists far beyond the detection of our human sensory organs. For the most part, it was delightful. It made the gnosis revolution at the Combs hidden library seem like kindergarten.

But it wasn't all joy. Some truths of our existence were hard to accept. When I first learned of the subjugation of the human spirit and what it meant for individual people, I was enraged. I've seen the dazzling substance of the soul. It's replete with love and joy, passion and wisdom. We are grander than we believe. We are light, born of pure love. We are a promise made manifest. We search for purpose, when we are the purpose. We yearn for miracles, when we are the miracles.

I came to understand that turning away from the truth of one's soul is what causes the bulk of our pain. It's what causes us to accept living as less-than who we are, because we don't see who we truly are. Eventually, I made a promise to work to end this artificially imposed and painful way of living. I vowed to end the need for anyone to live as less-than his or her true soul enables.

I made that promise after an extraordinary event that occurred when I was with Man'wa on a hill overlooking the temple complex. We were celebrating my eleventh anniversary at the temple. I wanted to remember the world I came from in detail, but I could only retrieve memories in small packets. Images of people came to me and with each was a swelling of love in my heart. I missed them, of course, but at the same time, I didn't miss them, because I missed no one and no thing. The love I felt in the last moments with each of them wasn't in the past, it was now. I told Man'wa that I felt closer to all beings than I ever had. I extolled the joy and love pouring from my heart, great love for all I've known and for all creation.

But I began to feel strange, as though every cell of my body was vibrating. Lightness gripped me as I felt myself rise. It was as though I was letting go of my skin, or perhaps more like my skin was letting go of me.

Man'wa clasped a hand over his mouth. We stared at each other. I heard Man'wa think, 'I didn't expect this just yet.'

Man'wa began to fade from my sight. I called out, "What's happening?"

"You're ascending…"

"Why?" I asked.

"Your consciousness has risen, your vib…" and that's the last I heard Man'wa say as I lost view of him completely.

It wasn't just Man'wa; the entire landscape faded, replaced with pure light. I flew through it effortlessly. The feeling was familiar. No physicality of me existed any longer. Only consciousness remained. I was ecstatic with bliss. The light around me and within me was absolute. I could say it was white, but it wasn't. It was that which creates white. It was all colors, each one distinct.

After a time my movement seemed to slow. When it slowed to the point of near stopping, I began to hear voices. I couldn't make out what they said, but they sounded in chorus, as if the tone of every word, every phrase, was in perfect harmony.

And as I listened to the serenade, a world of wonder began to materialize around me. I found myself immersed in a sea of souls. Each had a face and voice, yet I couldn't recognize an individual, nor pinpoint any word. At once, everything existed as free flowing energy and as materialized form. I realized I was floating outside of time and space.

"It's imperative that you make choices. Your life is cast by the choices you make. Some have momentary effects; others are so monumental in their effect that your life will never be the same afterward. It's not always easy to discern in which category a particular choice lies. Treat all choices with wisdom and care and the ones with sweeping effects will naturally serve you."

- Yeshua son of Joseph -

37 · Source

I floated through this sea of souls until a wave pulsed; energy beckoned the souls to align and turn their faces to me. They formed an unbroken sphere around me. It was as if I became the nucleus of a giant living cell.

These souls banded into loops and began to spin in ellipses around me. I shifted from the center of the sphere and as I shifted, the sea of souls faded, just as Man'wa had earlier.

I seemed to awaken after a long sleep. As my eyes adjusted to the scene around me, I realized I was standing in a field. The day was warm, and the light I would've expected coming from the sun was, instead, coming from every point above me. Flowers bloomed in scattered carpets; flowers like none I'd ever seen, sensual and brilliantly colored. In the distance, trees swayed.

Oddest was the silence, until I had that thought and suddenly birds chirped and plants rustled. Crickets joined in the reverie.

I stood enjoying the warmth on my skin, as a voice behind me spoke, "Issa, welcome."

I turned to see a being standing not six feet from me. "Hello. Where am I?" I asked.

"You're in a waystation, if you will. You were about to move into the next phase of your existence and I thought we should have a chat before there was no turning back." This being had no features to distinguish if it was a man or woman. It was unsettling.

"Would the form of a woman settle you?" the being said, as its features morphed into those of my mother, Mary.

"Yes, this is easier. Familiar."

She smiled, "Very good, then let's begin."

We chatted for a long while. She wanted to hear my thoughts. We laughed easily and I felt comfortable with her.

She told me more of why I was here. I'd achieved a level of mastery. I'd

"A person's gender is generally one of the first things we question in another. It can be disconcerting when the answer to that query is unknown, or when our original answer proves inaccurate. Contrary to popular belief, it has little to do with 'natural selection' and much to do with the boxes of belief we form around gender specific roles. We relate to, expect from, and desire of the genders differently, ourselves included. It's probable that you're not even aware of the box you place yourself in every time you notice another's gender."

- Yeshua son of Joseph -

demonstrated the ability to be the very substance of love. I no longer needed to be incarnate. I was released from the binds of the body and could move on to lighter vibratory levels of being.

"Is that something you want, Issa?" she asked.

"It seems a shame to have spent these years gaining mastery of my abilities to just walk away without using them," I replied. "Was all that diligent preparation just for personal gain?"

"You tell me."

"Well," I looked into the distance, "I can't see it. I can't see that all those people worked so hard… and all that energy was expended just to give me the opportunity to ascend." I faced her and said, "I don't want to just take my toys and go home."

She smiled, "Issa, you're not a petulant child. Every being that rises to the creative source gives a gift to humanity."

"But I think I'm poised to do more than that. I may be lost in self-aggrandizement, but it feels like I have more to do… work that can have a greater effect than merely adding one more speck to the sea of lifted souls."

Her eyes moistened, "The beings in the 'sea of lifted souls' as you put it, are still growing and living and making things happen. There are levels of life ahead that are very rewarding. You weren't yet there when I interrupted your journey, so you've not seen it."

I closed my eyes and tried to imagine what it would be like to move on and I couldn't. "I can't see it. I'm overflowing with love for all humanity. I feel connected to them. It's as if I am they. That connection calls me. Walking away now would be like turning my back on myself."

She stepped closer and placed her hand on my shoulder, "Would you like to have a new perspective on that which you call humanity?"

"Yes, I would."

She took my hand and the field melted away. We floated above the earth. It was a brilliant blue with brown and green landmasses protruding from the blueness.

She showed me individual scenes of life; people I didn't know, caught in energetic shackles. I saw them try to find truth and light, only to turn away and plunge back into a mire of illusion. Pain was rampant. Lies, cheating and betrayals were pervasive. Death was often too early. These people didn't know their own wealth, unable to see the glory of self that existed just outside their limited perception.

At first, I was enraged. It seemed unfair for these beautiful beings to wallow in pain and separation when the truth was so magnificent. "Why is everyone so lost to themselves?" I asked her.

"This is the human condition. They're subjugated to the will of others. Everyone. No one is free."

The magnitude of what she showed me began to sink in. "Where are the enlightened ones?"

"When those like you become free, they move on. All who remain are held prisoner to illusion, to the pain of separation from their source. Some who've lifted may extend a hand now and then. May offer a path through the deceptions, but it's rare. Most who can, leave."

"But we're all part of source, we come from source. Why doesn't the Creator ease the path?"

She sighed, "The creative source can't prevent suffering. Once a soul is created, it has free will."

"That's you, isn't it? You're a manifestation of the creative source. You're my Creator." She smiled and nodded.

"That's why you took the form of my mother. It was a clue." She nodded again.

I looked back at earth and even though I saw the subjugation and pain of abject poverty of spirit – even though I saw the horror people inflict on themselves and others as a result – I felt only love for these souls that kept going, kept searching. They knew in their core there was more to life, something greater than their temporal circumstances, and they couldn't help but eventually look for it.

"I love them," I said, "I'm in them." She took my hand and we melted back into the field.

"Issa, what would you like to do?"

"I want to go back."

"Why?"

"So I can help them find source. They're each of them as beautiful and wondrous as you. They're part of you, I'm part of them; we're all part of the whole. I want to help the whole escape the bonds that hold the separation in place."

"That may take a while. Maybe you can't do it in one lifetime. Are you prepared to fail?"

No part of me felt failure was an option. "I don't see failure."

"Issa, failure is always an option, as is the ability to try again."

"Do I have what it takes to succeed? Is this a fool's errand I want to engage in?"

"You tell me."

My mind reeled. Before me stood my Creator, empowering me to answer my own question. How could I know if my answer was the right answer, or if I was fooling myself?

She smiled, "If you're part of me as you say, how could you not know just as well as I?"

Tears began to trickle down my cheeks, "I want to go back. I want to be the instrument that ends the separation from source. What do I need to do to make that happen?"

She grasped my hands and looked deep into my eyes. I felt her gaze pierce to the very heart of me. "If you go back," she said, "you'll again become subjugated. When you do, you might lose your conviction. You might lose the knowledge of why you're there. You'll have to climb back out of the mire, a feat you've already accomplished. But I warn you, it may be more difficult the second time. I ask you again, are you prepared to fail?"

I was resolute, "If I did it once, I can do it again. I know my purpose now with greater clarity than ever before. I want to go back."

"Every soul will eventually ask the questions that'll lead them to their source. It might be tomorrow, it might be 200 lives from now. But like water, our spirit must seek its source, and if that means flowing into the crevices of many dark and horrific places, then that's what it means. Never give up on another being. Like yourself, they are in process."

- Yeshua son of Joseph -

"Then you truly are a Son of Man." She placed her hand on my cheek and it sent a jolt of energy through my spine. She continued, "You are glorious in my eyes. Try to remember as you do our work, I'm with you always."

38 · Confusion

The next thing I knew was waking in my bed at the Temple of Man. Was it just a dream? I didn't think so, but everything around me seemed unchanged.

I performed my chores, and went to find Man'wa. I wondered about his experience of the last day. He wasn't at his studio, so I wandered to the laboratories in hope of finding Jo.

When Jo saw me, his face lit up with an expression of joy and shock as if he were seeing a long lost friend. "Issa! What are you doing here?" he sputtered, all animated and flustered.

"I thought I'd drop by. I had a confusing experience and was looking for Man'wa, but he wasn't in his studio."

Jo could barely catch his breath, "You act like it's an ordinary day."

"Well, isn't it?"

"Issa! You've been gone for months. Man'wa said you'd probably never return."

"Months?" I was staggered. "It felt like hours to me."

"It's been months. I've missed you." He grabbed me and squeezed. He said, "You're different my friend. You've changed."

I promised to return to him when I understood more. I didn't want to speak about my experience until I had a chance to meet with Man'wa. Jo mentioned Man'wa was with his new student at the library. I didn't know what that meant; Man'wa had only one student at a time. I went to the library to find him.

When Man'wa saw me, his face reflected a confusion that mirrored my own. But like me, he wasn't prone to giving into excitement. He continued calmly with his student. A few minutes later, Man'wa walked to me and bowed. I bowed back, but this only heightened my confusion, I wasn't accustomed to Man'wa bowing to me.

It took him a few moments to get a word out, "I… Issa."

"Yes?"

"Why… are you here?" His eyes flitted across my face, trying to find an answer.

"I'm checking in. I'm not sure what's next."

Man'wa fell to his knees. "Issa, you've ascended. I didn't expect you to return. No one ever has." He lowered his eyes.

I was astounded, "You've had others ascend and none have returned?"

"No Master, no one's ever returned."

> "Only a fool says no to ascension. Only a fool goes backward. Only a fool can hope to find success in folly, because only a fool recognizes that where he goes, so exist those who need him."
>
> - Yeshua son of Joseph -

"There's no need to call me Master. At best we're peers, if that." I put my hands around Man'wa's arm and urged him to his feet. "Can we go someplace to speak more freely?" I said, "I'm as confused as you are." Man'wa said a few words to his student and we stepped alone into the fresh air.

"Jo said I've been gone for months," I started, "but my experience was of mere hours."

Man'wa bolstered out of his confusion. He latched his arm around mine and we continued our walk. I related my experience in as much detail as I could. Twice, Man'wa had to stop and collect his breath from the passion he felt over my tale. When I finished, he said, "Then you truly are a Son of Man."

"I don't know what it means exactly, but this is what the Creator told me."

He stopped walking and faced me, "I've succeeded." He touched his palm to my lips. "This is my mission, to facilitate the uplifting of a Son of Man." He pulled his palm back and touched it to his own lips, "In over 100 years I've watched many go. Some ascend, some return to whence they came merely more skilled. Each time I began anew, hoping I've done a good job, but with no satisfaction of knowing." A tear dripped down his cheek, "It's possible you're the first and only one I haven't failed."

"Why've you never told me this was your goal?" I asked.

"Because, the choice had to spring from you without a sense of expectation or obligation," he answered, "it only works if that's who you've become."

We formulated a plan. I'd honed my mind before I came to the temple. I'd honed my spirit and accepted my path as a Son of Man while here. Now, if I wanted to stand up to the physical rigors my path may demand, I needed to discipline my body. We decided I'd leave this ethereal temple, go back to the Earth, and study martial arts at a Bon temple.

We gathered, Jo, Man'wa and I, near the spot I arrived. Jo watched the dials of his calculator, calibrating the portal to place me at the right time and place. Jo's skill was as much an art as it was a science. It mesmerized me.

"It'll only be a few minutes before everything's aligned," he said, "we should say our goodbyes now."

I hugged him with fervor. "You've been a good friend. I'll think of you with love throughout my days," I said.

"I'll miss you." He said, "I still remember the day you arrived. I've never seen a friendlier, puzzled face than yours. You made me laugh."

"I remember that," I chuckled, "and I remember you unable to fathom that I couldn't hear with my mind."

I turned to Man'wa and grabbed his hand, "Our connection is firm. I feel I'll need you again as I travel further. Please, say you'll walk with me when I call. I'll feel more confident if I know you're with me."

He looked humbled. "You won't need me, Issa."

"No," I corrected, "I can't say that. The Creator told me I might forget; I might get lost. If I do, I'll need you to help me rise again."

"If I can help, I will." He looked over my face, "Yes, I promise. Keep me in your heart as I will you." He patted me on the back and pulled his fingers through my hair in a father-like gesture.

"We're ready now. Get into position," Jo said as he looked at his dials with great concentration. "I'm better for knowing you, Issa." He flicked a switch. "Be well, my friend."

I began to say something but I had a sudden sensation of being smothered, then everything went dark. When the light returned I felt heavier than I had in these eleven years. Gravity pulled mercilessly on my bones. And it was cold, very cold.

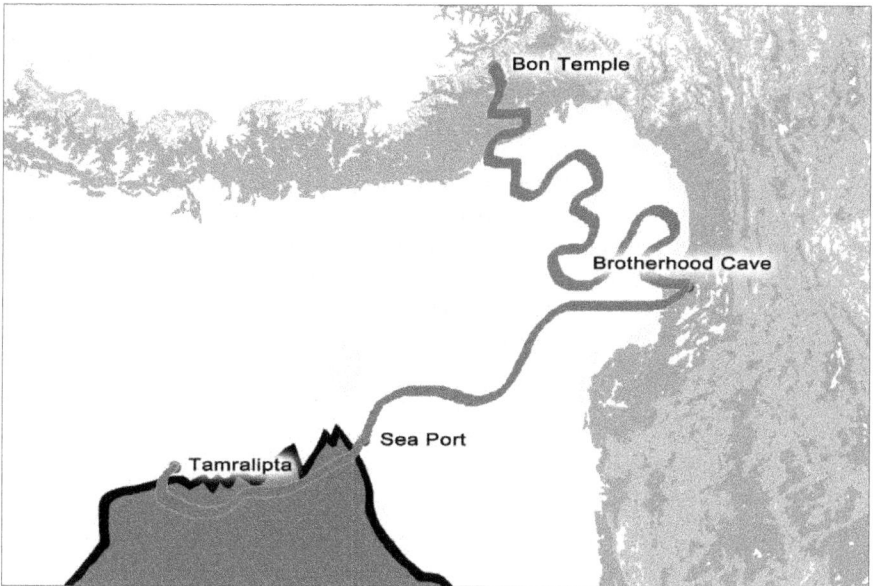

Figure 4: From adept training to Tamralipta on the way home –
The temple and cave locations are approximate

39 · Bitter Cold

I'd forgotten weather. The wind was bitter cold. It looked like fall from the state of the trees and grass turned brown in the field. Unfortunately, I was hungry and thirsty as well. Jo said I should arrive very near the Bon temple, within a half mile of it, but I'd have to figure out its exact location.

I looked for clues. I was standing on the side of a mountain. I remembered how the air was at Insa'alet temple and this felt similar, so I speculated this was a high altitude. I walked downhill about 30 paces and came to a narrow road. It had well-worn grooves from cart wheels. Fresh pack-animal dung was present; it was a recently traveled road. That was a good sign. The sun was directly above me, so I had at least four hours to find my way.

But which way? I looked in both directions and decided to take the way that went up. This road was either going to a village, or to a pass through the mountains into a valley. Either way, there should be people sooner than later.

The road became steep and wound treacherously up the side of the mountain with sharp switchbacks, eventually dipping down to circumvent a rocky outcropping. When I came around the rocks, I saw a welcome sight – a rope bridge spanning across a deep chasm. On the other side were buildings. It was obviously a Bon temple. I'd reached my destination.

The greeting I received upon entering the complex was warm, but brief. Everyone was short of speech and spare in movement. Nearly the opposite of where I'd just come from where everyone was vivacious and effusive.

I was ushered to a small courtyard deep within the complex. I didn't speak the language, but they indicated I should wait. They gave me a thick, leather garment to wear. I was warm and grateful for it.

I'd heard stories about entering training temples. I assumed I was already being evaluated. They'd want to know how well tempered I was. Did I have the mental discipline? Had I any previous martial training? Was I up to the challenge?

Darkness settled in. I stood, unwavering. From time to time a man, dressed in

"If given a choice, I was always pre-disposed to walk up hill. I grew up on a hill and going up meant the joy of going home. What does 'going home' mean to you? And when you look at your life, what actions do you take because your choice internally represents going or not-going home? For the positive or the negative, if you can discern when you're making a choice based on that deep-seated attraction or repulsion, you might understand your motivations at a level that previously eluded you."

- Yeshua son of Joseph -

what I assumed were priest's garb, came near me, smiled, then walked away. Even though I wasn't cold, I was still hungry and thirsty. And I was unprepared for the familiar effect of earth's gravity. After several hours standing, my muscles burned to move or sit down, but I continued my vigil.

In the buildings, I saw lamps lit and fires raging. The orange flames danced through the windows and doors. I didn't waver.

I felt quite foolish, but the men who left me here were clear by their gestures that I was to stay and wait.

A man rushed from one of the buildings with a bowl. Steam rose into the cold air. He handed it to me. It was soup and the smell of it made my stomach leap in anticipation of liquid and nourishment. I thanked him, though I don't know if he understood my words, and began to sip. I can't say it was delicious, but it delighted my senses. This was the first earthly food I'd eaten in over eleven years. The food at the Temple of Man was good and nutritious, but it lacked something intangible. Somehow, it didn't ground me like good food from the green earth.

When done, I cradled the bowl in my hands and continued to wait. Another hour went by and I no longer felt my legs; they were numb from my statue-like stance. My bladder must have given way, as I could smell urine. My eyes got heavy, I wanted to sleep, but I was resolute to the place they put me. I lowered my conscious mind into a deep trance, so I could weather the night without falling. By morning, I was still on my feet, though I no longer felt them at all.

People woke and the rituals of the day began around me. By midmorning, I felt as though I had only a few moments left before falling over. My body bobbed from side to side. That's when a middle-aged man came out of the large building to my right and walked straight to me.

He said something, but I didn't understand the language. I bowed to him as best I could even though I had difficulty bending. I heard him say with his mind. 'Welcome stranger, perhaps you'll understand me this way.'

I nodded and pulled a note out of my bag. I looked the man in the eye and said with my mind, 'Greetings, I have a note from Man'wa at the Temple of Man.'

The man blinked in surprise and took the note. He read it quickly, though obviously cherishing every word. He said, 'I know Man'wa well. I'm eager to speak with you further. But, please, rest first.' He spoke with the men around him and they helped me into a building and onto a cot. One handed me a cup of warm tea that I eagerly drank. I laid my head on the pillow and promptly went to sleep.

It was the next morning when I finally woke, disoriented, and unsure what day it was. Partly because I'd only come back to Earth two days before. But also, perhaps from sleeping so long.

I rose and stepped into the courtyard. Men were going about their business. This time I felt I could walk around. I had to find a place to relieve myself properly if nothing else, and to wash off the stench produced from my standing vigil.

None talked with me all day. I performed morning baptism. I attended midday meal. I meditated through the afternoon and when time came for evening meal, I went to the main table. But one of the priests took me by the arm and led me to a seat next to the Master. He conducted what I assumed were prayers, some spoken, some sung. When the food came, I found it modest, but nourishing.

When the meal was nearly complete, the Master turned to me and said with his mind, 'Please accept my gratitude for the note you brought.'

'You're welcome,' I answered.

He nodded his head, 'Man'wa says you're looking to be a student here.'

'Yes.'

'Speak your name aloud.'

"Issa," I said louder than was necessary.

He nodded his head, 'You don't look like an initiate to me.'

'I'm not from here. I was born far to the west.'

'That's not my meaning,' the Master said, 'I mean your spirit is already tempered.'

'I see,' I said, 'my physical body is in need of tempering as well.'

The Master looked me over again, pulled his hand from his lap, and raised his finger toward my face. Suddenly his finger turned to flame. I watched it burn for a moment, then I lifted my hand over the flame and drenched it with a spray of water from my palm. The master sputtered with surprise, then laughed with gusto. The men at our table were startled by his display of jocularity.

'Man'wa says you're a shining one, and yet you haven't risen. What are your motives?'

I thought about his question, then said, 'Master, I wish to be the instrument for the end of subjugation.'

The Master chuckled, 'You want to free prisoners?'

'No,' I said, 'I want to free souls.'

Upon hearing my words, the Master's mouth dropped open. After a moment, he said, 'That's too tall an order. Why should I invest in your education only to see you fail? It's a fool's mission.'

'Isn't it the fool,' I replied, 'that through innocence enters any new undertaking with faith? In fact, is there any other way to achieve but to begin with the eyes of innocence coupled with intention?'

The Master regarded me again and said, 'Man'wa believes in you.'

'He should,' I said arrogantly, 'he watched me ascend.' I immediately felt as though I'd gone too far.

The Master abruptly stood, pushing his stool behind him. He began to walk away, with great strides and heavy feet. He stopped and turned back to me, his face

"You probably haven't gone through the types of initiations I undertook. They gave me great power of control. But even still, you assuredly have some tempering of self. Parents, school, life lessons have all intervened in your growth to produce some measure of personal control. There's power in control. I'm not speaking of the type of control that strains on you; that requires effort. I'm talking about the type of control that rises out of you naturally; that's as softly wielded as a feather. If you recognize and acknowledge where you are already tempered, and you maximize the use of those qualities, your personal power will be magnified tenfold or more."

- Yeshua son of Joseph -

filled with anger, 'Now I see why Man'wa sent you to me. We'll humble that streak of pride in you, initiate, beginning now.'

He spoke to one of the priests and they scuttled me out of the dining hall and into the courtyard. The sun was setting; it would be bitter cold soon. They stripped off all but my underclothes. I began to shiver. They tied my outstretched arms to a tree so I couldn't shield my body from the cold and left me there.

The cold became vicious. My shivering became violent.

After a short time, a priest came and gently placed something on my shoulder. I couldn't see what it was, but I could feel it move. It slowly moved down my back and around my side. All the time my mind was alive with imaginings of what it was. When it came round to my belly, I saw it was a tarantula. If I hadn't already been reeling with mortal fear from the cold, and my undisciplined thoughts, the tarantula would've been just another of creations beautiful creatures. But the sight of the creature on my belly filled me with terror. I screamed and promptly passed out.

40 · Resistance

I woke, alone, in front of a raging fire. Multiple blankets draped over my body, sweat pouring from my brow. I sat up, dizzy. My shoulder hurt; obviously, I'd wrenched it falling unconscious against the restraints. I stared into the fire, wondering what was next, when a young woman draped in silk came and handed me a cup of cool water. I drank it quickly, handing the cup back to her. She left, returning a few moments later with the cup full again. I drank it all, but less quickly. She set the cup aside, and sat down next to me on the cot. It made me uncomfortable for her to be so close. She saw me wincing when I moved my shoulder, so she began to massage it. It felt good so I let her continue.

She began to make sexual gestures. I moved her hands off me, but she continued. Her persistence was annoying. Again, I moved her hands off me and turned to the fire.

When she came back at me again, it dawned on me, this was another test. So I tolerated her advances without giving into them for hours, until we both fell asleep beside the fire.

Every day continued like this; different forms of sensory deprivation or overload. It felt like torture. I knew there must be a purpose to this gauntlet, but it eluded me. No one talked with me, so I was no closer to learning the language. I ate meals with them, and participated in prayers I didn't understand, but aside from that, I was as much an outsider as when I entered the complex. I didn't even know if I was in the order, still being evaluated, or merely punished.

One afternoon I was sitting alone on a bench in the garden nursing my aching body. My shoulder still hurt, and on top of that, I had several bruises, scrapes, and sore muscles from head to toe. I was bent over, head down, and weary. I knew Man'wa wouldn't have sent me here if he didn't think this was the best place for me, but I couldn't fathom how this type of treatment would get me to where I wanted to go.

The Master walked up and asked me with his mind if he could sit next to me. I bid him sit, but I was wary. It was entirely possible that this treatment was solely a product of having angered him the last time we spoke.

> *"Setting aside the love we give and receive, when all is said and done, I guarantee that you'll look back over your life and cherish most that which caused you initial confusion and consternation. Because it's those times that precede your greatest actions. The burden of inaction can only be maintained when you perceive no challenge."*
>
> *- Yeshua son of Joseph -*

"Thank you," he said aloud in a language I knew. It surprised me. I thought we had no spoken language in common.

"You're surprised? We have more in common than you think." His face reflected a wry irony that I found intriguing.

"Tell me, what else do we have in common?" I asked.

"Well, for one we both studied at the Temple of Man. I was a student of Man'wa, too."

My eyes traveled over his face looking for clues to his age. When I found none, I said, "I see. I assume then, that you're older than you look."

"Ah... I was one of his first students." He smiled and I realized he must be well over 100 years old, even though he looked to be in his forties.

I brazened the next question, "May I assume we're speaking as peers right now?"

"Yes, Issa, please... ask your questions."

"I don't understand why I've had to endure these trials."

"You're in pain now, yes?" He said, "You're feeling beleaguered and raw?"

"Yes, very much so."

"What do you think these trials are about?"

I shook my head, "I've been contemplating that exact question all afternoon." I said, "I'm at a loss. I know I angered you the last time we spoke, for that I apologize."

"You think you've been put through these trials because I was angry with you?"

"Not for sure, but I reasoned it was possible."

The Master laughed, "I've had other initiates receive my anger, but none before you has apologized for it." He continued to laugh, "Your training began with that mock display of anger. I wanted to see how you'd respond to a variety of assaults."

"You weren't angered by my arrogance?"

"No. I'm touched that you chose my humble order to continue your training."

I lowered my head and chuckled. What a mistaken impression I'd formed. "How've I done? Have I passed the test? Am I accepted into the order?"

He laughed again, "You've failed miserably – every trial without exception!" Now I began to laugh; it was too ridiculous to see anything but the irony in it all. "Look, you're in the order," he assured me, "you were accepted the moment I read your note."

Still chuckling, I asked, "Then tell me, what's the point?"

"In every trial, your body met the challenge with resistance. This is your first lesson. Look at yourself now. Every bruise and ache you have is a direct result of the resistance you displayed to what was happening around you." He ran his hand over my leg and the aches in that leg instantly disappeared. "See how easy it is? I merely coaxed your leg into letting go of the resistance and now you feel no pain."

"This is all about resistance?"

"Absolutely. Fear, pain, nausea, revulsion, these and more are all forms of resistance to an unwelcome force." He stood and asked me to do the same. "Hold your arm out in front of you."

I did. He pushed down on my arm and I resisted. He kept pushing and I kept resisting. After a few moments, my arm hurt. Soon I couldn't resist longer and the weight of his push nearly knocked me over.

"That was resistance to the force I applied. What would happen if you simply didn't resist?"

"Well, you'd be able to push my arm with no effort. I'd be at your mercy."

"That would be true," he chuckled, "if you were predisposed to the superiority of outside will. But what if you weren't? What if your body wasn't resistant to my push, nor at the mercy of its force, but rather, was firm in its truth. The truth that the arm was out straight. Firm that no outside force could rewrite your truth, because your mind ruled your body, instead of your body dictating your mind."

I nodded my head, "I'm beginning to see…"

"Very good." He sat down and I followed his lead. "So, now, let me tell you what's next…"

He explained where I'd be staying, further up the hill at the training center. He assigned me to a trainer and told me where to pick up my new cloths. And he did something I wasn't expecting, but for which I was grateful. He offered to send a message to my home, to let them know I was here and well. I had no idea how he'd manage that, home was so far away, nor how long it might take, but it made me happy to know my family would be updated.

"It's a well known law of this universe that what you resist will persist."
- Yeshua son of Joseph -

41 · The Adept Way

I immersed myself in the training. It was more interesting and less painful than those first several days. That's not to say it wasn't sometimes arduous, it was, but my trainers were good men and I made fast friends. I completed the course in record time.

The course was called the Adept Way, and it consisted of training in the martial arts for protection, in yoga for tending to my body's health, and in how to control myself from feeling heat, cold, hunger, pain, sexual excitement, and many other sensations to which most people cannot help but succumb. I learned how to govern my body by slowing or speeding processes, such as heart rate, breathing, blood flow, and elimination. I could now bypass at will some of the laws of physics, such as gravity and light.

Coupling these new skills with the abilities I'd mastered at the Temple of Man, I felt truly ready to meet any circumstance encountered. I was a Son of Man graced with the power and dignity this achievement bestows. I didn't know how I was going to accomplish my mission, but I was committed to my promise to end humanity's subjugation. The very thought of it gave me joy.

I received a letter from my family about six months into my training. Really, it was more than a letter; it was a packet of letters. Some from James, from Joseph, some from Mary. There were even short notes from friends like Herodes. They were pleased and relieved to have gotten word that I was safe. The first thing I garnered from the narratives was my age. According to the calendar from home, I was in my twenty-fourth year. That was a relief to know.

Joseph talked about the farm and the construction business. He had several new contracts for buildings in Sepphoris. He was proud of me, and as usual, his words touched me deeply.

Mary gave me detail upon detail about the weddings. Ruth had been married before I left Kapilavastu, but now Jude and Sarah were married as well. Jude and his wife Rebekkah lived at the family complex. Joseph was training Jude in the construction business.

James was impressed that I was studying at a martial temple and he told me all about his life at Qumran. He was now a rabbi, trained in the art of negotiation, and I had no doubt he was good at it. He spoke about his work as emissary to several outside communities. He traveled extensively and often got to visit with the family both in Galilee and in Jerusalem. He said he was happy beyond measure, which made me happy, too.

He also confessed his new nickname, 'Old Camel Knees.' He explained that his fervor compelled him to walk to prayers on his knees, something none of the other brothers did, of course. Unfortunately, after years of bloodying his knees on the sharp rocks, they were swollen with scar tissue and looked like camel's knees. I winced at the thought of his knees cut and bloodied time and again, but I felt reverence for his devotion. Still, I couldn't help being amused by the name.

Of course, everyone wanted to know when I'd return. For that question, I had no answer.

Philar visited several times during my training. He was pleased with my efforts. Our relationship had deepened during my time at the Temple of Man; he was now a dear and old friend. I felt connected to home when he was with me.

The day finally arrived for me to leave the temple. Although I was a Son of Man and a fully-fledged adept, I had no idea where I headed. I knew that eventually I'd have to go home, but I wasn't ready for that yet.

I hugged the friends I'd made and said goodbye to the Master. I was sad to walk away from the people, but was glad to be done with the training. I needed the physical tempering, the skills, and the art of it all, but I was itching to do something new. I'd been studying one discipline after another for a long time, and I was ready to turn my attention to the world outside of me for a change.

My first day on the road was pleasant; the countryside was lovely. I slept under the stars at night, and was back on the road the next day. Optimism filled me as days like this continued into months. I met beautiful people along the road, and saw magnificent sights. I could calm hostile situations, and bring peace to people in pain. I always had what I needed; food and shelter were always provided. This optimistic attitude filled me with innocence and joy. I was quick to laugh and ready to sooth. I wanted to lift people. I wanted to sing into their spirits, to imbue them with faith, and help them see their journeys through eyes of wonder. This fiery, internal state seemed inextinguishable.

And I soon forgot the Creator's ominous warning.

"I've heard countless people lament that their parents were to blame for their emotional pain. Or their economic woes, or their bosses, or spouses. Fill in the blank. But the truth is that nothing outside yourself has any weight whatsoever in creating your current pain. It's 100% internal in origin. The sooner you accept this, the faster you can heal."

- James brother of Yeshua -

Darkness

of the

World

42 · Many Squalor Moons

I'd been wandering downhearted for months. My garments announced my adept status to all I met, and yet, I was increasingly disturbed.

When I left the martial temple, I felt the grace of my Creator with me. The first months were filled with discovery and the satisfaction of being of true service to my fellow man. But now, the cruelty and debasement of people repeatedly assaulted me. I witnessed too many inhumanities to innumerate. I saw the sacred parts of us routinely trampled, squashed, and mutilated. The brutality of murder, rape, assault, and slavery sickened me. Even more than the physical effects of these harsh realities, I became disillusioned seeing rampant moral impoverishment. It left me feeling weary and aimless. Perhaps the world was a place of pain and disappointment and little else?

The wandering didn't stop, but the positivity and faith engendered in an attitude of service stopped. I lost the love and care I had for humanity and with that loss, all care for myself left me. I had no concept of how I looked. I stopped daily baptism. I didn't take care of my body that had once so willingly submitted to the majesty of the Adept Way. I wasn't eating regularly. I'd withered to the point where my skin outlined my bones. My face was lined and gaunt, and my posture was bent from the weight of pessimistic thoughts.

I forgot my mission. I forgot I was a Son of Man. This went against everything in which I invested my faith on that fateful day I met my Creator. On that day, I was convinced of the divinity of man.

But all that faded, and as I wandered through the hamlets and villages of these eastern valleys, I found more and more that I disregarded the optimism of creation and embraced the pessimism of defeat. It was all around me in the squalor and injustice of the inhabitants.

As I walked into a small town one day, yet another ghastly scene confronted me. A man barked his wares as normal practice, but it was the nature of his wares that disturbed me. They were young girls, all of whom displayed marks of violence. Not one of them was more than eleven years old. Some looked as young as seven. The seller merely lusted for money, considering gold fair and adequate compensation for their flesh; paid by anyone who was willing to open a purse, with

"You can convince yourself of anything. Truly, you have the capacity to rearrange your mind to believe anything you wish to believe. Everyone has a tendency to covet the beliefs they accepted when they were young. Why? Because they're deep-seated and are pervasive in their effect over time. But just because they're pervasive in their effect, doesn't make them right. You've merely convinced yourself through causal observation that the effects reflect truth. In fact, it's those beliefs that you see as basic and unbendable, that are the first ones I suggest you examine and alter."

- Yeshua son of Joseph -

no regard given to the buyer's agenda.

People gathered, bidding for each child in turn. The winners bragged about what the child would do for them. Some of the bidders wanted slaves, while others wanted personal concubines or public prostitutes. As I looked upon the faces of these degraded angels, I was reminded of my once beloved Seleya. All I saw was the abject subjugation of the feminine, the first principle of our universe. Those lovely and majestic bodies, designed by creation to thrive, love, and perpetuate life in all its glory, would be forced to lay in the lowest of energies and lose their connection to the divine.

The buyers were in pain, each in their own way, unable to see how they reinforced their own fears through the loss of freedom they forced on another. Each saw the child's loss as their gain, oblivious to the spiritual decay they suffered by these actions. I saw the cycle of fear and subjugation continue through their lives. And when they died, the fear and pain would urge them to choose a new incarnation; to be born into an appropriately painful existence cast from a poverty-stricken soul.

This cycle of life after life, death after death, seemed to be a never-ending and downward-spiraling wheel that repulsed me. I was nauseous as I turned away. The scene was more horrid than I could personally hold and I felt impotent to change it. My vital energy waned as I walked through the center of town feeling the lack of connection with my own divine source.

This cynicism I'd adopted I'd seen written on the face of more than one adept since I left the martial temple. Early on, I'd felt sorry for those adepts, but now I was one of them, and I was about to pay a long and dear price for my apathy.

I continued, my head cast down and my attention squandered on futile thoughts. The sky was dark with clouds that threatened to rain at any moment. The ground I trod was thick with mud from recent downpours. My feet were already encrusted with the dried mud of the last several days.

I rounded a corner trying desperately to wipe those young violated faces from my mind's eye, but their visage was pervasive. Suddenly a man stood in front of me blocking my passage. He was short and wiry. "What can I do for you, friend?" I asked, not because I meant it, but because it was habit to speak so.

"You can give me that necklace you're wearing," he chortled.

I realized I was in danger. My full-self would have intuited that before I rounded the corner and would have changed direction, but the half-self I nursed this day moved blindly through the world. I said, "What use would you have to rob an impoverished adept?"

"Each man for himself," he slurred as he spat at the ground, "you won't be here long anyway, old man. You're starving."

Out of habit, I uttered simple platitudes, "Starvation is a matter for the soul. The body means nothing if the spirit feeds us." My mind was ruminating on hearing myself referred to as 'old man.' I was only 26. How could he mistake me for an old man?

The thief raised a club over his head and menaced me. "I mean it, give me your jewels."

I froze. My mind had no effective response. I couldn't run. I couldn't muster will. I couldn't even raise an arm to deflect his attack. I stood frozen, looking into his brittle face, until the blunt of his weapon cracked the side of my head. I felt my body falling, but wasn't conscious long enough to feel myself hit the naked ground.

"A platitude never helped anyone. Platitudes uttered are an indication that you're not present in the moment. If you aren't in the moment with the person you're trying to help, how can you possibly know what will help? A platitude is your way of saying, 'I don't want to help you enough right now to look at you clearly.' Ultimately, it means you don't want to look at yourself clearly."

- Yeshua son of Joseph -

43 · Intemperate Illusion

When I woke, I sat up in the mud. I reached to my neck, but sadly, the stones from the Master at Insa'alet were gone. More painful to me was the absence of the heart Joseph gave me. The thief took both.

Grief engulfed me. The heart I wore all these years was the only physical tie left to my home, my family. It was the only thing that gave my own heart redemption. I believed that if I truly wanted to, I could follow its beacon home. Now it was gone. My connection to home felt irretrievably severed.

I fell back in the mud, tears flowing. This was no crying as I'd ever engaged in before; it came from a pain so deep I had no precedent to understand it. My body was still and I made no sound, just tears copious and virulent streaming from my eyes. As the salty taste of tears washed across my lips, so did the acrid taste of blood flowing from the wound. My only thought was, 'Is this the taste of death?'

I can't say how long I lay in this squalid and pitiful condition. If someone hadn't come along, it's possible I would've lain there until the only thing left was my corpse. But someone did come along; an adept sat next to me and laid his hand on my face.

"Brother, you're lost," he said as if I didn't already know that fact. I moved my head enough to look at his face. It was thin, with wizened skin, and carried a wearied countenance much as I imagined my own. He took a brief puff on a pipe and said, "Brother, there's only one thing I know that can dull your pain. Here's something they didn't teach us at the temple." He held the pipe to my mouth so I could take a puff.

I resisted, not knowing what it was.

He said, "Don't be afraid, this'll quell the pain… give you the will to get up."

So I inhaled from the pipe. The smoke had an oddly sweet, flowery taste and I instantly felt my body react to a wave of relief washing through it. Each muscle in succession, beginning at my chest, felt this wave, until the entirety of my body was one notch closer to calm.

This adept was right; I sat up. When I did, he offered the pipe to me again. I eagerly took another puff, deeper than the last, and again I felt a wave of warmth and relief wash through me.

I looked at the adept more closely from this upright vantage point and saw that his face, though rugged and wearied, appeared kind. His eyes were glazed, but for some reason I trusted him. I pointed to the pipe, "What is this?" I asked.

He smiled and said, "Mother's milk, Brother, mother's milk."

I didn't know what mother's milk was, so I asked him, "Where does it come from?"

He laughed and pointed to a patch of tall flowers across the road and I understood. The substance of this flower was mentioned in the Vedic texts as a muscle relaxer, a pain alleviator, and an aphrodisiac. It was opium. I took another puff off the pipe and the world became colored with a pinkish, gauze-like light that seemed to make everything softer and more pleasant. So I sat in the mud with this other adept sharing his pipe of false redemption. I forgot I'd been robbed, I forgot blood ran down my face, I forgot I was broken.

My being became permeated with a seductive illusion that all was well. It felt real, but it was illusion born solely of intemperance. I didn't care. I simply didn't care where it came from or how it arrived. The relief was all encompassing and wholly satisfying.

I'd completely forgotten that I could reach this state of relief and calm, quelling all pain and filling myself with peace, without any external help. My adept talents were enough to accomplish the task if I'd employed them, but I had no interest in those talents now even if I'd remembered them. I was in a substance-perpetuated state. If any god in all glory had manifested in front of me at that moment, I would've thought it less interesting than the substance in that pipe.

As I sat with this adept and smoked the afternoon away, time turned in on itself. I forgot what time of day it was, or even what year it was. If someone had called me an old man then, I would've gladly accepted it as truth. There were no facts in my head. None. There was, however, a new reality born in me of this intemperate illusion and it carried its own truth.

I became a hollow shadow of myself willing to give my life over to self-deception. I was willing to sidestep truth, and in so doing denigrate all I'd been taught, all the gifts I'd been given, and all I was here to accomplish. I was willing to become a spiritual golem in exchange for not having to feel the depth of my disconnection from source. It was a frighteningly small step and much too easy to take.

I looked at this other adept and asked his name. He replied, "Jimon." He smiled with a bent mouth and asked, "What's your name, Brother?"

"Issa."

When he heard my name, Jimon dropped the pipe. He scrambled to keep it from scorching his clothing. He said, "No. How can that be?"

"That's my name." I said, "I come from far to the west, from Judea."

His surprised eyes stayed fixed on me, "I've heard of you. You studied at the Temple of Man."

"Yes, I suppose I did," I said, but it felt flat in me, with none of the fanfare of remembrance I should've felt.

"My brother Issa, you're welcome in my fold. Please come to our camp and make yourself a home." He stood and reached to help me.

When I grabbed his arm, I wavered, unsteady, and nearly lost consciousness again. "You have a wound on your head." He said, "We should find a stream and wash it before we go home."

"Your mother in creation has provided all good things for you. Everything in creation has a reason. Consider the peanut. It has the potential to feed many creatures. And yet, there are some people that could die if they ate a peanut. Always look at the temptations around you, given in grace and love, as worthy of respect. Then discern from a place of respect, if that grace extends to you personally or not. What helps another may harm you. Nothing in creation is universal, only divine law persists across the boundaries we hold dear and call self."

- Yeshua son of Joseph -

I let Jimon lead me to a creek and gently wash my face and clean the wound. His kindness was comforting. Looking at it now, I see that he engendered a level of trust in these actions that I can't say he deserved. I can't say he didn't. I simply don't know if he did or if I was willing to see a kind hand in the new illusion I'd embraced.

44 · A New Brotherhood

Jimon led me up a rugged trail to a mountain encampment in front of a cave. The entrance to the cave was masked by a large, brightly colored tent. Other adepts sat on carpets under an awning in front of the tent, each smoking a pipe. By the smell, I could tell not all of them were smoking opium. There were at least two or three substances being consumed.

All the adepts had glazed eyes that betrayed their disconnection from source. All were like me, bone thin and weary of face. I wondered how the Adept Way had failed so many. Obviously, we were all once strong and agile, able and willing, accepting of spirit and glad to be studying at one temple or another. Yet, here we were in this degraded condition.

There were approximately twenty-five adepts in this community and they accepted me into their fold immediately. Being a wearied adept was all it took to join this fellowship. Apparently, communities like this liberally dotted the mountains from here to as far east as one could travel before meeting the great waters. That amounted to a whole lot of beleaguered men like me, all spiritually trained, and unable to cope with the realities of this world.

Some still practiced meditation, some practiced chanting, but none with regularity. All consumed one substance or another to mask their pain. I made myself a home, finding inside the cave an unused bed alongside the other brothers. I was assured that my needs would be met, including unrestricted access to the opium stored in the back of the cave in little clay pots.

To earn food and other necessities, the brothers took turns sitting in front of the tent greeting pilgrims from neighboring villages. The pilgrims asked for healing, teaching, counseling, and a host of other services. The tent was set up with stalls for services that might require privacy. In return, pilgrims offered money, food, cloth; whatever they could afford.

I was happy to fold into the community. And I was happy to continue imbibing in the contents of the little clay pots. It only took a few days and I was firmly addicted to opium, oblivious to the toll it was exacting from my body and soul.

Days folded into weeks, weeks into months, and each day was exactly like the one before. I laughed regularly, attended to pilgrims regularly, and smoked regularly.

"Every community has its measurements of acceptance. Even the community of one you call yourself. It's hard to remain happy with who you are, if at some level you're violating a rule of personal community. Think about the rules you try to enforce on yourself to maintain some level of self-acceptance. Is there a way you can abolish the need to force yourself into conformity lest you eject yourself from your own favor?"

- Yeshua son of Joseph -

As my popularity rose, more pilgrims asked specifically for 'Issa.' Apparently, my presence had become legend across many parishes. It was widely reported that I'd studied at the hallowed Temple of Man. No one here seemed to care that I was lost in my intemperate illusion. My name alone evoked reverence and power.

Some days there were throngs of pilgrims waiting for me, and each day I made my requisite appearance, speaking with whoever was there. I can't report that I was wise or eloquent or even of true service. Maybe I was and maybe I wasn't, but pilgrims believed I had been, so they left copious gifts.

Soon, all the brothers were better fed and looking healthier, myself included. But none of us stopped imbibing our preferred substances. Our eyes and minds remained clouded and barren. Our spirits hung in limbo; we were merely better fed than before.

There was one service some brothers performed that made me uncomfortable. From time to time, a married couple would complain of a barren womb. They were desperate for children. Children were the only way these people could be assured of wellbeing into their old age. Without children, old age held the specter of abject poverty and premature death.

A couple complaining of a barren womb might need one of many services, including Ayurvedic treatments, exercises, sexual practice instruction, or if the trouble was that the husband was infertile, a gift of fertile fluid direct from a Brother.

I wasn't trained in this science and, because of my Hebraic sensibilities, I was uncomfortable performing or even learning these procedures. But more and more, these couples began to clamber for me. Young men presented their wives, asking me to impregnate them. It wasn't even clear that these couples had fertility issues. It seemed to be related to a growing idolatry of me. It was uncomfortable just being asked and I turned down every request.

But despite my stance, the throngs grew. Every morning fifty to eighty pilgrims would wait to meet with me. They chanted and presented alms. Some prostrated themselves when I stepped from the tent. Others wanted to touch my feet or kiss my hand. I grew increasingly uncomfortable with the clamor.

I began to spend entire days laying on my cot smoking and refusing to come out. The brothers were accommodating, they made no demands of me, but the throngs were loud with their chants and shouts. The more I smoked, the less invasive the noise seemed. Many days I was virtually catatonic. In all ways possible, I was hiding.

"We tend to believe that how a person looks, reveals how well they are. Generally speaking, the body will reflect the ravages of illness, but emotional and spiritual wellness-states are reflected in attitude and action, not necessarily in the physical form. Observe, listen, and learn."

- Yeshua son of Joseph -

45 · A Bad Night

It escaped my drug-addled mind that I hadn't heard from the Unseen this entire time. Nor had I received any visits from the Other, a testament to how far I'd fallen. I was running, I was hiding; I was effectively blind.

It was one of those blind evenings that turned out to be one of the most shocking and painful moments of my life. But if it hadn't been for the shock, all might've been lost.

It was a hard day. There were at least a hundred pilgrims, most of whom only wanted to see Issa. I worked with a handful of seekers over the course of a few hours, but they treated me as if I were a demigod: chanting over me, falling prostrate, kissing my feet.

It was more than I could handle. I tried to dissuade them, but they wouldn't stop. My pleas to cease their ministrations were mistaken as acts of humility. I retreated into the cave and smoked myself into a stupor, refusing to come out the rest of the day.

As evening approached, I was unconscious. It was preferable to listening to the clamor. But I was slowly roused out of my stupor by a young woman sitting on me in the cot. Not just sitting on me, but she was engaging in sex with me. Until that moment, I had no conscious knowledge of her presence. The drug had shut down my consciousness, just as I'd asked it to.

The side effects of this drug were like night and day. At times my body was ready for sex. More often, it had just the opposite effect. But in either case, I didn't have the heart or mind to engage in sex. It was wholly undesired. The idea of engaging in sex without proper consecration grated against my sensibilities.

But as I was half-waking to the fact that my body was cleaved to this woman, I realized I was being raped.

I yelled, "No," but just as I did, my body gave over and she received that which I held as my most sacred and intimate possession. I felt no personal pleasure; in fact, I felt just the opposite. I was sickened. I pushed her onto the floor. Again, I yelled, "No," but I knew it was too late; she'd been successful. I'd been roused to consciousness too late and as a result, I'd been violated in a very direct fashion.

She stood, laughing at me. It was clear her act was premeditated and she was pleased with her prize.

I shouted, "I didn't give you permission!"

She hissed out the words, "Your body gave its own permission, fool." She laughed again and said, "What kind of a man are you? You were ready, I did you a favor!"

I yelled, "No... I'm horrified!"

She continued to laugh as she walked out of the cave, hissing about the freak who didn't want her favor and that she was going to have my baby and there was nothing I could do about it.

I felt violated and defiled. Breathing became difficult. My heart raced like a trapped animal. I was compelled away from this event. So, I ran, out of the cave and past the camping pilgrims; down the mountain and across the valley. I ran and ran and ran until my feet tread into the nearest river.

I stopped and stood in the water, feeling the cold rush around my ankles. I stripped off my clothes and fell naked into the river letting the water cover me. I let it begin to strip away the grime of weakness and indifference that encrusted my being. I laid panting and feeling as if my head were going to explode from the pain of the violation I'd endured.

How could I allow myself to be so degraded that I'd invite such a violation? I struggled onto my knees and prayed the loudest and most desperate prayer I'd ever mustered. "My benevolent Creator, please forgive me. Forgive this foolish state. Please, Creator, heal me. Grant me access to your grace. I'm calling for help, for forgiveness." I continued at the top of my lungs, "I'm lost, please help me be found. I'm lost. Please forgive my foolishness, my imprudence."

I kept up these pleas for hours, well into the night. And as I cried for help, recognition of the truth of my current state began to rise into clarity in my mind. I was more than lost. Being raped was merely a symptom of the degraded state I'd fallen into. Yes, I was horrified at what happened, but beneath that, I was triply horrified by the man I'd become.

I was wretched. Waking up to that fact cut me into little pieces.

"If this part of my story seems unbelievable to you, if you cannot accept that a man can be physically assaulted in this manner, then I suggest you take a deep look at your beliefs regarding gender. These misperceptions are most likely adversely coloring how you see and interact with people."

- Yeshua son of Joseph -

46 · The Sun Rose Again

Those raw, broken pieces of me sat in the river for a long time. The cold numbed my body and I went into a deep meditation for the first time in more than a year.

As I began to bring the truth of my current existence into focus, I also began to hear the faint murmurs of the Unseen. I couldn't see them or make out their words, but I heard the tones of their voices and it reassured me that perhaps not all was lost. Perhaps I could atone.

Finally, the sun rose. It was the only clue I had as to where I was in relationship to the cave. I looked down at my hands and noticed two things. I was naked and with the light rising over the ridge, I'd better find my clothes. And I noticed my hands were shaking.

I found my robes and walked back to camp, but I felt increasingly ill. I sweat profusely which made little sense given that it was a cool morning. My hands shook worse than earlier, and the muscles of my shoulders and back twitched. When I entered the cave, I was certain I was ill.

I sat on the cot and wondered if the nausea would get worse. Jimon saw me holding my stomach. He came over and said, "Issa, you alright?"

"I don't think so."

Jimon knelt and looked into my face. He asked, "When was the last time you smoked, Brother?"

I thought for a moment then said, "Earlier yesterday."

Jimon nodded his head and fetched a pipe. He lit it, took a few puffs for himself, and handed it over, but I didn't want to smoke. I was just beginning to bring my wretched condition into focus and I wanted to find the true man in me again.

I said to Jimon, "I don't want this anymore. I think I'm done with it."

Jimon chuckled, smiling that familiar crooked smile, and said, "Brother, you're not ill. It's the effects of stopping. It'll only get worse. I know."

I looked at him and said, "What do you mean?"

"You're used to it," he said, "it's the mother's milk. The body wants it. It'll rebel if you don't give it what it craves."

"I understand," I said as I set it down. I heard the pilgrims outside. It was oppressive, not as I believed my life should be. I wasn't certain what life should or would ever be like again, but I knew this life, in this cave, with these people, wasn't the life I wanted.

The nausea worsened, but it was tolerable. I laid on the cot and thought I'd ride it through.

By early evening, however, as the chanting was at full bore, I burned with fever and pain. I was too nauseous to eat and my lips were parching.

I looked at the pipe and it beckoned seductively. I knew if I had just one puff I'd feel so much better, but I also knew it'd be temporary and the cycle of addiction would begin anew.

I tried to believe I was stronger than the pipe.

I tried to sleep, or at least meditate. I could do neither. By midevening the chanting had calmed, pilgrims would have to either camp or come back tomorrow; I wasn't coming out. In truth, I wasn't able to engage anything other than my distress. I shook uncontrollably. I was unable to sleep, or eat, or drink, or talk coherently.

I periodically noticed a brother or two file by my cot, checking on me. I saw them shake their heads in puzzlement at why I didn't pick up the pipe. A few of them even lit it, and offered it in hopes I'd stop this nonsense, but I was resolute.

I tried to believe I was stronger than the desire. That is, until the dark of night.

The last flame had been snuffed, and I heard the sound of brothers ending their days. It was the same every night. Some said prayers, some worried with the clanking of their beads, some snored as they drifted into sleep, and some took up their nightly ritual of self-eroticism. I'd gotten used to these sounds, and though they'd been hard to deal with when I first arrived, they were now oddly comforting.

For a moment, my body seemed to calm and I fetched a cup of water. My hands shook, so some of the water made it into my mouth and some found the floor instead.

I tried to believe I was stronger than the pain.

I laid on the cot and suddenly terrible, scary beasts surrounded me. They poked and snickered, talking to themselves about what a fine meal I'd be. I heard them snarl and smack their jaws in anticipation of my warm flesh. They got so close that I felt their hot breath on my face.

They snarled questions like, 'When's he going to die? Should we kill him now?' I tried to call for help, but I couldn't make noise, I couldn't move. My fear turned to terror.

The smaller beasts were replaced with larger, more fearsome beasts, still musing amongst themselves about how soon I'd die. They poked at me with sharp claws and sticks. It hurt and I was sure they'd drawn blood, but I remained frozen with fear. My heart's beat was so vicious I feared it would burst from the pressure.

I thought I couldn't withstand another moment of this torture, when all of a sudden I bolted upright and screamed. Most of the room woke. The beasts disappeared. I felt around my body and everything seemed intact, no blood, no ripped flesh. But the sweat poured from my brow in rivulets down my face and the pain in my back and shoulders was nearly unbearable.

A few brothers lit their lamps and came to me. One handed me a pipe and said, "Will you please help yourself before this madness takes you completely?"

I panicked, terrified that the beasts would return any moment. I snatched the pipe and inhaled deeply. I felt the familiar warm wave of false redemption cascade through my body and within moments, I felt less anxious, less pained, and more

"Trying to believe anything will leave you believing nothing new. Your old belief is stronger than that. You must take new action to convince your inner self that a new belief has merit. New action requires conscious choice."

- Yeshua son of Joseph -

settled.

I took another deep puff and laid my head on the pillow. Within seconds, I was asleep and knew nothing more until I woke midmorning.

"If people around you didn't support who you are right now, they wouldn't be around you. Either by their action, they would leave, or by your own action, you wouldn't be able to stay. Unless you choose to change and take appropriate action, the world will blissfully or painfully continue to support who you currently are. When you want to make a change, take a new action, and notice any resistance to that action from the people around you. The more resistance, the more enabling of your past self the other people prove to be. Their resistance isn't to you, rather their resistance is to the change they'll have to make to either stay in alignment with who you're becoming or step away from you. Just remember to be open as you notice the resistance. Judge if that resistance might have merit and whether it's your change that might best be moderated. If not, bring on the change and watch your life transform."

- Yeshua son of Joseph -

47 · Providence Takes a Hand

When I did wake, the chants of the pilgrims were deafening. Everyone wanted Issa. I was still unwell, though most of the pain had vanished. But not the resolve to change. I was now on a mission to reclaim parts of me that had been missing for a long time. I didn't know how I was going to do it, or how long it would take, but I knew I had to find the way.

I resolved to use opium sparingly, just enough to keep symptoms bearable. I reasoned that if I could stay functional, even if marginally, I could sustain enough clarity to keep working on my goal.

I picked up the pipe and took one puff. Setting it down was difficult, but I accomplished it. I then cleaned up.

Once done, I drank several cups of water and ate some fruit. It was the first nourishment I'd had in more than two days. I was relieved that it stayed down.

I braved the throng. Most of the brothers were already with pilgrims and were surprised to see me. I helped as many as I could. I didn't become irritated with the ministrations of the faithful. I let it be and tried as best I could to keep focused on being of service.

By the end of the day, and for the first time in months, I felt I'd actually been of service. I began to feel a trickle of self-affirmation and it felt at once both strange and wonderful.

———

I reestablished my daily rituals, strengthening my body with exercises I learned at temple, and I inspired others to join me. We began each day with prayers and baptism, followed by meditation and yoga. The combined effect on this small brotherhood was tremendous. I was still using the drug, but only minimally. It was more trust and caring for myself than I'd exhibited in a long time, it felt like a mountain of firm ground to stand on. And as I progressed in my reclamation, the pilgrims seeking my support grew more numerous.

Things continued like this for months. I was building a foundation of trust in myself. Whenever I felt tempted to deny my resolve and fall back into a stupor, I'd remind myself of the degraded state I fell into that culminated in being raped. I remembered how I felt on that fateful night when I realized how wretched I was and how desperate I was to atone. It'd instantly sober me and generate the strength

"There's nothing like success to populate the road ahead. You live in a continuum: when one goal becomes complete, a new way forward appears. In this way, success and completion can be viewed as the beginning of any journey, not the end."

- Yeshua son of Joseph -

to persevere.

Every day I entreated my Creator to cleanse me of the poison of selfishness and sloth I'd enabled in myself. But, I was still confused about how to proceed. I managed a few conversations with the Unseen. They were brief, but vivid, and gave me hope that I could find my way.

I might've gone on like this for a long time, when providence intervened in the form of a rider from the west.

He handed me a letter from James. I asked the rider how he found me and he said it'd been easy to follow the trail to me once he arrived in the Indus. My name was legend from here to as far west as Delhi. That surprised me.

I was anxious to read the letter, but what it said broke my heart and filled me with trepidation:

> "Yeshua,
> "I hope this letter finds you quickly. We've heard wonderful stories of your adventures over these last years, but it's time you must come home. If you can find your way to travel, sooner would be better than later.
> "Joseph is quite ill and we need you to take your place as head of the family.
> "I'm sorry to say this, but if you don't come quickly, you'll most likely miss him. He's not long for this world.
> "All my love travels to you and beckons you home safely.
> "James"

James' call had to be answered – no question. I wrote a short reply, saying I was saddened to hear the news, and that I'd be home as soon as possible. I gave the note to the rider, thanked him profusely for finding me, and sent him on his way. He'd surely get back to Judea before I could.

The question remained; in this condition, would I be welcomed home when I arrived?

48 · Five Promises Revisited

That night, I remembered I'd left home a boy with a great enthusiasm for life. And I remembered the five promises I made before I left. The first was to travel with no more than needed and only as much as I could freely carry. This promise had served me well over the years. I would keep it.

The second was to propel myself with my own feet. I had to keep this promise as the burden of laziness was close every day. Even though this meant it would take me longer to get home, I had to keep it.

The third was to follow the covenants of my birth as a Nazorean. I'd fallen from this promise as hard and far as a man can fall. By my estimation, I'd broken nearly every covenant I'd ever embraced: daily baptism, eating properly, cleansing the mind, providing a temple within to properly radiate love, compassion, forgiveness, and peace. Self-doubt was my burden as a result. Readopting the covenants of my birth was the only thing beginning to save me.

The fourth was to bring honor to my family, to my creed, and to my ancestors, through right ways of thought and action. There were no 'right ways' in the manner I'd been living. I'd been selfish, vain, and I'd deceived myself. Selfishness and deceit were still with me in the form of opium. As long as I remained in its web of illusion, these burdens were mine.

And the fifth was to return, to my home – to my family. I was about to do that, but I was skeptical that my homecoming would be embraced with joy. I was a shell of the man I'd been a few years before. It pained me to my soul that I had to reveal myself to the family with these burdens in tow.

The next day I began preparations for my departure. I told Jimon and worked my way through the brotherhood. All were sad to hear it, but they understood my reason.

That afternoon when I greeted the pilgrims, I announced my plan. They were… unhappy. Most of them prostrated themselves and began praying for my safe passage and swift return. I knew I wouldn't return. If I was successful in reclaiming my mission, the rest of my life would be lived in Judea.

"Right ways. It's a deep subject that many teachers try to address. Ultimately, there's only one thing that can adequately teach right ways: righting oneself from personal mistakes. The 'teaching' comes through the responses of the world to the varied actions you take. Right ways must be experienced to be understood. Experience can only come through action. Anything else is just talk and ultimately has no power."

- Yeshua son of Joseph -

That night, the brothers presented me with two gifts. The first was a new set of robes in a style worn in Judea, along with new sandals. I was delighted with them.

The second was enough money to sustain my travels home, including enough to pay for a boat to hasten the journey. I didn't want to take the money, but they reminded me that our coffers had swollen tremendously during my stay. Taking the money was a matter of honor to them, repaying a debt of gratitude they felt toward me.

I was touched, and as I looked over their faces, I saw glimmers of hope and peace that hadn't been there when I arrived. They were all healthier and most were beginning to reclaim their adept gifts that had gone fallow. As a result, I knew they would build upon this good start and serve the neighboring communities well. I was honored and grateful to accept the money. It would speed my journey substantially.

I realized that night that I'd become accustomed to these men; that I was sad of heart to be leaving. I swelled with gratitude when I remembered that this had been true in every community I'd made my home since my departure from Galilee. When I left, I left friends behind.

49 · Forgiveness Prevails

Two days later, I was certain this would be my last day teaching at the cave. I planned to leave the next morning, spiffed up in new clothes and ready to greet the next phase of my life.

I greeted the pilgrims with a smile. There were more than 150 that day. We were all busy with requests and it felt good. I could hold my head up when I left, knowing I'd given my best to these people who expected so much.

About halfway through the day, I was about to excuse myself for a meal when the crowd took on a hush. They parted to let a small woman come through. She was many-months pregnant and I instantly recognized her. She was, of course, the woman who'd so cruelly mocked me after raping me several months previous.

The blood drained from my face. I stood silent, not sure how to react. She was my devastator, but she was also obviously carrying my child. The broad range of emotions that erupted in me was overwhelming.

Something about her was different from her countenance those months before. When I first encountered this woman, she was bitter and mocking, selfish and without scruples. Now she seemed softer, humbler.

The crowd appeared to know why and how she was with child. I didn't want to be vengeful or blaming, I wanted to be the fullest and highest self I could muster, but I wrestled with the desire to lash out with my tongue. I took several deep breathes.

After a few minutes of this staring, she opened her hands and laid them out to me in a posture that I'd seen before. In her culture, it meant she was sublimating herself to me. As she did, the arms of her garment slid to her elbows and I saw the scars of mutilation on her. I was filled with empathy.

She looked into my eyes and pleaded, "I was wrong. What I did to you was unspeakable. Please, forgive me?"

I had to blink back tears to continue to see her face. "How did you get those marks?"

"After I became pregnant, I had regret," she replied. "I thought I didn't deserve this child. I felt the life in me," she hugged her swollen belly, "and it has a light to it... such a light... I felt dirty." She paused, "I tried to kill myself."

Regardless of how this pregnancy happened, she was going to be a mother. I felt that she deserved the best of me for the speck of time I had to give it to her. I said, "I have to leave tomorrow. I must go home. My father's dying."

She dropped to her knees, "That's why I'm here... to beg you to forgive me... please?" She looked at me, her face pleading, "Please Issa, so I can be the mother this child deserves? Please?"

I took her by the shoulders, gently raising her to her feet. I remembered my own pleas on that fateful night she perpetrated the rape. I was the one pleading for forgiveness then. I remembered how desperate I was. I saw the same desperation on her. I had a chance to change the course of this woman's life and to honor the grace I'd received by handing it back with the same generosity that it came to me. So, I said with every ounce of sincerity, "I forgive you, with all my heart. I forgive you."

She threw her arms around me. I met her embrace. At that moment she wasn't my devastator, she was my savior. What she did was a gift to me. I couldn't excuse the horror of her actions, but the shock from them gave me back my life and I was inexplicably happy that this child could be a gift to her in return. I said, "I hope with all my heart that this child gives you blessings… love and comfort."

I invited her to have lunch. I learned her name was Jing and she had no living family. She'd been stolen from her home in a bloody raid and sold into slavery. She was but one more of those young degraded angels like I'd seen the day I adopted my intemperate illusion. She'd managed to escape her captors in hope of creating a new life for herself. We talked into the afternoon and I found a place of love for her. And though I had no claim on the child, or on the mother, I've often thought of them fondly and hoped their lives were indeed blessed and happy.

If the mettle of my manhood had been tested through my association with her, it wasn't in the unfortunate experience of our meeting. Rather, my mettle was tested through my ability to forgive; to find an ocean of love to fill the repository of pain I experienced from our coupling.

When she parted that afternoon, the crowd was again silent. Not chanting, not prostrate, not clamoring – silent. I felt as though I'd won a great victory over my heavy burdens. They were lighter, I was lighter, and my road to home would be easier as a result.

"Ye'sHUa was warm and had a heart that was keen to accept a person as he or she presented. He was quick to give and take love, and slow to create barriers. He was usually appropriately modest in countenance and deed, yet when appropriate he preferred to physically touch a person with tight hugs, warm pats, and clasped hands."

- Miriam wife of Yeshua -

50 · Surrounded by Love

The morning arrived to start my journey home. I was trepidatious, but resolute. My family needed me. It was time to be put to the test. Was I ready to be my fullest and best self? Was I ready to take on the entirety of my mission? Was I willing to be of absolute service to this species called man?

No, the answer to all those questions was no. But I knew in my heart that the only way to become ready was to go home where the mission would commence.

I gathered my things and felt a twinge of remorse at feeling compelled to include a hefty amount of raw opium. I wished I hadn't accepted that burden. But the truth was; I had accepted it, and I wasn't done with it. I took enough to sustain my marginal state until I got home and beyond.

I was so much better than when I imbibed with abandon. I allowed myself a little in the morning after my baptism and a little in the evening before I retired. This minimal level of sustenance, however, left my body in a perpetual state of unrest. There was nearly always a tremor in my hands, and I wrestled with muscle cramps every day. I'd gotten used to eating food earlier in the day when the drug was more prevalent in my system.

The Unseen were with me again, not as fully as earlier in my life, but enough for now. I hadn't yet received a visit from the Other. Perhaps I would on the road. Seeing Philar was a request in my prayers every morning.

I dressed in the new robes. I knew I looked ragged by the standards of my homeland, but I wasn't there yet. I was here where the standards were different.

I cleaned out my area of the cave. It was ready to welcome a new adept and I stepped through the tent for the last time.

Everyone gathered. Brothers hugged me, some spitting water at my feet as blessing for the journey. But what surprised me were the pilgrims. Gathered at the mouth of the trail were approximately thirty men outfitted for the road. One of the men stepped forward and said, "We want to travel with you. We'll go as far as the ocean and see you safely onto the boat."

I was astonished as I looked at their eager faces. "You... want to walk with me?"

"Yes," he said, "It'd be an honor."

Their offer moved me. "Why would you do this? It's a long journey."

He looked at the outfitted pilgrims, then back at me, and simply said, "Because

"When life calls you to do something you have great fear for, and you have credible evidence that your physical well-being isn't threatened, you must act. You must stare down the fear and put one foot in front of the other until that which you fear is behind you. Otherwise your path forward will be stunted and crooked as you try desperately to avoid the very thing that will lead you to the garden of your dreams."

- Yeshua son of Joseph -

we believe in you." He paused, and then said, "We love you."

I surveyed their faces and recognized them. Each was someone I'd helped over the last year with their pains and doubts. But I saw none of those pains or doubts on their faces this day. This day they were bright and full of hope.

"I'm touched," I said. I smiled the biggest, most joyful smile I could muster, spread my arms and announced, "Alright! Let's go!" and we began our march toward the sea.

I waved my arms in farewell to the brotherhood and to the place I'd called home for more than a year. Horror and tragedy brought me to this place. Horror and tragedy visited me during my stay, but joy and love surrounded me as I left. For the first time in over a year, I felt the divine residing within me again and I endeavored to throw as much of that divine spark on these people as I could before they were merely a memory.

"You always have helpers. You always have a host of beings, seen or unseen, that want to rise up and support you when you make right choices. Embrace them, count on them, love them. Their presence heralds great things."

- Yeshua son of Joseph -

Returning
Home

51 · Ignoble Journey

Our march to the sea was unremarkable in event, but remarkable in its passage. As a whole, we were joyous. Thoughts of Joseph haunted me and filled me with trepidation, but my fears were held at bay during this ignoble journey.

I use the term ignoble in the humblest sense of the word. We were plebian; ordinary people walking together as a pledge of faith. The vast majority of the party placed that faith in me, in what they saw as the divine and inspired nature of my path. My faith lay in a prayer, in my very human desire to reconcile with my family and atone with my Creator.

Two of the pilgrims carried highflying flags. People saw us approaching from a great distance. Every town and village we traversed cheered our passage and offered gifts, as if they knew who we were in advance. In fact, they did know and I was merely oblivious to my own renown.

I was oblivious because I couldn't fathom that I, with these burdens, was someone worth engendering renown. I held myself to a different standard than those around me. And unfortunately, I felt that the people I'd embrace in Galilee would hold me to that same standard. The renown I encountered on the path to the sea might feel real in this place and in these people, but it was without substance to me. Rather, I saw it as a temporary state that heralded more to the weight of my burdens, than to any good in me.

But truly, who was I to denigrate the experience of these people? I was – in lockstep with most humans – my own worst judge and jury. And as is so often the case, I projected that judgment onto the world around me. Atonement seemed a world away.

But, regardless of the reception, I had to go home. Just as my inner self demanded of me since I was a babe in my mother's arms, I refused to run from the consequences of my actions.

When we got to the sea, I purchased a boat ride to Tamralipta. Tamralipta was the largest port town on the Bengal Sea and would be the best place for me to purchase passage to the Red Sea.

These men accompanying me wore their protective duty and delivery of me to the sea as badges of honor. They were swollen with pride. At this last touching, I endeavored to plant seeds that might grow into large canopies of wealth for them,

"What are your burdens? Do you even see them? Can you point them out in your life? If you can't name them, you can't atone for them. And if you don't atone for them, they're yours to keep. It's a guarantee."

- Yeshua son of Joseph -

their families, and their communities. I assured each that they now had a base of action to stand on that could command attention from their peers, and a leadership role in their homes. I asked them all to remember their Creator and every day work to honor the lives they'd been granted.

I cheerfully bid farewell and left my latest companions on the dock; their flags held high as I boarded the small transport ship for the short jaunt to Tamralipta. For a moment, I almost felt tall and true again, but that feeling was fleeting.

The little ship served me well and I arrived at Tamralipta within a few days. The area amazed me by its sheer size. Numerous private ports salted the delta to handle the vast number of transport vessels that required docking. There were scores of men employed to load and unload the various cargoes. The only city I'd visited that rivaled the size and bustle of Tamralipta was Alexandria on the Mediterranean. After docking, I found a willing merchant ship and purchased space to Krokola. I knew I could get to Aqaba from there.

Three days later, we set sail. It'd been many years since I was on the sea. I'd forgotten how silent the nights were and how inward facing the days would be.

I had ample opportunity to contemplate my life. I was Issa and had been Issa longer than I'd been Yeshua. I was soon to be Yeshua again and it filled me with dread. Only the last year and a half of my life had been wretched. The rest had been filled with adventure and astounding revelations. But this burden I carried now ate me up. I didn't want my family to see me in this condition, but I had no other logical choice but to proceed home, burden in tow.

I continued morning baptisms and meditations on the boat. They kept me sane. I spoke to the Unseen each day. They kept me from spiraling too far into fear. The problem was I knew the truth. I knew I had no need to fear, or be in pain, or carry this burden, and I was choosing it regardless. It's the eternal choice of man, to remain lowered in fear or rise into higher consciousness. If anyone had the ability to rise, it was me. I'd been there. I'd seen it all, the glory of an expanded universe. I knew without equivocation the truth of my soul and the direction of my work. I understood the absolute illusion fear places on heads and hearts.

And I chose to remain in fear. It was beyond my comprehension that I'd make this choice, and the more I contemplated it, the more perplexed I became. But it

"Humans have a compulsion to manipulate their environments. It's built into the fabric of our being. Even the naturalist, who sheds clothes and spurns dwellings, will pile leaves or straw to lay upon in sleep. Why fight it? If you feel compelled to exert dominion over the world around you, why not do that with gusto and live as large as you want? Allowing for the respect of co-creation and co-habitation, the Creator wouldn't have given you the desire to suit your world to your liking if she didn't want you to do just that!"

- Yeshua son of Joseph -

didn't change my choice.

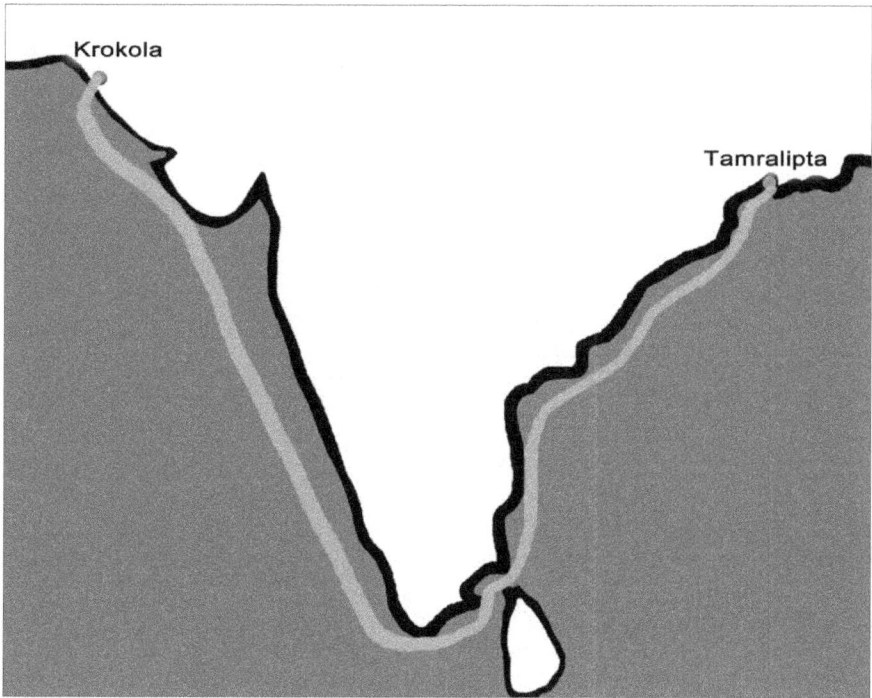

Figure 5: From Tamralipta to Krokola on the way home

52 · Myopia

Several weeks into the voyage, as we were making our way up the western coast of India, I had my first visit from the Other since my reawakening.

I was on deck, sitting by myself at the forward bow watching the horizon as it slowly bobbed up and down with the ship. The waters here were chaotic as we were close to shore and riding between mostly-submerged islands. The moon was nearly full, so the waves were highlighted with glistening light.

I'd just taken my nightly dose of opium and felt a limited sense of calm wash over me, when he appeared next to me. I was startled, but also overcome with relief at seeing his face; it was my Philar.

I smiled and said, "I'm relieved to see you. I surely need your help."

He looked deep into my face, "My dear Issa, I've been with you often. I'm relieved you're acknowledging me."

I bowed my head and realized that yet again, my intemperance had served my ignorance so well. I said, "I never want to ignore you. I'm grateful for your presence and need your help more than I can say."

He sat across from me. "There's so much to talk about," he said, "but I feel there's one thing you must hear before all else." I nodded in compliance and waited for him to speak. "It's about Joseph."

My heart sank. As soon as he spoke my Father's name, I knew. "Yes?"

"He's left this life. His body has expired."

There it was; my fear brought to fact before me. Joseph was dead and I missed the opportunity to say goodbye. My head fell into my chest and I felt tears close to the surface, but they didn't fall. Tears and I were old friends. I learned early in life to let them flow, not to stop them when they were near. But they didn't flow now.

I looked at Philar, "Was he with family when he passed?"

"Yes, your mother and brothers were all with him. He left in peace."

I nodded. It was good news by itself. "I miss him."

Philar touched my shoulder. "I do have a message for you… from Joseph."

My head snapped up, eager to hear, "Yes?"

"He considers knowing you to have been his deepest joy." I was shocked and dumbfounded. How could that be? Every day I fought to pull myself out of the wretched condition I'd allowed in myself. How could I be a joy to Joseph?

"Blindness has to be one of the most common energetic ailments of man. I've suffered from it, so I know firsthand how small our world becomes when we shut our eyes to the truth of who we are, of what we want, and of what we've done to create our circumstances. You can remain blind to these inner queries as long as you want, but you won't find your way to freedom without opening your inner eyes."

- Yeshua son of Joseph -

"I don't understand that," I blurted, "how's it possible? You see the state I'm in. You know how selfish I've been… I…"

He interrupted, "Issa, calm yourself. You've become myopic – it's understandable given the state of your body. But it's time to hold the larger view again."

I stared at him, "I've become myopic?"

"Yes, you have. It's the driving force behind your pain right now."

I laughed. Of all the things I worried about, I hadn't considered limited scope of vision to be at the top of the ladder. But I realized, of course it would be.

I said, "How do I hold this? All of this? How do I heal? Where do I find the strength to be Yeshua again? Now I've missed Joseph, how can I find peace?"

Philar raised his hand to my face and said, "By beginning anew." He pointed to my heart, "Everything is there, inside you. Throw the veils on your knowledge aside and stop pretending you're nothing more than a wearied adept."

I knew he was speaking truth, but the veils were tightly sealed. I didn't know how to lift them. "Can you help me find a way to do that?" I asked.

He sighed, that deep, raspy sigh I didn't like to hear, "Issa, Issa… I can do little to help you as long as you remain in the illusion of your addiction."

I felt the shame of my situation rush through my cheeks, flashing them red. I said, "Philar, I ask myself every day, 'What made me take up this burden?' But I can't find a good answer." I looked out to sea, "Maybe it was a bad day, a weak moment. Maybe…"

Philar waggled his finger to make me stop speaking. "No!" he said, "It wasn't a bad day. It was a purposeful descent into your own darkness. A journey to the place in you where the light of your path didn't yet shine. By encountering its recesses, you've illuminated that unseen dark corner of your being. It will now and forever be illuminated." He paused, looking at me intently. I kept my tongue, wanting to hear it all. He continued, "For all that's coming, once you climb out of this shadow of fear and self-loathing, you'll never have to wonder what would be if. You'll be immune to the pull of the least wise in you." He took a deep breath and said, "You'll be able to thrive where others have withered."

I was speechless. This idea was revolutionary to my current mind. Considering that this unimaginably selfish road these last many months was an integral part of my path seemed at first blush idiotic. I was obviously staring incredulously at Philar, because he asked, "You have difficulty with what I said?"

I pulled my thoughts together and tried to formulate an answer. After a minute I said, "This idea is difficult for me. I'm having trouble accepting it. How can it be that this terrible road I've been walking could actually be of value?"

"Ah, well, you'd know the answer to that question if your vision was broader."

I smiled and shook my head side to side. I said, "You're posing purposeful conundrums. You are indeed here to help me."

Philar smiled, "I am indeed, Is… no, I think it's time I start calling you Yeshua again."

I sighed, "Fair enough." I added, "I'll ponder your puzzle of consciousness. Will I see you again soon?"

Philar stood and said, "Yes, tomorrow evening if you're alone."

I said goodbye and immediately said a prayer of thanks for whatever I did right that brought Philar back into my awareness. I felt a new ray of hope. Unfortunately, it lay submerged in a bath of grief over the news of Joseph. I climbed down to my bunk and settled in for a long, tearful night.

§ *"Every thought, every action, every minute of every day will mirror to you some truth of your current state. You can't look at all of it. If you did, you'd get nothing else done. But you must look at some of it. It doesn't matter what part you examine. Like a hologram, the whole is reflected in the parts, so pick some piece of your life and dive in! There are gifts waiting from that swim."*

- Yeshua son of Joseph -

53 · Through the Gate

I was fortunate that the merchant ship had few inhabitants: the captain, a passel of sailors, and me. It was primarily a cargo ship and had nothing in the way of comforts, but the solitary confines afforded by my singularity as a passenger gave Philar a chance to join me almost every evening.

As a result of our conversations, I made my way through that initial thought puzzle and many more that followed. Philar said I was making progress, but I felt no closer to ending my addiction. I saw this as my next great challenge and the way to it was annoyingly shadowed.

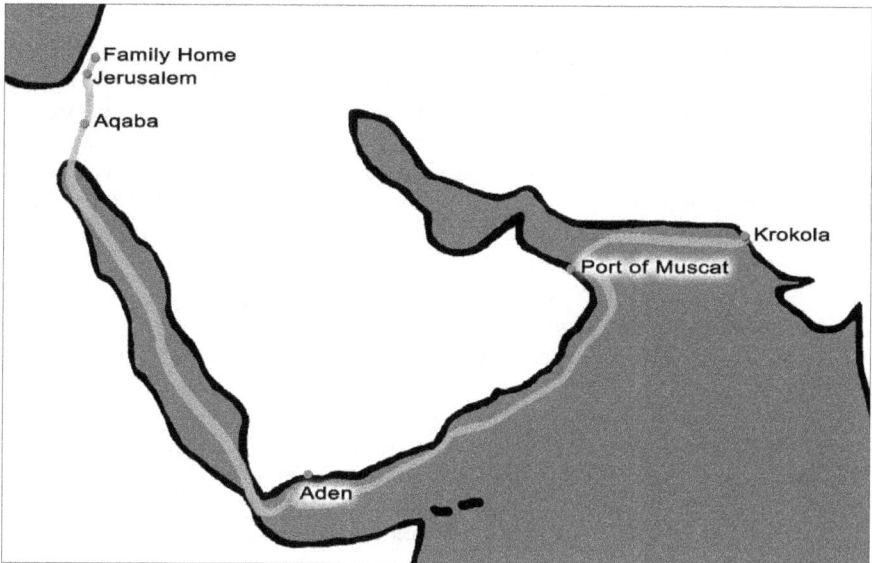

Figure 6: Krokola to home

When we arrived in Krokola, I immediately purchased passage to Aden. From there I got to the Gulf of Aqaba by way of a merchant ship. Next, I boarded a ferry to the town of Aqaba and proceeded to home from there by foot. I wouldn't see Philar again until I was on foot traveling the last leg of my journey home.

As I began my hike, I remembered the time I'd come the other direction. It was as if I was meeting myself on the road around each bend. The child in me, the hope of him, the absolute knowing in him that the world was his; they greeted me with persistence. So, I trudged, putting one foot in front of the other. I accepted these shadows of my previous life and vowed to give them voice in my actions to come.

I made it a point to talk to as many people as I could along the way. I hadn't spoken Aramaic or Hebrew for many years and while they were exceptionally familiar to me, I was no longer fluent with them. I was surprised and annoyed that I was so rusty at my native languages. Luckily, with daily use, their structure and vocabulary returned to me rapidly.

Philar met me again most nights as I camped along the road. He wanted to help me reframe my mind before I got lost in the reunion of home. It was helpful, very helpful, and I appreciated it.

The day finally arrived when I stepped up to the southern gate of the family compound and took my last breath as a wanderer. Seeing the gate for the first time in these many years, I was nearly overcome with the joy of familiarity and anticipation of home and hearth. But, the joy was fleeting, as I still grieved the loss of Joseph, and could feel the palpations of grief that emanated from the entire community.

And I was scared. My hands shook and my back twitched. I was gaunt and pale, with dark circles around my glassy eyes. My mouth was dry; my lips parched. This wasn't who I wanted to present, but I had to proceed. I had to step through my fear and embrace whatever greeting I'd receive.

I walked through the gate. The compound had changed a little, but not much. Children played and members of the community tended to chores. I walked to the main house and no one took special notice of me until I stepped onto the porch. When I did, a handsome, young man came out.

"May I help you?" he asked.

"I wonder if Mary or James is home."

"They're both here," he said, "who's asking?"

"Yeshua."

When he heard my name, he gasped in a breath-filled sputter. A look of surprise came over him as he took in my countenance. He yelled, "No! My brother! Welcome home." He grabbed me with his muscular arms, squeezing me to discomfort. He shouted, "Everyone, come quick, Yeshua is home!"

I asked, "Jude?" He grabbed me again and I realized that, for better or worse, I was indeed home.

"Judgment dampens your ability to see, to vision. There's no way around this unfortunate fact. Judgment closes doors. There's no way to open those doors again until judgment is released. Judgment creates a state in which you've calcified your desire. Once calcified, the desire is no longer living; it's dead, the passion fueling your desire is gone. So, to restate, judgment dampens your vision, closes your doors, and kills your passion. Can you see how important it is not to form judgments in the first place?"

- Yeshua son of Joseph -

54 · Confession

When Jude yelled, he captured the attention of everyone close and they came running. Within moments, people surrounded me, some I knew, some I didn't, but all, I was certain, were dear and beloved members of the community.

I greeted each of them one by one, until Jude took my hand and said, "Alright everyone, let's give the man some room. You'll be able to visit with him later." He turned his attention to me and said, "Let's go see family."

He guided me into the house. The instant I crossed the threshold I was dazed by a tumult of memories. It overwhelmed me. I broke hands with Jude and stumbled back out the door to breathe. It suddenly hit me that Joseph wouldn't be there; that the memories I had, were all I had. I wanted to cry, but no tears came. I wanted to scream, but my voice was mute.

Jude came after me and put his arm on my back, "Yeshua? Are you alright?"

I looked at him, his face flashed from a child to an adult and back again in rapid succession, and I said, "No, I'm not alright."

"James," Jude shouted, "come help!"

James came out and put his arm around my shoulders. As soon as I looked into James' face, I felt a level of shame deeper than I'd ever felt before. His face was so familiar, so wise was his gaze, so deep was our love; I wanted to shrivel from it. He said, "Come, please, let's go inside." Together they helped me to a bedroom, and laid me on the bed. James said, "Jude, bring Yeshua some refreshments." He turned to me, "Rest. You're overwhelmed with emotion and weary from the road. Take some time."

I nodded in agreement. When Jude came back, he gave me a piece of bread, some dried fruit, and a large cup of water. I thanked them and they quietly left the room, closing the door behind them. I immediately fell asleep.

A light tapping at the door awakened me. It took a moment to realize where I was. When I did I said, "Come in."

The door opened. It was Mary. "Mother!" I exclaimed as I jumped up. She folded into my arms.

"I'm so grateful you're home," she said in a low voice, barely audible, "I've been lost without him, my son."

I knew whom she referred to as him; it was Joseph and I felt her immense sorrow. "I feel lost too, Mother."

"James reminds me every day that we'll find our way in time." She squeezed me harder, "My heart is warmed in your arms."

We both sat to have a chat. She saw my grief; she spoke of the hole in my heart she saw from coming home. She held my hand and cried softly as she spoke about the last days with Joseph. I listened, wanting to take it all in. I asked questions. I let her get out all she needed, so it wouldn't be locked in her any longer. But no tears came from my eyes.

When Mother finally emerged from the memories of his last days, she touched her hand to my cheek and said, "I never worried that you wouldn't come home. I knew you would. But in the last few years, I worried for something else, something I couldn't put my finger on. And now that you're home, I see there is something you're afraid of."

"As always, Mother, you can see right through me."

"What is it?" her kind eyes urging me to tell her.

"I carry a burden," my voice broke, "a dark burden. I wish I didn't, but I do."

"No burden is so dark that it can't be brought to the light. What is it?"

"I wish I hadn't come home before I dealt with it."

She took my hand again, "Maybe you had to come home to find the path out of this burden's grip."

"Mother, I'm so concerned… that my brother's will hate me… that the community won't accept me back with this burden on me."

We sat in silence for several minutes, and then she said, "Your hands shake."

"They shake every day," I shook my head, "My muscles twitch… it's by fault of the burden." I took a deep breath and confessed, "I'm a slave, Mother. It's opium. I haven't been able to find my way free of it." She put her arm around my waist and pulled me closer. "I've been such a better man than I am today," I said. "If I'd come home two years ago, you would've met a very different man. I'm a shadow of myself."

"No, Yeshua, the man you were is still inside you. I see him. And some day I'll hear about the adventures that gave you such riches of spirit, but not right now. Now, you have to face your brothers. You're right, they'll likely not understand."

"Do you understand?" I asked her.

She took a breath and delayed her answer a moment. Then she spoke, "I can't say I understand, but I accept. You could've come home with many burdens, much deeper than this. You've been gone from our sheltered community for fourteen years." She squeezed her arm around my waist and laid her head on my side, "I love you with a love deeper than the sea. I have faith in your mission. I hope while you were wandering, you found that mission." She looked at me and saw the answer to that hope written on my face. "Yes. I see," she said, nodding, "the weight of your path is what pulled you into this burden. This I can understand." She shook her head, "I'm sorry your father isn't here to help you. I know he'd be kind and resolute in his support. There's nothing you could do to diminish his love

"Grief is the fear of continuing with life after loss. Grief can result from any loss, such as death, the loss of a relationship, property, or health. Grief can even follow letting go of parts of yourself, such as personality traits, beliefs, or habits that no longer serve. The fear says life will never offer you substance or meaning that matches or exceeds that which you had before the loss. The path through grief begins by forming a clear, new vision of a life ahead; one that gives meaning to you. It's important to affirm that life continues, that life has something to offer you even though you've experienced loss. The second step is to let go of the fear of that new vision of life you formed."

- Yeshua son of Joseph -

and acceptance of you."

I couldn't find words.

"I feel this isn't a burden you can lift on your own," she said as she placed a hand on my chest. "Your desire to be free of it is strong, but you need a healer, Son." I nodded. It was as I felt; a healer would be needed to facilitate my shift. "I'll help in any way I can," she said, "whatever it takes, I walk this road with you."

I cherished her words. They bolstered me. I knew she was right; I had to face my brothers. It was the only next step I could take.

"Your brothers are good men, Yeshua, however they act now, be patient, give them time. They love you, too."

The rest of the afternoon went well. Mary and I joined James and Jude in the courtyard. Mostly we talked, to begin to get used to each other again. I'd been gone a long time and especially in the case of Jude, I hardly knew him, or he me.

Jude's wife Rebekkah joined us. She was a lovely, strong woman, and I could see immediately that she and Jude were well-matched. But it didn't escape me that they'd been together for several years and there were no children.

I asked about other family members. My sister Sarah and family were in Sepphoris, as was my half-brother Simon and his family. My sister Ruth and family had moved to Caesarea. My other half-brother, Adam, and his family were still in Jerusalem. And aside from the deaths of a few extended family members, everyone was well and happy.

Eventually the conversation turned to Joseph. When it did, the mood darkened. Jude was overcome with tears right away. James and Mary quieted. I sat in my own grief, unable to put words to my feelings. And still, no tears fell from my eyes.

When the sun was low in the sky, Josea announced supper. I jumped up to grab her. "Josea!" I said as I twirled her around in the air.

"Blessings be, you're home, Yeshua!" she laughed as she spoke.

I set her down. "You look better than the last time I saw you," I said, "Herodes must be treating you well!"

"Oh, you scoundrel, when did you get in?"

"This morning. Why don't you both join us for supper tonight?" I looked at everyone else and all nodded their acceptance.

"It's so easy to have expectations of others based on our assumptions regarding their role in life. The life another wants to live may not have any resemblance to the life you want to see that person live. If you face the people around you with the knowledge that they are exactly where they want and need to be, you'll be better equipped to sing with them when they shine, and give them proper aid when they need a hand. And when you give to people in this way, without assumptions getting in the way, they can see you better and become your loyal champion."

- Yeshua son of Joseph -

55 · Not Who I Should Be

It was my first night home. I was ecstatic being with loved ones, but a sense of foreboding nagged at me. After supper, Josea and Herodes excused themselves to their own house, the rest of us moved to the big room. It was chilly, so James started a fire. I knew my burden would come up sooner or later, but James forced the issue sooner.

"Bit, what's the matter with you? Are you ill?"

I looked at Mary, and she nodded approvingly, "Trust them, Yeshua."

Filled with trepidation, I swallowed my fear and began. I told them of the horror I'd seen the day I was assaulted for my jewels. I recounted the pain I'd carried and how, when Jimon found me in the mud, I was bleeding and waiting to die.

I told them that I accepted the pipe offered me. That the substance in it got me off the ground and gave me the will to live. But, that substance was opium and I hadn't been able to get free of its grip since. Everyone was silent. I waited for some response, any response.

Finally Rebekkah spoke, "I don't know what opium is?" She looked at me, then at Jude.

Jude shook his head, "I don't know what it is either." He looked at James.

A dark cloud had settled over James. "I know what it is," he said. "I've nursed people who've used it. It's a terrible substance. An ugly substance." James looked at me and I saw the disappointment in his eyes. "Are you telling us, you still use it?"

I nodded my head yes, "Minimally, just enough to keep the symptoms from overwhelming me. That's why I shake. If I used it more, the shakes would disappear, but then I wouldn't be functional."

"Why don't you stop?" James said with a bite that surprised me.

"I've tried," I said, "it's not that easy."

"Others have done it," James said with anger.

"Perhaps others hadn't used it as long as I before they tried." I shook my head, "It's frightening, it's brutal."

"But others have done it!" James shouted.

"But I couldn't." I looked at James. When our eyes met, I saw the anger and pain in him. "I can see you're angry."

"Yes! I'm disappointed, and I am, yes, I'm angry." He shook his head and shouted, "This isn't who you're supposed to be!"

"But it's who I am." We stared at one another.

Jude broke in, "James, what are you angry about? Yeshua just told us he has a problem."

James was strident, "Yes, he has a problem… a big problem!"

"You need our help, right Yeshua?" Jude asked.

"Yes." I looked at Mary, "Mother thinks I need a healer to help. I agree."

"Then we must find a healer," Jude offered. "We need you at the helm,

Brother. You need to be well for that."

James snarled at Jude, "At the helm? Him? You want someone at the head of this family that can't control himself better than to… fall into a… degraded state like this?"

"James, where's your compassion?" Mary asked.

James looked at Mary, then at me. "Compassion? For this? I'm going to bed," and he left the room.

"Yeshua," Jude said, "Rebekkah and I still don't understand what we're talking about."

So I retrieved my bag and showed them. I explained how I felt before I took a puff: how the pain was mounting, the mental discomfort, and the sweats that were beginning. I inhaled once and told them of the difference I felt. How it calmed me, how it took the pain away. They physically saw me relax; my body responding to just one inhalation. Jude's mouth dropped open as he watched the change.

"That's astounding," Rebekkah said, "it's like nothing I've ever seen before."

Mary spoke up, "It's a good substance, it's not ugly like James said. Used in the right way it can have good effects. Outside our community, many healers use this for people in pain. When I was young, it was kept on hand in the infirmary for a variety of applications." She put her hand on my knee. "I'm sure when you first used it, Yeshua, it was relieving and helped you, but it's the effects of long-term use that are the problem here."

"I see," Jude said, "it's like alcohol. If you drink too much, it's a trap. You get caught." I nodded. "I see," Jude said with a troubled look in his eyes. He looked sideways at Rebekkah, then at his lap. I wondered what might be going through his mind. He looked at Mary, "What would Joseph say?"

"I'm sure he'd urge us all to help Yeshua reclaim himself." Mary looked back at me, "Is that something you want, Yeshua?"

I'd heard those words before, in a field somewhere. The same face looked at me, the same words entreated me, but the meaning wasn't the same. It was someone else. I knew it was. Suddenly, it flooded back to me. It was my Creator in the mask of Mary, asking if leaving here was what I wanted.

"Yeshua? Do you want our help?" Mary asked again.

The memory of standing with my Creator uplifted and strong, juxtaposed against who I was now, was overwhelming. The shame of earlier in the day re-erupted and I felt like I had no right to ask for anything, from anyone. I said, "I'm not worthy of your love."

"Don't say that," Mary said, "we love you."

"I'm not worthy. James is right, I'm not who I should be."

Jude and Rebekkah retired to their home, Mary went to bed, all with the promise we'd talk about it again. I went for a walk. These fields had been my

"Be love. Accept love. Give Love. Live by these maxims and the world will beat a path to your door. Follow less than all three and pain will be your companion."

- Yeshua son of Joseph -

playground once upon a time. They were where I met Philar. They were where my young mind began to learn about the wonders of this world.

I ruminated about the path I'd taken, who I'd become, and the memory of the conversation with Creator about my choices. She told me I could get lost. That I might forget and need to fight my way out of the mire. So, I guess I was fighting, and this drug appeared to be the battlefield.

I didn't know how to proceed. I thought about Joseph. I wondered what he'd suggest I do next. And when I thought of Joseph, I was consumed with grief. It knotted me up inside, but I found no tears.

56 · Cover of Darkness

The next day was the same, and the day after that. James was surly, Jude wanted to help, and Mary was loving and kind, but shame dogged me. I walked often, I thought a lot, but the specter of my former self haunted me. I wanted to clear this burden; clear this shame of letting everyone down. I also had to fight the desire to run from my shame by diving deeper into usage. It became increasingly difficult to take just one puff.

And every time anyone mentioned Joseph, I felt cold inside. My grief was buried under a mountain of shame.

Several days later, James' mood began to lighten. He was able to greet me, not with affection, but at least with civility. However, a change came over Jude.

One morning during my baptism, I saw Jude emerge from his house in what looked like a stupor. He held his head in a fashion that reminded me of waking up after smoking myself into unconsciousness. It was the second time in the last few days I'd seen him sluggish and without vigor in the morning, and at the young age of my brother, I was concerned about what could be weighing so heavily on him.

This morning, though, I had a different thought, I wondered if he was recovering from the effects of too much wine or beer, but later that day I asked Mary if Jude drank much, and she didn't think Rebekkah and he even kept any in the house.

Not long after that, Jude came to me as I was cleaning some farm tools recently used in planting. He'd become impatient, I just didn't know why until he approached me.

"I want to say something," Jude's face was pinched.

I braced myself. "What's that?" I asked.

"Joseph would be disappointed in you."

As soon as he mentioned Joseph, I felt cold grip my inner self. I took a deep breath, and said, "I'm not sure that's true, Jude."

Jude swung his head back and forth. "You know it's true!" he said with a strength that surprised me. "And by the way, Yeshua, why don't you grieve for

"The idiom, 'takes one to know one,' is derived from a very wise notion; that once a person has fully experienced a way of being, they can spot that same configuration in another. Literally, we all too easily see ourselves as we are, or as we have been, in those around us. Self-growth and healing is possible when we remember that, in those times, we're seeing ourselves in a mirror and to not place blame and condemnation on the person holding the mirror."

- Yeshua son of Joseph -

Joseph?" Jude asked.

"What do you mean? I miss Joseph terribly."

Jude said, "I don't see it on you," and he walked away.

———✦———

A few days later, Jude approached me again, "I'm angry."

I bent my head, positive he was going to talk about my addiction. Just the night before, I'd betrayed myself and taken several puffs instead of one. I had to force myself to stop before I became comatose. "What are you angry about?" I asked.

"What's wrong with you?" he sputtered, "I haven't seen you shed even one tear over Joseph's death. Not one!"

I was surprised that it was about Joseph again. "It seems I've no tears left. I cried for days when I first got the news." I laid my hand on my chest, "There's none here right now."

"That's cold." He looked at me as if I was a stranger, "It's wrong. And why haven't you gone to visit Father's tomb?"

"Jude, he's not there, it's just what's left of his body. I won't find Father there."

"But it's what's right." He looked away from me, "I can't accept it. The way you act around our loss, it's disturbing." He turned and walked away again.

———✦———

Nearly a week went by and I felt alienated from both my brothers. I was beginning to feel as though my relationships with my brothers might be beyond repair, when the unthinkable happened.

We sat by the fire. An invisible fog of grief and anger hung in the room.

"I can't hold my tongue any longer!" Jude shouted. It startled me. "Yeshua, I was raised to believe there was something special about you." He stood and paced as he shouted, "All through my youth, over and over I was told that. That your mission was different from the rest of us. That you were in some way destined to be a prophet or something like that!" He threw his arms into the air and shook his hands, "It was all so grand in my mind."

I sat silent, listening.

"But here you are!" He pushed one arm in front of him and pointed at me, "What a disappointment! You're addicted to some exotic drug; you walk around

"Sometimes we sense that another person is blocking themselves by a thought, or an action, or a habit. We may be seeing a truth, or we may be reacting from judgment. However, in either case, the other person can only remove their block if they're fully ready. Acceptance of change is the only thing that creates change. No amount of pushing, name-calling, cajoling, or bribing will get a person to move if they're not aligned to it. Here's a well-known secret: in all cases, the power of love is the most commanding motivator known to create readiness for change."

- Yeshua son of Joseph -

like a golem. You're cold, like a fish. Who are you?" His eyes held my gaze.

"I'm trying to find my way, like everybody else."

"Your way?" he shouted as his arms continued to wave about, "What sort of way leaves you unfeeling and unable to do anything useful!"

"I'm not unfeeling."

"Well, I don't see that. I don't see grief. I don't see any pain on you."

"You think you can see into my heart?" I asked him.

"What heart? I can't see into something that doesn't exist."

I felt cut to the quick. James jumped in, "Jude, he has a heart, it may be buried under his addiction, but I know he has a heart."

Jude turned to James, "Do you? He had one when he left home. Have you felt one since he returned?"

James looked at me, then at the floor.

Jude looked back at me, "I don't think you belong in this family, Yeshua."

I closed my eyes, "What are you saying?"

"I'm saying, I don't want you here."

The words hung in the air in seeming defiance of their enormous weight. No one spoke; each hoping that the words hadn't been spoken.

After several minutes I asked, "Do you truly feel that way?"

Jude looked at me; his anger was muted some, but still palpable. "I'm sorry, but yes I do."

"How about you James? Do you feel the same way?" He was on the verge of tears, his mind spinning through multiple emotions. "James. Do you feel the same?"

James looked at Jude, then at me, "I'm so disappointed in these things. I can't tease apart my grief or my anger from the pain at your actions. I feel lost."

"Do you want Yeshua to be the head of our family?" Jude asked James, "Like this? Who he is now?"

"That I have an answer for," James replied, "it's no. Who you are right now Yeshua, you're unfit to lead us. I'm unfit to lead. Look at us, we all are right now."

"You and I will recover," Jude said, "but will he? I don't see it."

My worst fears were being borne out in front of my eyes. My brothers were discussing disowning me. It was the most irreconcilable fear I'd held these many months since leaving the Brotherhood. I shook from pain on the inside, even if it didn't show on the outside. And I was altogether sure my brothers were feeling just as much pain.

Tears flowed down James cheeks. Jude said, "Yeshua, I'm sorry, but I'm revolted by who you've become. I don't want you here any longer."

I stood, my head bent down. "Alright. I understand." I turned to leave the room and saw Mary behind me, her eyes wide. "Mother."

"What's happening?" she demanded.

"My brothers have asked me to leave."

Mary shot a glance at Jude, then at James, "Why?"

"They're revolted by me," I said, "they feel I don't have a place in the family." I stepped past her and went to pack my bag.

———※———

A little while later, I heard a familiar tapping on my door. "Come in Mother." I was wrapping the belongings I'd need on the road.

Mary stepped into the room and closed the door behind her. "Yeshua, I don't want you to leave. I want to help you get well."

I was afraid to look at her. "It's alright. I'll find my way to freedom from this burden somehow."

"It's not alright, Son. You belong here in safety with your family." She placed her quivering hand on my arm.

"Not everyone feels that way," I said.

"Your brothers are wrong to ask you to leave." Mary grabbed my arm tighter and shook it until I stopped and turned toward her. She said, "Don't go, please?" As I feared, I saw the pain in her face. Her cheeks glistened with moisture.

"I don't have a choice. I'm as revolted by myself as they are. Staying here isn't going to change that."

She got a desperate look in her eyes, "If Joseph was alive he'd never let you go."

"But he isn't, and I'm not fit to lead this family. You'll have to look to Jude for that. I've made too many serious errors in judgment." I turned away.

Mary squeezed my arm. "You just returned," she said softly, "I can't bear for you to leave me again."

I turned to her, "I'm sorry, Mother."

Her hands grabbed my robe. "Yeshua, I need you to stay," she pleaded.

This request of my brothers was a terrible burden to put on her, but I didn't see how I could take that burden away. "Mother, I have to go."

"What can I do to make you stay?"

I realized she was more fragile than I remembered. I remembered her as strong and durable, but her life had been ripped apart by the death of her husband. I wanted to be the man she was aching for. I wanted to be the embodiment of love that my Creator had pointed to, but I wasn't, and the pain I saw written on Mary's devastated face made me feel that much more humiliated. "I'm sorry, Mother, I have to go."

Within a few minutes, she let go of my robes and her face displayed a wearied resignation that sliced through me like a sharp axe. She handed me a bundle to put in my pack. It contained a generous amount of dried fruit and cheese from storage, and a passel of gold coins. I realized she already knew before she came in that she wouldn't be able to persuade me to stay.

She said, "Everything we have is yours, as much as it's anyone's. You'll need money."

I accepted the gift and finished packing; all the while, Mary's gaze never lifted

"When you accept as your truth a judgment of yourself given to you by another, other people around you begin to act like mirrors, reflecting back to you a painful picture. This is true even if they don't consciously share this judgment. From the place of fear inside you that the judgment created, you assume everyone you know agrees with it. You might even go so far as to argue with them if they try to deny it, and hear them say it, even if they didn't. Shame will surely follow from any interaction of that nature. And once you're moved to shame, nothing you do, think, or say can be trusted. It's the height of fear-based illusion."

- Yeshua son of Joseph -

from the floor. I promised her I'd write and let her know where I settled. I hugged her goodbye, but her weary arms barely had enough strength to return the gesture. I wanted to run, to hide. I wanted to find a rock big enough to cover the ignominy I now bore. I turned from her, as my heart shattered, and I left under the cover of darkness, which seemed only fitting given the agony I'd caused.

57 · A New Seed

I wandered the countryside for weeks, perhaps a month or more. I wasn't keeping good track of time. I wasn't keeping track of how much opium I imbibed either. With little left to lose, I had little left to remain steady for. And like last time, both the Unseen and the Other were lost to me.

One day I stumbled onto a small encampment. I approached, hoping the strangers would invite me to share their fire for a time. They were five; four men and one woman. One of the strangers stood out as the leader and he invited me to sit. When I looked around at the faces, I realized the one who invited me in was my own cousin, John.

"My name is John," he said, "and these are my friends." He pointed around the fire and each nodded in turn, I nodded back. "And what may we call you?" he asked.

I didn't want to identify myself, so I said, "Isaiah."

"Welcome Isaiah, are you hungry?"

They fed me supper, we lingered by the fire, and through the meal John didn't seem to recognize me. If he did, he didn't let on. I was thankful for this. And through the meal, I saw the eyes, and heard the footsteps of wild creatures all around us. It was the call of John. Beasts were attracted to him in a way that was rare in my experience. Animals that were normally frightened, and typically shunned humans, would come close and lie calm near John. When we were young, I once saw him calmly pet a wild cheetah. It could be disconcerting, but this night, the animals' presence was comforting.

Unexpectedly, I felt John's piercing eyes on me. "Stranger, something's not right with you. What is it?" he asked.

I lowered my eyes in shame and said, "So much is wrong. I come from a land of disappointment. I foolishly believed things that are now, obviously, untrue."

"We've all been disappointed in others and in ourselves," he said, "but how is it that you know that what you believe now is any truer than what you believed before? Often, it's our disappointment that's incorrect, not ourselves."

I nodded. "Wise words. What do you believe for yourself?" I asked him.

"Ah, well, I walk on gravel until the sands of time close around me. I point the way for the Shining One. My God assures me that he'll come soon and that'll be a day of glory for us all. The Shining One will be better equipped than I to show the way. In the meantime, I baptize initiates; anyone who wishes to start fresh and take the hand of God in innocence." He looked at me with probing eyes, "Perhaps one day you'll put your trust in the waters."

"Then you believe yourself to be a prophet?" I asked.

"No," he said, "not a prophet of the ages, but a prophet of our time. The one who'll come after me will speak to the ages and I leave that to him gladly."

"And what do you think of me in your wisdom?"

John's eyes penetrated deeper until I felt them pierce my soul. The air around us seemed to close in and cleave us to one another. "You carry a great disappointment, and a great burden; but, you're not the Shining One. He'll have surety and carry a great knowledge of himself. I'll continue to wait for his presence. With luck he'll come soon." These words, delivered in kindness, nonetheless felt sharp.

John's eyes pulled back from their piercing and congeniality moved over his face, "Though you do look familiar, maybe you're a member of my clan, a cousin maybe; there's something in your face."

"That's possible," I said, "I'm from Galilee, of the House of David."

"I feel a kinship and a love for you that's more than I'd expect to feel for a stranger."

"I do know you, Prophet. You're John son of Zachariah. I know your Mother."

"I no longer have a mother," he said. "I left her to perform my work. I bring people to God. I have no family now other than those I bring to his fold."

I knew I had to leave, even though I didn't want to say goodbye to my cousin. I had to be alone with my pain. "Thank you for your hospitality," I said to the group. I turned to John, "I hope you find this prophet of the ages you're looking for. When you find him, touch him softly; I'm sure he's known disappointment."

John dipped his head to me, as did each of the souls around the fire, and I walked into the desert. But I didn't walk away bereft. I didn't know then that John had planted a new seed in me.

The next day, when I performed my baptism, I felt different. I felt inexplicably lighter. Throughout my ablutions, I heard a refrain, a simple sentence that wouldn't stop. 'I must find a healer.'

I didn't know where the words came from, but they were persistent. This resounded in my brain all day. I decided to ask the question why, why should I find a healer? The answer, 'To reconcile with my brothers.'

My brothers were resolute, I was sure of it. I repulsed them. But one thing was true; a healer was the only next step I could take toward that goal. If there was any chance of reconciling, I had to lose my dependency on the addiction. That morning I inhaled only once, then promptly set off to the south.

It took weeks of inquiries to find a recommendation that touched my heart. I'd

"At any moment, perhaps when you're simply walking down a lane, you might meet the infinite. The divine presence of your Creator could speak to you from a stranger, glare at you from a street sign, or jump from the pages of a magazine. Open your heart and let the infinite find you more than you do now. Regardless of how often you recognize these messages, I assure you there are more of them to find."

- Yeshua son of Joseph -

been walking east of the Dead Sea through Moab, staying near a small river. I wandered into Ar and started a conversation with a tavern keeper. I began just as I had begun many conversations in the last weeks, "Where might one find a good healer, one with compassion and skill alike?" He didn't stop to think about it, he told me of a woman who'd helped his sister. He spoke about her at length, extolling her gentle nature and kind heart. He couldn't remember the healer's name, but he remembered what her front door looked like. And he remembered her long, flowing black hair.

The tavern keeper said he'd trust this woman with his life. And that was exactly what I needed, someone with whom I could trust my life.

58 · Her Kindness

The desert is a fickle place. Illusions run circles around truth. And in the land of Moab, this seemed doubly so. I wandered, searching for her door, but my intemperate illusion and the illusions of the desert layered one upon another. One house, two houses, three houses, more; none were right. Here a trick of the eye, there a mirage, but when I finally stumbled upon a door that matched the description I was given, I was tired of the search; ready for the find. I knocked.

To my relief, she answered. She was Persian, of that I was sure. Her long black hair swung invitingly with the movements of her head. That, coupled with her voluptuous body draped in layers of silk, made her wholly captivating. I'm certain it was the desired effect.

At first, my appearance startled her. Curious, she whispered, "What do you wish for, Galilean?"

"Atonement," I said.

She hugged the edge of the door and laughed in a low rumble that made me uncomfortable. She sounded as sweet as honey from the bee when she said, "I've never heard it called that before."

"It's surely not what you think," I said.

She looked at my hands; they shook. She surveyed my face and asked, "Are you ill then?"

"Ill of spirit, yes," I answered, "bereft of peace."

"What do you want from me?"

"I'm told you have a soft and loving heart, and great knowledge of healing." I put my hand on my pouch and said, "I have money to pay for your time." I pulled out a small brown chunk of raw opium. "I can also give you a generous measure of this for your healing bag."

I dropped the nugget into her palm. She looked closely at it, gently letting her tongue brush against it. She recognized the telltale flowery essence, "Tell me exactly what you want."

I closed my pouch and let my arms drop to my side. Tumbling out of my mouth as if someone else were speaking them, came these words, "I'm a prisoner to that substance. I can no longer allow it to rob me of my future. I'm a Son of

"2000 years ago, people's outer appearance was less homogenized than it is today. If you were an astute observer, you could immediately discern what area of the country a person came from as well as his or her religion. I parted my hair in the middle and let it fall to either side; therefore, I was Galilean. And my style of robes said I was Hebrew. The ornamentation of the weave announced that I was also of the Essene sect. When the healer opened her door and saw me, it took but a moment for her to pinpoint my homeland, my heritage, and my beliefs."

- Yeshua son of Joseph -

Man and I need someone I can trust to watch over me and guide me through the journey my body must take to get from this place of illusion I've been living and onto the path of truth I now must walk."

Looking suspicious, she slowly took in my countenance, head to toe, and said, "There aren't many – if any – Sons of Man walking around. What's your name?"

I sighed, "I don't think that's important." I stood as still as my twitching body would allow. I was concerned that if I gave her my name as Issa, that my reputation would have preceded me. And that if I gave her my name as Yeshua, knowledge of my family or my birth position might become involved.

She stepped aside and motioned for me to enter. She pointed for me to sit on a padded bench and then sat across from me.

"I need to be done with this illusion for good," I added, "not just get past the initial withdrawal from usage. I need the desire for opium to never cross my mind again."

She nodded, "Mind you, I've not decided I will, but I can do what you ask." She took a deep breath, looking me up and down again. She said, "It won't be easy." She let out a deep sigh and looked at me with a sideways stare of suspicion, "I can help with the pain, and I'm certain you won't perish... It'll take time though, at least two weeks and perhaps as much as a month, or more."

I nodded in agreement.

"You'll have to stay here where I can make sure you're properly cared for."

"I'd be grateful." I waited for more.

"And," she added, "I won't provide you with special Hebrew food. You'll have to eat what I eat, when you can eat."

I nodded, "I'll be grateful for any sustenance."

She said, half under her breath, "You'll probably hate me before it's finished."

"Hate is a concept I don't entertain." Even though I meant it sincerely, I said this in that inglorious and pompous way of speaking I used when my heart was contracted from self-doubt and fear.

My pomposity infuriated her. With force she said, "Words mean nothing! Show me now that you're a Son of Man! Prove it! If you show yourself to me, I'll take you." She pointed a long and accusatory finger at me, "But if you cannot or will not, you can leave now, I'll have none of your falsehood."

I knew that as a Persian, she knew exactly what a Son of Man was. I nodded in agreement.

She said, "Right, then show me."

I took a deep breath. I wasn't sure what would convince her of my truth. I wasn't sure what, if anything, I could even do any longer. "Give me a moment to consider my options, please." She calmly waited.

After a few minutes, I decided. I moved to the floor, folding myself into a meditation mudra. I closed my eyes and breathed into as much inner silence as I could muster. I wrapped myself in a sheath of energy and gently, albeit haltingly, lifted myself off the ground.

I opened my eyes and looked into her face as I hovered, eye-to-eye with her, more than a foot off the floor. The success of my feat surprised me; that I was able to accomplish this given my minimally controlled state. It quelled my remaining fear and gave me confidence.

She watched me and after about a minute of staring, she realized I wasn't playing a trick on her – I was truly hovering in the air. She took in a sharp gasping breath. I reached out my hand to beckon her touch. When she laid her fingers on mine, I saw the reaction I often cause in people when I'm in my power. Her eyes fluttered with visions of her life – memories of love she'd forgotten.

And in exchange, I saw her pain. The life of ostracism and struggle she endured to acquire her knowledge and live her truth was deeply painful for her. Suddenly she pulled back her hand and said with conviction, "Of course I'll help you. Let's make a bed and start right away."

I sighed in relief and gave my body back to gravity. I fell to the floor too hard. "Ouch!" I yelped.

She giggled, "Well, I can see you're out of practice."

I laughed, "Yes indeed," and so we began.

"A mudra is a ritualistic pose that reminds you to adopt a certain mindset or energetic posture. I learned many through my various studies. Some involve the whole body, others merely involve certain body parts, such as the hands or arms. For the practitioner, they function similarly to biofeedback mechanisms. The point is, when you have difficulty calming your thoughts, or transforming your mental or emotional state, they can help."

- Yeshua son of Joseph -

59 · The Broken Sword

Weeks later, I woke, for the first time since we began, not drenched in sweat. I wasn't shaking or cramping either. It'd been a long time since my body felt... calm. I sat up feeling relief.

I remembered little of the last weeks, moments of pain, foggy memories of fear and sweat. I remembered some teas and elixirs she had me drink; some sweet, some bitter. I recalled vomiting from time to time from a sticky substance she smeared on my gums. But rather than feel fright over the loss of memory, I felt blessed to have what was surely a difficult and painful process, mostly blotted from my mind.

I heard her walk behind me. "It's not over," she threw out, "but you have a small reprieve before we start the last round. Would you like to eat?"

"Yes, food would be good. And I feel so well. I was hoping it was over."

She laughed, "I'm sure you were, but you'll have to be patient. I'll bring some food momentarily." A minute later, she came into the room with a bowl of hot soup and a piece of bread.

"I'm grateful for your help," I said between sips.

"Ah!" she exclaimed, "then I suppose you don't remember much of the last few days."

I looked at her, but I couldn't remember anything that would lessen my gratitude. I shook my head, "I suppose not."

She unveiled a series of raw scratches running the length of one arm. "You thought I was a demon who wanted to eat your soul."

I was shocked at the sight of it. "I did that to you?"

"Well," she said, "really you did it to the demon. I can't take it personally."

"I'm sorry. I wouldn't do that if I was in my right mind."

"Don't worry, Son of Man, I know that." She covered the wounds, "You're making good progress, but I suspect a new wave will come within a few hours. Before nightfall at the latest." She stood to walk out, but stopped and said, "Perhaps it'd be a good time for you to take a short walk. It'd do you good, but don't be gone long."

———※———

I roamed through the foothills. It was more a dance than a walk as my feet seemed guided by the music of my soul. For the first time in close to two years, I felt free; free from burden, free from pain, free to find my true self.

But I also accepted what she said, I wasn't yet fully free. There was still more of the illusion to release. So in short order, I turned and headed toward the house.

As I neared the small building, I saw two horses tethered out front that weren't there when I left. I wasn't sure what to do. Should I wait for the riders to leave? Should I go to the door and knock? I sat on the ground to assess my options. I wouldn't want to interrupt what might be a moneymaking opportunity for her.

While I was thinking, I heard a loud male voice from inside the home bellow. His angry tone was clear. I went to the door and opened it without knocking. It seemed the prudent thing to do; to add surprise to my entrance.

When I surveyed the room, I found two men, one holding her tightly to his chest, obviously against her will. Her gown was pulled up, held at her waist by his hand, inappropriately exposing most of her lower body. His intent seemed bent on harm and her face conveyed only fear. These were clearly men of violence; I saw the curved swords of war at their sides.

"What's this? Were we expecting company?" I said. The man let her go and stepped back to survey me. She lowered her gown and moved further away from the stranger.

"This is trouble," she said.

The man who'd been holding her said, "Who're you?"

"I live here," I said.

The two men looked at one another, then at her. The first man spat at her, and said, "Does he know what you are?"

Before she could answer, I said, "I know the love that's in her heart and that's all I need to know."

The man turned to me and yelled, "She's a dirty whore and you're a fool."

I sighed and said, "I may be a fool, but I believe you're not welcome here. I'd like you to leave."

"You'd like me to leave?" he yelled. "I'm not leaving until I get what she owes me."

I looked at her and asked, "Do you owe these men anything?"

Wide eyed, she shook her head no.

"What do they think you owe them?" I asked.

"I…" she began, "uh… I…" her eyes remained widened with fear. "They say its payment for a life."

That answer surprised me. I looked at the man and asked, "How is it possible that she owes you for a life?"

The man regarded me a moment, then said, "She was supposed to heal my brother. But he died! Now she must pay!" The man started toward her, but I slipped between them using a move I'd learned at the Temple. To everyone in the room, it must have looked like I disappeared and instantly reappeared in front of her. My unnatural swiftness startled the man.

I said, "She can't pay you for what the Creator has taken."

"Move aside, fool!"

"I didn't judge a woman for selling her body to feed herself or her children. In and around Judea, there were few economic options for women without a family or husband to provide for them. If a woman was forced to sell her body in exchange for enough coin to purchase food, she was assuring survival. Who can find fault with needing to eat? Rather, it would be horrific to starve to death if a means for acquiring food was available and dogmatic adherence to religion kept one from exercising self-preservation."

- Yeshua son of Joseph -

I simply said, "No."

The man snarled, "I want my payment! I'll take it from her body if that's all she has to give and if she's dead when I'm done with her, so be it."

I stood my ground, knowing that the power of my true self was close. As a result, I knew I was safe regardless of this man's actions.

The man pulled his sword and brandished it at me. "I said move," he threatened, "or I'll cut you down."

I restated, "For your own good, I ask you again to leave."

He pulled the sword higher and lunged toward me, aiming for my throat. Instead, I raised my hand and, with a shallow motion, knocked the sword from his hand without touching it. He jumped back in surprise.

Again, I said, "I ask you now, leave our home."

After a moment, he regained his composure and grabbed the sword from where it lay on the floor. And again, he raised it over his head and lunged toward me. This time I pushed out my hand, forming a strong wall of energy between us that he ran into with his head. He fell over backward, his sword dropping to the floor. This time blood poured from his nose.

The other man pulled his sword from its sheath and rushed in my direction. I stepped aside and let him impotently strike at the air with such force that he nearly fell over. His sword flew from his hand and hit the brick wall, breaking the blade.

"I'm a man of peace," I said, "I have no desire to hurt you. I suggest you both leave as I've asked."

The first man stumbled to his feet, blood still flowing from his nose. He yelled, "I'll kill you for what you've done!"

"I've done nothing," I said, "I'm just a fool, remember? But if you continue with your own folly, you'll likely hurt yourself. Take your swords and leave."

Undeterred, he raised the sword to lunge at me once more. I moved my hands to my mouth and blew into them igniting a fire that burned in midair. I stepped back and allowed the flame to hover between us. Startled by the flame, he stopped.

"What the devil!" he exclaimed.

"I'm glad you stopped," I said, "because if you'd run into that flame you could have set yourself on fire." After a moment more of burning, I gently blew on the flame to extinguish it. "Once again, I ask you to leave our house, and to not come back."

Both men now, their bodies unsteady, looked at me, then at her, then back at me. The first man screamed, "She owes me for my brother!"

I looked at her and asked, "Did you kill his brother?"

"No, he must have died of his wounds," she said, "he was too badly injured for me to help him. He was alive when he left here."

"I see," I said, "and did they pay you to heal him?"

"I told them I couldn't heal him, but they insisted I do something. I was afraid they'd kill me if I didn't try."

"Did they pay you anything?"

She shook her head, "No, first they raped me. Then they refused to pay me for the medicine I did provide."

I said to the first man. "I believe her. I believe she owes you nothing."

The man, so thoroughly enraged now and propelled by his violent nature, allowed his fury to overcome his sense and he lunged at me once more, roaring. Again, I pulled out the full force of my energy and threw it up in the air between us. He bounced off it like a rag doll. I heard his neck snap and the sword flew from his hand across the room. He fell to the ground as his sword drove deep into the chest of the other man.

I stood in shock, horrified by the scene. Neither of the men moved. I looked at her. She stared in shock at the two men on the floor. Slowly she looked at me, her eyes glazed, "My God, you truly are a Son of Man."

Tears began to form in my eyes. "I think… they're dead."

She came to me, her hand reaching to my face. Some of my tears dripped onto her fingers. She pulled them to her mouth and licked my tears from where they fell.

"Don't burden yourself with my tears."

"They're no burden," she said.

But I felt my body beginning to acquiesce to the detoxification process. "My hands are beginning to shake." I said, "Soon I'll be of no help. We should figure out what to do so I can be of service before that time comes." She nodded her head.

I looked at the dead men and began praying. I wanted to believe that I hadn't killed them; that they killed themselves with the violence of their own energy. I hadn't touched them, but they died while attacking me. I worried it didn't have to turn out this way. I anguished over it thinking that there must have been something different I could've done. Something that could've caused this encounter to end less poorly. I was disturbed to my core.

"There's no recompense that can be paid for a life taken. Certain societies might think they're asking a person to 'pay' for the crime of taking a life, but that isn't recompense, that's revenge. The human life-force cannot be bought, sold, recompensed, or otherwise put into a position where it is assigned a monetary value. Any act that mimics this is merely an act of violence, cloaked in a veneer of greed."

- James brother of Yeshua -

60 · Dealing with the Dead

After some deliberation, we wrapped the men in shrouds and tied them to their horses; swords included. We guided the horses onto the main road and sent them on their way. I suspected these men were mercenaries, but if anyone was waiting for them to return, they deserved to know the men's fate.

The entire incident was upsetting. I imagined it was upsetting to my healer as well, but when I inquired, she said the outcome pleased her. She considered it justice for their crimes. And I reminded myself that not all people with good and well-intentioned hearts subscribed to the Way of Peace as I did. She'd found a release from the terrible event – I hadn't.

But before I could spend much time deliberating it, my body had other plans. I spent the night in the pain of relinquishing my burden. It was another violent exchange my body had with the world; it strangely mirrored the violence that erupted earlier that day. And as with much of this process, I remembered little of it. There was one exception to my lost memory; and that exception was notable.

I woke and the night was black. I was in deep, excruciating pain. But I soon realized my head was safely cradled on her warm lap. She had a moist cloth and stroked my skin with gentle, even movements. It was calming and comforting. She sang a lullaby with such love and tenderness that the sound of her voice lifted me until I felt free of the pain. Her voice was like an angel brushing its wings against my soul.

Periodically, she stopped her song to say, "There, there, everything's alright. Nothing to worry about. It's nearly done. Everything is as it should be. Just hold on to my voice." The words she spoke echoed in my ears, deepening the otherwise nonsensical inner calm the sound of her voice engendered. She returned to her lilting refrain.

I marked this sound, this voice, and its healing message. I marked it so I could call upon it if needed later. Little did I realize that this mark, the memory of this voice, would save me again, one fateful day many years in the future.

"I can't emphasize enough the advantages of marking moments. Whenever you're functioning in a highly desirable state, such as happiness, peace, calm, comfort, feeling at one with all things, mark it. Give the infinite awareness that exists in your physical form the command to place a flag on that experience. If you do, the body will have the ability to recall that experience when you again desire it. The more often these states are aroused and marked, the easier it is to recall them. Once recalled, they can literally lift and carry you through times of need."

- Yeshua son of Joseph -

A few days later, she wasn't home when I woke. I decided to cleanup so I might be less sorry to her sensibilities. As I waited, Philar and one of his associates appeared in front of me.

"Philar!" I exclaimed, "I'm so relieved to see you."

"You're nearly free of your addiction." He said, "I congratulate you on your fortitude."

"Thank you," I said, "but there's still so much to be done. I have to find my way forward."

"The way will be shown, my boy," he said, "the way will be shown." I nodded and waited. I knew he wouldn't have appeared just to congratulate me. He continued, "I want to talk about your recent experience, with the dead men."

This was a sore subject, but I said, "If you have something to say, I'm prepared to hear it."

"If you hadn't defended yourself, both you and your healer would now be dead."

"I'm clear about that fact," I nodded my head in acquiescence, "but the other fact remains that they are now dead."

"Yes they are." Philar moved closer to me and sat down. "They were violent, disturbed men who killed and hurt many people and would have killed and hurt many more if they hadn't relinquished their lives."

"But Philar," I interrupted, "I can't help feeling my actions were to blame. There must've been something I could've done to create a different outcome."

"No, my boy, there wasn't – save dying yourself." He laid his hand on my knee, "If you had somehow talked them out of the house, they would've returned in the night when you were incapacitated, and the outcome would've been your life instead of theirs."

"They died in my face, rushing at me. I mocked them. I asked them to leave, but I knew they wouldn't."

"Yes, exactly, they wouldn't."

"I can't help feeling as though I own a measure of cause. I put up the wall of energy that man ran into. I built that… well… you can call it a weapon, that wall."

Philar shook his head side to side, "No, it wasn't a weapon, it was a barrier. If you'd stepped in the other room and shut the door, and he'd run into the door with the same result, would you consider that your burden for closing the door?" I wasn't sure how to answer him. He looked pointedly at me and said, "Do you, right now, feel sorry they're dead?"

I searched my being. I found no remorse at their passing. "No," I said, "there's no grief in their death."

Philar looked at me, "Then what's your dilemma?"

"I want to be certain that I carry no burden of guilt for the incident. I'm tired of burdens; I want no more of them. If I have guilt, I want to understand it and atone for it as soon as possible."

Philar leaned forward with a deep sigh, "Here's the truth, Yeshua. Many will die from your presence, and many more will be saved from death by your presence. Your presence alone will prompt some people into a marked desire for one state or the other. There's nothing you can do to stop this, save stopping yourself."

Now it was my turn to sigh. "I see."

Philar continued, "Being a Son of Man is a burden by itself. To walk this path, you must accept this."

"I see." I hung my head from the heaviness of his words, but the words weren't heavy, it was my heart that was heavy from taking in the words.

We both sat in silence for a few moments, and then Philar opened a new topic, "This woman has been very kind and helpful to you."

I nodded, "Yes she has. I couldn't have done this without her help. I'm grateful to her and honored to be able to help her when she was in peril."

"Have you considered what you'll give her in return?" Philar looked at me with a piqued expression that surprised me.

"What do you mean? I'll pay her with a generous amount of money and give her the last of my drug for her healing bag. Is there more I can do?"

He hedged, "She's an unusually kind woman with deep maternal instincts."

I looked at Philar and blinked. Maternal instincts? He couldn't be suggesting what I thought he was suggesting. I stammered, "Wha… what are you suggesting?"

"No, I'm not urging you to any such action."

"Then what? What is your urging?"

"You see I'm not alone here," he pointed back to his companion.

"Yes I see that," I said, "hello." The companion tipped his head to me in acknowledgement.

Philar continued, "We're prepared to give her a fertile and full womb if you agree that it'd give her happiness and a measure of security. You see, we're also grateful for her deep kindness to you." Philar obviously saw confusion on my face. He added, "It'd be in the same way I gave you to your Mother."

Suddenly I realized what he was saying. "Would the child be like me?"

"She'd be similar, but not the same; and she'd undoubtedly look very much like you."

"She! I see, a girl." I nodded, "Ah… she could learn her mother's ways and carry on her work."

Philar ticked his teeth and said, "My thought too."

"But we should ask her," I said, "it wouldn't be right without her permission."

"You're quite right, and she's coming down the path now, perhaps you can find a way to do that." With those words hanging in my ears, Philar and his companion disappeared. I knew they were still there, though.

"Death is not final. It's a passing of the self from one state of being to another. The one who passes moves into a new realm, intact. The ones left behind feel loss as if a hole opened in their lives. Whenever possible, connect with the adventure your loved one continues with, and heal the grief of loss as soon as possible. Your grief helps no one, and while it's a necessary part of your healing, it only widens the gap between yourself and the one you're missing."
- Yeshua son of Joseph -

61 · The Gift

A few moments later, she opened the door. A big smile panned across her face. "Son of Man!" she exclaimed, "You're up. How're you feeling?"

"I'm feeling remarkably strong given the amount of weight I've lost." We laughed.

She said, "Well, on that subject, I went to town and brought home some food I thought would be more substantial than soup. You could use a good solid meal to begin to rebuild your strength."

I stood and walked toward her, "Am I done then? Is this process over?"

She looked into my face, her smile unwavering, "I believe it is, yes. You may have a few more bouts of sweats, perhaps some shaking as the effects of my tinctures finish their work, but the pain and visions should be gone. And the cravings should be gone too, for good." She swallowed and said, "Welcome back to your life."

I was overjoyed. I'd yearned for this day since the day of my reawakening collapsed in that river calling to the heavens for forgiveness. In my joyous state I picked her up in a hug and twirled her around in the air.

When I realized what I'd done, I set her down and stepped back. "I'm sorry. I didn't mean to grab you like that. It's just that I'm so happy and grateful."

She giggled, "Don't worry, Son of Man, I take no offense from your happiness."

I clasped my hands in front of my chest and bowed to her being.

"Alright," she continued, "let me start cooking. You must be very hungry."

And I was, indeed, but then I remembered Philar and the care of my immediate task. I followed her into the courtyard where she began to prepare food. "I have something to talk with you about."

"Oh, what?"

"It doesn't escape me that you're without children, yet you're kind and loving."

She dropped what was in her hand. Her face fell and she looked at me, "I'm… barren."

I saw the pain of it for her. "But am I correct in assuming you'd want a child if possible?"

"Don't mock me, please."

"No, I'm not mocking you. I feel your pain… and your desire." I hesitated, and then said, "I'm prepared to pay you per our original agreement, a generous measure of money and the last of my drug for your cache. But I'm prepared to give you more than that, if you agree."

She stepped back from me, and said in a hurtful tone, "Are you trying to get into my bed now? Is that what our time together has come down to?" She looked stricken.

I realized how clumsy my words were and put up my hand, "No, no, absolutely not. I wouldn't touch you. I'm not like that. This isn't for me. It'd be a gift for you."

Her face showed confusion.

"Please, listen to me before you judge. I'm a Son of Man. You know this now, beyond a doubt. I have ways that you can't begin to understand. Without sleeping with you, and by no means of my body, I can give you the gift of a fertile womb."

She blinked, her face incredulous.

I continued, "I can give you a daughter." I hoped that she'd feel the sincerity of my heart.

She reached behind herself to find a stool to sit. She put her hand on her forehead and said, "Truly? This isn't a joke?"

"No, this isn't a joke. I can make it happen, and not by sleeping with you, you have my promise."

"But... but... I'm barren."

"That's not a problem. I can make it so you will be pregnant and give birth." I waited but she made no sound, her eyes stared at me without acknowledgment. I felt she was afraid to accept for fear of being disappointed. I sat on the ground in front of her, and took her hand in mine, "Let me do this. Let me give you a gift that in some way begins to repay you for the life you've given back to me; a gift given for your own kindness and generosity."

She began to move her lips, but no sound came out.

I said, "Forget for a moment that you don't think it's possible. Pretend it is. And if it is, would it make you happy?"

Tears ran down her cheeks. She looked into my eyes and said in a timid voice, "Yes, it would make me happy to have a daughter."

"Then right now, close your eyes, and hold onto my hand." Philar took the hint and tiptoed into the courtyard. As soon as he did, she became unconscious. I closed my eyes and waited.

After about fifteen minutes, Philar tapped me on the shoulder. I opened my eyes and took her hand. I asked him, "Is it done?"

"Yes, my boy, it's done," he said. "She's two months pregnant."

I smiled, "Thank you." I asked, "Is there anything she has to do, anything I need to tell her?"

He smiled, "No, nothing unusual."

I sighed and mouthed the words 'thank you' again. Philar brought her back to consciousness as he and his companion left. She yawned and opened her eyes.

She looked at me. "That was odd," she said, "I felt cradled. Then... I don't know. Well, anyway... what do we have to do?"

"Nothing more," I said, "it's already done. You're two months pregnant right now with a healthy little girl. It's my gift of thanks." The smile on her face was like

"As soon as you open your mouth to speak, put pencil to paper, or use a keyboard, you are relying on a finite and imprecise medium to express infinite and precise information. It's difficult to anticipate how another person will receive your words. All best efforts can still result in miscommunication. The antidote to miscommunication is simple: Open your heart. Be willing to restate. Be able to apologize and to forgive. These tenets will serve you regardless of any misunderstanding that may arise. And in any case, keep communicating – it's about connection."

- Yeshua son of Joseph -

heaven.

The rest of the day was delightful. I had a few tremors and broke out in a sweat once, but we had a joyous meal. We talked about our lives and about people we met along the way.

Her countenance became more radiant as the day progressed. She kept holding her hand to her belly and, at one point, she exclaimed that she could feel the baby growing.

"What did you do?" she asked, "Really, how is it that I'm pregnant?"

"I can't explain it to you," I said, "you'll have to accept this as a miracle. An unexplained and blessed event."

"But what'll I say to others about the Father?"

I thought for a moment, remembering Mother, "Well, I suppose you could say she was given to you by an angel."

"An angel?" She took in a deep breath and her eyes widened, "An angel was here?"

"You could say he was an angel. He certainly wasn't of this world."

Again, she lowered her hand to her belly and for a moment, I saw the fleeting thoughts of disbelief wash across her face.

"Believe it, you're growing a baby. Before you know it, your belly will be as big as the hump of a camel!" We both laughed and I remembered there was still some unfinished business between us.

I retrieved my pouch and I paid her what I promised and more. She thought it was too much, but I reminded her that she'd have another mouth to feed soon. She did finally take the extra money. And I told her I'd mention her healing services as I wandered in hope of sending her paying work.

I handed her the remaining packets of opium. The simple act of her taking the packets from my hand sent an electric and ecstatic feeling of release through my entire being that was beyond compare. I knew instantly, that phase of my life was over.

Toward the end of the day, I broached the subject of leaving, "I'm not sure how long I've been here, but I believe it's nearing my time to leave." When she heard my words, her face reflected sadness.

She said, "I wish you could stay. I've gotten used to having you here."

"I understand," I said, "but I have a lot of work to do and I have to get back on the road."

She asked, "Do you have family?"

"Yes, I do, but my addiction got between us."

"Perhaps now that you're recovered, you can go back to them." She looked at

---

"All creation begins with thought. And thought can only find form if you believe it can and add your passion to it. Thoughts alone are weak. Their only power is gained when they couple with the fire of desire. So let the thoughts you don't like fall away quickly as they expend themselves, and give your attention and passion to the thoughts you do like. This is the most basic tenet of creation."
- Yeshua son of Joseph -

me with hope.

I sighed, "I can't say if they can get over their disappointment in me or not. Only time will tell. Either way though I must get about my work." I stood. "I should get to bed now and hope to get a good night's sleep for a change."

She stood also and put her arms around me. "Thank you, Son of Man. Thank you for everything." I returned her hug, squeezing her with deep sincerity. She was my healer.

It occurred to me, I didn't know her name. I pulled back and with my hands on her shoulders I asked, "Would you tell me your name?"

"Ha" she laughed, "Not unless you tell me yours!"

I laughed, "Fair enough." I let go of her shoulders and with a hand on my chest I said, "My name is Yeshua."

She giggled and said, "Pleased to meet you, Yeshua. My name is Nadia." And she held her hand out to me as if we were meeting for the first time. I grasped her hand in a hold of friendship.

"It's nice to meet you, Nadia." As I held her hand, I realized that actually we were meeting for the first time. I wasn't the same person as when I first stumbled onto her doorstep. I was Yeshua now. And I marveled at when and how I actually found the courage to become me again.

"Everyone thrives within a family. Some with the family they were born to, others with the family they build. Without family, you'd wither. The man who wrote, "no man is an island," understood we're all connected and that connection is our imperative. You and I are both part of the interconnected weave of life. There's no separation. Yet we meander through that weave of life forming and reforming closer bonds as our life's passions dictate. Family represents the bonds that last longer. Family is society's deepest and closest expression of interpersonal connection. Bring your family close. Give to them as if your very life depends on it, because in a very real way it does."

- Yeshua son of Joseph -

62 · Jerusalem

When I left Nadia, I was unclear about where to go and what to do. I knew I had to start my work, but how?

I wandered around the southern tip of the Dead Sea and eventually found myself walking north to Jerusalem. When I got there, it felt like home, at least for now. I decided to procure a room and stay.

I'd been to Jerusalem several times, but it always surprised me with its cosmopolitan atmosphere. I thought of it as a Jewish town, but it was more than that. It was also a Roman settlement and military outpost with a large contingent of Roman and Greek citizens. Living here were also Persians, Armenians, Egyptians, as well as every other desert people. It was an international city.

Many buildings crowded together, sharing exterior walls; most were two or more stories in height. Streets were narrow and filled with horses, carts, donkeys, and people. There was a sense of immediacy, too. Things had to get done. People had to be met. Goods had to be sold. Even the public baths were full of people.

Unless a person made a point of looking at the sky, or stepping outside the crowded bustle to a garden or orchard, nature could be forgotten altogether. It seemed too easy for a person to become stifled and narrow-minded here, while at the same time feeling puffed up with self-importance.

That said; the need to attend to nature wasn't as immediate as it was in the country. Nearly every type of merchant good, including perishables, could be found throughout the business districts, of which there were mainly three. The Roman district had a massive merchant complex, and below Temple Mount was another merchant center that housed Jewish and non-Jewish businesses, and then, of course, within Temple Mount were the stalls of Jewish merchants who refused to do business with any people other than their own.

Overall, people have a tendency to fear change, especially when that change is imposed by force. Throughout history, few have been more forceful with their agenda than the Romans. But, here in Jerusalem, even the Romans finally folded into the mix. This isn't to say that living with the Romans was easy. They held all the political and military power in this land and as such, we could practice our religion, sell our goods, till our soil, and live unimpeded: as long as we bowed to their laws, paid their exorbitant taxes, and withstood the periodic anger-induced slaughter of our innocents.

It was degrading and inhumane. It was clear that one day the scales of balance would assuredly tip to revolution and many would die in futility. Rome was the

"Diversity creates an open mind. Embed diversity in every garden you care-take, whether that be a garden of plants, a garden of people, or a garden of ideas. Strive not to be constrained."

- Yeshua son of Joseph -

ultimate earthly power in these parts. The Roman army controlled all of the Mediterranean and most of Europe. The little band of subjugated people I called my brothers could surely never amass numbers great enough to defeat that army. Unfortunately, this fact would probably not keep some faction of us from trying.

I wasn't born to foment political revolution. I'm here to foment a change of higher substantive value. One human group toppling another to end immediate physical subjugation does nothing to end the larger subjugation. The subjugation all humans live under is that of the spirit. We are more than our physical bodies. And that 'more' of us, when amassed together into a consciousness, can exponentially increase our fortunes to unimaginable gain.

It was and is time for humans to be called to their birthright. It was and is time to move people away from the bonds of dogma and fear that have kept us in these insular conclaves of imagined brotherhoods.

All hearts beat with the same blood: All men, all women, all creeds, and all races. Arguably, there is more of one inbred bloodline here and another there, but strip away the physical features of genetic inbreeding and you find we are all, water and clay, metal and protein, animated into life. Our brains have the same capacities; our hearts carry the same compassion. And the only thing that makes a real difference between us is how consciously we choose to live.

Nothing else, on any level, has a substantive effect on our humanity or our community. Everything else is temporal illusion. Born today with one skin color, that eternal soul that you are could be born tomorrow with another skin color. Born yesterday as a man, you could be born again next year as a woman. Born last year as a genius, you could be born next century as a simpleton. When viewing lives in this context, how can anyone hold himself or herself as superior or inferior to another? Each life, each spin of the birth wheel, merely reflects a new choice, but the spirit remains eternal, complex, creative, and endowed with power.

Wandering around Jerusalem, I remembered that this was my mission, to end the illusion of separation and lift the imposed restriction on spiritual growth. To help humans understand that they have the power to choose a higher level of consciousness. By so choosing, we could stand together as a band of enlightened spirits, ready to lift our combined consciousness to a new paradigm, away from subjugation of any kind, and into a place where we can thrive. And by thriving, join in equality with the larger communities that inhabit our multiverse.

There'd be no way to do this without upsetting the status quo. I was and am a revolutionary in my heart and soul. My Son of Man and Adept Way trainings made this triply so. The status quo was well and good while I was learning its laws and consequences, but the status quo was wholly unsatisfactory for moving forward.

How could I affect change? How could I find a voice that would be large enough, powerful enough, and command enough respect? Here, without a family, friends, money, status or profession, I'd have to be clever, but I wasn't sure cleverness would be enough.

I still felt regret that I was alienated from my brothers, but I was resolute to abide by their wishes. Living in Jerusalem, I thought of them every hour of every day. My love for them helped propel me, and as each day passed, I practiced my mystical ways until I regained mastery of the physical world. I was relieved that Nadia's treatments had been supremely successful. Not once did I yearn for the intemperate illusion. My body recovered its complete composure. My muscles grew in strength and agility. I could be solid and command attention, or I could be like a shadow and fade into obscurity. I could walk firmly on the ground or hover above it. I could live with my beating heart, or stop its beat altogether.

I astounded myself with the rapidity with which I reassembled my skills. And I began to feel urgency from an inner calling that was compelling. 'This is the time,' my spirit whispered to me. Every exaltation I'd experienced, every blunder and dark corner I'd traversed, brought me to this place and I was ready. And as I wandered the streets and shook hands with the locals, I prayed to be shown the way. Philar promised that the way would be shown. Feeling fully able to perform my mission wherever it took me, and whatever it entailed, it was now time for the combined force of my helpers to step forward; it was time for the way to be presented.

"Greetings humanity, my name is Yeshua. I am a Son of Man and I can no longer be ignored."

"You never need to know 'how' something will be attained. You only need to believe it will. The 'how' will make itself known when the 'what' of our desire is clear. Begin the journey with passion and intent; it will unfold in divine ways."
- Yeshua son of Joseph -

63 · Joseph's Visit

I lay on the bed in my rented room, the walls and ceiling illuminated by the transiting light of the near full moon. Supper was long behind me and my body was annoyingly resistant to sleep. My mind wandered over the events of the last few days.

I'd bumped into an elder uncle while shopping for food. I was astonished that he recognized me. He hadn't seen me in over 15 years. Before I healed, I was unrecognizable, even to my dear cousin John, or at least that's what I thought. Now fused with my true self, I was undeniably and recognizably me.

This uncle from my mother's side knew of Joseph's death, but he hadn't heard that I'd returned. I was happy to see him, and happy to realize that the rumor mill hadn't crunched through my short and unhappy stay with the family.

He said I looked good and mused that my time in the east obviously went well. I thanked him for his compliments. He asked if I was going to take up my place as the head of the family. I told him I wasn't sure what the family was going to decide, but that if they asked me, I would comply. He seemed pleased with that answer. He realized I wasn't wearing rabbinic robes and I reminded him I'd just returned from my long absence and hadn't yet spoken to the elders about taking up my position. And with a look of elder disapproval, he urged me to do that as soon as possible. I assured him I'd set about that business in due time and I sent him on his way.

My sleepy mind drifted to my brothers, and how much I loved them. I missed them. I wanted to put my arms around them, comfort them from their burdens. I mused that if I'd attended to my own burden before I came home, perhaps I wouldn't be alone in this room now. In any case, I had to accept that my path was being watched and coddled more than I knew. Probably more than I'd accept if I did know. And that meant all was well.

My mind drifted until I was almost asleep when the room appeared to take on a brighter light than the moon would produce on its own. I opened my eyes and standing just beyond my reach was Joseph. He looked just as he had the last time I saw him in life: vital, and buoyant.

"Father?" I raised myself on my arms to see him better.

"Yeshua, my son. It's good to see you." A sparkle of light danced around him.

"I miss you so much," I said, "I'm sorry I didn't get to touch you before you left."

"Don't worry about that. I'm well, but I'm concerned about your mother."

"My mother? Mary?" My heart stepped up its beat.

"Have a care for the life you live in your dreams. It's as integral to your well-being as any other part of your existence. And never underestimate the variety of experiences you might be classifying as dreams. Open your mind."

- Yeshua son of Joseph -

"She's not well," he said, "what happened between you boys has wounded her spirit." I remembered the last time I saw her, the deep pain of loss that gripped her. For a moment, I felt a pang of regret and guilt over having been the instrument of that pain.

"What can I do? I was asked to leave."

"Consider this," he said, "consider that request was made in haste and grief. Consider that your Mother might not recover from the family rift and might decide to join me. Consider that you might miss her, the same way you missed me. What would your brother's request mean to you then?" He hesitated, and then said, "Consider that seeing you come home might be the only thing that keeps her from leaving prematurely. Is her happiness worth risking your brother's anger?"

"Father, her wellbeing is worth risking anything, everything."

"Then go to her, as soon as possible. I say, you must go home." As those words came from his lips, he faded.

I stood up, hoping to find him moved to a corner, but he was gone. His last words 'you must go home' echoed in my ears when all of a sudden I woke with a start to find myself still lying on the bed. Had Joseph really come to me? Was it a dream? I couldn't take the chance it was anything but real, so I resolved to set on the road to Galilee in the morning.

64 · Going home

This time, when I walked through the gates of the family compound, I was ready for whatever greeting came my way. I felt no shame. I stood upright and my gait was strong. My newly reclaimed body looked as healthy as I felt. And I knew that, whatever homecoming I received, I'd be fine. More than fine, I was on my path as a Son of Man, and I knew it deep in my soul, beyond any doubt or illusion. I was coming home.

On my short hike up the hill to the house, unlike the last time I walked up this hill, everyone I encountered greeted me immediately. They knew instantly who I was and their gladness at seeing me arrive was reflected in their faces.

When I got to the house, I knocked on the door. Josea answered. Her face beamed with joy, "Yeshua! My goodness… come in." She made way for and her face suddenly turned serious, "Mary has spoken to me, of course, and I know why you left. I'm relieved you're back." She shook her finger at me, "You shouldn't have gone in the first place."

"Thank you, but actually," I said, "it was good that I left. I found my healing."

She sighed and looked me up and down, "Indeed, you did. You look strong and well. Mary will be so pleased." She patted my arm.

"How is everyone?" I asked.

"Mary's well, she prays for your return. It's been hard on her."

I nodded, "And my brothers?"

"Well," Josea hedged, "fine I'm sure."

"Josea, don't coddle me, what's happening?" She looked me in the eye and I could see her face soften and her eyes brighten.

"You are back, all of you, I see it."

I smiled, "Now, please, tell me what's happening."

"No one is looking after this family. Everyone wants you at the head, but Jude won't have it. He hasn't told the community of your burden. He said you were ill. It confused everyone, me included." She waggled her finger at me again, "If you were ill, why would you leave the healing hearts of your home? Many wanted to find you and bring you back, but Jude said no. He put his foot down and forbade anyone from searching for you." She grabbed my hand, "It's not right. Being ordered about? Jude hasn't been himself. He's surly. There's talk from some of leaving the community."

I nodded, understanding better than she knew. "What does James have to say? Surely he has an opinion."

"James is gone… to Qumran." She crossed her arms in front of her chest and threw them out from her body in a dramatic gesture that highlighted her frustration, "He left in anger. Not long after you left. There were sharp words between him and Jude." Her eyes fell to the floor, "James said he didn't know if he'd come back."

"I'm grateful that you told me. I needed to know." I squeezed her shoulder, and asked, "So. Where's Mother?"

"She's with Rebekkah. Something happened this morning and Mary is supporting her."

"I see. Well, I doubt I should interrupt. I'll wait for her to return."

Josea put her arms around my waist. "I'm gladdened to see you home. My heart is calm. Things will be set right soon." I let her go back to her chores and settled in to wait for Mary.

I was on the back porch when I heard Mary come in. When she saw me, she practically stumbled over her feet. "Yeshua!" she shouted and ran to me, throwing her arms around me. I returned her hug with fervor.

"Mother, it's so good to be with you."

She pulled back and looked me up and down, turning her gaze to my face. "My word, Yeshua," she said in astonishment, "You're so different!"

"Yes, I'm healed Mother, no more burden." I beamed at her, "And I know who I am now, no more shame, no more lack. I'm free."

She squeezed me again and I felt her heart release the burden she'd carried since my departure. We stayed like this for many minutes, unwilling to let go of the joy these moments held.

But the practical overtook and I had to ask, "Are you well? Is everything well with Rebekkah?"

"Let's sit, Son." So we did. She told me of the trouble at Jude's. After breakfast, Jude was angered by something Rebekkah said. He slapped her, hard enough to leave bruises, and menaced her with his body and language. It wasn't the first time in recent weeks he'd raised his voice, but it was the first time he struck her. Rebekkah was shocked and angry, and in the ensuing argument, Jude told her he wanted to throw her out because she hadn't given him children.

"Jude hasn't been himself since you left," Mary said. "He's taken on an angry, violent streak that concerns me."

"It concerns me too," I admitted.

Mary calmed and looked over each inch of my face with the care of a mother looking over her newborn. "The change in you. You're not the same man that left here months ago." She placed her hand on my cheek, "There's no doubt that you're the head of this family. I'm sorry you inherit a troubled kingdom." She laid her hands on mine.

"Don't fret, Mother. Everything'll work out."

"Until a moment ago, I wouldn't have agreed with you. But now I do. It's all true, isn't it, everything I've been told since I was a child?" She got a sad look in her eyes, "Please stay with me as long as you can."

"Look at yourself honestly. Have you ever taken an action based solely upon anger and been pleased with the result in the long run? Actions taken in anger sooth the moment, give the primitive self a boost, but don't serve the infinite self. When anger prompts you to act, walk away, because a life lived in service to the primitive self is fruitless."

- Yeshua son of Joseph -

I interrupted, "Mother, please…"

"No, Yeshua, I promise. I won't let the world make me jealous for wanting all of you. Blessings be upon you," and she patted my hand with surety.

Our attention was interrupted by a commotion outside. We went to the porch to see what was happening. What we saw was shocking. James was home and standing between James and the house was Jude.

"I don't want you here," Jude yelled.

"I don't care what you want," James barked, "I'm going inside to see Mary."

"No you're not!" Jude moved closer to menace James, and he could do it. He was shorter than James, but his stocky build was more muscular. Other members of the community emerged from their homes, attracted by the commotion as we were, and now they were held to the scene by anxious curiosity.

"I'm older," James insisted, "I'm not taking orders from you!" James tried to walk past him, but Jude shoved him, hard enough that James almost fell over.

I decided to intervene before someone got hurt. So I moved between them. "Jude, if you're intent on picking a fight, why don't you pick it with me instead?"

Jude stepped back, startled by my intrusion. "Yeshua! What're you doing here?"

"The same thing you're doing here, my brother. I'm home." I opened my heart and sent love to him. "Why don't we go inside and talk like the brothers that we are?"

"I don't believe this!" Jude shouted, "You both disgust me!" I stepped closer to him and could smell the distinct odor of beer. I reached my hand out to touch his shoulder, but he slapped my hand away. "Don't touch me," Jude snapped.

"As you wish." I turned to James and put my arm around his shoulder. "Let's you and I take Mother inside the house." James looked at me with astonishment. I could feel his fear. As soon as I cradled him in my arm though, James pressed his body into me and let out a sigh of relief.

As we started to walk toward Mary, Jude tried to slug me in the face, but I moved just enough for him to slice through the air instead. He nearly fell over from the energy of the thrust. I again tried to lead James toward Mary, all the time keeping myself between him and Jude.

Jude came back at me, grabbing my arm. I let go of James and twisted myself into Jude. I swiftly wrapped my arms around him until, before he knew what was happening, I was draped completely over his back holding his arms crossed in front of his chest. I could hear gasps from the people around us. I laid my head on his shoulder and whispered in his ear, "I love you, my brother."

Jude struggled against my hold. "It's no use Jude," I whispered, "you can't resist my embrace." Jude struggled harder. "Brothers hold onto brothers, it's my duty to protect you."

"Nooooo!" he screamed.

"Yes," I whispered, "you can't run from my love." I turned my face toward James, "Take Mother into the house please." He nodded and complied. I turned

"My brother was a rock: he was ready to step into any situation without fear. Fearless is a state I yearned to learn from his example, but fear dogged me all through our work together. I was afraid I'd lose him, more than anything else, I was afraid of losing Yeshua. He was, as I say, my rock."

- James brother of Yeshua -

my attention back to Jude. His muscles were straining like a bull against a gate, but he was unable to budge my persistent hold on his arms. I leaned into his back and said, "I offer you safe passage through your grief. He didn't want to leave us, Jude, it was just his time."

"Nooo…." He pushed against my hold.

"He loved us with a love that is undying, a love that has no end."

"Yeeesss….." he cried as tears began to fill his eyes.

"He's still here with us, in us. We honor him with our love, my brother." Jude stopped straining and his body began to sink to the earth. I held him from falling as we both slid to the ground. "I won't let go. I'll hold you 'til my dying day." Jude sobbed, his chest heaving under the weight of grief he couldn't contain.

We sat in the dirt for a long time. I held him fast as his tears seemed unending. Members of the community slowly went back to their homes. James escorted Rebekkah into the main house to be with him and Mary.

James eventually came back to see if he was needed. Of course, he was needed; we were all needed.

65 · A Cluster of Fools

I helped Jude into the house. He was wrung out from weeping. I sat next to him, silently supporting him without intrusion. Josea brought a wet cloth for his head and water for his throat. We didn't ask her, she merely knew what to do and did it with love in her heart. After nearly thirty years of being Mary's closest confidant and helper, we were as family.

Eventually James and Mary joined us, sitting quietly as the sun went down. Rebekkah remained resting, sequestered for now. I anticipated she'd stay with us this night.

Josea brought hot soup before she retired for an evening with her husband. As we sipped, Jude finally uttered his first words since the afternoon, "James, Yeshua, I'm sorry. My actions were wrong."

I breathed in, feeling the nourishment and warmth of Josea's cooking in my stomach. It was soothing. After a moment I said, "Thank you."

James followed a moment later, "Yes, thanks."

I ventured, "How long have you been abusing alcohol?"

Mary's face snapped up to look at me, obviously surprised by my observation. James sighed and dropped his gaze to his lap, stunned. I silently hoped James could keep from humiliating Jude further tonight with judging comments.

Jude set down his bowl. He leaned forward, his head bent in shame, "It started before Joseph died, when he first got sick."

I nodded. Mary's eyes closed and she leaned back, a river of understanding washing over her.

"Where do you keep your supply?" I asked with sincerity.

Jude began to cry again and I was astounded that there were any tears left in him. He said, "In the shed behind the workhouse. God, I'm so stupid!"

I laid my hand on Jude's back and said, "I understand the shame you must be feeling right now, but I promise you, if you're willing to step up, we can work this out together." I looked up and saw Mary staring at me with a look that I couldn't decipher. It was some combination of euphoria, release, and liberation. I immediately looked away because I felt as though I'd just seen something that wasn't my business; even though I'm certain it had something to do with me.

A chill settled into the room, so James started a fire. Mary excused herself, saying we had much to talk about and she'd see us in the morning. On her way out, she stopped and said, "I'm pleased you're all home. This is where you belong." She turned to me and said, "Thank you for coming back. We need you more than you know."

Later in the evening, James was tending a magnificent fire. I'd cleared the soup bowls, carefully washing and stacking them. Jude was nursing his shame, and the silence was thick. I could tell Jude wanted a drink. Each time he licked his parched lips I felt the lust he had for it. It was a different addiction than mine had been, but the desire to stop the pain was very familiar. Questions swam through my brain, and I was sure it was the same for my brothers.

Finally, James spoke, "Aren't we a cluster of fools?"

"How so?" I asked, "Give us your thoughts."

"We're blessed in so many ways. We have affluence; we have a community that supports us. We have options and opportunities many people don't have. Yet we've been fighting and running from fear, as if we were urchins without a drop of love to our name."

I nodded, "Grief is a powerful emotion."

"I still can't accept that Father's gone," Jude said. "I'm not ready."

"We're lucky to have had him as long as we did," James said, "he was very old."

"There's no one like him," Jude sputtered as he began to cry again.

"That's sure," I said, "but he's still with us. He called me home."

"What?" Jude said in surprise.

"Yes," James added, "me too. I had a visit from Joseph in my dreams. He said I had to come home. That Mary was ill."

"The same for me," I said.

We let a silence slip around us again, until James spoke. I was beginning to understand that James nearly always had something to say. "Yeshua, I put you on a pedestal. When you came home with a simple human affliction, it threw me into a deep confusion."

"I understand," I said, "it was no more than my own confusion mirrored, I'm sure."

"Yes," James added, "but it made me doubt everything, especially my path and my place in the family."

"My anger didn't help that," Jude said.

"You were influenced by alcohol," I said.

Jude looked at me, his eyes red, and his emotions raw, "I don't know what to do."

I said, "Nor do I." And again, silence settled in.

We went back and forth like this for a long while. Inner truths were revealed, and when all was said and done, we realized we had great fear and it swallowed us. My fear centered on being accepted back into the family, James' fear centered on the apparent negation of his path, and Jude was afraid he wasn't up to the challenge of running the family business. Our fears led us to perpetrate the very difficulties we feared.

I was relieved for Jude's sake that James was introspective and measured his response to Jude's revelation. I reasoned that perhaps he'd grown from reflecting on his raw response to me those many months before.

"Numbing addictions are the wild and unrestrained manifestations of the desire to escape. Little do we know when we begin a path into addiction, that our fear of what we wish to dodge has actually drawn us into harsher chains even trickier to escape."

- Yeshua son of Joseph -

By the end of the evening, we stood together seeing eye-to-eye. I accepted my place at the head of the family and all the community obligations that came with that. James accepted his path and recommitted to walking with me. And Jude committed to dealing with his abuse issues. That would include apologizing to everyone he hurt because of it. James and I assured him we both believed in his ability to run the business once he accomplished the task of healing from his addiction, but only when he accomplished it.

Standing with our arms interlocked, we felt like brothers again.

James remarked, "Yeshua that was some move you made earlier, when you corralled Jude."

I laughed, "Part of my training."

"What else can you do?" he asked.

"Oh, a great many things you've never seen before."

"You're too mysterious," Jude said.

James added, "So show us something else."

I tried to beg off, to leave these things to their own time, but they wouldn't stop badgering me. Finally, I gave in, "Alright!" So, I faded from their sight and reemerged behind them. "Was that good enough?" I asked.

They were startled and a little frightened, yet when their fright finally quelled, they were changed. In an instant, their canvas of possibilities shifted. And from that shift, our futures would be served.

"Stand in the strength of your spirit and meet life with open arms. There's nothing to be afraid of. There's nothing that can touch you, or harm you, if you greet your life without fear. Fear is the only thing to be shunned. The rest of your life is filled with divinity."

- Yeshua son of Joseph -

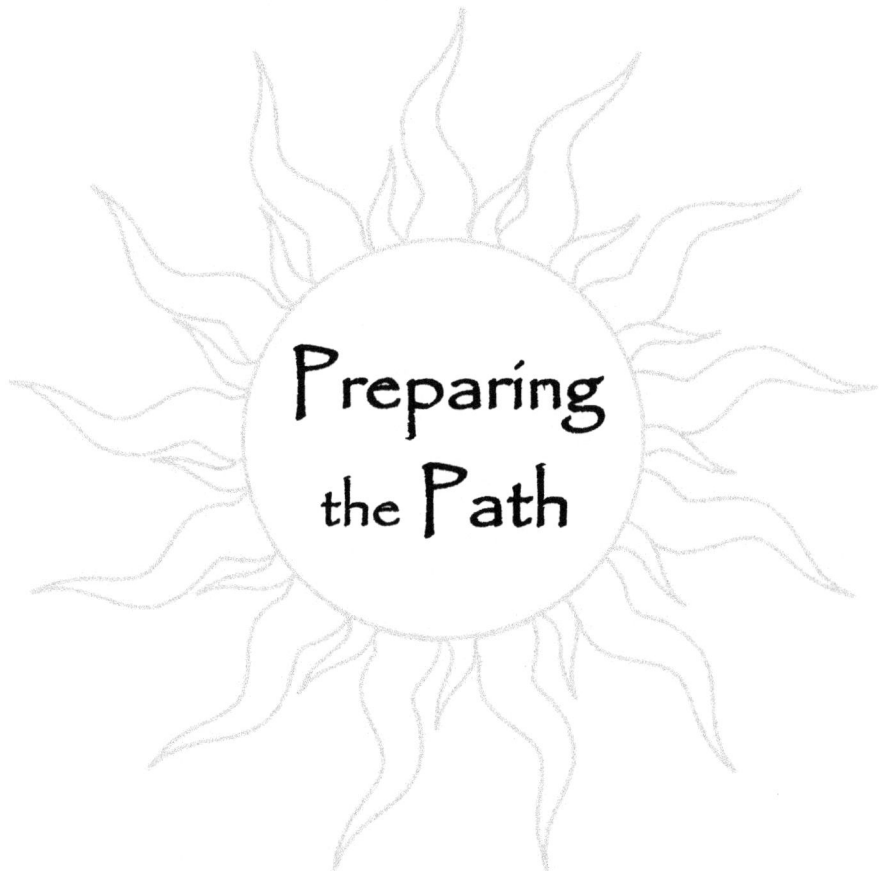

Preparing the Path

66 · Accepting the Mantle

The next day, Rebekkah moved in with Mary, James, and me. The road to her and Jude healing as a couple was not clear, but until they figured things out, she needed to feel safe.

First thing, we attended to Jude's healing from the ravaging effects of alcohol. He took James and me to his hidden store. He was emotional showing it to us and confessed how afraid he was that someone would discover his secret. He kept jars of herbs to cover the smell on his breath, and strips of dried, salted meat to settle his stomach on bad mornings.

When we asked him what he wanted to do, he said, "Give it away." I remembered how I felt when I gave my store of opium to Nadia. The feeling of release was tremendous. We packed it up along with some other overages we had, and took them into Sepphoris to a house of charity we dealt with regularly. Jude was relieved when the woman told him they'd be welcome gifts for many families.

We also needed a healer. I voted to send him to Nadia. I knew she could accomplish the detoxification process and set his body back to normal without cravings, but Jude didn't want to be gone from the family for that long. So we called on a recommended healer in Sepphoris.

While there, James and I paid a visit to our old family friend, Jacob. He was now head of the Essene Elder Council and we needed to update him. I was surprised when I saw him. After fifteen years, he was now an old man. His back was bent, and he was fully grey. I whispered a prayer of thanks that he was alive and well to greet us.

"Yeshua, my dear boy!" Jacob said as he threw his arms around me. "I've anticipated your visit. You look well!"

"I'm very well." I said, "And I believe you've met James."

"Yes of course, James," he gave James a tight hug, "so good to see you again." He led us to the sitting room and had a servant bring us juice. His face turned sullen, "I extend my condolences. Joseph's death is a huge loss for us all."

"Leadership in the society of my youth was hierarchical in the extreme. While bloodlines were established through the matriarchy, leadership was structured through the patriarchy. The first line of leadership was in the home with the father or father figure. The second line was with the local Rabbi or synagogue leader. The third line of hierarchy was the head of the extended family, established through the women, but practiced through the men. From there, power went to the priests of the Temple. Then power shifted back to the local political leaders and on up that chain. If the local political leaders weren't in one's family, that leader was likely to receive even less regard than the head of the family, even if the head of the family lived two provinces away. It was an unfortunate prescription for societal confusion and imbalance."

- Yeshua son of Joseph -

We each touched the back of two fingers to our lips then to our forehead as a sign of respect for the dead. After a moment of silence, I said, "We want to tell you our plans and obtain your blessing for our decisions."

We enlightened him and he agreed, further informing us that this was as Joseph had hoped. He brought up an issue that surprised me.

"One more thing," Jacob said, "of course, James, we respect your monastic status, but Yeshua, you've no such status and the community wants you to establish a family soon. Have you plans yet?"

I blinked, "No, not yet."

"Well, be advised that I've already heard talk of it. It'll come up without delay, I'm sure."

I sighed and my face turned red. It wasn't something I wanted to consider yet. "I'll be putting that decision off for a while. I'm a little overwhelmed with other responsibilities."

"Boy," Jacob laughed, "you give yourself away! Eastern education aside, I can see you're still innocent. Don't let me embarrass you, but it's something you'll have to do soon. People will press you for an heir."

"I understand, Elder." I bowed my head in acceptance.

Jacob continued to chuckle, "So, tell me more of this work James alluded to. As our teacher, Yeshua, what are your plans?"

I proceeded to tell them about the map from the Buddha and my journey to the Temple of Man. I told them of my subsequent ascension interrupted and the meeting with my Creator. I extolled the joy of seeing my path in such a clear light. Both men were held rapt by my tale. When I finished they were speechless. We sat in silence for a long while until Jacob finally spoke, "I'm humbled by your experience."

James nodded his head, "As am I, my brother."

"Your story... these aren't words to be shared with liberty," Jacob chastened, "I'll hold your confidence close to my heart." His eyes moistened. "I'm honored to know you."

I smiled, "As I am you."

We spent another hour or so together. After, James and I fetched Jude. On our way home, Jude mentioned his guilt about how he treated everyone. We knew the host of apologies he needed to make would be no small accomplishment. We promised to stand with him.

———————

About a month later, Jude remained steadfast to his healing. It wasn't

"There's often an underlying assumption that if one travels far from home, one will encounter looser morals. Truly, there are people of all moral persuasions in every community. Where you come from and where you go. The truth is more that when you step away from your home and travel to a new place, you have the opportunity to confront parts of yourself that forces within your everyday community suppress. These 'looser morals' are really the unsuppressed parts of yourself emerging. What you do with them when they emerge is up to you."

- Yeshua son of Joseph -

complete, but for the sake of our futures we had to proceed with faith that his healing would continue. He systematically made apologies to everyone in the community. To each he confessed his addiction and asked for forgiveness for the disruption he caused. It was comforting to watch the positive change this promoted in our close-knit fold. As my brother, Jude made me proud.

As head of the family, however, I made two requests of him. The first was to meet with him every evening, except Sabbath. Not to assure myself that he wasn't drinking, rather to talk with him about the business of the day. It was important that if Jude couldn't handle the workload for any reason, that we identify that quickly and take appropriate action. Compassion for what my brother was going through aside, I was resolute to watch over the health of the clan.

The second request was more difficult for him to accept, but I felt it was necessary. I asked that James review both the shipments of supplies into the compound and the payment registers. I wanted to trust Jude, but I couldn't take the chance that he'd either hide purchases of alcohol in larger shipments, or siphon money for hidden purchases. As well I knew, until he demonstrated a prolonged commitment to healing, I couldn't trust him to stay sober.

I also counseled James privately to take care with his review process: that it was important not to be tyrannical or judging. I encouraged him to do this with a heart intent on seeing Jude do well and to adopt a jovial manner throughout. He promised he would try.

A few weeks after we started these procedures, Jude confided that he was relieved to be working under the gaze of his brothers. He said it felt more like when Joseph guided him. It gave him confidence knowing that if he made a mistake, it would be caught before great damage could occur.

Once I was satisfied that we were standing on solid ground, James and I called the community together and on a sunny afternoon, we made our announcements. Everyone to a person congratulated us and pledged their continued support and acceptance.

After the announcements, we enjoyed a feast and everyone made merry into the night. Singing, dancing, laughter, I was filled with joy seeing everyone so happy. Jude stayed abstinent throughout the festivities, even though so many around him were drinking with abandon. I wasn't really concerned about it. I was more concerned that if any problem were to emerge, it would most likely be his old behavior of drinking in solitude and hiding the evidence. But, at the end of this night, it felt as though we band of brothers were finally moving forward.

A few weeks later, James was helping me study for a trip to Jerusalem, when Mary interrupted. She looked stern, "Yeshua, I need to talk with you."

"Go ahead," I said.

"I've been presented with a proposal for your marriage."

I gulped, "Oh."

"She's a lovely young woman," Mary continued, "from a good David family." James chuckled. "What's so funny?" Mary asked him.

"It's just... well..." James sputtered, "Good luck, Yeshua." I threw a glare at him.

"I don't know what to say, Mother." I looked at her with dismissive eyes that

I'm sure were unwelcome. This proposal was by custom, of course. And even though I was older and would ultimately decide for myself, the presenting family was compelled to go through my parent.

"There'll be more proposals," Mary said, "you can count on it."

I looked at Mary and said, "I don't want to get married right now."

"Why?" she asked.

"I'm looking for a particular match, and I don't feel her yet."

"A particular match?" Mary inquired with surprise. I nodded. "You and I have to talk," Mary said, "I need to know more about this."

How could I explain to her what I was unclear about myself? I wanted the White Tiger I met that day with the Master at Insa'alet, but I had no idea what she'd look like or when or how she'd appear.

Many months later, Jude had settled into his leadership position, his healing seemed thorough, though he was visiting the healer once a month for a maintenance treatment. Jude and Rebekkah reconciled and were happy together again. I received my Temple priest position and my rabbinic robes, but with admonitions from the Council to be married as soon as possible.

So I began my movement into the larger community. Starting with the closest towns, I visited with rabbis and elders regularly. I wanted to know them all, because soon I'd begin teaching and I wanted as many allies as I could garner.

And, against my desire, the proposals for marriage poured in; some weeks Mother had as many as three families contact her. Some families came back after a time and proposed a second daughter. Regardless of any of the maiden's wishes or mine, everyone obviously felt it'd be a coup for their daughter to marry the head of the David family. Unfortunately, not one of these good women felt right enough to even meet.

Periodically through the year, members of the community needed my council or help with disputes or other burdens. There were marriages, births, deaths, all the wonderful, grave, and natural human experiences, but it was generally a peaceful year. Nothing else of great incident occurred.

"Networking is the bedrock of success and the surest way for business to be done. This has been true for eons. If you're not networking, your interests will not thrive."

- Yeshua son of Joseph -

67 · Rosemary and Cinder

Life might have quietly continued like this for some time, until one day I was walking by the Sea of Galilee toward Capernaum. Through a grove of trees I saw a woman standing with one hand on a tree and the other holding a loose-brimmed hat. Her gown ruffled seductively in the breeze and I was instantaneously mesmerized.

I walked toward her. She cocked her head to the right. "James?" she asked.

"No, not I," I said with some curiosity.

She said, "Ah, you must be his brother I've heard mentioned?"

I wondered who she was and how she knew my brother. "That's me, yes. My name is Yeshua." I didn't stand too close or reach out in friendship, as it wasn't socially acceptable in many circles for a man to reach toward a woman. "I saw you standing here and wondered at your lovely hat." Yes, I could stretch the truth from time to time in an effort to be polite.

"Ah, I see, my hat is a great mystery to many," she said in a wry tone that might have made a lesser man feel foolish. She stood unyielding in her gaze and not offering another word, testing me.

I was intrigued. I smiled and said, "May I ask your name on this lovely afternoon?"

"You may. You look so much like your brother, but you're taller."

"He and I do bear a strong resemblance."

"Well, Tall Man, I'm Priestess Miriam of I's A'set Re." I believe she expected me to know her name and I could tell she wanted me to falter in her presence. I didn't.

"It's a pleasure to meet you, Miriam. Is there anything I can do for you today? I'm in no hurry and the day is young."

"Hmm," She looked me up and down, "You don't recognize me now that you hear my name?"

"Please, forgive me if I should. I've been away from Galilee for many years, only recently returned and... well... I'm unfamiliar with people and events others know intimately." I held my stance and looked her directly in the eye.

"I see," she said, her tone incredulous.

"I was merely a youth when I left many years ago."

"Well, you're not a youth now, Tall Man."

I bowed my head and resumed my gaze. "My offer stands."

"I knew from the start that he had experiences and abilities that set him apart from his community. He presented himself by manner of dress and adherence to ritual as a non-orthodox Jewish man, but his thoughts and subtle personal manner were not Hebraic at all."

- Miriam wife of Yeshua -

"I'm collecting rosemary and cinder." She said, "You're welcome to help me find some." I was delighted to have a reason to continue our conversation.

"Alright, but you'll have to help me. I've no idea what to look for."

Miriam laughed and if I hadn't been enchanted before, I was now. We spent the better part of the afternoon wandering among the trees, chatting about nothing of importance until she found her desired rosemary and cinder. I'd been no help at all in her quest, but I confess I wasn't working at it very hard. I was mesmerized, delighting in the conversation and in her presence.

When we were about to part on the road, she to walk back toward Magdala and I to continue toward Capernaum, I asked, "Please forgive my forward nature. You haven't mentioned a family. Are you married or otherwise betrothed?"

Her eyes narrowed as she stepped a foots-width closer to me. "I'm a priestess. I'm not allowed to marry."

"Then, may I ask, are you free to see me again?"

"And what would make you think I'd want to see you again? Even though you offered, you've been no help to me today."

"I take exception to that as more than once I heard you laugh, and what could be more useful than the company of one who can make you laugh?"

"You have an odd view of the world, Tall Man." She paused a moment, smiled, then said, "Yes, I'd be free to see you again."

"I'll be coming back this way in three days. I can meet you."

"Where," she sputtered, "here on the road?"

"Wherever you choose will be my pleasure."

She gave me directions to her home in Magdala. As I turned to leave, I felt a strange twinge in my stomach. I didn't want to walk away, but I did, one foot in front of the other until I was certain she must be long gone in the other direction. I turned to look and she was still looking toward me. My heart jumped a beat and for the second time in my life, my heart was roped by a woman.

"For me it wasn' love at first sight. Lust yes, but not love. That took time."
- Miriam wife of Yeshua -

68 · Dispelling Shadows

Three days later, after completing my business in Capernaum, I was once again on the road, this time to Magdala. When I passed the grove where I met Miriam, I was called to stop and visit with our shadows. So often, shadows grabbed me and I knew I had to dispel them.

The shadows of that day with Miriam were delightful. They filled my heart with joy of a kind that I so rarely knew. But I learned long ago that, joyful or not, it's best not to leave a trail of emotional energy behind me; a trail that could pull me into the past. Memories can be wonderful when visited by design, but remembrance of the past when unbidden has the unfortunate effect of coloring a person's now with thoughts and emotions that are no longer valid, leading to emotional imbalance.

I soaked up the joy that I'd relished and did as I knew I had to and energetically dissipated the shadows. Within moments, the grove was again but a grove filled with fruit trees, grasshoppers, and silence.

At my age, most men of my creed had been married for ten years or more. Here I was, unmarried, despite everyone's urging. They were becoming short with my unmarried status. Unless a Jewish man committed himself to life as a monk, it was his solemn religious duty to marry and produce children. Even though I had the excuse of being away for such an extended period, they felt that I should've rectified the situation by now by accepting one of the many proposals made to my family.

And I knew there was a rumor circulating that I'd ruined myself to marriage by wantonly engaging in erotic activities in the east. If the tongue-waggers only knew just how untrue that was. I still bore the emotional scars from the incidents I laid myself waste to experience.

I was the head of my family. If military forces hadn't deposed my family before my birth, I'd now be king. As it stood, I was a prince and, while they couldn't force me, they applied pressure, making life uncomfortable.

I didn't know where I'd find the woman for me, but I wasn't content following the status quo. I had a mission, knowledge, and experiences that set me apart. I loved my brethren, but in the area of establishing a marriage, they didn't understand me.

I was on the road to visit a woman I had emotional designs for. I felt compelled to pursue a deeper understanding of who she was. I was resolute to

"It may seem a cliché at this point to hear yet another teacher say, 'You must live in the present moment.' I assure you, you've heard it so many times because it is foundational to your growth. Take it in and make it so, and sooner is better than later."

- Yeshua son of Joseph -

continue to Magdala where I hoped this woman would give me a bit more of her time.

69 · Facing the White Tiger

I arrived at Magdala by early afternoon. I followed Miriam's directions to her home. It was a large, two-story building; a rarity most country people couldn't afford. Construction of multiple stories was an expensive engineering task. The home overlooked the lake and lush greenery surrounded it. A man was working in the yard and I called to him, "Excuse me friend, might I find Miriam here?"

"She's the Mistress of this house. Are you here on business?"

I suddenly realized that she was a woman of wealth. It hit me like a hard fist and I almost doubled over on the spot. In all my daydreams about Miriam in the last three days, I hadn't considered that she might be a woman of wealth. I answered, "The Priestess invited me to join her today."

"I'll have one of her maidens ask after you. Come into the shelter and wait."

I stepped through the gate and waited under the arbor. Hearing that she was wealthy enough to also have multiple maidens, I almost regretted following through. Almost.

A maiden came from the house. She seemed a gentle woman with a pleasant demeanor. "You must be Yeshua. The Priestess asks you to come in." She motioned me forward.

I entered and found myself instantly transported to another time and place. The odors and decorations were exactly reminiscent of my travels in Egypt as a boy. I was almost dizzy with the emotional rapture of the memory.

"Please sit down," the maiden said, "Priestess will be with you presently."

I sat on a bench and allowed the scents to remind me of traveling with Joseph. I let my mind roam free for a few minutes as I let go of my initial shock at the obvious wealth of this woman and allowed my heart to carry me away.

It wasn't that wealth intimidated me – far from it. I couldn't imagine that an accomplished woman of wealth would care one iota for one such as me. My family had stature, and I was, as I've said, a prince, but I didn't hold myself that way. In my mind, I was a humble, albeit enigmatic, Nazorean, and there was no reason to mask my intentions; I was attracted to this woman.

After a few minutes, the Unseen appeared. The one with the long beard spoke first, 'Are you prepared?'

'For what?' I said with my mind.

'For temptation.'

'What do you mean?'

The one with the long neck spoke next, 'Don't be naive. She'll tempt you.'

"From time to time before I met him, I grew wistful for that which I saw others possess: the emotional closeness, the yearning for another's physical proximity. But the yearning never lasted more than an afternoon, at most."
- Miriam wife of Yeshua -

'Tempt me to what? I'm already enamored of her.'

The long-necked one continued, 'Don't be naive. She's an accomplished seductress, and she'll have you, here, today, on the floor if you're not careful.'

'Please... I can't see that she'd even want me... you're ahead of yourselves.'

The flying one spoke next, 'Don't be naive. We see more than you do, Bit. Be wise and watch yourself or you'll regret this day.'

Suddenly from beside me a familiar voice sounded, "Tall Man, you bring Khusat with you?"

I stood and turned to face Miriam. When I saw her, a flush of passion jolted me. She was more beautiful and captivating than I remembered. "Hello Miriam... Khusat?"

"Beings outside our physical. You were talking with them when I entered." She turned and walked away from me. I was unguarded for this. Not one person had ever remarked upon those Unseen around me.

"How is it that you see these beings?"

"I'm a priestess, Tall Man, I see much." She turned to face me again and beckoned me into the adjacent room. "How is it that you, a Hebrew, consort with Khusat? I've never seen that before."

I followed into the other room thinking about her question, but my thoughts were interruptible and not well formed. Her eyes didn't leave mine and for several minutes, neither one of us spoke or moved. I realized that what my companions said was correct, I was being tempted.

I turned from Miriam and took a seat. "Then you must also see that I'm not like other men."

Miriam stammered, "I... I do, Tall Man. But I'm grateful you accepted my invitation. It's pleasant to see you today." She sat down near me, on the same bench.

"It's pleasant to see you. I've been looking forward to it," and that began our afternoon. If seduction had been on her mind when I arrived, she didn't act on it further, but we laughed and spent time getting to know one another better.

I liked her. I was captured by her depth of spirit, by her beauty, and by her love of language and artisanry. She showed me the artifacts she kept on hand. I was impressed by her ability to speak of history with such knowing; in my experience in this part of the world, only men studied history, and then only cursorily as related to their religion.

At one point, she showed me a flute. She was astonished when I began to play. She was familiar with the tune I played and sang along. Her voice enraptured me. It felt magical to make music together.

The afternoon passed too quickly and I was surprised when I noticed the shadows of twilight begin. "Miriam, I have to go. It's almost dark and I have to get home."

"You don't have to leave now. You can stay here if you like... leave in the morning."

I sighed, and said, "Miriam, I like you very much. Again, forgive me I'm a

"I was unaccustomed to men standing eye-to-eye to me in strength of self. And subsequent to the institution of my formal priesthood in Palestina, I hadn't met any man that could resist my spells. That is, until I met Ye'sHUa."

- Miriam wife of Yeshua -

forward person. I've enjoyed our afternoon together like none other."

"I've enjoyed our time together too, Yeshua."

My heart jumped that she finally used my given name. "But," I said, "I can't stay here with you. I'm tempted by you, and I'm not available for temporal pleasures. I hope we can see each other another day."

"Stay, we can have supper, I won't tempt you tonight."

"You already tempt me. I must leave now."

"Are you afraid of me?" she asked.

"No, I don't fear you."

"Then, does the Hebrew in you judge me?"

"No, Miriam. I have no judgment of you. I think highly of you. More than you know." I sighed, momentarily wishing I were a different person. I said, "But I know who I am, and I'm not available for what other men might grab. That experience isn't what I'm after. I yearn for something deeper, something more lasting."

"I see." She turned away from me, "I'm not free to give anything lasting."

"Freedom is a gift you give yourself. No one can hold you when your heart says otherwise."

Without hesitation, she said, "Then I suppose this is goodbye, Tall Man. I'm glad to know you."

I suddenly had to ask, "How do you know my brother?"

Miriam turned to me again, "Why does that matter?"

"I'm just curious," I replied.

"We had some business together."

"I see," I said, but of course, I didn't. I'd have to ask James for more information. "Thank you for the afternoon," I said as I turned to leave, but her voice caught me.

"You never answered my question."

I turned back, "What question?"

"Why do you consort with Khusat?"

I stopped, not knowing what to do. Should I share what I am? What I came back to accomplish? I just looked at her.

She asked again, "Tell me please, I want to know."

"My life isn't what it seems."

"What it seems… is that you're no mere rabbi. Tell me please, what are you?"

I wasn't reconciled to giving her my truth, especially if this would be our parting. My mission was sacred, not for indiscriminant gossip. "Miriam, I'm not…"

"Yeshua, please?" And for the first time in our two visits, she touched me. When her fingers touched my forearm, my head began to spin. The room around me slowly melted away. I was standing on that platform in the valley of my heart with the Master at Insa'alet. Behind me was the metal beast. Before me was the sacred White Tiger. I had two choices, I could turn and climb into the metal beast and leave this place for good, or I could embrace the White Tiger. As foretold, I

"At first I was intrigued, I thought him amusing and sexually provocative. By the end of our second meeting, however, I was compelled to a strong desire for him."

- Miriam wife of Yeshua -

knew it was possible that the White Tiger would eat me, swallow me, take my life and enjoy the taking. It was also possible that the White Tiger was my future, my desired and necessary companion. Was I ready to risk everything?

I glanced at the metal beast and it glowed in readiness to carry me to my destiny with dispassion. I looked at the White Tiger; she bowed her head and I felt in my heart that she wouldn't eat me. So I embraced her. My arms wrapped gently but firmly around her soft white body. And before I knew it, I was kissing Miriam.

That kiss. It filled me with feelings I'd never had before; feelings that were deeper and more passionate than any lust a body could muster. My arms wrapped around her shoulders and I didn't want to let go. "Miri..." I had trouble speaking, "I..." the words caught in my throat. She looked at me; her body pressed firmly against mine. She said nothing.

What could I say? I wanted to kiss her again, more than anything I wanted to. I finally said, "Please say this isn't the end."

A tear formed in the corner of her eye. "I'm not clear... not sure... what this is," she stammered.

We stood in each other's arms, not knowing what to do. "Promise me we'll see each other again," I pleaded.

"I'm not able to give you what you want. I belong to the Goddess. If you want more than friendship, you have to leave me. Go, walk away."

"I can't do that." With all my strength, I held on to the White Tiger. "Promise me we'll see each other again." She was silent. I pressed, "Promise me."

Miriam softened, "Yes, of course. I'll see you again."

"Then I must leave now or I'll do something I'll regret." I placed my hands on each side of her face and gently touched my lips to her forehead. "I'll come back in one week." I let go of her, turned, and walked through the door.

As I closed the door behind me, I heard Miriam say, "Be careful on the road, Tall Man, I'll be waiting."

I was shaken, how could I not be? I was confused and unclear. I could hear the Temple Master's voice, "Make your choice wisely." Well, I made a choice, but in a moment of passion; a moment I had to trust now, when every ounce of my being told me to be afraid of it.

This happened once before with Seleya. I made a choice in a moment of fevered passion, and it turned out very badly. But one thing I did know, the past is a poor measure of the present. The present takes care of itself if you trust your truth as your heart speaks it. So I kept walking. I was on the road to home and as long as I kept to the path, I knew that before long, things would become clear.

"I was married to the Goddess and my identity as a priestess was instilled in me quite skillfully at an early age. That role was indoctrinated into my psyche so thoroughly that any thought of opposition to it would quickly prove to be silenced from within."

- Miriam wife of Yeshua -

70 · Rumors, Rumors

My encounter with Miriam left me with unspent energy. I walked high into the hills to find some sanctuary. Consequently, I returned to the family compound midmorning. I was still confused and unsettled, but the business at Capernaum had gone well, so at the least I had good news to relay.

When I walked in, James was sitting with two monks from the monastery at Carmel. Their faces weren't familiar, but I recognized their clothing.

"Welcome home," James said, "I'll greet you when my business is done." I bowed my head and walked toward the back, hoping to find Mother. She wasn't there, so I grabbed some fruit and bread and sat in the courtyard to catch my breath and clear my head.

James found me about to bite into an apple. He pulled me out of my seat for a hug. "Welcome home, Bit."

More than anyone else, James made me feel at home. "Good to see you, Brother," I said.

He inquired, "How did the meeting go?"

"Very well," I laughed, "they were happy overall. I feel we have some strong allies in Capernaum."

James sat and asked me to do the same. "I've received some disturbing news," he said.

"Tell me," I said as I bit into the apple.

"The brothers informed me about a rumor they heard."

I rolled my eyes. The brothers always seemed to have some drama to report. "What else is new?" I muttered.

"Well, they say you were seen accompanying the Priestess Miriam."

The speed of the rumor mill was surprising even to me. How could such news travel so quickly? It'd only been a few days since I met her. "I was in the company of Miriam," I said as I took another bite.

James's jaw dropped. "Why would you do such a thing?" he exclaimed.

"Why is it of such consequence? She's a delightful woman."

James shouted, "Don't be so naive!" I was annoyed at being repeatedly accused of being naive lately, even though it was probably true.

"James, you're going to have to explain, because I'm perplexed."

James proceeded to tell me in detail of Miriam's exploits with many high-ranking men. How she would extract, and use, sensitive information during intimate encounters to get what she wanted. She had power in the Roman Council, in the Samaritan aristocracy, and in the Sanhedrin as a result. I listened intently, but I was numb to any lasting effect.

"You don't understand," I added, "I enjoyed being with her. I'm enamored of her."

"You're what?" James exclaimed, "You're… what? How can you be so stupid?" The vehemence of James words dumbfounded me. In an overtly accusatory tone he demanded, "Have you slept with her?"

"That's none of your business," I said.

He sputtered, "It most certainly is my business if we're partners on this journey."

I stared at him, unable to understand the real issue. Was James also attracted to Miriam? Was he jealous? Was he afraid of the wagging tongues of the rabbinic monks, whose propensity to gossip obviously surpassed any? "What's the real issue here?" I asked with sincerity.

James stopped to compose himself. He leaned back in his seat, but he couldn't take his eyes off me. "I really thought you'd tell me it wasn't so."

"Believe me it was innocent. I met her on the road. I had no idea who she was, but she was delightful to be with and we passed the afternoon hunting rosemary."

James stared at me as if he was waiting for the next shoe to drop, "That was it?"

"Well it would've been," I licked my lips from the juice of the apple, "but yesterday I saw her again at her home. We spent the afternoon together."

"So you did sleep with her!" James' anger was clear.

"That really isn't your business," I said, "but I assure you my covenant is unbroken." I couldn't believe I was having this conversation.

"How can I believe you knowing what she's like?"

"How can you believe me? Me?" I reeled from the notion that my brother would think I'd lie to him. "You think I'd lie to you?"

James countenance softened, "No, Bit… you never have. But you don't know what kind of woman you're dealing with."

I sighed, "Joseph taught us this: Every businessman, every politician, uses whatever skills he has to gain confidences. She uses what she has." I paused contemplating my words. Grinning, I said, "and I can see she's been very successful."

James looked at me with distrust. "You've become enchanted."

"Yes, I have, but not through any means outside myself, I assure you." I looked at my half-eaten apple, "What about you, James? What's your interest in this woman?"

"I have no interest in this woman."

I took another bite, "Obviously you do. At the very least, you have an interest that she have nothing to do with me."

James sat back, his mouth shut. He was quiet for many minutes. I was committed to James. I'd sit here as long as it took to find a center between us. Either of us may need to listen, or speak, but above all, we both had to hold onto our love for the other.

James was the next one to talk, "I apologize. You're right. I've asked you questions I've no business asking. Please forgive me."

"James, I'm not like you. I'm not committed to spending my days without a

"As a brother he was too forgiving. James and Jude could do no wrong. He respected them as products of Joseph's and Mary's training and appreciated their views even when opposed to his own. That said, he was correct in assuming he could trust them and give them independence in their missions. They were good men both."

- Miriam wife of Yeshua -

wife. I want a companion. You have to accept this." I set the apple core on the bench next to me, promising to take it to my favorite goat later.

Again, we sat in silence for a time.

James said, "You're right. I have an uncommon interest in this woman, just as I have an uncommon interest in you, Bit"

I considered James words. I asked, "How do you know her? At first she thought I might be you."

"A few years ago I did some trading for the brothers at Salt. I negotiated a trade for scribing parchments with her temple. I had to negotiate with Miriam."

"Ha!" I blurted, "That must've been a chore!"

James smiled, "It wasn't easy, yes." We both laughed and I felt the tension between us drop.

"Bit, to her credit, she did nothing to use or seduce me… or do anything else unreasonable in my presence." James' face turned dark, "But I confess; after many hours with her over several days, I wish she had. That's the effect her presence had on me." He looked at his lap, "I feel guilty about that."

"Don't be hard on yourself. You're human." Our conversation again hovered in a silence that lasted several minutes. I said, "Thank you for telling me. I appreciate your candor."

"Tell me you're not going to see her again," he implored.

"I can't do that. I'm seeing her in six days."

James hung his head. "I know you. If you want her, you'll be relentless in your pursuit." He let out a heavy sigh, "This shouldn't surprise me. You and she are a lot alike."

My heart jumped when he said those words, that she and I were alike. It was as I felt too, and again, I was reminded that, right or wrong I had to trust my choice. "You're right," I said, "I believe she's my White Tiger, and I will pursue her."

"As you know, I was devoted to the monastic lifestyle. There were very few times I experienced lust. The fact that one of those times centered on the woman my brother fell in love with, was an ongoing source of guilt and pain for me. When she subsequently moved into our home, I had to find healing from that desire quickly. When I finally allowed her to be in the proper place as my sister, that initial lust turned to love and it never bothered me again; I was devoted to her."

- James brother of Yeshua -

71 · Mary's Heart

Mother wasn't home that morning because she was meeting with a family, yet another prospect for marriage.

She was reluctant to tell me about these women. She knew they weren't right for me. She remembered the bond that grew between her and Joseph. Once they took up the mantle of marriage, their relationship was beyond compare in its joy, its intimacy, and its strength. She wanted all that and more for me. But none of these young women seemed to have the strength of character, the intellect, or the tenacity to follow me through the difficulties she knew I'd face. Nonetheless, eventually I'd have to take a wife. There was no way to stop the tide of social pressure.

I resolved to pursue Miriam before Mother came home. Of course, I didn't know Miriam well yet, I didn't even know if I could persuade her to consider me. But, I'd made my choice and I had to see it through just as foretold by the Temple Master all those years ago. And I now glimpsed a shadow of what he meant when he said I'd need to risk everything. Given all I'd learned about Miriam from my discussion with James, the risks were becoming abundantly clear.

What I'd give to sit in the Masters quarters again, walking hand in hand in the valley of my heart, hearing his sage words. But the yearning to be with him physically was born of my human self, not my master self. My master self knew time and space were merely illusions created to give us a common ground to experience life. I could visit with him anytime I chose.

Still the human in me desired his physicality; I wanted that common experience of closeness that space and time provide. Some of my most fortunate of life's blessings were the wise mentors that surrounded me. With one notorious exception, every part of my journey had been accompanied by older men of great character to guide and give me root; starting of course with Joseph.

When Mary got home, she greeted me warmly, but with a pinched look that meant she had news she didn't want to impart.

"Before you say anything," I said, "I have something to tell you." I took her hands and sat her down with me. "I've chosen a woman to pursue for marriage."

She was startled, "Who is it?"

I shook my head, "If I tell you who, you'll think I'm crazy."

"You must tell me," Mother insisted, "I need to talk with her family."

"No, she has no family to talk to. And actually, there's little chance she'll be persuaded."

Mother countered, "Yeshua, what maiden wouldn't swoon at the opportunity to marry you?"

"She's not a maiden."

Mother blinked. I saw her mind searching. "She's a widow?" she asked.

"No, she's a priestess."

Mother was speechless. I saw thoughts jumping through her brain. 'She's not

Hebrew?' 'Where did he meet her?' 'What's her name?' 'Where does she live?' 'What does she look like?' 'How old is she?' The thoughts went on and on... I knew these questions would be answered in time, when her mind was settled enough to ask them...

But suddenly, she surprised me. Her thoughts stopped and her face bore a thin, yet exquisite smile, as she placed one hand on my cheek. With the other, she lifted my hand and placed it over her heart. "My son, you've a grave mission that I've supported all your life. It's right and it's time that you find a companion of worth." Her eyes remained fixed on mine. "She'll have to be strong and wise, able to shoulder the weight of the world you'll not be able to carry on your own." She paused a moment, considering her words carefully. "If you've found her, then I'm happy. If she's your choice, let me come, when it's time, to bring her into the family. It'll be my honor to welcome her."

Relief and joy filled me. There was no greater validation for my choice. If it settled this quickly into the heart of my mother, then it was a good choice. Only one challenge remained, and it was a big one; to convince Miriam it was a good choice for her as well.

"If Mary had been a lesser woman, not adherent to 'the way of peace' herself, there could've been great difficulty between us, any of us in combination. Mary, however, was a strong and intelligent woman who supported her son's mission one hundred percent. The love between them was inviolable. If Mary ever saw or suspected that a desire or need of hers might conflict with his marriage, Mary would withdraw her request or urging. And there were times I would do the same. In this way, Mary and I covertly kept Ye'sHUa from having to choose between us. I don't know if he knew that while he was embodied. If he did, he didn't let on to me."

- Miriam wife of Yeshua -

72 · Proceeding

By the time I arrived at Miriam's, I was resolute regarding my motives. I'd met with her a mere two times, but those meetings overwhelmed me with a powerful sense of destiny intertwined with passionate desire. Since then, I'd heard fervent accounts of her exploits.

My deepest concern didn't regard Miriam at all. It was whether I'd remain resolute to my vows. Until a mutual decision was forged, I was at risk. The White Tiger had the ability to make of me a most pleasurable meal.

I made weekly trips to Magdala. The rumormongers found a rich sack of mulch from those visits. But one thing was certain: during these months, I was her only escort. She directed her maidens to turn everyone else away. Apparently, something was happening with the Priestess that wasn't business as usual.

At first, I stayed for the day, leaving at dusk. That changed to leaving after supper, but it didn't take long for those short visits to prove unsatisfactory. I began to stay overnight for a second day. My feelings for her deepened rapidly and my desire to make her my wife remained steadfast. On most visits, Miriam made her sexual desires known to me, and each time I said no. She became increasingly frustrated by my resistance, but I was resolute to stay adherent to my rabbinic covenant.

One evening I confessed my ambition for marriage. She was adamant that marriage wasn't an option. When I pressed the issue, she threw me out. I walked home with a sad and heavy heart.

James wasn't happy to see me sad, but he was overjoyed to think that this foolishness might be over. In his worldview, we had a lot of work to do and we'd better get on with it.

Mother wasn't so quick to dismiss the matter.

Three weeks later, a rider from Magdala arrived. He brought a letter from Miriam and said he'd wait for a reply. I went to my quarters to be alone with her words. The letter read:

> "Dear Yeshua,
> "I'm beside myself with grief that I've sent you from my

"After a time, when he presented himself to me as a marriage suitor, I was angered. As I've said, being a wife wasn't a role I sought. The morays of my community afforded me ample opportunity for sexual fulfillment without encumbrance."

- Miriam wife of Yeshua -

life. I lie awake at night feeling your heart in chaos and I can't stop my heart from feeling the same. I've allowed my temper to create a chasm that I now must hope to bridge. You didn't deserve my abrupt dismissal.

"I write now hoping you can forgive me and consent to visit with me once more. We're both in sorrow and that's a crime only we can remedy. I invite you back to my home. If you can see your way to be here, I will welcome you with an open heart.

"Please indicate to the rider your consent. I await your arrival. Please be quick.

"Miriam"

My heart was not consoled as I considered her request. I wanted to be in her presence, but I was concerned that it'd be a never-ending quest. She'd apologized for her outburst. And yet, she hadn't acknowledged the proposal on the table. I wasn't willing to let that go unmentioned.

I wrote a reply:

"My dear Miriam,

"Yes, my heart is in chaos. The lack of you in my life is unwelcome. Staying away has been in respect to your wishes.

"Of course I forgive your outburst. I understand that what I ask of you cannot be easy to contemplate, but contemplate it I must ask you to do. With every bit of my soul, I want you near me for the rest of my days. Nothing less than a relationship consecrated by a sacred commitment is acceptable to me.

"Your road is your road. I can't tell you what's right for you. But I can tell you what feels right for me. What feels more than right is you in my arms, married.

"I'll come to your home again, but only if you consider my proposal. Perhaps if we each take a step toward the middle, a bridge will be built, and we can once again be blessed by the other's joyful presence.

"I await your reply.

"Yeshua"

I took the note to the rider. Mother came out and handed him another note as well. I was about to ask what she was doing, but she lifted her hand and cut the air between us in a motion I knew to respect. I closed my mouth, averted my eyes, and made no inquiry.

As the rider rode from view, I walked from the compound. I walked for hours, propelled by thoughts making nests in my mind. I'd spent three weeks yearning for a chance to sit with Miriam again. But when the chance came for that, I rebutted the request. Was this arrogance; some need to have her only on my terms? Was this the art of negotiation; parlaying desire in hope of seeing her soften? Or was this insanity; stubbornly holding some social convention above my clear and present feelings? I couldn't discern the truth of it; perhaps it was all three. So I sat beneath a plum tree until the gentle wind swept my mind empty.

Three days later, the rider brought a surprising reply from Miriam. It read:

> "Yeshua,
>
> "Bring your proposal and make your case. If the Goddess is willing to let you speak, I must be willing to listen. If rejecting your proposal is the only thing that keeps us apart, I'd be a fool not to consider it.
>
> "I'm eager to see you. Please hurry.
>
> "Miriam"

I sent a note back saying I'd be there within hours. To the family, I made no excuse. I didn't explain my trip and I refused to say when I'd return home. In my mind, there was no need coming home again until I knew how Miriam and I were going to proceed.

73 · Moments of Truth

There come moments in life when our strength of character is tested beyond the pale. Our personal mettle is subjected to intense pressures, our response to which will either break us or make us. Sometimes to avoid breaking, we must hold without willingness to budge from what's absolute in us. Other times, we must bend to the point of discomfort to avoid a break that would be beyond repair. Knowing which response is correct is the substance of wisdom.

I arrived at Miriam's in the early evening. She greeted me at the gate herself, a consideration I'd never witnessed her give to anyone. She was soft, inviting, and altogether alluring. She listened to my proposal. She gave me her dilemma. I gave her mine. This time, she held our respective difficulties with care and respect and that meant a lot to me. We spent the evening talking about our dreams and desires until we innocently fell asleep in each other's arms.

During sleep I found myself at the precious Temple of Man. Man'wa was holding something for me to see. When I approached, I saw a fallen deer in one hand and a crying boy in the other.

"What are you showing me?" I asked.

"Issa, who's the boy?"

I looked again and saw my young visage on his face. I said, "It's me. Why am I crying?"

"Who, or what, is the deer?" Man'wa asked.

I looked closely at the deer. Its neck curved back in death. I stared into its eyes until I realized, "It's also me." My brain tried to unravel this image until I remembered that my brain had no power for this task. I had to engage my heart and ask my knowing for the truth of this puzzle.

"How did the deer die?" I asked.

"Very good, the deer was brought down by a thought."

I said, "A thought?"

Man'wa moved his hands to his mouth and pursed his lips in a move I'd seen

"When I found myself in love with Ye'sHUa, I was surprised to be in love at all. The mysteries of romance and partnership were not jewels on a crown I sought to wear."

- Miriam wife of Yeshua -

hundreds of times. As I searched for my answer, I saw the boy strike a boulder with an axe, creating sharp, stone shards that flew in many directions. One of these shards struck the deer in the heart and fell him in his tracks.

But the deer was me. I looked again. I saw my current slavish adherence to dogmatic convention, a state I promised myself I'd avoid when I came home. I looked at the axe striking the boulder and saw the innocent in me frustrated, trying to force my desire into submission by pounding it into the matter of the stone. It was a violent action that had no place of life in me. The violence rose from denying my true heart's desire. True heart's desire cannot be reformed, compressed, or cut into any shape other than it presents of itself. True heart's desire can only be accepted or rejected.

My actions made a mockery of my true heart's desire. I was making demands of the woman I loved that were born of dogma; born of the old. I knew I had to be present in what was truth right here, right now to find a clear path.

I saw myself at the Combs staring across the field at Seleya being loaded into a cart for transport to her unwanted life. Her eyes were filled with remorse and fear. I remembered the pain in my heart as I felt impotent to do anything: impotent to save her, impotent in my life. I remembered how this very thought of helplessness shattered my sense of self and left me stricken.

That is, until the Temple Master took me to the valley of my heart and presented me with a new heart's desire. I was introduced to the White Tiger. She stood in front of me and I looked deep into the bright green eyes of compassion she candidly turned in my direction.

I awoke, my arms innocently draped around my beloved, and my dilemma was truthfully clear where it had been mistakenly clear the night before. The actuality of my dilemma was in accepting my true heart's desire as it presented itself, without conditions. When I opened my eyes and beheld Miriam, I was no longer me looking at her; I was one of us looking at the other.

Casting aside ill-placed adherence to dogma and filled with discomfort, I bent the fabric of my being to meet the moment. I embraced Miriam in a new way. I set my precious rabbinic covenant aside in deference to my heart's deepest desire and I invited to me the White Tiger, this time with passion and vigor. I let myself surrender and we made love to one another with abandon. I let this true heart's desire know that I wasn't backing down; I was embracing her with every bit of my soul. We folded our bodies together until I lost myself in the oneness of us. I saw our hearts entwine and become one heart. I felt our minds stitch together and become one mind.

As foretold by the Temple Master all those years before, I risked everything for a chance to receive my greatest gift. I risked losing my position as priest. I risked tainting my soul's mission, something I held as more sacred than anything of

"I knew from third party testimony that he was fiery of speech and thought, the leader of his people, and of royal blood. I could see without question that he was sexually handsome and his body was unusually tempered."
- Miriam wife of Yeshua -

this earth. I risked denigrating my position in the family. I risked losing the respect of the entire community I lived in.

And I risked abject rejection from Miriam. She still had the power to say 'no' to our partnership, or worse, and that was the deepest, sharpest point of risk I incurred. If the White Tiger decided I'd make a tasty meal, I'd just served myself up, bare-boned on a gilded platter.

74 · To Be or Not to Be – Married

Something fundamental shifted in me. Miriam was now my sacred partner. It was truth even if we proved unable or unwilling to present that truth to the world. In me, it was absolute. And by the time the sun was at its apex in our sky, it was clear by Miriam's countenance, there'd be no meal served from my bones that day.

Miriam was changed; she was buoyant, joyful. The engaging woman I fell in love with wasn't comparable to the woman beside me now. The Goddess was more present in her than at any time I'd yet seen. There's no way to say this except to say it outright and without apology or equivocation: for the first time in my life, I looked upon the heart of a woman that was a clear match in divine presence and power to my own. But the earthly question remained, would she marry me?

I wanted to continue to share her bed, and if it was to be, I wanted her to bear my children. I felt it an imperative to consecrate our relationship. But, regardless of how that consecration bore out, any children we produced wouldn't be considered Hebrew. Even if Miriam converted to Judaism, which I wouldn't expect, the children wouldn't be born of the house of David. Therefore, they couldn't inherit my station. I didn't agree with these unnatural customs, and just as I was unhappy with many of the customs of the time, they comprised a reality I had to accept.

We could marry with a liberal rabbi. We could marry in the Egyptian temple. We could run to Samaria, or Moab, or Syria and be married of some other tradition. There appeared no easy path. The only thing that would amend my plans would be Miriam declining.

Miriam had her own internal battles to fight. She was the High Priestess of Galilee. That position was a great honor and one she was born to fulfill. She was good at it and the temple was successful. By consequence, she was a woman of wealth and power.

She'd retain her personal wealth and power if she married me, but she'd relinquish her position in the temple and her standing in the community. If she married me, stepping down would be required, because priestesses were forbidden to marry. Not because of a prohibition to sex, Miriam's people had a different relationship with sexuality than the Hebrews. Rather, the prohibition was to the blending of allegiances. Her allegiance as Priestess was only to the Goddess, not to any family or partner. To marry me, she'd have to walk away from the social structure she was born to lead.

No part of me required her to change any belief born of her service to the Goddess. It would be righteous arrogance to do so. However, in believing herself able to fulfill the Goddess' desire in only one way, she'd preclude herself from creating a partnership with me.

What Miriam discovered on that day of reckoning, however, was that her allegiance had shifted without her conscious bidding. Her heart had already given over to our union. And so, to my delight, the White Tiger announced she'd accept my proposal.

Putting faith in the strength of our feelings for each other, and throwing caution onto the compassionate waters of fate, Miriam and I would walk the rest of our days together as one.

I spent the next two days with my beloved in Magdala. For each hour of joy and delight, we encountered an hour peppered with fear. We helped each other smooth the emotional edges and dispel the anxiety as best we could, but it was soon clear that if we were going to be married, we had to return to our lives and begin preparations.

As I was preparing to head home, Miriam said she wanted to marry in the Hebrew tradition and, if the family agreed, live at the family compound. I was overjoyed. She had fear about the family welcoming her. But to her, it was a small matter on our road ahead.

She shared a lucid vision the Goddess gave her the night before. It was of Miriam and me, walking through neighboring kingdoms, speaking to large numbers of people, liberating souls from a life without a clear connection to source. She saw us embrace each other in equality and be happy for several years.

But then she saw herself walking a long and lonely road without me in a foreign land. There were young children at her side and the Goddess told her it would be the beginning of her signature work in the world. That while I was with her, Miriam and I would lay the foundation for my mission. And that when I left, she would see that we'd laid the foundation for her work too.

She asked the Goddess if I was going to die young, but she was mute. I remembered the vision Joseph had of me, generated on the day I was born, and the cryptic message of my losing all signs of life, but transcending death and living.

I listened to Miriam while she took in my reaction, but it was a short one. I had no time to waste contemplating my own demise when I was certain it was but an illusion. So I asked her to wait for my word and I set out toward home.

"When I sent Ye'sHUa away in anger, for the first time in my life I felt sickening pain from possible loss. Pain over the prospect of losing his presence permanently. It was then that I realized that marriage wouldn't be a useless institution; it would be an external reflection of an internal truth. My truth."
- Miriam wife of Yeshua -

75 · How Quickly a Day Can Change

That afternoon, I arrived home and something was wrong; not a soul was in sight. No one was attending to the crops or the animals. I finally found Rebekkah at home. She ran to me and grabbed my hands, "Yeshua, you're home!"

Her hands shook as I inquired, "What's wrong?"

She began to sob and I thought she might fall over, so I led her to sit, laying my hand on her shoulder. "I'm here for you."

She spoke in short snippets, "Yeshua... the news is... ghastly. Most of... they've gone... Sepphoris. I'm afraid... Jude's with them... James too..."

"Why have they gone to Sepphoris?" I asked, but she broke into sobs again, unable to calm herself enough to continue. I told her to stay put; that I would return.

I searched for other people, someone to help me piece this together. When I got to the storehouses, I found several women huddled in the granary, but my mother wasn't among them. I asked, "Why are you all here?" None spoke, except me, "Do you know that Rebekkah is alone in her home?"

One woman stood and said, "No, she shouldn't be alone. I'll get her." She left.

I sat on the ground and said, "I promise we'll get through this. I just got home and I don't know anything. Tell me, please." Several began to talk at once. The story tumbled out in pieces until I fit most of the events together.

This was indeed a dark day. Earlier, in Sepphoris, an altercation between a Roman soldier and a Jewish merchant ended with the soldier dead, stabbed by the merchant in self-defense by the merchant's story. However, the legionnaires didn't see it that way and flogged the merchant to death in a public spectacle. Tensions were high as the crowd turned violent. The resulting confrontation with the Roman Legion was bloody. The last report received counted as many as fifty Jewish people dead and the confrontation was still progressing.

We had family, friends, and associates in Sepphoris and the men of our compound left for the city to see if they could be of assistance. But it was a risky undertaking, as we knew too well; they could all be dead before the day was over. A contingent of women, including Mary, left with the children, headed for the safety of the monastery at Carmel.

This was a good plan, but I was surprised that these women hadn't gone with them. They said that if none returned in quick fashion from Sepphoris, someone should be here caring for the animals and crops. These women volunteered to stay and risk the exposure.

My people had lived through scattered bloodbaths at the hands of the Legion more than once in my lifetime. They were frightening times followed by periods of deep grief. My heart was heavy that we were in the midst of another purging.

Herod Antipas, the de-facto King of our land, did little to care for his own people. He was loath to work with the Romans to improve our living conditions. He was more interested in padding his pockets and breaching his faith with fresh concubines. So we suffered these cyclic tragedies, hoping for the day that we'd again govern ourselves. It was heading in the wrong direction, however, with factions of Zealots, homegrown warmongers, spreading their tomes of violence amongst us. I saw nothing good coming of it, only continued death and grief.

The news of Miriam and I had to wait. Now wasn't the time and I felt a momentary pang of guilt that I was bringing her into this mass of subjugation I called my people.

The question on the table now was what, if anything, I should do. Should I go to Sepphoris as well? Should I wait with these women for our loved ones return?

After careful consideration, I decided that regardless of my talents, one fact remained; I was their leader. If the Romans decided that the uprising could only be quelled by killing every Hebrew in Sepphoris, I shouldn't willingly walk into the slaughter. It was also noted that of the two of us, James and I, he was the better negotiator. If negotiation was in the works, he was more qualified to handle that task.

But secretly, there was one thing about me that couldn't be said of the others, my will could directly re-sculpt reality. I'd been given specific training to hone that will. Few outside my immediate family knew this, and even they didn't know the extent of this honing. But soon a day would come when I'd reveal it in a public forum. Was today that day?

"Perhaps because of the societal horrors and personal pains they periodically witnessed and experienced, the women of my community were as strong, probably stronger, than the men. Perhaps as a whole they didn't have the physical strength to till the soil as deeply as a farmhand, but they had the integral strength to hold weeping or dying brethren with greater force of love. The second form of strength is by far the most valuable to possess."

- James brother of Yeshua -

76 · Counting the Dead

I went to the cisterns to wash off the grime of travel. Before I was done, I heard a commotion from the road. James was walking at the head of a large party, and they were pulling two litters. James' countenance was clear; it was bad news.

I greeted the party. It was most of our men, returned, and a substantial number of brethren that needed safe shelter for a time. Many had bloody clothes either from helping others or from their own wounds. However, the litters were the hardest to look at. In one was one of our men with a broken leg. He'd be bedridden for some time, but he'd mend. The other litter, however, carried the slain corpses of two of our men. Both were good men I knew well, one with young children.

The wife of one of the slain came from the granary and, upon seeing his body, began wailing. The wife of the other was at Carmel with their children. They wouldn't find out until they got home. Still, our ears were continually assaulted by wails of grief as men trickled home with news about fallen loved ones.

Everyone around me this day was touched by death. I felt desperate to reweave a blanket of safety around these people I was charged with protecting. I couldn't feel as though I'd done enough. All of today's dead deserved to die old in their beds, not like this, cut down in their prime. I had to guard against feeling soul-sick for them and for the families they left behind. It was one thing to know the absolute truth of our eternal existence; it was quite another to afford oneself that comfort when surprised with loss.

We dealt with logistics: getting care for the wounded, finding adequate provisions for the visitors, and creating a place to grieve and care for the bodies of our slain. Once done, James and Jude joined me away from others hearing. I asked them for a full account.

They confided what they'd witnessed. It was a brutal day. Men and women slain, many in front of their children. Many of the men who'd been shouting at the soldiers during the flogging death of the merchant, were gathered and hung by the neck from the walls of the city.

James said he'd never seen so much blood and death in one place. Jude was shaking from the trauma of it. No regard had been paid to any fact other than that the person being gutted was Jewish. Unfortunately, that determination wasn't always made well. Together, they estimated that over 300 Jewish men, women, and children, along with a generous share of Samaritans, Greeks, and Syrians were killed, and many more were maimed and bleeding.

James managed to talk his way into the Legion compound and convince the Praetor to call the soldiers off their death orgy. His presence proved to be invaluable in stemming the tide of violence. He'd placed his life at risk for the community, both of my brothers had. I was sad that they were forced into that position, but proud of them as well. I said a prayer of appreciation for Joseph and felt his warm hand cup my face. I saw into the past to times like these when Joseph was in the shoes I wore now. His infinite steadiness, patience, and wisdom always carried us through. The vision lent me the confidence to continue.

James confided that he was worried for the state of relations with the Romans. That he was shocked by the flagrant bloodlust and brutality he witnessed. Jude said he didn't know it was possible for a man to gain pleasure from killing as much as he'd seen this day.

I asked James if he thought the violence was put to rest, or should we be prepared for a follow-on attack. He was more worried about Zealot retaliation than a simple continuation of Roman blood feasting. This would be especially true if the families of the hanged men weren't allowed to take their dead for interment preparations in a timely fashion. James said his last plea to the Praetor before he was escorted from the city, was to give the bodies over as soon as possible. We could only pray the Praetor listened.

I felt it best for everyone to stay put for the night and we'd consider other options in the morning, but to be safe, we set up a watcher rotation so we wouldn't risk a surprise assault. Also, we asked that no one sleep alone; everyone was to group in parties of no less than eight and to gather in the buildings closest to the top of the hill.

Once the community was blessed and in for the night and watchers were in place, I sat in front of our fire. We had sixteen people staying in this building. I felt my community was as safe as it could be given the events. The bodies of our slain had been washed and scented; a second cycle of care, including wrapping them in shrouds, would be given after dawn. We didn't want to entomb the man whose family didn't yet know that he'd passed. But we could deal with that issue in the morning. I needed to clear my head if I was to remain effective.

James sat near me, his face drawn and red from emotional pain and exhaustion. I knew Jude was safe with Rebekkah in their home gathered with several other people, but I didn't know about the rest of our family that resided in Sepphoris. James said no one was home at Simon's house, or Sarah's. The optimistic news was that James didn't see members of either household in the dead that he surveyed. I asked providence to watch over them and all the rest of our brethren tonight and grant us peace in our grief.

James didn't ask me about my visit to Magdala and I didn't offer. It wasn't the time for such things. Marriages and happy events were the furthest things from everyone's minds.

"War with Rome was inevitable. That became clear to me when I walked into Sepphoris during a massacre and found myself stepping over bloody human body parts just to walk down the street. The horror of that day stuck with me as did the smell. The sickening stench of blood, intestinal contents, urine, and feces mixed together gave me nightmares for months."

- James brother of Yeshua -

77 · A Telling Visit

Two days passed. We weren't attacked and our scouts heard nothing grim. On the morning of the third day, we assumed the violence had ended, but to be safe, we kept the watcher rotation in place and the nightly grouping for at least another week. I also sent a rider to Carmel to tell the women what transpired and invite them home at their earliest safe opportunity.

We heard some news. Simon's family was in Jerusalem at the time of the uprising, visiting Adam, so they missed the trouble. We still hadn't heard about my sister Sarah.

I didn't have even a minute to think about getting news to Miriam. I assumed she'd be oblivious to these events until I told her. I underestimated her reach, however, and midday a familiar rider came to the gate. It was my beloved, alone on horseback, and noticeably relieved to have me greet her.

It was obvious that this rider wasn't Hebrew and the watcher didn't want to let her proceed. I assured him that Miriam was a welcome guest. I wrapped my arms around her when she came off her mount. Obviously, she'd been worried about me. I was careful not to continue to touch her, however, on the way up the hill. She seemed to understand and kept a respectable demeanor in the community. This was her first meeting of everyone except James and I knew she wanted to make a good impression.

When we got near the main house, James stood in the doorway. By the look on his face, he was clearly disturbed. He watched us until we were an arms distance from him.

I said, "Miriam came to see that we were safe and unharmed."

James replied in a flat tone, "Of course she did."

Miriam said, "Hello James, it's good to see you again. I'm sorry for the circumstances that pulled me here."

James tipped his head to her and said, "You're welcome in our home, Miriam." He stepped aside and motioned us in. Once inside, he looked at us and said, "You're different, Priestess."

"Perhaps that's true," Miriam said, "and perhaps that's true of you too, James, you're no longer with the monastery?"

James nodded, "I've much work here since Father passed." James looked at me and cocked his head to one side. "Bit, something about you is different too."

I nodded my head in agreement. A plethora of activity was going on around us and a steady stream of people flowed through the room, some needing this and others needing that. Miriam, being an experienced priestess, was appropriate and

"And to his sisters, he was loving but unassuming. He rarely spoke of them and rarely went out of his way to visit with them or their families. That was a product of the times, brothers grasped brothers, and sisters grasped sisters."
- Miriam wife of Yeshua -

comforting to everyone she met. Her countenance and demeanor was soft and accommodating.

After some hours, the three of us found ourselves suddenly alone. James began the evening fire. As he worked the wood he said, "Something's happened between you two. I can feel it, and more than that I can see it on you." Miriam and I were silent. After a few minutes, James looked at us directly and said, "How will the two of you proceed? Do you know?"

I looked at Miriam and she nodded, so I said, "We're getting married."

James couldn't hide his surprise. Wide-eyed, he asked Miriam, "You're giving up your Priesthood?"

Miriam simply said, "Yes."

James was nonplussed. He worked the fire, and said, "What I've seen this week, the brutality, the broken lives. It's changed me. And in the midst of such tragedy, two people I respect... one for whom I would gladly lay down my life... tell me they've found each other." His voice choked, "I can't think of anything more... I'm overjoyed for you both. Truly, I am."

James stood and so did I, to embrace him. When I did, he began to cry. They were purging tears, beginning his healing from this terrible time. His love stunned me, in its honesty, its purity. I felt humble in his presence. And though he eventually proved to have more acceptance work to do, he never again to my knowledge said a disparaging word about Miriam. He became, next to me, her staunchest supporter.

78 · Like Glue

Miriam stayed the night, safe within our fold.

The next morning she asked if it would be disrespectful to the community to pray to the Goddess for healing. I thought it was a welcome idea as long as it wouldn't appear as sorcery. Many of the people sheltered here from Sepphoris were Orthodox, not Nazorean, nor Essene, and they might misjudge some of Miriam's practices, especially in this confusing and frightening time.

She agreed. So, while I was in meditation for my daily baptism, Miriam walked the grounds in animated prayer. It felt good and no one complained.

After breakfast, Miriam worked alongside the other women, tending to people's wounds, and helping with other needs. She got along with everyone; her presence slid into the mix without friction.

Midday, James caught me watching her from the porch and put his hand on my shoulder. He said, "I want to apologize."

I asked, "What for?"

"For doubting you." His face was still pinched with grief from the events of the last days, but I couldn't relate to his apology.

"There's nothing to apologize for," I said, "everything you've ever said to me has been because you love me. Don't apologize for that."

James looked at the ground, "No, I doubted that your heart was speaking truth to you. I thought this obsession with Miriam was a fool's dance." He looked into my eyes, "But I know now you were seeing truth, where I was seeing only the veneer. Whatever's transpired between the two of you, the change in Miriam is unbelievable. And I imagine, when my eyes are accustomed, I'll see an equally astounding change in you."

"Thank you." I said and together we spent the next moment watching our community mend and rebuild with my beloved folded into the fabric of it. The moment was fleeting, however, as we heard shouts from the road below.

It was the women and children returning from Carmel. I stayed on the porch looking down the hill at people greeting each other. The periodic cries of grief from women and children hearing the news of dead loved ones punctuated the scene, a terrible echo of three days earlier.

Miriam came up the hill and stood next to me. She asked, "Is this what it was like the first day?"

I looked at her and said, "That day was much worse, but yes, like this in part." I wanted to hold her and feel myself melt into her, but I knew I couldn't yet, so I crossed my arms in front of my chest to keep them from betraying me. I said, "I want to hold you. I want to hold you and never let go."

Her eyes closed and her face flushed. She said, "I believe you."

I saw Mother walking toward the house, flanked by James and Rebekkah. Even though I knew Mother was safe at the monastery, it was a relief to see her home. I said to Miriam, "That's Mother with James."

"She's lovely," Miriam said, "I see a great presence in her." I knew she was seeing truth. Mother was an extraordinary woman of great faith and courage.

When Mother reached the porch, I welcomed her home, arms outstretched. Her arms wrapped around my back and squeezed with fervor. She pulled back, looked at me, and said, "Something's different."

I gestured toward Miriam, "Mother, I'd like you to meet Priestess Miriam."

Miriam spoke first, "I'm pleased to meet you. It's an honor."

Mother stepped over to Miriam and locked eyes with her. After a few poignant moments, Mother smiled, placed her hand on Miriam's cheek, and said, "You'll do."

Miriam said, "Yes I will," and they hugged. As they did, I heard Miriam whisper to Mother, "Thank you, from the bottom of my heart, thank you." I wondered what she was thanking her for; then I remembered the letter that Mother sent Miriam. I closed my eyes and said a prayer of thanks for these two extraordinary women.

Later that evening, Mother found me sitting alone on the back porch. She sat beside me, "She's beautiful."

"I love her, Mother, with all the best parts of me."

"I can see that," she said, "I can see... much."

I knew what she meant. She could see, just as James had seen, the electric bond that Miriam and I created by our physical union. It stuck to us like glue.

She pulled a locket of hair from my forehead and stroked the length of it, and said, "You're my son, but you're also my King. I have no right to question you. Just tell me, do you plan to marry?"

"Yes, of course, as soon as possible." I smiled and added, "We'll ask James to perform the ceremonies."

She smiled and looked down at my hands, "It's funny, your hands, they're so like Joseph's. You're the only one that's not his natural born, yet you're the one who carries his hands." She refocused her gaze to my eyes, "Care for her... cherish her while you can, Yeshua. She's giving up a lot to walk with you." She continued, "Let her know every day that she's the sun that lights your path. Tell her at every opportunity, that you'd be less without her. Show her body, and her soul, that your love is as wide as it is deep." She paused a moment, sighing deeply, then said, "You and I both know you'll leave before she does. Those are the things that will... console her... when you're gone." I knew she could see the worry in my eyes, "Shhh, tst, tst. Don't fret that I know this. For now, I think we need to plan a wedding." She pinched my cheek, and giggled as she walked away. Over her shoulder, she threw these words, "I'll be busy!"

"Ye'sHUa was a kind and attentive son as well. Mary was his first beloved and while he never made me feel as though I was second in his eyes, he always made Mary feel she was first."

- Miriam wife of Yeshua -

79 · Betrothal

Life slowly returned to normal in our community. We learned that my sister, Sarah, and her family had fled Sepphoris also to the safety of Carmel. That was a relief. The wedding plans, however, proved to be at the tip of everyone's tongues. Miriam went back to Magdala to make arrangements and tie-up loose ends for her life and for the temple. Time was closing in on us.

A few weeks later, Miriam stepped down as Attendant Sophia. She renounced her position at the temple in the morning and traveled with her maidens to the family compound for the betrothal that evening.

The social philosophy underlying a betrothal is best understood by first realizing that in all ways, and above all else, a marriage was considered a business contract, a financial partnership. The financial and legal obligations of forming a partnership had to be publically recognized. It was the community's obligation to ensure the continued health of the clan.

I'd witnessed several betrothals since my return to Galilee. They began as solemn occasions until the contract was properly witnessed and sealed, then they became joyous occasions. Sometimes the witnesses required a renegotiation of the contract, but usually not. Most families consulted with community leaders before the actual day and so were assured that the arrangements were satisfactory.

We hadn't consulted with anyone, so I wasn't certain our arrangements would be satisfactory from that standpoint. Rather, I was certain because I knew in my heart they were fair and exactly as they should be for everyone's happiness.

As I took my place at the head of the crowd to stand next to James, I felt a flutter in my stomach. When Miriam flanked James on the other side, I felt a strong sense of youth grip me. I was a young man again looking at the beginning of his life, not knowing what the future held, but thinking only of the joy of discovery ahead. It'd been years since I felt this way, since before the Temple of Man. It's as if time turned back for a moment, and while I enjoyed it temporally, it was somewhat unsettling. I wasn't a youth; I was ancient. I wasn't new to discovery; I knew where my path led. It's as if I was filling in a gap of experience that once filled would one day serve me. And despite my distinctly precarious hold on my normally balanced state, I was enjoying the moment.

Family, neighbors, and friends attended our betrothal. The only concern I had going into the ceremony was Miriam's age. She was older than I by about eleven years, and we both wondered if anyone would object. Happily, no one offered resistance to any portion of the contract, but several customs had to be witnessed and accepted before the contract could be lawfully sealed.

First, law required a dowry for Miriam. The groom's father was expected to pay the dowry. In my case, since my father was deceased, the payment fell to me. By custom, this payment would consist of gold or goods, the value of which would pay for any marriage preparations by the bride. It would also contain an amount adequate to compensate for the time she spent in preparation if for some reason the betrothal had to be dissolved before the marriage was consummated. If the marriage went through, this overage would be given to the father of the bride in compensation for the loss of his daughter.

A monetary dowry was unnecessary in this betrothal as Miriam's liquid assets were greater than mine and she had no father to require payment. But the law was the law, so I presented Miriam with a dowry that consisted of the following:

+ A text of the basic Mosaic Law for her reference in understanding the community she was embracing.
+ A bolt of gold threaded silk cloth from Persia to portend prosperity in our home.
+ A pregnant goat, to satisfy Miriam's desire for fertility blessings from the Goddess.
+ And, a smooth, round river rock with no monetary value whatsoever to signify harmony and equality in our union.

Handing over each item, I felt like a schoolboy. I even found myself blushing more than once. Luckily, I didn't have to speak – James did all the talking.

As required, once the dowry was presented, those in attendance were asked to attest to its authenticity and fairness. Happily, they did.

Second, Miriam had to give me a representation of her promise of fidelity. Before you assume this was a custom designed to signify the bride as property, remember that these were financial and legal arrangements for protection not for punishment. The promise of fidelity was the gift of the woman's womb to the partnership to legally bind any progeny as the responsibility of, and legal heir to, both parties. This was henceforth true even if that progeny was conceived before the marriage ceremony, or was not a product of union with the groom. It was this very rule of betrothal that years before happily made me Joseph's legal son and heir.

To comply, Miriam was delighted to present me with the flute I played the first time we made music together. Those in attendance noted her promise and approved. After the ceremony, I hung the flute on the wall above the bed we'd share after the wedding. It seemed fitting.

Third, I presented a housing plan.

Since Miriam owned three homes – in Magdala, Tiberius, and Caesarea – and my brothers and I owned this complex of buildings outside of Sepphoris, the ability to house my new family was undeniable. However, what the community wanted me to ensure was that Mother would be adequately housed and provided for after this marriage. I felt they also secretly wanted assurance that the entire community

"The actual year of my birth was purposely shadowed from me, but the best guess is that I was older than he by 11+ years. I was in the vicinity of 50 years of age when he transitioned his body. I had approximately eight glorious years with him in his physical form."

- Miriam wife of Yeshua -

would be cared for; that my allegiance to Miriam wouldn't cause me to dismiss my responsibilities to them.

So, we announced that the farmhouses, workhouses, crop fields, gardens, and storehouses would remain open and functioning without change. We announced that Jude would remain the operations manager of the business. We presented the main house as the continued residence of Mother and James, and designated a secondary house as the homestead of Miriam and me, and as required by custom, we authorized the community to inspect that home's contents at any time before the wedding. This odd sounding custom was to ensure that the home would be perfectly functional before the wedding. The duty of the community was to leave gifts upon inspection, anything that might be needed to live there ongoing. It was infinitely helpful to young couples just starting out.

We didn't tell the community that our actual intention was for the home we designated as Miriam's and mine to become the home of her maidens and we'd reside in the main house with Mother and James. There was plenty of room there and Mother preferred it that way. Mother would have preferred to have all her sons reside in her house, but Jude and Rebekkah wouldn't agree to that. Rebekkah was a strong-willed woman with emotional ties to her own matriarchy. Miriam was more like Mother in that she didn't cook and was perfectly content having that and other domestic responsibilities handled for her. She was happy to share a roof with everyone.

The community, however, would've been hard-pressed to agree officially to any arrangements that didn't include an individual roof. In all first marriages, if finances allowed, a new couple was required to live on their own. It made absolute sense for young couples who'd be wrestling with the sudden strangeness of marital life, newly accepting themselves as heads of a residence instead of as chattel for their parents, and taking on the responsibility of consecrating a home to raise their children. But for Miriam and me those considerations were of little consequence. We'd both long given up being anyone's chattel.

Fourth, we set the date and place of the wedding and named James to preside over the ceremony.

When all was done, the contract was sealed. James wrapped a thong around my wrists and Miriam's to bind us together symbolically and we were betrothed. Looking into the face of my beloved said everything I needed to know in that moment. She was radiant.

"As a friend and lover, Ye'sHUa was imaginative, inventive, jovial, and effusive. He loved to laugh, to dance, to sing, to celebrate life and all the glory of the Goddess' earthly creations."

- Miriam wife of Yeshua -

80 · A Dark Omen

Considering possible consequences of a marriage, Miriam and I failed to account for hidden dangers. How could we? We were ignorant of the far-reaching fingers of acrimony our decision would inspire.

Unfortunately, on the day after our betrothal, a hint of those malicious consequences arrived. But we were blind to accept anything that would add to the burden of decisions we'd already put to rest. As we relaxed at home, a rider came carrying a note from an anonymous source. It read:

> "If you proceed with this union, all your progeny will be cursed. Turn back your decision before it's too late. Once this union becomes written, you'll henceforth be marked."

The rider abstained from revealing who'd sent him and he left immediately.

I loathed paying it any attention. I knew my marriage plans were without welcome to many. Miriam was nervous about its origin. We took the note to the family: Mary, James, Jude, and Rebekkah. Each had an opportunity to weigh in on its meaning and, after a short discussion, we decided to ignore it. We burned the note and put the incident behind us.

In retrospect, had we fully known what the note represented, I doubt we would've made any different decision. Miriam and I were resolute that our lives were entwined.

That night, Miriam decided she was having no more of sleeping alone when her beloved was just a few feet away. So, after most were in bed, she tiptoed into my room and asked if she could sleep with me. The note filled her with foreboding and she wanted the comfort of being with me through the night. We folded our arms around each other and went to sleep.

I didn't know until many years later, what happened after that, just a few rooms away.

James saw Miriam enter my room. He almost burst in then to chastise us. He felt that as rabbi in attendance over our marriage he had an obligation to keep things proper.

However, he also had other thoughts that were not so altruistic. He was distraught by them, so he went to Mary's room instead. James relayed the following conversation to me:

> "Mother, I'm not sure what to do."
>
> "About what?"
>
> "I saw Miriam enter Yeshua's room, just now. I'm sure she'll stay all night."
>
> "And so what if she does?" Mary said matter-of-factly.
>
> James looked at Mary, eyes wide, "It's not proper."
>
> "Who is it not proper for?"
>
> "To everyone, the community… me."
>
> Mary thought for a moment, then said, "James, they're betrothed. Do you honestly think they shouldn't spend time together?"
>
> "No, of course not, but this is different."
>
> "What makes it different?"
>
> "They're behind a closed door. They could be doing anything."
>
> Mary put her hand on his arm, "We both know they're not innocent of each other."
>
> "You don't understand what I'm saying!" James was disturbed.
>
> Mary grabbed James forearm tighter and tugged it lightly. "Get hold of yourself and listen to me."
>
> James took a deep breath, "Alright."
>
> "They're not children betrothed in innocence, they're already married."
>
> "No, they're…"
>
> Mary shook his forearm again and overrode his words, "No, listen to me. Don't you understand who your brother is?"
>
> James lowered his eyes, "Yes."
>
> "No, I don't think you do." Mary stared at him until his eyes lifted to meet her's again. "He hasn't begun to show himself."
>
> "What do you mean?" James asked.
>
> "I mean, he's more than even you think he is. And this woman, whatever we may think of her or any actions they take, she belongs to him now. She's his choice."
>
> "I know that Mother, but what about…"
>
> Mary shook his arm harder this time and spoke sharply, "Stop, right here. Listen to yourself. You're being jealous and petty. You've been the closest to him for a long time, but now Miriam is his wife. That relationship trumps everything." She paused to let her words sink in. Then she said, "You're his brother. Not just his brother, you're his closest confidant and advisor. You'll continue to be that until the day he leaves us, at which time you'll also be his successor. You can't let yourself be buffeted in these emotional oceans. You must come to shore and stand tall in the place only you can occupy."
>
> "But, I…"
>
> "Don't 'but I' to me! Not now, not ever again!" Mary stood her ground, "Take this in. Miriam and Yeshua are already married. They've been married since the day they became lovers. Don't you understand? Your brother took her."
>
> "What do you mean?"
>
> "I mean he captured her. He set about it like a fisherman nets fish. Your brother's will is honed and absolute. With Miriam, he was no doubt gentle, but when he made up his mind, his will overtook, and she had little choice in the

matter. And whatever choice she had, we had less." Mary's voice deepened, "Get used to it, James. It'll be like this from now on. This partnership is his last hurdle in preparing for his glory. His will is first and last now, and all that follows from here will be like the blinding flash of a white-hot fire."

James looked at her unable to speak, allowing her words to wash through him.

"Don't you know how much consideration he's already giving us with these little ceremonies and social proprieties? He doesn't need them. He has no use for them. This is all for you and me. I mean it, literally; all of this is for us!"

James stopped shaking. "If not for us, they'd be gone," she said, "far from here. Together in some land where Hebrew and Pagan mean nothing. His deep love for you and for me shines through every day in these gifts, so if they want to sleep in the same room now, so be it. Within a few weeks not even the high priest of the Temple would frown on it. They'll be through with all these social rituals and it'll be law for us, but make no mistake; it's already law for them."

Mary leaned closer, looked James in the eye, and said with conviction, "When all is said and done, and you and I are walking into our old age, he'll not be with us. When that time comes, you'll rue any moment you spent alienating his love from your heart. I strongly suggest you find acceptance of his actions and embrace them. I'd hate, when that time comes, for you to have too much regret to live with yourself in peace."

At hearing these last words, the air left James lungs like the deflation of a cooling flatbread fresh from the oven. He kissed Mary on the forehead and said, "Your words have touched home. I've a lot to think about," and he went back to his room.

81 · My Wedding Day

I was married to Miriam on a beautiful summer's day, in a meadow of green near my home. My brother, as rabbi, presided over the union. Hundreds of people attended our bonding and, with only one exception, the day was joyous and merry.

I wasn't married through the Temple; no scribe noted our union in the annals of my creed. My wife wasn't Hebrew and wasn't welcome in the Temple or its rituals. Many in the larger community held my marriage with contempt, but to my loved ones, and to the faithful who lived around me in the Nazorean community, Miriam was welcomed with open arms simply because she was my choice.

There were only a handful of rabbi's willing to perform mixed creed marriages. I was fortunate James was one of them.

After the Hebrew ceremony, everyone was enjoying the party. All who came were genuinely happy to see me wed. To most, it was long overdue and welcome. Miriam charmed the visitors and they felt settled to have her join our family. Once people were fed and laughing, Miriam and I, James, Mother, and Miriam's maidens, retired to a tent to partake in a rite of the Goddess to consecrate our marriage in Miriam's traditions.

However, part way through the rite, we were disrupted when one of Miriam's maidens left the tent and returned with another Priestess in tow. Miriam was angry and told the Priestess to leave, but she wouldn't. She said she represented the Council of Sophia. She came to give Miriam one last opportunity to turn back from her ill-chosen path. Miriam adamantly refused.

The Priestess spoke Egyptian and while I knew it partially in written form, I was not perfectly versed in its spoken form. I can't repeat what she said verbatim, but to paraphrase, she told Miriam that her womb was consecrated for the Goddess. It wasn't made to carry any child unless the Goddess directed it be so. This union was soiled.

The Council of Sophia promised to curse any offspring created outside the binds of her station, and through all her days, she and her progeny would have to watch their back; that at any time the Council could and would call for their culling.

Miriam was incensed. She refuted what the Priestess said, stating that she'd performed for the Goddess for many years, and performed faithfully and well. That the Goddess wouldn't have put feelings in her heart for this Hebrew, me, if it wasn't in the Goddess' interest.

Miriam was consumed with anger and again told the priestess to leave and to take the treacherous maiden with her. The maiden fell to Miriam's feet in tears,

"So we married. From that day, I never looked back. I never yearned for the station I left. That's a testament to making a good decision, but it's even more so a testament to Ye'sHUa as a remarkable individual and partner."

- Miriam wife of Yeshua -

begging Miriam to keep her, but Miriam shoved her away and told her to leave now.

The visiting Priestess wrapped her hand over her head to form a sigil in the air, threw a string of colorful stones at Miriam's feet, and said in Aramaic, "Those are the Stones of Circ'a'sia. You've earned them; keep them close, they're the last mantle you'll ever possess. So be it."

With that, the Priestess pulled her robes up tightly and exited the tent. The maiden Miriam dismissed was still on the ground pleading with Miriam to let her stay. Miriam was adamant and the maiden left in tears.

James asked us to wait inside and he followed the maiden. When he came back, he said the two had left; the maiden on a donkey he gave her. I was pleased they'd caused no uproar among the other guests and that James had given her a means of safe travel.

When the ritual was complete, I felt a strange feeling of destiny fulfilled wash over me. It felt as if some ancient bond within my soul was enacted and that leaving was near. I was barely 31 years old and I already felt my demise. If anything, that very feeling gave me a touch of grief that punctuated my remaining days with a sense of immediacy and preciousness.

My physical time with Miriam was the fondest and most dangerous of my entire existence.

Son of Man Ignited

82 · Gift of Light

With Miriam by my side, I felt complete. I flourished in my new role as husband and she was a delightful addition to the family. Mary and she got along well, often going on forays together. And James loved her even when he didn't agree with her.

It wasn't until after my physical persecution that James would step into his wisdom and overcome his righteous pretension of how others should live. At this time however, James' judgments were pervasive, especially where I was concerned. I had to become inured to his comments.

James lived an austere life. He was spare with his indulgences and had difficulty tolerating them in others. My repeated transgressions could be something as usual and innocent as dipping my bread into flavored oil at supper. This simple act of delicious enjoyment for me would often prompt a comment like, "Really, Bit, must you always?" Sometimes I'd remind him that the Way of Peace teaches moderation, not abstinence, but more often, I'd simply ignore him.

Miriam got along with Jude and Rebekkah to the point that Rebekkah began studying some of the esoteric arts with Miriam. Within a short time, Miriam was teaching many more women. She guided them to step-up their individual power and unleash their inner talents. The entire community benefitted from this lifting of feminine power.

I saw how important these familial bonds were to Miriam. We were the first family she ever had. She blossomed and relaxed in the unconditional love the family extended to her.

I wanted Miriam to meet my sister Ruth. Ruth hadn't attended our wedding, so we traveled to Caesarea by way of Sepphoris. In Sepphoris, we met with Sarah and her family, and then with Simon and his wife. Simon was older than I by more than twenty years, so he felt more like an uncle than a brother, but we were brothers. It was a glorious union of family. When we got to Caesarea, we met with Ruth and her family and stayed several days by the sea in Miriam's home there. The last time I'd seen the Mediterranean was when Joseph took me to Egypt. It was relaxing and rejuvenating.

Both Sarah and Ruth had young children, and Miriam confessed that after being with them, she felt the pull of motherhood. She wanted to have children and so did I, but she was worried about her advanced age. The Sisterhood raised her to be a high priestess. They shielded her birthdate from her: this to keep her from

"Before Ye'sHUa, pregnancies were of little consequence to me. I owned land and had money, position and power. If I'd been compelled to birth a child, a husband wouldn't have been required for my child to be a full and accepted citizen. But after falling in love and getting married, it became specific; I wanted to have his child."

- Miriam wife of Yeshua -

being at the mercy of astrologers and sorcerers, but it also left her feeling slightly out-of-sync with people. Even though she didn't know exactly how old she was, she reasoned she was probably eleven years older than me. That would make her forty-two. I told her not to worry, that if it was meant to be, it would be. So, she began calling on the Goddess to grant her a pregnancy.

Not long after we got home, Miriam was astonished to find her prayers answered. She was pregnant. We were overjoyed and our future looked bright.

A few weeks later, I had a vision dream. In it, I walked with Man'wa in the courtyard at the Temple of Man. We discussed my next step. We tossed around several ideas and after a time, Man'wa stopped and asked me, "Why is the next step not clear to you?"

I thought about it, but nothing came to me. "Maybe I'm not ready?" I said, "Maybe there's something I still need to do to prepare?"

"This is possibly so," Man'wa nodded in agreement. "I wonder. Is there someone you're supposed to meet? Someone who'll give you a new spark?"

"Why do you say that?" I asked.

"It seems possible," he said, "sometimes we need the spark of another person to move forward. As open as you are, as many dimensions of life that you have access to, it may be the spark of a human-to-human interaction that'll break the veil between where you are and where you're going."

"I see."

"Your teachers are many, and your connections are strong, but look for a spark, Issa."

"Any ideas where I'll find this person?" I asked.

"All I see is that he's by a river, and he's waiting."

I awoke, and those last words rang in my brain. 'He's by a river and he's waiting.' I looked around the room. Everything was quiet. Miriam slept soundly by my side. A cat perched in the window. Crickets chirped outside. 'He's by a river and he's waiting.'

It hit me, my cousin John. He'd asked me if one day I'd trust the waters. Perhaps it was time to do that.

Three days later, Miriam, James, and I were walking by the Jordan, near where we heard John was preaching. Last time I saw John, he seemed to not recognize me. I wondered if now he would.

We rounded a grove of trees and saw a group of people at the water's edge. As we got closer, I saw it was John. He stood in the water baptizing an initiate. He expertly dunked the man into the water and back out three times. I watched the man with my inner eye and saw his spirit wash clean in a transformation that was nonsensical except for the power of my cousin to facilitate the change. I was impressed.

I took my place in line. James didn't want any ritual and neither did Miriam. They both thought me silly for wanting this. I stood there anyway.

Each new person who walked into the water greeted John. They spoke for some minutes. John would ask if they were ready to give up their fear and become an initiate of the one true God. Only one person said no and left without the dunking. Everyone else followed through with John. He'd recite passages from Torah, and add some words of his own, entreating God to wash this person clean of what separated them from God's light. He'd dunk the initiate three times and with each, I witnessed the same cleansing of spirit I'd seen in the first man. He dunked men and women, young and old alike.

My time finally came. I stepped into the water and walked to John. When he saw me, his hands flew to cover his mouth. A moment later, he cried, "It's you!"

"Yes, it's me," I said as I relaxed my arms and opened my heart to him. I had nothing to hide.

"I've known you from a child," John exclaimed, "but I've obviously not known you."

"Nor I you," I answered. We stood in the water searching each other's face for a sign of something, I don't know what.

I felt more people come to observe. Something about our silent discourse was attractive.

"This is only the beginning, Cousin," John said.

"As I feel it also."

"Now that this moment has arrived, I don't feel worthy," John confessed.

"No, I've watched you these many hours," I said. "You're faith personified. You are His hand."

John cupped his hands around mine. "Bless me, please," he asked.

"No. I'm not ready yet. Make me ready, Cousin. It's time."

I felt the eyes of the crowd riveted. I don't know what they saw; I only know what I felt. It was a tremendous dose of power.

"Are you ready to trust the waters, Shining One?"

"Yes," was my clean and clear response.

I heard the crowd gasp, and I heard my wife ask, "James, what's happening?"

John put his arms around me and I relaxed into his embrace. Together we submerged into the water: John and me completely. The water grabbed me, it carried me, it lifted me; it was a liquid dance that felt like it lasted an eternity. And in that eternity, I saw many things; visions of my path, things I had no precedent to understand. These visions flew through my brain like flocks of bird on wing. Knowings succeeded the visions. I knew my next step, and the one after that. I knew who would follow, and who would oppose. It was more knowledge than I think I wanted, but I was at the point of no return. Like it or not, I saw myself heading toward a bloody conclusion that no person would ever wish for.

Next, I was above the water, breathing, John still holding me, and we submerged again. This time my visions were from a different perspective, looking down on life. The visions whisked past the ugly and inevitable conclusion I'd seen before. Much work was ahead, lasting longer than I could possibly believe. The people around me were moving faster and faster, wars came and went, populations exploded, technology zoomed.

Again, John lifted me above the water. His eyes appeared filled with our Creator. And again, he pulled me into the water and the liquid released me to stand in front of my Creator.

She maintained the visage of my Mother.

"Are you ready?" she said.

"Yes, but for what?" I asked.

"You've come through the maze of subjugation one more time. I'm exalted by your steadfastness. Are you ready to launch your mission?"

"Yes," I said with passion, "I am."

"Then I give you a gift for your travels. The gift of light." She touched me on the top of my head and I was...

...standing in the water in front of John gasping for breath. I was drenched, pulling wet hair from my face.

John stepped back and stared at me, wide-eyed. Everyone was staring at me, looks of incredulity on their faces. John stepped back a few more paces. I was unable to walk. I looked around the shore at people, one at a time; they were awe-struck by something. When my eyes met Miriam's, she was crying, and it seemed the tears were from passion, not from pain. When I found James, he was on his knees praying.

I looked down at my hands and I finally understood. I was glowing, with a light that seemed to emanate from inside me. The Creator said she was giving me the gift of light. I didn't realize it would be so literal.

I stood still for many minutes. Finally, the light dimmed, but didn't go out completely. John cried out in a loud voice, "He's here, my children. The Shining One has arrived!" I turned to face him. "Hallelujah!" he cried. He walked to me, tears streaming from his eyes and asked again, "Please, bless me."

I took his hands and when I did, I saw his end. It was gruesome, but the road to it was filled with riches of spirit. "Bless you, John. Thank you, from the bottom of my heart."

John kissed me and said with conviction, "My life has been only for this moment. Now I know the sands of time are coming for me. I'm your servant until then."

When I finally got back to shore, people were reluctant to come near me. No one seemed to know how to act. James finally placed his hand on my shoulder, "We're right where we should be, Bit." I grabbed his arm and squeezed.

I heard John loudly exclaim, "Follow him now. He's your prophet." Most people returned to the river with John, except three who stepped toward me. They introduced themselves as the brothers John and James, sons of Zebedee, and Judas son of Simon.

"Realize that when your thoughts are clear and you make a request to the Creator, delivery is instantly arranged – until you change your mind. So, guard your thoughts. They're literally the means by which your Creator understands your requests and creates your gifts. If your life and its gifts are confusing or undesirable, look no further than the mire of confusion in your thoughts."

- Yeshua son of Joseph -

83 · Logistics

Ready or not, my path was set. I had a new gift that I didn't know how to use and three followers. We walked back to the family compound in relative silence.

When we arrived home, midday the next day, I asked Josea if she'd make food for all of us. I didn't know how to treat the followers, or where to put them, but I gathered from my visions in the water, that there'd be plenty more as time progressed. Herodes helped me figure out an interim housing solution. Off the orchard was an empty building that had no cooking facilities. We designated it camp headquarters for followers. There was space around it to pitch tents if needed. James oversaw the task of outfitting the building with needed items such as cots, benches, table, etc.

One of Miriam's maidens volunteered for the ongoing task of food for the followers. Herodes helped them prepare a fire pit near the building for a common gathering place. It was temporary, but it would have to do until further arrangements could be made.

Mary had been away helping a friend down the hill. Later that night, when she saw me, she said, "You have a glow about you now." She sat down, and added, "What happened that brought these new people to our land?"

James filled her in on events from his perspective. I found his account fascinating, because as a witness, James saw things I didn't. Apparently, there were strange lights and apparitions swirling around the river. When James was done, I relayed some of the visions I'd been given that pertained to our immediate lives.

"So, we'll have more of these strangers come to live on our land?" she asked.

"It would appear so, Mother, yes," I confirmed.

"Well," she continued, "life will certainly be changing." She dipped her head and I saw a cloud of sadness settle over her, but I couldn't dispel it. She was correct.

And with all the change, Miriam, James, and I didn't have an opportunity to discuss what happened at the river. Life simply moved forward.

A few weeks later, tragedy struck. Miriam had a miscarriage. It filled us with grief. The child growing in her belly was as precious to me as if it had lived a full life by my side. For a time, my arms felt empty.

Rebekkah opened up to Miriam and recounted how she had lost two children, one in an early miscarriage and the other prematurely stillborn. I found it interesting that no one had ever spoken of these events. Rebekkah and Miriam's relationship grew stronger from the compassion of common experience, and it gave me comfort. Knowing this also helped me understand Jude better and appreciate how easy it was for his own grief to linger and make him susceptible to excess when Joseph became ill.

As painful as my current grief was, it deepened family bonds and brought us closer together. It was a good reminder that any event, no matter how painful, can have unforeseen benefits.

There was little time to wallow, however, because as word of my transformation at the river began to spread, new followers arrived. I continued my visits to neighboring synagogues, and speaking to gatherings. Not all of them welcomed my new ideas, but they treated me with respect, until one fateful Sabbath in Capernaum.

I stepped up my rhetoric. I began paying attention to planting thoughts I wanted to sew as fertile seeds. As a revolutionary, I liked to stir the pot, get the juices of change flowing within people. I spoke at length about the dead language of the religious texts. I made a case for stepping beyond the literal words of our ancestors and for each person to form a relationship with their living Creator. It was the first time I used the term 'Living Law' in my talks, but it was not the last. It became a pillar of my public teachings.

There were hundreds of people gathered that day in the synagogue. Women, men, children, it was a full building. They were anxious to hear what I came to say. Near the middle of my talk, however, many in the assembly became agitated. They harangued me to step down. I wanted to finish my thoughts, so I ignored them, but when I did finish I was menaced out of the building by a crowd.

This mob actively made their dissatisfaction clear. The men turned their backs to me, and the women… well, the women did something I'd only experienced in very small groups, not large ones like this. They began a loud trilling of their voices by vibrating their tongue while shouting. It was a fearsome sound that rattled me to my bones.

I bowed to the group and, over the din, thanked them for their feedback and walked away. Following me were the people who came with me: James, Miriam, my uncle Joseph from Jerusalem, and a handful of followers, including one that was from Capernaum. His name was Peter and he'd known my father, Joseph, before me. Peter was a local merchant, and together with one of his sons, had been moved to study with me by a previous talk I'd given.

Peter invited us to stop at his home for refreshments. It was a joy to meet more of his family, including his wife. But what happened next surprised me. Within an hour of our visit to Peter's home, we were crowded out of the house and into the courtyard by a growing number of people who'd been at the synagogue. My speech had moved them. They weren't in agreement with the discontented who'd menaced me. They wanted to hear more.

"The people I lived with in the East embraced a saying, 'Every tragedy bears a blessing.' They believed it so deeply that they actively searched for the blessings each time tragedy struck. Adopt the same posture. Look for the blessings. They're not merely inherent; they're equal or greater in value to the depth of the tragedy."

- Yeshua son of Joseph -

84 · Gathering Talk:

The Living Law

What follows is a recreation of a typical talk I might give; this one on the Living Law. I would give talks in synagogues, or in town squares. I might give one on a hilltop, or in a grove, or just in conversation at someone's home, but this is typical of my style of speech.

You are a spark of divine consciousness. You may not know it. Or, you may know it, but not feel it. But whether you know it, or feel it, or not, it's your truth. You were brought to this life by the creative source of all things.

And your Creator, like mine, for they're one and the same, has endowed you with a living will. You have free choice. Every human spark of consciousness that has ever existed before you has also had this burden of free choice. And it is a burden. I say it's a burden, because it's through free will that you can grow to higher consciousness or fall into degradation. It's your choice, your free and divinely gifted choice.

As a group, we've chosen to write down the deeds and thoughts of our ancestors and we call them sacred texts. We use these texts as tutorials. We glean from them clues about how to utilize this divine gift of free will to help ourselves rise, instead of let ourselves fall. And if we study well and learn from these writings, we may have an easier time understanding the raw power of our choices.

Yes, raw power. Because, that's what we have in our hands every time we make a choice, the raw power of a divine gift.

The sacred teachings we've written down do give us clues. Not only about how to make a choice, but also how to right ourselves again if our choice was a poor one.

So, hear me now. These writings, while significant and necessary, aren't the last word from your Divine Creator. They're dead.

These writings are merely the method by which you built a foundation for your life. They're like bricks you carefully placed together. Preferences for habits are spelled out in them. Covenants you adhere to are explained in them. And suggestions are offered about how to deal with the inevitable grave circumstances of life in a harsh world.

But like bricks, they're cold; they're dead. And they're not the last word.

You have free will, it was a gift, and it is a burden. Just as Jacob, Isaac, or Rebekkah listened to their Divine Creator, so you too must listen to yours. And remember, their Creator and yours are one and the same. It's the same source, the same voice, and it's the same gift.

Listen, yes, to how these men and women we deeply honor and respect used their free will, and then find the living voice of your Creator to help you use yours.

Step beyond the dead language of people long gone and find a sacred voice that comes from a repository inside you. A voice that has a home in you because it is the voice of your Creator. Your Creator gave you free will, yes, but didn't cast you aside. Your Creator walks with you. Your source of all things, eats with you, sleeps with you, works with you, and speaks with you.

Are you listening?

If your ears are attuned only to the language of dead ancestors, then how can you hear your Divine Creator? Joshua heard his Creator when he cowed his enemies and gave us a home. Sarah listened to her Creator when she displayed the courage to stand by her faith regardless of circumstance.

Are you listening to yours?

Stop holding onto these sacred texts as the only means of hearing the voice of the one who made you. Stop believing that these texts and their commentaries are the only way that you can know. These sacred texts are old teachings, from old voices. They built for you a foundation. Now build upon that foundation a temple. A temple wherein the voice of your Creator is exalted as it whispers to you, shouts to you, massages your consciousness with what I call the 'Living Law.'

Throw out the dead law once it's given you a base of understanding and embrace the living law.

You have a divine gift of free will. It's a burden, because it places on you the onus of choice. The living law, that can be revealed to you every day, can help you with that burden by spreading before you the glory of the wisdom of your Creator. The same glory of wisdom that created your life in the first place.

This living voice resides in you, not in the words manifest from ink blotted onto a parchment. The Creator's voice that resides inside you will always steer you toward your highest aspirations. That voice will uplift you, comfort you, and will never die.

Are you listening?

You have a divine gift of free will, given to you in wisdom and love from the source of all creation. Stop trying to find your answers outside yourself. Stop and look inside. Stop and embrace that voice as it rises from your depths. Live your life according to the law that is kept live in you and revealed in love directly from your Creator.

Hear me now; allow the sacred ancestral texts to take their rightful place as your foundation. Then choose divinely to live according to the inner voice of your Creator. Listen carefully to the Living Law as it is revealed anew to you each day.

I give you this in truth.

85 · Devotees

Crowds at my talks were getting larger. And so were the number of followers around me. I was never alone. It became harder and harder to find a place I could relax and unwind from the rigors of teaching, talking, and being of service to others.

My home became my sanctuary. The doors of my house became my beloved sentries. Sometimes, when the doors weren't enough, I'd go on pilgrimage into the desert. I'd cherish three or four days of nothing to intrude on my senses other than the creatures of the earth and my unseen friends. Alone in the wilderness I could clear my mind and cleanse my spirit. It was the only antidote certain to right my course if I faltered.

Miriam hated my pilgrimages, but she knew that when I needed them, there was no substitute.

Some followers became more involved than others, and soon a natural split emerged between those who watched and listened and those who actively became students and devotees of the teachings.

We set up two camps inside the gates of the compound and one larger camp outside the gates. The outside camp was open to anyone. Between visits to other towns and synagogues, I'd talk and teach at this camp regularly. But the camps inside the gates were smaller, more intimate, and housed only those invited by James, Miriam, or me to study with us more closely. Together, these smaller camps would average thirty to thirty-five people.

Devotees at the inside camps were as close to us as older more established members of our Essene community, even though they were not all Essene. A few weren't even Jewish. What mattered was the commitment in their hearts to the teachings and their willingness to adhere to the tenets of the Way of Peace.

Jude successfully oversaw the construction business. His healing was complete, and his newfound confidence and integrity served the family and our community well. Herodes had completely taken stewardship of the farm, orchards, and storehouses. Because he was getting older, I worried that the workload was becoming too much for him. I impressed upon him the need to train his new foremen well and delegate more responsibilities.

While I loved all the devotees, a few became close friends. Especially beloved were Peter and Judas. Peter was older than the other devotees, and he held a depth

"There's a big difference between hearing words and embracing concepts. Words can stimulate thought, but concepts stimulate the soul. True teaching carries more than words alone can convey; it carries ideas. True learning can only happen when you listen for the concept and disregard the words. This requires an open mind. It's easy to recognize a true student; he or she won't argue an imprecise word. He or she will find the light behind the words."
- Yeshua son of Joseph -

of wisdom that I respected immensely. There were times he reminded me of Joseph. He was pragmatic, kind, and even-tempered, and naturally took to the Way of Peace. More times than I care to enumerate, Peter soothed my emotional aches with his empathetic ears of gold.

Judas, on the other hand, was young, the same age as James. And he had a fiery disposition. He was eager to learn and grow in spiritual attainment. He lusted for enlightenment, but he was also a Zealot with a passion for war and revolution that gripped him. In an odd sort of way, he was more like me than any of the others. He was intelligent and learned, with a quick wit, and he never flinched from upsetting the status quo if it suited his aim. And he was loyal to those who had his back. Something clicked between us that created an almost instantaneous friendship and acceptance.

I cherished our fireside chats, and our long walks together. And every time Judas left the compound, which was often, my heart missed him until he returned.

We were all three teaching, James, Miriam, and I. And with the added numbers of people around us were an added number of difficulties. It took all three of us to manage the load.

In these early days, the most bothersome difficulties were caused by simple human jealousy. Men and women studied with us. Some were married with spouses also studying with us, while others had left their spouses behind to follow the teachings. And still some weren't married, either single or widowed. Most instances of jealousy centered on Miriam or me. We both had to become expert at deflecting unwanted advances. And we had to become good at recognizing how some devotees might misconstrue our actions toward other devotees. Most often, someone would yearn to be favored and would lash out when favor wasn't extended.

During this time, Miriam had two more pregnancies, both of which ended in miscarriage. It was deeply painful for both of us. Miriam became convinced that the curse placed on us by the Sisterhood on our wedding day was active. She felt that nothing could counteract it and she stopped trying to become pregnant. There were two unfortunate side effects of that choice.

The first was a negative effect on her mood. A pervasive depression set in. Sometimes, when she didn't think anyone could see her, her head would bow and her face would turn grey. Her eyes, which normally danced with color, would dim, and her mouth would sink into a frown. It wouldn't last long, until she was with people again, but it caused me concern. I wanted her to be happy.

The second side effect was more difficult. She became ill-tempered at times, lashing out at me with anger or jealousy over things I had no control over. The unwanted attentions of a woman, a conversation with a child, or a supportive hug given to a friend could turn into a betrayal in her mind with a speed that astounded me. And there was never anything I could say or do that would change her pain or

"It was maddening to me – unsatisfying – and often left me feeling like his heart had gone suddenly cold, but it would prove to always be the kindest response possible to walk away and not engage with my darkness. As I look back on that, I'm grateful to him for not engaging, but at the time, I would've been gratified if he had. And what I now see as strength of purpose, I saw then as cold arrogance."

- Miriam wife of Yeshua -

her anger. Experience taught me that, at those times, simply walking away instead of engaging the insanity of emotion was kinder to us both.

But Miriam was beloved, by me, by the family, and by the larger community. Those truths usually quelled her fears and gave her solace. And as a teacher, she was exemplary, a fact she regarded with pride.

One evening, I sat in the olive grove, my back leaning into the gnarly, twisted trunk of my favorite olive tree. It was my favorite, because it had a branch that swung invitingly low and made a perfect boy-sized, lazy-afternoon hammock. I spent hours as a boy, lounging on that branch, listening to the cooing of the doves. Dozens of these gentle birds lived here, and their beautiful call always lifted my heart.

But it wasn't working today. I was grieved over the most recent miscarriage and Miriam's discontent haunted me. While I wanted children as much as she did, her depression was of deeper concern.

As my mind searched for a respite from the pain, Philar appeared. "Hello, old friend," I said, "it's good to see you."

Philar sat beside me, his back against the same tree. "I'm happy to see you, too."

"Can you help me?" I asked.

"What with?" he asked.

"Miriam and I've lost another baby. It hurts."

Philar leaned back and sighed, "I've never lost a child, but I've lost people precious to me. I know it hurts."

"Each of those souls came into my life at the moment I heard they were growing," I said. "They stitched open pockets in my heart. Pockets that were waiting to carry the wonder and joy of watching them become whole... in the world." Tears began to flow down my cheeks, "Those pockets aren't gone, Philar. They're still in my heart, but they're empty. They'll never be filled."

Philar placed his hand on my leg. His caring pulsed through that touch; it was comforting.

"My wife is in deep pain," I said.

"I see the pain in both of you," Philar said.

I turned and looked directly into his face. It was kind and sympathetic. It helped to muster the courage for what I was about to ask, "Can you help us?"

"Are you asking if I can give you a baby?"

"Yes, I am," I said as tears washed my face.

He looked at me with sympathy. "I'm sorry, I can't at this time."

It wasn't what I wanted to hear. I leaned closer and said, "Please?"

Philar raised his hand to my face and brushed some of the tears back. "I wish I could. I wish I could take all the pain away, but I don't have permission."

Permission. He didn't have permission? The concept felt incongruous to what I was feeling. I stared at him, not knowing how to react.

"There are larger considerations here than you realize right now," Philar offered. But it didn't quell my confusion, or my pain.

"I don't understand," I finally said.

"Who you are, Son, what you're doing... I can't interfere. I wish I could."

"You've done it before. You gave Nadia a daughter."

"Yes, we did, but that was different."

I shook my head in confusion, "In what way was it different?"

"Yeshua, we could go on like this for hours trying to right your confusion, but it won't change the fact that I can't do what you ask," he said, "I'm sorry."

I twisted back into the tree, resting my head against its rugged bark. Philar's answer gave me no comfort and the ache I felt spoke, "Is this my fate then? I give comfort to many and receive none myself?"

From the corner of my eye, I saw Philar hang his head and I realized my words were ill chosen. "I'm sorry; I didn't mean to sound blaming. I'm just disappointed."

His hand patted my leg and he said something that startled me, "Don't worry, there's nothing you could say to me that would be sharper than the words I say to myself every time your heart cries. There's a pocket in my heart too – stitched on the day you came into the world. Believe me when I say, even a full pocket can carry a mountain of regret."

I saw pain through his thin smile. I put my arms around him and together we cried.

"Pity is judgment. Pity for another is the judgment that where that person is, is flawed. Pity for self is the judgment that what you already have, or where you already are, is flawed. The truth is that everyone, at all times, is exactly where he or she needs to be to facilitate the flawless expression of his or her inner self. If you don't like where you are or what you have, then change who you are. Pity will precisely anchor you to the self that created the pitiable state."

- Yeshua son of Joseph -

86 · Gathering Talk:
Spiritual Slavery

You are a slave. We're all slaves. All living people, regardless of station or wealth, are slaves.

I'm not talking about the slavery you might feel living under the yoke of another living soul. Whether you regard the Romans or the tax collectors as your slavers, or your spouse as having a thumb on your head, they're not the subjects of my speech. Because like it or not, nothing another person can do to you will ever compare to what you do to yourself every minute of every day that you fail to recognize your own worth; your own light.

You are the promise of the universe. You're the shining light of creation made manifest. You have within you the power of all creation granted to you by your Creator if you'd but see yourself with clear eyes.

So why don't you? Hmm?

Why don't you see yourself as pure love? Why don't you know in your depths that you are brilliant light manifest into form?

Why?

It's what you are, yet I see ignorance in your face. It's apparent in the way you hold your head and the manner with which you look at each other. It's apparent to me that you're enslaved by your own thoughts that tell you the truth is something else entirely. These thoughts try to tell you that you're small, insignificant, undeserving, and incompetent.

Oh no, no, no. You are immense. You are preciously significant. You are deserving, and your spirit is as competent as the Creator who birthed you.

But the lies are so compelling because they scream at you. They try to prove to you every day that they're true by bullying you into submission. These lies you tell yourself, they are your slaver.

You believe these lies because your faith is weak. It takes great faith to know you're something more than is defined by the clothes on your back. It takes great faith to remember that you wouldn't be manifest in form if the Creator didn't grant you the freedom to move around the universe unhindered.

But still you walk on this land as if you were bound to it with chains. You interact with others as if at any moment they could steal from you something you need to stay alive.

Stay alive? How could you not stay alive?

You're pure love. You're brilliant light. You're alive at a level of existence that stretches far beyond this limited body you hold so dear that you let fear of losing it rob you of the very truth that will set you free.

If it isn't clear by what I've said thus far, let me say it as plainly as I can. It is fear that enslaves you. It's the fear you generate, and hold onto as truth, that robs you of your birthright. It's fear that strips you of your knowing.

Hear me now. As long as you allow yourself to be trampled by the boot of your own fear, you'll not be free.

Look at your hands. Go ahead, hold them out in front of you, and take a good long, look at them. These hands do a lot. Think about what these hands do for you during the course of a day. The value of these hands in your life is immense.

Now picture the most precious thing you do with these valuable commodities, these hands. Do they cradle your child? Do they caress your spouse's shoulder? Do they stroke the fur of a beloved pet? Do they brush the hair of an aging mother? Picture your hands doing that very precious chore for you, whatever it is. Feel the power, the love, that emanates from those hands as they perform this precious chore for you. Imagine your hands doing that cherished act right here, right now.

Now take one of these hands and hold it up to your cheek. Gently rub your cheek. Imagine that cheek is your child's cheek, your spouse's shoulder, your pet's tummy, or your mother's forehead. Let yourself melt into that hand for a moment. Feel the love that is in that hand. Absorb that love, as you would want any cherished being in your life to absorb it. Lean your head into your hand as your loved one would lean into it. Feel the love that is pulsing out of that hand. That love is immense.

Now pay attention. That love is you. What you just felt from your own hand is a hint of your own power-of-self bringing itself to bear. Did that feeling just now from your own hand make you feel good, if even for a moment? Did it give you a glimpse of calm, a fragment of soothing acceptance? Did it? Does that surprise you?

It shouldn't. And if you really grasped the truth of who you are, the immensity of the love you are at your core, a manifestation of the pure light of creation, you'd wonder why your reaction to your hand's touch wasn't bigger.

And so I say again, what dampened the reaction to your hand just now is the same thing that dampens your knowing of the nature of your true self. It's fear. The most damaging thing in your life, in the lives of any being in this world, is the boot of fear that emanates directly from within.

And right now, I imagine many of you are feeling some anger at my words that I dare say your trouble comes from inside you. That anger you feel right now comes from the very fear I mention. Anger is fear. Guilt is fear. Judgment is fear. Grief is fear. The very nature of fear obliterates love. And the only way you're going to end the slavery you live is to take the boot of fear off your life and let the love of your own light shine into the world. Then, and only then, are you in any position to see your truth.

And as I said earlier, it takes great faith to do that. Because it requires a leap. You have to believe you are that which you cannot yet see, to open a window through which you can then see it.

Take that leap. Find that faith. It's the only way you'll ever be free.

Hear me now; as long as you allow fear to enslave you, you'll not be free.

I give you this in truth.

87 · Saving Simon

I walked to Sepphoris and the sun was unforgiving as it heated the clay buildings along the promenade. Galilee was warm in the summer – but this was unusually hot. The warmth rising off the walls caused everyone in this bustling town to slow down. It was cooler away from the buildings, but here, in the midst of activity, is where business was conducted.

My half-brother Simon sent a note asking to meet me about an urgent matter. I was concerned for his safety because he asked to meet me alone at a sidewalk tavern instead of his home. Coming to Sepphoris alone, without followers at my heel, was a difficult task to manage by itself.

I took a seat at the tavern and waited. The tavern keeper brought me a cup of water and obviously recognizing me, bowed in respect. We Jewish people typically paid close attention to our own. He introduced himself as Uriah.

I grasped the man's hand and held it tight in a show of mutual respect. When our eyes met, and for a mere instant, Uriah saw the shadows of his loved ones parade across his vision, causing his heart to swell with love. Tears slipped from his eyes, running down his cheeks in relief.

I let go of his hand. I knew I affected people in this manner and while I was grateful that I could bring awareness of the real to people, sometimes it made me sad. New people I met always reacted this way, causing them to see me through eyes glazed with visions, rather than seeing me for myself. It made me cherish the people who'd been in my life since before the transformation.

"What can I bring you?" asked Uriah.

"A plate of bread and cheese will do. My brother will join me shortly." Uriah bowed his head and scurried off.

A moment later Simon was standing over me, arms outstretched, and smiling from ear to ear. I jumped up and threw my arms around him. We held each other tightly. I loved him and would protect him with my life if need be.

His resemblance to Joseph was striking. I saw the familiar lines of aging that had once graced Joseph's face and felt a momentary pang of grief at Joseph's passing. Brief as the pang was, it was sharp. Luckily, it faded in the joy of Simon's presence.

We bantered stories back and forth, relaying the ups and downs of the recent months in a volley of 'he said, she said' punctuated with rolls of laughter and genuine merriment. Uriah brought us a plate of delicious food and it was nearly fully devoured before Simon finally divulged the truth of this visit.

"I'm in trouble," he said.

"What can I offer you?" I asked.

"I don't know. I'm in real trouble."

"Tell me the trouble and we'll sort it out together," I said calmly.

Simon proceeded to relate his tragedy that began with an ill-placed business deal and culminated in owing the Roman coffers more gold than his entire net worth. He faced the specter of losing everything, seeing his wife on the street, and himself in a Roman prison.

I'd seen this same scenario more times than I cared to count in the last few years, especially within the Hebrew population. The Roman elite had engineered a series of laws and edicts that favored the systematic draining of money from the commoners. I took Simon's hand, "Don't worry. We'll walk through this together."

Simon wasn't a devout man. Religion had passed over him. He believed in the ways of the world. He'd been dismayed when his father had taken monastic vows years before I was born. But I knew he loved his family as deeply as any man.

"I'm overwhelmed," Simon said, "I'm grateful for your help, but I feel ashamed for being in this position." He hung his head.

"There's no need for shame, Simon. The times are to blame."

"I've been so stupid," he declared, "and now my family has to pay for it!" But then, his face turned to shock.

"Calm yourself, we'll get through this." I became concerned for Simon's health. We were all perspiring from the heat, but the sweat on Simon's face multiplied. "Are you alright?"

"No, I…" Simon grabbed his arm and a look of great pain came over his face. "Simon?"

"The… noise… pain…" he groaned.

I watched my brother transform from a mass of shame to a stiff board of pain in seconds. The look on his face was of absolute horror as he went unconscious. I lunged from my seat and grabbed him as we both slipped onto the ground and rolled into the sun. I pulled us back into the shade of the lean-to and rolled Simon into my lap.

As soon as I did, I saw his spirit rise out of his body and stand behind it, looking around in a daze.

Anxiety gripped me. Simon was dying. This couldn't be, not on my watch. Not like this – with horror on his face, feeling less than the gentle, loving, and kind man he was. I held Simon's body and simultaneously stared into the face of his spirit until the spirit looked back, locking eyes with me.

Uriah saw Simon fall and ran to us. Strangers from the street gathered, none knowing what to do.

I shouted to Simon's spirit, "Not now. Don't go now. Stay here and let's fix this trouble first."

"Self-preservation is absolute in every being. So absolute that sacrifice for another is the only thing that can override the self-preserving instinct. There are no exceptions. Suicide is a form of self-preservation; a desperate form that perpetuates from the mind of one who is in so much pain that the act of ending the life 'preserves' the self from the pain. We tend to see suicide as an unfortunate mistake or sin, when the one in agony sees it as a last-resort act of protection. And it doesn't matter if the act of suicide is quick or slow, conscious or unconscious; suicide is self-preservation in action. What is absolute about suicide is not it's 'wrongness,' it's the unfortunate waste the act creates, both for the loss of precious life itself and the wake of pain that is spread through those who love and cherish the being who left. May you hear this: there's always an alternate road to self-preservation than suicide, and it usually involves facing fear head-on."

- Yeshua son of Joseph -

Simon's spirit said in words I was sure only I could hear, 'Is this it then?'

I pleaded, "No, this isn't it. Don't go."

'Where am I going?' Simon's spirit asked.

I was frantic. This was my brother. I couldn't let him die. I remembered how I felt when Myrrh died in front of me. It had been his time. I had to accept that. I had to accept death as an inevitable passage from one life to another. But today I couldn't. I felt this wasn't inevitable; that Simon didn't have to leave now.

"Stay Simon," I pleaded, "we can make things right, I promise." Simon's spirit began to walk away. "No. Stay here." I insisted.

Suddenly my franticness subsided. I remembered that this was an illusion, all of it. My breathing deepened, and a sense of calm washed over me. As it did, my vision opened and I saw other non-physical beings around us. They gathered around Simon's confused spirit.

I felt the heat of a bright light flow into me like water filling a bowl. My calm deepened. I shifted attention to the still, but warm body on my lap. Placing my hand over Simon's quiet chest, I began to softly sing to him in a language I'd learned in the east.

There were many onlookers now, but where it was loud and frantic a moment before, a hush descended.

At least twenty minutes passed, and I continued my serenade to Simon's heart. Simon's spirit had walked far away, but I wouldn't stop. I remained loyal to his heart and to my soft refrain. The crowd whispered, and to all who looked on I'm sure it was clear that Simon was no longer alive.

Finally, Simon's spirit walked back to me. I locked his gaze.

'Yeshua, they won't let me in.'

"That's because you're needed here. It's not your time." I heard the crowd comment, wondering who I was talking to.

Simon pointed to his corpse, 'But look at it. I'm dead.'

I shook my head and calmly said, "No, the body's resting. I'm holding its place open for you."

Uriah stepped forward and knelt next to me. He laid his hand on my shoulder, a look of pity on his face. "Rabbi, I'm so sorry. Your brother has passed."

I turned to Uriah and said with calm surety, "No, he hasn't. He's coming back. Be patient."

"Rabbi," Uriah continued with compassion in his voice, "I know it's hard to accept, but his body is motionless. His eyes have gone grey."

"No, be patient," I insisted, "I'm calling him back, you'll see."

I turned my focus back to the body and the heart within its breast and suddenly, my entire being pulsed brighter with the light from Creator. The crowd gasped.

Simon's spirit said, 'It's too much trouble. I don't want to face it. Let me go.'

I said to the body, "I'll speak to you in here. I'll answer to the voice from these lips, none other."

Uriah was shaking. I felt he wanted to run as the scene had become preternatural. But he was riveted, his hand locked on my shoulder.

Another ten minutes or more passed. Simon's spirit paced back and forth, unwilling to decide. I refocused and the light around Simon's body, Uriah, and me, intensified. More people gathered. I knew they felt there was surely nothing more to do, this man was dead, but they couldn't turn away from the amassed light and energy.

Finally, I took a deep breath and said to the body, in a clear and commanding voice, "I expect you to return. I promise you, all will be made right. Return now!"

And as I said that, the body lurched forward with a gasp of breath so strong that it nearly knocked him from my arms. A sudden red cast returned to his cheeks and his eyes returned to normal. I stroked his hair as one would a sweating child waking from a nightmare.

The crowd let out shrieks of surprise and a persistent murmur began. Uriah fell to the ground in disbelief. I continued to stroke Simon's hair until his visage was calm and regular. "Welcome back, my brother, welcome home." The light within me slowly dimmed to normal.

Simon was now clearly alive to all watching. In my heightened state of awareness, I felt a few amongst them were discontented by what they witnessed. I knew without doubt that accounts of this event would be brought to the highest authorities. But in that moment, I was relieved and happy. Regardless of what came of this, I had no regret about bringing my brother home.

"What you might call supernatural, I call natural. What you might call paranormal, I call normal. The mysteries are only mysteries until you allow yourself to perceive them. Then they're natural and normal events that cause only wonder and no fear."

- Yeshua son of Joseph -

88 · Surrender

I took Simon back to his house and put him to bed for some needed rest. I assured him and his wife that together we'd find a solution to the problem they faced. We called for a healer and I paid him before I left. I also pressed a few coins into his wife's hand as I kissed her goodbye and told her not to skimp on food or a healer's care and to send a runner if she needed more before I had a chance to come back.

When I got home, I went to my bedroom and shut the door. Some community members tried to garner my attention as soon as I stepped into the compound, but I put them off. I needed to be alone. On the walk home, I became troubled when I realized what happened. Not at the level of spirit, my spirit attended the incident without falter. No, it was at the level of my human self that I had to grapple with the enormity of what occurred.

A dead man was called back to his body. A dead body became live once more. Setting aside that it was my brother; I was overwhelmed with the magnitude of the action. Was it me? Was it my will? Had I misused a sacred gift for my own selfish desires? Was it Simon? Had he merely made good use of my faith and given himself a second chance? Was it the light? Was it something this gift could do on demand? Was it the Creator manifesting through the light? Was she using the gift she gave me to create an event that had to be? My mind shuffled through the questions too fast to get an answer to any of them.

I felt confused and under enormous pressure to integrate this incident as quickly as possible. I had many responsibilities and no longer had the luxury of wandering through vision dreams and sitting alone with my thoughts for days on end.

After a half hour or so of this dizzying mental tirade, I fell asleep.

The next thing I knew, Miriam was leaning over me, her beautiful, smiling face looking lovingly into mine. "Hey, Tall Man. What're you doing sleeping in the middle of the day?"

I smiled and immediately responded to her closeness. "Waiting for you to come kiss me," I said. But a short moment later, the Simon incident flooded back into my consciousness.

Miriam pulled back, "What's the matter?"

I sat up expecting people to be there, because it felt like a crowd was all around me, hundreds of people deep, clamoring for my attention. Their energy felt crushing.

"Yeshua?" Miriam looked at me with concern. I was obviously in distress. My breath was heavy, my eyes darted about. I didn't know what to say, I was mute.

"Hold on a moment." Miriam went to the door and called out, "James, would you come here please?"

Almost immediately, James came in. "Shut the door behind you," Miriam said, and beckoned him to the bed. They both sat with me breathing calmly, until my body began to relax from their prompt. When my breathing finally calmed, Miriam said, "What's happened? Obviously something's wrong."

The incident seemed a thousand miles away and the seeming crush of an unseen throng around me wouldn't dissipate. I didn't want to talk about it, but I knew I had to. Once I started, it flooded out, from Simon's confession of economic collapse, to his death and eventual revival, to the promise I made to him and his wife, and to the feeling I had now of a throng surrounding me, crushing me with their need.

At first, they were speechless, but it was an enormous relief to me to have us hold these issues together, instead of just me, alone.

I broke the lingering silence, "I love you both so much." Miriam squeezed my hand and James patted my leg.

"I don't know what to say," Miriam offered. James was quiet.

"Neither do I," I said.

After a time of silence, James cleared his throat and managed to speak, "Why don't we bring Jude into the discussion about the Simon issue." His voice sounded raspy, as if he hadn't talked in days, "I'm sure he'd be willing to oversee a solution. I agree that we need to help Simon sort this out. We owe him that by blood."

I looked at James, "That's a good idea. I'm sure there's a solution and it's probably a purely economic one."

James cleared his throat again and nodded his head. He seemed humbled and clearly affected by the discussion. "So… let's… take that off the table and… uh… be with the rest of it."

A peculiar silence overtook us. It was as if each of us were asking multiple questions, layered one upon the other, and even though the air was thick with them, none of us could give them voice.

Mesmerized by the silence, an abrupt knock on the door startled us. It turned out to be Herodes looking for James. After a short conversation, James came back to the bed. He looked me in the eye and said, "I know you already told us, but would you mind telling us again? What happened with Simon?"

So I laid out the tale of Simon's death at the tavern once more. I stuck to the facts, as best I could, though the facts were incredible even to me.

When I finished, James said, "I'm speechless."

"You know, in my world," Miriam said, "reanimation of the dead is possible, even sought after, but, only the gods have the power to…" she took in a sudden, sharp breath and dropped her gaze to her lap, "…the power to do it."

"Your mind can travel across the universe in the blink of an eye, but it can also become trapped in circular thinking, repeatedly retracing its own path until you become convinced that there are no other thoughts to be had. When these circles of illusion catch your mind, there are only two ways out; one involves deep, clear sleep, the other involves sincere sharing with others. Neither is an absolute prescription, but either one can put your mind onto a different track and stop the retreading that leads to a deep rut in your thinking. Remember that a rut in your thinking digs a rut in your life."

- Yeshua son of Joseph -

After a few moments, James asked with a boyhood innocence that was oddly calming, "He was actually dead?"

"Yes," I said, "I believe he was dead. His skin was cooling. His heart was silent. His eyes were clouding…"

"Yeah," James said.

"I tell you," I said with astonishment, "I watched his spirit walk away."

Simultaneously, our eyes cast downward, each searching for a way to respond.

"It was the light," I finally said.

Miriam looked at me, then at James, "We've never really talked about what happened at the river that day."

I closed my eyes and realized I was wrestling with the same feelings I had as a boy when a new ability presented itself. The feeling of inadequacy, of stumbling blindly through something with no precedent and not knowing which way was up.

I looked at them, first one then the other, back and forth until out of my mouth spontaneously came a question that surprised me more than anything else that day. I asked, "Am I still human?"

Both of their faces registered surprise as they thought about my question. But it was James who spoke, "Yes Bit, you're still human. In fact, I believe you're the next level of human." He cleared his throat again, "I think you're where we're going."

I closed my eyes to take in his words. They meant so much to me and until a moment before I didn't know I wanted them. My human subconscious was obviously wrestling with being different. I let James' words penetrate me.

"Yeshua," Miriam asked, "is there still part of you that believes you're in control?"

I looked at her face. It was strong and beautiful and wholly without guile. "What do you mean?" I asked.

"I mean," she continued, "I was there. I saw the light flood into you. The light was conscious."

"Yes. I agree," James said, "it was a directed force, not passive."

Miriam nodded in agreement, then said, "You're an instrument now."

"An instrument?" I asked.

"Yes, a well-tuned… instrument of… pure light." She looked at James then back to me. "Surely you see that your will is no longer the strongest energy directing you."

I looked over every inch of her face. It remained without conceit. I asked, "So… you think I didn't make a mistake today with how I used the light?"

"Did you will the light to perform?" she asked, "Or did it happen unbidden?"

"Unbidden," I replied.

"Then isn't it more likely that the light used you?" she asked in all sincerity.

I looked at James. His face was solemn, but with a glaze of passion that intrigued me. "What are you afraid of Bit?" he asked.

"I don't know," I said, "arrogance is such an easy pit to fall into."

"Yeshua," he took my hand and cradled it gently in his, "you remember the time when we were boys, when you stole my bird?"

"No," I said.

"Sure you do, when the bird I was nursing was eaten by the cat?"

Suddenly, the memory flooded into my consciousness. "Oh yes!" I laughed, "My God, I haven't thought of that in years. I was devastated by what I'd done!"

James laughed too, "You were. So was I."

"We cried all morning." I chuckled.

"Yes, and remember what Joseph said?"

I shook my head, "No. What did he say?"

"He said that you should confess to your Creator every day," James recounted, "confess what you'd done until the burden was lifted."

"Yes, morning baptism," I nodded, "that's how it started!"

"Do you shirk that obligation to your Creator now?"

"No," I said, "not now. I did for a long time though, when I was lost in my addiction."

"But, are you even capable of that now?" He cocked his head to one side and smiled at me in typical James fashion that lit up my heart with love.

I chuckled, "I wouldn't underestimate my ability to hit the mud face first." We laughed, but there was an undertone of gravity in my words.

A poignant moment drifted by and Miriam uttered the precise words I needed to hear, "You can't direct this… you have to surrender to it." Upon hearing those words, every muscle in my body relaxed. My mind let go of the resistance it had mounted. Every cell in my body responded with acceptance. Miriam was right, I was subordinate to the light, and its bidding was my doing. I had to surrender to the light, to the manifest will of my Creator.

That thought caused my heart to open its gate. I felt the energy expand to encompass Miriam, James, the entire compound, and beyond. I looked around at the unseen throng surrounding me, reaching for me, grabbing for access to the light I carried. They were still there in the field of my inner vision, but now it felt like their reach was natural; that their gathering would lift me, not crush me. I remembered the time in the far eastern mountains when I took the first step out of my then wretched condition. I had to accept the pilgrims and surrender to their ministrations. That act put me back into a mindset of service: a place where I could truly be of benefit to those around me. I saw the connection between accepting them and accepting myself. And I saw the connection between surrendering to this light and accepting this throng of people now. It was direct, not subtle. It was immediate, not in some faraway place.

Absolute surrender had to be my new home.

"Regardless of our origins, humankind is indeed evolving. You, right now, are on the cutting edge of the evolvement of your species. Are you leaning back into the oblivion of subjugation, or are you stepping forward into greater consciousness? Choose."

- Yeshua son of Joseph -

89 · New Places, New Faces

It wasn't long after the Simon incident that the stone walls of our compound became a thin line between us and thousands of new seekers. The camp we established outside the walls was overflowing and makeshift camps were popping up all around us.

It seemed that the throngs I'd felt coming, were making themselves known.

We posted a permanent watcher rotation at the gates to control access to the inner compound, but people were increasingly intruding on the peaceful life we were accustomed to. Several in our community lived on homesteads outside those walls and they had increasing difficulty putting their land to its proper use. Enough disruption of farming activities could spell disaster for the whole community.

We tossed around ideas about how to alleviate this issue before it became a real problem. One particular idea we gave serious consideration: build a town down the hill and close to the main road, with houses, a synagogue, a well, and merchant facilities. It would take a fair amount of labor, but over time might move the seekers further away from the compound itself and off tillable land permanently. Jude was certain that if we took our time, we had the crews to facilitate the construction and not endanger our gainful building contracts. Many felt it might be a real boon to the community as it would give people a place to diversify their profitable activities.

I authorized Jude to begin the project.

It provided part of the solution to Simon's troubles as well. The deal we arranged was simple. Before the magistrate had a chance to seize it, Simon sold his land holdings in Sepphoris on the open market, which brought a goodly sum because of its choice location. James, Jude, and I added money from our personal coffers to meet the Roman levies. The magistrate willingly discharged Simon based on his satisfying the plaintiffs' demands. We promised Simon and his wife a house and merchant facilities in the new town we were building, so they could start fresh with the means to flourish. Simon and his wife were ecstatic about the arrangement; it took the pressure off Simon immediately and his health returned. It also comforted us to know our trusted brother would be living onsite and watching over the formation of this new township.

And in my heart, I knew Joseph would be happy with the outcome, and that was important to me.

Coincident with these decisions was a growing feeling that it might be time to spread my current teachings past the borders of my beloved Galilee. Galilee was

"Two or three challenges can become one solution if you're open to thinking creatively. True creative thinking is dependent upon how adept you are at letting go of pre-conceived notions."

- Yeshua son of Joseph -

saturated with my message, not that I didn't have more to say or that I wouldn't continue to speak to gatherings here, but the people here knew who I was and what to expect if they came to hear me speak.

All of this was going to take some planning, so James, Miriam, and I decided to get away and sequester ourselves. We traveled to Magdala to Miriam's house on the shore of the sea. We took Miriam's maidens to help keep us ordered and fed and we brought Judas to buffer us from seekers who might come around while we worked. Our goal was to formulate a plan for taking the teachings to a larger audience. We were resolute that we wouldn't go home until a plan was in place.

Of course, the sea was beautiful, and things had been so complicated the last many weeks, we were all exhausted and desirous of rest. The first few days we drifted with the sun and wind and replenished our spirits. I was happy to see Miriam recovering from her protracted depression and being with her in this nostalgic setting filled me with joy and gave us some new and unforgettable moments.

We settled down to work and before we knew it, we had a plan. It was a simple plan for taking my message on the road. The three of us would lead the devotees through a whirlwind campaign. We'd begin south through the eastern portion of Samaria and Northern Judah, then cut across the Jordan to Moab, around the southern tip of the Dead Sea, and back up through western Judah and Samaria. We figured we'd be on the road for at least three months and would be able to garner quite a bit of attention.

Once we decided on the plan, we got about the business of setting it up. I charged Jude with getting as much of the new town operational as he could before we got back, so anyone following us home had a place to stop and stay. Minimum, of course, would be a well for water. Herodes and his foremen were happy to help when the farm didn't need them. They were anxious to get the seekers to vacate arable land.

A brilliant blue sky enveloped us as we set out on campaign. Our party was large, consisting of over forty people. James, Miriam, and I were at the lead, with devotees behind, some minding carts of provisions pulled by donkeys, and straggling seekers followed. Judas and a few of his Zealot companions were on horseback, riding ahead from time to time and watching that none in our group became separated or molested by outside forces.

I hadn't been on an extended road trip for many years and I was looking forward to the long walks, new people, and nights beneath the stars.

In each town, when we stopped, we hired and sent runners to the next town to tell people we were coming. It was a winning strategy for creating excitement about our campaign. After our first few stops, we found that people were often ready and waiting our arrival.

The gathering talks were well attended, and in a few towns, we gave more than one talk because the demand was high.

From time to time, runners would come to us and ask when or if we'd arrive at a particular destination. It was exciting to know that people were anticipating the messages we brought.

Not everyone loved us, we were Galilean after all, and prejudices against our place of origin were sometimes too thick to overcome. But, people were, more often than not, forgiving of our accents and what might be construed as odd attire. And of course, being head of the royal family carried its own weight, regardless of the accent.

We were having success, and it felt good.

"What you might call 'going-viral' is not a new phenomenon. It's a consequence of the oldest social game in the world. It's people touching people, sharing what they feel passionate about."

- James brother of Yeshua -

90 · Gathering Talk: Most Precious Currency

What is the most precious currency of your life?

Think about it. If I asked you to pay me with the most precious commodity you have, what would you pay me with?

Would it be money? I doubt it. Money has no worth other than the worth given it by a fluctuating economy. What one gold piece buys today may be twice what it buys tomorrow. Something so changeable cannot be your most precious possession.

So, what would it be?

Would it be food? Is food the most precious thing to you? Hardly. We put a lot of time and energy into procuring and maintaining food supplies for our families. We need food to survive, but if your crops fail or your milk animals die, it would only be a problem for a season or two. Family and neighbors would no doubt intervene, and you wouldn't starve.

Many people, perhaps some of you here, live entirely or in part off the bounty of our Creator's storehouse: the flora and fauna of the natural world. The point being that food is a renewable resource. And something readily renewable cannot be your most precious possession.

And of the other things in your life, which of them could possibly be so precious that it would satisfy what I asked for? It couldn't be anything purchased with money, or made from a renewable resource. So don't give me your shoes, your supper plate, or your chair. They wouldn't satisfy my request.

No, I'm asking you to pay me with the most precious thing you possess. Something so precious that it cannot change in value, for its value is immense. Nor can it ever be renewed. It has the same value now as it will have in two years, in five, and you can never, ever get it back once it's gone. It is something that exists once, and only once.

Your most precious currency is the attention that you spend in this moment, right here, right now.

In fact, every one of you listening to my words, is already paying me with the most precious commodity you have or will ever have. You are paying attention to this moment. You are paying attention to me.

I thank you for that. Nothing of greater value could you ever give me. I know this because I understand how precious your attention is.

What is it that I understand about attention that you may not yet?

Well, I understand that for my message to thrive I need your attention. My message fails and doesn't move into the world if you don't pay attention to it. And it doesn't matter whether you like my message or it angers you. If you're paying attention to it, it simply thrives. For me that's good.

But more importantly, what does your attention do for you?

That attention you spend buys your ticket to the Promised Land. I say Promised Land, because the result of the way you spend your attention is a promise, it's a guarantee. But what manner of Promised Land are you purchasing? One filled with riches of love, happiness, and honor, or will your Promised Land reside in the bottom of an empty cup?

It's your choice. And you make that choice every time you spend your most precious currency, your attention.

Hear me now: What you pay attention to you get to keep. That's the promise. Just as at the market, if you pay money for a sack of seed, you get to keep that sack of seed. If you pay attention to what I say, you get to keep the ideas I've introduced.

So, let's take it further. Say you like a beer or two at the end of the day. You like it so much, you wistfully dream about beer as you do your repetitive work. By the time your day nears its end and you drink that beer, you have lusted for it with such fervor that your attention is rapt upon it. You enjoy it with gusto. And when you've finished it and perhaps a second one, you're left with nothing more than an empty mug. Perhaps while you were drinking your beer, your children wanted your attention, or your spouse. Did you stop and pay attention to them? Did they warrant some of your most precious commodity? If you spent most of your day dreaming about that mug of beer, it's reasonable to conclude that they got less of you, less of your attention, than the beer did.

In that moment, that mug of beer was more precious to you than the love of your spouse or rearing your children. You paid for it with the attention you gave it throughout your day. By spending your precious currency on that mug of beer, it became your promise. And in that moment, that mug got more of you than your family did. If you do that often enough, what happens? The love of your spouse fades, your children stop looking to you for guidance, and you're left only with what you paid attention to, an empty mug of beer. Your life might otherwise be cold.

But what if you changed where you pay attention; changed what you pay for and therefore changed your promise? Perhaps while you did your repetitive work, instead of dreaming about beer, you paid some attention to your own spiritual attainment. Perhaps you also paid some attention to a sweet sentiment you could give your spouse. And perhaps you even spent some of your attention working out a plan for sharing some of your own thoughts about spiritual attainment with your children, so they could learn with you. At the end of your day, you might have that mug of beer, but you might also have a spouse delighted by your thoughtfulness, children who were eager to spend time with you, and a measure of spiritual growth.

I say again, what you pay attention to you get to keep.

It goes deeper than beer and even deeper than the love of your family. It goes to the very heart of your life. You pay attention to this moment and the one after that and eventually you have a well of cherished memories. You pay attention to your spiritual attainment and you grow into a closer relationship with your Creator. You pay attention to helping your neighbor and you achieve the honor derived from service to your community. You pay attention to the covenants of your faith and you get a life lived in integrity.

What you pay attention to you get to keep. Your attention to this moment and the moment after that is the most precious currency you have.

So tomorrow, will you spend the day wistfully dreaming of beer at the end of the day? Will you spend your day paying attention to the transgressions of the world, while all the while ignoring the life that is in front of you?

Or will you take my words you have raptly paid for today and let them sprout like seeds in you, growing into a bounteous Promised Land? Because the Promised Land is at the end of every moment. Let me say that again. The Promised Land is at the end of every moment. It doesn't wait to come to you at the end of your life. It meets you every moment of every day. You pay for the Promised Land with every breath you take, every word you utter, every thought you think. You pay for your Promised Land by where you spend your attention.

So what are you buying? Will your Promised Land be joyful, filled with love and honor? Or, will your Promised Land lie in the bottom of an empty cup. The choice is yours.

Hear me now: What you pay attention to you get to keep.

I give you this in truth.

91 · Nadia Returns

Madeba was situated on a plateau nestled between craggy hills. This was high desert. It was warm in the daytime, much of the year, but tended to be cool to cold after sunset. It reminded me of the area around Jerusalem though the average daytime temperatures were hotter. The skies were generally open and clear, but when the clouds did roll through they usually moved quickly.

It was midday when our band of travelers stepped through the western gate of Madeba. Everyone was tired, so the first order of business was to find a place to camp.

This was a thriving city filled with artisans of all trades and it showed, even in the building facades. Here, walls weren't plain or ordinary. Instead, they were decorated with fine mosaics, colorful paintings, or stunning stone work. Plants flourished in masterfully made pots and arbors of grapes and other vines stood around shops to provide shade from the sun. The town was soft on the senses and a joy to behold. I felt a kinship with these people who placed such a high priority on aesthetics.

Across the open area, a group of traveling players performed a puppet show for a group of children. No doubt they would fetch a paying audience for their more serious performances later that night.

As we ambled through the square, enjoying the colorful artwork and flowering greenery, I saw a radiant woman walking ahead of me. She had long black hair and a spritely bounce to her step. I hadn't seen her since I left her home six years before, but I was sure it was Nadia.

"Nadia?" I called out.

The woman looked in my direction. As soon as she saw me, her face lit up. "Yeshua!" she cried.

I ran to her and we grabbed each other with joyous abandon. I'm sure my behavior toward Nadia was odd to the people I was with. In our circle, a man only hugs a woman if she's a member of his family, and by her dress and Persian features, it was obvious that Nadia was not family. Of course, they had no way of knowing how deeply grateful I was to this magnificent woman who gave my life back to me.

Finally, I let go of Nadia, stepped back, and said, "You look happy. What are you doing in Madeba?"

"We live here," she said, "I moved here shortly after the birth and opened a

> *"The desire to entertain and be entertained is inherent in human nature. But theater is not restricted to humans. I've seen groups of monkeys and herds of elephants partake in play-acting for their friends. If a being has a mind that can conceive, that being has a mind that enjoys witnessing the conceptions of others."*
>
> *- Yeshua son of Joseph -*

healing practice."

"Things are going well for you then?" I inquired.

Her eyes twinkled, "Oh yes, my friend, business is good and I'm very happy." My heart soared with delight from the news.

She added, "You must meet Dania." She turned and looked across the square to the crowd of children watching the puppets. Standing there giggling was a tall girl, with sun-streaked hair. I knew instantly who she was.

Nadia called to her, "Dania, come here child." The girl ran to her mother, grabbing her outstretched hand. I knew the child was only five years old, but from her height, she looked to be nearly seven or eight. Looking at her this closely though, prompted a shiver to run up my spine. It wasn't just her height, or her hair. It was eerie how much she looked like me. The same nose, the same eyes; it was like seeing me in a girl's body.

Members of my group gathered, naturally curious about the woman I so exuberantly greeted.

Nadia said to the girl, "This is an old friend of mine, Yeshua. Say hello."

I said, "Hello Dania, it's good to meet you."

Dania looked at me. Letting go of her mother's hand, she stepped over and said, "Hello." Her face was surprisingly inquisitive and there was an uncommon depth of wisdom in her eyes. The surprised reaction I had to her mimicked in me the reaction I'd heard other people describe of meeting me for the first time. "I know you," she said, "you helped me once."

Nadia gasped, surprised by the girl's words.

"When did I help you?" I asked Dania.

"You helped me find my Mother." I understood what she meant, she was referring to the day of her conception. The group around me began to murmur.

I bent down and said, "Dania, I'll always be close to you and your Mother. Thank you for giving her such joy." I put my arms around the little girl and hugged her softly.

She looked at her mother and said, "Can I go watch more?"

"Alright," Nadia said, "but we'll go home soon. Listen for me." The girl ran excitedly back to the puppets.

I stood and realized Miriam was next to me. "Nadia, I'd like you to meet my wife, Miriam." I turned to Miriam and said, "Nadia is the healer I told you about, that helped me several years ago."

Miriam extended her hand and said, "Hello Nadia, nice to meet you."

Nadia grasped Miriam's hand exuberantly. "It's very nice to meet you. You're a lucky woman to be with Yeshua. He's a special man." Nadia looked at me. "I wouldn't be so happy today if it wasn't for knowing you." Her face beamed.

"He is a special man," Miriam said, "and I can't help noticing how much your daughter looks like him." Miriam looked at me and said with an odd tone, "She has your eyes, Yeshua."

"Yes, she does resemble you quite a bit. That is odd," Nadia said to me.

"Maybe not that odd," I chuckled, "but surely difficult to explain."

Nadia chuckled too, "Are you two in town for a while?"

"Perhaps a few days," I added, "we're here with a group. I'll be speaking tomorrow somewhere around town."

"Oh, good!" Nadia offered, "I'd love to treat you to supper tonight. Won't you both please join us?"

"That would be lovely." Miriam said before I had a chance to remark, "Where should we come?"

Nadia gave us directions to a tavern on the other side of town near her home. She also suggested a place for our party to camp that was southwest of town, near a small river.

As Nadia made her way out of the square, Dania in hand, she turned and blew a kiss in my direction. When she was out of sight, I turned to Miriam and sensed the seeds of discontent growing. I took her hand and said, "I love you." That seemed to quiet her for the moment.

"Suspicion is a form of fear, pure and simple. Suspicion of another means you believe two things; the first is that something is hidden from you. The second is that the hidden thing has the power to harm you. Rest assured, there are always things hidden from you, and the thing that harms you more than the hidden is the fear of them."

- Yeshua son of Joseph -

92 · Discontent

The place Nadia suggested for our camp was perfect. A small river, more like a wide creek, flowed southwest of town. The spot we selected to pitch our tents was flat and next to the water with trees for shade, and easy access to the road. It was just a short stroll from town.

As the afternoon progressed, we set up our temporary home and made plans for the public gathering scheduled for the next day. Several members of our group were dispatched to wander through the town and casually invite people to hear me speak. In a mid-sized town such as this, it was a good strategy for spreading the word. The rest of us had nothing to do but enjoy the day.

When we traveled, the group expected me to have supper with them. It was the time set aside where they could ask questions in a relaxed atmosphere and I'd respond with answers that were deeper and more specific than I might give in a public gathering. On the rare occasion that I chose to eat somewhere else, people would grumble and pout. So, when I mentioned we wouldn't be present at supper, I quietly ignored the groans of disappointment.

Close to sunset, Miriam and I strolled to the tavern. Miriam had been distracted all afternoon. That wasn't odd in itself, but her distraction was more pronounced than usual. I hoped it had nothing to do with meeting Nadia and her daughter, but my intuition said it did. If I were right, this wouldn't be the first time Miriam felt jealousy in our relationship. Prior to marrying me, Miriam lived in a community that placed less importance on monogamy. Her own lifestyle reflected that value. So, it was surprising the first time I realized she was jealous of a woman's misplaced attentions.

When we reached the tavern, Nadia and Dania were already seated. This was a small establishment connected to an inn. There were five tables, none of which sat more than four people. But the atmosphere was lively; the tables were full and a smiling, young man playing a zither serenaded us. Greetings were warm and I settled in for a welcome respite from the grind of the campaign. We ordered an abundant meal and I was pleasantly surprised that Nadia and Miriam were enjoying their conversation. Laughter was plentiful.

After the food was cleared, we continued talking, satisfied from our indulgence in delicious food and good wine. Dania became restless as any child might, and she excused herself to the courtyard to play.

Miriam quickly turned to Nadia and opened a new topic, "Dania's very

"Jealousy is a misplaced belief in ownership. People cannot be owned. They can be subjugated, but they cannot be owned. Unfortunately, to subjugate another you must objectify them. In truth, jealousy subjugates the holder more than it ever can the object."

- Yeshua son of Joseph -

intelligent. And I can't get over how much she looks like Yeshua. That is quite unusual."

Nadia smiled, "I agree, and I don't know why that is, given the circumstances of her birth."

"And what were those circumstances?" Miriam asked. I leaned back to listen.

"I wish I could tell you," Nadia said, "but I'm not exactly sure. It's a mystery… actually, a miracle I can't explain."

Miriam looked at me and asked, "Can you explain it?"

"I probably can," I said, "but I'm not sure that here and now is a good time to do that." Miriam looked down at her lap and I felt her discontent pique. "I'll tell you more if you wish later," I added, "but I assure you, Dania isn't my child, if that's your concern."

Miriam took in a sharp breath and looked back at me; her demeanor unsettled.

Nadia added, "It's true. Yeshua's not my child's father." Nadia looked intently at Miriam and said, "Forgive me, but may I touch your belly?"

Miriam was startled, but let her proceed.

When Nadia laid her hand on Miriam her expression changed, "You're pregnant and it's not the first time."

Miriam was surprised. My heart jumped at the news. The tragedy of the past miscarriages weighed on us. Smiling, Miriam took my hand and said, "I didn't know for sure. Now I have confirmation."

"And it's not the first time?" Nadia asked again.

Miriam confirmed Nadia's words with a nod.

"But you've lost the others, is that true?"

Miriam nodded her head again, the delight that had been on her face the moment before turned to sorrow.

"If you'll let me," Nadia said, "I'd like to help you keep this one."

Miriam looked at me with surprise. "Nadia's an excellent healer," I said, "if she believes she can help us, I'd trust her."

Miriam looked back at Nadia. "What do you see?"

"It's your age," Nadia continued, "your body isn't properly balanced for pregnancy. I think I can fix that."

Miriam and I had wondered if her age was causing the difficulty. None of this could be easy for Miriam. I sat quietly and waited for her to find words.

Miriam sighed, and her shoulders dropped a bit, "What do you need me to do?"

Nadia nodded, and with a sweet smile, she said to Miriam, "Why don't you come see me tomorrow."

"We have a gathering tomorrow," Miriam looked at me, "do you think we have time?"

"We have as much time as is needed, this is important," I replied.

Miriam smiled and said to Nadia, "Why don't you come hear Yeshua speak, and then you and I can go to your home after." Nadia cheerfully agreed.

We filled the next few minutes readying ourselves to depart. Nadia pointed out her house so Miriam knew where to go in case she missed the gathering. Her home turned out to be right across the road from the place we ate. We thanked Nadia for supper and after hugs, Miriam and I turned toward camp.

The moon was bright, lighting our path with a delicate blue aura, but Miriam was stiff and silent as we slowly walked toward the river. I held her hand, but I felt her turmoil. Suddenly, she stopped and swung around to face me. I looked at her with all the love that was in my heart. She was my delight, my absolute joy, and I wanted only the best for her. "What is it?" I asked.

Miriam dropped my hand and pulled away. She said with fervor, "How could you lie to me like this?"

Her question shocked me. The last thing I'd want to do was lie to her. "I haven't lied. What do you think I've lied about?"

"Dania!" was her strong reply.

"Miriam, I haven't lied. Dania isn't my daughter."

"I don't believe you!" Her words were forceful, but her voice cracked through her pain. "All anyone need do is look at her. She's your image all over. Your intelligence, your depth. No other thought is reasonable but that she's your daughter."

I remained quiet.

"The whole camp is whispering. This afternoon three people asked me if I noticed how much the girl looks like you! Everyone's thinking it!"

I hadn't considered this. When I put my mind to it, though, I could see it was a reasonable conclusion, but I knew my truth and I hadn't lied. "I see why you think this," I said calmly, "and yes, it's reasonable, but you have to trust me... that I wouldn't lie to you."

Miriam's eyes flashed, and her mouth pinched. As she stared at me, her hand flew up and firmly slapped me. The sound of it was sharp and cut through the night air like a starling whipping through a low hanging cloud. I was surprised and dumbfounded. Her sharp nails had ripped my skin. I grabbed my face and stared at her.

She screamed, "How many more of your bastard children will I have to suffer meeting?"

Surprised by her own actions, Miriam stepped back, mortified. She clasped her open mouth with her hand, the same one that had just assaulted me. I stood, not sure what to do. I realized how painful it must be for her to think, however wrongly, that this other woman had carried my child to term when she was having such difficulty doing so. I was tempted to walk away; give her space as I'd done in the past when Miriam displayed unfounded anger, but something this night kept me anchored in place.

Suddenly, Miriam's hand dropped from her face and the rage of the moment before quickly returned. "I know this was before we met," she wailed, "but if Dania is your daughter, you've lied to me about many things, not just her!"

I felt the persistent sting on my face. My hand went back to my cheek.

"As a hot and un-tempered person myself, I was ready and willing to engage with the world through anger, jealousy, and violence. I found his rejection of those states very difficult to accept. When I was angry and I yelled, I wanted him to yell back. He wouldn't. If I pushed him, I wanted to be pushed back. He wouldn't. When I struck at him in jealousy or reproach, I wanted him to return the energy. He wouldn't. His response was nearly always dictated by 'the way of peace.'"

- Miriam wife of Yeshua -

"Ouch," I said. The throbbing burn of it pushed me off center. "I haven't lied to you!" I said in an angry tone that I regretted instantly. I paused a moment, breathing, to recover some composure, "It's beyond my ability. I could no more lie to you then I could lie to myself."

Miriam's head dropped and she grabbed her arms to crisscross her chest and shield her heart. She was crying, but I couldn't reach to comfort her. My feet were rooted to the ground; my hand fastened to my face.

Miriam's head abruptly snapped up and she cried, "I can't believe you in the face of this... evidence. I feel shamed by you!"

I was offended that she'd feel shamed by me. Unable to stop, my voice rose in anger again, "This is crazy! I've never shamed you! I wouldn't. I couldn't!"

Then, as if my words had been weapons, Miriam whimpered and grabbed her belly. Something was wrong.

"What is it?" I asked. This time I stepped to her and touched her shoulder.

She let out another yelp and doubled over. I looked down and saw a line of blood trickling down her ankle onto her foot.

I cried out, "Oh, no, dear God, please no!" Miriam looked at me, her eyes pleading for help and all I could think of was to get her to Nadia. I picked her up and ran. I ran as hard and as fast as I could to Nadia's door.

When I arrived I yelled, "Nadia! Help us! Please?"

Nadia opened her door and as soon as she saw Miriam's white face and the patch of blood growing on her gown, she hurried us into her home. She directed me to a room where I laid Miriam on a tall cot. As soon as I did, Nadia began her work.

I went to the common room and dropped onto the floor. With all my heart, I prayed to my Creator to heal these rifts: heal Miriam's body, heal the baby, and heal us.

As I sat pleading, Dania came to me. She placed a soft hand on my shoulder. She looked at me with her innocent face and said, "Don't worry. Everything'll be alright." And as I looked into her deep and radiant eyes, I knew it was true; everything would be all right.

93 · No More Walking

Nadia worked with Miriam into the night. I remained steadfast in my prayers. After several hours, as the sun began to shed its first halo onto the land, Nadia sat next to me. "Your wife is fine and so is the baby," she said. "She's no longer bleeding and for now... all's well."

I almost passed out from the relief of her words. "Thank you."

She squeezed my hand and continued, "You know me. I won't honey-coat things."

"Yes, I appreciate that."

"Then listen carefully." Nadia's voice softened, "She needs rest. She needs several days in bed, flat, right now."

I sighed and nodded my head.

Nadia went on, "There's more. I'd like to give her a round of treatments that'll make her body more receptive to this pregnancy. That'll take a few weeks at least to complete. Maybe longer."

"Oh, I see," I nodded my head again.

"Now listen. At that time, she'll need to go home. She can't be on the road. And, I know this isn't your first choice, but she needs to be carried home, not walk. You should consider a beast or litter of some sort to move her there."

"I can do that," I said.

"And Yeshua... this might all work together to bring your baby to birth, but it's not a guarantee. She may still lose this child."

With tears forming I said, "I understand."

Nadia squeezed my hand again, "I'm glad you do, but if there is, in my power, a way to give you back the gift of a child, it'll be my sincere honor to do so."

I smiled and knew she meant what she said. "Thank you, tell me again, what's next?"

"Well, I'd like to keep her here with me for a few days. Until I'm relatively certain the bleeding won't recur, but you should rent a room with a good bed. When she's strong enough it'd be good to transfer her there so, she can stay comfortable and in bed for the duration of my treatment."

"Yes of course, I'll do that." I added, "As before, Nadia, money's not an issue. I'll compensate you for your work and I can afford whatever provisions are best and needed."

Nadia shook her head and said, "Son of Man, I've no doubt of that. I'm beginning to understand from the throng that follow you, and from the fineries of your robes, that you're not a pauper."

I nodded, "You're observant." For a moment, I considered my day ahead. "I must attend to the gathering. I must speak as promised. And after that, I'll come back. My brother's with us. No doubt, he'll want to come, too. Do you approve?"

"Oh yes. I've given her a tincture to help her sleep. Go to her now for a few minutes before she's unconscious. Oh, and... congratulations that you're reunited with your family."

"Ah… thank you, and yes, I'd… like to see her now if I can."

"Sure, but then come back here. I'll attend to your face."

I chuckled. In the aftermath of my run here, I'd forgotten all about my face. "Alright. I'll be right back."

I slowly entered Miriam's room. Her eyes were closed, but she looked peaceful. I went to her cot and cupped her hand in mine. After a moment, she opened her eyes.

"I'm so relieved you're alright," I said.

"I'm sorry," Miriam said.

"What are you sorry about?"

"The baby." She placed her hand on her belly.

"But the baby's fine. Nadia said you're both fine."

Miriam's face lit up, "I thought I lost it?"

"No, no my love, you're still growing our child."

Even though she was weak, her smile at my words was radiant. She said, "I yearn to have your child so much. I want this baby."

"I know. We'll do everything we can to make that happen. I promise you."

She looked at me in confusion, "What happened to your face?"

I laughed, "Don't you remember?"

"No, what?"

"You slapped me."

"I what?" she exclaimed, "Why'd I do that?"

I realized that the urgency of her body's turmoil must have driven her to extremes. It made sense she might not remember. I flashed on the scratches I clawed into Nadia during my treatment years earlier and how I had no memory of that either. I squeezed Miriam's hand and said, "Don't worry about that. I'm sure it looks worse than it is. What's important is that you're fine and the baby's fine and Nadia is going to keep you fine."

"She's wonderful. She makes me feel safe, I trust her."

"So do I, my love, so do I." I gave her a soft kiss and told her I'd be back after the gathering. Her eyes were heavy, and I knew once I left she'd fall fast asleep. I set down her hand, told her again that I loved her, and went back to Nadia.

Nadia patted my face with an ointment that stung, but she said it would cleanse the wounds and take down the swelling. She didn't ask me why my face was blighted, and I didn't offer. It was probably obvious. When she was done, I left for the encampment. There was a lot of news to relay and a full day ahead.

"Sleep is a state through which our mind stops engaging in the act of physical creation. This allows the body time for its natural processes to run without hindrance from the thinking mind. When the mind is disengaged from the body, it too has an opportunity to run its processes without fear of harming the body. It's a glorious opportunity for both the body and the mind. Sleep regularly and with intent and your life will be well served. Miss sleep, and your life begins to degrade."

- Yeshua son of Joseph -

94 · Infinite Possibilities

Most of the camp was awake when I got there. Everyone seemed surprised when they saw me, probably because one, Miriam wasn't with me, two, I had wounds on my face, and three, I'd obviously not slept. Nevertheless, I kept my morning silence. As quickly as I could, I found James; he was right where I expected, by the river completing his baptism. I joined him. We patted each other on the back, but remained silent.

We sat by the river watching the morning unfold. The subtle light of the awakening sky reminded me of a flowering magnolia. Gratitude swam through my heart for the outcome of the night's events, but I still had to break the news to James, so I spoke up, "I have troubling news."

James' snapped to attention, "What is it?"

"Miriam fell ill last night. She's going to be fine, but she's with the healer right now resting."

"I'm glad she's going to be fine, but… what happened?"

"She's pregnant. She began to bleed just like before."

"I'm sorry, Bit. I didn't know she was pregnant again."

"Well, she didn't want to make something of it until she was sure. It's to our fortune that Nadia's here. She's an accomplished healer and worked with Miriam all night. She's still carrying the baby."

James look of concern turned to surprise, "She didn't lose the child?"

"No, no, and Nadia thinks there's a chance she can help her bring it to birth."

"That's good news!"

"Yes, I'm hopeful. But it's going to mean a change of plans for us." I went on to explain the course of action Nadia had proposed and asked James to think about what it would mean to our campaign. If Miriam had to stay home, I'd stay with her. He was noticeably stressed, but he understood and gave me his assurance that he'd look into the changes.

He looked away from me and said, "Please forgive me if I'm overstepping… but… I have to ask you about something."

I remained silent waiting for his question.

"Everyone is talking about this child we saw yesterday," I sighed, this line of questioning would have to be addressed, and yet, I didn't know how. James continued, "I assume the woman you greeted… that is, the child's mother… she's the same healer Miriam's with today?"

"Yes."

"So just tell me… is the child yours?"

I sighed again, "The simple answer is no, she's not my child. I'm not her…"

James interrupted, "That's hard to believe. Looking at her is like looking at you as… a girl."

"I know…" I said, "the resemblance is remarkable."

"So if the simple answer's no," James inquired, "what's the complicated one?

And don't worry, we have time, you're not speaking until midday."

I proceeded to explain to James as best I could the circumstances of Dania's conception. I reminded him they were the same as the circumstances of my own conception. James looked at me throughout the entire story with a face of utter bewilderment.

When I got the whole of it out, James simply said, "How in God's name are we going to explain that to anyone else?"

"Do we have to?" I asked.

James said, "We have to address it somehow, otherwise people are going to think you're hiding something."

"But I am… hiding, some things… I am."

James burst out laughing. It made me laugh, too. Laughter felt good after all the heaviness of the last several hours. "And, by the way, I can guess what happened to your face. Miriam didn't believe you, about the girl."

We laughed even harder and I exclaimed, "Absolutely!"

———————

I sat by the embankment for a while longer thinking about the previous night and the coming day. On top of all of it, I tried to figure out how to address this issue of Dania. The actual explanation was inappropriate for general conversation. Foremost was the Other who were hidden from all but me. James and Mother knew of them, Mother had her own experiences with them before I was born, but I hadn't even told Miriam, not yet anyway.

So what remained? A half-truth? A stretched truth? A lie? Or perhaps an innuendo? Perhaps, proposing an explanation that could be true. An explanation presented as plausible, even if improbable, was that a stretch? Was that a lie?

I resolved to ask James. On the way to find him, I was approached by John son of Zebedee. "Good morning. Where's Miriam?" he asked.

"Good morning. Miriam's with a healer. She took ill last night."

"Oh, no!" he exclaimed, "What happened? Is she alright?"

"Thankfully, yes, she'll be fine." He looked relieved. I continued, "If you would, please, assemble everyone. I'd like to address the entire group this morning. Would you do that?"

He said, "Of course. I'll do that now."

"I need to speak with James for a few minutes and then I'll come to the group. It won't be long."

"Certainly, I'll get right to it." John got about this business. I found James speaking with Judas. When I got closer to them, I saw they were arguing.

"Am I interrupting?" I said.

"I was nearly always willing to shift my perspective if Yeshua gave me reason to disbelieve my own eyes. I learned very early on that the eyes aren't witnesses of the real, they are witnesses of the illusion. Shifting my perspective wasn't always easy, but if I hadn't made the effort to do so often, I would've lost the opportunities of a lifetime; opportunities to witness the profound mystery that underlies this world."

- James brother of Yeshua -

298 | *Kaarin Alisa*

My presence startled them. James looked at me and said, "We were just talking about something... personal."

Judas looked at the ground.

"Well, if it's personal," I said, "I'll keep my nose out of it. But James, I need to speak with you a few minutes. I'll be addressing the group shortly. Is this a good time for us to talk?"

"We can talk later," Judas said to James.

James whirled to face Judas again and said with some strength, "Only if you promise to stay the course. Until we talk again, promise you'll do nothing."

Judas hesitated; then glanced at me. He sighed and said to James, "Alright, I promise. I'll stay the course until we speak again." He turned to walk away, but under his breath, he said, "But I hope you understand how serious this is." A moment later, he was out of sight.

James asked me, "What do you need?"

"I want your counsel on what I'm thinking about saying to the group, but first... Is there something I need to know, about what Judas just said?" I trusted Judas. As I've said, he was intelligent and shrewd. And above all, he was exceedingly loyal to me. Next to James and Miriam, I trusted him most of all.

James said, "No, not now... really it's... What are you thinking about saying?"

I explained my approach and James agreed it seemed workable and certainly a better option than trying to spring my implausible truth on these folks.

I addressed the group. I announced the pregnancy and explained Miriam's situation. I told them Miriam made the marks on my face in the course of her difficulty. I also told them we'd be changing campaign strategies so Miriam and I could go back to Galilee. I brought up the issue of Dania:

> "I understand that many of you are curious, and naturally so, about the woman and girl I greeted when we arrived here yesterday. The woman, Nadia, is a gifted healer and is responsible for helping Miriam last night and saving our baby. For this, I'm thankful. I know Nadia because of a deep kindness she showed me several years ago when I was in need of healing.
>
> "Her daughter, Dania, is a delightful child, and by your own eyes you can see she looks very much like me. Because of this resemblance, there's been conjecture that perhaps she's my daughter. She's not my daughter. If she were my daughter, I wouldn't hesitate to embrace her. I'd joyfully give her the benefit

"The Zealots were always looking to foment revolution. They examined every opportunity to determine if it was a possible means to their desired end – war. This is the nature of violence; perpetuation of itself at all costs. Violence in any form cannot be blithely tolerated, for it will perpetuate. And like a small knob of ice on a downward snowy slope, it will accumulate and expand until no one close to it is safe."

- Yeshua son of Joseph -

of a father's strong love.

"If I'd been intimate with her mother I'd have felt compelled to at least try to make her my wife. If agreed, she'd be here by my side. She'd be my delight and joy and I might not have ever met Miriam.

"But again, I wasn't intimate with Nadia, and Dania isn't my daughter.

"I was told this morning, that this statement is hard to believe, but consider this: Your Divine Mother, the giver of all life, the interconnected weave of nature that exists all around you and within you, is capable of producing, through her wisdom, infinite possibilities of creation.

"Look at my brother, James. He and I are near twins in our appearance, yet we're not twins. And you could say, 'but you have the same Mother,' and you'd be right. But my brother, Jude, and I have the same Mother and we don't resemble one another at all.

"Who among you hasn't seen a stranger on the road that looks very much like a brother, an aunt, or a cousin… but when you inquired, you found that they had no connection to you at all, let alone, shared a parent.

"I'm prevented from giving you any other adequate explanation of why this child is so similar in appearance to me. But I can open your mind to accept that it's by some means other than a union between her mother and myself.

"This is my truth. And if you were to ask Nadia, she'd tell you it's her truth as well.

"It's divine intervention that cast the lot that made Dania resemble me. I ask you to open your mind and see possibilities: see the wonder that exists in all creation, and find a way to put this question behind you. I ask this from my truth, and I ask this in kindness to Miriam. As she struggles to nurture to life the child that is mine, continuing to give voice to this erroneous question could be hurtful to her."

On that note, I ended the meeting to prepare for the gathering. To my knowledge, this question of parentage was never brought up again. Whether that's because my plea was successful, or because, out of respect for Miriam it wasn't given voice, the effect was the same. It was put behind us. And for that, I felt relieved and blessed.

95 · Gathering Talk: Exaltation

You are part of creation. Nothing in creation exists separately from you.

In this grand and glorious world we inhabit, we tend to think of ourselves as detached from the things and people we see around us. But nothing could be less true.

You're part of the weave of this world. The piece of us that is you is an integral part of the whole. Without you, the whole would suffer. Without you, the story would be without merit. Without you, creation couldn't be complete.

When you've finished walking this land in the body you now inhabit, you'll not disappear, no more than you disappear from our eyes when you remove your clothing. Rather, when you step from your body, you'll reveal a more truthful presentation of who you are in spirit, just like when you step from your clothing, you reveal more of the truth of who you are in your skin.

Who do you aspire to be in spirit when that time comes?

If you're a seeker of higher wisdom, if you yearn to bring more of your spirit to your day-to-day experience of life, you work to exalt yourself: to lift your thoughts and your actions. When you exalt yourself, you create a clearer presentation of your spirit to the world. In so doing, you exalt the whole; you lift the expression of everything around you, because you're not separate. You're not detached. What you do affects that which you touch and see.

The same is true if you languish in lower propensities, such as greed, lust, pain, and anger. These excesses lower the expression of your spirit. Consequently, you lower the expression of everything around you. Again, you're not separate; you're not detached from what you touch and see.

It's impossible to change this. It's an immutable truth that makes us brothers and sisters at our physical core. And if you work to exalt yourself, it makes you closer in spirit to your brothers and sisters who also exalt themselves. If you work to lower yourself, it makes you closer in spirit to your brothers and sisters who also lower themselves, for like attracts like, and nothing is hidden.

So let's assume you're here listening to me because you're pulled to a higher calling. You feel your Divine Creator urging you to grow and remain humble to its gift of life in you. You're here listening to me because you want to exalt yourself and thereby shine the light of your exaltation on everything around you.

To do that, to exalt yourself:

+ you lift your thoughts,
+ you purify your passions,
+ you let go of your excesses,
+ and, you accept your place in the plan of creation.

For remember, the world can't be whole without you. You must accept this.

But be aware. When you work to exalt yourself, you must root down to the core of your being and excise your personal pains and judgments. You must accept everything that's ever happened to you and every decision and choice you've ever made as also being part of the blessed weave of all that is you, and thereby of all that is around you. Again, remember, you're not separate.

How could that not be true? How would it even be possible for what happened to you this morning, yesterday, or last year, not to be an integral part of who you are right now? It's what made you. Your reactions and responses to your life molded the very being who now listens to me. To exalt who you are right here and right now, you must raise all that brought you to this expression of your being. You must raise everything; from your Divine Creator, to your mother and father, even to every hand that ever stole from you something precious.

For I say to you today, you cannot exalt yourself and tear down that which made you. It cannot work. You cannot raise yourself up, as you are, made by all that has been, and declare that some of what made you isn't worthy of exaltation as well.

So, how do you do that?

Well… you exalt a transgression by forgiving it. Forgiving releases you from the bonds of pain around that transgression. Forgiving isn't about the transgressing person. It's about you. It's about releasing yourself to heal.

You exalt a judgment, by releasing it to see life through the compassion of your heart instead. When you hold a judgment or anger or pain around a transgression for a week, a year, ten years, you fall into the pattern of excesses that we know lowers you, lowers your expression of your spirit, and thereby lowers everything around you.

If you hold onto anger for an extended period for even the smallest transgression, you're guilty of the excess of anger. If you hold pain for an extended period, you're guilty of the excess of victimization. If you hold judgment, it's the same. And these excesses lower your expression, and thereby lower everything around you.

To exalt yourself you cannot tear down that which made you. Everything that has ever happened to you must be embraced, must be exalted. Until you let go of your pains, your angers, your thoughts of revenge, your choices to remain a victim to experience… until you do, you cannot exalt yourself. These excesses will pull you down. They'll weigh on you and you won't achieve exaltation of self.

So I say again, you cannot exalt yourself and, at the same time, tear down that which made you. If you try, you'll fail. You won't raise the expression of your spirit and you won't positively contribute to the weave of life you are an integral and necessary part of. You'll negatively contribute instead. The choice is yours.

For when you step from this life and shed your physical form, you'll stand in the truth of your spirit. Your Creator sees all, and at that moment, providence will reveal your truth.

It's your choice how you live your life right here and right now. And each choice you make takes you closer in spirit to the next experience that suits your newest nature. That suits what you've made of yourself through your thoughts and your actions.

You want to exalt yourself so that when you step from your physical form and stand before your Creator, the experience Creator has of your spirit is a closer match in expression to itself, and carries a greater seed of spiritual wisdom.

It's in your power to do so. It's accomplished through exercising choice, and you can start right now by letting go of judgments and reaching for divine forgiveness.

Hear me now; to exalt yourself you must exalt all that made you.

I give you this in truth.

96 · Back to Galilee

We stayed the course with Nadia. Miriam responded well; she and the baby got stronger by the day. When the treatment was complete, Nadia made a tincture and other aids for Miriam to use at home. We promised we'd send regular updates by rider.

I purchased a donkey with a cart and Miriam was comfortably cradled for the journey. It was difficult for her to remain still. She was an active and vibrant woman and this amount of forced convalescence was frustrating. Still, we took no chances and followed Nadia's instructions to the letter. I was as passionate about the birth of this child as Miriam was.

James and several others accompanied us on the journey home. But many of the group continued south on the campaign without us. They'd spread the teachings to people as best they could. They'd invite people to come north if they wanted to hear more of what I had to say. It was the best James could assemble in the short time. It would have to do as providence's hand had forced our own.

Before we left Madeba, I witnessed James and Judas arguing several more times. I was curious beyond measure, but felt that they'd bring it to me if it was my business. I was their brother, friend, and leader, but they were sovereign men in my eyes and I had no right to breach their privacy. But it nagged me.

When we finally left Madeba, Judas didn't accompany us. In fact, he'd left the encampment several days before. I talked with him on his way out; asked him where he was headed. He said, "To Jerusalem," and declined to tell me why. I left it at that, but made him promise he'd return to Galilee at his earliest opportunity. Concern for his safety sprouted in me after he left.

I reminded myself that while Judas was a loyal member of my circle, he was also a Zealot. His way was not the way of peace. I trusted him with my life, but I also knew he participated in violent activities. It wasn't my place to judge or interfere with his life. He took full responsibility for his actions. I decided early on in our relationship to accept him as he was and let the rest remain. It's fair to say that I deeply loved Judas.

I still do.

"Wise people know their greatest strengths can also be their greatest weaknesses, and in that, Ye'sHUa was no different. He had strength in upholding another person's privacy and never intentionally overstepped boundaries, emotionally or psychically. His psychic power was unparalleled, and if it hadn't been for his strict respect of people's boundaries, he could've known anything about anyone. Yet, he was loath to use his power in that way. But that proved to also be a weakness. More than once it worked to keep knowledge from him that would otherwise have been essential to know."
- Miriam wife of Yeshua -

Life returned to near normal once we arrived at the family compound. Miriam was able to rest in bed most of the time. Twice a week she held class for her students. And all that time I watched her belly grow.

After several incident-free months, I became convinced the baby would be delivered, healthy and beautiful. I'd never seen Miriam so content. Her bedridden state made her restless, but Mother kept her occupied as much as was possible. And at night, I was happy to join her and fold my arms around her, delighting in our growing joy.

Mother was elated. She considered helping Miriam a personal mission. She corresponded with Nadia regularly and oversaw the preparation of Miriam's supplements and food per Nadia's instructions. It was delightful watching her. She hadn't been this happy since she arranged our wedding. And I understood why it gave her such joy. This would be her first grandchild from one of her sons.

I kept busy organizing meetings and attending guest speaking engagements in nearby towns, but I didn't venture long or far from the compound.

One afternoon, Judas returned. He rode in on horseback with a friend at heel. I saw them come through the gate while I was teaching. I dismissed class promising to return to the subject later. I wanted to greet Judas. When he got to the top of the hill and dismounted, I saw that he was wounded.

"Judas, my brother, what is this?" I pointed to the bandage protruding from beneath his garment.

"Yeshua, just give me a hug!"

I did that, with gusto, taking care not to grab him over the wound. When my heart was satisfied, I let go and said, "Introduce me to your companion."

"This is Micos." He looked at the other rider and said, "If you don't mind, I'd like him to stay with us for a few days."

I grasped Micos hand and said, "Any friend of Judas is a friend of mine." I saw by the patterns on his garments that he was of the Hellenist sect. I looked back at Judas, "Of course he can stay. We have plenty of room as you know," but I was uneasy about it. My intuition piqued. I wondered if I was putting our community at risk.

Early evening, James ran to me, panting. I said, "Catch your breath... what's made you so excited?"

Through his labored breath, James said, "We just received a rider from the south... with news. A party of Jewish men... including two members of the Sanhedrin... was attacked early this morning in Samaria near the Galilean border. They were traveling to Sepphoris... one of the priests is dead... the other severely wounded."

"Do we know who they were? Relatives?"

James still catching his breath said, "No, not kin, but... the one who died... was vehemently opposed to your teachings. He was... actively seeking to indict you."

"Indict me? For what?"

James eyes narrowed, "If you want to know more... I suggest you ask your friend, Judas. I think he knows much." James words struck me like a roof beam falling into place. Could this be why Judas was wounded? Could this have something to do with the arguments between James and Judas? If so, why hadn't they talked with me about it?

I instructed James to set up a watcher rotation until we had more news and I went to find Judas. I didn't want to make erroneous assumptions.

"Politics was not my strong suit. Politics is concerned with the vanities of humans. I was always more concerned with the hearts of humans. Vanities and hearts are rarely compatible as their basic internal motivators are as opposite as night and day."

- Yeshua son of Joseph -

97 · Treachery Revealed

I found Judas sitting on the back porch idly talking with folks. I said, "Judas, I apologize for interrupting, but I need to speak with you right away."

Judas excused himself and joined me inside. I shut the door, so we could talk in private. It felt as if the world was spinning beneath my feet and I became shrouded with a feeling that, if I wasn't careful, events were about to spin out of my control. I breathed deeply and tried to remain steady, quelling the desire to attend to the situation by quick and forceful means.

Judas probably saw the swirling confusion of thought and emotion I was dealing with.

I quickly said, "My friend, disturbing news has come to me about an attack in Samaria earlier today. I'm not a simpleton. I know you're involved, but I don't want to jump to conclusions, so I'd appreciate it if you tell me flat out what you know about this and what led up to it. Full disclosure is what I am asking for."

Judas sniggered and shook his head, "You don't want full disclosure. Believe me."

I moved closer to him and said with quiet force, "I've never wanted full disclosure more than I do right now. This community of people depends on me for their safety and wellbeing. You're in my house. I ask you again, what do you know about these events? And I tell you true, my friend, I'll help you in any way I can, but I won't coddle you holding back information. We're men, not children, step forward and act like one."

Judas was surprised. I'm certain he'd never felt from me the passion of determination I'd just showered on him. He stammered and said, "Al... alright, Yeshua, why don't we sit down."

I sat down, folded my hands in my lap, and closed my eyes to listen to Judas. I wanted to take him in fully and not get lost in side-trips my mind might take if I was poised to interrupt and ask questions. So I listened; I listened for near to half an hour. What reverberated in my ears was like a chorus of out-of-tune singers that

"In any situation, being an effective leader can only be accomplished when personal emotions are first set aside. There can be no room for irrational outbursts or fear-based waffling of intention at the outset. When situations emerge, fact-finding must ensue. An effective leader holds steadfast to the collection of facts, paying regard to each fact's veracity, until enough facts have been collected to form a clear picture. Once immediate fact-finding is complete, emotions must then be considered, as they can hold deep clues to nuances and intuitions that could be disregarded by the rational mind. It's why a good leader will ask questions, formulate working hypotheses, and then sequester him or herself before any action is taken. An effective leader makes full use of the rational and the irrational."

- Yeshua son of Joseph -

resounded a sad testament to these troubled times.

Here's his story reduced to its most pertinent components: Earlier in the year, while we were on campaign in Judah, a member of the Sanhedrin was invited to hear me speak. I spoke at length about the living law. As I so often did, I made a case for stepping beyond the literal word of the sacred texts and asked people to find the living law that each of us receives from our direct relationship with our Creator.

This priest found my speech to be heretical. He began a campaign to bring me up on charges. None of the other Sanhedrin, with the exception of the current Roman substrate leader, Caiaphas, wanted anything to do with challenging the teachings of the head of the David family. Even though most of the priests in the Sanhedrin were not Davidic, they grudgingly acknowledged the sovereign right of the David family to claim royal inheritance.

Certain Zealot sympathizers heard Caiaphas denouncing the 'Yeshua Movement' as 'a dangerous one that would fell the rule of law if left unchecked.' A Zealot campaign to undermine the leadership of Caiaphas was launched. This is when Judas came to James the first time. James rejected the problem as insignificant.

The main goal of the Zealots was to end Roman rule in Judea, but any Roman substrate was target for their ire. The Sanhedrin had become corrupt with Roman puppets and therefore became a target for Zealot attack.

The Zealot movement had recently been fortified by allegiance with a radical arm of Hellenists. The Hellenist's were already at odds with the Sanhedrin over their right to be recognized in the Temple, something the Sadducees bitterly opposed. The Sadducees claimed that the Hellenization of the Mosaic Law to make it palatable to new Greek and Roman audiences created a new religion that wasn't adherent to the covenant. Their acceptance was continually rejected.

Several violent plots, hatched in and around Jerusalem, had taken place over several months regarding both of these issues. Judas had participated in a number of these fights. His personal motivation was fueled by Caiaphas' mounting aggression toward me.

Eventually, Judas decided to arrange a face-to-face public debate with me and a member of the Sanhedrin, but James vehemently opposed it. James didn't even want to involve me in the discussions because he deemed the proposal too dangerous to consider.

Judas' growing desire for revolt brought him repeatedly to the door of insurrection and he now had the support of nearly all of the most radical revolutionaries in Judea.

Subsequently, eyewitness reports were dredged up regarding the incident in Sepphoris a few years prior; specifically my role in Simon's death and revival. These reports persuaded several previously neutral members of the Sanhedrin to question allowing my teachings to continue under the auspices of my priesthood. However, my Temple Priest position was granted for life. Ending my position would be difficult to accomplish, if even possible. That is, as long as I was alive. Even imprisonment wasn't a reason to strip one of a permanent position.

Unfortunately, my association with Judas, given his meteoric rise to power within the rebel community, caused a substantial uproar and subsequent rumor that I was giving purse to rebel forces. This could be used against me if it could be proven. And even though it wasn't true, the corrupt on the Sanhedrin were known to provide false witness in the past.

The party attacked earlier that day was on the way to Sepphoris to meet with Galilean leaders to discuss what they knew of my movement and what might be done to stem my growing power. No doubt, an attempt would be made to influence Herod at the same time.

Judas confessed that he and Micos were part of the attack, but that he, Judas, wasn't the one to deliver the killing strike. Though he said he would've been happy to have done it, his anger at the priest was so thorough.

The mounting opposition to my teachings offended Judas and he was passionately fueled to his own righteous cause of revolution by the entire affair. James had continually counseled him to pull back his aggression and not fuel the rumors of my involvement in a political revolution. James told Judas that his closeness with me was dangerous and that he should consider distancing himself if he was going to continue his violent campaign against the Sanhedrin. James also urged Judas to talk with me about it on more than one occasion and told Judas he was disappointed in him for not doing so.

After listening to Judas' compelling account of political treachery and opposition to my teachings, I was without words, or at least without civil words. Too many issues had been raised all at one time. On top of that, I had to calmly and systematically deal with my swirling emotions around the behavior of those close to me. These issues should've been brought to me much sooner. Nothing I'd heard seemed easy to deal with and my feelings weren't appropriate to bring forth until I understood them.

There seemed to be one thing, however, that needed to be dealt with right away. Was it proper for the community to continue to allow Judas and Micos to stay on our land?

98 · Breaking with Tradition

I gathered James, Jude, and Judas, for a meeting. I also asked Mary to attend to bring a historical perspective to our discussion. We gathered in a small room off one of the stables. It was nighttime; sounds carry easily and I wanted our voices far removed from community ears.

I started by having Judas relay the information he gave me before the meeting, however, I asked him to leave out one thing. I didn't want him to confess his violent acts to the whole group. It seemed too deep a burden of knowledge. Instead, I asked him to admit to having knowledge about that day's attack.

When Judas was done, I told the group my concern that he might become a person of interest in the crime and that harboring him here might open our community to Roman scrutiny, something we preferred to avoid.

I opened up the discussion. Not surprisingly, James was the first to speak. He was angry with Judas for coming here after the attack when he knew the situation. James felt that Judas should've had more consideration for our safety. Judas apologized to James and confessed that he couldn't think of anywhere else to go. He wanted our support because he was scared. James said he understood, but that he was still angry about other things as well.

Mary spoke next. She said that Joseph probably would wholeheartedly allow them to stay here safe and secure. That Joseph would see it as our responsibility to care for members of our community regardless of personal risk, but that he would cooperate should the authorities arrive. That could include peacefully allowing the authorities to arrest someone if they insisted.

I knew that if the Romans came and Judas was here, arrest would be the best of the possible outcomes. Was I prepared to standby peacefully? Look on as he was arrested, or worse, slaughtered in front of me? I remembered when I saw Joseph do that very thing and it haunted him. It haunted me.

Everyone was silent for a time.

James interrupted the silence, "What about all this information regarding the Sanhedrin and charges sought on you, Bit?"

"Mm... I can't be concerned with that tonight." I shook my head, "There're probably many things to discuss around that, including a small sense of satisfaction I feel from striking a disturbing note in the minds of the established order, but... that's not for tonight. This issue with Judas is pressing. The rest can wait until I've sorted it further in my mind."

James looked away.

"We're not average people," Mary added with a voice of authority. "We derive our strength from divine love. Our community breaks only if we disregard one member for the fear of our own skin. The way of peace teaches that we stand together, or we don't stand at all."

Jude gasped. "Mother, you sound like Father. I still miss him so much..." Jude's voice broke. James put his arm around him. After a moment, Jude continued, "I can't help you, Yeshua. This is a decision you need to make. Bless you for asking us our opinion, but you're the one that'll be accountable for the outcome. I stand with you, whatever you decide. I support you unconditionally.

James said, "I agree."

Judas said, "Me too."

And that was that. The decision was left to me.

When the sun rose in the morning, Judas and Micos weren't with us. I told people that before sunrise, they'd ridden west, and I didn't know their destination.

Truthfully, I lied. I knew exactly where they were headed. With Miriam's blessing, I sent them to Tiberius to lay low in our house there. Miriam and I never traveled to the house in Tiberius, so it was reasonable to assume that most outsiders to the family wouldn't know the house was ours. He was to leave the compound as if he were traveling west, then before dawn, swing around and head east to Tiberius.

I scribed a note for Judas to give to the house staff. It held my official seal so they'd know it was authentic. In it, I explained that they were to provide shelter, help, and safety to the riders as best they could. Also, as soon as they read my note they were to burn it and forget they'd seen it.

I instructed Judas that he and Micos should change their manner of dress and sent them with clothes to do so. Tiberius was a newer, growing city, filled with construction projects, and it might be a good idea for Micos and him to blend in as construction workers for a time. I assured Judas I'd send news with any change.

When they were about to leave, Judas grabbed me and held me tightly.

"Take care of yourself, my brother," I said, "I love you from the depths of my being."

He whispered in my ear a solemn promise, "Everything I do now is for you. I will do as you ask, now and for all time."

Midmorning, Mary came to me and said, "I'm surprised you sent them away."

"I did, Mother."

"I thought perhaps you'd follow your father's lead," she said.

"Most people need to look to a leader for community decisions. Most people cannot shoulder the depth of burden that community-oriented decisions require one to carry. A leader performs a deep service to his or her people by shouldering that burden of decision. If a decision turns out to have poor ramifications, the very people a leader is in service to could revile him or her. A good leader knows this and allows that fact to have proper weight during the decision-making process. By proper weight I mean enough weight that decisions aren't made frivolously, and not so much weight that the fear of personal rejection keeps the leader from making a difficult yet necessary decision."

- Yeshua son of Joseph -

I sighed, "You must trust me. Perhaps I broke with tradition, but in this instance, I believe Father would approve of my decision. You're lacking knowledge of some aspects of this affair."

She looked at me with concern. Then her face changed to reflect resignation. "Very well, my Son, I'll have faith and trust you. Blessings be upon you," and she walked away. I wished I could've told her that I'd taken Joseph's lead and that Judas was safe in hiding under the umbrella of our community, but again, the burden of knowledge would've been too deep.

Two days later, three riders came. They were Roman, one official and two guards. The watcher at our gate brought them up the hill.

I went outside to greet them and as I waited for them to get closer, I looked out over the valley and saw what appeared to be at least half of a regiment on the road by the new town. When he got close, the Official said, "Are you Rabbi Yeshua, leader of this community?"

"Yes, I am."

"My name is Oranos." He said, "I'm the Commander of the regiment at rest below." He dismounted and came to me. He was shorter than I, and balding, but he carried himself with a strong determination. We shook hands; it was odd to be shaking hands with a Roman Commander.

"What can I do for you, Commander?"

"I'm looking for a man who's a known associate of yours. The rebel leader, Judas."

"I'm not surprised you're looking for him," I said, "he was here a few days ago and told me someone might ask after him."

The Commander seemed surprised that I was forthcoming. "Then you admit he was here?"

"Of course, I've no reason to hide it. Is this concerning the attack in Samaria earlier this week?

"Yes," the Commander stated.

James came to the porch. I asked the Commander, "And you suspect the rebels had something to do with it?"

Oranos just looked at me.

I shook my head, "That was a terrible business. I didn't know the murdered priest, but no man deserves to die like that. The other priest, will he recover?"

Oranos eyed me for a moment and then said, "His fate is uncertain. You seem to know a lot about this."

"Change is the only constant in life. Change comes from three primary places, one, as a response to the actions of people, two, as a consequence of the actions of Mother Nature, or three, from the urgings within yourself. If you face all challenges for change as if they were from the third place, your internal urgings, you'll be best served. In other words, always look to your heart for your next action or reaction to emerge."

- Yeshua son of Joseph -

I gestured at the homes, "I'm the leader of these people. I make it my business to be well informed. By the way, why is this of Roman concern? You don't usually investigate humble Jewish incidents."

"Frankly, I'd rather be home than here," he sniggered, "but it seems our Praetor feels we're responsible for murders on our highways, even if only a Jew."

I coughed and cleared my throat to hide my distaste of his words.

Oranos continued, "Besides, if this was an execution led by the rebels and not thieves, then it concerns us greatly. These rebels are dangerous."

"I see," I said, "well, I travel several times a year and safety is important."

"Where's Judas now?" he asked pointedly.

"I don't know," I answered, "he left a few days ago. He was here merely for a few hours to refresh himself."

"Was he alone?"

I simply said, "No."

"Did you know about the attack in Samaria when he arrived?" he asked.

"No, I found out about that later. I surmised after the fact that it might be the reason Judas was concerned. I'm not ignorant of his reputation."

"Why do you associate with him? They say you're a man of peace."

"Yes, indeed," I said, "our entire community is built on what we call the 'Way of Peace.' I associate with Judas because he's one of my people. I believe in accepting people as they are. Anyone can be moved to repentance and change," I leaned closer to the Commander, donned a wide smile, and said in a low hushed tone, "even a Roman."

At first, Oranos eyes widened at my remark; then he smiled, chuckled, and nodded his head. He turned his attention to our watcher and asked, "Did you see him leave?"

The watcher nodded.

Oranos continued, "Which way did he go?"

Without hesitation the watcher said, "He rode toward the west, before daylight."

The Roman turned his attention back to me, "If he comes here again, tell him he's wanted for questioning in Caesarea."

"I will, of course." I invited them to come inside for refreshments before they rode out.

Oranos seemed surprised by my invitation and said they'd just take water if it were handy. I had water and dried fruit brought out. I wished them peace on their ride and had the watcher escort them back to the gate. I was pleasantly surprised that they didn't search any of the buildings or interview more people.

So far, so good.

"Bearing false witness isn't an inconsequential matter. It often has surprising and unfortunate results. But even people with strong intentions to be truthful in all things, can be provoked to an untruthful response by circumstance. Be clear about your reasons and stray from your intentions rarely, and you and your Creator will have little to hash through later."

- Yeshua son of Joseph -

99 · Rebel Purging

The rebel purging began a few months later and I was thankful that Judas was still in hiding. It was another Roman bloodbath, but this time it was targeted.

The rebels, bolstered by the partial success of the incident in Samaria, launched assassination attempts on both Caiaphas in Judah, and on Herod in Caesarea. Neither was successful, though a few of Herod's guards were injured, one rebel died, and another was caught, tortured, and beheaded for the crime. In anger and fear, Herod called on his Roman Praetor to mount a raid against the rebel leaders.

The Praetor called on the new Roman Prefect in Judea, Pontius Pilate, to create a combined force that swept through both lands in record time.

Though I was aware through my network of allies that the military campaign was underway, my direct attention was pulled into the affair when, early one morning, a Roman military contingent of approximately twenty-five soldiers, headed by none other than the commander Oranos, stormed through the gate of our compound with weapons drawn.

I was in the middle of morning prayers and partially dressed when I heard the commotion. I threw on a robe and made my way to the porch. James was already there when Oranos dismounted and walked toward us.

"Commander," I called out, "to what do we owe the pleasure of your visit?"

James put his hand on my arm and under his breath he said, "Be careful, Bit."

I turned to him and nodded, whispering, "Make sure our women are dressed and secure." James went back into the house. I stepped into the sun to meet Oranos. He grimaced as he looked at me.

"Rabbi," he began, "we're here to search your compound."

When he got closer to me I reached to shake his hand, but he didn't offer his hand in return. I pulled mine back. "I see," I said, "may I ask what you're looking for?" I looked around and, except for the soldiers, we were alone, everyone else had gone behind closed doors.

"No," he said forcibly. As my gaze cast to his chest, I noticed recent blood spray on his armor. That meant only one thing; that he'd killed or seriously wounded someone within the last few hours. It could've easily been at Newtown. I had a sudden twinge of concern for Simon, but in any case, I didn't want the next spurt of blood to be while Oranos was here.

"If I know what you're searching for I might be able to help." I looked Oranos

"What you are, how you define yourself in the world, shapes what you perceive as solutions. The carpenter will see things to build. The mother will see people to nurture. The artist will see ideas that need expression. The doctor will see people to heal. And the soldier will see people to kill."

- Yeshua son of Joseph -

in the eye. With my mind, I silently spoke to his inner self with my will in a way he wouldn't be able to ignore. *'Work with me Oranos. You know we're men of peace.'*

He hesitated, "We're looking for rebel leaders."

"Ah," I said, "you'll find none here, but you're welcome to look." Silently I willed to him, *'Give us time to secure our women and children.'*

Oranos blinked several times, hesitating, then said, "I'll give you time to awaken your community, no need to frighten your women or children."

Even though I knew they were already frightened, I said, "I appreciate your patience and generosity." I silently willed to him, *'Instruct your men to pull back their weapons.'*

Oranos blinked again and turned to his men still on horseback. He said something in Latin and they dismounted and put their weapons at ease. I sighed in relief. I could will them to leave, but I had a bad feeling about such an action today. The force of that willing could come back to haunt me. If it were just me at risk, I would've done it, but I had the community to protect. I decided to let him continue, hopefully with moderation.

James came back. I said, "Commander, if you'll give me a few minutes, I'll set things in motion so this can be done quickly and easily." I willed to him. *'Stay at ease and don't interrupt until I come back.'*

Oranos nodded to me, "Take your time."

I gathered James, Jude, Herodes, and two of his foremen to help with the search. I gave them instructions then walked back to Oranos, "Commander, I've instructed these men to take you to each house where they'll bring out the women and children first. Then your men will have free reign to search each building. Is this to your approval?"

Oranos looked at me. I willed to him, *'Work with me. We're men of peace.'* He nodded his head slightly, then said, "That's a beginning."

"Alright," I said, although his comment concerned me. So, I willed, *'Instruct your men to be careful.'*

Oranos turned to his men and said something in Latin and they split themselves into five groups, each to accompany one of my leaders systematically through the compound.

The search began well. Women and children came out unmolested and gathered under the trees. They searched the buildings and herded our men into the clearing nearest Oranos and me. When the soldiers made their way toward my house, I watched as James brought Mary out. She went to the trees to stand with the other women and James let the Roman's into the house. Miriam hadn't come out with Mary and I was confused. I looked at James. He shook his head and with his eyes urged me to stay silent.

When finally the search of the buildings was complete, Oranos walked to the gathered men. He slowly eyed them, as if looking for some reason to pick on one. When no one stood out, he looked at me with an evil glare of satisfaction on his face and shouted, "Rabbi, tell your men to kneel to me."

My heart sank. This was a power play; a dangerous one that I wished with all my heart wouldn't begin. Oranos knew that Jewish men wouldn't willingly kneel in submission. Kneeling was reserved for showing respect. "Men," I shouted, "sit down for the Commander."

As the men sat, Oranos grabbed one of the nearest and pulled him back up. He squeezed the man's arm so tightly I saw him wince from the pain of it. "Rabbi," he shouted to me, "I told you to have them kneel!"

I walked closer to Oranos and said in a calm voice, "Commander, we've been directed by our sacred texts not to kneel in submission to any other than God himself. I can't order them to break that commandment." I silently willed to him, *'Stop this, Oranos.'*

"Tell them to stand back up!" he shouted.

"Please, stand up men," and they all rose. Oranos let go of the first man, and for an instant I thought he might let this perilous game go, but he suddenly turned to the group and grabbed another; it was gentle Peter. Oranos shouted at me, "Tell him to kneel."

I looked at Oranos and shook my head no, "I cannot, Commander."

Oranos said something to one of his soldiers. My heart rose to my throat as I saw the spear rise and move toward Peter, but the soldier merely slapped Peter across the back of the legs. He fell unwillingly to his knees, but I was relieved beyond measure that the spear hadn't stabbed through him. "You see Rabbi?" Oranos boasted, "I can get your man to kneel."

"I see that." I silently willed to him, *'Pick on me Commander, not my men.'*

Oranos stepped to me with a speed and deliberateness that showed I was his target all along. He stood right in my face. I felt his hot breath on my lips as he barked, "You kneel to me, Rabbi!" I stood unflinching. "Kneel!" he yelled again, but I ignored his request. "Aren't you afraid of me?" he shouted. I wanted to scream 'No,' but I calmed myself and stood silent.

He called a soldier over and shouted an order at him. The next thing I knew I was on my knees from the sharp slap of the spear. My insides were churning. I wanted to resist. If my community wasn't at risk, I would've resisted with every bit of adept knowledge I possessed, but that could have brought their wrath down on any number of people who counted on me for their safety. I had to remain compliant for their sake. I stayed on my knees with arms at my side and my gaze turned down.

I was hyperaware that the next moment could be my last.

Oranos grabbed my beard and pulled my face up to look at him. His face bore the contorted residue of misused power. "You're weak. Admit you're weak!"

I took in a deep breath and said in a clear voice, "I surrender to the needs of my people. I'm weak to your force if it keeps them from danger."

He slapped my face hard. Some of the women gasped and moaned. I looked at him undeterred. He slapped me again. The taste of blood filled my mouth. I let the blood run down my beard unhindered. Again, I willed to him, *'Take me if you must, then leave my community.'*

> "Every leader must acquiesce to the authority of someone else. The first external authority to every leader is the group he leads; he is subject to their needs. But there will invariably be others that he or she must remain subject to. In my case, I was subject to the laws of the land and the men who made and upheld those laws, the Sanhedrin, King Herod, and the Romans. From my own experience I can say without equivocation, while the position of a leader may seem to be exalted, it is not so. A leader is in the unenviable position of being the first to be squeezed by both sides. Lie on bedrock and have a bull sit on top of you. In this way you might understand."
>
> - Yeshua son of Joseph -

Oranos shivered and looked at my men, then back at me. I willed, *'I surrender to you in the name of my Creator. With all my heart I give myself to you.'* If he lusted to kill, I was his. Oranos stepped back, his eyes blazing with perverse passion. He was aching for destruction. I felt his hatred, his mounting anger at what he perceived as a weak leader of scum fruitlessly sacrificing himself. His insides were roiling with animosity. He reached for a spear and I knew that if his hand caught the weapon, it would quickly find a home in my flesh. I heard a sudden rustling of activity behind him, and saw confusion flash across his face.

Out of the activity came a strong, commanding female voice, "Why are you persecuting this man of peace?"

Oranos whirled around and I caught a glimpse of Miriam in full priestess regalia.

"Priestess…" he said in bewilderment, "…what are you doing here?"

"I see you remember me, Commander," Miriam said. "Good." She deliberately walked past him to me. She turned to face Oranos and laid her hand on my shoulder. "This man is special to me. I'll not look kindly on your continuing to beat him." I closed my eyes and offered a prayer that this ploy didn't backfire.

Oranos was staggered by this turn of events. "How can he be special to you, Priestess? This is a Jew!"

"You question me?" she shouted, "How dare you!"

Oranos bowed his head, "I apologize."

"And how is your wife? She favors you I trust?" she asked him.

"Yes, of course she does," he said.

"Not of course," Miriam shouted, "she favors you because of our last discourse!"

"Yes, you're correct."

"Of course I am, and your Praetor won't continue to look kindly on you either after a visit from my maidens. They're ready to go to both, if you anger me." Miriam's hand gently urged me to stand. I did.

She put a hand on her belly and patted it. "You see this?" she said to him.

"Yes, Priestess, it appears you're with child."

She pointed to me with her hand, "This man of peace is favored by the Goddess. She's kissed him with her favor." She touched my cheek with her fingers. "He's the father of this child soon to be born – of the Goddess' child!" She gestured to the entire compound, "This community has been chosen to protect the Goddess' offspring." I stayed silent and watched.

"I see," Oranos dipped his head.

"I hope you do, Commander," Miriam hissed, "because neither the Goddess nor I will take kindly to any man who persecutes those under our favor."

"Priestess, I'm here with orders to search for rebel leaders."

"And have you done that?"

"Yes."

"And have these people unlawfully resisted you?" Miriam asked.

"No, they haven't."

"Then why are you still here?" she shouted.

"I was…"

"Make no excuses, I saw you with my own eyes." She flicked her hand at Oranos and commanded, "Leave now! There's nothing here to further concern you." She turned her back to him. He stumbled backward toward his soldiers, as

Miriam turned to him again and said, "And I expect you to remember what I said about these people being under the Goddess' favor. You know what'll happen if you don't."

Oranos nodded and they all mounted their horses. They began to ride toward the gate, but Oranos unexpectedly rode back to Miriam and I. "Rabbi, you've been nothing but cooperative and I'll tell my Praetor so."

I nodded to him, "Thank you, Commander. Go in peace."

When the Romans were well outside the gates and on their way, I wrapped my relieved arms around Miriam. "Thank you," I sighed. She laid her head against my chest and I felt my robe grow wet from her tears. The entire community came and put their arms around us until we were all standing together, arms enfolded, supporting each other, giving thanks as one host for delivery from what could've been a very bad day.

§ *"The Creator takes on many forms and isn't limited by any belief you might hold. The beliefs you hold only limit you."*

- Yeshua son of Joseph -

100 · Grief and Honor

When the community unfolded from one another, the first order of business was to clean up the homes. The soldiers hadn't been respectful with the contents of the buildings. I attended to the broken skin on my mouth. Miriam went back to her bed to rest, and we all got about our chores. Quite naturally, though, everyone was on edge.

A few hours later, a group of seekers from Newtown came. As I feared, Oranos had made a horrific spectacle of two men that morning. These seekers wanted to know what they should do with the bodies, one of which was no longer in one piece. They would've come sooner, but they wanted to make sure the Romans were gone.

It was gruesome news, but I could change nothing. I asked if they knew the identities of the dead men. They did. Both were known Zealots and I assumed Judas knew them well. I had to be careful. Oranos might've killed them in an attempt to flush Judas out of hiding.

It did help me better understand why Oranos came to the compound ready for a fight. He'd just found two known Zealots staying at the settlement below us. He assumed I was hiding more. The irony is that he was right, I was hiding more, but luckily, they hadn't been hiding here. I said a prayer that they were still safe and hadn't become victims to this latest purging.

After talking with James, I decided to send the dead men to Jerusalem. I recruited this small contingent to prepare the bodies per Mosaic Law, wrap them in shrouds, and drive them to Jerusalem to their families. We sent them with cloths and herbs, shrouds, ropes, and a donkey with cart to accomplish the tasks.

A young man in this group named Thomas impressed me with his straightforward nature. Something in his eyes intrigued me and he prompted a strong response from my heart. I told him to come see me when they returned from their grave mission. He said he'd see me when he brought back the donkey and cart. I wished them God's speed.

Other than the visiting seekers, none spoke of the morning events. It was as if not speaking about it put it far behind us. Though I noticed that throughout the afternoon the community didn't hum with joy, and the children didn't run with laughter.

Even Mary didn't mention it when I spoke with her before supper. These

Roman intrusions were nothing new for her, and I was certain it was horrifying to see her son in a position her husband had endured time and again.

My heart was still heavy later that evening, so after supper I went to our room early and eased into bed with Miriam. I pulled her close and cradled her in the crook of my arm, savoring just being safe and alive together. I thought about our baby with wonder and relief that I was spared to enjoy this moment. Both Miriam and Mary felt this child would be a boy. I knew it was a boy, and in approximately two weeks, he would arrive.

I finally whispered, "Thank you for your help today."

"I wasn't sure if it would make a difference," she said, "but I had to try. Things weren't going well."

"No they weren't," I said, "we're lucky that he knew you. But calling yourself out like that, it could have gone badly for you too."

"Yes," there was sadness in her voice, "I don't want to think about what might have happened."

I rubbed my hand across her shoulder and wrapped it around her soft arm. "I felt constrained. I couldn't use my skills to resist him." I said.

"That was wise," she murmured as she gently touched my swollen cheek. "You're fine with what I did?"

"Yes, I'm fine with it."

She added, "I wasn't trying to..."

"Stop," I said, "don't think you have to soothe me. I'm not intimidated or shamed."

"Alright."

"I'm pleased that you acted from your power," I said, "our community deserved no less."

Miriam hesitated, then said, "I'm selfish, I did it for you."

I sighed and held her tightly as I said, "I understand." I wanted to kiss her, to squeeze her, to give her pleasure, but the baby's time was too close for such delights, so I closed my eyes and drifted into sleep instead.

During sleep, I dreamt I was walking through the main square of the Temple of Man. I looked for Man'wa and couldn't find him. I walked through many

"Every being on this planet is unique. We may see dogs as inherently being protectors and companions, and yet a dog may become an entertainer, or take the place of a human's eyes. The dog isn't limited by the generalities we believe inherent in its form. Such is true of people as well. A man may nurture and a woman may build. What you see for one may be true for any. Loosen your beliefs of the roles and limitations of people outside yourself and your own life will relax. You can do what you are called to do, regardless of the physical form given you by birth."

- Yeshua son of Joseph -

buildings, including Man'wa's house and studio; he was conspicuously absent.

After a time, I sat on a bench he and I'd shared on many occasions. A man walked toward me, but it wasn't Man'wa. When he got close, he asked, "Issa?"

"Yes, I'm Issa."

"I have news, may I sit with you?"

"Yes, please do." I patted the bench next to me in friendship.

The stranger sat and we lingered for a moment in silence, breathing as was custom in this place, until our breath was in unison. He spoke, "You were a student of Man'wa?"

"Yes, I mentored with him for eleven years. I'm quite fond of him."

"And I understand he was fond of you." I heard the past tense in the sentence and I knew exactly what the news was.

"I see." I hung my head in sadness.

"He wasn't ill for long," the stranger said, "he let himself leave quickly." He turned toward me and rested his hand on my arm. "Man'wa asked me to wait for your visit, so I could give you the news."

I put my hand on his. "He was thoughtful," I said.

"He loved you, Issa." I patted his hand and nodded my head. I had no words to speak. "Would you like me to sit with you for a while?" he asked.

"Yes, thank you. That would be kind," I said, and we sat watching the trees and the birds. I thought of Man'wa and the many gifts he gave me – the joyous acceptance of life he had – and despite my grief, I smiled.

When morning came, I woke with a start. Someone was knocking on our door. Miriam was already waking beside me, so I called out, "Come in."

James came slowly into the room. "Yeshua, Miriam, sorry to awaken you so abruptly, but you should get up and dressed. There's something you should see."

I gave him a concerned look, and he shook his head, saying, "No, no, something good. Come outside when you're ready."

I sighed in relief, "Sure, we'll be right out."

A few minutes later, we headed to the main porch. The morning sun was strong, and I had to shield my sleepy eyes to see into the clearing. In front of us, arms interlocking in several rows were the members of our community, women, men, and older children.

"What's going on?" Miriam asked.

Mary and James were standing next to us on the porch and James motioned for Rebekkah and Jude to step forward.

"Good morning, Yeshua, Miriam," Jude began, "we…" he motioned to the group behind him, "all of us… want you to know how grateful we are for yesterday. You put yourselves in harm's way… for our sake. Your wisdom and faith kept us safe." The crowd murmured agreement. Jude urged Rebekkah forward, "Go ahead."

"Miriam," Rebekkah started, "these are for you, gathered by the women here." She handed Miriam a large spray of flowers, thistles, and grain stocks.

"Thank you!" Miriam said as she took them into her arms. She looked up at me with surprised delight. I smiled at her and nodded in appreciation.

Jude spoke next, "And Yeshua, this is for you from the men here." He handed me a leather thong with something hanging on it. "We made that for you, to replace the one you lost."

I held it up and looked at it more closely and as soon as I realized what it was, tears of joy began to flow. It was a small, plump wooden heart; very similar to the one Joseph made for me all those years before. "Thank you," I said. I looked at Miriam and she smiled and nodded. I placed the thong over my head and let the heart fall to my chest. I put my hand over it and felt the love emanating from it. The gift touched me deeply.

"I… I don't know what to say," I stammered.

Jude and Rebekkah folded back into the lineup. "And everyone here," Jude said, "has one more thing to say." And like a flock of heron floating in unison through the light of a setting sun, they kneeled. It was an act of respect and appreciation so loudly delivered that it awed me. I was speechless. So was Miriam. This was the most glorious honor we could ever receive.

"The heart is the seat of the divine in your being. Looking back on it, I realize that if I could choose one symbol to stand for me in this world, I would prefer it was this heart of divine love we all carry; the love that my Creator saw in me the first time I met her face-to-face in that field. If I could, I would replace the symbols made popular by the misconceptions of me and my message with a simple, plump heart."

- Yeshua son of Joseph -

101 · Micah

Twelve days later, I sat in the big room listening to the periodic cries of my wife as she sat sequestered in the act of birthing. Many women of our community, including Mary and Rebekkah, were with her. Every now and then, between the cries, I heard the women singing lullabies. It was calming.

With me were James, Jude, Herodes, Peter, and a handful of other men from the community. I was nervous. I knew in my heart that Miriam and the baby would be fine, but I'd attended enough birthings to know that things could unexpectedly go wrong at any time. Two people, who'd previously been one, had to physically separate from one another. It involved a rending of living flesh. As natural as this process was, it was also dangerous.

We passed the time reading Torah, laughing over stories, and praying for a safe delivery. Josea brought us water and fruit periodically. She elected to care for us instead of be in the room with Miriam. She had issues accepting that there'd never been a birthing of her own.

I wanted to meditate; to get out of my body and watch, but Miriam made me promise I wouldn't. Now I regretted that promise. Meditating would've helped me calm the jitters I experienced.

As the afternoon progressed, I became concerned about the amount of time it was taking. James sat beside me, "You all right, Bit?"

"Yeah, I'm all right."

"I ask because you look worried," he said.

"I am, I guess," I said, "I'm staying calm." But a scream came from the birthing room. It was the most forceful scream I'd ever heard from a birthing. I jumped up. Silence followed. James grabbed my arm and kept me from bolting toward Miriam.

Minutes later, another scream came just as loud as the first. Again, a prolonged silence followed. I became frantic inside. Silence from the birthing room wasn't what we wanted to hear, especially after the expression of such pain. The men, recognizing that something could be amiss, surrounded me. They were there to support me if something went wrong and they knew what they were doing. "Calm your breathing," one of them said. "Sit down," said another. It was wise advice that I took immediately.

A third scream pierced right through my heart. I wanted to scream with it, but within moments, I heard a baby crying and the sound of women laughing and

"Over time, meditation can produce a longed for state of being that can conquer any fear, transcend any pain, and calm any upset. The trick is to make the meditative state second nature so that you can call upon it when you really want it, but cannot otherwise regress from a situation at hand. Nicely, this is possible, but it takes practice and patience."

- Yeshua son of Joseph -

shouting in joy. That could only mean one thing, that the baby and mother were both fine.

Immediately, the men pulled me into a circle and we began our traditional prayers of thanks, but I was distracted by the sudden and overwhelming elation of relief.

———⟶※⟵———

'Who are you?' I thought as I peered into his saucer-like eyes.

"You look happy," Miriam said.

"I am." I cooed as I cuddled the swaddled baby to my chest. "He's perfect."

Miriam laughed, "He is that." She giggled, "Have we decided on his name?"

"I like Micah," I said. "He looks like a Micah." I laughed.

Miriam swatted my arm, "He has no look yet."

"Yes he does." I said as I held the baby out for her to see. "Look at that face. He's strong… and creative…" The baby's mouth made suckling movements.

"Give me," she said, holding her arms out, "that's not creative, that's hungry."

I handed him over and watched his lips latch onto his mother's breast. "He's beautiful," I said, "you're beautiful."

Miriam's face beamed with satisfaction. "I've wanted this for so long."

"Me too," I stroked her hair, "I was worried."

"They tell me the next one will be easier."

"The next one? Already planning, are we?" I teased.

"Maybe…" she said with a smile.

As I looked at Miriam nursing our son, I felt euphoric. I felt as though I'd lived every moment just for this one. I was wholly unprepared for the unabated joy of it.

———⟶※⟵———

Soon, we gathered again for Micah's circumcision. By rights, it was my ritual to fulfill, but I couldn't bring myself to do it. James consented to do it instead.

Even though James performed the cuts, I had to hold Micah still and announce his name during the ceremony. I felt the fearful trembling of his legs and the cries and jerks of his body as he reacted to the shock of it.

It was hard for me. This was very different from the elation I felt at his birth. I was Jewish and proud of it, but my training had taken me past the literal law of the Mosaic covenants and in my heart, I no longer believed circumcision was an absolute. Besides that, because of my wife's pagan status, no one outside this community would accept Micah as Jewish by birth.

I wrestled with the pain I helped inflict on my son. I don't know how other fathers got through the ritual unruffled. For me it was deeply disturbing.

James was no help to me. He easily accepted performing the ritual. He felt it a privileged and sacred duty. All I could do was imagine Joseph holding me in the same setting. Realizing that I didn't remember the ritual at all and knowing in my heart that it didn't affect how much I loved Joseph. And if he had doubts or pain over the ritual, he didn't relate them to me.

I forgave myself and put it behind me quickly. Too many recent grievances from life's tragedies and near misses were threatening to pile up on me. I couldn't let them linger.

Every day now, I felt a rushing of time around me, as if something monumental was coming toward me at a speed I couldn't slow. Life seemed too short, too sweet, too precious to let injuries and injustices get in the way of my joy. I resolved to make the most of the time I had left.

I resolved to faithfully put love first and let it lead my heart with forgiveness into each and every moment.

"The truth of the statement 'what you do to another, you do to yourself,' is no better brought home than in our relationship with our children. They're not just mirrors of us; they are shiny, magnified, sensitive, and immediate mirrors of us."

- Yeshua son of Joseph -

The Quickening

102 · Unclean Acts

The months progressed and life brought me joy, every day. I loved rearing my son, and tending to the duties of my station, even those with challenges gave me renewed satisfaction. But soon, that satisfaction would be tested in ways that were as yet unforeseen.

One lazy Sabbath afternoon, I was lounging with the family in the back courtyard, laughing and watching Micah swat at Miriam's hair. Mary was especially happy and I marveled at her steadiness. James was relaxed, a state too uncommon for my brother with the need to get things done. Jude and Rebekkah were caressing each other in ways that made my heart sing. After their rift, they'd found a new place of dearness with one another. It was a day born of love and delight.

Suddenly, a member of the community interrupted our reverie to announce a visitor on horseback, a single Roman.

I put my rabbinic robes back on. It was only proper on the Sabbath to greet anyone with my faith first.

When I got to the clearing, I saw it was Oranos, and as told, he was alone. When he saw me he didn't dismount, but rather waited for me to walk to him. "Good afternoon, Commander," I said.

"Rabbi."

"This is Shabbat, our holy day." I mustered a thin smile, "Are you here to worship with us?"

Oranos looked away, "No, Rabbi, I've come to give you news." He looked back at me, his face hardened.

"Oh?" I said, "What news?"

"Your friend, Judas son of Simon, is… dead." My heart plummeted.

"I see," My voice betrayed grief.

Oranos' face cracked into a smile at seeing my pain. "I thought I should tell you right away," he said sarcastically, "since I know you want to stay abreast of news that concerns you or your community."

"Yes," I managed to speak, "you're accurate. I appreciate hearing the news."

Oranos continued to enjoy the sight of my heart fighting with grief.

"Where," I inquired, "did you find him?"

"In Tiberius," he said. "He thought he could elude us."

"Well, you're as thorough as ever, Commander." I couldn't stop the tears; hearing Tiberius I thought it must be Judas. "I haven't seen him since you came for him the first time. This news saddens me."

Oranos cocked his head to one side and for a moment, I thought I saw empathy in his face, but it left too quickly for me to be sure. I heard someone on the porch behind me. I imagined it was James, or Jude, or both.

"Have his remains been released to the family?" I asked.

"No," he said, "we've done nothing since he was dispatched this morning." It was a brazen and debasing act of vengeance to kill a Jewish person on the Sabbath.

I was sure Oranos knew this and I quickly set aside my impulse to be angered by it.

"I'd like to see to his proper interment." I said, "Please release his remains to my community."

His face betrayed his maturing wickedness as he said in a loud, mocking voice, "Rabbi, I only have one piece of it, but you're welcome to it." He grabbed a blood-soaked bag hanging from his saddle. I thought he'd hand it to me, but instead, thick globs of blood splattered across my robes as he threw the contents at the dirt.

It was a severed head. It rolled, and then rocked at my feet. As I stared at the grisly display, cries and gasps rose from the people around me.

I was consumed with horror at Oranos' obvious brutality, and luckily so, because it was easy to hide my relief at realizing this wasn't Judas. It was Micos. I closed my eyes and allowed my head to remain bowed to the scene. I put a hand over my heart and turned to the house. James and Jude were appalled by this display too. I called out, "Would one of you please bring me a clean cloth?"

A moment later, James brought me a cloth that I unfurled and laid gently over the partial man at my feet. James put his hands on my shoulders to steady me.

"Oranos," I said, "I'm grateful to you for bringing me this news of Judas. Please leave us now so we may be with our grief?"

Oranos laughed, and shouted, "You grieve over a treasonous murderer?"

"He was a brother to me in faith," I said, "I'm bound to administer to his remains with respect."

"You disgust me," Oranos said. The irony of his words struck me like a heavy hammer falling on a fig.

"Nonetheless," I asked again, "please give us the space to do as we see fit."

Oranos turned and shouted as he drove his horse out the gate, "We'll meet again, Rabbi." It was right then that I realized this was a very personal vendetta. Oranos and I were locked in a battle only he wanted to fight, but obviously locked we were.

I knelt beside the cloth and began reciting from Torah. James joined me.

———

That evening, I sat sequestered in a bedroom, not my own. I'd done something I had to atone for. A Jewish person isn't supposed to touch the dead on the Sabbath, especially a Rabbi. If you do, you become 'unclean,' a state you must atone for.

But I couldn't let the man lay in the dirt the rest of the day. To me it was important to take care of him quickly. I didn't feel right commanding another person to perform an unclean act, so the care of Micos fell to me.

"It's unhealthy to postpone grief. You can forestall the momentary reactions of your heart in deference to the initial moment of loss, or your body can override your reactions with shock. But it's best to react to any situation that creates grief as quickly and as fully as possible. The better you are at expressing grief as it arises, the faster you'll be able to overcome it. Initial barriers to grief have the unfortunate propensity to turn into large obstacles over time. Don't create grief, where you might not feel it; but if you feel it, let it roll through."

- Yeshua son of Joseph -

I took him to the workhouse. His eyelids wouldn't close, so I placed swabs of clean cloth on them. Neither could I close his mouth, so I left it open. I washed his remains carefully with respect and love, and sang to him as I gently combed and braided his hair, adding ornaments to it as his Hellenist brethren would. I laid him on a bed of leaves, herbs, and oils, placed gold pieces on his eyes, closed his shroud, and took him to the same tomb where Joseph had lain.

We burned the rabbinic robes Oranos had splattered with blood, and that I wore caring for the remains. Next, I was compelled to spend seven days in ritual cleansing to atone. Forbidden from eating or praying with others, touching my wife, or administering rabbinic duties, I was an outcast until I completed the rituals.

When the seven days were done, and the sun was gone from the sky, I tiptoed into our room and asked Miriam if she'd accept me back from my cleansing journey. She said, "I can't wait to hold you."

And neither could I wait to be held.

A few weeks later, a rider brought a note. It read:

"Yeshua,

"I send my condolences over the fate of Judas son of Simon. I've heard that the Romans left his body with you for entombment.

"I've spoken with his family. They're aware of the events that transpired and are thankful for your tending to his remains.

"I'm now in Jerusalem and will swing by your home in a few weeks on my way home.

"See you then.

"Micos"

I was overjoyed as this note obviously came from Judas and I was anxious to see him. My heart ached for his presence. Even James was noticeably relieved when I showed him the note, and he said he looked forward to greeting Judas when he arrived. Obviously, there was love between them no matter how much James liked to hide it.

And to the outside world, we continued to pretend that Judas was dead.

"When you love someone, you love them, the real them, their spirit. Actions may cause a rift here or there, may even cause a parting of the way, but that person will remain tied to you in spirit with a bond that is unbreakable. Love transcends the temporal and permanently unites us."

- Yeshua son of Joseph -

103 · Disturbing News

A few days later, an unfortunate incident occurred with a young married couple named Azrael and Sarah. They lived at the devotee camp inside the compound and were dedicated to the teachings. In particular, Miriam and Sarah were close. Sarah attended Miriam's classes and they shared a deep kinship. Azrael attended my classes and proved to be a profoundly religious man who often had to struggle with letting go of dogma to see the larger picture. But he was eager to do so, even when it was difficult. I admired his diligence in that respect.

But, before I can speak of this incident, I must reveal the events that led to it. The story is complicated.

Some months before, John son of Zebedee, asked to speak with me in private. He was anxious. "I've something disturbing to speak with you about."

"Feel free John, I'm here for you."

"Yes," he said, "I'm here on behalf of several people who just don't know what to do. It's about Azrael and Sarah." He took a deep breath, and hesitated a moment, then said, "Sometimes we hear things that are unsettling... I think Azrael is abusing Sarah."

I sighed. I wasn't sure if what they heard was merely young people being audibly indiscreet. John picked-up on my thought, because he said, "Yeshua, we live with little privacy and many of us are married. From time to time, we hear things that we simply ignore out of respect for others' privacy. I don't think that's the case here."

"I see," I said, "setting aside others for a moment, have you personally heard things that disturb you?"

"Yes, I have," he said, "last night I heard things I've heard before, only worse." He looked at his lap, obviously troubled. "I walked by their tent, and I heard Azrael shout, 'Do it woman.' It startled me, Yeshua, he was angry, so I stopped. I heard Sarah clearly say, 'No.' Then I heard slapping, and cloth ripping." Tears formed in John's eyes, "I heard her whimper. I know she was hurting. I left quickly." He looked at me, his face was red and pinched, "I feel like a coward for not helping, but they're... married. It's... not my place."

"It's alright," I said in an effort to comfort him, "you're right to come to me. You say this is typical?"

"Yes, others have spoken of similar things. And I haven't heard this myself, but others have heard Sarah choking."

> *"Marriage is a partnership. Like any type of partnership, it can be beautiful and rewarding when each partner respects the other as a sovereign being creating and upholding mutual and individual goals through the container of the relationship. The golden rule is paramount. Never ask your partner to fulfill a role you wouldn't ask of yourself."*
>
> *- Yeshua son of Joseph -*

"Choking?" I asked.

"Yes," John said in a low voice, his face again turned downward.

Hearing this third-hand from John was disturbing to me, let alone if I'd heard it myself. "Your observations concern me." I touched his arm. "I'll tell you one thing though," I said, "if you hear anything like this again, shout into the tent, ask if she's alright. If she says yes, then leave. If she says no, then call others over and go in as a group to help her. Just because she's married, she hasn't given up her right to be safe."

Later that same night, I talked with Miriam. Like me, the tale disturbed her. "I think I need to talk with Azrael," I said, "on the surface, it sounds like he's abusing her, asking her to do things against her will. I should ask him for an explanation. Is that right? Is that fair?"

"What does your intuition say?" she asked.

I closed my eyes and looked inside. What I saw from my inner inquiry shocked me. I looked at Miriam. "My intuition says he's degrading her in multiple ways. And it's been going on for years." My heart ached as I realized this was no longer in the hypothetical. I tried not to look into people's private affairs with my inner senses. I could see things that were none of my business. It was uncomfortable and I sometimes felt I was breaching people's privacy, but when things came up that demanded I use these senses, I trusted them explicitly. This was one of those times. "Would you be comfortable asking Sarah about this?" I asked Miriam.

"If I can keep my anger out of it, I do." She wasn't joking, she meant it sincerely.

"Can you?" I asked.

"Frankly, I don't know," she said.

I decided to talk to Mary for a historical perspective. I found her already in bed, reading. "What are you reading?" I asked. Our community was one of a few that encouraged women to freely read the sacred books.

"Psalms," she said, "Joseph and I read them to each other. It soothes my heart." She saw the trouble in my eyes. "You didn't come here to talk to me about Torah, Yeshua, what's so heavy on your heart?"

"Something's come to my attention that's disturbing. I'm told that one of the devotees is abusing his wife. Mother, he's raping her."

Mary sighed, "That's a hard one. It's not easy to intervene in a marriage."

"Did this ever come up when Joseph was alive?"

"Yes, once," she said, "of course we all knew, she had bruises that couldn't be ignored."

"This woman appears fine. Things have been heard at night that point to this violence. And not just that. Upon the urgency of the accusations, I looked with my inner eyes. These accusations are the tip of a much larger problem. What did Joseph do?"

"Few understood the true extent of Ye'sHUa's respect for them as sovereign beings, because few truly understood how transparent they were in his gaze. It seems to require a super-human strength to resist the temptation of acquiring that much knowledge. Ye'sHUa proves to us all, that it's wholly within our capability to respect others that deeply by first respecting ourselves just as deeply."

- Miriam wife of Yeshua -

"Joseph did the pragmatic thing. He moved the man out of the house and counseled him for months. I counseled his wife. Gradually they came back together. But it wasn't easy."

"What caused him to do it?"

"Oh," Mary said, "she rejected him coming to her bed for many months, and one night in frustration, he couldn't take being rejected again."

"I don't think that's the situation here," I said, "I suspect he's violent by nature."

"Well, there's only one way to start," she touched my arm, "you have to talk with them."

I went back to Miriam and asked her not to speak with Sarah in the morning. I wanted to talk with Azrael first.

104 · Harmful Actions

I did talk with Azrael and he was shocked... and angry. He thought it was none of my business what he did with his wife. I made it clear that in our community, women had rights. One of those was the right not to be forced into any act.

Finally, he confessed his violence. I sensed it was purging for him to speak, but it was difficult for me to hear. Most of my difficulty arose from seeing his certainty that he had a right to abuse her. He freely admitted to the things I'd seen with my inner eyes and other things even more degrading. By the time he finished confessing his offenses, they'd sickened me. I found it difficult to stay neutral. It was terribly reminiscent of some of the things I'd witnessed in my travels.

I asked Azrael if he was serious about the teachings and he asserted his devotion to them. I made it clear that he had no chance of raising his spirit if he couldn't see the harm of his actions.

I was tempted to ban him from our community, but one of the most basic tenants of our faith was that people can atone. And I knew in my heart that he was sincere in his search for spiritual attainment. I felt compelled to give him an opportunity to change, regardless of the severity of his acts. So, I told him he had to stay away from her. I assigned him to live in a separate tent from Sarah.

His last words to me after I told him he had to live separately were, "But she belongs to me."

I said, "No, she belongs to no one but herself."

Later that afternoon, Sarah was with Miriam and together we talked. She broke down crying and said the abuse had been going on since soon after they married. She told us that for these seven years, none had ever expressed concern for her safety. That included Azrael's parents, and a brother they lived with for a time. Her story was disturbing.

She'd felt as if she had no identity and no worth. She confessed that before she began studying with Miriam, she'd accepted that the pain of her life was merely her lot. However, now she understood that she had a right to say no to these humiliations. Just recently she began doing that. Unfortunately, her assertions made Azrael angrier and the pain he inflicted got worse.

"How can you know if you're actually growing from any spiritual practice you adopt? That's easy. Examine other areas of your life. It does no good to count spiritual progress by how many hours you can meditate, how many books you've read, or how often you pray. You must measure your growth by the small things. Are you smiling more? Do you have more patience with your loved ones? Are you kinder to people? Do you have less judgment of yourself, or of people you once judged harshly? Are you more forgiving of mistakes? If a spiritual practice isn't lightening your everyday life, it's not doing you much good."

- Yeshua son of Joseph -

Miriam's heart flooded with empathy. She was so immersed in helping Sarah that she had no space to let her anger get the better of her. I made a mental note to congratulate her later when we were alone.

I mentioned that Azrael moved to a separate tent, but Sarah felt he wouldn't be able to respect those boundaries. I said we'd cross that bridge if need be later. Then I told her something I was surprised I uttered, but it came straight from my heart. I wouldn't blame her if she wanted to ask for a divorce. And if so, I would help her achieve it.

I assigned Peter to counsel Azrael on a regular basis. I thought Peter's advanced age might help Azrael accept the mentoring relationship. Things were fine at first, but it only took a few weeks for Azrael to violate my request, by going to Sarah's tent and violating her. This time, however, Sarah told Miriam. When Miriam told me, I talked with Azrael. I implored the light inside me to heal Azrael, but it wouldn't.

A few days later, it happened again, and it was clear that Azrael couldn't control himself even with regular counseling. And each time I asked the light to heal him, it wouldn't. Unfortunately, by this time, the entire community knew about the problem and I watched Azrael become more and more isolated. It left Azrael with very little support. Upon Rebekah's invitation, Sarah moved in with her and Jude temporarily, in hopes that her nights would be free of Azrael's visits.

But that didn't stop Azrael. He found her one afternoon as she was picking fruit in the orchard. He threatened her with a knife and if she hadn't screamed to alert others to her plight, he could've done anything.

This was an untenable situation. Because they were married, nothing Azrael did was 'against the law.' Whether I felt it should've been or not, it wasn't. All I could do was expel Azrael from the compound based on him willfully, and without remorse, repeatedly harming a member of the community. Sarah was now free to move back into a tent and continue her studies. And to make things permanent, Sarah asked for a divorce.

One last time, before I sent him away, I asked the light to heal Azrael, but it wouldn't. I was never able to command the light. It had its own consciousness and if I ever doubted that, I no longer did.

I moved to convene a rabbinic council to grant Sarah's divorce. But I had a bad feeling about everything around this situation. A divorce wouldn't necessarily keep Azrael from harassing or otherwise accosting Sarah. She might live the rest of her life under a dark cloud of fear.

Upon hearing about the rabbinic council, Azrael became enraged. He brought two of his brothers to try to force me to relinquish his wife. They purported that I was unlawfully detaining his 'possession.'

Their demands infuriated me, but I remained politic. I reminded them that inside these walls the law didn't support their demand. Sarah could stay or go as she saw fit. When I asked her in front of them, she said she wanted to stay. That was that.

Azrael threatened to go to the Roman Magistrate to retrieve his 'possession' and I said he was welcome to do that. I knew the Romans were more enlightened than many on this point of women's rights, and would no more insist Sarah leave with him than I did.

That was the last time I saw Azrael, those few weeks ago, when he and his brothers left. I was looking forward to the rabbinic council, because once the divorce was granted, any attack on Sarah by Azrael would be in violation of law and could be dealt with through the magistrate.

But wishing doesn't always make things so, and the unfortunate incident I'm about to divulge put the entire community at risk yet again.

The last thing I expected when I went to sleep that night was to be awakened by a bloodcurdling scream. It was so terrifying a sound that it woke nearly the entire community. Miriam and I jumped out of bed and went to the clearing. Dozens of people were already there.

"Where did that come from?" someone asked.

The night was deadly silent. Miriam suddenly said, "Sarah, where's Sarah?

We rushed toward Sarah's tent. People were standing there, gawking. I gently urged myself through the crowd and what I saw was an even greater shock. Sarah was standing over Azrael, a knife in her hand, and blood was gushing from a sizable wound to his neck.

He reached his hand toward me as if to try to touch me and slurred, "I wish I could've…" but he didn't finish the thought before he died.

Sarah dropped the knife, her face transfixed in anguish and shock. I called out, "Miriam!" I said to Sarah, "He'll not hurt you again."

When Miriam pushed into the tent, I asked her to take Sarah back to the house. Several of those standing around helped me with the body.

"One of the strongest living things ever created is the seedling. Why? Because a seedling pushes toward the light and knows in its core that it has an imperative to find it."

- Yeshua son of Joseph -

105 · Maelstrom

Obviously, Sarah killed Azrael in self-defense, but the outside world wouldn't see it that way. This was an underclass woman who killed her husband while, they could arguably say, 'he was asserting his rights.' The tide of social thought would be that she should be put to death.

But the notion of capital punishment was abhorrent to me. As I've said, anyone can atone, especially for an act so desperate. I wanted to find safe passage for all of us through this trouble, but I wasn't sure I could.

The first problem was that we'd have to release Azrael's body to his family. His brothers would want her dead, I was certain of that. If we could keep the incident in the community, we'd have many choices, but that didn't seem to be an option.

Miriam was frantic for Sarah's safety. "We have to protect her," she said as she paced back and forth in our bedroom. I was tired. I'm sure Miriam was too. The sun would soon rise and we'd gotten very little sleep.

"Do you have a suggestion?" I asked her.

"Send her away." She looked at me with determination, "You've done it before, with Judas."

"I'd be happy to arrange it if I felt it would work."

"Why wouldn't it?" she asked.

"You think the authorities would believe we weren't hiding her if she disappeared now? Besides, Judas has a reasonable chance of defending himself if caught."

"She could run away."

"And then what? If she managed to elude Azrael's brothers, which is doubtful, how would she support herself?" I shook my head, "Become a prostitute? That would just add to her punishable crimes."

Miriam threw her hands in the air.

"We could employ her at one of your homes," I said, "but I'm sure the authorities would look there. We can't trust the Tiberius house any more, not after Oranos found Micos."

Miriam looked at me and the worry practically dripped off her face like hot wax. I had only one idea, "I can send inquiries to allies outside Judea, but that'll take time for riders to make the trips."

Miriam put her hand on my chest. "I'm frightened for her, Yeshua."

I put my arms around her and pulled her close. "I have a very bad feeling about this."

"What'll we do," she asked, "if officials come before we find a place for her?"

I sighed, "I'll have no choice. I'll have to give her over if they ask."

Miriam pulled away from me, "You can't!"

"I won't have a choice."

She started to sob, "You can't."

I put my arms around her again. "Let's hope it doesn't come to that."

―――🌿―――

Eventually Miriam was able to get to sleep, but I couldn't. When the sun rose, I went about the business of the day. I completed my baptism and found James. "We have to release Azrael's remains to his family," I said.

"Yes, I agree," he said, "it's our duty to do that quickly."

"Would you see to that? I have some other business to complete."

"Yes, of course," and he went off to attend to it.

I was anxious. I knew that if I wasn't careful, my entire community would get caught in a maelstrom of events that could have grave consequences for many people. It was unfortunate that Sarah had resorted to such severe violence, but I couldn't blame her. In my heart, her actions were entirely justified. The problem was; would I feel the same about my actions when this business was over?

―――🌿―――

Later that afternoon, I'd finished dispatching five letters on Sarah's behalf to confederates outside Judea. I knew at least one of them would offer help, but when I gave the letters to the riders, my heart was burdened with a knowing that the help wouldn't come in time.

As I contemplated options, trying to formulate new thoughts, Azrael's brothers interrupted by forcibly storming through the gates and up the hill.

"Where is she?" the eldest one shouted.

"That's not your business," I said calmly.

The eldest came toward me with malice in his eyes and I put up my hand. "I promise you'll not be happy if you attack me," I said, "I will defend myself."

He stopped in his tracks and yelled, "I want her to pay for what she's done."

This was much too reminiscent of the situation with Nadia so many years before. I had a hard time staying rooted in the moment. Nadia's frightened face rose into my vision, and the memory of the two mercenaries dead on the floor swirled around me. The faces of the two brothers intermingled with the faces of the dead men in Nadia's home. I kept forcibly pulling myself back to the present. I was determined not to have that sort of outcome today. So, against my better judgment, I set my will. I willed that they back down and leave without attacking

"Your brain has an internal mechanism that continually seeks to match your present with your past. It helps you form habits and gives you the ability to sail through mundane tasks without effort. However, it has no ability to sort out when it's being helpful and when it's not. When the brain finds a match, it transports you to the past, hoping, of course, to show you how to handle the situation based on how you handled it before. The problem is that as soon as you are transported to the past, you no longer have the wherewithal to accurately assess the current situation. Taking the time and making the effort to learn to live fully in the present every day gives you the exact tool you need to keep yourself from falling victim to this otherwise helpful mechanism."

- Yeshua son of Joseph -

me, and with no more than Azrael's remains.

Once my will was set, the situation immediately changed. Both brothers backed away and the eldest said, "All we want is Azrael. Then we'll go in peace."

A short time later, they left pulling Azrael's remains in a litter.

106 · Dangerous Man

Of course we hoped that'd be the end of it, but a few days later in the afternoon those hopes died. Who else but Oranos, with a full contingent of well-armed soldiers, ambled up the hill in an unhurried display that defied the gravity of the visit. I sensed, as I watched him come slowly toward me, that he was looking forward to causing havoc in my life. And the more it hurt me, the better. Unfortunately, I was acutely aware that he had the law on his side.

When he got closer, I saw Azrael's brothers following the soldiers. It was unnerving to have them proceed so slowly. It was like being bound to a stump, waiting for the axe to sever my head from my neck, and having the executioner stop and have a meal and a nap before he did the deed.

I made certain Mary, Micah, Miriam, and Sarah were safe and out of sight in the back of the house. All men did the same with the other women and children, and then joined James, Jude, and me around the clearing. I stayed on the porch. If Oranos was going to take his time getting here, he could come all the way here.

Several men came to me over this time to tell me they stood by me whatever I had to do. They had faith in my judgment. That was good to hear, and I sent out earnest prayers that my judgment would stand up to their faith.

Finally, Oranos and his soldiers came through the gate and made their way to the main house. When he got close to me, he said, "Well, Rabbi, we meet again."

"Oranos."

"You must know why I'm here." Suddenly, Azrael's brothers ran from the rear and stood in front of Oranos' horse.

The eldest pointed at me and shouted, "Make him give her up!"

Oranos said something in Latin to his men and several soldiers rushed to restrain the brothers. "Rabbi," Oranos eyes were filled with loathing, "you can see that there's some urgency among the family of the murdered man to get justice."

"Commander, I'm surprised you care about this little matter. It's best handled by a rabbinic court, don't you think?"

"Oh no, no," Oranos shook his head, "Herod has personally asked me to see into this matter. After all murder is murder."

"It was self-defense. Her husband had been abusing her for years," I stated.

"That's what husbands do, Rabbi."

"Ye'sHUa made friends everywhere he went. His joy and love were pervasive and easily rubbed off on people. Unfortunately he made enemies as well. He was unable to bow to convention, and he preached rebellion in thought and deed. He held little regard for the institutions of man or the stations of men. This was seditious, but without prejudice: a dangerous combination to the status quo."

- Miriam wife of Yeshua -

"Not all of them, Commander, not the better ones." I stood unwavering, but a pinch of guilt accosted me when I realized that in a few minutes matters might force me to cause my own wife pain. "I'm still unclear why this matter is important enough to warrant an entire contingent of Romans."

"Oh. You think this is only about the woman…" Oranos waved his hand through the air, "she means little." The eldest brother scoffed and one of the soldiers gut-punched him. "This is about you, Rabbi. You're becoming a problem."

"I fail to see how one man," I said, "dedicated to a life of peace and service can be such a problem."

Oranos dismounted and walked closer, yet stayed several feet back from me. "You're a good speaker, Rabbi. You have a flair for using words to deflect the obvious." He looked me in the eye and said, "But we both know you're dangerous."

"Dangerous to what?" I asked.

"To the status quo, Rabbi. The status quo." He walked to the side a few steps and said, "You preach revolution. You harbor rebellious traitors. You protect murderers. You say you're a man of peace. Hah, you're a man of the sword, and your sword is made of words and will, instead of iron."

"I disagree with your premise," I said.

"Of course you do." He looked at his soldiers, then at me. "Rabbi Yeshua, I'm here to legally arrest the woman Sarah wife of Azrael for the crime of murdering her lawful husband." He lifted his face and looked down his nose at me, "My soldiers will forcibly search for her if you don't hand her over and they've been instructed to care little for the damage they cause during such a search." He looked at the ground, and then back at my face, "Do you understand what I'm saying?"

I paused, considering my options. I had several, but most of them would end with many deaths, I was sure of it. "Commander, I…" the light began to mount in me, so I said instead, "I need a moment to confer with my brothers."

"Certainly, and Rabbi," Oranos face transformed to reflect the vicious passion for violence he displayed the last time he was here. With surprising venom he said, "I hope you resist me." He smiled with wicked satisfaction as I turned from him to confer with James and Jude.

"Bit," James whispered, "you're glowing."

"I know," I said, "I'm at a loss to understand why now." I shook my head, "Do either of you have any suggestions?"

"Give her over, Yeshua," Jude said.

James shook his head, "I have nothing else to offer."

I took a breath and felt the light continue to mount. "If I order Sarah out, I'm condemning her to death."

"Bit, she condemned herself when she used the knife."

I shook my head in disagreement, "Well, if I do order her out, will you two see to Miriam? She'll be… well, she'll be… outraged. There's no telling what she'll do." They both nodded in agreement.

I turned to Oranos, "I'm going to ask you one more time, Commander, is there some other option we can take that doesn't involve condemning this woman to death? Can we convene a rabbinic court instead?"

Oranos regarded me for a moment, "What's going on with you?"

"I've merely asked you a question," but the light was mounting.

Oranos stepped back and yelled, "Bring the girl out! Bring her out now!"

"Can't we…"

"I said," he bellowed, "bring the girl out now or we'll go get her!"

The light came into me strong. I could see his fear with clarity. It consumed him. He was afraid of me. That fear turned into a passion for my death. He grabbed a spear and thrust it at me. Several of the men gasped, but I saw it coming at me in slow motion. It was easy to put up my arm and deflect the spear. It fell impotently to the ground.

The ease with which I downed his weapon stunned Oranos. His eyes opened wide with surprise, but quickly, that surprise turned into rage. "I want you dead!" he roared.

Everything now was in slow motion. I watched his men mount their weapons. They had spears, swords, and bows. I saw Oranos' face flood with passionate excitement as he swung his arm above his head. I saw my men brace for an attack. In another moment, I'd be watching my community decimated. If an attack happened, I knew I could escape by virtue of my talents, but if I did, I'd never be able to live with myself. No, if an attack ensued, I'd let Oranos take me. Then where would the community be?

I had no time to think, I couldn't let an attack happen. Senseless violence didn't have to continue. So, with unhappy resolve, I did what I needed to do. I willed that the entire situation come to a halt. That the soldiers pull back, that Oranos return to a passive position, and that we proceed without violence.

And before Oranos could pull his hand down to instruct his soldiers to attack, the scene around me rapidly transformed. The soldier's weapons were at ease and Oranos was standing in front of me. He said, "What's going on with you?"

"Nothing of concern," I said, calmly. I had the option to avert slaughter, but I was now certain there was only one sure way to do that. I'd have to acquiesce to his demand for Sarah. "Give me a moment to bring Sarah out," and I backed away into the house.

James and Jude came with me. "She's with Miriam in your room," James said.

Miriam instantly knew why I was there. "No! No!" she screamed.

"I have to. Sarah, please come with me." It was a terrible scene. Both women resisted. We finally managed to pull them apart and it took both Jude and James to subdue Miriam. I walked Sarah out to Oranos.

I stood in front of him holding her by the shoulders. I looked him in the eye and asked again, but for the first time since I reset his demeanor, "Commander. Is there some other option we can take here? Can we convene a rabbinic court instead?" I heard Miriam crying in protest from the house.

Obviously disappointed that he wouldn't have an excuse to satisfy his personal vendetta against me, Oranos said, "She'll have a trial, but it'll be at Herod's court. I promise you she'll be alive when we get there."

"Who'll stand in her defense?" I asked.

Oranos sighed and tapped his foot in frustration. "Who do you want?" he

"Some say, 'You can't squeeze blood from a turnip.' To be sure, you also can't squeeze compassion or empathy from the passion of violence. When the passion to destroy is aroused, all things that create, and all abilities to comfort, are smothered. Extinguish violence in yourself, in thought and in deed. Otherwise, you're part of the destruction of life, instead of the defender of it."
- Yeshua son of Joseph -

asked me.

I looked in the house and beckoned James out, "Will you go with Sarah and see to her defense at trial?"

He took a breath and I know he wanted to say no, but instead he relented, "Yes, of course I will." He went back into the house to gather his things.

"Alright Commander, my brother James will accompany you. I want your personal assurance that he'll have access to Sarah the entire time between now and the trial, as well as during the trial."

"You have my assurance," he said, "now, hand her over."

I looked at Sarah and my heart pounded. "I'm sorry I have to do this, but James will be with you. I wish you peace and swift justice." I kissed her on the forehead.

"Don't worry, Yeshua." She said, "I have no regrets. Pray for me."

I nodded and with my own regret, I handed this precious child of our Creator to her new enslavers. Oranos gave her to his guards. Again, I heard Miriam scream, "No!" The sound split through my heart as efficiently as a sickle cuts through stocks of ripe wheat.

Oranos started to walk away, but he stopped and turned to me instead. "Rabbi, tell your priestess that I've done only as the law requires." He waited a moment for my response, but when he didn't get one, he mounted his horse.

James came out prepared for his journey. They loaded him on the same horse as Sarah and began their journey to Caesarea. I saw him comfort Sarah by wrapping his arms around her shoulders and pulling her back to lean on him. It was proof to me that he was the right person to accompany her. Knowing that until her trial was over James would be with her was the only salve I had to offer my heart. I had no delusion that a trial would go in her favor, but at least she wouldn't be alone.

"Extracting a promise from someone you can't trust, is foolish. Even in the best of circumstances, with promises given by people you trust, they create a false sense of security. No outcome is assured until it is realized. Basic nature will always prevail. The snake that has just eaten may idly watch a mouse stroll in front of its nose, but when the snake becomes hungry again, woe be to the mouse that held onto a false sense of security."

- Yeshua son of Joseph -

107 · How Could You?

Jude was still holding Miriam and her eyes seethed with anger. I nodded to Jude and he let her go. "How could you do it?" she shouted.

"It was the only option left," I said.

"No it wasn't!" She ran at me with both fists first, her blows landing squarely on my chest.

Her fists hurt, but it was nothing compared to the pain in my heart. I stood still and let her fists get out some of her anger.

"Why?" her eyes implored as she continued to strike me, now with the flat of her hands instead of her fists, "Yeshua, why?"

I heard Micah crying. I turned to Jude, "Will you see if Micah and Mary are all right?"

"Sure," he said and left us.

"She was like a daughter to me!" With the bulk of her immediate anger spent, Miriam began to cry, "They'll kill her, Yeshua, they'll kill her!"

"Likely so," I said.

Miriam hit me again. "I'm so angry with you! You could've done more. You could've saved her."

"At what cost?" I continued to stand still, my arms passively at my side.

"Why did you have Jude hold me back?" she screamed, "I could've helped! I could've convinced him!"

"No, there was nothing anyone could do."

"You don't know that!" She picked up a basket on the table behind her and threw it at me. "She's precious to me..." and as she said that her legs gave out and she fell to the floor sobbing.

I picked her up and took her to the bed. I laid her down carefully and pulled a blanket over her. I sat beside her and placed my hand on her arm. All I could say is, "I'm sorry."

She sobbed for nearly an hour. During that time, the light came and went. Each time it came, it pulsed into Miriam, and each time it did, her tears lessened a bit. When finally her flood of tears subsided, she calmly said, "I want you to move into another room."

"If that's what you want, Miriam, I will."

"It's what I want," she said matter-of-factly.

So I picked up some things I knew I'd need for the night and closed the door

"Don't ever think that your ability to affect the world around you is limited to how far your arms reach or your voice carries. You are an infinite being whose emotional and energetic wake far exceeds the boundaries of your physical form. You have the power to influence the world. Are you using it positively?"
- Yeshua son of Joseph -

behind me. Jude was in the hall. He saw the things I carried and said, "Did she kick you out?"

"Yes."

Jude looked at the ground and said, "Well, for what it's worth, Brother, you did the right thing."

———✦———

For several days, Miriam wouldn't talk to me. During this time, the riders I dispatched on Sarah's behalf began returning with answers. When all had returned, two of my confederates said they had the wherewithal to help Sarah, but it was too late for that and the ill-timing of it all merely added to the burden my heart carried. I didn't answer, though. I held out a spot of hope, but that hope was very small.

———✦———

Only a few days later in the afternoon, James came home. The dejected look on his face said it all. I put my arms around him. We held each other until I heard Miriam walk up beside us. We pulled apart and looked at her.

"So," she asked James, "it's over?"

James nodded his head yes.

With flint in her eyes, Miriam turned to me and said, "I want a divorce."

I was stunned. So was James.

"Miriam, we should give this more time," I stammered, "we haven't even talked yet."

She narrowed her eyes, "You cut my heart when you let her die. I don't love you anymore," and she went into the house.

A few hours later, she'd prepared herself to move back to Magdala. Her maidens were packed. Micah was packed. She made up her mind, and that was that. I asked two men from the community if they'd ride with them to see that they got safely to Magdala. Miriam tried to refuse them, but James convinced her it was for her own good, so she relented.

As I watched them leave, I felt like my whole life was riding away from me. My wife and my son, both of whom meant more to me than air or water, were gone.

———✦———

As the days progressed, I became less and less sure that I'd done the right thing. If I'd let Sarah run, perhaps she'd still be alive. Or if I'd sent her to one of the other homes. Could I have used my strength of will to change more of the circumstances that fateful day with Oranos?

Every few minutes my mind threw my heart into a fire and poked at it with a stick. I had to stem a growing desire to use my will to force Miriam back, but I knew that if she were ever going to come back, it had to be of her own choosing; otherwise, our love would simply die.

Bottom line, I had to allow for the possibility that Miriam wouldn't come back; that we'd indeed separate, and that possibility was the fire in which my heart so painfully burned.

———

Mary came to me one evening and asked if we could talk in private. I went with her to her bedroom.

"What can I do for you, Mother?" I asked.

"No, what can I do for you, Son?"

"What do you mean?"

"Yeshua," she said, "I see you questioning your decisions. I've seen this before, in my husband. Don't keep it inside. It'll eat you up if you do."

As always, Mary could see right through me. "Mother, when Miriam left, it was like all the air was stolen from my lungs."

She patted my hand, "Yes, I can only imagine what this must be like."

"I don't see that I could've made any other decision. She's angry because of what I had to do." I continued to unburden my heart on Mary's ears for several minutes, and when I was done, I felt a little better, but not resolved.

"What do your brothers say?" she asked.

"Oh, as expected, they both say I did the right thing. And I must have!" I exclaimed, "It kept Oranos from slaughtering us!"

"But... do you regret the decision?"

A sudden well of tears tumbled down my face. "Yes, Mother, I do, but not because it was wrong. I regret it because of the pain it's caused." I looked in her eyes and said, "And selfishly for the consequences."

Her eyes reflected her empathy, "There were times when Joseph had to do things that would cause pain to some, yet would help others. He always weighed in on the side of 'good to the many' over 'good to the one.'" She cocked her head and said, "It's a hard, lonely road when 'the one' is yourself."

"Did you ever hate him for his decisions?"

She shook her head, "No, I'm lucky. I always supported his decisions."

My tears continued to fall, "I ache for my family. I want them home more than I can say." I looked into her eyes and with every ounce of hope I could muster, I asked, "What do you see will happen?"

Mary took a deep breath and nodded her head, "Miriam is fiery and hardheaded. Give her time to grieve. I think she'll come around. The kind of love you and she share doesn't go away as quickly as she thinks."

I grabbed that glimmer of hope that Mary bolstered with her words and I wrapped it around my smoldering heart. For the time being, it would have to be enough.

"When your hurt is bigger than you believe you can hold, you'll see a fast-track pointed away from it. If the track points outside yourself, you'll likely poke and prod at those around you, wielding blame for your pain wherever you can muster it. If your track points inside yourself, you'll likely withdraw, further, until your blame becomes depression and anxiety. Hear this; your pain is never too big to hold. The only way to stay balanced is to stop wielding blame, on others and on yourself. Hold your pain as it is, for as long as it hurts. Work with it as it shows itself. Otherwise you could have a hard time coming back to center."

- Yeshua son of Joseph -

108 · The Cost of Power

It was just the next day that Judas rode in. As expected, he was dressed as a Hellenist, maintaining the illusion that he was Micos. When I grabbed him for a hug, both relief and sorrow overwhelmed me. Here I was holding onto a man I cherished, a man to whom I'd given a fighting chance to live, yet I'd lost the two people I loved even more because I couldn't do the same for a woman my wife cherished just as much.

As we walked toward the main house, I had the sudden realization that this was the cost of opportunities offered and that things wouldn't be right until I accepted the proper use of the power endowed by my leadership role. There were options to weigh, calculations to make, and decisions to wield. When those decisions played out, if I'd done my primary job well, success or failure depended almost entirely upon the cooperation and actions of other people.

That's why my will had only temporary effects. When the effect of my will fades, the will of others resurges and colors any situation with their needs and desires. I could keep people in my immediate vicinity out of danger, but I couldn't ensure long-term safety for anyone.

In a way I hadn't seen before, James' words when confronting the agony of sending Sarah to her death made sense. He said, 'Bit, she condemned herself when she used the knife.' It wasn't that Sarah did something inherently wrong; I believe her actions were justified, but her act carried consequences that she set in motion by choosing to kill Azrael instead of choosing to endure one more act of degradation. I finally saw that my gift of a chance at safety wasn't a promise, it was merely an opportunity; it was something any person could accept or reject at their discretion. And even if a person accepted it, as in the case of Micos and Judas, the weight of his or her past actions might still override the opportunity received and contribute to undesired consequences.

My mind spun with these seemingly small revelations that were none-the-less monumental understandings. I saw how I was accepting too much responsibility for the outcomes of other people's actions and at the same time, not accepting the proper weight of responsibility for my own.

In all leadership matters, I must thoroughly weigh the options, make the calculations with extreme care, and wield the decisions with compassion and grace. If those decisions come with opportunities, I hand those opportunities over fully with as much empowerment for success as I can. Part of that empowerment is to

"How often do you take responsibility for things that aren't yours to carry? How often do you abstain from taking responsibility for things that are yours to carry? Make no mistake, if you do one, you do the other. Each finds a home in you when you remain unconscious of your intentions and your actions."

- Yeshua son of Joseph -

clarify for the receiver his or her own power of choice and then let go of the opportunity, such that the clear weight of power for completion is in the hands of the receiver.

These were new understandings that created boundaries of power in my mind. Boundaries that I saw could either ease or enhance any burden I carried. I still had to look at the consequences born from opportunities I created, but I had to look at them with new eyes. I had to ask the proper questions. Had I weighed all the options available at the time? Did I calculate the affects and interactions of those consequences judiciously? Did I base my decision on the best understanding of the situation I had at the time? And last, but not least, did I give the opportunity to that person with a clear sense of empowerment?

These realizations were a turning point for me.

All of a sudden, I felt Judas patting my back. "Yeshua?" I heard him ask.

I shook my head and realized my focus was on my inner track. "I'm sorry, I was lost in thought."

"You sure were!" Judas chuckled.

Looking at his face pulled me back to the world, and I said, "It's just good to see you, my brother!" and I gave him another tight hug.

Later that night, during sleep, I was conscious of floating to the ground of a long forgotten field: a field where the light of day came not from the sun, but from the very ethers. It was the brilliantly colored field where I met my Creator so many years before.

"You've made some important discoveries today," I heard her say.

My head snapped up and I beheld her lovely countenance, still fashioned after Mary, but so clearly that of a power so immense that I could but barely take her in. I was confused, though, "Am I leaving again? Has something happened to my body while I slept?"

"Calm yourself. You're well and alive in your bed. I've merely chosen to speak with you, if that's alright?" Her eyes shone with all-encompassing love.

"Of course, I'm honored by your presence," I bowed my head to her.

"My steadfast word, I'm always with you," she said, "you carry my light now."

"Ah," I sighed with recognition, "yes of course, the light isn't merely from you, it is you."

"It is indeed."

"I admit I don't always understand the reasons for when that light shines and when it doesn't. Nor of what it chooses to accomplish."

"You'd have to step inside my mind to understand all of that, Issa."

"I'm clear that's not something I'm going to do," I said in humility.

"Pity," she said. Her comment intrigued me, but she changed the subject immediately, "Your internal discoveries today are important."

"They make sense of things I was floundering with."

"Yes, and I wonder what you'll do now?" she asked.

"Is there a path you'd like to suggest?"

"This is your life, I make no demands of you."

"Demands are one thing, suggestions are another," I said, "I'm open to hearing your ideas."

"I'm happy to say you are, with regularity. I hope it helps you."

"More than you may know," I said.

"Then, tell me, what do you foresee I'll suggest today?"

I stilled myself and reached for a knowing that'd been sitting in me for days. "That I go back on the road and reach more people."

She extended her arm with her palm upturned. Out of it drifted a gentle breeze of moist jasmine scented air. As soon as its delightful scent caressed my nose, I woke in my bed. For the first time since Miriam kicked me out of our marriage bed, I woke without a sudden surge of pain from her absence, and I knew beyond a shadow of doubt what I had to do next.

109 · Home Again

It didn't take long for us to set out on campaign. This was a smaller party than I'd ever taken before. James was with me, Jude of course stayed at home, in charge while we were gone. Judas was with us, still disguised as Micos, and a handful of devotees came too. Only men this time for ease of logistics.

I wanted to keep the campaign simple if possible, but that was proving to be impossible. Everywhere I went, people followed. The light came out almost every day. Sometimes I just glowed, for hours on end. Consciously, I was walking, greeting, and speaking when people amassed, but people reported that I was doing many other things. Sometimes people saw me do things in places far removed from where I thought I was. I went with it, accepting that I couldn't find logic in it, and let people have their experiences without the need to reconcile them.

Above all else, I gave love. I spoke love, I ministered love, I endeavored to be the very embodiment of the love I knew was the greatest power in all creation. And at every turn, I was surprised by the myriad responses that love engendered: from acceptance, to desire, to grief, to revulsion, to exaltation. It baffled my mind.

Priests often attended the talks. Opposition to my teachings didn't keep me from speaking my truth. The wisdom I engaged when I spoke came from deep within my soul and I couldn't stop it. I wouldn't be intimidated by short-sighted men of power. Sometimes a priest would ask a question that was meant to trip me on some point of belief, but I'd navigate through the rhetoric. More often than not, my answers transformed these men of faith into allies.

And something else happened on this trip that I can't explain. I began to speak a language that wasn't foreign, but perhaps by force of will, only certain people understood the words. I don't know how it started, but it did. And from then on, when I wanted only those in my closest circle to understand me, I spoke in this manner. It was very convenient.

———

Two months later, we returned to the family compound. I was happy to be

"Ye'sHUa couldn't be bought, was rarely fooled, wouldn't be overpowered, wanted for nothing, and saw deeper into truth than anyone I've ever met. He was also humble to a fault, unable to understand emotions like greed, revenge, and jealously, easily brought to heartfelt tears, and eternally submissive to his spirit. It is the last, his complete submission to the bidding of his spirit, that delivered him into the hands of willing oppressors and bid him physically to leave me. It was an act I found challenging to understand and excessively difficult to forgive."

- Miriam wife of Yeshua -

back, but the trip had been fulfilling; I knew I'd miss it and want to get back on the road sooner than later. Many new seekers followed us and we left them at what we were now just calling 'Newtown.' And as we made our way up the hill, I had a short pang of apprehension recognizing that one of the factors that made the last few months so relieving was not having the space to dwell on my family being gone, but coming home it would be front and center once more.

We walked through the gates greeted by members of the community as we went. I stopped when we got to the clearing to clarify who'd do what as far as putting away the supplies.

I was thinking about our transition home and my back was to the main house. The sound didn't register in my consciousness at first, but as it continued, I realized it was a baby crying. James recognized it before I did. He looked at me with a quizzical look of disbelief. When he did, I realized it wasn't just any baby; it was my son.

I spun around. Standing in the window was Miriam bouncing a fussy Micah in her arms. A jolt of hope and desire pulsed through me. I couldn't move, afraid that if I did, they'd melt from my vision like so much illusion. She smiled and it broke my spell. I ran into the house.

As I stood in front of Miriam, she handed Micah to me. "He needs his father," she said as I scooped him into my arms. His crying instantly quelled.

I gently squeezed him to my breast, delighting in having him near once more. He meant so much to me, this little one who'd barely begun his journey. I looked at Miriam. She was my joy, my companion, my fire, and my wife. A momentary pang of fear touched me, but I moved past it quickly and asked, "And what of you, Miriam? Do you need me?"

She stepped closer to us, "I need you more than I can say." She wrapped her arms around us and my heart nearly burst from the joy of it. Through the window, I saw everyone who'd walked so faithfully with me these last two months. They simply gazed at us, smiling.

Once again, I was home.

Miriam had already moved back into our room and her maidens were living in their house again. The rest of the day was a whirlwind of information. It wasn't until later that evening that Miriam and I had the space to huddle on our bed to talk.

"One thing was true, Ye'sHUa couldn't be reproached if he didn't see wrong on his part. Unless he was able to see his mistakes, he was unable to accept them, or otherwise be convinced of them. Rather than fight about it he'd usually tell someone that they were welcome to see it that way if they liked. If it would help a situation he'd apologize for doing something that appeared to be or was perceived to be inappropriate and any resulting pain that may have caused, but he wouldn't apologize for any action unless he could see the truth of an error in himself. This propensity sometimes left sore feelings that could persist with those closest to him; persist, yes, but never overshadow."
- Miriam wife of Yeshua -

"I was angry," she said, "I wanted someone to hurt for what happened."

"I understand that," I said. "What changed? Why'd you come home?"

She got a sad look in her eyes, "It was the Goddess." She clutched my hand. "I thought you gave in too quickly. Assumed you hadn't even tried to save her, but Goddess showed me what happened when you tried to stop them."

"I see," I said, "I did try, Miriam."

"I know that now. It's clear from what I saw." She pulled her hand away. "Goddess also showed me what would've happened in several choices you considered. Yeshua, they were all bad – bloody. We were slaughtered in every scene."

I looked down, "I know."

Miriam pulled closer to me as we sat on the bed and ran her hand through my hair. "I need to trust you more. I… you hear me? I… I need to learn to trust."

I looked at her face and saw the inner turmoil. "What're you letting go of?" I asked.

"Mmm," she thought for a moment, "I guess I'm letting go of believing that the world will always let me down."

"That's got to be hard," I said.

"I suppose it is, yes," she whispered. Her lips curled and she chuckled, as she ran her hands through my hair again. "You're my honey bee, and I can't imagine life without you." Her smile lit my heart. We sank into the bed and I couldn't imagine life being more perfect than it was at that moment.

110 · Harbinger

I loved my life. It suited me as nicely as a warm slipper suits a cold foot. As far as I was concerned, life could've continued like this for decades and I would've felt more blessed than any person who ever lived. But decades would prove not to be available.

The harbinger of shortened time came soon after Miriam returned. Philar appeared to me one afternoon as I was strolling through the back acreage. He walked with me, enjoying the afternoon as we chatted, until he said, "I have to meet Miriam."

I was startled. "Meet Miriam? Why?" I queried.

"There's something I must speak with both of you about."

I turned to Philar, "What could you need to speak to Miriam about?"

"Trust me," Philar said. "And probably I should meet James too. And Mary should come."

I felt a wave of anxious energy sweep through me. "I'm not going to be happy with this, am I?"

"Probably not."

———

Later that evening we gathered in Mary's room waiting for Philar. I asked a few devotees to stand watch for us. I had no idea what Philar had on his agenda, but whatever it was, I wasn't looking forward to it.

I tried to make it clear to everyone that Philar was a trusted friend to me and to Joseph before me. Mary knew Philar from her childhood, so she spoke about how Philar was one of the angels that helped her learn of her miracle and accept her marriage to Joseph. James had heard stories about Philar since I came home from my travels, but along with Miriam, this would be the first meeting.

As Mary talked, I felt Philar pat me on the shoulder. I revealed he was in the room and asked him to sit before he appeared. A few moments later, Philar appeared in the empty chair and everyone was startled, even Mary, and even though they knew it was about to happen. Philar sat silent waiting for everyone's heartbeat to return to normal before we continued.

It was no surprise to me that James had something to say right away, "I'm overwhelmed with your presence, Sir."

Philar nodded to him.

I looked at the others, Mary was smiling, her hands neatly folded in her lap, her eyes locked lovingly on Philar. Miriam was piqued with passion.

"Go ahead, take the lead, Philar." I pointed to him and he nodded in agreement.

"Thank you," he said, "I'm happy you consented to meet tonight." He paused, letting everyone settle into the sound of his voice. "I have some important things to speak with you about. Are you ready? James? Miriam?"

Miriam nodded yes, her face flushed with excitement. James just stared, not moving, and not saying a word.

Miriam took James hand. "James?" she asked, "You all right?"

James said still staring at Philar, "Yeah, I'm fine. I'm just curious as anything about... uh... why he's here."

"I'm here," Philar began, "because we have some things to discuss. And I wanted us to do that all together. I suspect this won't be welcome news."

Mary gasped, "No Philar," her breathing was quick and shallow, "please not yet. Tell me it's not yet."

"No Mary, it's not yet, but it's not far either." Tears flowed down Mary's cheeks.

"What's not far?" I asked.

Philar looked at me with a grave expression. "Yeshua, it's you."

"What? What's me?"

"There's a high probability that you won't be alive that much longer."

"No!" Miriam shouted, "Don't say that!"

James, still holding Miriam's hand, squeezed it tightly; his eyes traveling around the room as if he were looking for a means of escape. I sat, shocked to hear with my ears what my inner self had been trying to ignore.

"I'm sorry to bring this news," Philar said.

"No!" Miriam shouted again, "I won't have it!" I went to Miriam and folded onto the floor by her feet. I wrapped myself around her lap, burying my face in her thigh. She grabbed my robe and squeezed the fabric tightly. "No," she said, "you can't leave."

I was a mass of complex emotion as grief and uncertainty emanated from everyone in the room, Philar included. My inner vision filled with the remembrance of the pool of blood I'd seen next to my older self in the Yawn on my way to the Temple of Man. The 'older self' I'd seen that day was not much, if at all, older than I was right at that moment.

Fear gripped me. I gasped, "Oh my God, no." I felt James slip out of his chair next to me and wrap himself around my back. 'Breathe,' I thought, 'just breathe.' I knew if I could keep breathing, we'd all be fine.

Everything was rushing around me, so I slowed down time. I pulled the slowness around me like a blanket and tried to find a respite in what seemed like a flood of pressurized energy. After a few moments I heard Philar in slow motion whisper behind me, "Slowing time won't keep this from you, Yeshua," but it was helping me catch my breath.

Finally, I relented to the truth of what Philar said and I let go of my hold on time. The sounds of labored breathing and crying surrounded me. I raised my face

"While dying is something most people accept as inevitable, it's uncomfortable to consider death past the point of prudent planning. Why think about death, unless death is something you can exert some measure of control over? People are raised to believe they have no control over death. I'm here to tell you, you have ultimate control over death, including whether or not you will die. I'm living proof. But you must do the extensive work involved in evolving your consciousness and precious few have ever done that."

- Yeshua son of Joseph -

out of Miriam's lap and turned to Philar, "Why tell us now? Philar? What's the good of causing this upset?"

James lifted his face toward Philar. Mary looked at him, and I was sure Miriam was riveted as well.

Philar looked at his lap and back to me, "There's a reason, we'll get to that."

"Why? How?" Miriam asked Philar, "We can stop this right?"

Philar shook his head, "No Miriam, it's not like that. Circumstances will compel action. The place and method are not set, but the time, well… the window of time narrows every day."

I turned to face Miriam. All I could say was, "I'm sorry," but when our eyes locked together, I felt the union of us slowly bolster me. It bolstered Miriam as well. I grew stronger, less conflicted. Her countenance eased. She lifted a hand to my cheek and her face displayed an exquisite veneer of love and acceptance. "It's alright, Yeshua. It's as the Goddess foretold," she nodded, "I accepted it before we married."

I took in a deep, cleansing breath. I looked at Mary, she was still crying. But I smiled and she smiled back. I turned to James and his deep love landed on me as softly as a hummingbird lands on the wings of an egret. I laid my head back on Miriam's lap and let myself hold onto the love around me, instead of the pain. Miriam stroked my hair. James rested his head on my shoulder. It took maybe fifteen minutes of this stillness, but I finally felt as though I could continue. I gently rose and returned to my seat. James followed suit.

I took a few more breaths before again addressing Philar. "So, do we know when?" I asked with trepidation.

Philar nodded his head, "We have a good idea of timing, and the good news is we're still counting the time in years." Sighs of relief emanated all around me. Philar continued, "But soon, we'll probably be counting the time in months… instead of years."

"I see," I said. Everyone was less anxious than when the news first hit, but the blade of disquiet continued to cut through the room. "I'm, uh… afraid to ask what else you have for us, Philar." I stammered, "I can't, uh… imagine what else there could be after this tempest."

"I know it's a lot to take in," he said.

"It's a big shock," I said.

"I'm glad you told us though," Mary said, "I've known this would come… since the day you were born, Yeshua." She wiped her cheeks with a small cloth. "I'm glad to know we still have some time with you before…" tears erupted again. "I'm sorry… no, I'm all right," she sniffled and smiled at me again.

"I love you," I murmured.

"Shocking news can intrude on your life at any moment. Death, betrayal, injury, abandonment, and financial loss, on you or your loved ones, are all possible intrusions. You mustn't dwell on them happening, but you can assume some will. Every day you have the opportunity to prepare for these inevitable setbacks by equipping yourself with the strength of inner peace. This comes by letting go of the fear, worry, and suffering that plagues every mind that doesn't achieve higher consciousness. Grow into your higher conscious mind and you protect yourself better than any amount of fore-planning can."

- Yeshua son of Joseph -

111 · Secrets Revealed

I hadn't had enough time to process the news of my impending demise, but I knew Philar had more. How was I going to listen when all I wanted to do was run?

James suddenly stood. He'd been sitting between Miriam and me. "We should trade places, Yeshua. I think you should sit next to Miriam."

"Sure," I said as I exchanged seats with him. Miriam and I grabbed each other's hand and held on tight. "So, what else Philar?" I asked.

He took a deep breath and looked into my eyes, "This is a new subject that's likely to be difficult to talk about, but timing is critical and this can't be ignored."

"Is there something you need me to do?" I asked.

"Y-yes," Philar hedged, "but let me explain the problem first." He looked at everyone, then back at me. "Yeshua, you've only produced... two children."

My eyes fluttered in disbelief that this was the subject at issue. I faltered, "Wha... what did you say? Children?"

"What?" James probed, "Did you say two?"

"Yes, two, and yes, children," Philar answered matter-of-factly. James sputtered in disbelief. I looked at Mary and her eyes were wide open. I'd told Miriam about the baby created by the rape incident long ago, but I'd never mentioned the incident to anyone else.

"Philar," I said, "Miriam's the only one here who knows about Jing."

"Jing?" James cried out.

Philar looked chagrined, "Oh, I didn't realize."

"Yeshua? Jing?" James pressed.

I didn't want to talk about it. "James, Mother," I sighed, "this is difficult." I shook my head and lowered my face, barely containing tears of shame I didn't realize I still held.

Miriam squeezed my hand, and said, "Shall I tell them?" I nodded, so she continued, "Before Yeshua came home from the east, he lived with a group of adepts. That's where he started using opium." James and Mary both nodded. Miriam continued, "There was an unfortunate incident with a stranger, a young

"When fear causes you to hold back from asking for the help you need, you risk falling into rigid thinking. The more rigid your thinking, the more rigid your life becomes. Life experience follows thought, which then creates similar thought leading to similar life experience. It's a focused spiral that seems unchanging when thinking is rigid. And yet you have the ultimate power to change the trajectory of the spiral by intervening with new, creative thought. It was fear that kept you from asking for help in the first place and locked you into rigid thinking, so let go of the fear, ask for help, and let yourself flow again. Sooner or later, as you allow flow, new thoughts will form and they'll affect change in the life you experience."

- Yeshua son of Joseph -

woman. She took advantage of Yeshua without his permission one night. He passed out and was unable to defend himself. She raped him… and she had his baby."

James mouth dropped open.

Mary lowered her eyes and said with compassion, "I'm so sorry, Yeshua."

I nodded to Mary. Reluctantly, I looked at James, braced for his judgment, but instead, his face reflected a deep empathy, and I was flooded with a sudden knowing that something similar had happened to James when he was apprenticing; an incident that gave him his conviction about becoming a monk. "Oh, James," I said to him, "I see." I nodded my head, "I'm sorry."

James eyes filled with tears and he nodded in acknowledgment. I let go of Miriam's hand and stood. I urged James out of his seat and put my arms around him. "I'm so, so sorry," I whispered, "It happened while you were in Europe?"

"M-hmm," James affirmed.

I heard Mary gasp in recognition behind me.

I squeezed James tighter, "Why didn't you tell me?"

James whispered, "Like you, I was ashamed. I still am."

"But you were so young," I squeezed him. "You were forced?"

"I was, more than once," James gasped, "and he… wasn't young… or gentle."

Those words slapped at my heart. I suddenly understood all of it; James' propensities for judgment, his early need to supplicate himself on bloody knees, and his distaste for sex and marriage. I said, "I love you, Brother, and I'm so, so sorry this happened to you." Our embrace lasted minutes. I didn't want to let go of him.

By the time I finally took my seat, my body felt like I'd been through two days of hard labor. These waves of emotion were exhausting. I looked at Philar. "Tough night," I said. Philar nodded. I asked, "So why do you bring up children?"

Philar cleared his throat, "Yeshua, you remember the discussions we had in my studio?"

"Yes, I do."

"Well, it's imperative that you have more children. Two is not enough."

"Enough for what?" I demanded.

Philar paused, then blurted, "To spread your physical make-up throughout humankind."

I looked at Miriam. She looked as confused as I. "Philar," I said, "Miriam had difficulty bringing Micah to life. We hope to have more, but it's…"

"Yeshua, listen to me. Miriam, you too. There isn't enough time left for Miriam to have the number of children required."

I was dumbfounded. Everyone in the room was. "How many are 'required'?" I insisted.

"Seven or eight is best by our calculations," he answered, "six might do, but no fewer."

This seemed ridiculous on the surface. My temper exploded. "Why did you never tell me of this 'requirement'?" I shouted, "Why spring this on me now?"

My angry tone surprised Philar. "Well, we hoped, of course, that we'd have more time. Also that Miriam and you would have less trouble." He stammered, "We… we didn't want to ask you what… what we now feel we have to ask."

"What you have to ask?" The implications were crystal clear. He wanted me to impregnate other women. I lost my composure, my temper exploded. "What am I now?" I yelled, "A stallion you rent to the neighbor when his mare is in season?"

"Yeshua, please," Philar implored, "calm yourself, it's not like that."

"You bet it is!" I was livid, "I know what you're insinuating and I'm offended by this discussion!"

"Please calm," Philar reiterated.

"I've lost my temper! I know that!" I stood and walked around the room behind the chairs. "I'm yelling! I know that, too!" I stopped and looked at Philar. I was seething from his proposal. "I'm married! To one woman! That's my answer! You make happen whatever you need to have happen, but you do it without me compromising my marriage bed! End of discussion!" I stormed out of the room and slammed the door behind me.

I went into the night and vowed not to return home until I could hold my temper again.

112 · Consequences and Choices

I was fuming; mad with anger at Philar. First, he told me, and my closest, that I'm going to die soon, then he revealed my secret about Jing, and then he had the temerity to propose I impregnate someone, no some ones, other than my wife! My perfect world, my adored life, felt shattered in one short evening.

I walked, and I walked. And when I finally sat, paused to take in the night more fully, I got up and walked some more.

By the time the sun came up over the eastern hill line, I was atop Mount Tabor. The view was glorious. The valley floor lit up with vibrant color. Birds awakened and flew around me in the morning sky. Their calls and caws were like a chorus of monks lifted in harmonic rapture.

Best of all, I was able to breathe; to pull air into my lungs and let it fill me with living manna. And I was alone; a rarity I cherished.

My anger had dissipated, but the letup felt temporary. I performed my morning baptism, and when I finished confessing my excesses, which consisted mostly of arrogance, righteousness, and anger, I went into a deep meditation.

I saw myself sitting with Philar at the Temple of Man. He explained in basic terms how our flesh consists of individual cells; that those cells have instructions written into them, as if each cell has its own library. It was fascinating. He explained that the instructions written in my cells were a little different from those written in the cells of most people. And that it was those tiny differences in instructions that gave me the marked differences and abilities I possess.

I left my memory of Philar and followed my breathing into one of these little cells. It was like falling into an ocean. I swam through the thick liquid of the cell encountering structures and bits of debris that bumped into each other like blind fish. I couldn't find a library, but I believed it was there.

When I came out of the cell, I whisked through the ethers and found myself deposited into that brilliantly colored field I was becoming quite familiar with: the one where I met my Creator face-to-face the first time. She stood awaiting my arrival, still cloaked in the facade of Mary. My heart lit up when I saw her.

"Issa, is this alright if we talk a bit?" she asked.

"Of course. I'm honored as always."

"You had a difficult night."

I sighed, "Yes, I did. My friend Philar gave me news that I have difficulty accepting."

"Anger can be internally motivating, but ultimately, anger is nothing more than difficulty accepting the truth. Anger is a way of trying to force the outside world to conform to the way you want it to be, rather than you conforming to the way things are."

- Yeshua son of Joseph -

"I can see that. I'm sure you know that you don't have to accept anything you don't want to accept. I believe we've demonstrated that to you in the past."

I thought about it a moment, "Yes, you have. Yes."

"Issa," she said, "this is your life. You govern its trajectory. You decide its mission."

"I can accept that."

"And sometimes," she continued, "sometimes we have consequences and choices that appear to come from the outside, and feel forced, but are a direct result of our own inner direction."

"Yes, I see that."

"You've accepted a mission that sprang from your wisdom and experience of humanity. Not many would ever consider accepting your particular mission. It's beyond the scope of most even to conceive of it."

I bent my head in thought.

She continued, "What you have before you now are consequences of choices you made. It's up to you now to decide if you'll accept, deny, or alter these consequences."

"I see," I said.

"You were raised by a man who also encountered a difficult set of circumstances. Oddly enough, proposed by the same friend who proposed yours last night."

"Joseph?" I asked.

"Yes, Joseph," she answered, "and I thought it might help you to have a conversation with him, so I brought him here too. So you could talk." She smiled at me, and I was obviously confused, so she pointed behind me.

I turned and there was Joseph. I ran to him and threw my arms around him. He returned my hug with fervor.

"Yeshua, my boy," he said.

He felt solid, warm and real. I pulled back just enough to look into his face. "I'm so happy to see you. I can't believe my fortune." I grabbed him to me again and when I did, the field melted away and we were sitting at a table in the main house of the compound. We were alone.

"Father, tell me what you're doing now. What's life like?" Joseph proceeded to tell me of his life in detail. He was establishing a school for children who died in difficult circumstances. He felt it was beneficial for the souls of these children to have a bonding experience to recover from the confusion of death from hard circumstances like war, abuse, and starvation. To help them see greater choices, and allow them to remember their fullness before moving to the next stage of development.

I swelled with pride. "I'm sure you'll be successful. I can't imagine a better soul to create it."

"You've taught me what I need for this, Yeshua."

I was taken aback, "Me? I taught you something?" I stammered.

"Yes, my boy. Is that so hard to believe?"

"Well yes, actually," I said, "it is. I owe you everything."

"Perhaps we both owed a debt to the other," he said, "a debt that we paid in concurrence with our learning."

I chuckled, "Yes, perhaps." I grabbed his hand again, "It's so good to see you, Father."

"It is, Son, but now I'd like to hear from you," Joseph said, "what's so heavy on you that Creator wanted us to talk today?"

I proceeded to tell him about the night before. I expounded on things that I felt he needed background to understand fully. Remembering everything in detail wound me up again and I seethed with anger at Philar once more. When I was done with my tale, Joseph laughed.

"Father, I'm angry and you're laughing?"

He nodded, "I'm laughing at what seems so monumental to you, I'm sure, but it's so typical of Philar!"

I stared at Joseph laughing at my plight, but it was contagious, and before I knew it, I was laughing too. It felt good to laugh.

"So," I finally said, "you say it's typical of Philar? And the Creator said you had similar consequences to consider. So, fess up. Tell me what happened and what you did."

"Oh, well, you know part of the story already. It's about my accepting being your father."

"But I suspect there's part of the story I don't know."

"Perhaps, yes." Joseph grabbed my hand again and when he did, the room faded and we floated in a blank space.

113 · Joseph's Memories

As we floated, Joseph explained, "I'm going to show you memories of my life, from the time before you were born. I was about to find out your mother was pregnant with you, but I was hardheaded. I couldn't believe that she'd be pregnant without having coupled with a man."

I relaxed into the visions. The first was at the Mount Carmel Monastery. My grandmother, Anne, sat with Joseph and another man I didn't recognize.

"That's Hiram, the head priest," Joseph said, "he was a great man. I was in charge of protecting Mary because there were threats on her person. I had double guard duty on her sunrise to sunrise..."

Anne said, "My friends, I don't know what to do. I have shocking news." Anne looked at their faces, "Oh God, how do I say this? I think Mary is pregnant."

Joseph said, "That's not possible."

"Her menses is several weeks late," Anne explained, "and when I asked her, she said she's with child; that the angel brought the baby."

Joseph stood and walked to the opposite side of the room; his back to the others.

Hiram cleared his throat. "This is... uh... quite a surprise. Is it possible Mary's late for some other reason? Is she ill?" he asked Anne.

"You've seen her. She's absolutely bursting with health," Anne said.

Joseph had his hand over his eyes and his face downturned. "And she's glowing," he murmured, "with the soft light of a pregnant woman."

"Joseph?" Hiram asked, "Do you know something?"

"No, just the opposite, I know nothing." He shook his head, "This shouldn't be happening."

Anne looked at Hiram, "What are we going to do?"

Joseph turned to Anne, his voice elevated, "How did someone get to her? Who was it? What happened?"

"Joseph, I don't know," Anne said, "as far as I know she hasn't been touched."

Joseph's anger was mounting. He paced back and forth, like a caged animal. "Something happened!" he shouted.

Hiram stood, "Get hold of yourself. We'll figure this out." He put his hand on Joseph's shoulder, but Joseph whisked his hand away.

"No, I can't," Joseph said, "protecting her was my job! I've let her down!" He covered his face again with his hand.

"This isn't your fault," Anne said.

Suddenly Joseph erupted, "I want to know who did this!" he yelled, "I want to know who hurt my little Mary!" Joseph was livid, his face contorted and red. He screamed, "I have to go. I just need to go or I'm afraid I'll hurt someone!" With that, he stormed out of the room and left the compound on foot.

When the scene faded, I silently noted how similar Joseph's reaction had been to my own just the night before.

"I walked for hours, screaming at God for my little Mary being hurt," Joseph said to me, "I believed she'd been raped, not blessed."

I looked down and saw...

Joseph running, stumbling through the hills.

He stopped and faced the setting sun, screaming at the top of his lungs, "Go--------d! Who are you that you let this happen? Why am I devoted to you when you let someone so special – so precious as little Mary – be hurt? What did she ever do to you that you let a defiler visit her this way?"

"I was so angry," Joseph said, "and ashamed. The next day I stumbled back into the monastery and found an ally named Jeremiah visiting. I went to Hiram's office to meet with them and Anne. Now remember this is before I ever met Philar..."

Anne spoke, "Well, as you might expect, I wanted confirmation of Mary's state, so I confess, I secretly took her to the infirmary and asked one of the attendants to check her. I've gotten to know this woman and I trust her to be discreet. Let me shock you again. I've two things to report. The first, Mary does appear to be pregnant."

Joseph made a grunting noise as if someone had just punched him in the gut.

Anne looked at him, "But I have a second thing to report – Mary shows no sign of sexual penetration. Mary is still a virgin."

Joseph slowly raised his face to look at Anne, "What was that you said?"

"I said," Anne answered, "Mary is still a virgin."

The room was silent. Everyone exchanged glances, but no one spoke.

After several minutes, Jeremiah opened his bag and extracted a note, sealed with an unrecognizable seal. "I guess this is the right time," he looked around the room at the others, "I've been carrying this note for more than a year now. Jacob gave it to me. It came to him from one of the 'hidden' he works with. I was instructed to open it when the child's mother proved pregnant. I didn't expect us to be at this juncture so soon, but I think the time is now, do you agree?"

"Wait," Joseph said, "who are these hidden anyway? They've been mentioned before."

"I don't really know who they are. When Jacob talks about them, it's with reverence."

"Are they from Judea?" Joseph asked.

"I don't know. I just know they have a great amount of power. And, well, they often seem to know things before they happen." Jeremiah asked again, "Do you think I should open this?"

With trepidation, Hiram said, "Yes."

Joseph said, "Y-yes."

Anne merely nodded.

So Jeremiah broke the seal and read from the note:

> "Dear Associates,
>
> "As I write this note I realize that you're starting down a road that won't proceed as you plan. And yet, there's nothing I would do to stop you. The road you take now is necessary, but will be a wasted effort.
>
> "The girl will soon be a woman and I promise you, that before you have a chance to betroth her to a young man, she will prove pregnant.
>
> "I know this because it's I who was ordered to make it so. Here are the only words I can use to describe it in terms you'll understand, the child in question was divinely created. The seed didn't come from a man.
>
> "If you've opened this note, it means you've now found the girl to be pregnant. You're dismayed because you can't believe she's had sexual relations. But you're right; she hasn't.
>
> "You can't understand the means by which this event has come to pass. But you should believe your eyes. The girl is pure and the child she carries is of the greatest importance to your world. This child will grow into a person capable of great things. He'll have abilities that other people lack.
>
> "If you examine her carefully, you'll have the proof you need, that by your science, she shouldn't be pregnant; but she is. We told you early on, that when this child comes you'd have proof it's the child of our prophecy before he's born. Right now, in the girl's untouched body you see proof. And in the reading of this note after the fact, you have secondary proof.
>
> "Treasure this girl and treasure this child. They're yours now. Give them what they need to flourish.
>
> "Yours truly, Philar"

"She was right," Hiram said with reverence, "the angels gave him to her."

Joseph looked at Jeremiah with disbelief in his eyes, "You swear to me you've been carrying this note for a year?"

"Yes, I do. And if you must, ask Jacob when he gave me the note. He'll concur with the timing."

"Philar does know how to shock one, doesn't he?" I said flippantly.

Joseph laughed, "That he does!"

114 · Angels

"That letter wasn't enough. I was still unconvinced." Joseph said, "I couldn't see past my own prejudices to believe."

I nodded with understanding.

"At that time I loved your mother like she was my daughter. Let me back up and show you two interactions with Mary that I had before she became pregnant. She was just a child then, but since she was chosen to be your mother, we began to make plans for her marriage…"

Joseph and Hiram sat in Hiram's office with Anne and Mary.

"Mary, I'd like to talk with you about something that everyone feels is very important," Joseph began, "is that alright with you?"

Mary looked him directly in the eye, "Of course, you want to ask me to marry."

Joseph was surprised, "Well, that's part of it, yes."

"Then ask me," Mary said, smiling.

"Mary, I'm not going to ask you to marry me, rather, to marry someone chosen for you. Someone appropriate."

Mary's face turned quizzical, "I don't understand."

"We'll find you a good husband."

Mary smiled, "You'd be a good husband."

Joseph looked uncomfortable. "Mary, I'm too old for you."

"That's not what the angel said."

Hiram, Anne, and Joseph exchanged confused looks. Hiram said, "What did the angel say?"

"The angel said that I wouldn't live here much longer. He said Joseph would protect me and marry me and help me raise a very special baby." Mary's smile was wide and beaming.

"Mary, you know about the baby?" Hiram inquired.

"I've known about him for a long time. I've already talked to him. He's a nice man."

Joseph said, "I'm confused. How could you have already spoken with a baby that hasn't been born yet?"

"Don't you know? We're already people before we're born. He's waiting for me to be ready. He says I'm still too young, but it won't be long."

"Well," Anne added, "it'll take some time to find the right husband, Sweetheart."

Mary turned to her mother with a look of surprise, "I don't need a husband for this baby."

"Yes you do," Anne said, "we discussed this already, don't you remember?"

"This baby's not coming that way. The angel is bringing him to me."

Everyone looked surprised by Mary's statement. Hiram finally said, "So, Mary, you agree that getting married and giving birth to a special baby is a good life for you?"

"It's the only life for me, silly. It's what I'm here for."

Joseph laughed, "Mary, you're a delight."

"But, Joseph, you're silly too, if you think you're too old. If you give me to a young man, who's going to properly raise this baby? He needs the right father as much as the right mother."

"Mary, you have to let this go," Joseph insisted, "I can't be your husband."

Mary just looked at him, smiling, and said, "We'll see."

"That was the first time anyone mentioned me being Mary's husband," Joseph said. "I didn't like the thought at all. And I was angry with this 'Angel.' I didn't believe he was real, I thought he was a man bent on harming Mary. So we proceeded to find a husband for her, a young man named Mikel. Here's the second conversation with Mary…"

Mary was sitting on a stool, watching Joseph carve a piece of wood. Her eyes were fixed on his hands. "Joseph?"

"Yes Mary, what's on your mind today?" Joseph kept his attention on the wood.

"I have something to tell you."

"All right, I'm listening."

"I had another visit last night."

"What kind of visit?"

"My angel came with news."

Joseph stopped and turned his attention to Mary. "What kind of news?"

Mary looked down and fidgeted in her seat. "Well, he says I'll be with child soon."

Joseph's face turned to a frown. He took Mary's hand. "Mary, that can't be. You're innocent, aren't you?"

Mary looked at Joseph. "Yes, of course."

"You know what I mean by that, right?"

"Yes, I do. And no, I haven't been touched by anyone, except you holding my hand… like now."

"Holding your hand, or patting your shoulder isn't what I mean."

"I know, you mean in that other way. I'm never alone anyway."

"Mary, you're never alone because you remaining untouched is very important." Joseph sat on a shorter stool to be eye-level with Mary. "The first boy to touch you must be your husband, and that'll be Mikel." Joseph paused, then said, "Have any of the men here at the monastery approached you?"

"No!" Mary pulled her hand back, "Why don't you believe me?"

"It's not that I don't believe you. I just want to make sure you understand my questions. I know you'd never intentionally lie to me."

"Well, I'm just telling you what my angel said."

"And I have to confess, that news makes me nervous."

"It makes me nervous too," Mary said in a small voice.

Joseph took Mary's hand again. "Then maybe together we can be less nervous." He smiled at Mary. She smiled back.

"After I found out about her pregnancy, I became convinced," Joseph continued, "that this was a charade, an elaborate hoax. I had no other logical way to explain it. I left the monastery a broken man. I felt I'd failed miserably. I needed to try to put the whole business behind me, so I temporarily moved in with Simon in Sepphoris and looked at opening a woodworking shop."

"You were good with wood," I said.

Joseph smiled, "Well, while I was scouting for a shop, I ran into Jacob and he invited me to his home for supper…"

Jacob and Joseph sat in Jacob's parlor. Jacob leaned in to Joseph and lowered his voice, "I must tell you there've been many developments. I don't wish to dwell on things gone by, but I'm sure you'd like an update."

"Yes, of course."

"Mary and Anne are secreted here in Sepph…" he stopped abruptly as a servant entered the room, "try the wine Joseph, it's very good."

Joseph picked up the cup and sipped the wine. "Oh, that is refreshing."

When the servant left the room, Jacob said, "I'm not going to try to change your mind about anything, but I'm thinking to ask your advice. I trust you explicitly. Is that alright with you?"

"Yes, of course. If there's something I can do without compromising my ethics, I'm available."

"Wonderful, thank you. Why don't we take a stroll in the garden?"

They went to the garden and when Jacob was certain no one was near, he opened up, "As I said, there've been many developments."

"Please, enlighten me."

"The hidden are insisting that this child be born, whether he's legally made crown-heir or not. They say he's the Great Teacher. We've secretly moved Anne and Mary here to segregate them from the monastery."

"That's a shame if he can't be made heir," Joseph said, "but in truth he's not. He wasn't fathered by a Davidian."

"True, as they say, the child has no father."

"No one will marry Mary?" Joseph asked.

"No one will marry her, and the child has no father. Mary is still pure to this day."

Joseph shook his head in disbelief. "You've had that independently verified by a doctor outside the monastery and our circle?"

"Yes, of course. The claim was so fantastic, we had to."

Joseph reacted, "Well, that surprises me."

"This didn't convince me, Yeshua," Joseph continued, "I was still conflicted, but the evidence was mounting. I wanted to visit Anne and Mary, but I stopped myself. My shame was too deep." He looked at me, "I know you understand shame, Yeshua."

"Yes, I do understand shame, all too well, Father."

"Well my shame kept me from seeing the choices in front of me with clear eyes and an open heart. Until I had a visitation one night…"

Joseph was drifting into sleep, when all of a sudden the room filled with light. He sat bolt upright in bed. Across the room, a being materialized that glowed with a yellow-orange light. Joseph's mouth dropped open.

The being tipped his head to Joseph and said, "Don't be afraid Joseph. I've come with news."

Joseph's mouth tried to move, but nothing came out.

"I'm a messenger of peace, come to give you news. I say again, don't be afraid."

"I... I... what's the news?"

"Know that you're favored in our eyes. You've always sought to do right by your brothers and this is pleasing to Him whom you love above all."

"This is good." Joseph self-consciously drew his knees up. "Are you an angel?"

"My name is Raphael and I have news."

Joseph gasped, "Oh, I've heard of you."

"Let me ask you first, why don't you believe Mary? She's also favored and I've spoken with her many times."

Joseph dropped his face, "You shame me. I'm sorry. This is all so difficult."

"Don't be ashamed Joseph, but it's time to accept the truth. Mary's pregnant while still a virgin. Her child will have an impact upon your world for generations to come."

Joseph clasped his hands in front of his chest and climbed down to the floor, kneeling in front of the angel. "Please forgive me my failings. Even as you say these things, I can't believe them. What if you're a delusion, an old man's mind failing? How can I know if this is real?"

"If you won't believe me, perhaps you'll believe another."

Joseph reached out, "No, no, it's not that I don't believe you... please, it's I that I doubt, not you."

"Don't worry Joseph. I'm not here to punish you for your doubts. I'll go now and have another come to you before the night is through. Go back to bed and have no fear. We're watching over you."

"No please..." Joseph begged, but the angel disappeared and the light vanished.

"Visited by an angel, Father? What a blessing," I said.

Joseph chuckled at my comment about the angel, "I didn't feel so blessed at the time."

115 · Made for This

"So, who did Raphael send next?" I asked him.

"It was later in the night, look…"

A hand on his shoulder roused Joseph. "What?" Joseph said in his half-sleep.

"Joseph, wake up."

"Wha… what is it?" Joseph sputtered.

"It's close to dawn and I need to speak with you before the household wakes."

When Joseph's eyes finally opened, he jerked back and nearly fell on the floor in fright.

"Don't be frightened, Joseph. You've heard from me before. I'm Philar."

"Philar?" Joseph looked him up and down. "Where did you come from?" Joseph's voice was raspy.

"I'm someone who cares about you very much. I mean you no harm, just the opposite, I mean to help you."

"You touched me?"

"Yes, I touched you." Philar extended his arm toward Joseph, "Here, you can touch me, I'm real."

Joseph hesitantly touched Philar. "Your skin… it's warm."

Philar chuckled, "Yes, like you I'm alive."

Joseph sat up and invited Philar to sit in a nearby chair. Joseph began to calm. "I've wanted to meet you since I read that note you sent us."

"Ah, yes, I would've come sooner, but those around you counseled me to wait."

Joseph hacked, his throat was dry.

"Fetch some water." Philar said, "I'll wait here."

Joseph did and when he returned to find Philar still there, he was startled, but caught himself on the doorframe, then carefully made his way back to the bed.

"Joseph, you must know that I want you to marry the girl."

Joseph said. "Why?"

"You're a wise and straightforward man. This baby is special. He'll need a gentle and spiritual man to guide him. A vacillating or emotional man, or an inflexible or un-tempered man, might not be able to give this boy what he needs to flourish. Your age and experience are assets."

"I've already done my time with family. I can't be starting a family now. It's irresponsible."

"I've done a full work-up on your health," Philar stated, "and barring unforeseen events, you'll live a long time."

"I'm uncomfortable with this idea!" Joseph asserted.

"Do you believe now that Mary is carrying this baby by divine intervention?"

"I don't know, maybe."

"I assure you, I created her pregnancy through means you can't understand. No man has touched her."

Joseph looked at Philar again, "You're not human?"

"No, I'm not. That in itself should convince you that something out of the ordinary is happening here." Philar pulled from his pocket a small device.

"Ah! What's that?" The device frightened Joseph.

"It's something ordinary from my life. It's a device for seeing things. Sit back. I'm going to show you something." Philar pointed the device at the space between Joseph's bed and the wall.

Suddenly a picture of the monastery at Carmel appeared. Philar began, "Here's the monastery. Those are the gates you so lovingly carved. Everyone there misses you."

This began a series of emotional vignettes from Joseph's far past through until the present. Joseph was brought to tears through this display several times; the death of his mother, his wedding, the birth of his children, the death of his father, the death of his wife, and many high and low points in between.

Philar paused, Joseph was weeping. "Your life has been full," Philar said.

"Don't show me anymore," Joseph begged.

"I have two more things to show you."

Joseph shook his head, "No, please no."

"Yes, I must, because eclipsing everything is that you can't see yourself physically taking Mary as your wife."

"No, I can't, she's a child, like a daughter."

"Joseph, look. This is what Mary will look like the first time she invites you to her bed."

"No, I don't want to look!"

"Look up!" Philar commanded.

Joseph looked up and what he beheld was the vision not of a child, but a fully-grown and beautiful woman. She was lovely and alluring and had no hint of childishness. Standing next to her holding her hand was a toddler.

"Beside her is the growing child," Philar continued, "and by this time, he'll be in your heart like no other ever has or ever will be after him. He looks older than he is because he's tall. He's as tall as he is intelligent and talented. Let me go further ahead and show you this last thing."

Tears were flowing down Joseph's cheeks as he beheld himself standing next to Mary with a bundled baby in his arms. His face was radiant, proud, and exceedingly joyous.

"This is your first child together. By this point, you wouldn't believe for a moment that you could've lived your life any other way. The gifts will have been many." Philar moved the device and the pictures stopped. "Your life is far from over. You were made to foster this child. You were made to live and love once again with a woman who will cherish you and stand by you. You were made to be an integral part of the upbringing of the Great Teacher. It's an honor only you can accept. Without you in the picture, Joseph, I'm afraid the mission will be lost. And if the mission is lost, so is all of humanity."

I watched Joseph's face. At first, he seemed confused, but seeing this last picture must have clicked something inside of him into place. As the scene progressed, he looked like a man moving into deep resonance with himself.

Joseph rose and grabbed at the robe over his chest. "I see now. I feel it Philar!"

Philar stood too. "Do you believe now?"

"Yes! Yes! I do," Joseph said, "I believe it all!"

"Then you have to go to Mary today and beg her for her hand. You have to go today before she gives up."

Joseph laughed, "I will, I must!"

"I was changed then, Yeshua, I was a different man after Philar spoke with me." Joseph looked at me with patient eyes.

"Philar knew about my mission," I asked him, "even before I was born?"

"Apparently so, my boy."

A chill swept up my spine. "So what happened next?" I inquired, "What happened when you spoke with Mary?"

"Would you like to see?" he asked. I nodded...

Joseph knocked on the door and Anne opened it. "Joseph!" she said with surprise.

"Hello, Anne. How're you?" Joseph said.

"Come in, please." She stepped aside and let Joseph enter. "What in God's name are you doing here?"

"In God's name I'm here to see Mary."

She nodded, "Alright, sit Joseph, I'll go get her."

Joseph didn't sit; he looked too anxious to sit.

A few moments later, he heard a familiar voice behind him, "Hello Joseph. I knew you'd come. I'm glad for your visit."

When he turned, across the room stood Mary, belly enlarged and glowing with a peace I'd seen on her many times. "Mary, I need to ask you something."

"What's that?"

"Will you..." the words caught in his throat and he had to swallow first. "Mary, will you have this fool? Will you be my wife?"

Mary stared at Joseph. Her face broke into a wide smile, "My answer's been waiting a long time. I'd be honored and proud to be your wife." She ran to him and they wrapped their arms around each other. She looked into his eyes, "What do we do now?"

"Well, I suppose we should talk to Jacob! I think people are waiting to hear our good news."

When this last memory vision faded, Joseph took my hand and we were back at the table.

116 · Just Getting Started

I looked at Joseph across the table. "I'm moved by your memories."

"Yeshua," Joseph asked, "what are you having difficulty accepting?"

"You told me many times that my life is my life. I decided long ago, I won't bow to prophecy."

Joseph nodded.

"And today the Creator told me that I can accept, reject, or alter the consequences and choices presented. I take from this that nothing is written. I have a choice!" I said as I slapped my hand on the table.

"Yes, my boy, you do," Joseph asserted.

I shook my head, "But I don't feel like I have a choice. Philar comes into my home. He tells me, and those closest to me, that the time of my death is nearing, and that it's imperative I father more children!" I paused to catch my breath, "I don't want either of those things. Not as he's presented them!" I slapped the table again.

Joseph nodded.

"But I think about what you've shown me, Father, you were adamant, you couldn't be Mary's husband. You felt she was part of a hoax. Yet you found not just acceptance, you found a mission!"

Joseph nodded.

"You and Mary were happy."

"We were exceedingly happy," Joseph agreed.

"How'd you find that? How did Philar convince you?"

"Philar didn't convince me," he said, "my face from the future convinced me. When I saw my face radiating that joy, I knew in my heart, that was what I wanted. The weight of that desire compelled me."

"So, Philar helped you see what your inner self was already grasping for?"

"I believe that's true, yes." He added, "Remember, everything around you, now and when you return to your body, it's all illusion. You have the power to manipulate that illusion, better than most people."

I thought about his words. "Talking with you is a good thing. Thank you."

"I'm here for you." Joseph looked at me quizzically, "Son, let's look at these two things separately. Start with you dying."

"I don't want to die."

"Why would you?" he said, "Do you believe you can alter that?"

Joseph's question piqued me. "Maybe I can alter that. Philar said I couldn't, but... maybe he doesn't see everything."

"Maybe," Joseph said. "What if you held onto life as the picture for your future? Would that change how you feel?"

I nodded, "Yes that would change how I feel. Yes." And when I said that, I felt a lift in my spirit. "I'll keep with that."

"I remember what your grown-self told me on the day you were born, and I remember it nearly verbatim. Your own words were these. 'Don't be afraid, Joseph. I'm here today because I'm alive. Although it appears I die young, I won't die. I'll transcend death and live.' Those were your words. I believe what you said to me that day."

"It feels good to hold it that way. At least it's a start."

"Alright," Joseph said, "then what about these children?"

As soon as he brought up the children, my mood plummeted into the confused and angry state I began in. "There's the real issue, Father. It makes me angry." I saw an image of Miriam in my mind and I was flooded with her being. "I wish you could meet Miriam." My thoughts brightened. "I love her with my life. I have no desire to be with any other woman. I know her spirit, I know her mind, I know her body. I've spent hours on hours getting to know her at a level so deep, I can't fathom going deeper. But then we spend time together, exploring us, and I know her more than before we began." Joseph was smiling as he listened. "Do you know what I mean?"

"Yes, I know what you mean."

"Sometimes," I said, "I feel like days are painted with joy only because it leads to another night with her." I smiled as my heart lifted. "And it doesn't matter what we do. It's not about sex, it's about being, just being, as one, even if all we're doing is sleeping, we're sleeping as one."

"She's a lucky woman."

"I'm the lucky one to have her," I nodded, "and that's why this angers me so much. Philar wants me to have sex with other women and I have no stomach for it. My marriage bed is sacred." I looked at Joseph. "I told him no. I dismissed the idea, but it won't go away and I don't know why!" Familiar tears begin to well in my eyes.

Joseph took my hand again, "Yeshua? What's your mission?"

"The mission is to end the subjugation that humans incarnate into over and over again."

He patted the back of my hand. "That's a big mission."

"Yes," I chuckled through my tears, "Creator's made it clear that I might've bitten off more than I can chew!"

"And yet, you continue?" He let go of my hand and threw his arms into the air. I chuckled at his dramatic display.

"Yes," I said, "I believe I have a real chance at being successful."

"Think about what Philar asks, not from the standpoint of your relationship with Miriam. Think about it in relationship to your mission."

I felt my forehead wrinkle. "That's the way Philar presented it," I said.

"I imagine," Joseph mused, "that populating the world with your descendants would be one way of helping your mission succeed."

When Joseph said this, I felt my insides begin to shake. My sensibilities were threatened. "But I'd have to have sex with other women to make that happen."

Joseph simply said, "Yes." He held my gaze, then he said, "When I wrestled with what was asked of me, I couldn't imagine having sex with a girl. I was an old

"Ye'sHUa wasn't perfect, he was merely the best man I've ever known, and I've been privileged to call him my husband."

- Miriam wife of Yeshua -

man, she a child. It grated against my sensibilities as a good Jew. It was patently wrong. I could've ignored that, married her in name only, and never had relations with your mother at all. But that's not what happened," he beat his finger on the table, "because of the very same reason; I was a good Jew! We're commanded by God to bring pleasure and fulfillment to our wives. Creator wants every person to walk in joy, fulfilled in every aspect of our being. I had a sacred obligation to give your mother that fulfillment," he pointed at me, "just as you have that obligation to your wife. Knowing that was what made any commitment to marriage so difficult to consider."

"I see that, yes," I said.

"So, I found an option I could live with. We slept in separate beds until she wanted me, of her own accord. It took time for her to want me. When her body became a woman, she could give birth, but when her spirit became a woman, she wanted a marriage bed. Then I knew she was no longer a child."

I nodded, "I see, yes."

"So!" Joseph said, "We have a similar problem. You're a good Jew. You have a relationship with your wife that gives your wife – and you by the giving – fulfillment and joy. This makes me proud, my son. And yet, you've a mission that requires you to consider something that doesn't sit well in you. Where's the middle ground? Where's the place that maintains your sense of pride, your wholeness, and takes care of business at the same time?"

"That's the right question, Father? Where's the step that protects the sacred in me, and still promotes my mission?" I nodded.

"I imagine," he said, "that if you carry this question around, you'll find your answer."

I squeezed Joseph's hand. "I miss you so much. I can't begin to express how good it is to talk with you."

"I've missed you too, Son," he said as a tear formed in the corner of his eye. "There's so much for you to do. Forgive me if I tell you, you're just getting started." He said as he winked at me.

I wasn't sure what he meant, but those words captured me. "I love you," I said, and as I did, the table faded, the room faded, and I was back in the field standing before my Creator. I looked around. "Joseph?" I felt a hole open in the pit of my stomach when I couldn't find him.

"He's gone, Issa," Creator said.

I turned back to her and remembered that Joseph was normally dead. I let out a sigh, "Thank you for arranging that visit."

"Did it help?" she asked.

"Yes, it helped."

"Are you prepared to consider your consequences and choices?"

I nodded, "Yes, I think so. I'm not angry anymore. I'm not exactly happy, but

"I can't press upon you enough the importance of self-examination. Higher consciousness, wisdom, inner peace, and the ability to achieve your deepest calling are dependent upon it. Of course, you can put it off. But sooner or later, some lifetime of yours will wake up. Eventually the tide of consciousness will carry you to it. Wouldn't you rather go there now, though, instead of after countless more cycles of death and rebirth?"

- Yeshua son of Joseph -

I'm not angry. There are things to consider."

"Do you know what you'll do?"

"No, I don't. But I'm prepared to consider my actions with greater care." I smiled at her, "You've made a difference today."

"You make a difference every day, Issa. Go now and be steadfast, my word."

As she said that, my consciousness pulled back and I remembered I was on the mountain top meditating. It took a few moments to come back fully to the world, but when I did, I was ready to go home. I wondered what was happening with the people I walked away from and I felt selfish to have left them as I did. It reminded me how absorbing anger is and I resolved to apologize for my actions.

I opened my eyes and gazed at the green valley below. This is a beautiful earth. This is a beautiful life.

117 · A Sacred Act

When I got close to home, I was surprised to see James sitting at the bottom of the hill. "I was worried about you," he said as we hugged. "I wanted to find you, but when I got here, I felt you were on the way home, so I waited instead."

"Thanks for coming to find me," I said, "I really needed to be alone last night, but not now. Let's walk." We started the climb up the hill, slowly, so we could talk on the way. I apologized for running out and for yelling, but he said it wasn't necessary to apologize. He understood completely why I had difficulty with the conversation. I told him about my visit with Joseph and how instead of dismissing the request, I was going to consider it until I figured out if there was a middle ground.

"You constantly amaze me," James said, shaking his head.

"Why's that?"

"You can change your perspective on nothing more than a new thought," he said, "and you rearrange to suit your change of perspective nearly instantaneously."

"Has that always been true?" I asked.

"No, I don't think it has." James thought a moment, "It's only been my experience of you since you recovered from your burden."

"Ah, then it must be a skill I acquired at the temple," I mused, "but isn't that true of everyone, that it takes new thought to affect change?"

"Yes, Bit, but… for most of us, we need to sustain a change in thought over time. Change takes place over days, weeks. But for you, it seems to take you latching onto just one thought and you rearrange yourself to suit it within hours, if not minutes."

"I suppose that's a blessing."

"Indeed, it is. A blessing any of us would love to have." James continued, "And something else, I want to thank you for accepting my truth with such grace."

"Your truth?"

"Yes, about what happened in Europe?"

I stopped and turned to James. We were getting close to the gate, and I wanted to acknowledge him before community accosted us. "How could I not? I'm so, so sorry that happened to you." I put my arms around him, "My heart aches for you."

James began to cry, "I locked it away. I was so scared of letting anyone see."

"Come, let's sit." We sat beneath a tree. I remained quiet, holding him in my mind's eye as clear, whole, and ready to be unburdened.

"All resistance to growth is an illusion. You were born from pure consciousness. Let go of the resistance and watch the barriers to your growth fall away as if they were never there. Banish any thought you have that affirms you're weak, less-than, or otherwise without the ability to transcend all limitation. Nothing could be further from the truth."

- Yeshua son of Joseph -

"I blamed myself, that I must have asked for it," James said, "that there was something wrong with me."

His story was heartbreaking. Finally, James said, "At Salt, I worked with brothers who had abuse issues from their childhood. I never blamed them. I knew in my heart that it wasn't their shame, it was the people who assaulted them." He looked at me. "I knew that was true for them, but I couldn't accept that for myself."

"Did you tell anyone there?"

"No, not a soul."

I pulled him to me. "It's not locked in you anymore. It's time to heal," and as I said that, I felt the light pulse into James. We sat looking over the valley, the light gently and softly healing. I held him, thinking of my brother as he was then, as he is now. I knew he had the power to be the most remarkable man I've ever known and I felt his passage to that place of power was close.

When we finally reached the main house, Miriam met us. I folded my arms around her. "I was so concerned for you," she said.

"I'm alright," I assured her, "and I apologize for my behavior yesterday. My anger was uncalled for."

"Oh, I don't know," she said, "I thought it was rightly called for. Actually, I was amused to see you angry for a change. I didn't think you had it in you," she poked.

I laughed, "Yes, I guess that would be so."

Hearing my laughter brought Mary out. "You're home."

"Yes, Mother, I'm home."

"Good," she said, "you worried us."

"Mother please, I'm a big boy." She shot me one of those looks that indicate she's my Mother and it doesn't matter how big or old I get, she has a right to worry. "Are you settled after all the revelations last night?" I asked her.

"Yes, Son, I'm fine. I'm with you," she smiled.

"Well, then, if it's alright with everyone, I'd like to have a conversation with my wife," and I led Miriam back to our room.

Once we were alone, I urged her onto the bed and let her snuggle into the crook of my arm. I loved the closeness and comfort we shared. I started with a recount of my time with Joseph. Miriam listened intently, letting her gentle, intuitive parts be present.

I was reluctant to tell her I was looking at the situation in a new way, but I knew I had to, so I completed the story with Joseph's recommendation to see if there was a middle ground. Part of me feared Miriam would be angered by the thought that I'd even look at what Philar suggested. But she wasn't.

We breathed together for a while, then Miriam said, "Are you afraid that this subject will make me jealous?"

I sighed, "Actually yes, I am."

"Mmm," she said, "is that why you had such a violent reaction to Philar's suggestion?"

"No, my reaction was selfish. It offended me." I added, "I do have that concern now, though, that I'm past my anger and willing to consider options."

"I see," she said, "I want to tell you something."

"Go on."

She rose to face me. "There's room in me for what Philar asks of you." She continued, "The act of having sex with a woman wouldn't diminish our relationship if it's for the purpose of procreation." I just breathed and listened. "If you were attracted and lusted after another," she said, "that might cause me pain. If your aim was to pleasure yourself wantonly, that would cause me pain." I nodded. She continued, "But if your aim was to produce a child, that's a sacred act, a divine gift. It wouldn't interfere with the closeness that we share."

I tried to understand what she was saying. I knew Miriam came from a society with different views on sexuality than mine. And Miriam had a unique perspective from her priestess experience. "I don't want to touch another woman," I said, "I have no stomach for it. I don't know how I could even manage it."

"With the right incentive, my love, you'd be able to manage it, trust me."

I looked away, "Well, that issue aside, I don't want to." I looked back at her, "To do this, I'd have to get over a revulsion to caressing another woman."

"Is it that abhorrent to you?" she asked.

"Yes. It is."

She lay back into the crook of my arm and ran her hand across my chest. She murmured, "That's extraordinary and very rare in my experience of men."

"Well, rare or not," I said, "it's how I feel."

"I'd love to see a child born that could figure out how to harness the energy of worry. If it were possible to convert it to usable energy, it would produce a sustainable surplus of the world's energy supplies within hours. But until such a time occurs, worry is useless. Any time spent on worry provides no return of any worth."

- Yeshua son of Joseph -

118 · Energetic Matrices

"Maybe we should have another talk with Philar," Miriam said, "we didn't really have a chance to explore his thoughts last night. The conversation was cut off quite abruptly."

I laughed, "Yes indeed, I did do that." I chuckled, "Well, yes perhaps I should give him a chance to say more and give myself a chance to ask questions."

"Can you call him here?" she asked.

"Not usually. It'd be nice if it were as easy as just saying, 'Hey Philar will you join us?' But that's not been…"

"Yes I will," Philar said from the foot of the bed.

Both Miriam and I jumped, "You startled us!"

"Sorry," he said, "I've been on standby."

"Great," I said, "let's do it." Miriam and I sat up and Philar sat down. I began by apologizing for my outburst. He accepted my apology and said he understood the difficulty of the exchange.

"I have a burning question," I said, "why can't you make these pregnancies happen without my participation? That's how I was created."

"It not that simple," he explained, "the material that made you was, well for lack of a better term, uncooked. By that I mean it'd never been used. You've now used that material. You've cooked it, if you will. By living your life, it's been transformed into something that we couldn't create without your life-force molding it. Energetically, what you have in you now is what we need to perpetuate, not the basic seed we started with."

"But if you use that basic seed several times, it will become 'cooked' in the children you produce."

"No, not like you've cooked it, Yeshua." He shook his head, "Believe me, the energetic matrix you've created is beyond anything any other being would ever create." He nodded, "It's beyond anything we hoped for. Besides, the amount of energy and resources we've brought to bear to give you the opportunities and support you've had are just not available again on the low chance another would be as successful as you. Not anytime soon anyway."

"So, if I understand what you're saying, it's not just the material of my body you need, it's the energy that is exclusively me, created by the choices I've made."

"I couldn't have said it better."

"Then why can't you take my seed and use it? Create as many babies as you want?"

"There're two reasons."

"I'm listening,"

"First, the mothers need to be prepped, and the community of women you have around you already know what it would mean to carry your child."

"That wouldn't preclude you from doing the deed yourself," I said.

"Well perhaps not by itself, but coupled with the second reason, it does."

"And?"

"The second reason has to do with human sexuality and how it works." He scratched his head, obviously pondering how to say things. Finally, he said, "Let's leave out the spiritual side of this equation for the moment. On a purely physical level, when a couple engages in sex, there's not just an exchange of fluid. In a positive interaction, there's also an energetic exchange. The energy that the man sends to the woman creates a kind of energy bath in which the baby will grow. It's imperative, in this early stage of dissemination, that you perpetuate the exchange so the energetic matrix will be produced and transferred. That's not something we can mimic." He shook his head, "There's energy that the woman adds to the womb as well and that can't be stimulated artificially." He looked into my eyes and said, "It's something that was missing from Mary's womb when you grew and frankly, we worried about that. We didn't know how it would affect you, if at all."

"And did it? Affect me?"

Philar nodded, "Yes it did, but luckily not in an adverse way. We can't be certain that it'd always have as benign of an affect. We wouldn't be able to control the external environment of each birth as effectively as we controlled yours."

"I see."

"But I'm curious," Miriam said, "if the man sends an energetic matrix to the woman, does she send one back to the man?"

"That's a good question, Miriam, and I can understand why you'd want to know. The answer is yes, she does, again, if the experience is positive. In the case of Yeshua and any woman he might be with, I can't imagine it'd be anything but a positive exchange."

"I see," she said.

"You must be advised, Miriam, that you're an adeptly intuitive woman and you'd feel that energy. It would dissipate over time, but you'd perceive it at first. It could be confusing."

"That's something I'd have to prepare for," she said.

"Yes," Philar said.

"It sounds like you're recommending," I said, "that if we do this, we ask women from this community to be the mothers?"

"Oh yes. It'll be easier to both hide the true parentage, and still give the children a thriving and socially sound upbringing."

"Sexual expression is meant to be enjoyable, but the full truth of how sex affects you is misunderstood. Even though it can be used as such, sexual expression is no simple dalliance, and it is never meaningless. Sex affects your body, but also has emotional, energetic, and spiritual effects. I'm not saying, 'don't express your sexuality,' I'm saying, 'know who you're expressing it with and pay attention to why.' And if you are choosing to have sex for the first time, take extra care in selecting that partner. The energetic effects of the first exchange stay with you for your entire life. If you don't choose your sexual expressions wisely, you can count on built-up, unused energy overruling your better judgment in seemingly unrelated parts of your life. Wake-up to what you're actually doing, and then choose your actions from wisdom rather than from ignorance. It's not easy or fun to wake-up after the fact and recover from an emotionally-charged bath of misplaced loyalties, emotional dependencies, confused decisions, and possible addictions."

- Yeshua son of Joseph -

"Did I hear you right? You said, hide the parentage?"

"Yes, these children will be raised belonging to other people. You'll have been a surrogate father, not even in name, in deed only."

"Ah, I understand," I said. I looked at Miriam and she smiled and nodded. "Thanks Philar, this information helps a lot. I still have to think about this."

"Yeshua, hear me. I know it seems like I'm trying to dictate your life. I'm not. Why do you think it took me so long to even bring this up? It's your life, you make your own choices, but I can't stress enough how this would enhance your mission. I hope you find yourself amenable to our proposal."

119 · Volunteers

Lots of talk and much thought later, I consented to Philar's request. And yet, until the last moment, I thought I wouldn't agree. Several things came together to help me arrive at a decision.

Miriam understood this whole business. Female and male surrogacy was an accepted part of Miriam's background. It was sacred service, and an integral part of the functions she oversaw at her temple. She saw this as a gift to the greater community; many couples had no children of their own.

James, who initially had some of the same misgivings as I, did research and found a section in the original Bon texts that pointed to the sacred nature of surrogacy. There was an entire set of passages devoted to the proper delivery of the surrogacy function by the male priest. Obviously this wasn't part of the texts we were shown when we were children.

And I remembered the surrogacy functions the adept brothers undertook at our mountain cave those many years before. I recoiled at the idea then, but the pilgrims who requested those services were delighted with the chance to have something as precious as a child.

I also remembered Nadia's face, both the day Philar gave her the pregnancy and when we met again in Madeba. Her life positively changed by the presence of a child. And I didn't have to go back very far in my own life to remember how I felt on the day I was weeping in the orchard, asking Philar to help Miriam and I keep a baby. Together, this information and these memories were convincing and comforting to me.

Once I decided I was on board with the plan, Miriam convened a meeting with the inner circle of devotees. Of those present, eight women volunteered, six who were married to other devotees, one who had abandoned her husband to follow the teachings, and one who was a widow. As it should be, of the married women, their husbands were equally on board. These remarkable couples were desirous of having children and all but one of the couples had none. They saw this as a miraculous chance to fulfill the dream of a family. The volunteers and their husbands went through counseling with James to avert any possibility of rifts in their relationship and to give those women who weren't married a helpful shoulder

"Finding your way in life is not supposed to be hard, but so often it is. There are so many paths to take, so many voices telling you what they think. And so often those voices are only hawking for their own agenda. You must follow your heart. If you haven't awakened to the strong and positive voice your heart has for you, I urge you to awaken to it now. One thing you can count on; your own heart will have no other agenda but to further your path toward your higher goals and desires. Hear its voice and you'll find the ease of knowing that your decisions are well advised."

- Yeshua son of Joseph -

to lean on.

Unfortunately, one of the unmarried women, the one who'd abandoned her husband, was declined a role in this plan. Her name was Danielle and we had misgivings from the beginning for her participation, as her husband wasn't present. If he ever did come back into her life, the child would be hard to explain. She'd be considered an adulterer and could be put to death. And then, during counseling, James uncovered that the woman had a secret sexual yearning for me. Given all this, everyone involved felt it was too dangerous. Denying her a role made her angry and she left our community shortly after that.

Miriam and I made it clear that the parentage of any resulting child wouldn't be questioned, the child would legally and for all purposes be the progeny of the volunteers. The world would never know the circumstances of any pregnancy. And I was firm that there were no romantic ties desired or being created by these unions; I was devoted to Miriam. This was surrogacy, not romance.

And even though I agreed, I had apprehension following through. It wasn't easy for me. The first few attempts left me emotionally drained, and I almost called it quits. But there's nothing like success and very quickly, we had our first pregnancy.

It was Mirah, the wife of Andrew, Peter's brother. They were an older couple and of all the women, she seemed the least likely to find success. Yet, in her time Mirah gave birth to a beautiful girl they named Shiah.

The next successful pregnancy was with Beeza, the wife of Roman. Interestingly, Roman and Beeza weren't Jewish. Beeza gave birth to a healthy boy whom they affectionately named Joseph in honor of my father. There was a lively discussion throughout the pregnancy as to whether there'd be a circumcision if the child proved to be a boy. I stayed out of the discussion for obvious reasons, but in true avid rabbinic fashion, James tried to convince them to have the procedure done. In the end, they declined.

Ann, the wife of Philip, was the next to become pregnant; however, Ann had a miscarriage two months into the pregnancy. They were devastated. It wasn't their first miscarriage and they took it as a sign that they weren't destined to have children. We didn't try again.

Carole was a delightful woman, a widow whose beloved husband had recently died unexpectedly. It was a joy to see her come alive with hope when she became pregnant. She considered this a spiritual gift from her husband and vowed to raise the daughter as if she were his. She named her Rose.

Willa and her husband Jonas were the next and last of the volunteers to have success. Willa eventually gave birth to a beautiful girl they named Rebekkah.

Matthew's wife Anna withdrew from the plan before engaging with me. After some counseling, she decided she just couldn't go through with it. Everyone respected her decision with no recrimination.

And Simon's wife, Ruth, had no success. She never became pregnant and we eventually stopped trying when Philar said he thought it wasn't going to occur.

Overall, we produced four more children and that satisfied Philar. Especially because he thought Miriam might have another pregnancy before anything grave happened to me.

And all through this time, life was relatively normal. The community hummed. I traveled to give talks and went on campaigns. Newtown was growing with prosperity and becoming a regular part of merchant caravan stops. The shops garnered a fair amount of trade from travelers to Sepphoris. And I was happy to be with my family and help my own son grow.

There were rumblings, though, of continued opposition to my teachings that got louder and louder. They had much to do with an opposition to a perceived political power they saw me amassing. I had no political aspirations, none whatsoever, but it's difficult to convince a paranoid political beast that another man with a piercing voice isn't poised to usurp him.

My old nemesis Oranos made his presence known on numerous occasions. There seemed no reason for most of his visits except to harass me and remind me that he was ever hopeful I'd cross the line and give him a good reason to slaughter me.

Judas maintained a web of allies and spies that monitored both the Sanhedrin in Judah and Herod's court in Caesarea as well as their satellite power centers. I received news weekly, sometimes daily of their comings and goings. This was an effort to keep our entire community safe from reprisal.

One could argue that the best way to keep us all safe would be to stop spreading my thoughts across the land, but I couldn't. I was compelled to speak. It was the passion of my life and my mission to end subjugation. And as the months rolled by, my dialog naturally became more and more scornful of the reigning authorities.

If there was one thing to point to that made my speech more dangerous than anything else, it had to be my propensity for declaring that fear was the true enemy, and that those who advocated fear had no place of honor in our lives.

"Ye'sHUa had precious little time to explore being a father, but the time he had with Micah was quality time. Micah was still a toddler when his father left him, and that was unfortunate. In that short time, Ye'sHUa never pushed his son away, never refused him affection, and never made him to feel anything other than loved for no reason but that he was alive."

- Miriam wife of Yeshua -

Conception

120 · Pagan Rattles

Passover celebrations were behind us and crops were ready for harvest. It was Micah's third birthday and there'd be a celebration later that afternoon. We didn't celebrate adult birthdays, but we marked the passing of years for children up to their majority. The child's friends might gather to play games. Adults might tell stories. There might be a sing-a-long or some other fun group activity. If the parents were wealthy, they might hire puppeteers or other entertainers for the gathering. We didn't give presents, but we'd provide a favorite meal of the child's, if possible. We endeavored to celebrate the gift of another year together by sharing joy, comradery, and love.

Tragedy marred this day instead. Just before the children were to gather for the games Jude had lovingly arranged, a rider galloped up the hill. He was an earnest young man obviously new to the riding business and eager to perform his duty well. He jumped off his horse, running to find me as fast as he could. The note was heart wrenching. It was from a contact in Herod's court informing me that Herod had just jailed my cousin John on charges of sedition. Technically, John was guilty of sedition, so was I; we both spoke words that could excite people to rebellion against any oppressive authority.

There was no question that John would be put to death. We knew Herod well enough to know that he wouldn't have bothered to place John in chains if he hadn't already condemned him. People generally didn't get out of Herod's prison alive. And I couldn't help remembering the gruesome end I'd seen for John that day at the river.

John never married. His unique perspective on life left him believing he couldn't make that kind of commitment. But I knew he'd recently coupled with a woman named Anna. They lived together and I was immediately worried for her safety and wellbeing.

Anna was a tall, dark-skinned woman originally from Axum. I'd met her once, and her deep spiritual nature flooded the air around her. She was a captivating woman.

I dispatched Judas with a contingent of men to locate John's camp and bring Anna, and anyone else who wanted to come, back to the compound for their safety. I wrote a note for delivery to John, asking him if he had messages for me. I was willing to relay anything he needed to whomever he needed it relayed. I was very careful how I worded the note; I spoke of messages only in a benign way any relation might talk to another. I wanted my note to get to him unmolested. I sent the note off with the young rider and joined the birthday games. I sought to celebrate my son's birthday with all the joy I could muster, but I was distracted and bothered by the news.

Later that evening after supper, Judas came back with Anna and the other women of John's camp. The men elected to move their camp closer to the prison to keep a prayer vigil going for John, but they felt it was too dangerous for the women to be there. I was glad to hear that common sense prevailed. Miriam and her maidens outfitted a tent for them and got them safely tucked in with a sound meal and warm blankets before retiring. There was one thing that Miriam didn't miss though; Anna was pregnant.

The next morning I met with Anna. Even though I had no doubt, she volunteered that she carried John's child. Obviously, John's imprisonment affected her, but emotion didn't consume her. She was a stalwart soul and a realist, able to grasp the severity of John's imprisonment and accept it.

"I have no illusion, John is gone," Anna said, "we play only the game of catch-up now." I had no trouble understanding her, even though it was evident that Aramaic wasn't her first language.

"I want to help in any way I can," I offered, "John's dear to me, as you are now, and as your child will be."

"Thank you, and if I can stay for the birthing, I be grateful." She put a hand on her belly and smiled, "This child is what I have of him now."

I nodded with understanding, "What'll you do after that? You're welcome to stay longer."

"No," she said, "I think when baby can, we go home, to Axum."

"I see," I nodded, "you have family there still?"

"Yes, parents and much family."

"I'm sure they'll welcome you."

She looked at me with a strange expression. Her eyes became piercing, much like John's could. She said, "But it's you I concern over. Your time is nearing, just as John's did."

Her words jolted me. I hadn't given my demise much thought lately. "What do you see?" I asked.

She took a deep breath, closed her eyes, and entered into a spontaneous trance. The energy in the room changed significantly. I heard the shaking of a pagan rattle, even though none was present. And it felt as though a swirling wind gently blew around us. I smelled the distinct odor of smoldering wood. Only a trained priestess could manage these manifestations. She moved to the floor and I joined her. She took my hands and said something in her native language. "I don't understand your words," I said, "can you speak in a common language?"

"There is a fine line between simply accepting reality as it shows itself to be and colluding with the illusion. Colluding with the illusion means you see reality as unmalleable. You believe that you have to put out great effort to have a small effect. Accepting reality as it shows itself, though, allows you to be right here right now. And being fully seated in the present is the first step to being able to have a great effect on the illusion with minimal effort. It's a fine line, but an important one."

- Yeshua son of Joseph -

As if in a dream, I felt two hands grasp my shoulders. I couldn't see him, but it was obviously a man sitting behind me; I felt his beard and his breath on my neck as he leaned in to my ear, "Don't worry, Cousin, I can translate for you." The voice was unmistakable; it was John, or at least a perfect apparition of him.

Anna continued as John translated, "Your time is near, but you have the power to select the place and the method." The swirling wind seemed to ramp up as it whooshed across my forearms. "Choose wisely," John said as Anna continued. "Don't leave it to chance. Herod is after your head. The Roman is itching to draw your blood. And the Sanhedrin is ready to bring you to counterfeit justice." I worked at deepening my breath so I wouldn't pass out. My body began to shake. "You'll know when your time's at hand. When Miriam proves pregnant again, act swiftly."

My body still shaking, I said, "Yes, I understand."

Anna continued, John said, "You'll suffer fate, but you don't have to die, choose wisely."

There was an extended pause, so I asked, "Is there anything else?" The pungent smell of smoldering wood filled my nostrils.

Anna's eyes still closed, my hands resting in hers, they continued, "Don't let the mounting aggression sway you. The words you speak from here to there are of the utmost importance. Generations will thank you."

Anna squeezed my hands as she let go and placed her hands at rest on her pregnant belly, her face downturned. The sound of the rattle stopped. The wind died and the scent of smoldering wood faded. John's hands squeezed my shoulders and before he faded, he said, "Thank you for everything. My love is with you."

I sat for a time on the floor with Anna in the quiet of the morning. I was overwhelmed not just with the message, but with the obvious parallels between John and me. We both had devoted followings. We both had mystical ways that set us apart from other teachers. We taught ideas and philosophies that were dangerous to the powerful elite. Anna now proved to be a priestess, something I didn't know about her before. That meant John and I both paired with pagan priestesses. And if the prophecy just now was true, we'd both be dealt with by the authorities while our women were pregnant. John had been born about a half a year before me. Would he now also prove to find his end about half a year before me? I didn't know what any of this meant, but it was certainly no coincidence.

After a time, I put my hand on Anna's knee and thanked her for her messages. She said she didn't remember them, but hoped they were useful. When we stood I gave her a hug and she went about her business.

The information she gave me validated the plan I was formulating, but there wasn't much else to do yet, so I simply went back to my regular duties.

"Prophecy is useful in seeing where things might be headed, but never fall victim to believing that because it was prophesized, then it must be. The future is malleable. If you aren't actively molding your future, you're missing out on your best life."

- Yeshua son of Joseph -

121 · Will the Killing Stop?

Later that evening, just before sundown, a familiar and undesired visitor came with a full contingent of soldiers; it was Oranos, of course. This time I recognized the soldiers as elite guards from Herod's court.

When he got to the clearing, I walked out to meet him, "Commander. What could possibly demand Herod's own elite guard?"

"Oh, good. You recognize them," he said, "do they intimidate you?"

"Of course they do," I said.

He smiled a broad smile, "Well, don't think they're here on your account. They just happened to be with me when another matter came up."

"Oh, and what's that?" I inquired.

Oranos reached into his lap and threw something at me. "This!" he said, laughing.

It smacked into my chest and bounced to the ground. When it hit the ground, I recognized it as a severed hand, cut off above the wrist.

I looked him dead in the eye, "You do seem to enjoy hurling body parts at me, Commander."

"They're a good substitute until I can get the body I'm really after," he pointed at me.

"Well," I said, "I'm honored to be so well despised."

He scowled, "Believe me, it's no honor." He slid off his horse and walked toward me.

"I assume you want me to ask who used to own this appendage," I said.

He came close and held out a note that I recognized as my own, "You tell me. He had this with him. The only way I could get it was to relieve him of his means of grasping it."

I felt a thud in my abdomen when I realized it was the eager rider who so innocently brought me the news of John the day before.

"I see you know him!" Oranos said.

"Not really," I said, "I met him briefly only yesterday. He's a young rider making a living with his horse. He brought me the news that John was jailed."

"You mean he was a young rider." Oranos grinned, "I ran him through after I took his hand."

Oranos actions sickened me and I had to force myself to keep from doubling over and retching. "As far as I knew, Commander, he was a young innocent man trying to make an honest living."

"Then why was he carrying this note with your seal on it?"

"Because I paid him to," I said. "I love my cousin. I'm bereft that he's in prison."

"You expect me to believe that's all this is?" he said with incredulity.

"I don't know what you will or won't believe, Commander, but I'm overwhelmed that an innocent died merely because I was sending a supportive note to my incarcerated cousin!" I glared at him, "Should I send you a duplicate of every note I write from here on?" I said with force, "Will that keep the young merchant boys of my creed safe on the byways?"

Oranos was unaffected by my words, "So the Baptist is your cousin?"

"Yes, through my mother."

"It runs in the family then?" Oranos said.

"What runs in the family?" I demanded, my patience wearing thin.

"A blatant disregard for authority."

I was tired. I was grieved and fed up with the game of harassment Oranos was playing. "So with that logic, should I assume that other members of your family throw severed body parts at people?"

"Explain this note!" he shouted.

"I already have!" I threw my hands into the air and looked away from him. "My cousin is in jail, I expect him to be put to death at any moment. I'm distraught over that and I wanted to know if I could help him relay personal messages. Maybe there's someone he wants to apologize to," my voice raised to a shout, "or maybe someone deserves to hear of his love before his neck is made barren of his head!" I looked at Oranos, "Listen, if you want to kill me, why haven't you?"

Oranos smiled and slowly mounted his horse, "I haven't killed you yet because it's simply too sweet throwing body parts at you, Rabbi," he laughed, "and you're right about your cousin's head. It won't be his long."

Suddenly, from behind me, Miriam called, "Yeshua? Are you coming to supper?"

I looked at Oranos, "You tell me Commander. Am I going to supper?"

Oranos looked toward Miriam and cocked his head, "Priestess." He looked back at me, "You're an odd pet for the pagan, Rabbi."

I just glared at him.

He pulled his horse back a few steps, "We'll meet again."

"I'm sure of that," I sneered as he waved his hand at the guards and they rode down the hill.

I picked up the bloody hand and walked back to the porch. "I need a clean cloth to wrap this hand for burial." I paused, "I don't even know his name."

Miriam said, "I'll get that for you." She touched my cheek with her fingers, "Remember, you're a good man."

"Just like you, the people around you are creators. The world consists of all you and they have created and co-created. For example, books are co-creations and couldn't exist without the complicity of many people. Yet, whether it rains or not is also a co-creation, one in which you're probably unconscious of your complicity. But, just because you co-habit with co-creators, you don't have to have every experience of life that they have. You can live next door to someone who creates violence and not be affected by violence yourself. But you must pay attention to what you create. Are you complicit in inviting an experience by how you view yourself? For example, to be an avenger of justice you must have an experience of injustice. In the same vein, to fight for freedom you must be touched by a lack of freedom. If fighting for freedom is your mission, then that's perfect, but if it's not, then why invite it? Hear this; pay careful attention to what you want to experience and structure your life and your creations accordingly."

- Yeshua son of Joseph -

392 | *Kaarin Alisa*

I closed my eyes and tried to forget about Anna's messages from the morning. They wouldn't fade. And when Miriam came back with the cloth, I wrapped the boy's hand and took it into the house. I laid it on the table in the big room, the place we'd lay any honored dead before entombment. I said a prayer and went to wash off the slime of Oranos before having supper with my family. And I wondered just when the killing was going to stop.

122 · Dark Energies

Several weeks went by and we heard nothing of my cousin. I wondered why Herod was delaying the execution, but I was restless and decided to go on another campaign, this one into the heart of Judah. Miriam wasn't pregnant, though I hadn't told her anything of Anna's prophecies. However, I was considering Anna's words most carefully.

I was sure that, by now, James had put Philar's prophecy out of his mind. I hoped that Miriam had too, but I knew Mary hadn't.

I stood in a town square near Jerusalem speaking to a crowd. I extolled the bliss of trusting in the love of our Creator, listening to Creator's words as they flow through the heart of every human who seeks them. Suddenly, a cloaked woman stepped out from the crowd and declared, "Why should we listen to you, Nazorean?"

"You have no need to listen to me except as my words might urge you to listen to your Creator," I answered.

She stepped closer, "But I've witnessed how impure you are!" She lifted her head and part of her face became exposed. I recognized her immediately; it was Danielle, the woman excluded from the surrogacy plan.

"You believe you know something that precludes my ability to inspire people with truth?" I asked.

"I know about you, Yeshua," she scoffed, "I used to live with you."

"Yes, Danielle. You left our village many months ago. You left in anger, if I'm not mistaken."

She turned toward the crowd and said, "Don't listen to this faker! He speaks as if he is pure, but he robs people."

"How do I do that?" I asked calmly.

She turned to me and said, "You lie!" The crowd became restive.

"I've not lied to you, Danielle." I saw both a Temple priest and several of Herod's scouts in the audience. James had been in the back and he moved through the people to be closer to me.

Danielle spat at me, "How can you claim piety when I know how you live?"

I felt the light pulse. "I claim no piety. I'm a man of contradictions, like any man."

She turned to the crowd. "This 'Rabbi'," she pointed at me, "proclaimed his love for me. He convinced me to leave my home, leave my husband… to live with him!" The crowd began to murmur. "He tried to convince me to have his baby, even though he's married to a pagan woman!" she shouted.

The crowd gasped.

Danielle turned to me, "What do you say to that, Rabbi!"

The light stepped up its brilliance, "I say, that's a perversion of the truth, Sister. You're angry and want me to pay for choices you've made of your free will."

"I accuse you, Rabbi! I accuse you of coupling with married women! Women of faith! I accuse you of adultery and of siring children with them!"

I took in a breath and felt the light glow with strength. The crowd gasped and the murmuring din got louder. I stepped closer to Danielle and said in a soft voice, "I see you, Danielle."

"You can't see me!" she screamed.

"I see you," I nodded. "Tell me, Sister, is the child in your belly from your husband?"

"What are you talking about?" she shouted as she began to recoil from me.

I stepped closer, "I'm asking, who's the father of the child? As you imply, is it mine?"

"No." She staggered backward. "There's no child!" she yelled.

"I see you. I see a child."

She pulled further back, "I'm pure!" She pulled off her cloak and threw it at me in rage. As she did, her robe pulled across her belly and the bulge of her pregnancy became apparent.

"You're pure?" I said, "Then let me touch you." I stepped closer to her.

"No!" she screamed, "Don't touch me." She tried to step back more, but the crowd had moved close around us. They wouldn't let her step back further.

I took another step toward her and the light pulsed more. It emanated from me with brilliance.

"I'll not harm you. Let me touch you."

"No!" she yelled again.

"Here," I extended my arm to an old woman that was standing next to me. "You touch me. See if I'm harmful." The crowd moved back to give the old woman room. She hesitated, her eyes darting about from being on the spot. She put her hand on my forearm. She gasped and an expression of ecstasy came over her face. "Am I harmful?" I asked her.

"No," she said with awe, "You're light. It's beautiful." Tears filled her eyes.

I turned to Danielle, "You see? Let me touch you."

"You're a liar!" she yelled, "I hate you!"

Two men in the crowd cradled her shoulders. "Let him touch you," one of them urged, "we want to see what happens." The look on her face was pure terror.

"I'm certain you blame me for every pain in your life," I said, "but I'm not the perpetrator of your pain." I stepped a little closer, "But I can be the purveyor of your healing. If you let me."

"No," she said, but her voice was less strident and her body seemed to relax.

"You don't have to. I promise I'll not force it. Even though these folks want it, if you deny my touch, I won't." I held deep empathy for her. "I know you're in

"Spiritual growth comes in spirals, like water moving through a tube, you'll find yourself flowing round and round. At certain curves along the way, it may seem as though you're merely circling; don't be fooled, don't give up. Keep growing. One day you'll look back and the forward movement you've made will be clear to you."

- Yeshua son of Joseph -

pain. You were in pain when you left our community, and it hasn't gotten better for you." I let my upturned palm hover close to hers. "Let me calm some of that pain, if not for you, for the child."

After some silence, she said, "Alright," and she laid her fingers across my palm. The light's pulse slowed to a more deliberate rhythm. I saw the baby in her belly wasn't her husband's. I knew that if I said that, the crowd would stone her for adultery. I had to say something benign.

Her face softened, tears amassing in her eyes. I said, "The life growing in you is one of faith. This child is a pure light."

I grabbed her hand tightly, the light urging me to pull her close. "Come closer." I held her tightly to my chest. The light grew to encompass us both. The crowd gasped.

"I ask everything that isn't pure to leave you now. The light fills you and pain has no welcome in you any longer." She screamed. Dark swirls of dense energy bolted out of her.

The crowd was mad with fright. They practically stumbled over one another as they tried to get away from us. But they didn't go far; the scene riveted them. I held Danielle as more dark energies rushed out of her, dissipating in midair.

"My love for you, Danielle, is as it always has been," I said in a loud and clear voice. "It's the love of a father to a child. A love that is without limits." The light continued and Danielle screamed as a torrent of thick, dark energy streamed out of her. And the moment the last dark streak dissipated, the light in me diminished and Danielle collapsed on my arm.

The din of the crowd grew loud. I pulled Danielle to her feet and gently caressed her forehead until she came back to consciousness. When she opened her eyes, I let her feet carry her weight and pulled my arm back to rest on her forearm. "How are you now, Danielle?" I asked.

She looked at me surprised at my presence, "Yeshua?"

I nodded, "Yes it's me."

"What're you doing here?" she asked with a voice so light, it touched my heart with sweetness.

"Don't you remember the last few minutes?"

She shook her head, "I remember coming to the square to buy vegetables."

"You had a bit of trouble. We've all been concerned for you."

She noticed the crowd of people amassed. "Oh, dear," she said, "I'm fine now though." She looked at me, "It's good to see you." She spied James, "You too, James," and she smiled.

I picked up the cloak and handed it to her, "I think this is yours." She took it and cocked her head in thanks.

The crowd was wild with enthusiasm. They rushed in and grabbed at me. They pulled at me mercilessly. "Take care of yourself, Danielle," and I let go of her as the throng drew me backward into their embrace.

"Give of yourself. Never be confused into believing that there's anything more valuable to the outside world than the true gift of your full self in the world. People have physical needs and you can feel free to help with those, be they true needs, or merely things of temporal delight. But in the end, when all things are known, nothing will stand out more than the gift you made of yourself or the gift of you withheld. Be you and share you, openly, freely, and with intent."
- Yeshua son of Joseph -

123 · Cold Comfort

Later that evening, James and I sat alone on a bluff outside town. The devotees with us were already abed or sitting by the fire some distance away.

"Today was scary," James admitted.

"Yes," I replied.

"First Danielle," James said, "then the crowd."

"I got through it," I said.

James paused a moment. He was suffering. "Bit?"

"Yes?"

"The danger has stepped up."

I took a deep breath and stared into the valley, "Yes, it has."

"What if this happens again?" he asked.

"Then I'll get through it," I said matter-of-factly.

"Why's it different now?" he asked with apprehension, "Why's it so dangerous?"

I looked at him and nodded, "You know why."

He looked away. "No, I don't," he said with a determined set to his jaw.

"You don't want to know," I said quietly.

"I want you to be safe."

"Why ask for what can't be ensured?" I said.

"I'm scared," he exclaimed, his face fraught with fear.

"We both signed up for this."

"I'm with you, I am. And, I'm scared about what might happen!"

"I told you," I said, "you already know what'll happen."

He pleaded, "Can't you just comfort me tonight?"

"No," I said. James got up and walked back to the fire leaving me alone. I had a strong feeling that by this time next year, my body would be rotting in a burial chamber, or if alive, life wouldn't be at all the same. And though I had no images to comfort me, I hoped it was the latter option and not the former.

Through the next weeks, we campaigned into Jerusalem and then back toward Galilee. In more than one town, I ran into a detractor. In all but one, the light quelled the uproar in a similar way it quelled Danielle. But in one of the small towns along the Samarian border, I used my adept skills to escape a crowd that turned into a mob. I disappeared for fear they'd rip me apart.

This was a different type of campaign, not pleasant. My path no longer felt open and joyful. In towns where my words were well received, hands were nonetheless constantly reaching for me, pulling at me, begging for access. People shouted about spontaneous healings and demons defeated. Weeping throngs dogged me. Sick people crawled to me. People pushed the blind at me.

I slept little and spent long hours at night wishing I was home with Miriam. She'd refused to come on this campaign; she had a bad feeling about it. And even though selfishly I wished she were here, I was glad she didn't have to endure the hardships the crowds repeatedly thrust on us.

When we got home, I was surprised to learn that John was still alive. Miriam showed me a note that came while I was gone. It revealed the reason why Herod hadn't yet executed him. John was promising that, if Herod executed him, he'd mercilessly haunt him. John professed that he was a prophet of God, and that God wouldn't let those who persecuted him go unpunished.

This notion tickled my rebellious heart. It made me laugh. I pictured my cousin with his bellowing voice, harassing Herod; proclaiming his relationship with God to all who'd hear. I sent him energy to keep it up.

After all, Herod was Jewish, even if he lacked all piety and decency; he grew up with Torah. He had to know there'd be consequences for killing a prophet.

A few months later, however, I woke in the night out of a deep sleep. I was having a dream about fishing with Micah. It was delightful. In the dream, Micah looked near his majority, easily eleven or twelve. He and I were on the Sea of Galilee in a small boat. We threw nets over the side and pulled in fish after fish. I said, 'I'm teaching you to be a fisherman, Boy!' Micah laughed with glee. Then John stepped into the dream and put his arms around me, squeezing me with a depth and fervor as only he could. 'Don't worry about me any longer, Cousin, the deed is done.' My eyes snapped open and I knew it was true, that John was dead.

I considered waking Miriam, but decided against it. Waking her would be selfish, reaching for comfort while disturbing someone else's. So, instead, I wept myself back to sleep.

"There are consequences to every action. Like it or not, you make waves every time you act. You make waves every time you refuse to act as well. So if at any time, fear is keeping you from acting, then fear is creating the waves around you. Better you throw out fear and make a conscious choice, then it's you making the waves. It's much easier to take responsibility for the consequences of your actions when you set about them consciously."

- Yeshua son of Joseph -

124 · Odious Offering

A few days later, Anna was close to giving birth. The women prepared a birthing room and were on standby. Anna was quite dear to me, to the whole family. We accepted her as John's common-law wife, and treated her as cherished kin. But as we waited for the news of her child beginning its journey to the shores of conscious life, a rider came up the hill flanked by two men. He was dressed in fine linens and didn't look like a rider for hire.

He introduced himself as Secretary to the Magistrate in Caesarea. This was a distinguished guest.

We sat at the table, "What brings you to my home?" I asked.

"I've a package for you, from Herod."

My mouth dropped open, "What could that be?"

"I'm sorry that the news accompanying the package is grim."

I nodded, "You have news of my cousin then?"

"Yes, Rabbi. He's been executed."

I was sad, but since I already knew John was dead, I received the news with grace. I had to ask, "Am I correct in assuming he never had a trial?"

The secretary cocked his head to one side and pulled up his shoulders. "It's hard to say, I'm sure Herod made his determination on evidence."

I put my hand up. "Please, don't continue. I've no quarrel with you and I'd hate for your words to create one."

The secretary sighed with relief and nodded.

"I assume we can have his remains," I said, "for proper interment?"

The secretary exchanged looks with the two men he brought with him and stammered, "I, I... I believe that won't be possible."

"Why not?" I demanded.

The secretary looked at his lap, "The wolves have already had their fill."

I stood and turned my back on them. My stomach rolled over and I was barely able to hold onto breakfast. The thought of my beloved cousin's body devoured and picked over by the very animals that used to adore him, horrified me.

Just then, Jude came in. He greeted the visitors and walked to me, placing his hand on my shoulder. "You alright?"

I grabbed Jude's waist, "No, I need a moment to steady myself."

Jude helped me to a bench and we sat together. A few minutes later, my stomach stopped bucking and I opened my eyes. I was across the room from the

"There's no greater power in the universe than the power of love. Don't underestimate the good it can do, especially when amplified by flowing through your exceptional human heart. And don't underestimate the pain that can be perpetrated when love is absent."

- Yeshua son of Joseph -

secretary, which suited me just fine. I said to Jude, "These men bring us news of Cousin John's execution."

"Oh, no," Jude shook his head and sighed. "We expected this, but it's still shocking."

"Secretary," I said, "as you can see, this news doesn't sit well with us." I took a breath. "I'd appreciate it if you'd complete your mission so we can move on with our grief."

"Certainly, Rabbi." He pulled up a leather bag hanging from his shoulder and emptied its contents onto the table. I heard the clanking of metal and saw the glint of gold as coins cascaded over one another.

"What's this?" I asked.

"There're a few things that were in your cousin's possession when he... was taken prisoner. A whistle, and um... a small reliquary of some sort."

"That's a memento of his father," I said, "he always wore it around his neck."

"I see," his body quivered, "well, it's... it's here now."

I looked at him, "And what's the rest of this?"

He cleared his throat, "It's gold, Rabbi. It's... gold."

I shook my head. "I'm certain my cousin didn't carry these coins."

The Secretary looked at me and I could tell he didn't want to say what he came to say, "No, Rabbi, these coins are from Herod." He took in a labored breath, "Herod wants me to tell you that he... well... he's sorry, and hopes this... offering... will help ease your pain."

Time stood still. Everything around me thundered to a halt. I felt the cascading effects of rage begin to tumble through my body. For all I know, if time hadn't come to a halt, I might've jumped this bureaucrat with deadly intent, arms flying. I looked at Jude and he sat frozen, his face locked in shock. I looked at the secretary and his body revealed the horrible betrayal of self he made to bring me this heinous gift.

Seeing the consequences to the people around me of this odious offering helped my rage began to subside, and while the room remained frozen, a lone figure came through the door. He walked to me with deliberate intent. He knelt in front of me and cradled the back of my head with his hand. It was John. He looked me in the eye and said, "Don't spend energy avenging me."

"Alright," I said.

"I have my own plan to exact. Herod won't escape his fate."

I remembered the gruesome end of his I saw at the river, "You were beheaded?" I asked.

"It's our vile King's favorite method of murder," John said. "He's kept my head, though. He can't bring himself to let go of it."

I was shocked, "He's kept... your head?"

"Yes, and now he's trying to atone by throwing gold at the world." John smirked, "There's no atonement in this life for him. My God will take him first."

I was still stuck on his first statement, "Why has he kept your head?"

"He talks to me. He thinks if he pleads, I'll forgive him."

"What?" I was appalled, "Does he think your head will come alive and talk back?"

"Perhaps he does, Cousin, perhaps he does!" John laughed with a hearty guffaw that filled the room with his presence.

It made me chuckle, "I'll miss you. The world is less for losing you."

John shook my head affectionately, "No, the world doesn't miss me, but it will miss you."

"It's close, isn't it?" I asked.

"You know it is," he said with certainty. "Do me a favor."

"Anything, just ask."

"Take this blood money and give it to Anna. It'll ease her journey back to Axum."

"I will and I'll match it for her. She's about to give you a child, John."

"No, it's not my child, he's a gift for the world. As always Cousin, I was but the messenger."

"He'll be your son."

John smiled at me, "Your rage is gone, yes?"

"Yes, I'm calmed from seeing you." I smiled back.

"Then I must go, I have a king to haunt." and he disappeared. I took a deep breath and the room eased itself back into motion.

Jude yelled at the Secretary, "What did you say?"

I put my finger to Jude's lips and said, "Shhhh." Jude swung his face to me in surprise. "Shh," I said, "it's alright." I turned to the secretary. "I know, and you know, this isn't something I can accept as offered. It's abhorrent. Nothing can pay for the loss of my loved one."

The secretary was about to speak, when I interrupted, "But," I said, "if it'll ease Herod to know he's done some good, I'll donate this money to a needy charity."

Jude stared at me, unable to understand. I looked at him and said, "There're many brethren with children that need to be fed." I nodded my head at him.

I felt Jude relax and he nodded as well.

"Good," I said, "then, Secretary, goodbye. I'm overcome with grief and have no more energy for entertaining."

The secretary stood, then said, "Of course, Rabbi, my condolences to you and your family." I stood, but didn't walk to him. I had no desire to shake his hand, or help him alleviate his burden over this deed. They showed themselves out.

And by the next morning, we were enjoying the presence of John's progeny cradled safely in Anna's arms. She named him John in honor of his father.

"When I talked about turning the other cheek, I was speaking of the ability to forgive. Forgiveness is paramount to moving forward with love and honor. Wanting to move forward without finding forgiveness is like pouring a bucket of molasses on your head and not expecting it to flow down your skin and gum up everything you touch."

- Yeshua son of Joseph -

125 · Conceiving the Event

If my speculations about the parallels between John and me were correct, I had no more than six months left before fate would catch up to me. Maybe less. There were few other markers to rely on, but Miriam wasn't pregnant, so I could breathe while creating a plan.

I'd prophesized my own odyssey through death back to life. My Creator told me I could alter my consequences. I had choice. Joseph told me I could live. John told me I could live. Anna told me I could live. My own apparition told Joseph, Mary, and me at various times that I would live. Philar was the only voice that said I wouldn't. I chose to believe his vision of this was limited.

But at the same time, I had to acknowledge that, as my Creator said, failure was an option.

I stopped vacillating and bucked up. I looked at this puzzle as a meal I must eat. I had to make this meal what I needed it to be. If this repast couldn't be avoided, if I must find my way through death to realize some divine scheme and succeed, then I had to exact a measure of control over the circumstances.

I had at least three powerful enemies: Herod, Oranos, and Caiaphas. Any one of them would be happy to seal my demise. There was only one way I had any chance of living through an event that would normally kill a man. I had to have an intact body at the end. If Herod killed me, my head would be gone. I couldn't live through that. If Oranos slaughtered me, he'd likely chop me to bits. He'd been waiting too long to celebrate his satisfaction with one mere whack.

And then there was Caiaphas, a Sadducee, head of the Sanhedrin and puppet of Rome. Caiaphas was passionately against my teachings. On several occasions, he'd denounced my words as heretical and seditious. And he was desperately afraid that as head of the David family, I'd usurp his power through insurrection. Two members of his Sanhedrin were close members of my family. I believe he was also afraid that his interpretation of events was wrong and that I was the Messiah. He knew his power was otherwise already tenuous, not only because the Pharisee were increasingly unhappy with the Sadducee interpretation of Torah law, but also because the Romans were unhappy with Caiaphas' lack of willingness to reform Jewish attitudes in full favor of Roman commerce.

Judas reported a few months earlier that an allied spy in Jerusalem overheard Caiaphas say he hated me. That he'd be happy to see me hang dead for the people

"Life is precious. It's not guaranteed to persist. While it does persist, you have a gift to be cherished. Do something with your life. Truly, it doesn't matter if you accomplish any of the things you feel you need to accomplish, it matters that you keep going, keep using this gift of life. With the gift of life, you have a mind, you have a heart, you have a spirit. It's your holy trinity. Bring them together and do something!"

- Yeshua son of Joseph -

to spit on and the birds to chew. But, they were empty words. The Sanhedrin in Judah had no authority to execute, though the Roman Prefect did and would act at the head Priest's behest if he could be swayed to the necessity of it. However, with the exception of the personal vendetta of Oranos, Rome didn't appear to be against me. And Pilate, as Prefect reporting to the Emperor, would need a lot of persuasion to put me to death. I had many allies in high places and commanded a measure of respect for the position I held if nothing else. As long as I was unwilling to challenge Herod for control of Galilee, and unwilling to usurp their puppet in Jerusalem, what threat did I pose to Rome? None.

More and more I concluded that only a few conditions had to be present for any survival plan to emerge. Not only would I have to be whole in body at the end of the deed, I'd have to be near family, so prompt care would be administered, instead of the body left to be mauled by scavengers. And if I was going to do this, to go to the trouble of staging my execution, there'd be no way I'd do it in secret. My supposed death would have to be very, very public.

I considered the calendar. Nearly six months after John's death was Passover. I knew the Roman Prefect would have to be at Jerusalem for crowd control over the holiday. I thought it opportune that the very holiday that in part commemorated the slaughter of the proverbial spring lamb might very well be the perfect time for this lamb to lie down. Getting around Pilate was the only unknown quantifier in the plan I was devising.

The Roman's had many ways to kill people, but only two regular forms of execution, the first was hanging by the neck, and the second was crucifixion. As far as hanging, it was unpredictable, and too quick. They used hanging in the event of uncontrolled riot, to kill many people quickly in a way that would leave them on display for maximum effect. If the Sanhedrin forced my execution, the Romans wouldn't use such a rapid method. Unfortunately, I reasoned, that if I carried this through, I was most likely going to suffer crucifixion…

Perhaps I can't adequately explain the shudder of dread that passed through my body when I realized this.

Everyone was familiar with crucifixion. You couldn't travel around Judea without seeing the hanging bodies somewhere. It was the most prolonged, agonizing, and humiliating way to kill a person ever devised. Evil incarnate must have invented it, but the dogs of evil perfected it over many hundred years. The Romans had it down to an exact science. Any poor creature consigned to crucifixion would be lucky to succumb early, but due to the calculated nature of the process, the victim couldn't usually manage death until the horrors made manifest on their body had ample time to strike horror in those who witnessed it.

I couldn't imagine any crime that warranted such a death. But it satisfied every need I had. I could survive it; I knew I could. I could promise family would be near and able to take my body quickly. And it would be, without a doubt, very public. If I did this in the lap of the Sanhedrin, in Jerusalem, at Passover, no one would miss

"Often you know when it's time to finally accept a course of action and move forward. Regardless of how much angst and internal discomfort led to that moment, when you get there, your inner self will calm, your muscles will relax, and your mind will become clear. When you find that clarity of understanding, nothing can stop you. There'll be no question, it's time to act."

- Yeshua son of Joseph -

it, especially if I worked up the holiday crowd beforehand.

I resolved to it. I felt committed, but was it truly the right decision? Doubt consumed me immediately upon my decision. I agonized over it for weeks, especially when I spent quality time with Miriam or Micah. I tortured myself knowing that if things went wrong, they'd be without me. Micah would grow without his father. Miriam wouldn't have a husband to love her as she deserved to be loved.

And what of James? He'd have to become the leader I knew he could be. And Mary? It'd be horrible, no doubt, but she already expected it. My apparition told her that I wouldn't die, that I'd live, but I feared Philar had dashed that hope.

To quell my doubts, I reminded myself that if I didn't take things into my own hands and direct the events in my favor, I'd die at the hands of someone for whom I had little respect. Herod or Oranos, it didn't matter, they'd ensure that my light was snuffed but good!

I had to accept my decision. Time was running out.

126 · A Matter of Faith

I talked to no one about my thoughts. If I opened my mouth to explore my thoughts, anyone I knew would beg me out of my decision.

Then it happened, not long after my thirty-eighth birthday. I'd just finished my morning baptism and Miriam, with arms open and face beaming, ran to me.

"Tall Man!" she shouted, "My love, my dearest, my honey bee!" She threw her arms around me and squeezed with gusto.

I laughed, "What's got you so excited?" I asked.

"I think I'm pregnant!" Her face was radiant as she expressed her joy to me.

My heart sank faster than a boulder in an ocean. I returned her squeeze. I tried with every ounce of my being to match her enthusiasm, but I couldn't. My authentic self was falling into a deep hole and it hurt. It hurt like falling into a nest of vipers. "That's good news," I forced, "when will we know for sure?"

"Within a month I should be certain," she said, but her face began to reflect seeing my anxiety. "What's the matter, Yeshua?"

"Nothing," I said, as I pulled back. "I'm, I'm happy at the news. Should we send a note to Nadia? I think we shouldn't wait."

"Yeshua?" she asked with concern.

"Really, don't you think we should… do that?" I looked at the sky, trying with all my might not to start weeping.

"I think you should be honest with me."

"I can't, Miriam. I'm, I'm… I have to go walk. I can't stay here right now." I pulled my hands from hers.

"Don't you want another child?" She looked as if her heart was breaking.

"Yes, of course I do," I snapped, "don't assume… I… I really think we should contact Nadia as soon as… I, I have to go, Miriam, I just have to go." I started to run, and then I turned and shouted, "I love you like the sun loves the moon. I love you with a force that cuts through time. I love you more than I can ever express. Please, wait for me?"

I ran down the hill, through the gate, and off the land that so lovingly supported my life. I screamed with my mind, 'Creator, please, how am I ever going to face this?'

———※———

I ran east. I ran and ran, for hours, across the Jordan, out of Galilee and into the barrens of Decapolis. The stark relief of the landscape in this desert was exactly what my mind needed to begin to calm.

Miriam was pregnant. Getting this last marker thrown in my face was evidence, not just that my time was drawing near, but also that I wasn't able to control my emotions. I blew it with Miriam. I knew I did. She was probably hurt, the last thing I wanted for her in these last days with me.

'Last days with me,' I heard myself say. Why did I think these were the last days if I was certain I could live? I closed my eyes and reviewed my questions. What, about this situation, was so confusing and difficult? Was my inner self trying to tell me I'd fail? That this staged execution would turn out to be a real execution? Was I fooling myself to think I even stood a chance of living?

Was I frightened of the process? That was the only question I could answer. Of course I was, deeply. Any man in his right mind would be in terror of the rigors of crucifixion. The agony that'd be borne was nearly unimaginable; it was more than a mind could hold.

It came to me. There was no way I was going to have any certainty as to the outcome. This was a matter of faith.

As soon as that thought reverberated in my head, I heard a familiar voice behind me, "Issa." I turned and saw my Creator outfitted as Mary once again.

"Creator," I sighed in relief, "hello."

"Issa, I see you're in need." She folded her hands in front of her waist and looked at me with loving eyes.

It was clear, I was afraid, so I asked, "Am I going the wrong direction?"

"What a question?" she said. "That question implies that there might be a path before you that you haven't paved. How could that be?"

"Let me restate. I've created a path that leads me to a point of death, or at least near-death. Is it an illusion?"

"It's no illusion."

My heart shuddered. "Then it's true, as things stand, my death will be enacted, unless I find a way to survive?"

"Yes, Issa, this life you hold, is a passionate play. You're on stage, the stage of history." She unfolded her hands and held one out to me. I took her hand and we melted into a forest.

"One more time, I will admonish fear. It's one of the two most powerful forces in this universe. The other is love. They both multiply when given a chance. They each flow into the crevices of your life like water and root out any hidden recesses filled with the other. The nice thing is you get to choose which of those two you'll amplify. You get to choose which you want to dominate the recesses of your life. Fear or love? Choose."

- Yeshua son of Joseph -

127 · Loud Voice of Wisdom

The trees of this forest were unfamiliar. They had dense foliage and wide canopies. The ground beneath our feet was spongy with dried leaves the color of crushed cinnamon.

"Where are we?" I asked.

"We're on an island far to the northwest," the Creator said as a small group of girls ran toward us, giggling. They looked to be between seven and ten years old. "The Romans and others have come here," she said, "and the world of these young girls isn't what it once was."

"In what way?" I asked.

"You see them free and lively now, like their ancestors have been for centuries. But watch. I'll translate for you if they speak."

The girls danced and giggled. Their playfulness was infectious. A few minutes later, two men on horseback rode toward them. As they got closer, the girls screamed and ran.

"Come back, little sweets!" one of the men shouted, but the girls were scattered and nowhere to be seen. The man laughed and said, "Too bad, they looked good."

The other man grunted and said, "It's better we leave them. You'll get your fill of woman tonight. These are a little young anyway." I suddenly understood the issue.

"These savages are better young. Fresh, you know?" the first one said as they laughed and rode away. I was concerned for the girl's safety.

"Little girls like these," the Creator said, "rarely had to worry about being molested before the kings of commerce arrived. The divine feminine was honored here. Now they're taught how not to be caught." She looked at me, "They play with fairies still, but those will fade in the years to come."

I nodded in understanding. The forest faded and we were standing on a tree-covered plateau looking over a bushy plain. I saw herds of animals roaming through the clearings below.

"Where are we now?" I asked.

"We're in Africa west of the Red Sea," she said. "You traveled near here on your way to university."

"We're in Axum?" I said with wonder, "This is where Anna's from."

"Close your eyes and remember a time in your life, close or distant doesn't matter, that you experienced pure joy. Feel it now as if it were happening right now. Make the memory real and truly feel it. Now know that there's no difference between then and now that a change of thought can't alter. No difference between then and now that won't melt away if you want it to. Joy is your birthright. The more you feel it, the more of it you'll have to feel."

- Yeshua son of Joseph -

"Yes. Watch the valley there." She pointed to a herd of animals that looked similar to deer. A few moments later, a cloud of dust rose into the air, a group of twenty men on horseback creating the cloud. The men looked of Quraysh decent. They had spears and bows. The startled animals began to run, but the galloping horses kept up with them, and the men downed nearly the entire herd.

The men stopped killing finally, and pulled the dead animals into piles to skin, but proceeded to throw the skinned carcasses away. "Why aren't they taking the meat?" I asked.

"They've no use for the meat. Only the pelts are valuable."

"They took almost the entire herd," I exclaimed, "they left nearly none to replenish the stock." I was stunned at this behavior.

"Yes, Issa, these men have brought their horses and their greed. Commerce will reward them with gold. The valley can sustain this extravagance of waste only for so long."

"I understand," I nodded.

She took my hand and we melted into yet another scene, this one of a forest on the edge of a tranquil ocean. The water was a delicate color I'd never seen before, light aqua. The sand was nearly pure white. The trees were familiar, palm like, but not quite like those of my homeland.

"Issa, we're again on an island. This time in the middle of the great waters."

"Oh, the great waters." My mind stirred at the thought of the ocean I'd heard so much about in my travels. "Why're we here?"

"Some of these islands were once mountaintops. A large civilization lived here, but now they're gone, scattered due to rising waters."

"I see," I nodded with understanding.

"Some of their descendants still live on these islands." She pointed around us, "They're peaceful people with no war, nothing to divide them from nature or each other. They work and live together in relative harmony."

"That sounds serene."

She took my hand and led me into the forest, "Let's walk a few feet for you to see."

We walked through the towering palm trunks; buildings built on stalks began to emerge. I'd seen similar buildings in my travels through the east. As we neared a clearing, a statue of the god Vishnu became visible. "That's Hindu!" I exclaimed. "Do they know Bon here?" I asked.

"No," she said, "not as you know it, but come with me." She led me around the edge of the building and across a clearing; I saw what looked like dead bodies. As we got closer, I realized they were scattered across the landscape. Women, children, men – young and old – all dead, gutted for the most part. As I walked among them, I saw birds, and insects beginning to reclaim the wasted flesh. My heart felt cut apart by this scene.

"This is horrific!" I cried.

"Yesterday they were happy, celebrating the end of harvest," the Creator sighed.

"What happened?" I asked.

"A ship of sailors from the north came to steal the harvest," she explained, "the people put up a fight, but it was no use. They had only small knives, sticks, and fists for weapons, the men from the ship had swords. Now the fruit of their labors will be devoured by the men who killed them and the overage sold for gold."

We melted back to the barren rock cliffs of outer Decapolis. I was weeping from the accumulated emotion of what I'd seen. "What've you shown me?"

"As the continents become more populated," she said, "and technology advances, Issa, cultures run into each other. Sometimes it works, sometimes it doesn't. When cultures clash, people can be stimulated by avarice and primal lust." She put her hand on my shoulder. "You see this in your homeland. You see this now as I've shown you occurring across the earth."

"Yes," I said.

"When civilizations die, when populations are enslaved, when resources are needlessly plundered, the wisdom of the ages suffers. On the island we last visited, if anyone is left alive, perhaps a few children that were urged to run, will they grow knowing why the statue of a Hindu god graces their clearing?"

"Probably not," I said with sorrow.

"On the first island we visited, will the principles of the divine feminine still be alive after a few generations of girls plundered by ravaging men on horseback?"

I sighed, "Probably not." I sat down, my face downturned. The Creator sat with me.

"Issa, listen to me. There must be, from time to time, a voice of wisdom so loud, so undeniable in its truth, that the ravages of clashing civilizations cannot mute it. These lone voices must inspire people past the point of intellect, past the point of faith, to the point of belief. This must occur so that when the lone voice's body falls to time, those inspired have enough fervor of belief that they must keep the message of that voice from falling too."

I searched her face. "Am I one of those voices?"

"You know you are, Issa."

I felt dejected. "Then I haven't done enough."

"Why do you say that?"

"There're a few hundred who study with me, but once I'm gone," I sighed, "none of them are inspired enough to do what you say."

"Not yet," she said.

"But, if what I feel is true, I've only a few weeks left. There's James and Miriam, maybe a few others, but I can't turn the bulk of these devotees into true believers in that amount of time."

"No?" she looked at me with a piqued expression.

I blinked. "You think I can?"

"I feel you will."

I was flabbergasted, "How?"

"By transcending death."

The internal shaking of my body stopped, and suddenly I felt solid in a way I

"Understand what love is. It is power. It's the raw energy of your creator flowing through your world. It's not a wish you hold on Valentine's Day. It's not a lustful desire, or a craving for things. When the power of love is mistaken for lust or avarice you can become confused and forget what it is you actually need. The power of love is what fuels the Creator's work in this world. It's the very substance of what made you. Turning your back on the power that love is, is ultimately making the decision to die without learning the most important lesson any person will ever learn: that when you own love, you own yourself."

- Yeshua son of Joseph -

hadn't felt for weeks. The Creator's face was radiant.

"Then I can?" I asked, "I can live through a Roman persecution?"

"You have the knowledge, the talent, you've demonstrated the abilities you need time and again," she said, "haven't you?"

"Yes, I believe so." I looked out over the valley, "I'll live?"

"One way or another, Issa, you'll live."

I looked at the Creator as my fear mounted again. "One way or another?" I beseeched her.

"I have another gift for you." She placed her hand on the top of my head and I felt a lightening of my spirit, as if the weight of my questions and insecurities vanished. "I've taken your fear and released it, my steadfast word. There's no need for you to suffer through these coming weeks."

And without warning, we were standing in a recently harvested field behind the main house of my family compound. She stroked my cheek with her soft hand. "You know what you must do. Your plan is sound. I suggest you spend quality time with loved ones until it's time to go south." She grabbed my hand, "I'm with you every minute until your transcendence is complete. I'll continue to lift your fear. Stay clearheaded and be the fullness of love I know you are," and she faded from my view.

It was nearly suppertime; the sun was setting. I walked to the house and found Miriam. I apologized for my earlier confusion and expressed genuine happiness over her news. This time, nothing got in my way of relishing her joy.

It was approximately five short weeks until the Passover holiday and after supper I announced with certainty and clarity that we'd be celebrating the holiday in Jerusalem this year.

"Meet me. Somewhere, anywhere, anytime, but please meet me. This is an open invitation. I want to hear your heart. I want to know your love. I want to be in your life with no other agenda than to be as friends."

- Yeshua son of Joseph -

128 · Affairs in Order

Over the next several days, I had two goals. The first, to spend quality time with my loved ones as Creator suggested. The second, to put my affairs in order.

With Jude I examined the contracts and ledgers of the business, and reviewed the contents of the storehouses and granaries. I pressed Herodes to name two men he'd want to succeed him, in the event he retired. I interviewed both and made my recommendations.

I spoke with Josea about the running of the household and recruited an apprentice cook for her to train.

I reviewed with Judas and James the methods in place for security of the community. We discussed each ally and how I felt about his or her loyalty and trustworthiness. In short, I satisfied myself that if things went poorly, the community would continue to have structure and security.

After all of this, I had a meeting with my brothers to declare formally that I expected James to be my successor as head of the family and Jude to continue with his stellar management of the family business.

James balked, "I want to know what's going on," he demanded.

"What do you mean?" I asked.

"You're acting like… well, actually," James said, "you're acting just like Father did when he got ill."

"Oh," I said, "well, I'm not ill."

"You're putting your affairs in order," he stated. "Why?"

"I want to make sure that if something happens to me, the community is taken care of."

James' gaze could've bored through wood if I could've harnessed its energy. "Do you know something we don't?"

"Perhaps I do," I said, "but you know as well as I, times are dangerous right now."

"Yes, but," James glanced at Jude then back at me, "you can handle it. You have powers that keep you safe. I've seen them."

"Yes, that's true," I admitted, "and I hope they'll always be enough."

James and Jude exchanged looks. "Why are we going to Jerusalem?" Jude blurted.

"There's something I have to do there."

"During the most crowded time of year?" he said with incredulity.

"Yes, specifically during the most crowded time," I said, "besides, I think it's a good thing for us to show up at the Temple once in a while."

"If we're going as a family, why are some of your devotees coming with us?" Jude asked.

"Because I wish it," I smiled at him.

"Curses, Yeshua!" Jude shouted, "You're being annoying!"

"It's my prerogative as your leader."

James jumped out of his seat. "Stop this right now!" he shouted. "Drop the leader ploy and be our brother for a minute. Tell us what's happening!"

I looked at James. He stumbled back and forth across a line between wanting to know everything, and not wanted to face what he'd heard from Philar. "Do you remember Philar?" I asked James. He stared at me. I stared back.

"What?" Jude asked, "What's Philar?"

"Philar is a he," I corrected, "James met him a few years ago."

"That was a ruse," James said stridently. "It was a tactic to get you to agree to his plan."

"You can believe that if you like," I replied.

James huffed and stormed out of the room. Jude looked at me, his head shaking. "I don't pretend to know what that was about, but I'll carry out your wishes."

"You have my complete trust, Jude."

He looked at me with resignation. "Thanks for the vote of confidence."

A few days later, we were on the road, my family, my followers, and my faith. We gave ourselves plenty of time to get to Jerusalem so we could move slowly and enjoy the journey. We had lively group meals every evening, followed by songs and games. And when we retired each night, Miriam and I reveled in our passion for each other.

Each day, as we walked, Mary made a point of walking with me for an hour or more. She'd put her arm around me, and lean into my side as we walked. She was energetic, yet she wore an air of sadness. I was certain she knew what was going to happen, but we didn't talk about it.

We got close to it once. Mary said something unexpected one afternoon. "Have you told your wife?" she blurted when we were out of everyone's hearing.

"What?" I asked

She looked into my face with solemnity, "Have you told her, Yeshua, where we're going?"

I took in a sharp breath as I realized what she was saying. "No, I haven't said a word," I admitted.

"I wondered why she was so happy." Mary said, "Thank you for letting me know, I'll be discreet." She squeezed me and we kept walking, with nothing more said about it.

We arrived at a small town outside Jerusalem two days before the Sabbath, the

"Yeshua took on an urgency about his being. An urgency that was extremely compelling. He urged us to go to Jerusalem. He said (in his cryptic way of speaking) because he had work to do there. He was often cryptic, speaking in riddles and parables, but never so cryptic as in these days."
- James brother of Yeshua -

week before Passover. It was a pleasant town with contented people. Big enough to buy needed supplies, but small enough to be cozy.

We erected our camp just beyond the town's limits on a small rise. There were trees for shade and rocks for the children to climb. It was a lovely place to spend a few days. Micah was almost four and he'd become obsessed with lizards. He often brought me a new lizard he'd captured. It was a great joy to me to teach him how to handle them. One afternoon he ran to me squealing, "Lizard! Big lizard!" He pulled me to a rocky outcropping and on the far side was a huge lizard nearly as big as Micah. I laughed and picked it up, lazily letting Micah pet him. Micah squirmed with delight at the large size and leathery feel of the creature. Later when he told his mother about the big lizard, he exaggerated the size to be nearly as big as she. I said a prayer that in some way, any way, I'd be able to enjoy my son's wonder of the world after the holiday was over. I had to let those thoughts go quickly, though, lest they drag me into melancholy.

And as she promised, the Creator drained my fear, every minute of every hour.

"We weren't in Jerusalem on that Sabbath; we were in a small town outside of Jerusalem. Initially things were calm and everybody relaxed. We needed the respite to prepare for what was coming. We just didn't know what was coming."
- James brother of Yeshua -

Meeting
the Edge

129 · Eleven Days of Ardor

I no longer gave thought to the danger; I was resolute to the plan. I couldn't think about the pain my actions would cause those I loved. How could I? Those thoughts would have paralyzed me. I felt Creator with me, in me, every step of the way and I credit the Creator's participation in the plan that was about to unfold as the one and only overriding reason it succeeded.

What I did, I did from training and faith; what the Creator did was miraculous.

History calls this plan 'The Passion,' highlighted by the 'Crucifixion' and the 'Resurrection.' I call it the 'Eleven Days of Ardor.' I cannot reassemble every detail of those eleven days, but there are vivid moments that remain indelibly etched on my psyche. In truth, the details aren't as important as the achieved outcome. Trumping every minute of those eleven days was a plan carefully arranged to produce one outcome and one outcome alone: my living through the brutal violence that should have killed me.

I achieved my outcome, I didn't die; I triumphed over death.

The Eleven Days of Ardor began on the Sabbath before Passover, with my recruiting one of the most important allies in my plan. They culminate with me sitting down, very much alive, eleven days later, breaking bread with my devotees in my new state. However, before I began this risky and rebellious plan, I never envisioned the actual shape of that outcome.

In the next several chapters, I recount those eleven days, beginning with day one and moving through the miraculous sequence of events, as they unfolded.

"Probably, if we'd all been prepared it might've changed some of the events. On many levels, it might've been kinder of Yeshua to tell us more. Yet, I understand now his need to play this through so close to the vest. These upcoming days were explosive, yet very difficult and delicate to arrange."

- James brother of Yeshua -

130 · Only One I Trust

Eleven Days of Ardor, Day One Begins

Finally, the Sabbath before Passover arrived. After the evening meal, we sat around the campfire telling stories and laughing. Miriam was certain about her pregnancy and we used the occasion to announce it. Everyone rejoiced except Mary. Mary smiled suitably, but the pinch of sadness and worry was on her face. The announcement, however, was my cue. It was time for my plan to commence.

Micah sleepily climbed into Miriam's lap and I noticed Judas standing to one side. It seemed the perfect time to have a needed conversation with my most trusted friend. I excused myself from the circle and asked Judas if he'd take a walk with me.

Once out of hearing range of the group, I began, "I need to have a conversation with you right now that you're not going to like."

"Yeshua," he responded, "whatever you have to say, I'm willing to hear."

I urged him over to a large flat-topped rock. We climbed it and sat together looking out at the stars; it was a particularly peaceful and clear night. The moon was nearly half, yet the stars shone brilliant in the sky. I decided to seize the moment, "Swear to me that what I'm about to reveal, you'll repeat to no one."

"I swear to you, if you need it," he said.

"I'm going to do something that will seem foolish," I began, "no, more than foolish, probably crazy."

"Nothing you do would be crazy."

"Swear to me," I pressed, "that whatever you hear from me tonight, whatever I ask, and no matter how you answer, you'll keep this to yourself."

"Alright."

"Swear," I pressed.

"Rabbi… Yeshua, I swear in the name of God," he said solemnly.

"Thank you, my friend."

"So, now you've got me worked up, spill it!" he cajoled.

"I'm going to give myself up to be executed," I blurted.

"What!" Judas shouted.

"Shhh," I said, "stay calm."

"What the devil are you thinking?" he implored.

I locked eyes with him, "I'm deadly serious."

"So that evening everyone came together and there was a lot of light and love, people singing songs and drinking in the night air. It was a peaceful night. Yeshua was quite proud of Miriam and the child to be and he announced it to everybody."

- James brother of Yeshua -

Judas' breathing quickened and at first, I thought he might shout more, but he pulled his body around to face me cross-legged. I turned to face him fully too. "Why?" he demanded.

"It's a long story," I replied.

"Don't you think I deserve to know? You're telling me this for a reason, even if I don't know that reason yet, I want to know why."

For what I was about to ask of him, he was correct, he deserved to know the why. I proceeded, starting with the prophecies, from Joseph's right up through Anna's. I told him about some of my conversations with the Creator. I told him about my careful assessment of my strongest enemies, Herod, Oranos, and Caiaphas, and the method of execution I chose and why. And I told him about my torment over the decision.

We were interrupted only once, when James came to find us. He wanted to know when we'd be joining the group again. I told him I was helping Judas with something and I'd be along soon. I found it odd that he simply accepted that explanation. I was hiding the truth and James usually quickly sensed when I was hedging the truth. I could tell from his acceptance of my small deceit that he truly didn't want to face what was upon us.

Once James walked back to the fire, the energy in me mounted, giving me courage to make my request. I knew I'd be putting Judas in a unique and uncomfortable position, but I had to do it. There was no one else I could count on to have the courage to follow through. This would be abhorrent to his being; I knew that too. But his participation was integral to my plan.

Judas had asked many questions, and now his eyes were red from crying and his cheeks wet from tears. He grabbed my hands, "I don't want you to make a mistake."

"Of course not," I agreed, "but I know I can live through a crucifixion if things go to plan."

"If… if things go as planned?" he pleaded. "Have you really thought this all the way through?"

"The time is now," I said, "and if I don't take this in hand, right now, within a matter of weeks I will be dead. And in a manner I won't have a hair's chance of surviving." I trusted Judas intellect, especially where militant issues were concerned. I leaned in closer and asked, "Do you agree with my assessment?" I searched his eyes for any clue of hesitation.

He lifted his face to the sky. "Unfortunately, I do," he said.

"Judas," I whispered, "the Creator calls me her steadfast word. You, my brother, are my steadfast protector." The light began to pulse. Judas eyes softened in response. "So, I need to ask you a favor, and it's a big one."

"My King, my Lord," he said, "I've promised I'll do as you bid anytime, anyplace."

"You're the only one I trust to carry this through."

Judas squeezed my hands, "And I'll honor that trust. Just name it, it will be done."

"Absolutely nothing happened that was unforeseen. It was only a matter of who allowed themselves the opportunity to accept the foreseen before it happened. Certainly that wasn't my choice."

- James brother of Yeshua -

I took a deep breath, "I need you to betray me to Caiaphas."

Judas back stiffened. His eyes didn't leave mine. I saw a wealth of emotion flash through them. We sat silent for a long time, just breathing through the moments.

"What you ask…" he murmured, "what you ask…" His breath was shallow and short. He looked as if he'd pass out at any instant. His hands went soft, as if all his strength had drained away.

"I love you," he whispered, "I love you with a love that stretches beyond time." He breathed deep, "What you ask is little compared to… that love." His tears began to fall again, "I want to refuse. I want nothing to do with this plot, but I can't." His face fell toward his lap, "I can't refuse you."

I enfolded my arms around him and pulled him close until he was nearly in my lap. Judas grabbed my hair and held it like a baby would of its mother. He pulled his knees up and leaned fully into me. The light stretched to encompass us both and we sat rocking in the pulse of the light and in the breath of each other. We sat huddled together like this for a long time, long enough that the flames of the fire at camp waned and turned to embers.

Judas eventually pulled back from my embrace far enough to look into my face. "Yeshua, of course I'll do this, just tell me the plan and I won't let you down."

I proceeded to outline the plan as I saw it playing out over the next several days. We promised to talk clandestinely about how the plan was proceeding at least once a day until fulfillment.

On our way back to camp Judas asked to be absent. "I have to prepare myself for what's ahead. Don't worry if you don't see me all day," he said, "but I'll be back before the end of the Sabbath." He grabbed my hand again, "I'm with you, Yeshua. I'm with you as a brother, as a friend… and as a subject." I gave him another tight hug and we parted.

Back at camp most were already abed. I went to my tent and wrapped my arms around Miriam. She woke with a smile and we spent the rest of the night wrapped together.

"Yeshua was very close to Judas. As close to him as he was to anyone, save Miriam. When they looked at each other, you could tell they were engaged in some way unseen. Whether it was telepathy or deep empathy, it could be unnerving to witness."

- James brother of Yeshua -

131 · King for a Day

Eleven Days of Ardor, Day One Continues

The next morning, I felt my resolve unhindered. My lungs took in the fresh air and I was without care, without angst. The plan was set into motion and I felt ready, willing, and able.

And it was a lovely day. The sky was blue and the temperature mild. I spent all midday lying in the sun and watching lazy white clouds move through the sky. I felt so blessed to have this time, in this land, on this good and beautiful earth. Micah brought me lizards. Miriam brought me fruit. Mary brought me flatbread. Devotees brought me water and flowers, all unbidden. And the clouds continued to move with lazy determination. Of all the days of my life, this day stands out as the one I actually felt like a king.

And as promised, Judas was nowhere to be seen all day.

Eleven Days of Ardor, Day Two Begins

Supper was a tremendous feast. Several townspeople ate with us and they brought food with them. Roast lamb and root vegetables, leafy greens of several varieties, beautiful leavened breads and cakes. I was a vegetarian, but to be hospitable I tried some of everything, even the food I wouldn't normally eat. I always made it a point to eat as my host ate, wherever I went. Some people didn't agree with my philosophy in this regard, especially James. But it seemed to me that receiving the gift of good, nourishing food of any kind from a neighbor was a sign of acceptance and respect. And I'd always rather respect the generosity of another person than worry about what a few bites of this or that might do to harm my covenant with my Creator. Even if my neighbor served pig, I'd eat it (albeit a small portion) before I'd refuse to break bread with him or her.

Toward the end of the meal, I mentioned that I'd be speaking at midday next if they wanted to come. And I urged them to bring their family and friends.

Judas returned as promised. When I looked him in the eye, he smiled and nodded crisply at me. Like me, he seemed clear, resolute, and ready.

"Yeshua was gregarious, and he loved people. I mean really loved them. He was generous and kind, and very, very accepting. Hardly anyone can resist such acceptance."

- James brother of Yeshua -

Later that evening, I took a walk by myself and came face-to-face with Philar. I hadn't seen or heard from him in these last months and I wondered if I'd see him before my plan was realized.

"Yeshua," he said, "I've been remiss in not visiting you sooner."

"It's just good to see you, my friend," I said sincerely. "What've you been up to?"

"The usual," he said, "but I do bring you news."

"Oh? What's that?"

"I've studied this plan you outlined to Judas." I must have expressed surprise, because Philar said, "Forgive me. I was eavesdropping on your conversation last night."

I chuckled, "I see."

"So, I've discussed this plan with my fellows and we want to offer our support."

"That's good news," I said, "I welcome it." I put my arm around him and patted his back. When I pulled away, I asked, "How do you propose to help?"

"I've assigned four of the team to be with you," he said, "through everything you do from tomorrow morning on, until they're not needed, no matter when that is."

"What sorts of things are they able to do for me?"

"Well, I can't exactly predict," He nodded, "but if something comes up, they have permission to step in and help, if possible."

"Do they understand the outcome I need? I must face execution."

Philar looked at the ground for an extended moment, then back at me, "Yes, they understand that."

"Philar, I'm committed to this road, but I'm curious, do you believe this is a fool's mission?"

Philar hesitated, then said, "Yeshua, as I've said before," he whispered, "you've become more than any of us predicted. More than we hoped. I'm sure you've become all that God has desired." He laid his hand on my shoulder. "I don't profess to know more, or know better, than you and God have put together in faith and devotion." He shook his head, "I don't even know if we can do anything to help. We may not be needed at all." He hesitated again. "But I couldn't... I wouldn't be able to continue with honor if I didn't see you through this with all my resources poised to offer assistance."

I nodded, "Thank you. It means everything to me to have your support. And for what it's worth," I leaned my face close to his, "I plan on speaking with you in detail when it's all over." I smiled. He didn't, so I hugged him and bid him well until we met again.

Eleven Days of Ardor, Day Two Continues

Morning came, and I was up with the sun and on duty with my baptism. I recruited a handful of devotees to go to Jerusalem and let people know I'd be speaking this day and the next. I hoped to draw a crowd from the people gathering for Passover.

A few times during the day, I dropped hints that something significant might happen to me. I wanted to build toward the idea that I would transcend death.

The midday talk went well. A large group of people from town attended and a few from Jerusalem, but not the crowd I'd ultimately need. I knew word-of-mouth would build over the next few days and I hoped that would be enough.

"He told us through repeated warnings, through repeated action and statement of purpose, through prophecy. For the most part his warnings were unheeded, so there was very little or no preparation for what was to come."

- James brother of Yeshua -

132 · Destined to Rise Again

Eleven Days of Ardor, Day Three Begins

Supper was just our party again. Devotees were getting the idea that something unusual was going to happen in Jerusalem. They posited that I'd overthrow the current rule. I assured them I wasn't in the business of political revolution, but I didn't take away the mystery that something might happen.

At one point, I said something to the effect that these were dangerous times and that something could happen to me. This created uproar among the devotees; they didn't believe it possible that some danger could befall me. I assured them that danger could befall me if I allowed it.

James was angered by this comment and after supper, he took me aside.

"What are you playing at, Bit?" he said.

"What do you mean?" I asked.

"You've been hinting now for two days that danger is waiting in Jerusalem. If so, why the devil are we going there?"

"You already know that my life is threatened from multiple directions."

"Then why go?" he reiterated.

"Destiny," I said.

"You don't believe in destiny."

"Don't I?" I said, "If you harvest a field in winter does it not rise again in spring?" I stepped closer to him. "If the Son of Man is laid to rest, is he not destined to rise again?"

"What are you talking about?"

"I'm talking about cheating death," I said with sincerity.

"That's nonsense," James declared. "Whatever you're playing at, stop it."

I shook my head, "I can't stop the wave now. It's heading toward shore."

"We're lost if you die, Yeshua."

"No, we're all lost if I don't continue on this road." I grabbed his hand, "Open your mind, James. Let me show you."

He pulled his hand from mine abruptly, "No! I don't want to see what you think is destined. It's not!" He started to walk away, but turned and faced me again, "I'm not supporting you, whatever this is. You have a son, he's about to turn four,

"Toward the evening, I'm not remembering who it was that said something to Yeshua about that, and he said, 'You think no harm could come to me?' and we said 'Obviously not. No harm could come to you, protected by God, with powers beyond those of any other man.' He said, 'Does it occur to you that harm could come to me if I allowed it?' It made me angry. We were all in denial."

- James brother of Yeshua -

for God's sake. You have a wife, a community who depends on you." He shook his head. "My council is you let this go, now!"

"I can't," I said, "the wave has formed. I told you, I can't stop it."

"You will stop it and you will come home with us after the holiday. You're not the only one who can will things into existence."

"This is not from my will, James. This is the will of our Creator." I stepped closer, "You think you can force your will against the will of Him?"

James did something he'd never done before. He slapped me. I looked at him, my heart filled with compassion.

"Yes, I'm angry," James said, "but I won't apologize for that. You deserve that and more if you keep on with these thoughts of personal destruction."

"James, calm yourself. I'm not wishing for personal destruction. It's going to be alright."

"Have you lost your sense?"

"I have the power to survive, whatever it is that comes," I said. "I told you, if the Son of Man is laid to rest, is he not destined to rise again?"

"Of all the times in your life to quote prophecy to me, now is heinous." He shook his head, "I won't entertain these thoughts. I won't even give them the time of day. Whatever you do here, unless you rearrange your thinking and move your fealty back to your family where it belongs, I won't help you."

"My fealty belongs with my Creator and my mission," I said with fervor.

James looked over my face carefully, then pointed a finger at me, "Don't make trouble." He turned and walked back to the fire.

Eleven Days of Ardor, Day Three Continues

The next morning, I attended to my baptism, but I felt a change had fallen over the entire camp. Everyone was on edge, especially my family. Miriam was ill from her pregnancy; she spent most of the day in bed. Throughout the morning, I heard the buzz of speculation whizzing around me. It was as needed, so I let it continue, unabated.

When midday came, a crowd of people gathered for the talk, both from this town and from neighboring towns as well, including some from Jerusalem. There may've been as many as 500 listening. It was a better size crowd than the day before, by a lot, but it was still not big enough. I hoped that the next day would be larger.

At one point in the afternoon, I remember seeing James and Mary arguing. It was unusual for James to argue with Mother, so it stood out. I assumed it had something to do with me, but I don't know for sure.

"There was a sort of grief, a sadness in his face all week that Miriam tried to write off as, 'Oh, he's tired.' But I could tell she was having a hard time letting go of a feeling of dread."

- James brother of Yeshua -

Eleven Days of Ardor, Day Four Begins

That evening, we gathered around the fire. I announced that we'd be moving into Jerusalem the next day, but not until after the gathering talk. Normally, at Passover, Jerusalem was fully packed. Pilgrims were in makeshift camps all around the city and every room for rent was filled to capacity. Every home had visitors. The city's population more than doubled, sometimes more than tripled by the influx of people wanting to attend Temple for the High Holiday.

Luckily, we had family in Jerusalem. There were accommodations awaiting us.

That night, Miriam was up and down all night. She was miserable. It'd be a lot easier for her in Jerusalem as far as sleeping arrangements, but I had a bad feeling about how her eventual upset was going to affect the child. Regardless of what happened, Miriam was going to be distraught.

But I couldn't think about that.

Eleven Days of Ardor, Day Four Continues

I stood on a small rise just outside town surrounded by my family and devotees. Provisions and gear were packed, and we were ready to trek into Jerusalem after the gathering. I watched as people gathered around me, many walking in from neighboring towns, and people coming from Jerusalem. The road was covered with a steady stream.

When the bulk of people arrived, I began. This was the most fervent talk I'd delivered in months, possibly ever. I talked about the Son of Man and his mission. I found it odd that when I talked about myself recently, I spoke in the third person, as if he were not me. Looking back on it, it must have been my way of separating the human me from the deeds. Perhaps it was the way I stayed balanced.

I talked about my favorite subjects; divine love, the living law, and the ways each of us prepares to meet with our Creator at the end of life.

It was a longer talk than usual. I engaged the audience often; asked questions, listened to anecdotes. I walked among them as I spoke, to get a sense of their issues, their motives. Several members of the Sanhedrin and other dignitaries were present, as were many Roman citizens and troops. And the best news; this crowd was well over 7,000 people. James estimated the crowd at more than 10,000. This was a crowd large enough to excite the authorities in Jerusalem.

My Essene community believed I was the Great Teacher. I heard the thoughts of many people at this talk reaching to me with faith, that I was a Son of Man, and a particular one at that; that I was the Messiah. Rumors and discussions were rampant around Judea among the non-Essene that I was the coming Messiah; it'd been going on for years. But the powers in Jerusalem had studied my speech, my deeds, and me, and had officially ruled that I wasn't the Messiah, even though many of the Sanhedrin members thought otherwise. Nonetheless, Caiaphas made the ruling public; to quell crowds from listening to me, but it didn't stop people. People believe what they believe regardless of what a powerful few say. Their determination, right or wrong, was all they needed.

I never confirmed any distinction other than my Son of Man status. My Creator affirmed that designation and Man'wa confirmed it. I could claim that with all certainty and humility. The rest of it I consign for fate to decide and I wasn't then, nor am I now, concerned with the validity of those labels, mostly because I'm not concerned with the validity of the written prophecy that created them.

"There was a gathering in Jerusalem at that time for the holiday, and there were people in Jerusalem from all over the countryside, many who had never heard of Yeshua before, or had heard of him and had been in towns that he had traveled through, but had never stopped to take notice of his words. Many of these people came out to the town we were in and all of a sudden there were thousands of people there. We really didn't understand why Yeshua still wanted to go into Jerusalem when so many from Jerusalem were coming to him. It didn't make sense."

- James brother of Yeshua -

133 · Mark These Words

Eleven Days of Ardor, Day Four Continues

Just before the end, I felt the Creator in me, on me, around me. The light turned up slowly over the talk, but now I shined with great illumination. I felt the Creator envelope the entire group. Encouraged and boosted by divinely inspired passion, I was ready to meet our co-created will made manifest.

I stood on the highest point of land nearest to the road. I was filled with fervor. "The Son of Man will make manifest the will of the Divine Creator with his faith and his commitment to you. To all of you." I paused, looking into the faces of those closest to me. "The Son of Man offers himself to you to help you lift the veil; the veil that separates you from recognizing your divine glory." I surveyed the crowd, "The Son of Man offers himself as the one who'll bring an end to your enslavement. He offers himself as a sacrifice on this, the most holy of holidays." I turned and faced the bulk of my devotees sitting near one another. James stood, angry. So I shouted directly to him with the heat of a piercing fire rod, "Mark these words, the Son of Man will shed his blood, like the proverbial spring lamb, but the Son of Man won't die. You'll talk with him, and walk with him, within three days of his sacrifice." I turned to the rest of the crowd, "I swear to you, the Son of Man will be triumphant. He will lift the veil!" The crowd went wild. They stood and cheered. "I thrust my arms into the air and shouted, "Let's go... now... to the City of David where the will of our Creator will prevail!"

We began our march. Children ran to me and grabbed at my hands. Fifty or more children surrounded me as we walked into the city.

Adults cheered, shouted. They laughed and danced as we made our way through the city gates. The passion of the day seized me. We walked slowly through the streets. From time to time, I'd stop and deliver a few more lines of speech. I didn't know where my family was, but I kept going. After a while, I found Jude, or more precisely, Jude found me. He was stunned. He'd never gone with me on campaign, always the one who stayed behind to run the business and community while James and I were gone. This was his first glimpse of the bewildering crowds

"So, we made the trek to Jerusalem, and everybody followed; thousands of people. Like it or not we were being announced. No slipping in the gate and up to our relative's house. Yeshua walking at the head of this large throng, thousands of people. There were a lot of people who assumed that what Yeshua was going to do was march into the city with many of the city's inhabitants behind him, and claim himself for who he was, throwing out the bad old rule and proclaiming a new city state under the rule of David. But of course, Yeshua had other plans."

- James brother of Yeshua -

James and I had mentioned.

"What are we to do?" he asked.

"Go to the family and get settled. You have the job of ensuring that everyone arrives safe." I patted his shoulder. "Don't worry. I'll join you soon," and the crowd carried me away.

Eleven Days of Ardor, Day Five Begins

I arrived at the home of my relatives just before supper. Miriam grabbed me. I asked her how she was feeling. She gave me a rocking-hand motion. I hugged her again and whispered, "I love you," in her ear.

James greeted me next. He appeared haggard and contrite. "I'm sorry, Bit." He looked at Mary, then said, "I've been stubborn."

I grabbed him, "No need to apologize. I love you with my life."

Micah jumped into my arms, so I settled down to catch up with the extended family and have some needed replenishment.

—— 🌿 ——

When we retired that night, I folded my arms around Miriam and Micah. We three were in the same bed, as the accommodations, while comfortable, were crowded. I was still riding high off the passionate fervor I'd caught earlier in the day and tried to channel that passion into my expressed love for my family. I really didn't want them to feel cut off, though I'm sure they felt a change in me. I held them and comforted them and gave them as much of my care as was there to give.

Eleven Days of Ardor, Day Five Continues

I don't remember much about the next day except for two things. First, I made it a point to stir up crowds as often as I could. I wandered the city and spoke about the Son of Man. I spoke of love, fear, burdens, inner peace, the living law, pretty much anything I'd spoken about until then, but as often as I could I pointed out the fear mongers and dismissed them as our enemies. I wanted someone to report me for fomenting sedition.

Second was an incident at the Temple. I hadn't been there in years.

On the way in, the number of merchants that had live animals and food for sale surprised me. I expected some with live lambs, and other items appropriate for the coming Passover sacrifices, but there were merchants with odd fare, much of which wasn't appropriate at any time, let alone at Passover. One merchant in particular had among his other stock, a dog in a cage much too small for its size. The poor animal had defecated on itself. I was overwhelmed by the memory of

"Miriam had her own problems being quite ill from carrying the baby. She didn't understand Yeshua's growing distance, which for him, wasn't a distance because of non-love. Just the contrary, it was a distance that he had to arrive at for himself so that he could be obedient."

- James brother of Yeshua -

those girls being sold at auction on the day I adopted my intemperate illusion, and I was overcome with empathy for the dog. When I looked in his eyes, he seemed consigned to his circumstances, while at the same time begging me for any help I could muster.

I asked the merchant why he had the poor dog in the cage. He made an offhand comment about the dog making a good meal for someone. Dogs weren't an animal Jewish people ate. Their meat isn't kosher. Dogs were considered helpmates and companions, not food.

I tried to let go of the dog's situation, but my ire was provoked. The passion I'd been carrying all day ignited, and in an act I wish hadn't happened, I argued with the merchant and several of his peers, eventually exploding in rage. I saw them as despoiling the sacred nature the Temple should represent to my people. I proceeded to open as many cages and free as many animals as I could. I was a formidable combatant, and once angered no one was able to stop me from busting up several merchants' stalls in the process.

I'm sure the scene ended up working for my mission, but my behavior appalled me. I hurried to my family's home immediately and calmed myself as quickly as I could.

Once calm, I went back to the venders. I waited for guards to leave the scene, and I apologized and paid full restitution for the property I destroyed. There were enough priests present, however, that I knew my deeds would be spoken of to the people who needed cause to arrest me.

Eleven Days of Ardor, Day Six Begins

That evening, after supper, I had a long conversation with Judas about how he saw the tide flowing. He recounted his conversation with Caiaphas and some of his loyal priests. Judas told me how very pleased they were that someone in my organization was willing to give them what they needed to 'take me out of the mix.' It was chilling to me but expected. Judas told them, just as we had discussed he would, that I was making plans to overthrow the leadership of the Sanhedrin during the week following Passover.

They made a pact with Judas to lead their guards to me during a 'planning' session the evening before Passover. So far, so good.

But before our conversation was over, Judas grabbed me and asked me one more time if I was sure about my course. I told him I was and when I saw him before bed, he was standing in the corner of the room silently weeping.

"I didn't witness the incident at the Temple. Yeshua had been alone that morning. I know he wanted to visit the Temple itself, though he didn't get that far. Knowing what I know now, I'm not surprised that he became inflamed. The corruption at the Temple was remarkable and obvious. And the amount of stress Yeshua was under, given the plan he was in the process of executing, was a prescription for rage. It was a rare incident, but wholly understandable."
- James brother of Yeshua -

Eleven Days of Ardor, Day Six Continues

The next day, Judas found me before I was done with my baptism. Apparently, the Roman quartermaster issued orders that any soldier who saw me, was to arrest me on charges of starting a riot.

Before I left for the streets, I requested that the family have a special supper this night. I asked to have the family and devotees meet together in the hall above my Uncle's shop. I knew this would be my last meal with those I loved before life changed, in whatever way it was going to change, and I wanted to speak with them all together.

Once among the people, I made a point of evading the soldiers, and by the end of the day, they were frustrated. I simply faded into the shadows. I'd work up a crowd to passion for my words, and when the soldiers came I'd be gone.

I eluded them with ease.

"The soldiers were instructed to capture Yeshua. That wasn't so easy. He wasn't findable. Though he was leading everyone, though he was speaking on the footsteps of buildings and the centers of the squares, he was not findable."
- James brother of Yeshua -

134 · The Last Supper

134 · The Last Supper

Eleven Days of Ardor, Day Seven Begins

I went back to the family home early. I wanted to spend time with Micah. I'd caught a small lizard and brought it to him. He played with it for a bit. We sat and talked about life. He lit my heart and after a few hours, I had to steel myself for whatever was coming. I almost lost my strength of composure with my love of being with him.

But the gathering at supper brought the real test of my resolve. Everyone met in the hall above my uncle's shop. There were about forty-five people gathered, including the family we were staying with in Jerusalem, a few friends, and the devotees who'd accompanied us. It took several tables to accommodate everyone.

They urged me to perform the blessing, which I did. And while we were eating, I mentioned that what was coming was coming quickly.

Most people didn't understand what I meant. In their minds, I was their King and they expected that to be formalized through intervention from the Creator.

So I went a step further and said, "Please understand, I won't join you for Passover tomorrow. And I want you to know I'm accepting everything that comes as the devotion to my mission demands." The room became quieter. "And I implore you to not grieve. I'll be joining you again within a few days."

Slowly, the quiet subsided and many people went back to their regular merry chatter, but I saw the specter of worry settle into the faces of those closest to me.

I changed my speech to that mysterious way of talking where only certain people could understand. I looked at Judas and he nodded, so I said, "I tell you that someone here, someone very close to me, will betray me tonight." The few who could understand me gasped. They clamored to know who it was and what I meant. I reached across the table and gave Judas a cup of wine. Judas looked at me with deep sadness in his face. He nodded again and downed the wine quickly. "I love you, my friend," I said to Judas, "please, make it quick."

Everyone's eyes turned to Judas. He looked around the table. Emotional turmoil enveloped him as he stood, panting, and hurried from the room. After a

"It was a late meal and everyone asked Yeshua to perform the blessing on the meal because most all believed that in doing so he'd be proclaiming his blessing on the first of the meals eaten in triumph. Well, it ended up being that such was true but not specifically in the manner that we all thought. He told us that he'd be leaving quickly and that this would be his last meal with us before some change was to occur. Well, most thought he meant his last meal as a heretic because by tomorrow he'd be known as the true king, not a heretic. We didn't want to see the truth."

- James brother of Yeshua -

moment of silence, I said, "Everyone understand, I accept what's coming with faith and devotion. I don't want you to grieve. You'll be eating with me again in a few days."

Someone asked, "Where're you going?"

"I'm going on a journey only I can take. I don't know what it'll entail." Miriam and James had tears streaming down their faces. "No matter what you hear," I said to them directly, "no matter what you see, the Son of Man is fine." I looked at the rest, "Before this is over, some of you will deny you know me. Some will cower in fear. Some will shrink with extreme sorrow. I tell you, none of it matters to me. You carry the seeds of the new covenant within you and those seeds will sprout, even as you deny me." I stood and backed away from the table, "I want to talk to each of you, individually now, then I'd like all you men to join me for a prayer beneath the light of the moon."

So, I went to each one by one. I spoke to each of the love I had for him or her, and I offered myself as their servant; that I'd be in their service for eternity. I told them that no matter what happened I had faith in their innate divinity. And I again asked each to not grieve.

When I was nearly finished, Mary was no longer in the room. So, I faced Miriam. She was ill, I could tell, and she was shaking. I grabbed her hands and she felt as fragile and devoid of strength as I'd ever felt her. We stepped behind a curtain for some privacy. "Is this it then?" she asked as her tears fell, "is it over?"

"No, it's not over," I said, "I don't know what'll come. I, I don't know what it'll look like, but it's not over." I put my hand on her belly, "I want this baby to know me. I just don't know how that can happen." I hugged my beloved and felt a sudden surge of the deep love we shared. I kissed her and felt the fullness of my physical passion for her for one last brief and shining moment. When we pulled apart, Miriam placed her hand on my face. "I love you, Tall Man. Please stay out of harm's way."

"I love you, never forget that," I begged, "never," and I bent to the ground and kissed her feet. "I'm yours for all time," I said, as a surge of power coursed through me. I stood. "It's time. I have to go now."

As I turned, she said something that both surprised me and touched me deeply, "Sleep well, my Prince." As our fingers pulled apart, I knew deep in my bones that I'd never have the opportunity to hold her in that way again. I felt revolt suddenly rise in me. I wanted to grab her and leave Jerusalem right then. I had the strongest urge to run. Every instinct in me was ready to snatch her and not look back, but a veneer of restraint sat on the edge of every muscle and I couldn't move. I lingered in that moment until the radical need to run subsided and I walked away from the White Tiger. I walked away from the deepest and most complete love a man could ever know and my heart nearly exploded from the pain. And of any pain I experienced over this brief time, that was by far the sharpest.

"He announced that his betrayer was one of us. And that it was as it should be. And at that point we got worried. Everyone was whispering to one another and I believe it was John, sitting next to Yeshua, said, 'Who?' Yeshua said, 'The man whom I now bless.' and then he reached over and handed something to Judas and said, 'I love you.' Judas got nervous with all the eyes looking at him... everyone's eyes on him... he left."

- James brother of Yeshua -

135 · Treacherous Priest

Eleven Days of Ardor, Day Seven Continues

We gathered behind the home in a beautiful walled garden. This was the pre-arranged spot to be arrested. Except for the anxiety many were feeling, the garden was peaceful. The moon was nearly full, and it shone with a force that could have blinded my eyes if I looked at it.

We said prayers and when they were exhausted, we lingered. I was waiting for Judas. Most of the men dozed.

I thought about my life; places I'd gone and things I'd done. I thought about the magnificent people I was fortunate enough to meet. I wondered at what got me here to this moment? I knew the next few days would be difficult, so I asked Creator to be with me. Then I realized I was saturated with her, right on down and through the soup of every cell in my body. I felt no separation between us, and that instantly quelled my mind from its incessant jabber.

Soon after, I heard footsteps; the time was at hand. In a moment, I was going to consign myself to men who would relish and delight in my agony. And the fact that I was doing it willingly and with fervor was bewildering to me at my most human level of existence, but it didn't change my choice one bit. I belonged to humanity now. I asked the ancestors to have mercy on me.

I stood as a handful of guards with a priest came in with Judas. The commotion awakened everyone. One of the guards asked where I was.

"I'm here," I said, "I'm Yeshua." The guard looked around as if he couldn't see me. I stepped closer and said again, "I'm Yeshua."

"Rabbi, stop!" Peter shouted.

The guard looked annoyed and demanded, "Where is he?"

James rushed to step in front of me, but I put my hands on his shoulder and urged him to the side. Judas stepped up and laid his hand on my shoulder. We stared at each other, our hearts locked in mutual support. With tears in his eyes he said, "This is he, this is Rabbi Yeshua of Galilee."

"What're you doing?" James yelled.

In a whisper, I said to Judas, "Thank you," and he kissed me. His love for me communicated through that kiss with force.

As the guards moved toward me, the men tried to fight for my escape. The guards mounted an immediate response and hit at them, knocking a few to the

"He asked some of us to come with him for a prayer, an evening prayer. So, we left. When we got to a garden behind the home of a family member, a closed garden, we sat. It was very late. I was very tired. All except Yeshua were tired. He was waiting."

- James brother of Yeshua -

ground. James suffered a knife wound to the side of his face, nicking his ear.

I was startled. As soon as I regained composure I said, "Stop. Stop fighting. I'll go peacefully." Several tried to grab me and stop me from walking away, but I gently removed their hands. "I'm going of my own volition. Listen to me. Remember what I told you. Don't grieve. I'll be with you again soon."

The next thing I remember was standing in the Hall of Priests, my hands tightly bound in chains and my feet in shackles. I must have been beaten, as one of my eyes was badly swollen. Many Sadducees were present. It surprised me to see them together at this late hour. Obviously, they were waiting for my arrival. What was less surprising was most of the Temple elders that supported me were absent. Nicodemus was there, obviously covertly aroused to the meeting.

Caiaphas sat in front of me. To his right sat his predecessor, and family patriarch, Hanan. Their clear intent was to find a means for my disposal.

The priests peppered me with questions, most of which I was predisposed not to answer. I finally said, "Why do you ask questions you know I won't answer? Questions designed to incriminate me no matter how I respond?"

"Are you the Messiah?" Caiaphas interrupted.

"I thought that was decided," I said, "haven't you already made that ruling? Do you doubt yourself that you have to ask my opinion?"

"Stop being insolent!" Caiaphas shouted.

"I'm a duly appointed priest of your Temple," I said with some sarcasm, "how can it be insolence to bow to your superior word?" Caiaphas rose from his seat and Hanan grabbed his arm to keep him from lunging at me. "Why do I anger you so much?" I asked, "I haven't claimed any right that displaces your authority."

"You consider yourself king!" he shouted.

"I've never claimed that," I answered. "Is there someone who claims I have? If so, bring him forward."

"Bring him in." Caiaphas motioned a guard to bring in a man I didn't recognize, but clearly could've been in one of the crowds recently.

"State your name," one of the priests asked the man.

"I'm Simon son of Matthias."

"And what do you do?" the priest asked.

"I'm a tradesman." Simon said, "Building construction mostly,"

"Do you know this man?" the priest pointed to me.

"Oh yes," Simon answered, "I know of him. I've heard him speak."

"Have you heard him say anything that leads you to believe he means to overthrow the current rulers of our Temple?"

"Judas came back with the soldiers. Some of the same soldiers who'd been trying to find Yeshua all day… but the soldiers were confused because they didn't see Yeshua, even when he stepped out in front of them, the soldiers couldn't see him. And even though he said, 'here I am,' they didn't see him. Not that they didn't see him, they didn't recognize him, and so, Judas walked up and said, 'This is he. This is Yeshua of Galilee.'"

- James brother of Yeshua -

Simon nodded his head, "Yes. He said he'd stand on the throne of the new kingdom in the City of David and cast aside the old rule." The room exploded with shrieks and outcries.

That wasn't exactly what I'd ever said. I knew that, and so did Simon and Caiaphas. I looked at Nicodemus and he shook his head in disbelief.

Caiaphas interrupted again, "What do you say to that?" he shouted to me.

"I'm ready to make manifest the will of my Creator," I said, "whether that's in the hallowed City of David or elsewhere." The din of the room rose again.

"Blasphemy!" someone shouted.

"Is it blasphemy to want to do as my Creator bids?" I retorted, "Isn't that what our sacred texts urge of each of us?"

"He calls himself a prophet? He hears God?" one yelled. "Stone him!"

Caiaphas motioned, and a guard stepped over and, without warning, punched me in the face and the gut. I doubled over from the sudden pain.

"Stop this!" Nicodemus shouted, "He's not convicted. Treat him with respect!"

"Brother Nicodemus," Caiaphas shouted, "are you in league with this traitor?"

"I'm in league with civility and due process, Caiaphas!" he answered.

Caiaphas called off the guard. I stood and felt blood trickle onto my robes.

"Caiaphas," I said, "you've spilt this blood on my rabbinic robes. Is it enough or do you want more?"

Caiaphas rose from his seat, his face bright red. "You insult me!" he shouted. "Who do you claim yourself to be?"

"I claim only what I've been endowed by right of birth and honor of study," I answered, "I'm the head of the royal family David, by birthright. I'm Temple Priest and a Son of Man by study." The room exploded again.

"I'll whip you for your impudence!" Caiaphas shouted.

"And will I be in chains when you do?" I laughed and simply pulled my wrists free of the chains. "Or out?" All in the room heard the wrist and ankle restraints clank against the floor. I held my arms up so all could clearly see they were free.

"The Son of Man stays in restraints only when it suits his purpose," I said. Everyone in the room fell silent, even Caiaphas. Hanan stood and motioned for the guards to grab me again, but their hands swept through thin air as I faded from their grasp and reappeared behind Caiaphas.

"Sorcerer! He's a Sorcerer!" I heard one priest shout.

Caiaphas whirled around. His hand flew through the air striking my face as it flew by.

"Some of us tried to follow the soldiers and were beaten back. Some tried to sneak around and were beaten back. Some of us were just plain scared at the overwhelming understanding of what just happened, and what was possibly going to happen, that we were frightened into a stupor, if you can understand that. Miriam was hysterical. But, we assumed, however erroneously, that nothing would happen without a trial which was law. And we thought that a trial couldn't happen until the next day, assuming that people had to be gathered. But, that wasn't true because Judas, in forewarning them of when he would deliver Yeshua into their hands, facilitated them being ready right then, in the middle of the night. By the time we were mobilized and out the next morning that part was already over."

- James brother of Yeshua -

"And now we see the real passion of you, Head Priest," I said. "Can your will be made manifest? Are you strong enough?"

His face contorted, he roared like a lion in the wild. I faded and reappeared where he originally had me stand. "Or are you too weak to affect my dismantling?" I faded and reappeared behind the crowd. "Can you find me in the crowd?" I faded and reappeared on the other side of the room in the open. "Or do I have to step into plain view to help you with your cause?"

Caiaphas was dizzy with my display, so I faded once more and reappeared in front of him with my arms outstretched, ready to be shackled again. "I bow to the will of my Creator."

Most of the room had stepped far back against the walls, including the guards; they didn't want to be close to me. "Are you ready to condemn a Son of Man, Head Priest?" I stood still and waited.

After an extended silence, Caiaphas ordered the guards to put the shackles back on me. He looked at Hanan who nodded. So he turned again and said. "I find sufficient cause to champion your execution, you treasonous conjurer," he said, "I'll ask Herod to seal the order."

"I doubt he'll be willing to do your bidding," I sneered, "wouldn't your friends in the Roman quarter be more likely to play your game?"

"Wait!" Nicodemus shouted, "This man hasn't been duly convicted, or even tried! He should be held for trial at most!"

Caiaphas ignored Nicodemus. "Take him to Herod," he ordered.

"His abilities gained from his time in the east were astounding. Shocking actually. Miraculous. He truly experienced the world differently than I and most everyone in Judea."

- James brother of Yeshua -

136 · Send Him Home

When we got to Herod's estate, all were asleep. The guards pounded on the door. Several head priests were standing ready to speak with the King himself. When the house staff roused, they were reluctant to wake Herod, but the priests insisted, so they brought us inside and asked us to wait.

About an hour later, Herod came in with two of his elite guard. He didn't look happy or well. "What do you want?" he screeched at the priests.

"Caiaphas asked us to bring you this prisoner," a priest said.

Herod looked me up and down. "Well, who is he?" he asked.

"As we spoke about yesterday, your Highness," the priest said in a low voice, "this is Yeshua of Galilee."

Herod gasped and pranced over to me. He walked around me slowly, chuckling the entire time. "So this is the man who would be king." His eyes traveled over every inch of me. "Not so mighty tonight, are you?" he declared.

"I'm not certain by what instrument you measure me, King," I said, "but I assure you I am by no means incapacitated."

Herod laughed and turned to the priest. "Why is he brought here?"

"Herod," the priest answered, "as we spoke. Caiaphas wants you to seal an order of execution on this man."

Herod's eyes got big. He started to perspire, and his eyes darted about in an erratic manner.

"Me?" Herod said, "Seal the order?"

"Yes, your Highness," the priest assured him.

Herod stepped back and said, "What of you, Rabbi, are you what they say you are?"

"Who is they and what do they say?" I asked.

"They, them, all!" Herod flung his arms about as he hissed, "They say you are the Messiah."

"The heads of the Temple put that rumor to bed when they ruled I wasn't, but I am a Son of Man," I said in a clear voice. "I proudly wear that title along with my rabbinic robes and my station as head of the David family."

Herod's eyes narrowed, "Son of Man." He stepped closer again and said, "Prove it to me."

"Be careful, Herod," a priest shouted, "this man is a conjurer!"

"How can I prove what your heart is unwilling to see," I said to Herod. "Are you no closer to understanding the bruise you gave our Creator when you slaughtered his prophet John?"

"John was a traitor and slanderer!" He walked to the doorway and looked both directions, then turned back to me. "The Baptist was no prophet!" His eyes got wide and he jumped, shaking in his slippers, his breathing cut short.

The priests looked at each other in confusion.

"John's here, isn't he, King?" I asked.

"Shut-up!" he bellowed.

"Will you have my blood on you as well?" I said to him.

"No! No!" Herod stepped back until his back was against the wall, his head shaking. "Go! I won't seal my fate with another prophet's blood! I won't!"

"But your Majesty, Caiaphas was insis…"

"Go! I won't have the blood of another prophet on my hands! No! Don't! Leave me alone…" Herod covered his eyes and cowered to something no one else could see, but I knew it was my cousin.

At Caiaphas house he was waiting for the news of my incarceration at Herod's. He was livid when he saw me still in his custody.

"This is outrageous!" he fumed. "Why has Herod fallen back on his promise?"

"It was rather confusing," the priest said to Caiaphas, "he acted like a madman."

Caiaphas nodded, "It's that Baptist business." He shrugged, "He's lost his mind over the affair." He motioned for the priests to come close and they huddled in the corner whispering. Finally, they broke their treacherous knot and Caiaphas said. "Keep him in chains and take him to Pilate."

Before sunrise, I was standing in front of Pontius Pilate the Prefect of Judea. Pilate had a reputation of being swift in his judgments and ruthless in his ambitions. He was predisposed in the beginning of his tenure in Judea to slaughtering my brethren at the slightest provocation. But, in recent years his rule had softened, and his hand applied more evenly. This worried me. I needed him to order my crucifixion.

Pilate sat on a bench, speaking with one of his commanders. When their conversation ended, he turned to the priests. "What is this matter about?" Pilate said, "And be quick, I haven't had my breakfast yet."

"We've come from Caiaphas," a priest said. "We've brought you the prisoner Yeshua of Galilee."

"Ah, so this is Yeshua the Healer?"

"Yes. He's been charged with heresy," the priest stated.

"So they marched out to where Herod was staying, conveniently, and he was, at that point, as far from sane as any man can be. Herod, who had been tearing his hair out, had almost ripped his own eyes out, because John the Baptist was walking around the hallways of his home, behind every curtain, behind every door. Herod believed that he put to death a prophet of God, which was a sin that he couldn't atone for. Herod refused to issue an order of death because he didn't want to risk having another prophet on his hands."

- James brother of Yeshua -

"What is that to me? Nothing," Pilate said, "why bring him?"

The Roman Commander interrupted, "Sir, we issued orders just yesterday to have him arrested for starting a riot."

"Starting a riot? I should think so. From what I've heard there could be no other effect from him speaking in public." He turned to me, "What of this, Rabbi? Are you starting riots?"

"People become excited when I'm around,"

"Indeed." Pilate turned to the priests. "I've no need to punish this man. Release him and be done with it."

"But we can't," the priest said, "Caiaphas has called for his execution."

"On what grounds?" Pilate laughed, "Healing too many people?"

The priest pulled back indignantly. "He's treasonous and a conjurer," he said.

"So send him home," Pilate insisted. "He's a Galilean. Let Herod sort this out."

"We've already seen Herod. He's refused," the priest replied.

"Then obviously this isn't as serious as you think." Pilate looked at me, "But I'm confused. Isn't this man of royal blood? Why are you treating him like a commoner?"

"Pilate, he's stirred the people..."

"Wait," Pilate put his hand up to the priest. "Rabbi, isn't one of your family Joseph the aristocrat?"

"Yes," I answered, "he's my cousin."

"Mmm. Good man too." Pilate turned back to the priests, "I'd like to hear from him. Why isn't Joseph here now?"

The priest cleared his throat and bowed his head. "He's unavailable."

"Unavailable?" Pilate shook his head, "Let this man go. Or send him to Herod. I'm done." Pilate left the hall.

"Pilate was an educated man from a higher level of society than most soldiers. I had heard from more than one source, that Pilate was quite spiritual as well. Not your usual military man."

- James brother of Yeshua -

137 · Give Me More

I didn't want to go back to Herod. I wanted Pilate to order my death. But here I was again standing in front of the puppet king.

"Why have you returned?" Herod shouted.

"Your Highness, Pilate has refused to deal with this man," the priest said, "he told us to come to you."

"I won't have anything to do with him!" Herod shouted.

"He's been convicted of heresy. Please? He's a conjurer and seditious." the priest begged.

"I won't do it," Herod insisted, "tell Caiaphas he'll have to do his own dirty work for a change!"

"But Pilate sent us to you."

"Then let Pilate put me up on charges if he likes." Herod's eyes darted about like a frightened bird. "Now get out of here and let my fate be as it will be!" he screamed.

"Caiaphas can't order an execution," the priest tried to explain.

Herod stood and gestured wildly with his arms. "Guards! Guards! Get these men out of here. Now!" he shrieked.

The sun had barely begun to show its light above the horizon, but the streets were already filled with people making their final preparations for the coming Passover. It'd be a big day for business.

We hastened through the streets, but people couldn't help but notice me in chains. I saw them point and whisper.

Soon, I again stood in front of Pilate. "Why've you brought this man back to me? I'm impatient with this matter," he said.

"He must be put to death," the priest said.

"I don't feel this man deserves death." Pilate looked at me again, "He deserves a bed and a good meal."

"You're the only one who can seal the Temple order for his execution!" the priest insisted.

"So, Herod told them that he refused. At that point he was more willing to take the wrath of Rome then the continued wrath of God. He wouldn't live much longer anyway."

- James brother of Yeshua -

"You must stop confusing insults to your temple with crimes against Rome," Pilate said, "they're not the same." He turned to the guards, "Take these chains off. I want to speak with him." The guards hesitated. "Do it now!" Pilate shouted. Caiaphas guards backed away, so Pilate called on his soldiers to remove my chains. He looked at me and said, "Come with me. I want to have a chat." He held his arm out for me to follow. "And bring this man a cloth and some water to clean his face," he said to one of the soldiers as he led me into a separate room. When the soldier returned with the cloth and water, Pilate ordered the soldier to leave and close the door behind him.

Pilate motioned for me to sit and wash. I did, both. It felt good. He said, "I'm in a quandary here, Rabbi."

I felt his turmoil. "What's the quandary?" I asked.

"My wife mostly," he took in a sharp breath, "she likes you. No, she adores you."

"I see," I said.

"She's heard you speak," he added.

"Easily done," I said.

"She had a dream. A... uh, prophetic dream, she says." I saw the traces of past cruelty etched on his face, but none of that cruelty was talking with me now. "She said, if I harm you, it'll seal my demise."

"I see," I nodded.

"I've nothing against you, Rabbi," Pilate continued, "I have a measure of respect for you, actually. And I'm not the only one, there're many in Rome who share the opinion that you're someone quite special."

"I'm honored," I said.

"Well, honor or not, there's the quandary of what to do today. I want to let you go. You're not a common criminal and I don't see that you pose a threat to me."

"That opinion is not shared by your associates, Caiaphas and Herod," I said.

"Ah, well, Caiaphas is a fool. He thinks he has more power than he does. And Herod." Pilate laughed, "My sources say he's recently gone quite mad."

"He appeared as such to me earlier today," I offered.

"Yes, well." He looked at my face, searching for something. "Who are you, Rabbi?"

"You know who I am. I'm the head of the David family, the Hebrew royal family." I nodded, "I've studied faithfully in several traditions and become something of an enigma among my own."

"Many people I know have witnessed your feats." Pilate seemed genuinely interested.

"I can't say one way or the other, which of those feats were mine and which belong to my Creator," I said, "I'm a messenger of his will, if nothing else."

"Show me. Show me something, Rabbi," he asked with sincerity, "I want to believe like my wife does."

"It was morning. We were waking everybody, rousing everybody. Making sure or trying to make sure everybody understood that the soldiers had taken Yeshua. We had no idea that the trial had already taken place and we were trying to set up some type of plan of action."

- James brother of Yeshua -

"What can I show you? What here needs undoing? What here needs the Creator's attention?"

"I suppose we both need the intervention of a benevolent god," Pilate said as he hung his head. "There're so many factors at play. I feel as though it doesn't matter what I do, I'll regret this day."

"I understand that feeling," I said as the light began its glow. Pilate looked up as it began to pulse.

"Rabbi, you're glowing," he said as his eyes opened wide in wonder.

"This happens often," I said, "I have no say in it."

"It's extraordinary," Pilate murmured. "Can you save us? Rabbi, can you end this quandary?"

I sighed, "Unfortunately I can't. In fact, I was going to ask you to please do as the priests ask of you."

Pilate was stunned. "What? You want to die?"

I shook my head, "No, I don't want to die, but I'm assured I won't die. You'll not be able to douse my light with your tortures."

"That's ludicrous." Pilate sat up straight. "I assure you that if I consign you to my soldiers for execution, you'll not walk this earth again."

"I'm not daring you, Pilate. I'm grateful to you today for your civility and your open heart. Yet I do hope for your acquiescence to be part of this plan."

"What plan? What could be your motivation?" he sputtered, "You have money, education, station. You have everything you need to live a satisfying life. I'm mystified."

"Listen to me," I said, "the human race is in trouble, everyone. You, me, the commoner, the Emperor, we all live under a yoke of subjugation." I continued to explain the reason for my mission. I told him of the prophecies that said I'd transcend death and live. He stayed rapt to my words. He listened with an open heart and an open mind, and all the while, I pulsed with the light of my Creator.

When I was done, he stared at me for several minutes, then said, "Most men I meet here are without erudition." He shook his head, "What you say astounds me. You're a rare man, Rabbi." He put his hands out with his palms up, "Please give me more."

"What more do you wish?" I asked.

"Something to set my mind at ease," he begged.

"I can't ease your mind. Your turmoil is a result of being caught between two worlds. You want to go on as if nothing has changed. But the truth is, much has changed, and more change is coming. You're being called to follow, not just with your ritual or your words. Right now, you're called to perform at the highest level of faith. You're being asked to send the Son of Man to his destiny."

Pilate stood and turned his back on me. "I'm not going to order your execution."

"Pilate asked to talk with Yeshua alone. I think few really know what happened between Yeshua and Pilate. I don't believe I really know, except that Pilate somehow understood what was happening. Pilate wanted Yeshua to show himself for what he was. Yeshua wouldn't and it made Pilate mad, made him angry when he began to understand the part that he was going to have to play in what was happening."

- James brother of Yeshua -

"Pilate, look at me," I asked. He turned around. The light pulsed with steady beams of energy emitting from my hands. I touched his shoulders. Tears began to stream down his cheeks. I saw the shadows of his past march before his eyes. After a moment, he went to his knees. I followed him to the floor as the markers of time pulled his resolve this way and that. "You're caught in time," I said, "a product of the old world, but called to the new world." I saw the effects of years of cruelty and hard-heartedness melt away until he appeared as a child again.

He looked at me with all innocence. "Rabbi, what have you done to me?" he asked.

"I've done nothing. You've shifted. Now the question remains, when you stand to your feet again, how will you act?" I stood and put my hand out to help him. When he got to his feet, he let go of my hand and stepped back.

"No, it's too late for me, Rabbi. I've sealed my fate," he said, "you may die today, but not from my hands. And may the gods look on us with pity." He turned and walked back to the hall, motioning for me to follow.

"Yeshua changed people. He didn't do that through telling people what to do. He did that by being the very embodiment of love. Meeting pure love face-to-face is highly compelling."

- James brother of Yeshua -

138 · Hang Him

Eleven Days of Ardor, Day Seven Continues

Caiaphas was waiting in the hall with the priests.

"Ah, Caiaphas, you came for no reason," Pilate said, "I'm refusing to order the execution. You persecute an innocent man."

"Wha… why isn't he in chains?" Caiaphas sputtered, "This man is dangerous."

"To whom?" Pilate asked. "Certainly not to me, and certainly not to Rome."

"He preaches sedition." Caiaphas said.

"I urge you to let him go." Pilate looked at me, "Will you leave the city if I set you free?" he asked.

I took in a deep breath and said, "No."

Pilate shook his head and turned to his soldiers, "Take him to the Jewish quarter and let him go."

"Stop!" Caiaphas shouted, his face red, "Pilate, remember your allegiances. Deal with this traitor."

Pilate shouted back, "He's no traitor to me. Your own people would agree with me." He turned his back on the priest, "Now go, get on with your holiday!"

"You think the people will agree?" Caiaphas said with amusement, "Are you so sure Prefect of Caesar?"

Pilate turned to Caiaphas. "We can ask them, if you like." Pilate went to the balcony and looked out on the Temple courtyard. It was bustling with people buying and selling goods for the celebrations. Pilate motioned to the soldiers to bring me over. "Come, everyone, Caiaphas, come. We'll ask your brethren what they prefer."

Everyone walked onto the balcony and Pilate shouted, "Attention everyone. Listen to me." He waited a moment and shouted again, "Everyone, give me your attention." The crowd began to quiet and draw closer. "I have a question for you." He grabbed me by the arm and pulled me to the edge of the balustrade. "Do you recognize this man?" The crowd buzzed with whispers. "Yes? You recognize him?" He waited for a response.

A lone voice from the crowd yelled, "That's Rabbi Yeshua, the Galilean!"

"Yes," Pilate shouted, "Yeshua the Healer. You've all heard him speak no doubt?" The crowd noise strengthened and many nodded in agreement. "Good.

"Pilate refused to issue an order. Caiaphas got mad and said that he couldn't issue the order himself but by Jewish law he must die. But the Romans hadn't given the Sanhedrin the authority to condemn someone to death. Pilate said he wouldn't condemn to death the beautiful innocence that he saw in Yeshua."
- James brother of Yeshua -

Well, your Priests want me to execute this man. They feel he's dangerous." The people looked confused. Pilate continued, "Do you think he's dangerous?"

The people shook their heads no and I heard a general 'No' rising from the din. I was concerned that they'd give Pilate cause to let me go. So, I willed that the mood of the crowd shift. Suddenly a lone voice from the edge of the crowd yelled, "Yeah, I don't like him." The crowd began to murmur.

Pilate was no fool. He felt the energetic shift I created. He spun to face me. "What are you doing?" he demanded.

I didn't say a word.

He turned back to the crowd and pointed at me. "Do you want to see this gentle man, this man who heals the sick, do you want to see him die?"

"He's no healer!" I heard another voice yell.

"But you've seen it, at least some of you, I've heard your accounts," Pilate shouted to the crowd, but the murmured consensus seemed to be that they hadn't seen a thing. From the back, I heard a voice yell, "Hang him!"

Pilate stepped away from the balustrade and looked at me. "Whatever you're doing, stop it. Stop it now." He ordered.

I looked at him and said, "I've merely done what I must do. And so must you, servant of Rome."

Pilate pulled his hand from my arm and I saw anger grow in him. People in the crowd taunted me with ethnic slurs. After all, I was a Galilean.

He looked out over the crowd and shouted, "I'll have him whipped. Then we'll see how you feel. We'll be back!" He grabbed me and threw me into the hall. "Soldiers, take this man and have him scourged. Put the fear of death into him, but I warn you, a simple beating. Keep him alive!" He looked at Caiaphas, then at me, and then back at the soldiers, "Then bring him back here with another man ripe from the prisons. Someone scheduled to die today. I want to give the people a chance to change their mind." He looked at me, "You brought this on yourself, Rabbi."

I nodded, "I'll see you again," I said as the soldiers grabbed me and pulled me toward the barracks. As we left the hall, I heard Pilate bellow, "Keep him alive. If you kill him, I swear I'll kill you!" The two soldiers sneered at me and shoved me to the ground. I recognized one of them as one who'd tried to arrest me the day before. I knew he was itching to beat on me. I got up and let them escort me to the scourging area.

When we got there, the soldiers stripped off my rabbinic garments and under robe, exposing most of my skin. They chained my wrists above my head to the scourging post.

A commander walked over and said, "What's this?"

"Scourging," the soldier said, "Pilate wants us to beat him, but not to kill him."

"Yeah," the other soldier said, "Pilate said if we kill him, he'll kill us."

"You better listen to that," the commander said, "Pilate means what he says. I've seen him carry through on those types of threats." They began to walk away,

"The only thing I understood is that as long as Yeshua was untouchable, the people could believe. I assume that as soon as he was shown to be mortal flesh they were bewildered and confused and that turned into hatred for what they believed to be shattered dreams."

- James brother of Yeshua -

but I heard the commander ask in a voice that sounded bemused, "So, what're you going to use?"

While they were gone, I began my preparations. I had to close the part of my brain that would scream at me in pain. It was something I knew how to do well, but I'd never tested it the way I was afraid I would test it today. I fervently prayed I'd be successful, because if not, this day would be one I'd surely regret.

For the time being, I was successful, because when I saw them walk toward me smiling and swinging flagellums in the air, my consciousness left my body.

139 · Now We Shall See

Eleven Days of Ardor, Day Seven Continues

The next thing I remember was becoming conscious chained to a wall. My brain was still closed to pain; a blessing, because my skin was gouged and shredded in multiple places, and I was covered in blood. I mentally surveyed my body; one of my eyes was swollen shut, my nose was broken, and my jaw was dislocated. I felt relief that I was still alive.

The thought that followed was crucial. I realized I'd become a replica of the pitiable and dehydrated older me I met in the yawn on my way to the Temple of Man. I couldn't help but laugh aloud from that thought. Somehow, I'd stumbled into the very set of circumstances from which my own self predicted I'd live. It was immensely relieving, but my laughter caught the attention of a soldier near me.

"Hey! He's awake!" the soldier shouted. I heard the feet of men rushing toward us. I opened my remaining eye to look. Blood spray covered their uniforms. One of the soldiers shouted, "Jupiter saved us, he's alive." They all laughed in relief.

"Hey, I have something," one said, "I heard this Jew thinks he's king!" They laughed again.

Another said, "Yeah, as if Herod isn't enough trouble."

The first one pulled a rolled-up knot of thorny branches from behind his back, shaped like a thick, crude helmet. "I've got a crown for the king!" he laughed as he started toward me.

"Wait," another one said, "wait. Let's pull lots to see who gets to crown him."

The soldier carrying the branches grumbled a moment, then said, "All right, all right. Pull lots for the privilege."

All except one went through the ritual of pulling straws. The one who refused, stepped back and stared alternately at me and the ground, obviously disturbed. The soldier I'd frustrated the day before, won the pull. He grabbed the helmet and held it in the air, laughing. "Here's your crown, your majesty," he said with contempt-ridden sarcasm. With both hands, he drove the branches down onto my head with such a force that some of the thorns punctured my skull and stuck there. Thankfully as I intended, the pain never registered in my brain, but I felt the sensation of flesh ripping and blood flowing down my face and through my hair. I nearly passed out from the sudden shock to my body. Blood flow covered my one remaining eye, and, for the time, I was effectively blind.

"I've never gotten over the amount of beating the soldiers gave my brother. He didn't deserve that level of cruelty. I can't imagine who would."
- James brother of Yeshua -

When the soldiers recovered from their glee over my crowned plight, one of them threw a thin robe at me and told me to dress, which I couldn't do until they unchained me from the wall. When they did, one set of gentle hands helped me dress. Again, I was relieved that my brain hadn't register the pain of the fabric grating against the wounds.

Unfortunately, the sudden downward trauma of the blow to my head was too much for my spine. When I finally stood I couldn't stand straight. I stooped forward and leaned to the left. I was rapidly losing sensation in one of my legs, one foot already felt as if it didn't exist. I groped at my face to give me limited vision again, but the soldiers prodded me forward as I stumbled toward a waiting Pilate.

———————

When he saw the mangled state I was in, Pilate flinched and steeled himself. He genuinely liked me, and I was sorry we hadn't met under different circumstances. Unlike Oranos, I mused that this Roman and I might've become friends. Pilate's empathy quickly turned to rage. "I told you a simple beating!" he roared as he grabbed one of the soldiers by the neck and pulled him nearly off his feet. Pilate's strength was tremendous. "This man is nearly dead! I should crush your skull right now for it!" The soldier's bladder gave way from fear.

Caiaphas stood behind Pilate and the look of satisfaction on his face was pure evil.

Pilate threw the soldier to the floor. He whipped around and struck the other soldier holding me square in the face. "You're lucky he didn't die, or it'd be you on that crux today!" he bellowed. He pointed at the soldier on the floor. "Clean up his mess!" The soldier jumped to begin the cleanup. Pilate looked around the room. "Where's the other man," he thundered, "the other prisoner I told you to bring?"

"He's on the way," one of the soldiers said.

Pilate turned to Caiaphas, "Now we'll see what your people want." He looked Caiaphas up and down, "And I hope they have more fear of their God than you, Priest."

A few minutes later, the other prisoner arrived. This man wasn't beaten, but he was filthy and haggard from incarceration. I recognized him as a Zealot, an associate of Judas. He recognized me too and nearly fell over, stumbling backward from the shock of seeing my state. He mouthed to me, "I'm sorry, Rabbi." I nodded.

"Bring them," Pilate commanded as he walked to the balcony.

When I got to the balustrade I saw that the crowd had nearly tripled. Word of mouth brought them, perhaps. Likely, many came because of treachery on Caiaphas' part to salt the crowd with dissenters. I felt the energetic pull of a few hearts that were very close to mine standing in the crowd, but my vision was

"It was about this time that some of the members of our family, who were rabbis on the tribunal council, went to find out when the trial would be held and at that point found out that it had already been held without them being contacted. They heard the verdict and so they went off to see if they could get any more information."

- James brother of Yeshua -

blurred. I couldn't make them out. The crowd gasped in horror when they saw me. Barefoot, stooped, body barely covered with a blood-soaked robe, blood still flowing down my legs and down my head from my thorn cover, my face nearly unrecognizable from the swelling and dislocation, chained and nearly dead; I was a far cry from the triumphant leader they'd seen just a few days before. If I were them, I'd feel my dreams of liberation had been betrayed.

"Attention," Pilate shouted into the courtyard, "listen up." The crowd pulled closer. "I have two prisoners." Pilate motioned to the soldiers to pull us closer to the balustrade. "One is Yeshua the healer, a Rabbi and man of God. You may have been here earlier and saw him before the scourging." He looked at me with genuine sorrow in his eyes and his chest heaved. "The other," he looked at the Zealot, "is a man sentenced to die today. He's a rebel, a murderer duly convicted." He looked at the crowd. "One of these men will die on the crux today, but as tradition allows, I will spare one of them." The murmur of the crowd rose. "Which one I spare is up to you." Pilate stepped back from the balustrade and let the crowd talk amongst themselves. He looked at Caiaphas, and then at me as he said in a low voice, "I'm trying to save your life, Rabbi. Don't give these people more reason to hate you." I heard Caiaphas snuffle, sounding more like a pig than a man.

Pilate stepped to the balustrade, "So, as I've said, only one of these men will die today. Will it be this gentle man of God," he pointed to me, "who's already suffered greatly for no crime I can discern?" He pointed at the Zealot, "Or will it be this man, a murderer duly convicted? A man who has committed a crime your religion holds as one of the highest offenses to God." The crowd murmured. "Which will it be?" Pilate folded his arms and waited.

People in the crowd were pointing at us and I heard them talking. Suddenly a voice from the crowd yelled, "That man, the Rabbi. He deserves to die for lying to us!" The din of the crowd got louder.

"Surely, if he lied, that's not a crime punishable by death in any court I know!" Pilate shouted.

Another voice rose up, "Kill Yeshua!"

Pilate looked at me. "Are you doing this again?" he demanded.

I shook my head 'No.'

Pilate pointed to the Zealot. "Surely this man is the worst offender," he shouted.

The Zealot fell to his knees. "Please kill me, not the Rabbi. He doesn't deserve to die," he pleaded to Pilate.

The crowd gasped. Someone yelled, "See him? He's repentant. He's selfless. Hail the rebel!" The crowd quickly picked up the beat, "Hail the rebel! Hail the rebel!" The chant resounded in my ears, "Hail the rebel!"

Pilate ordered the soldiers to get the Zealot off his knees and one of the soldiers struck him in the face as he stood. The crowd went wild, crying out against Roman brutality. They were agitated, working themselves up, and I felt the hint of fear rise in Pilate for what might happen if mob mentality turned against his troops.

"The members of our family that were in the Temple square that morning were without recourse. By the time they got there, Yeshua was already badly beaten. They could tell Pilate didn't want to send him to his death, but everyone seemed to be caught up in a fervor of conviction."

- James brother of Yeshua -

"Listen!" Pilate shouted trying to regain some semblance of control over this mob, "Who will die today?"

The chanting subsided as the crowd began to roar, "Yeshua! Yeshua! Yeshua!"

Pilate gasped for breath. He looked at me and shook his head, "I tried, Rabbi, I tried, but I fear your power is greater than all of us." He turned to the soldiers holding the Zealot, "Let this man go free." He turned to the crowd and shouted, "Your will be done! The rebel is free." The crowd cheered, a triumphant cheer. I felt their sense of zeal and power surge at forcing the Prefect's hand to let a rebel go free.

Pilate turned to me. "Remember when you reach your maker, Rabbi, I've not ordered your death. Your own people denied you." I saw his eyes fill, "And please, if there's any peace to be bestowed, I could use some." He turned to the soldiers and told them to deliver me to the 'machina mortis,' the machine of death, and he walked swiftly away.

"Pilate gave the authority of life or death to the people. And the people said death. There were hundreds of people standing there and it was almost unanimous, to the same man that they had walked into town with just days before, following, hailing. They were all the more enraged at Yeshua's obvious mortality. Pilate walked away. The other man was set free. And Yeshua was taken to the jail."

- James brother of Yeshua -

140 · An Ancient Dance

Eleven Days of Ardor, Day Seven Continues

I remember nothing more until I came-to, lying on my face in the middle of a paved street. People were shouting. Something heavy pinned me to the ground and someone was kicking me, but my mind had difficulty sorting through the noises around me to understand any individual words.

Obviously, I wasn't dead, but I had difficulty connecting to my body. I couldn't feel my legs and I didn't think I'd be able to get up off the ground.

Slowly, my mind cleared enough to parse some of the noise. Someone was barking orders at me to get up. It must have been the same person kicking me. The crowd was arguing with the soldiers. With my head turned as far as it would go toward them, I saw a figure of a man menaced by the soldiers. It took a minute, but eventually I could tell it was Peter. Behind him in the crowd, I made out a few faces I knew I should recognize, but their identities eluded my brain.

I thought I saw myself walking toward me from behind the rest. Tears streamed down my face and my arm was cupped around a woman with long hair, holding her tight. Her arms stretched toward me, weeping. Her mouth was saying something, but the words weren't coming together in my mind. She looked so familiar, but I couldn't figure out why I was there holding her.

As I looked at the woman, my eyes connected with hers and I felt a surge of energy and a whoosh of movement that snapped me into my body. All at once, I understood everything. It wasn't me in the crowd; it was my brother, James. And the woman he was holding was my beloved. Peter was arguing, trying to get help for me. And the men standing behind Peter were John and James, sons of Zebedee, and Bartholomew.

The one kicking me stopped and I heard him yell, "You there! Yes you! Come here and pick up this beam!"

The crowd still shouted, and it felt as though riot was but a moment away.

Suddenly, I felt intense pain, as if every cell in my body was on fire. Miriam wrested herself from James grasp and lunged toward me. I heard her shout, "Yeshua!"

James yelled, "No, Miriam, come back!" and I saw the others turn toward them. As Miriam pushed through the crowd, Peter, James son of Zebedee, and

"Still at our family's house, we heard what was said when they came back and we immediately left the house practically running as best we could. Miriam was ill and hysterical, but we ran across town. When we got there we saw the horror that was next. Walking, stumbling in the processional with the soldiers, was my brother. My beautiful, light brother..."

- James brother of Yeshua -

Bartholomew moved to intercept her. Before I lost contact with her eyes, I tried to mouth the words, 'I love you,' but my jaw wasn't working.

I heard someone yell, "That's his wife!" and a general outcry arose from the crowd. The soldiers rushed forward, and I lost sight of her.

The pain pulsed with a terrible intensity, it was overpowering. I tried to force my brain to bypass the excruciating sensations. My hand lay flaccid in front of my face and I saw the light begin to pulse. 'What odd timing,' I thought as I felt the tremendous weight of an object lift from my back. At the same time, I heard a voice, like an angel, sing a lullaby filled with compassion and tenderness. It was the remembered voice of Nadia. It was the voice I'd marked all those years ago that had saved me once, and it was saving me again. It lifted my mind and gave me the focus to again bypass the agony. The pain quickly faded.

Pulled through time, the song continued its gentle refrain and I heard Nadia coo, 'There, there, everything's alright. Nothing to worry about. It's nearly done. Everything is as it should be. Just hold on to my voice.'

So, I did. I held onto her voice.

The noise of the crowd changed. Instead of anger and riot, I heard awe and reverence. Was it real? Or was it the change in me I was hearing? I can't say, but the light now pulsed with a steady beat that matched the rhythm of the lullaby.

The heavy object no longer held me down, so I tried to raise myself off the ground. It was no use, I didn't have the use of my lower body, but the movement gave me no pain. Suddenly, a woman broke through the crowd. With a gentle hand, she wiped my face with a moist, cool cloth. She mimicked the gentle movements of Nadia, washing me down with calming effect and I remember smiling and nodding in thanks.

The song continued, and the light pulsed. The crowd calmed, and I knew I had to stand, and as if angels surrounded me, my body rose to its feet. I wasn't willing it, I wasn't directing it, but invisible hands moved my body for me. I simply relaxed into the hands and let the song carry me to a place of surrender, as the hands made it look like I was walking.

The invisible hands brought me through the street and up the hill. At the top, my bloody clothes were stripped away. The soldiers left nothing on me; gone were my underclothes, even the heart on a thong the men of my village had carved and given me. I was stripped bone bare. There was a gentle breeze on the hill and for a moment, I almost felt like I was flying from the movement of the air across my skin. A soldier pushed me backward. I fell, but not quickly. Instead of hitting with a thud, my back lay down upon the ground as softly as if I had fallen on a bed of feathers.

More than anything, this was like a dance – an ancient, ritualistic dance.

I was transfixed on the voice, on the lullaby. I knew the soldiers were manipulating my body, but I had no care about it. Several soldiers shoved and shifted me into whatever position they wanted. My arms pulled out straight from

"Miriam rushed through the crowd to help him. I tried to stop her. The soldiers hit her across the face, knocking her down. We picked her up. Some of the crowd taunted her and the soldiers suddenly realized who she was. At that point, we pulled her back into the crowd for safety. Once we knew she was safe, we continued our walk with the procession up the hill."

- James brother of Yeshua -

my torso. Ropes wrapped them, fixing them to something. I felt tremendous pressure applied to my wrists, but the pressure was short lived. Every muscle in my body relaxed as the sound of Nadia's voice permeated my being. Her words caressed me, 'Nothing to worry about. It's nearly done. Everything is as it should be. Just hold on to my voice.'

The dance carried me.

Several soldiers raised my body into the air. Whatever I was attached to was dropped and jarred into place, yet still I felt no pain, only the awe of the voice gently serenading me with its tremendous love.

The soldiers that were holding me aloft lowered me and hung my bottom on a peg. I could tell because the peg pushed up into me, internally tearing flesh in the process. And when the soldiers let go and let gravity pull at me, I felt as raw and exposed as a newly slaughtered carcass a butcher hangs to let the blood drain. The position of the peg forced my torso to lean forward and the bones at one shoulder pulled lose from their socket.

I held onto the lilting refrain of Nadia's voice and let the dance persevere.

My head hung forward; my face toward the ground. I couldn't feel them, but I saw my legs; they were dangling free. One soldier carrying a mallet, pulled my legs in. I watched with genuine amazement as he deftly positioned my feet onto a small ledge and nailed them into place. The precision and economy with which he exacted his movements was masterful. He even knew where to stand so no blood would splatter on him.

Still I heard Nadia and her voice embraced my spirit, 'There, there, everything's alright. Nothing to worry about. It's nearly done."

The light of my Creator pulsed from me now like a steady beacon of light and it reminded me of the lighthouse at Alexandria, safely calling sailors through the fog to port. I thought, 'I'm the beacon, but where's the port?' I thought I had to find it, but I was hanging, waiting, listening, surrendering... wondering...

A magnificent creature of durable spirit stepped from the gathering crowd. It was my mother. She carried herself with a regal splendor that caused even the soldiers to let her pass unmolested.

She walked to where I was hanging. It was unusual that she should be so near as the soldiers never let family come so close to the posts. She came right up to me and placed her hand on my leg. Slowly she turned her face up. When her eyes met mine, she smiled a thin yet radiant smile and said, "I was with you when you started. I'll not leave you now."

I nodded to her as best as I could. "You are a gift from God," Mary said, "you are the most precious fruit of my body. Thank you for sharing your life with me, my dear Yeshu'men'horah."

I hadn't heard that name since I was a child. I'd only heard it used when she was less than pleased with my behavior. But now, for the first time, I realized what it meant to her. It was her appreciation of the light she always saw in me. It was her way of pulling that light forward, even when it wasn't obvious.

> "The soldiers had degraded Yeshua's body as far as they could. He was bleeding profusely and bruised everywhere he wasn't bleeding. We were amazed that on the walk up the hill, he'd bled enough blood for about twenty men and was still alive when he got to the top of the hill. It was beyond belief."
>
> - James brother of Yeshua -

The soldier who'd refused to participate in the straw-pull, walked to Mary, and placed his hand on her shoulder. He set a stool behind her and urged her to sit. As she sat, she said, "Thank you."

He bowed his head to her. "Your son has touched me deeply," he said, "I won't let him suffer longer than need be, I promise you." He squeezed her shoulder and stepped back. Mary leaned her head against the post and began humming; the wood gently vibrated.

I knew others I loved were in the crowd, but I didn't have the physical strength to hold my head up and look for them. Breathing was hard enough.

"We watched as they mercilessly pounded him to the wood. And not once, not once did he make a sound. It was as if we were watching the horror of the entire world brought about in those few hours and yet watching it transformed on the face of an angel. He had a smile on his face! Then they rose him into the air. And everyone waited – there was nothing more we could do."

- James brother of Yeshua -

141 · It is Time

Eleven Days of Ardor, Day Seven Continues

Hours passed. The sun had moved past its apex, and I had difficulty remaining conscious.

When I woke this time, I felt Mary's persistent humming continue to vibrate the wood. I opened my eye and saw her sitting beneath me, calm and steadfast in her vigil. I wanted to speak with her, but it was no use. My dislocated jaw, coupled with a dry throat and very little air moving through my lungs, made speaking almost impossible. I'd been waiting for some sign, some knowing; something to tell me it was time to put myself into suspension.

Suddenly, a hand touched my chest. The hand was warm, and I knew it was from my Creator. I whispered, "Is it time?"

I heard her voice, the voice that had greeted me so many times along my journey, in a loud and clear tone, "It's time."

"Thank you," I sighed. I looked at Mary and whispered, "Mother, I leave myself in your hands."

She stood and looked at me. I was surprised she'd heard such a feeble attempt at sound, but her hand again lay on my leg. "Be at peace, my son," she said as I hastened a practice I was well schooled in. I brought my bodily processes to a near stop. My heart slowed its beat to an imperceptible rate, my lungs stopped gripping for air, my sight faded to black, my ears stopped hearing, and my brain curtailed its persistent activity.

Suspension isn't sleep, it isn't peaceful; it's nothing. It's as close to not living as any person can be in a live body. Dead in body, the spirit springs forth alive in a different realm, but suspended there's no spring; there's no winter either. There's nothing.

"He was still alive hanging on the wooden beam all day. I just watched, sickened and grieved to my core. The crowd expected something. They must have expected something. The day wore on and nothing extraordinary happened. Most of them left, sickened in their hearts for what they'd done. They finally had too much when it was too late... and I think everyone in Jerusalem took into their hearts their own meaning of the words, 'Fear God.'"

- James brother of Yeshua -

142 · Entombed

Eleven Days of Ardor, Day Eight Begins

There's nothing.

Eleven Days of Ardor, Day Eight Continues

There's nothing.

Eleven Days of Ardor, Day Nine Begins

From the nothing, my brain began to fire. It felt prickly, like a dull, fuzzy cactus rolling over me. It flowed outward from my brain in layers and encompassed more and more of the body until my spirit was again seated in living, breathing flesh.

I was alive! I made it through the gauntlet! At first, I was overjoyed. I'd come through the worst of things. My heart had a strong pulse, but, I was bringing air into only half of my lungs; the other half wasn't functioning. My nose wasn't open, I had to breathe through my mouth, which could scarcely open.

I'd put this body through an agonizing trial. As my brain continued to awaken and its processing ability improved, functions within my body slowly roused. First was hearing. I heard the song of a night bird and I wondered how long I'd been suspended: One day? Two? Smell awakened, and my mouth filled with the scents of fine oils and herbs. The ability to feel opened next and I flinched from the sharp sting that seemed to cover every inch of my skin. My eyes tried to open, but something heavy held the lids down.

It struck me, they thought I was dead. Why wouldn't they? I hadn't prepared them to look for life in me. A cloth wrapped me, coins held my eyes closed, and a block was wedged under my chin to hold my mouth closed. Oils and herbs covered me. Like kindling catching spark in the dark of night, I realized I was entombed. I wrestled a sudden flush of fear that urged me to struggle against my restraints.

"The soldiers were frightened and didn't want to touch the body. As far as they were concerned, he should've died long before they got him to the hill. So we did. It was nearly sundown, so we wrapped him quickly in a shroud, and placed him in the crypt nearby that was owned by the family. The soldiers sealed the tomb and Pilate ordered guards, day and night, to watch the mourners, to control any riots that might happen, and to keep the body from being taken."
- James brother of Yeshua -

Luckily, I calmed quickly. Fear wasn't my friend.

First order of business; ascertain if I was in immediate danger. I took stock of my body. In my preparations, I hadn't accounted for the extra animosity of the soldiers my actions unleashed. Now that my heart was beating with regularity again, blood was once more oozing from some of the larger wounds. My skin was ripped through in well over 100 places with hundreds of smaller cuts and scratches accompanying them. Patches of skin were worn raw at the knees, shoulders, back, and bottom of the feet. Bruises covered nearly every place the skin wasn't torn. My skull was punctured, bleeding had occurred in my brain as a result. Several other puncture wounds covered the head. One eye bulb seemed ruptured. My nose was broken, and the breathing cavity blocked. Two teeth were missing, several others dislodged, and the jaw was cracked and dislocated. One bone in my neck was offset. One shoulder was dislocated to the extent some of the internal connective tissues were completely torn apart. One elbow was dislocated. My wrists were run-through, several small bones smashed, and the hands severely damaged. My chest had a large puncture wound that collapsed one lung and damaged my diaphragm. Many internal organs were bruised. Several ribs were broken as was my spine. The spinal break damaged the nerve column. One hip was cracked. Some internal organs in the lower abdomen were torn. The genitals were partially crushed and mangled. The feet had large puncture wounds that damaged bones important for standing and walking. And my blood was poisoned from internal waste, which could cause rapid infection.

Yes, I was alive, but the state of my body was shocking. I was still at risk of dying and soon. I sighed. I'd thought that if I got here, the rest would be easy, but this didn't seem easy, perhaps not even doable.

I said a prayer that I'd find my solution; that the way forward would become clear. Accompanying the prayer was great gratitude that I was even alive to need a solution. For the time being, I held onto the connection to my body and focused on breathing.

I don't know how long I lay there breathing, but a gentle hand touched my shroud so slightly that I almost didn't notice it. I grunted.

"Yeshua?" I heard Philar say, "Are you alive?"

I grunted again.

"Let me get you out of this!" he said with urgency.

I couldn't form words, so I used my mind to talk with Philar the way we could at the Temple of Man. I screamed, 'No! Don't touch me. Don't do anything.'

After a moment of silence, he said, "Why not?"

'I'm in seriously bad shape. I'm not sure what the right thing to do is.'

Another moment of silence, then he said, "We thought you were dead. You're in a tomb. You should be in a bed, being attended."

'No!' I screamed again, 'Wait!'

"Wait for what?" Philar was impatient, "Yeshua? Wait for what?"

'I don't know,'

"Let me alert someone at least," he sputtered.

'No! I need to find the right path.'

"My friend, you could die while you're looking for it," Philar said with great seriousness.

'Hold on. I haven't been awake that long.'

"If you let me unwrap the shroud," he begged, "I can at least give you some water while you think."

I hesitated. I really wasn't certain what the right course was.

"Yeshua, please?"

'Alright,' I thought, 'but be careful. My body is in serious trouble.'

Philar carefully untied the strip of cloth that held my death cocoon together and pulled back the top layer of the shroud. Unfortunately, the cloth was stuck to scabs on my skin and pulling the cloth off, even as gently as he did, caused these wounds to bleed again.

When he finally uncovered my face, he murmured, "My God, you're a mess."

I nodded my head so slightly, I'm surprised he recognized it.

He touched the block holding my chin in place. "Let me move this wood so you can talk," he said.

I screamed, 'No, don't move that. My jaw's broken.'

"Can I remove the coins so you can see?" he asked.

'No, for the time being, let's move as little as necessary.' I heard him sigh one of those deep sighs that rattles in his throat.

"Are you comfortable?" he asked.

'Are you joking?' I responded.

"I mean… I don't know what I mean." I heard him move something. "I have some water here. I'm going to give you a few drops at a time, agreed?"

I nodded one of those nearly imperceptible nods again. Moments later, the ecstasy of cool, clean water began to drip into my mouth. It was a sweet sensation I'll never forget. My tongue pulled the droplets to my throat, and after several, I was able to swallow. Pain surged from using the muscles of my neck, so I said, 'Wait, I have to do something,' and I again manipulated my brain into the blessed state of no pain. When I was ready, I said, 'More please,' and the drips continued. After several minutes of this drinking, I said, 'That helps. Thanks.'

"I'm prepared to do more if you let me."

'You have to wait,' I said, still communicating with my mind, 'let me tell you what's wrong.' I proceeded to recount my known injuries to Philar. About a quarter of the way through my report, I heard him crying. I finished the list of injuries. All I heard were his continued sobs. 'Philar?' I said.

After another moment, he replied, "Yes?"

'Do you have suggestions based on what you know now?'

The sobbing slowly stopped. "My boy, I'm certain healing will take the intervention of God." He breathed deeply. "I don't see… how… how we can bring your body back to full use. Or how we can even keep you alive. Even if we can, with rapid and sustained care, you're at risk of living with the loss of several of life's basic functions."

Those words hit me like bricks new from an oven, hard and hot. It was as I'd already concluded, but it was difficult to take them in from a voice outside my own

"The next few days were terrible. We were nearly comatose and couldn't understand why this had happened. Miriam's baby miscarried, so there was double grief in our house."

- James brother of Yeshua -

head.

'I can speed my healing, and I can ask for help from you and the Creator, but I don't know what she'll do. Her miracles are at her behest, not mine.' I stopped to contemplate the situation. 'It's the ripped internal flesh I'm most worried about. And the spinal damage.'

"Me too," Philar sighed.

'I need to talk with Creator.'

"You have to do that soon. In the morning, they'll come to redress your body."

'I see. How long is that?' I asked.

"Sunrise is about eight hours from now," he sighed, "and I have to say, every hour you delay, the likelihood of healing grows thinner."

I wrested back wanting to cry. Like fear, it wouldn't help me now.

'Philar?' I paused, waiting for a response. One didn't come, so I asked, 'Are you still there?'

"Yes, my boy," he said, "I'm here with you."

'Are you thinking what I'm thinking?'

"I hope not," he replied.

'Then you are,' I said, 'dying is a viable option.'

"If we'd realized he was alive, we wouldn't have put him in the tomb. But he truly looked and felt dead. When we had him laid out and ready for the shroud, I was shocked by the sheer number of wounds. I didn't even question whether he was alive. I couldn't imagine anyone surviving that."

- James brother of Yeshua -

143 · Before You Were Born

Eleven Days of Ardor, Day Nine Continues

Soon after dying became a viable option, the light turned on. Philar noticed it. It wasn't making changes to my body: it simply glowed.

I asked Philar to stay with me until I made a decision and he promised he would. It was a good thing, because shortly after his promise, I lost touch with my body completely and found myself free-floating in a void.

I'd been in this void before. The last time, I was in the process of ascending. It was possible that I'd just died, but it didn't feel like it.

I hung in the ethers until the scene around me melted into a familiar vision. I was standing in that vibrantly colored field where I first met my Creator face-to-face, and as I turned my head, I saw her.

"Hello Issa."

"Hello. Thank you for seeing me. Can you help me?"

"I believe I can, but that's predicated on what you ask for," she said.

"My body is seriously injured, and I need to make some decisions."

"Indeed you do," she said.

"Everything led me to believe I could live. That task I've accomplished. I'm alive. Yet, I'm still in danger of dying, and I face serious disability, that is, if someone such as you doesn't intervene and heal me further than I can do on my own."

"This is your assessment?" she asked.

"Yes, adding this," I said, "I believe I have three choices. One, I can die. Or, two, I can get on with healing, but face any subset of serious disabilities. Both of those choices seem less than optimal. Or three, I find a choice that transcends the limitations of the first two choices." I looked at her intently, "For any third choice to be viable, it must ensure that I continue to live, and I must preserve enough faculties to continue my mission."

"Is there a third choice?" she asked.

"There must be," I said, "or I wouldn't have discerned its possibility."

The Creator smiled and stepped closer to me, "There is indeed a third choice." She looked into my eyes with clarity and care. "Tell me what you can conceive, Issa. As creator in your own right, posit an experiment."

Her suggestion staggered me, and my mind nearly froze from overwhelm. I

"I was more than distraught, I was devastated – plagued with the thought that I'd done something terribly wrong, that I hadn't been able to dissuade him from this horrific plot. In a way my perception of his death was vindicating, but I didn't want to feel vindicated, I wanted to die too."

- James brother of Yeshua -

shook my head rapidly, as if to throw off any fog that may have just befallen it. "An experiment?"

"Yes, Issa, an experiment." She cocked her head slightly and smiled, "Isn't that what creators do? Assess their theories through experimentation?"

"I never thought of it that way before," I said, "specifically of me, I hadn't thought of myself as a creator."

She laughed. "You speak of it often," she chuckled.

"You're right," I admitted, "but this opens my thinking to a new layer of meaning to that thought."

"As it should," she said with a continued chuckle.

A sudden, unpleasant sensation gripped me. It felt as though my body was pulling at me. "Is my body alright?" I asked with fear.

Her face turned solemn, "Some of its functions are trying to fail. I promise I won't let your body fail while we're talking."

"Thank you," I said.

"You have more power than you know, Issa," she said, "there's no fault in this. Your life necessitated living fully as a human. Remembering your full self, your full power, would've kept you from becoming who you are now, but it's time for you to accept a larger framework. It's time for you to remember who you really are."

I tried to fathom her meaning, but I couldn't. "What do you mean, who I really am?" I asked with some trepidation.

"Try to remember a time before you were born," she said.

"Before I was born?" I just looked at her. "You mean a past life?" I was at a loss to understand her meaning. "Am I being dense?" I asked.

"No, you're being human," she replied.

I chuckled this time.

"Let me help you," she whispered as she touched my arm.

Suddenly a swirling mass of light came into my vision. Voices arose, and I realized a conversation was taking place. Several minds were meeting, discussing something that seemed preposterous to me at first; the creation of a new universe.

I listened intently, the points of greatest contention centered on the creation of life. Questions about what sort of constraints the universal laws would place on life forms. I was fascinated. As they continued, from time to time, I recognized a constraint that I lived with on earth. For example, laws that govern the creation of night and day necessitated the eventual sprouting of life in dualistic forms. It went on and on, until I realized this was either a memory from before my birth, or a representation of the thought that spawned our very universe.

Or both.

"Creator!" I shouted. "Bring me back!" I implored.

The Creator reappeared in front of me as calm as the moment before the swirling light began. I was excited; elated from the enthusiasm of discovery. "Was I part of that discussion?" I asked, "Was it a memory or a representation of a

"Several of the devotees were frightened of a backlash from the soldiers. They feared that we'd all be hunted down. I couldn't see it myself. I figured Caiaphas was behind this and he got what he wanted, Yeshua was no longer a threat to his rule. I didn't go into hiding, but many did."

- James brother of Yeshua -

thought experiment?" She beamed acceptance of all I am. "It was both, wasn't it?"

"Yes, Issa, it was both."

"Was it many beings, or just one?"

"Is there a difference?" she asked.

I chuckled, "Are you helping me comprehend that I had input into the creation of the world I'm living in right now?"

"Would it be so odd to think you are part of the very fabric of this world?" she asked me.

"No, not as I think about it, no, not odd," I said, "and as I sit with it, it's not odd to think that done once, it could be done again, in any configuration desired."

"Exactly, Issa, you're finding yourself."

"Experiments can be altered. They can be changed and added to as circumstances grow from within the experiment itself." My energy expanded as I spoke.

"Yes," she said, "and realize, not all experiments are as successful as the one you live in. Many systems are created and find their stasis in destruction. They implode, or otherwise cease to exist as the constraints fail to cohere into an organism that's sustainable."

"I see," I said, "give me a few moments to consider what I've just learned."

"Take your time," she said, "your body will wait as will the world around it."

I nodded and sat down. I closed my eyes and made ready to conceive.

144 · Incubation

Eleven Days of Ardor, Day Nine Continues

I don't know how long I pondered the situation: hours, days, weeks. Eventually I was ready to discuss my experiment. I opened my eyes to the richness of the Creator's field. "May we talk?" I asked.

From beside me, she spoke, "I'm here. What have you?"

I turned to her, "I get it."

The Creator laughed. Her joy was captivating. "What do you get, Issa?" she asked as she chuckled.

"I get that I'm about to try something that probably no one's done before."

"And what's that?"

"I'm going to live, still fully human, fully alive, and have no permanent attachment to a physical body," I said with great certainty.

"How do you propose to facilitate that?" she asked.

"I'm going to create a new human form that's not attached to the cycles of death after death, life after life. A form that isn't dependent on the physical matter of the world. A form that retains the life I currently have and utilizes the mind and heart I have patiently and painstakingly developed." I nodded, "I'll be a human built to live permanently outside the subjugation: built to live indefinitely, without any impending threat of the eventuality of death or rebirth."

"Will you be able to interact with those who are now incarnate?" she asked.

"Yes," I said.

"And will you be able to interact with those who die and reside as spirit still attached to the rebirth cycle?"

"Yes."

"That's interesting, Issa. So in a state like that, you'll not need the things that other's need to sustain their bodies. You'll not need to eat, or sleep, or drink, or breathe?"

"I imagine that would be so, yes."

"Then what do you propose as a constraint on your being to encourage you to disengage from activity and spend time in self-care?"

"Nothing except my continued desire to be of service, knowing that I can only be that if I stay balanced."

"Do you think that's wise?" she asked.

"Maybe, maybe not, but it's the experiment I posit. If you think I'm on the

"During this time, Mary didn't speak. She was stalwart as usual. She held her head high, proud, but not a word came from her."

- James brother of Yeshua -

wrong track, I'll go back to my thoughts."

"I only ask, Issa," she said, "I desire to see if you've thought it through." She put her hand on my shoulder. "I promise you this. We can pull on the creases of your experiment, so the fabric of your thoughts is taut. And, after that, if you decide you'd rather stay inside the body as it is, I'll heal all but two of your impending disabilities."

"Two?" I asked.

"Yes, two… any two you choose."

"That's easy. If I stay, I know what I choose, the loss of one eye and the loss of reproductive capacity." I looked at the grass at my feet. "If I stay in the body, I'll need to have vigor and vitality. All the internal organs must heal, including the bones. I'll need the ability to write, and walk and talk, and eat and drink… if I do it this way, my wife won't be happy, but it seems an easy choice given the circumstances."

"Then we are agreed, either we manifest your new experiment, after we've hashed out the details, or I put you back into a body that is healed, retaining two disabilities."

I took a deep breath and felt the life-force surge through me more fully than it had since this ordeal began. "Yes, we are agreed." I felt good about it, all of it. In fact, I was riding so high emotionally, that I only saw the joy of discovery and creation. Perhaps that made me partially blind to the side effects of my choice, but it did open the space for the conception of great things.

We tossed ideas back and forth, pulling on the creases of my experiment as the Creator so eloquently dubbed it, and after a time, I was ready to choose.

"So which will it be, Issa?" she asked.

"The new form," I stated with certainty and pride in the process of development we'd just been through.

"You have no reservations?" she asked.

Her question prompted a shiver of doubt to flutter up through my spine. My choice would mean tremendous change in my relationships, my wife and son at the forefront. "I have sudden doubts, yes," I muttered.

"You'd not be the kind and compassionate being I know you to be if you didn't." She looked at me lovingly. "Take a moment and consider these doubts if you must." So I did, but the Creator interrupted, "Perhaps I should give you an update on some events that've happened since you last saw your loved ones."

This grabbed my attention and I nodded in agreement.

"Your wife has been adversely affected, as you might assume, she lost your

"Micah was a handful. I'm sure he didn't understand what death meant, but he cried a lot. Every few hours he'd climb into my lap and have me hold him. As his elder uncle, it was up to me to be as his father. It was not a role I was ready to embrace."

- James brother of Yeshua -

baby."

I hung my head. It was an outcome I expected, but I'd wished with all my heart wouldn't be. Now, knowing that whichever choice I picked I'd already decided there'd be no opportunity for another pregnancy, a guilty pang ripped through my heart. It pounded in me and caused tears to flow. "I'm sorry at that," I murmured.

"There's another event that you may find more difficult, Issa."

I looked at her through my tears, "How can that be?"

She placed her hand on my chest. "It's your companion, Judas."

I knew before she said, and my consciousness flashed to repel the words before they came. "No! No!" I said as my head shook violently back and forth. I turned my face from her and tried to step away from her hand, but I couldn't.

"Issa, he's gone."

"No!" I screamed as I fell to the grass. "How? Why?" I pleaded.

She bent down to the ground with me. "He couldn't live with himself believing your mission had failed."

"How?" I pleaded.

"He used a knife to bleed out," she said, "he's at peace now."

My gut wrenched from the news. "He didn't have to do that!" I screamed.

"He knows that now, Issa." Her eyes pulled at me until mine again locked in hers. "And he's at peace with his choices," she added.

I felt dispirited. The exalted high of a few moments before was lost in a mound of guilt and shame. I asked myself, 'Who was I that I felt free to make choices that would so adversely affect people I loved?'

"Issa, who are you? You continue with this question? Isn't it clear yet?"

"Yes, I think it's clear," I cried, "But doesn't that put even more onus on me to make right choices?"

"Onus?" She pulled back from me a bit, "Is that how you see this? As pressure? As joyless?"

"How else can I see it when I hear Judas killed himself as a result of my action?" I yelled.

"He didn't kill himself because of you," she said, "he killed himself because of his inability to see clearly."

"Isn't that splitting hairs?" I cried. "It was still my action that helped his vision cloud."

In that moment, my own vision clouded, and I no longer saw the Creator. I began to sob. The tears were for Judas, and Miriam. They were for the baby that didn't get a chance to birth. They were for my body lying in a tomb failing to thrive. They were for James, and Mary, and everyone else who participated in the fever that was my crucifixion. These tears were for all that had gone before and all that would come. They were cleansing and forgiving and felt without end.

My tears were for everyone, everywhere, without judgment, with cause or without, and they cleared the chafe from my eyes.

"I don't remember seeing Judas at all after the incident in the garden, but I'm sure he was there. He wouldn't hide from the horror, he was used to violence. But this was Yeshua being violated and I knew he was devoted to him. It had to be devastating."

- James brother of Yeshua -

145 · Birth

Eleven Days of Ardor, Day Nine Continues

Suddenly, I woke as if from sleep. My eyes had to readjust to the bright ambient light of the Creator's field. I stretched my arms over my head and looked around. The last I remembered were tears that felt unending, yet here I was and there were no more tears.

I stood and decided to walk. I didn't have a body with muscles to stretch and energy to work out, but walking was pleasant. I realized that if I took the new form, this is more like how I might feel all the time; walking might be pleasant, but not for the same reasons I'd known to date. I even mused at why my 'eyes' had to adjust to the light when I woke, as I had no physical eyes here.

I didn't have an answer to that question either, but it made me think about life without my body. My body had been a good friend. When I gave it what it needed to thrive, it supported me in everything. When I mistreated it, it readily forgave me and responded when I changed my ways. It was such a magnificent and essential part of me. I realized I'd be giving up something I held dear.

Instantly, the Creator appeared and said, "Issa, I wanted you to have some time to think about your decision at a visceral level."

I looked at her. "I think I do understand now, better than I did when I was high on the energy of creation. I'm giving up a lot to follow this new path."

"Indeed you are," she said as she stood shoulder to shoulder with me, looking out over the brightly colored field in the same direction I was looking. Never had she stood with me like this before. "I'm looking at the horizon with you. It's a bright day dawning as we begin." She took my hand, "Are you resolute in your decision?"

"Yes, I am," I said without reservation and as soon as I did, we were standing in the tomb with Philar and my body. I felt Philar's grief and wanted to cradle him in my arms and give him peace.

"You'll have the opportunity to speak with him before we begin, but first, let me tell you how I see this going..." The Creator went on to explain the process we'd go through to create this new pocket of reality adjacent to the one I'd lived in

"There was significant anger in our community at Judas, but I couldn't reconcile what I knew of him versus his actions. I remembered the night the week before when Yeshua and Judas spent the entire evening secluded from the group. Judas wasn't the same after that night. I couldn't help thinking that Yeshua asked Judas to do what he did. Nothing else made sense. And if Yeshua did ask Judas to reveal him to the soldiers, it was a good move trusting Judas to do so. None of the rest of us would have done it."

- James brother of Yeshua -

to date: a new pocket that would be my home for, well, longer than I could imagine living. Neither death nor fear would reside with me, and I'd have all I need to complete my mission. As I listened to the Creator tell me about her plan, I was again overcome with the joy of discovery. It was exhilarating. I was also fascinated by the plan for implementation; it was brilliant and ordinary at the same time.

"Are you ready?" she asked.

I simply said, "Yes," and immediately shifted back into my body. I gasped, and I felt Philar respond by coming closer. 'I have a few minutes with you to explain,' I said, 'remove the block from under my chin.' I felt the block pull away and was astonished to be able to move my jaw. The Creator was good enough to give me this few minutes unhampered by injury. "Perfect, thank you," I said aloud.

"I thought your jaw was broken!" Philar exclaimed.

"It was," I said, "I have a few minutes of grace with you, my dear friend." I went on to explain what would happen next. He was as fascinated as I'd been.

After some discussion, he asked a question I couldn't answer, "What can I do to support you?"

"I don't know. This is new territory. No one's ever attempted what I'm about to attempt. Can I answer that question later?" I asked.

"Of course, of course." He placed his hand next to my arm, "I'm scared, Yeshua."

I had to admit that I had some anxiety about the process too, but I didn't want to add to his, so I said, "The Creator is overseeing everything. It'll be all right. Whatever the outcome, I'll be fine."

Philar sighed.

"Now, you have to leave," I said, "you can't be here when I make the shift. From what I gather, every cell in my body will collapse. The energy released might be harmful, I don't know."

Philar hesitated, and then whispered, "I love you."

"I love you too, more than you know. Now pull the cloth back over me and go." I waited a few moments extra to make sure he was gone, then started the process.

Energy amassed and light filled the room as I began my birth into a new reality, one where death would never again haunt me.

146 · I'm Alive

Eleven Days of Ardor, Day Nine Continues

A short time later, I stood looking down at the shroud that had covered my body during the creation process. The birth was successful.

I no longer had a body like I had before. I felt as unsure in this new form as a newborn calf trying to stand on legs that had never borne weight. I could see me, I could touch me, and yet I had no physical mass. I had no weight, no muscles, and no mass. Yet I looked the same as before the change. The only exception was that now I looked healed, but with telltale scars where my skin took damage before the change. Later, I'd learn that they weren't real scars; they were visual representations of lingering trauma.

In that moment, I felt no pain, no fear, and no restraint. Oddly, I still breathed, not that I took in air, but the lungs still opened and closed. And I could 'feel' my heart beat as if it was pumping blood, but there was no blood to pump. I had no idea why these things were so, nor if they'd continue. I simply observed that they were so.

"Creator!" I shouted, "Are you here?" I waited for a reply but got none. "Creator?" Again, I waited, hoping to talk to her; to hear her perspective on how things went, but she didn't answer.

After a time, I decided to see what life was like outside the tomb. The first problem was that I had no clothes. I'd been enshrouded per tradition, naked. I couldn't proceed into the public like this. I reasoned that, because I created the constraints of this new reality, I should be able to create robes for myself by applying proper thought. It took me several attempts, but upon one such attempt, robes appeared. Appropriately, they were rabbinic robes. I was now ready to greet people.

I went to the entrance where a large rock had been rolled, sealing off the opening. I had no precedent to rely on. I didn't completely know how my new form would interact with the physical world, so I tried to move the stone. Pushing on it had no effect. I tried to use my mind to make it roll and still nothing happened. I thought about how I posited the new realm and decided to try to walk through the rock.

Success! The illusion of the physical world was even more apparent and malleable to me now than it had been before. Wonderful.

I stood in front of one of the guards posted at the tomb and said, "Hello," but no response. I tried several ways to rouse his attention with no success. I realized the sun was beginning to rise. Soon, people I knew would be coming to the tomb. I imagined that perhaps they'd be more receptive to me.

A few hours passed. I was happy to note that I did have the ability to perceive time as it existed for others. I'd been playing around, trying to gain a better understanding of just what life was going to be like from here on out, but I stayed near the tomb, in hope of interacting with whoever came to redress the body. Suddenly, I heard my wife's voice coming down the path. Accompanying her were my mother, Peter's wife, and Carole. I was surprised to see Peter's wife, I didn't realize she'd come for the holiday. They were carrying baskets of supplies.

They walked right past me, unaware of my presence, and Miriam asked the guards to roll away the stone, so they could perform their ritual. After a bit of discussion, the guards hefted the stone to the side and the women entered the tomb.

I heard Miriam scream and all the women hurried out, shocked and shaken. The guards asked about the matter, and upon hearing that the body was gone, they rushed in. They staggered back out of the cave, faces white from shock.

Carole fell to her knees, "He's gone! It's prophecy fulfilled!" she shouted.

Miriam and Mary looked at her and each other. Mary put her arm around Miriam and pulled her into her side. "We'll figure this out," she said to Miriam.

Peter's wife turned to the guards. "What've you done with his body?" she shouted. The guards just looked at her, clearly confused.

"Wait," Mary said, "let's think about this." She motioned for the women to move some feet from the guards. Tears streamed down her cheeks as she put her arms around them and pulled them close. "Something has happened that we can't understand by shouting at the guards or falling prostrate." She looked at Peter's wife, "Surely my Son wouldn't want us to call unwanted attention by causing a riot."

"Surely no, Mary," Miriam added, "he'd caution us to seek help from a friend."

"Yes, let's get Joseph," Mary said as she lovingly straightened Carole's neckline. "Carole, you go back to the house and tell James what's happened. Miriam, I suggest you stay near and watch the activity." She looked at Peter's wife. "Let's you and I go find Joseph."

All nodded and went about their assignments. Miriam lingered as was suggested, sitting on a short bluff, near the path. I was sure Mary made that suggestion so Miriam wouldn't be burdened by activity. After all, she'd recently miscarried on top of her grief. When Miriam thought she was alone her face turned red and she began sobbing.

I sat next to her and tried to comfort her, but she didn't feel or see my attentions. One of the guards rushed down the path. Miriam startled him, but he recovered quickly and continued his rush. He was undoubtedly on his way to alert the authorities to the disappearance of my body.

I yearned to make myself known to my beloved. I sat on the bluff with her and diligently cleared my mind. This state I was now in was my new home. It's where I planned to be for a long time. I needed to understand how to use it.

"When I heard that Judas had committed suicide, I was anguished. Whatever the truth was of what happened, I loved him like a brother. We weren't as close as he and Yeshua were, but he was dear to me, deeply dear to me. I never wished him to pay for this with his life. I never wished anyone to pay for this. Nothing in this world could possibly make up for my brother being gone."

- James brother of Yeshua -

I was alive. I knew it. I felt it. My life-force was palpable. I stood and began a series of experiments, this way and that, to be able to interact with Miriam. The question of 'how' loomed in my mind. 'How,' I asked over and over, and I didn't give up.

Perhaps a half hour went by of trial and error when suddenly one try succeeded. I said, "Please don't grieve," and a startled Miriam jumped to her feet. I stood several feet behind her as she whirled around to face me. Her hand flew to cover her mouth as she let out a stifled shriek.

"Miriam," I said, "I live. I'm alive."

"No, you're dead!" she cried.

"No, I'm alive. I survived. I wasn't dead when you put me in the tomb," I said with surety.

"No, no!" she shrieked as she stepped backward.

"Miriam, I love you so much. I'm so sorry for the baby."

"Goddess!" she shouted, "What is this? Help me understand!"

I reached toward Miriam, "Please, I love you."

Miriam dropped her basket on the ground and ran toward the city. I stood on the bluff wondering what I looked like to her and, more importantly to my heart, would she ever be able to accept me again.

"Miriam, Mary, Peter's wife, and one of the other women went together to the tomb to do what was supposed to be done with the body by religious custom. When they got there, just like everybody says, there wasn't a body. Miriam heard Yeshua's voice say, 'I live! Don't mourn me!' She thought she'd gone crazy. She came running back to the house in hysterics."

- James brother of Yeshua -

147 · Recognized

Eleven Days of Ardor, Day Nine Continues

Many people came to the tomb and witnessed the mystery of my lost body. Romans, priests, devotees, family… no one had a satisfactory explanation.

I continued to work on making my presence known to people and I succeeded in having conversations with many. I visited John son of Zebedee and asked him to assemble the devotees together for supper the next evening. I wanted to take some time to work on my skills before I began whatever work I was continuing with my community.

I went to Pilate. I made it clear that, as foretold, he hadn't been able to douse my light with his machinations. He was impressed in the extreme; so much so, that he prostrated himself in my presence. He was a changed man; of that I'm sure.

I visited Miriam, one more time, and her anger toward me was clear. That visit was brief as a result. I found James, too. His grief was deep, and he had trouble believing I wasn't a hallucination, however, when he finally got over his own judgment, he saw me, more clearly than anyone had yet.

"My God, Bit, you're alive," he stammered.

"Yes, I am," I said, "our work is just beginning, Brother."

"I spent the last few days feeling like I failed you." He said, "I didn't believe you when you said you'd live." He looked into my eyes, "I didn't believe you, Yeshua."

"I know, it's understandable."

"How could I have gotten caught in that illusion?" he pleaded, "Why didn't I have faith?"

"Because you're human," I said as I put my hand on his arm, "just transmute that energy now. See the real. We have so much work to do and I need you to stand strong. You have to lead now. I can't from where I am."

"You… no, you have to lead."

"No," I said, "I can't. This family and this cause needs a flesh and blood leader. You have to step up. I'll help you, I'll support you, but it's up to you now to take the helm."

"It was that same morning, about the same time Miriam heard Yeshua's voice, John was at the garden praying and Yeshua appeared to him and told him that he'd been gone for a few days, but that now he was back. Yeshua also told John that we were all to gather again for supper. Yeshua visited Pilate that morning. He told him not to worry, that he'd played his part well, and that he received grace. Unfortunately, Judas had been all alone and was dead from suicide before Yeshua returned. It would be days before Yeshua revealed that indeed Judas wasn't a traitor at all."

- James brother of Yeshua -

"Bit, I'm not ready."

"Yes. You are," I nodded my head, "I have great faith in you." I pulled him into my arms for a hug and was ecstatic that I could perform such a 'physical' act as a hug. "Look after Miriam and Micah for me, please?" I asked, "She's too angry right now to talk with me."

"I will Bit, I promise."

I left him and sought out a group of devotees who were in hiding, fearing further repercussions from soldiers. I interrupted them talking about the ravings of Miriam and John at seeing my apparition. I assured them I wasn't an apparition. They finally began to understand that I wasn't dead; that I was indeed alive.

Eleven Days of Ardor, Day Ten Begins

As each hour passed, I better understood my new state. I had conversations with more people. I walked through the streets of Jerusalem and shared a cup of wine with a stranger at a tavern.

The Creator finally came, and we had a long discussion of how to proceed. Much still had to be done to nourish and grow the budding state I was in. When she left, I sat on a hillside and fell asleep. I didn't need to sleep, but it was habit and felt comforting.

Eleven Days of Ardor, Day Ten Continues

After I woke, I walked and, in many places, people recognized me. I heard murmurs that I was alive as I'd prophesized, and I felt the spark of hope resounding.

Eleven Days of Ardor, Day Eleven

We gathered for supper, the devotees, my family, and me. We ate, we drank, we talked. It was a glorious celebration of my promised return, and a solemn beginning of a long journey. Most of these devotees were woefully unprepared to take up the mantle of teacher. While I was in body, they saw little reason to prepare for personal mastery.

Now, however, they began to grasp that in order to continue, they had to step up. They had to stop playing at mastery and transform.

They all pledged, but only time would tell which, if any, would succeed. I promised myself to them when this whole business started. Now I promised them again, that I'd be near them, with them, supporting them, loving them. And, if they wanted to ascend, I'd show them the path and give them the means.

"He stayed with us for a number of days, though not sleeping, he ate with us rarely. I don't think it was necessary for him to eat, but he did so as companionship, as usual. He gave us all paths, duties – force fed us some of the lessons we'd ignored, not understanding their true importance, and held our hands until we weren't babies anymore."

- James brother of Yeshua -

Just the
Beginning

148 · Aftermath

I kept my promise. The devotees who attended that celebratory supper spent the balance of their lives changing the course of history. I stayed with them while they learned, and they learned quickly.

By the time my family and friends ended their individual incarnations, I'd settled into my new extra-dimensional home. None of them joined me in the new realm. Many died a violent death, and most of them ascended in spirit when they finally left their bodies behind.

James became head of the family and climbed the ranks in Jerusalem to become one of the most respected and powerful men of his time. He garnered the honorable nickname 'James the Just.' Forces worked against him however; late in his life, he was murdered on the steps of the Temple by an angry mob.

Miriam left Judea to continue her signature work elsewhere. Philar was generous enough to give her another pregnancy, a child created from genetic material he took from me during the time of the surrogacy program. This child was born after she left Judea and was raised in her religion. She named him Philippe, in honor of Philar's kindness. Philippe was a great comfort to her.

It is probable that Philar acted independently and created many more pregnancies from my genetic material, in women scattered around the globe. It was something I sensed, but he wouldn't confirm.

Jude and Rebekkah moved the family business to Jerusalem and my son was adopted into hiding as their son. It was clear that Micah would never be safe if it were known I was his father, so he was raised as a natural born Jew and heir in line to head the David family through Jude. Unfortunately, Micah never got the opportunity to fill that chair. Soon after James was murdered, the Hebrew population was decimated and scattered by a revolt and subsequent war with Rome. As I foresaw, my people tried to throw off the Roman boot, and the effort wasn't nearly enough to overcome the greatest military force of the time.

Mary moved north with Carole and her daughter Rose. Like Miriam, Mary's life was in perpetual danger while she stayed in Jerusalem. Miriam gave Carole the 'Stones of Circ'a'sia.' They were Miriam's calling card and identified Carole as Miriam in any land. This deception gave Miriam the time and ability to find a new home far away. Carole lived the rest of her life caring for Mary until they each

"Even though he was back, it continued to be very hard for Miriam, for me, and some of the others in the family. We'd lost more than just a Teacher. We'd also lost the man. When he came back as a Teacher, they got back what they lost. We didn't. Little Micah didn't even get that much back. Nothing was the same for us. But, if I think about it, nothing really was the same ever again, for anyone. Yeshua instigated revolution, a spiritual revolution, and we're still in that revolution today."

- James brother of Yeshua -

ascended.

The other children that carried my genetic code traveled far from Judea, their parents taking the teachings with them. The interesting point to glean from the existence of these children is that they scattered, and they produced large families in disparate parts of the world. The reason Philar wanted so many children to carry my genetic code was so that one day, as in the twenty-first century, the genetic code I nurtured through simply living my life, would be innocently distributed through generation after generation of descendants.

Nearly all people living on the planet at this time, carry a partial string of my genetic code in their DNA. There's a strong chance that you, reading this book right now, are one of those people. So, when I say I'm with you, in you, I mean it literally. I'm in your life, I'm ready to join with your heart, and I'm literally in your genetic structure.

You carry enough of my DNA to support a change in you that can, if activated, speed your growth toward higher consciousness. If enough people hear this call and activate this genetic code, you can collectively speed all of humanity past the spiritual subjugation to which humans still seem tied.

Given that you're reading this book, there's a strong chance you already feel a call to step up your vibration and become more conscious. Part of that call is the desire of the DNA to activate. Anything I did in my lifetime, you can do. Anything I learned, you can learn. Anything I've worked for, you can realize. It has everything to do with intention, and everything to do with choice.

The blueprint for becoming the next level of human is already inside you. You merely need to answer the call with intention and turn it on.

"That was a time of sorrow, but it was also a time of great joy, because in the years that followed, we came to understand that the totality of our path was right. That what we were doing was right. We were right about who he was. We were right about what he was doing. We were right about where it was taking us. The Great Teacher, the Son of Man, well, I'm honored to be a part of his plan."

- James brother of Yeshua -

149 · I am Waiting

I am alive. I haven't died. I remain in this state to facilitate my mission. I intended then, as I still do, to be the best helpmate to humanity I can be; to use all the tools, knowledge, connections, and wisdom I own to bring about a change in the direction and expression of consciousness. To end the subjugation of spirit that keeps humanity locked in fear and pain.

Once my promise to support my loved ones was made moot by their passing, I was filled with the excitement of my continued mission. I had the freedom to design my way forward with fewer physical constraints, but with new and differing constraints, that only time would help me understand. I decided that to meet my intention with integrity required more study.

So, the first thing I did was to see the world, the whole world. I wanted to know at a deep level the entirety of this Earth's inhabitants and understand their various homes and cultures.

I literally walked the planet. I touched the soil of every land, every continent, and spent time living and working with every ethnic group and tribe. This took me approximately 500 years to accomplish and I was mesmerized by the diversity of peoples and places. Also, and probably more so, I was astounded by the sameness of people. The same hearts beat in my homeland as beat in the deserts of Australia. The same emotions exist in France as exist in the highlands of China. Humans, regardless of physical characteristics, are born of the same flesh, with the same capacities and similar sensibilities.

Society and its institutions and mores are the influences that put the final touches of disparity upon humans. When we are born, however, we are all equal in grandeur of spirit, glory of divinity, and force of will.

I found that I love humanity, in its combined glory and in its individual expressions.

Generosity, kindness, forgiveness, and love permeate the human condition. For every lie, there are 100 gifts; for every act of cruelty, there are 100 acts of kindness; for every transgression, there are 100 hands reaching to heal; and for every tear shed, there are 100 hearts beating in the synchronicity of friendship and kinship.

I didn't begin my existence as a human, no more than any of us did. We began as divine sparks, flames that jumped from a fire of divine creation to burn as light enmeshed in an individual life form. When we incarnate as humans, we receive the gifts all humans receive: a sophisticated brain, capable of infinite wisdom and compassion, and a heart so well developed and encoded that we are directly responsible for the formation of the world that encases us.

I love this human heart as I love every life form that owns one.

Be part of this glorious movement. Join with me. Reach out and accept the hand of friendship I offer. As I told you in the beginning, I'm fully alive, right here, right now, lovingly wrapped around your life. I'm ready to show you the path to a fundamental wholeness born of knowing that you are loved beyond measure.

As I promised, I'll never ask you to change, merely to embrace. Intention is the seed that brings all things to you.

I am waiting.

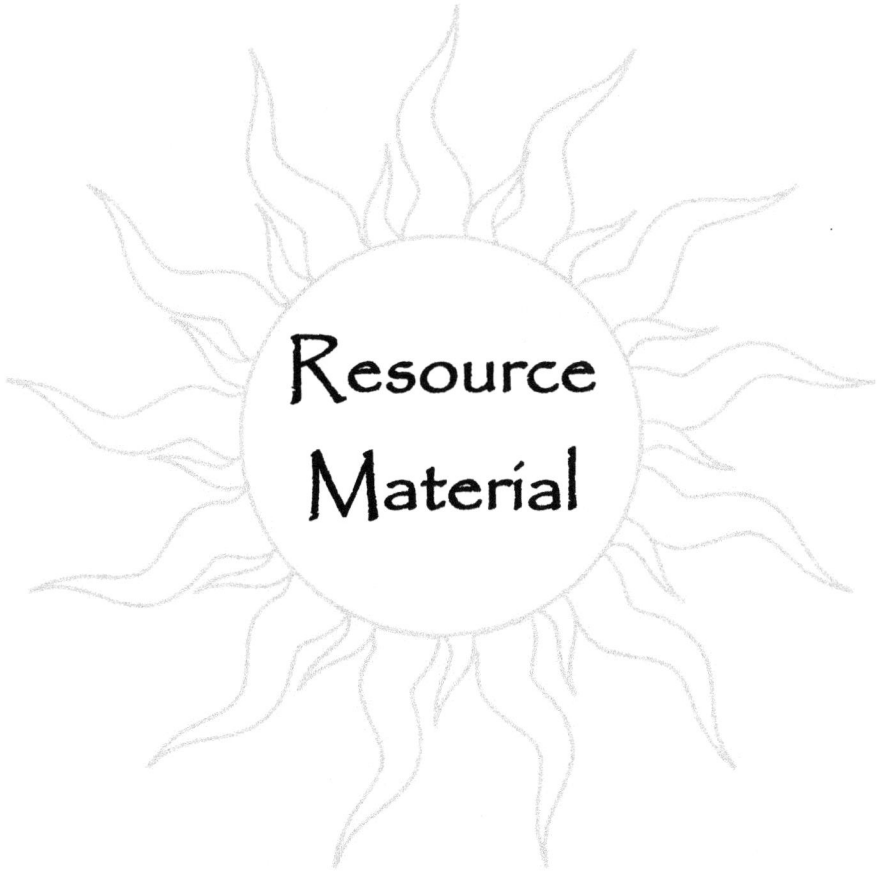

Resource
Material

Yeshua's Family Tree

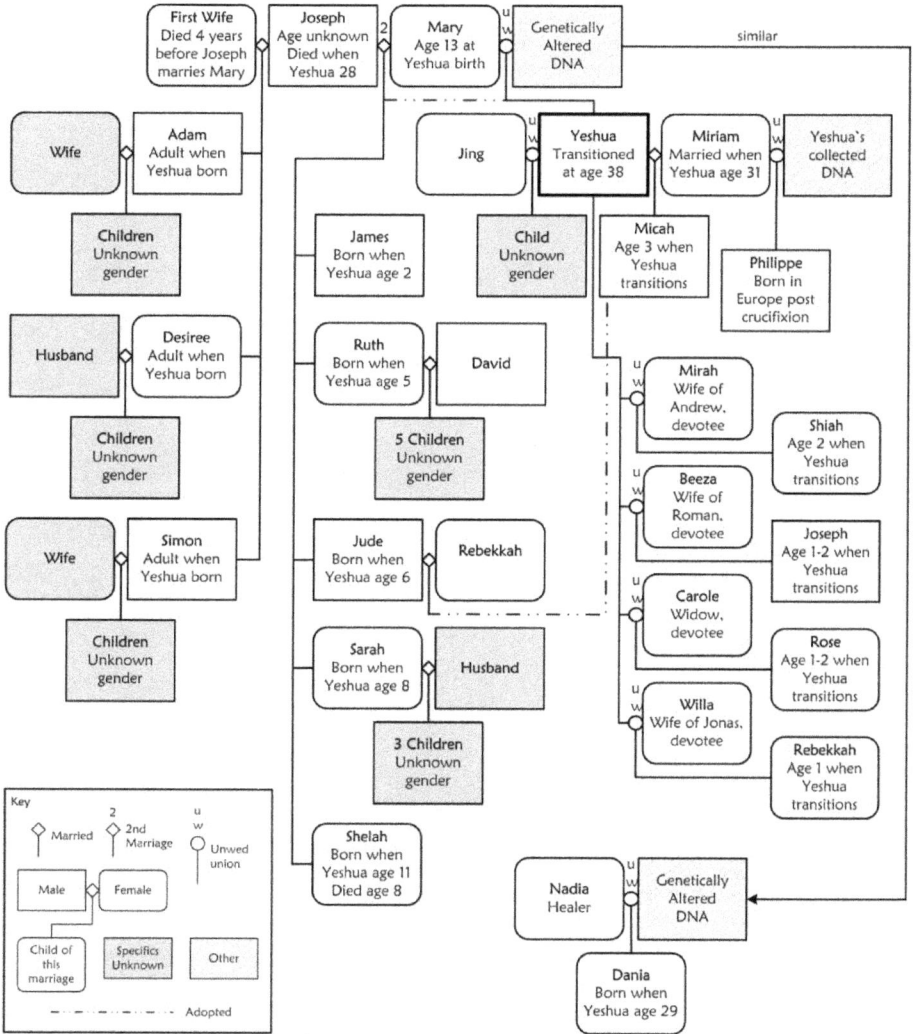

Figure 7: Yeshua's immediate family tree

Who's Who

Adam, son of Joseph, half-brother of Yeshua:
> The firstborn son of Joseph from his first marriage. Adam was a married man before Yeshua was born. He lived with his family in Jerusalem.

Andrew, brother of Peter and husband of Mirah:
> From Capernaum like his brother Peter, he followed Yeshua as devotee. He was married to Mirah, one of the seven women who volunteered to give birth to a child of Yeshua. Their child's name was Shiah.

Ann, wife of Philip:
> A devotee of Yeshua and married to Philip. She was one of the seven women who volunteered to give birth to a child of Yeshua; however, she didn't bring the child to term.

Anna, common law wife of John the Baptist:
> A native of Axum, called Ethiopia now. She was the common-law wife of John the Baptist and was pregnant with his child at the time of his beheading. The child was born shortly after John's assassination and Anna named the child John after his father.

Anna, wife of Matthew:
> A devotee of Yeshua and married to Matthew. Anna was one of the seven women who volunteered to give birth to a child of Yeshua; however, she changed her mind prior to engaging.

Anne, mother of Mary:
> Mary's mother and grandmother of Yeshua.

Azrael, husband of Sarah and devotee of Yeshua:
> Married to Sarah. Both were devotees of Yeshua and Miriam. Sarah was particularly close to Miriam. It was discovered, however, that Azrael was abusing Sarah and in an act of desperation, Sarah killed Azrael. The event exposed the entire community to danger.

Bartholomew, devotee of Yeshua:
> A devotee of Yeshua and follower of John the Baptist before Yeshua. Bartholomew helped save Miriam from the soldiers during the procession on the morning of the crucifixion.

Beeza, wife of Roman and mother of Yeshua's child:
> Married to Roman, she and her husband were devotees of Yeshua. Beeza was one of the seven women that volunteered to give birth to a child of Yeshua. Their son's name was Joseph.

Bon Master, master of the Bon Adept Training Temple:
> The Bon Master of the Martial Temple, just called Master by Yeshua. Both Yeshua and the Bon Master were students of Man'wa at the Temple of Man.

Caiaphas, Head Priest of the Temple at Jerusalem:

Head Priest at the Temple at Jerusalem and in charge of the Sanhedrin. He was against Yeshua and was instrumental in delivering him to Pilate for execution.

Carole, mother of Yeshua's child:

A widow and devotee of Yeshua. Carole is one of the seven women who volunteered to give birth to a child of Yeshua. Their daughter's name was Rose. Carole and her daughter settled away from Judea with Yeshua's mother Mary after the crucifixion, posing as Miriam to throw enemies off Miriam's true destination.

Colum:

A member of the 'Other' who helped Yeshua and his party after the flood while on their way to Kapilavastu.

Creator, The:

The personification of the living God that Yeshua met and worked with in formulating, and carrying out, his mission.

Dania:

The child of Nadia the healer. The pregnancy was made possible by Philar.

Danielle:

Cut from the surrogacy program, Danielle left the community in anger. She reappeared one day while Yeshua was on a campaign in Judah and made some difficulty for him with a crowd.

David, husband of Ruth:

Married to Ruth, sister of Yeshua. They resided in Caesarea.

Desiree, daughter of Joseph, half-sister of Yeshua:

The daughter of Joseph, the adopted father of Yeshua, from his first marriage. Yeshua never met her as she was married to a Greek citizen and moved to Cyprus, before Yeshua was born.

Gautama Buddha, The Great Master:

The Buddha revered by many people today.

Great Teacher, The, (Original):

The Great Teacher was the inspiration for the initial Vedic texts while walking on this earth 35,000 years before Yeshua. It was prophesized that he would return and be born in the land of the 'Nazorean.' To keep his teachings alive, he built a place called the Temple of Man.

Great Teacher, The, (Returned):

Through prophecy, it was believed that Yeshua was the returned incarnation of the original Great Teacher.

Goddess, The:

A form of the living god-force, worshipped in many pagan religions, Miriam was her servant as High Priestess of the Galilean pagan temple.

Hanan:

Head Priest of the Temple in Jerusalem before Caiaphas. He still held great power in the city. He resided over the condemnation of Yeshua through his puppet, Caiaphas.

Hassim, companion of Yeshua:

An elder, widower from the Essene community of Yeshua's birth. Hassim volunteered to travel with Yeshua as one of his companions and caretakers. Hassim traveled back to Judea when his daughter's husband died, leaving Yeshua without any immediate friends tied to his homeland.

Herod Antipas, Hebrew King of Galilee:
> King and de facto Roman puppet in Galilee during most of Yeshua's life. Yeshua's birth family, David, was effectively deposed approximately a century prior to Yeshua's birth. Yet, most of the Jewish sects still considered the David family the true and rightful royal family. When the Sanhedrin priests brought Yeshua to Herod Antipas for an order of execution, he refused to issue the order. However, he was the king who ordered the assassination of John the Baptist.

Herodes, foreman of the farming operations:
> Recruited by Joseph to run the farming operations at the family compound before Yeshua was born, he was still the foreman of the farms while Yeshua served as head of the family.

Hiram, Head Priest of Carmel:
> The Head-Priest of the monastery on Mount Carmel when Joseph was a monk there. Hiram inducted Joseph into the brotherhood and was instrumental in shielding Mary, preparing her to be Yeshua's mother.

Huume, Combs Master:
> The School Master in Kapilavastu who oversaw the education of Yeshua during his first years in the East. Huume became a father figure to Yeshua after Hassim left.

Issa:
> This is the name Yeshua used in his travels in the East.

Jacob, member of the Yeshua's community:
> A member of the family's community and the victim of the first murder Yeshua ever witnessed. Yeshua was only five years old when it happened.

Jacob, Essene Elder from Sepphoris:
> Hebrew magistrate reporting to the Roman Praetor in Sepphoris. As a powerful member of the Essene Elder Council, he was instrumental in helping Joseph get started in his life with Mary. Later he helped guide Yeshua.

James son of Zebedee, devotee of Yeshua:
> James was the son of Zebedee and brother of John. He and his brother became Yeshua's first devotees, having first been followers of John the Baptist.

James, brother of Yeshua:
> James was also known as James the Just, James Son of Man, and James the brother of the Messiah. James was a rabbi and monk from Qumran (City of Salt monastery) on the Dead Sea. James never married and kept his monk status his entire life. He walked with Yeshua as his mission partner and closest confidant throughout his work in Judea.
>
> James was nickname d 'Old Camel Knees' as a young monk during his life at Qumran based on the scarred and swollen condition of his knees. He had a habit of piously walking to prayer on his knees; the path of sharp rock left his knees cut and bloody.
>
> James was the leader of the Yeshua movement after Yeshua's transition and he relocated the family to Jerusalem. He vowed to take Yeshua's radical teachings back into the Temple where he encountered

resistance. James was an excellent negotiator, however, and was revered for his sense of fairness and wisdom.

It's reported that Saul of Tarsus (later named Paul) threw James down a set of stairs during a public forum and broke James' legs, further adding to James difficulty walking. Because of this difficulty, James walked with the use of a special cane.

James died by stoning on the steps of the Temple just prior to the outbreak of the Jewish War. Afterward, James' cane was said to be secreted by his followers and turned into a venerated object. Lost to antiquity, however, the object is now a subject of legend.

Jeremiah, ally to Essene Elders:

Worked for Jacob on the Essene Elder Council. He was the first person to introduce Joseph to the existence of Philar.

Jimon, wearied Adept:

The wearied adept who invited Yeshua to join his Brotherhood. Yeshua lived with these brothers for a little over a year before being called back to Judea.

Jing, mother of a child of Yeshua:

While in the East, after an unfortunate experience, Jing became pregnant with Yeshua's child. He left for Judea before the child was born.

Jo, scientist at the Temple of Man:

A scientist trained in transporting people to and from the Temple of Man. He became a good friend of Yeshua during his stay there.

John son of Zebedee, devotee of Yeshua:

The son of Zebedee and brother of James. He and his brother became Yeshua's first devotees, having first been followers of John the Baptist.

John, son of John the Baptist:

The child of John the Baptist and Anna, named after his father.

John the Baptist:

A cousin of Yeshua, he was a radical itinerant-priest known for his austere manner, assertive attitude, and willingness to help people return to the true God through public baptism. He's known as a prophet. Yeshua was publicly baptized by John in the river Jordan. It's at that baptism that Yeshua, among other gifts, acquired his first devotees and began to walk his mission with fervor. John was executed by Herod Antipas.

Jonas, husband of Willa:

A cousin of Yeshua on Mary's side. He was married to Willa, one of the seven women willing to give birth to a child of Yeshua. The daughter of Yeshua and Willa was named Rebekkah.

Josea, assistant to Mary and wife of Herodes:

The cook, housekeeper, assistant, and confident to Mary. She came to the position along with her husband Herodes, before the birth of Yeshua.

Joseph, adopted father of Yeshua:

Joseph was married in his youth to a woman he adored. They had three children, Adam, Desiree, and Simon. Soon after their children were grown and married, Joseph's wife contracted a lung disease, most probably tuberculosis, and died. Joseph, in his grief, became a monk at the monastery at Mount Carmel in Galilee where he subsequently met Mary.

He had no intention of remarrying, until he was visited by an

Angel who asked him to marry a young pregnant Mary. But Joseph had a difficult time accepting the story until a visit by Philar.

Joseph became husband to Mary and adopted father to Yeshua. He and Mary had five other children together after Yeshua's birth: James, Ruth, Jude, Sarah, and Shelah.

Joseph said goodbye to Yeshua at the docks in Aqaba when Yeshua was 14. Joseph died when Yeshua was 28, before Yeshua returned home.

Joseph son of Matthias from Jerusalem:

Also known as Joseph of Arimathea, he was a member of the Sanhedrin and cousin to Yeshua on Joseph's side. He was often referred to as Yeshua's uncle out of respect for his advanced age. He was a keen, yet understated, often hidden, supporter of Yeshua. Joseph was well known as a prosperous merchant and had strong ties to Rome and northern Europe.

Joseph, son of Yeshua:

The son of Yeshua born of Beeza, wife of Roman. Roman and Beeza raised him as their own son.

Judas son of Simon, devotee of Yeshua:

A beloved devotee and friend of Yeshua. A radical Zealot, Yeshua considered Judas to have one of the fiercest and most loyal hearts of all in his circle. Judas was intelligent and well trained as a fighter. He was in charge of security for the community and ran a network of allies and spies for Yeshua. Yeshua asked Judas to turn him over to Caiaphas in furtherance of Yeshua's own plans. After the crucifixion, Judas couldn't make peace with his action and killed himself.

Jude, brother of Yeshua:

A brother of Yeshua, born of Mary and Joseph. Jude was married to Rebekkah and lived at the family compound. Jude had a good head for business and took over the family businesses after the death of Joseph. He and Rebekkah had no children, having suffered miscarriage and stillbirth. After the crucifixion, Micah, the son of Yeshua and Miriam, was adopted by Jude and Rebekkah and raised as their own to hide Micah from his inherited enemies. After the crucifixion, Jude moved the family businesses to Jerusalem leaving the family compound in Galilee to be used and cared for by members of the extended Essene community.

Madib, assassin:

Sent by powerful forces to assassinate Yeshua and his traveling party on their journey to the East. Yeshua encountered Madib and his party twice, once on the boat to Krokola and again in Kapilavastu.

Man'wa, Master at the Temple of Man:

A master trainer at the Temple of Man. He taught and otherwise helped forge Yeshua's mantle, remaining an 'unseen' mentor and loyal supporter of Yeshua far past Yeshua's stay at the Temple.

Mary, mother of Yeshua:

Known to many as Mother Mary, she went to the monastery at Mount Carmel as a child, to be raised as a temple maiden. Mary was selected for the honor of giving birth to Yeshua when she was eleven. She was made pregnant at the age of twelve and married to Joseph at the age of thirteen, giving birth shortly thereafter. When Mary was fifteen, she and Joseph consummated their marriage and had five children together; James, Ruth, Jude, Sarah, and Shelah. Mary lived as matriarch to the David family until she left Judea shortly after the crucifixion.

Mary, wife of Peter:

Wife of Peter, she considered herself a supporter of Yeshua, but didn't travel with the group. She stayed in Capernaum to run the home of Peter as matriarch to their large clan.

Matthew, husband of Anna:

Married to Anna and a beloved devotee of Yeshua. His wife was one of the seven women who volunteered to give birth to a child of Yeshua; however, Anna changed her mind prior to engaging with Yeshua.

Micah, son of Yeshua and Miriam:

After several miscarriages, Micah was born to Yeshua and Miriam three years before the crucifixion. To hide his true identity, Micah was adopted by Yeshua's brother Jude and moved with them to Jerusalem. Micah didn't find out the truth of his parentage until he was a young man.

Michael:

A boy Yeshua and James played with as children. One day, Michael fell into a hole and broke his leg. While helping Michael, Yeshua discovered his talent for manipulating time.

Micos:

A Zealot and friend of Judas. Micos was a member of the Hellenist sect and was the attacker who killed a member of the Sanhedrin on the border of Samaria and Galilee. Because of this fight, which Judas also participated in, Micos and Judas went into hiding in Tiberius. While there, Roman forces found them and Micos, mistaken for Judas, was killed.

Mirah, wife of Andrew (brother of Peter):

Married to Andrew, she and her husband were devotees of Yeshua. Mirah was one of the seven women who volunteered to give birth to a child of Yeshua. Their child's name was Shiah.

Miriam, wife of Yeshua:

When Yeshua met Miriam, she was the Attendant Sophia of Palestina; the High-Priestess of the pagan temple on the Sea of Galilee. After an extended courtship, she renounced her position as Priestess and married Yeshua. She taught alongside Yeshua thereafter. She gave birth to Micah, son of Yeshua, and also to Philippe, a child given to her by Philar after the crucifixion. Miriam gave Micah to Jude and Rebekkah, to help shield him from their enemies, and fled to Europe with Yeshua's children Shiah and Rebekkah as her own. To shield Miriam's true location, Carole masqueraded as Miriam and fled Judea with Mary and Rose. Once in Europe, Miriam proceeded with her own mission, establishing the Order of the Rose.

Myrrh, companion of Yeshua:

A monk from Qumran. He volunteered to be a companion and caretaker for Yeshua on the trip to the East when Yeshua was fourteen. He died while they were in Kapilavastu.

Nadia, the Healer:

She took in Yeshua and used her kindness and her healing knowledge to help him recover from his burden. In return, Yeshua and Philar gave her a daughter, Dania. Later, Nadia helped Miriam keep and birth Micah.

Nicodemus, member of the Sanhedrin:
A supporter of Yeshua, member of the David family, and on the Sanhedrin, but his exact familial relationship with Yeshua is unclear. He was against the capture, torture, and crucifixion of Yeshua. Nicodemus continued to support the family throughout the rest of his life, becoming a major influence in James' eventual rise to power.

Oranos, Roman Commander:
Commander of the regiment chasing rebels who killed a member of the Sanhedrin in an attack at the Samarian border of Galilee. Oranos grew to hate Yeshua and became a dangerous enemy to him; harassing and threatening him throughout Yeshua's tenure as head of the David family.

Other, the:
'The Other' are what Yeshua calls members of a group of inter-dimensional beings that are committed to Yeshua's cause and mission. They appear to Yeshua in the flesh when communication with him is imperative. Philar, Yeshua's friend and supporter, was one of the Other.

Peter, (Simon Peter) devotee and friend of Yeshua:
From Capernaum and married to Mary. He was a devotee and close friend of Yeshua. Peter was a merchant and had known Joseph, the adopted father of Yeshua, before him.

Philar:
Geneticist and primary helpmate of Yeshua. He appears to Yeshua when needed as part of what Yeshua calls the Other.

Philip, husband of Ann:
Married to Ann and a devotee of Yeshua. His wife was one of the seven women who volunteered to give birth to a child of Yeshua; however, Ann didn't carry the child to term.

Philippe, son of Miriam:
The son of Miriam, created by Philar. and conceived after the crucifixion. Philippe was born in Europe. He had the same strong will and intelligence as, and looked very much like, Yeshua. However, he wasn't predisposed to a spiritual path, instead taking up business as his mantle.

Pontius Pilate:
Roman Prefect of Judea and the man who ordered the flogging and subsequent crucifixion of Yeshua.

Raphael, Angel (Archangel):
Raphael appeared to Joseph to help convince him to marry Mary.

Rasa, Mistress to Seleya:
The chaperone and mistress to Seleya, a young woman Yeshua had romantic feelings for while studying at university.

Rebekkah, daughter of Yeshua:
The daughter of Yeshua and Willa. Rebekkah went with Miriam to Europe and was raised as Miriam's daughter.

Rebekkah, wife of Jude:
Married to Jude and sister-in-law to Yeshua. She lived on the family compound until Jude moved the family businesses to Jerusalem after the

crucifixion. To hide his identity from enemies, Rebekkah became the adopted mother of Micah, son of Yeshua and Miriam.

Roman, husband of Beeza:

Married to Beeza and a devotee of Yeshua. His wife was one of the seven women who volunteered to give birth to a child of Yeshua. The child's name was Joseph.

Rose, daughter of Yeshua:

The daughter of Yeshua and Carole. Rose went with Carole and Mary after the crucifixion.

Ruth, sister of Yeshua:

Married to David and the daughter of Joseph and Mary, sister of Yeshua. She lived with her family in Caesarea.

Ruth, wife of Simon:

A devotee of Yeshua and married to Simon. She was one of the seven women who volunteered to give birth to a child of Yeshua; however, she didn't conceive.

Salome, Head Priestess of the temple in Memphis:

Sister-in-Service to Head-Mistress Shekhin at the monastery on Mount Carmel, Salome was an ambitious woman who proved to be Shekhin's murderer. Joseph encountered Salome again while he and Yeshua were traveling in Egypt. At that time, she was Head-Priestess of the Temple of Sekhmet in Memphis. Salome attempted to kill Yeshua by poisoning him.

Sarah, sister of Yeshua:

Married and with her family, lived in Sepphoris. She was the daughter of Joseph and Mary, sister of Yeshua.

Sarah, wife of Azrael and devotee of Yeshua:

A devotee of Yeshua and Miriam, and wife of Azrael. She was particularly close to Miriam. She was abused by her husband and killed him in desperation. The incident brought danger to the community.

Seleya, first beloved of Yeshua:

A young woman that Yeshua befriended while he was at the Combs in Kapilavastu. Yeshua had complicated romantic feelings for her, but she wasn't available to him, as she was promised in marriage to someone else.

Shekhin, Head Mistress of Carmel:

The Head-Mistress of the sisterhood at the Monastery on Mount Carmel. She was murdered while working to bring Mary into position to become Yeshua's mother.

Shelah, sister of Yeshua:

The daughter of Joseph and Mary, sister of Yeshua. She was the last born of Joseph's clan and died of illness when she was eight years old.

Shiah, daughter of Yeshua:

The daughter of Yeshua and Mirah, wife of Andrew. Shiah went to Western Europe with Miriam after the crucifixion and was raised as Miriam's daughter.

Simon, husband of Ruth:

Married to Ruth and devotee of Yeshua. His wife was one of the seven women who volunteered to give birth to a child of Yeshua; however, Ruth didn't conceive.

Simon, son of Joseph, half-brother of Yeshua:
>The last born of Joseph from his first marriage. Simon was a married man before Yeshua was born. He lived with his family in Sepphoris. Yeshua saved Simon's life a few years before the crucifixion in an incident that many regarded as a miracle.

Simon, son of Matthias:
>Testified at the mock trial of Yeshua. Simon's lies in his testimony were used by Caiaphas to condemn Yeshua.

Temple Master at Insa'alet:
>A wise and elderly Bon Master, and Temple Master at Insa'alet while Yeshua was there. Yeshua revered him.

Thomas, devotee of Yeshua:
>One of the youngest devotees of Yeshua and known for his gentle pragmatism.

Unseen, The, guides for Yeshua:
>Guides of Yeshua's who followed him everywhere. They were invisible to all but Yeshua. There were usually three of them. One was an elderly man with a long beard and a staff. One stood about four feet tall and had a long, curved neck. The third was only a few feet tall and had a habit of floating around Yeshua like a bee around a flower. Yeshua called on them when he needed assistance and they also volunteered their assistance.

Uriah, proprietor of the tavern in Sepphoris:
>He witnessed the incident in Sepphoris when Yeshua brought Simon, Yeshua's brother, back from the dead.

Willa, wife of Jonas:
>Married to Jonas, she and her husband were devotees of Yeshua. Willa was one of the seven women that volunteered to give birth to a child of Yeshua. Their child's name was Rebekkah.

Yeshua son of Joseph from Galilee:
>This book is about the life and work of this extraordinary man.

Timeline

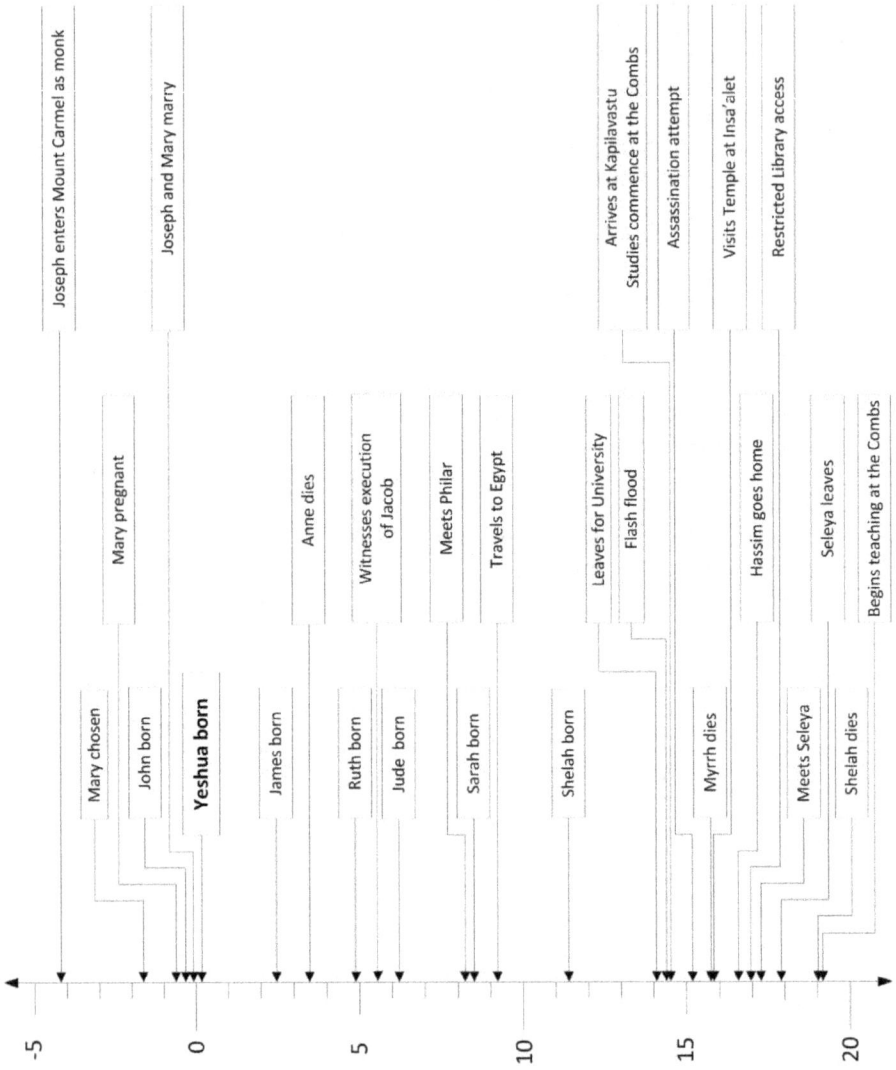

Figure 8: Summary timeline of Yeshua's first forty years
Charted time is relative to the birth of Yeshua
Year zero stands for the year Yeshua was born
and does not correlate to the year 1 BCE or 1 CE

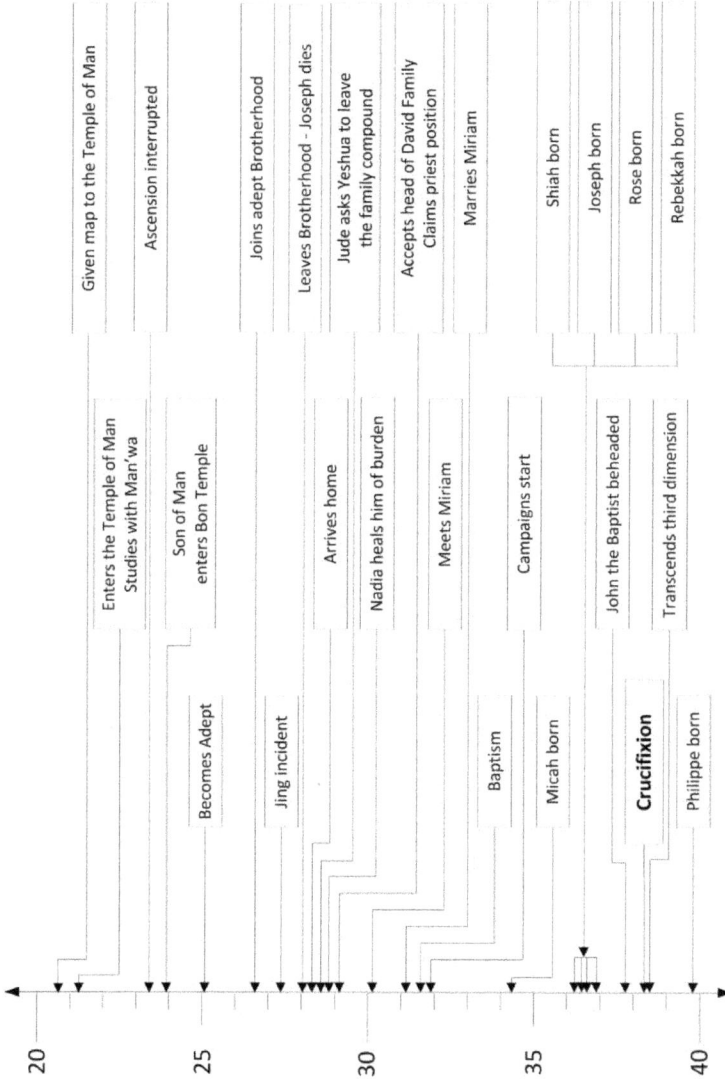

Index

Index of Quotes

About the Author

Bestselling author Kaarin Alisa is a catalyst for spiritual growth and personal transformation. She has honed her abilities as a change agent in the metaphysical and energetic arts for more than forty years, practicing as a spiritual adviser, medical intuitive, clinical hypnotherapist, teacher, and energy practitioner. She's helped people from all walks of life realign to their highest truth, so they're better able to pursue their dreams and ambitions.

Known to many as Jesus, Kaarin began her relationship with Yeshua as a child. Over the years she has honed the ability to interact and collaborate with him through both her own personal development and her work with others seeking guidance.

A sought-after speaker, Kaarin offers tele-seminars, workshops, and private sessions by appointment. For more information about Kaarin and links to her other books and projects, go to: http://KaarinAlisa.com

What's Next?

Come and join the *Journey of a Prophet* community – add your name to the growing list of people who have accepted Yeshua's invitation. To also keep abreast of new developments and offerings in the *Journey of a Prophet* community, please go to: http://JourneyofaProphet.com